Teach
Yourself
IntraBuilder
in 21 days

D1427549

Teach Yourself
INTRABUILDER
in 21 days

Paul Mahar
Ken Henderson

201 West 103rd Street
Indianapolis, Indiana 46290

For Toni, who is simply the best. And in memory of Jack Nance. —PDM

For Genie and a lifetime of dreams come true. —TEG

For Lottie, who loved the written word, and taught me to. —AAK

Copyright © 1997 by Sams.net Publishing

FIRST EDITION

International Standard Book Number: 1-57521-224-2

Library of Congress Catalog Card Number: 96-70714

2000   99   98   97   4   3   2

Interpretation of the printing code: the rightmost double-digit number is the year of the book's printing; the rightmost single-digit, the number of the book's printing. For example, a printing code of 97-1 shows that the first printing of the book occurred in 1997.

Composed in AGaramond and MCPdigital by Macmillan Computer Publishing

Printed in the United States of America

Trademarks

Publisher and President Richard K. Swadley
Publishing Manager Greg Wiegand
Director of Editorial Services Cindy Morrow
Managing Editor Mary Inderstrodt
Director of Marketing Kelli S. Spencer
Assistant Marketing Managers Kristina Perry, Rachel Wolfe

Acquisitions Editor
Christopher Denny

Development Editor
Jeffrey J. Koch

Software Development Specialist
Brad Myers

Production Editors
Ryan Rader
Katherine Stuart Ewing

Copy Editor
Marla Reece

Indexer
Cheryl Dietsch

Technical Reviewers
Corinne Cottle
Chris Andersen
David Neff

Editorial Coordinator
Katie Wise

Technical Edit Coordinator
Deborah Frisby

Editorial Assistants
Carol Ackerman
Andi Richter
Rhonda Tinch-Mize

Cover Designer
Tim Amrhein

Book Designer
Gary Adair

Copy Writer
Peter Fuller

Production Team Supervisors
Brad Chinn
Charlotte Clapp

Production
Elizabeth Deeter
Chris Livengood
Deirdre Smith
Ian A. Smith

Overview

Contents

6 Scripts, Events, and Methods 117

7 Tables, Queries, and Database Administration 135

Acknowledgments

To my wife, Toni, for her recommendations and dedication as my "alpha" reader. Thank you once again, for spending weekends going over chapters and examples instead of enjoying the California sun, sand, and sea. —*PDM*

Special thanks to Paul, Ken, Alan, and Chris for all their patience and help. I couldn't have done this without the Spirit of Christ in my heart, although the encouragement of my family and that great gang in California sure didn't hurt. —*TEG*

We would like to extend our thanks to all who made this possible and recognize members of the IntraBuilder development team. Randy Solton is the product architect who took us gently into the land of webs and honey. The core development team is Bruce Bundy, Bill Joy, Charles Overbeck, David Miyachi, Dondi Gaskill, Helen Bershadskaya, Hin Boen, Liz Stevenson, Peter Johnson, and Ray Kiuchi. Michael Gardner, Robert Pirani, Paul Johnson, Curt Patrick, Pete Lindberg, Ross Dembecki, Leanne Goulding, and Tony de la Lama provided the many teams an environment for creative experimentation within a framework of ever-present schedules.

Lastly, a big thanks to Chris Denny, Jeff Koch, Ryan Rader, Marla Reece, Kathy Ewing, and all at Sams.net who helped turn a mass of words and images into a book.

About the Authors

Lead Author

Paul Mahar is a developer on the IntraBuilder R&D team. Paul lives in Scotts Valley with his wife, Toni, whose editing helps bring clarity and conciseness to his writings. Paul is also the author of *Visual dBASE 5.5 Unleashed*, published by Sams. He has been a speaker at several Borland International Conferences and has a bachelor's degree from DeVry Institute of Technology. For *Teach Yourself IntraBuilder in 21 Days*, Paul wrote Chapters 8 through 14, as well as Chapters 18 and 21. If you have questions about *Teach Yourself IntraBuilder in 21 Days* or suggestions for future revisions, you can contact Paul at pmahar@corp.borland.com or on CompuServe at 73422,2200. For more information about this book or Paul, visit his Web site at

http://ourworld.compuserve.com/homepages/mahar/

Contributing Authors

Ken Henderson is a database developer and DBA with more than 10 years of experience. He is the author of several commercial software packages, including programmer productivity aids and software libraries. He is also a frequent speaker at industry trade shows. Currently, he is a consultant specializing in database administration and client/server architecture. Ken can be reached at 74763.2305@compuserve.com.

Ted Graham, after spending five years at Borland, is now beginning the life of an independent contractor. He lives in Cleveland, Ohio, with his beautiful wife, Genie, and a slightly overweight tabby cat named Chester. As a member of the IntraBuilder R&D team, Ted developed many of the prebuilt business solutions and samples that ship with IntraBuilder. Ted is the author of Chapters 16, 17, and 19 of *Teach Yourself IntraBuilder in 21 Days*. He is an active participant in the IntraBuilder online discussion forum (www.borland.com/intrabuilder), and he can also be reached at IBuilder@aol.com.

A. A. Katz (Alan) is CEO of Ksoft, Inc., a custom software developer and publisher in Johnson City, NY. Alan left a 16-year career in architecture in 1983 to indulge his passion for the emerging personal computer. He spent more than a decade at ApTECH, Inc., where he authored the nationally distributed Abraxas accounting/management software. He's a proud member of Borland's TeamB; the editor of the *Visual dBASE Web Magazine* (http://www.wji.com/vdb/homepage.html); and the author of more than a dozen magazine articles for *dBASE Advisor, DataBased Advisor, Internet and Java Advisor*, and *Computer Reseller News*. Alan wrote Chapter 20 of *Teach Yourself IntraBuilder in 21 Days*. You can contact Alan at aakatz@worldnet.att.net.

Tell Us What You Think!

As a reader, you are the most important critic and commentator of our books. We value your opinion and want to know what we're doing right, what we could do better, what areas you'd like to see us publish in, and any other words of wisdom you're willing to pass our way. You can help us make strong books that meet your needs and give you the computer guidance you require.

Do you have access to CompuServe or the World Wide Web? Then check out our CompuServe forum by typing GO SAMS at any prompt. If you prefer the World Wide Web, check out our site at http://www.mcp.com.

 NOTE

> If you have a technical question about this book, call the technical support line at 317-581-3833.

As the publishing manager of the group that created this book, I welcome your comments. You can fax, e-mail, or write me directly to let me know what you did or didn't like about this book—as well as what we can do to make our books stronger. Here's the information:

Fax: 317-581-4669

E-mail: programming_mgr@sams.samspublishing.com

Mail: Greg Wiegand
           Sams.net Publishing
           201 W. 103rd Street
           Indianapolis, IN 46290

Introduction

IntraBuilder offers a vast array of classes, tools, and designers to help create dynamic Web pages. This book will help you learn how to create Web applications using IntraBuilder's visual designers and the JavaScript language. You do not need to know or learn any CGI, NSAPI, ISAPI, or even HTML to create Web applications with IntraBuilder.

This book assumes some basic knowledge of programming, Windows, and browsers. If you have ever worked with a rapid application development environment such as Visual Basic, Delphi, or Visual dBASE, you will feel right at home when using the IntraBuilder designers. If you know what a variable and a loop are, you know enough to start working with JavaScript.

Practice and Experiment

The best way to learn an application development environment is to create applications. During the course of this book, you will be instructed to create forms, reports, and scripts that demonstrate various aspects of IntraBuilder. You are encouraged to experiment with the examples and expand on them where appropriate.

Week by Week Coverage

The book is divided into three weeks, of seven chapters (or days) each. The first week describes the many tools and data connectivity features found in IntraBuilder. If you are already comfortable with RAD environments and other products that use BDE (Borland Database Engine), feel free to scan the first seven chapters with a focus on unfamiliar topics.

When you have a good feel for the tools at your disposal, you can put them into action during the second week. Days 8 through 14 guide you through the creation of a shopping cart application, from the ground up. Although you can use the files on the CD-ROM to start developing the application at any point, these chapters make more sense when read in order.

The third week covers advanced topics such as ActiveX controls and the dynamic object model. As with Week 1, you can read these chapters in any order. The topics covered in the third week assume you are familiar enough with IntraBuilder to build a simple application that uses dBASE or Paradox tables.

At the beginning of each week, you find a Week at a Glance section that describes the topics for the week. Similarly, each week ends with a summary called Week in Review. Refer to those sections for more information on the contents of each chapter.

Although the chapters are called Days and sets of seven chapters are called Weeks, do not feel compelled to work through exactly one chapter each day. Some chapters will go faster than others. If you have worked with other RAD environments, you will likely find yourself working through the first week in less than a week. Conversely, if you step through every exercise in the second week to build the shopping cart application and perform the related benchmarks, do not be surprised if you get a day or two behind. The last week is the most likely to take an actual calendar week.

Q&As and Workshops

To get the most from *Teach Yourself IntraBuilder in 21 Days*, be sure to try out the Q&A and Workshop sections. These sections appear at the end of each chapter. The Q&A includes answers to common questions that you might have after reading the chapter. The Workshops consist of a quiz and some exercises. Appendix A lists the answers for all quiz questions. The exercises provide ideas for further experimentation with subjects covered in the chapter.

Conventions Used in This Book

NOTE

A Note box presents interesting pieces of information related to the surrounding discussion.

TIP

A Tip box offers advice or teaches an easier way to do something.

WARNING

A Warning box advises you about potential problems and helps you steer clear of rough surf.

 A New Term box introduces and defines words and phrases that might be unfamiliar.

ANALYSIS An Analysis icon identifies the explanation of a JavaScript source code listing.

The Companion CD-ROM

This book comes with a CD-ROM containing all the source code for the examples, a complete IntraBuilder shopping cart application, and a 60-day trial version of IntraBuilder Client/Server. There is a folder of source files for each day's chapter. Some folders such as the Tables folder contain files that you will use over several days. The book contains instructions on how to create most of the example files. You can use the example files to verify your work. The files also allow you to jump to any section of the book and start without creating supporting files.

TIP

I recommend using the example tables provided. The example tables are already populated with data that shows the linking and image-handling capabilities of IntraBuilder.

The 60-day IntraBuilder 1.01 Client/Server Trial works as an upgrade from 1.0 and as a trial version. If the setup program locates version 1.0, it installs an upgrade with no date restrictions. The upgrade works only for the certified version of 1.0. If you installed a beta test version of IntraBuilder, you should remove it before attempting to install the Client/Server Trial.

The Client/Server edition allows you to work with SQL-Links to connect to Oracle, Sybase, DB2, Informix, InterBase, and Microsoft SQL Server. The trial CD does not contain the SQL-Link drivers. You can use the IntraBuilder trial with 32-bit SQL-Link drivers that ship with the Client/Server versions of Delphi, C++ Builder, JBuilder, or Visual dBASE 6. The SQL-Link drivers also come with the non-trial version of IntraBuilder Client/Server.

At a Glance

During the first week, you take a tour of the various tools that comprise IntraBuilder. The first seven days provide a foundation of knowledge that you can use to build the shopping cart application during Week 2. IntraBuilder is a data-centric development tool, and these first seven chapters help you quickly create dynamic Web pages for client/server, ODBC, and native BDE tables.

The first two days get you up and running with the IntraBuilder Designer, the IntraBuilder Server, and the Borland Database Engine. The first day is an overview of the IntraBuilder Designer and a step-by-step guide for connecting to Access tables through ODBC and connecting to InterBase tables through SQL-Links. You can also use this chapter as a guide for connecting to other data sources such as Oracle, Sybase, and Microsoft SQL Server. Day 2 describes the sample files and solution applications that come with IntraBuilder. You learn how to configure a Web server to work with IntraBuilder and see how JavaScript forms can run within IntraBuilder Designer as well as through a browser.

The primary component of an IntraBuilder application is the JavaScript form. Days 3 and 4 show you how to create your own JavaScript forms. Day 3 includes an overview of the Form Expert, the Form Designer, and many of the components you can place on a JavaScript form. Advanced layout features and multiple page forms are topics for Day 4.

Day 5 introduces you to JavaScript reports. You learn about the Report Expert, the Report Designer, and how to create groups and summary fields within the Report Designer.

On Day 6, you learn about the Method Editor, Script Editor, and Script Pad. These tools assist you with the writing of JavaScript methods. This chapter also describes application partitioning through client-side and server-side JavaScript.

NOTE

This book does not contain a tutorial or reference for the JavaScript language. For more information about the JavaScript language, refer to Chapter 2 of the *IntraBuilder Language Reference*. Sams.net also publishes several JavaScript books including *Teach Yourself JavaScript in a Week* (ISBN: 1-57521-073-8) and *JavaScript Unleashed* (ISBN: 1-57521-118-1).

The first week wraps up with a discussion of tables, queries, and database administration. On Day 7, you learn the pros and cons of various data sources including the native BDE tables, ODBC, and SQL-Link connections. You also learn how to create new tables using the Table Expert and Table Designer.

Day 1

IntraBuilder and Data Connections

by Ken Henderson

Today you learn how to get around in IntraBuilder as well as how to set up database connections. I'll give you a brief overview of how IntraBuilder works, and then you can delve into a task that IntraBuilder excels at—connecting Web pages with information from databases. I'll show you how to establish ODBC connections (including connections to Access databases), as well as native Borland Database Engine–based connections. You'll also learn the first steps of doing constructive work with IntraBuilder.

An Overview of IntraBuilder

No discussion of IntraBuilder basics would be complete without at least mentioning the technologies that comprise IntraBuilder's underlying architecture. In addition to the IntraBuilder visual designer, IntraBuilder also relies on two other elements to pull off its server-side magic successfully. These two technologies are known as IntraBuilder Brokers and IntraBuilder Agents. I'll discuss each of them separately.

IntraBuilder Brokers

An IntraBuilder Broker facilitates communication between your Web server software and IntraBuilder. It lives on your Web server and supplies "live" data to Web pages without client Web browsers even being aware that it is there.

Out of the box, the Professional and Client/Server versions of IntraBuilder include brokers for WINCGI, NSAPI, and ISAPI, so you can choose the broker that works best for you. IntraBuilder's support for WINCGI allows it to work with a number of Web server packages, including O'Reilly & Associates' WebSite. NSAPI, of course, is Netscape's Web server API, so IntraBuilder can interface with Netscape's FastTrack Web server as well. Finally, because IntraBuilder provides an ISAPI broker, it can also interoperate with Microsoft's Internet Information Server (IIS). The completeness of IntraBuilder's server support helps ensure that you won't have to switch Web server packages just to deploy IntraBuilder applications.

IntraBuilder Agents

IntraBuilder Agents allow the server's workload to be distributed among several machines. By spreading processing over multiple machines, your IntraBuilder-enabled Web server will be able to support a larger number of concurrent connections and a heavier workload. IntraBuilder Professional includes support for multiple local IntraBuilder Agents, while IntraBuilder Client/Server includes support for multiple local *and* remote IntraBuilder Agents.

Establishing a Database Connection

Because the whole purpose of IntraBuilder is to allow you to easily connect Web pages with databases, it seems fitting to begin with a discussion of just how to do that. IntraBuilder applications connect to databases using the Borland Database Engine (BDE). The BDE ships with native support for Paradox and dBASE tables and can access SQL Server (Sybase and Microsoft), Oracle, Informix, DB2, and InterBase databases via Borland's SQL Links, which ships with IntraBuilder. (The Professional version of IntraBuilder includes drivers for InterBase and Microsoft SQL Server only; the Client/Server version includes drivers for all six platforms.) In addition to its native and SQL Links–based connections, the BDE also supports connecting via ODBC drivers. Any DBMS or file format for which a 32-bit ODBC driver can be obtained can be accessed from IntraBuilder.

Establishing an ODBC Connection

Though you will probably prefer native SQL Link driver connections to ODBC connections, you might still need to make use of ODBC drivers from time to time. For example, if you wish to connect to a Microsoft Access database, you'll have to do so via ODBC because there's no native SQL Links driver for Access.

 ODBC stands for Open DataBase Connectivity. It is Microsoft's generic API for accessing databases and database-like file formats. The original idea behind ODBC was to provide a uniform API that software developers could use to communicate with database servers and manipulate database files. This uniformity allows applications to be somewhat independent of the databases they access and allows the back-end database to be changed without forcing the application to be rewritten. For the most part, ODBC has lived up to its original intent and is quite pervasive throughout the database world.

Acquiring ODBC Drivers

ODBC drivers can be acquired from a number of different sources. First and foremost, Database Management System (DBMS) vendors themselves usually provide ODBC drivers for their respective databases. Often, these drivers are included free of charge (and sometimes automatically installed) with DBMS products.

You can also acquire ODBC drivers from third parties. Intersolv, for example, markets a comprehensive ODBC package that includes drivers for most popular DBMSs. If your DBMS vendor does not provide its own ODBC driver set, chances are the vendor will direct you to someone who can.

NOTE

Because IntraBuilder is a 32-bit product, you can't use 16-bit ODBC drivers with it. IntraBuilder uses the 32-bit version of the Borland Database Engine, and the 32-bit BDE requires 32-bit ODBC drivers.

Defining ODBC Data Sources

Connecting to a database using an ODBC driver requires a data source definition. An ODBC data source is simply a collection of parameters that the driver requires. Data sources provide a level of abstraction between applications and the ODBC drivers they use. They allow applications and the databases they reference to be much more loosely bound. When you make use of data sources, details regarding ODBC connections can be changed without modifying your applications. If, for example, you have two applications that each utilize a different Microsoft Access database, you could define two separate ODBC data sources, each one referencing your Access ODBC driver. This way, your applications are insulated from the details that the Access driver might require. ODBC data sources are located externally to your applications and can vary from machine to machine.

You create ODBC data sources using the ODBC Administrator. I'll give you a brief tour of the ODBC Administrator before actually defining a data source. You should be able to locate its icon in the Control Panel. As Figure 1.1 shows, it's in the upper-left corner of the Windows 95 Control Panel.

Figure 1.1.

You can start the ODBC Administrator from Control Panel.

You can double-click the 32-bit ODBC icon to start the ODBC Administrator. After you do, you'll be presented with a list of currently defined data sources, as Figure 1.2 shows.

Figure 1.2.

The opening dialog of the ODBC Adminis-trator lists your currently defined data sources.

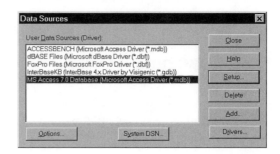

Because these data sources function as intermediaries between your applications and ODBC drivers, it's helpful to know what ODBC drivers are actually available. Click the Drivers button to list the currently available ODBC drivers. Figure 1.3 shows an example of what you might see. Your driver list will vary based on the ODBC drivers actually installed on your machine.

Figure 1.3.

Clicking the Drivers button lists the available ODBC drivers.

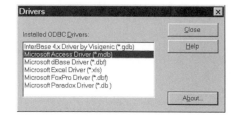

You can click the About button in the driver list to view background information about a particular ODBC driver, as shown in Figure 1.4. You can, for example, view the name of the actual driver file from this dialog. This can be handy when troubleshooting ODBC connection problems.

Figure 1.4.

The ODBC Administrator's Drivers/About dialog lists important driver-specific details.

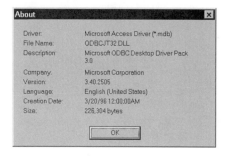

WARNING

BDE does not support all versions of the ODBC Access driver. Check the IntraBuilder `readme.txt` file for a list of certified drivers.

Click OK to close the About dialog and click Close to exit the Drivers dialog. After you're back in the ODBC Administrator's opening dialog, click the Add button to add a new data source. You'll then be asked to select a driver on which to base the data source, as Figure 1.5 illustrates.

Figure 1.5.

The first step in defining an ODBC data source is to select an ODBC driver.

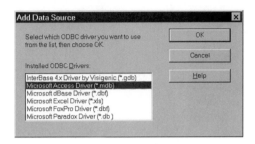

Within the Add Data Source dialog, double-click a driver to specify it as the basis for the new data source. After you do, you'll see the Setup dialog shown in Figure 1.6.

Figure 1.6.

You use the Setup dialog to specify ODBC data source details.

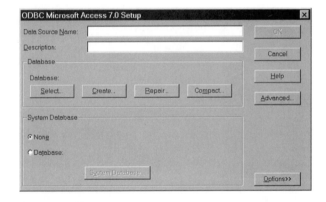

Click the Cancel button to exit the Setup dialog and return to the ODBC Administrator's opening dialog. Now that you've finished your cursory tour of the Administrator program, you'll define an ODBC data source that you can use from within IntraBuilder.

Creating an Access ODBC Data Source

Because it accompanies Word and Excel in Microsoft Office Professional, Microsoft Access is one of the more popular local DBMSs. In this section, I'll show you how to create an Access data source that you can use in IntraBuilder. If you want to use an existing ODBC data source instead of creating a new one, skip to the next section, "Configuring ODBC Data Sources for IntraBuilder."

To begin creating your new Access data source, click the Add button in the ODBC Administrator's Data Source dialog. After you've done this, double-click the Microsoft Access Driver in the Drivers dialog to use it as the basis for your new data source.

NOTE The ODBC Access driver comes with Access and other Microsoft Office products. If the driver is missing, you'll need to install it before proceeding.

Next, you are presented with the ODBC Microsoft Access 7.0 Setup dialog. Type a one-word name into the Data Source Name field and a description into the Description field. The name and description you enter will vary, of course, based on what database you intend to use. A common convention is to name the data source after the database it will reference.

Next, click the Database button and select the Access database file (it should have an .MDB extension) that you want the new data source to reference. After you've selected a database, the data source definition is basically complete, and you're ready to move on. Figure 1.7 shows an example of what your Setup dialog should look like.

Figure 1.7.

You use the ODBC Data Source Setup dialog to configure new data sources.

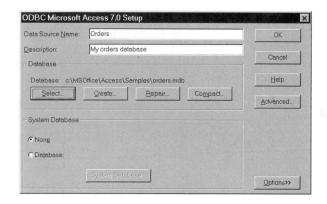

Now that the data source definition is complete, click the OK button to create it and return to the Data Sources dialog. You should see your new data source listed, as shown in Figure 1.8.

Figure 1.8.

Your new data source shows up in the ODBC Administrator's Data Sources dialog.

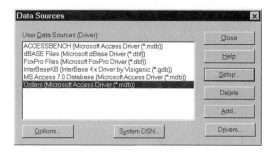

After you have an ODBC data source, you're ready to get on with the business of utilizing it from within IntraBuilder. To do this, you'll need to configure a BDE alias that references the data source.

 A BDE alias is very similar to an ODBC data source. It consists of a collection of parameters that correspond to a particular database or DBMS connection.

Configuring ODBC Data Sources for IntraBuilder

BDE aliases are created using the BDE Configuration Utility. You should be able to locate the configuration utility in your IntraBuilder folder. Double-click its icon to start it now.

There are two ways to create a BDE alias for a given ODBC data source. The easiest way is to simply enable the AUTO ODBC option on the System page of the BDE Configuration Utility. This will cause the BDE to create aliases automatically for each currently defined ODBC data source. The only downside to this is that you might get a number of new BDE aliases that you do not actually need. Click the System tab now and set the AUTO ODBC option to TRUE. (See Figure 1.9.)

Figure 1.9.

AUTO ODBC *allows*
you to create ODBC-
based aliases easily.

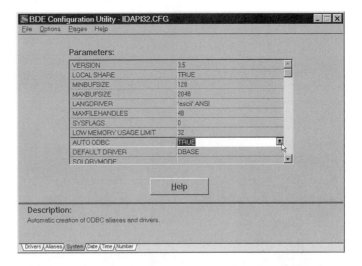

If you click the Aliases page tab now, you should see your new ODBC-based aliases.

The second method of creating a BDE alias for an ODBC data source involves two steps. First, you configure the data source as a BDE database driver, and then you create a BDE alias that references this new driver.

If you want to create an alias using this method rather than via AUTO ODBC, follow these steps:

1. Click the Drivers tab in the BDE Configuration Utility.

2. Click the New ODBC Driver button.

3. Type a name for your new driver into the SQL Link Driver field. The configuration program will prefix whatever you type with ODBC_.

4. Select the ODBC driver and data source that you wish to use. These should correspond to your entries in the ODBC Administrator program.

Figure 1.10 shows what the completed Add ODBC Driver dialog looks like.

Figure 1.10.

To establish ODBC-based aliases, begin by creating BDE driver entries for your ODBC data source.

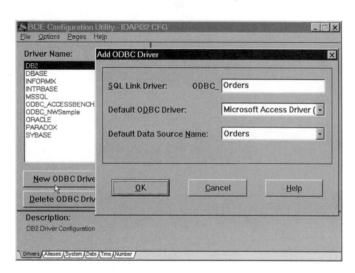

After you've created a driver entry for the data source, you're ready to proceed with creating an alias for it. To do this, follow these steps:

1. Click the Aliases tab.

2. Click the New Alias button.

3. Type in a name for your new alias.

4. Click the drop-down list in the Alias type field and select the driver entry you just created.

5. Click OK. You'll notice that the ODBC DSN (Data Source Name) field changes to reflect the data source you specified when you defined the ODBC driver entry.

Figure 1.11 shows the completed alias definition.

Figure 1.11.

After you've created an ODBC driver entry, you can create a BDE alias that references it.

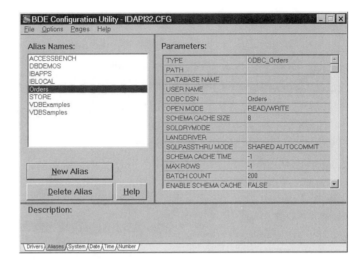

Now that your ODBC-based alias is created, click the File|Save option to save your changes, and then exit the BDE Configuration Utility.

Opening an ODBC Table from IntraBuilder

Making use of tables contained in the database referenced by your new alias is a snap in IntraBuilder. If you haven't already done so, start IntraBuilder now and click the Tables tab in the IntraBuilder Explorer. (See Figure 1.12.)

Figure 1.12.

You can use the IntraBuilder Explorer to open database tables.

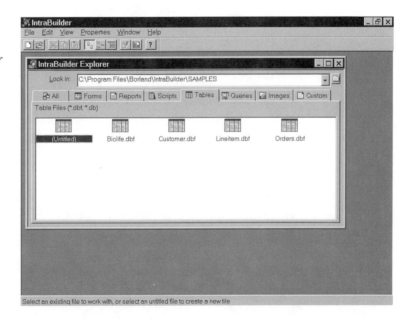

Next, click the Look In drop-down list and select your new alias from the list, as illustrated in Figure 1.13.

Figure 1.13.
You can select BDE aliases from IntraBuilder Explorer's Look In list.

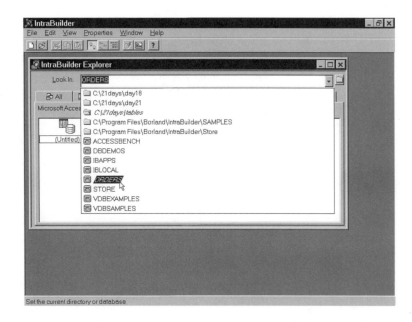

After you've selected your new alias, you should see the tables contained in the database it references listed in the Explorer, as shown in Figure 1.14.

Figure 1.14.
IntraBuilder Explorer lists the tables in your alias.

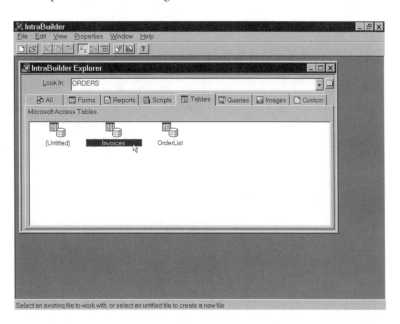

Double-click one of the listed tables, and IntraBuilder creates and runs a default form for it, as illustrated in Figure 1.15.

Figure 1.15.

IntraBuilder builds default forms for tables you open.

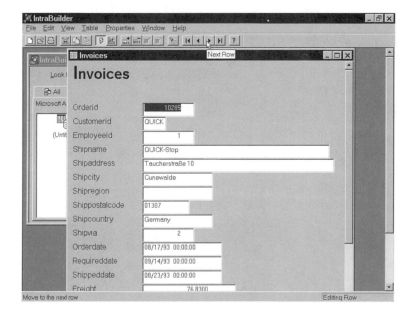

You can now click the default form's Close button and return to the IntraBuilder Explorer. For more information about working with Access tables, see Day 10, "Querying for the Quickest Searches."

Getting Connected with SQL Links

As mentioned previously, in addition to being able to establish database connections using ODBC drivers, IntraBuilder can also connect using Borland's SQL Links drivers. Out of the box, IntraBuilder Professional includes drivers for the Microsoft SQL Server and InterBase platforms. IntraBuilder Client/Server includes SQL Links drivers for Sybase SQL Server, Oracle, IBM DB2, and Informix, in addition to the Microsoft and InterBase drivers. The fact that IntraBuilder already comes with drivers for the more popular DBMS platforms means that you can connect to them without needing ODBC drivers.

The process of creating an SQL Links BDE alias and connecting to it from within IntraBuilder differs very little from ODBC data sources. I'll take you through the process of establishing SQL Link DBMS connections just as I did with ODBC data sources.

Defining a BDE Alias for SQL Links

As mentioned previously, you define an alias for an SQL Links connection much the same way that you define one for ODBC data sources. Begin by firing up the BDE Configuration Utility (which you should be able to locate in your IntraBuilder folder). Then click the Aliases tab, as shown in Figure 1.16.

Figure 1.16.

You begin defining SQL Links aliases by selecting the Aliases page in the BDE Configuration Utility.

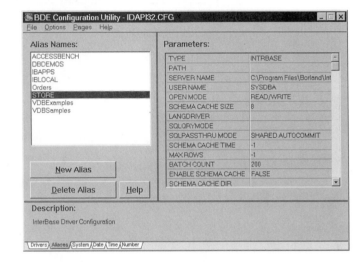

Next, click the New Alias button on the Aliases page. You should then see the Add New Alias dialog. Figure 1.17 shows where to key in a name for your new alias. Then select the SQL Links driver you wish to use in the dialog's Alias type field.

Figure 1.17.

Set up new aliases using the Add New Alias dialog.

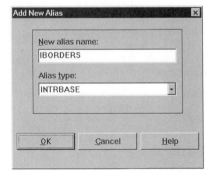

After you've named your alias and specified a driver type for it, click OK. At this point, you're ready to define additional alias-specific parameters as necessary. You'll at least need to specify a server name, and, depending on your selected SQL Links driver, you also might need to specify a user name, and possibly a database name. Figure 1.18 shows some sample parameters for an InterBase alias.

Figure 1.18.

You can define alias-specific parameters for SQL Links connections.

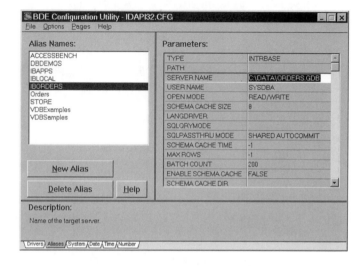

After you've finished defining your new alias, click File|Save to save your configuration to disk, and then exit the BDE Configuration Utility and return to IntraBuilder.

Opening a Table Using an SQL-Link Connection

Now that your SQL Links alias is defined, you're ready to open the database and access its tables from within IntraBuilder. Click the Tables tab in the IntraBuilder Explorer, and then select your new alias from the Look In drop-down list. At this point, you'll probably be prompted to enter a password, as Figure 1.19 illustrates.

Figure 1.19.

Most remote databases require an access password.

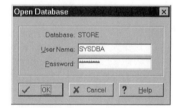

Key your password and click OK. You should then see the table contained in your database listed in the IntraBuilder Explorer, as shown in Figure 1.20.

Figure 1.20.
The IntraBuilder Explorer lists the tables in your SQL Links database.

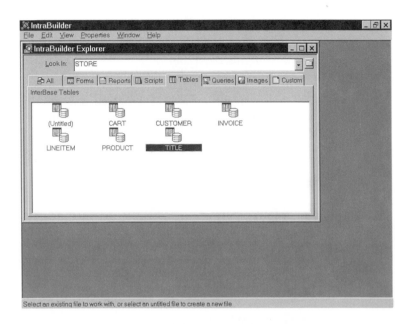

As with the ODBC data source–based connection, double-clicking any of the tables listed creates and runs a default edit form for the table, as you can see in Figure 1.21.

Figure 1.21.
You can double-click an SQL table to instantly create an edit form for it.

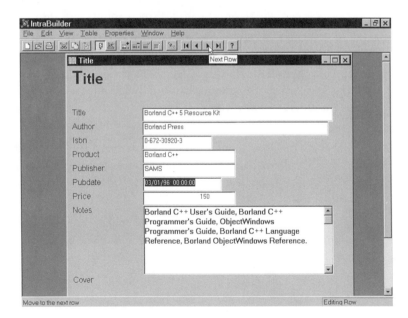

You've now successfully connected to and created a form for an SQL Links–based table. You can now close the edit form that IntraBuilder constructed for you. For more information about working with InterBase and SQL Links, see Day 21, "Building Client/Server Applications."

As you can see, opening tables over ODBC data source and SQL Links connections is quite painless. Add to this the ease with which you can build edit forms over those tables, and you have a development tool that is a pleasure to use.

The IntraBuilder Development Environment

In this section, I'll take you on a guided tour of the IntraBuilder development environment. Though you've already had a few excursions into the environment, you've yet to explore it in a comprehensive, step-by-step fashion. You'll do that next.

The IntraBuilder Explorer

As with Windows itself, the heart and soul of the IntraBuilder development environment is the IntraBuilder Explorer. From the Explorer, you can navigate IntraBuilder forms, reports, scripts, queries, and so on. If you close the Explorer and wish to reopen it, just select the IntraBuilder Explorer option on IntraBuilder's View menu. Figure 1.22 shows the IntraBuilder Explorer.

Within each page tab of the Explorer, double-clicking the left mouse button on an item opens it. For form objects, this means that IntraBuilder runs the form. For table objects, it means that IntraBuilder creates a default form (if one does not already exist) and runs it. Note that you can also press F2 while an object is selected to open it.

Double-clicking the right mouse button on an item opens it for modification. For forms, this means you're placed in IntraBuilder's Form Designer. For tables, you're placed in IntraBuilder's Table Designer. Note that you can also press Shift+F2 while an object is selected to open it in the Designer.

Right-clicking an object displays its shortcut menu. From this menu, you can do a number of things that are based on the type of object you've selected. Figure 1.23 shows the shortcut menu for form objects.

Figure 1.22.

Use the IntraBuilder Explorer to navigate IntraBuilder.

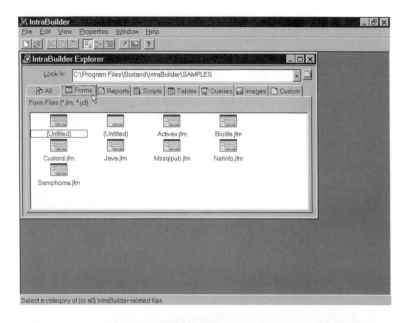

Figure 1.23.

You can right-click an object to display its shortcut menu.

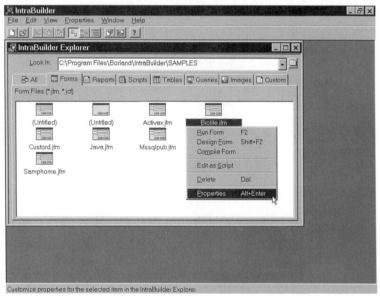

In keeping with the standard established by Windows 95, one element you'll always find on the shortcut menu of existing objects is the Properties item. Selecting it displays a variety of background information about the currently selected object, as Figure 1.24 illustrates.

Figure 1.24.

You can view an item's properties via its shortcut menu.

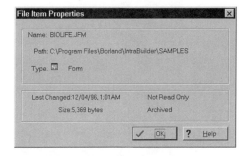

Note that you can also press Alt+Enter while positioned on an object to view its properties.

The IntraBuilder Explorer also supports drag-and-drop. When designing a report, for instance, you can drag a table object from the Explorer to the Report Designer, and IntraBuilder will add the table to the report.

Menus

As you can see, IntraBuilder includes the type of menu system you would normally expect in a Windows application. Though most things can be done without the need of menus, you'll have to use the menu system for some of IntraBuilder's less common tasks.

Six basic menus are available regardless of the page tab or type of object you currently have selected. These are the File, Edit, View, Properties, Window, and Help menus. Each one has submenus and items of its own, so I'll cover them separately.

File Menu

From the File menu, you can create new objects, edit and run existing ones, and perform other miscellaneous tasks such as database administration. Figure 1.25 shows the default File menu.

When you select the File menu's New option, you can create any of the object types that IntraBuilder supports. Note that Query objects come in two different flavors—Query Builder queries and SQL Statement queries. You can use the New submenu to create either of them. Figure 1.26 shows the New submenu.

1

Figure 1.25.

The default IntraBuilder File menu.

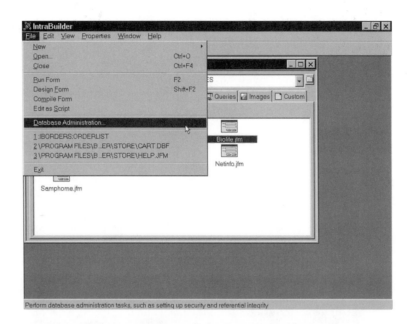

Figure 1.26.

You can create new objects using the File menu's New option.

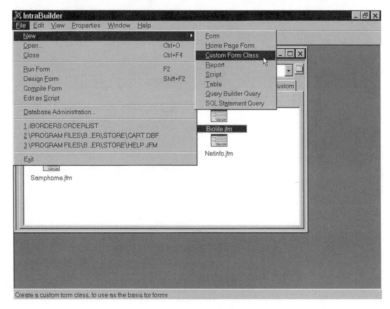

Another interesting option on the default File menu is the Database Administration item. Selecting it enables you to perform certain database administration tasks on local tables, as Figure 1.27 illustrates.

Figure 1.27.

Use the File menu's Database Administration item to manage your local databases.

 NOTE

The Database Administration dialog is sensitive to the current database. For example, the security options are not available when the table type is INTRBASE.

Keep in mind that the items on the File menu will change based on what type of object (if any) you are currently designing or running. For example, Figure 1.28 shows what the File menu looks like when a form is being edited.

Figure 1.28.

The File menu as it appears during form design.

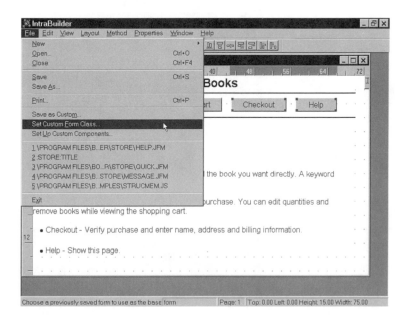

Edit Menu

By default, the Edit menu is fairly typical. It mimics what you'd expect from the Edit menu in any Windows application. (See Figure 1.29.)

Figure 1.29.

The Edit menu as it appears by default.

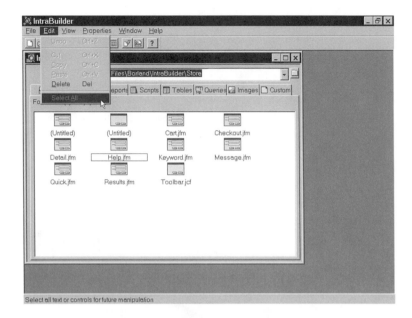

As with the File menu, things change dramatically when an object is being edited or executed. Figure 1.30 shows what the Edit menu looks like when a form is open in the Form Designer.

Figure 1.30.

The Edit menu as it appears during form design.

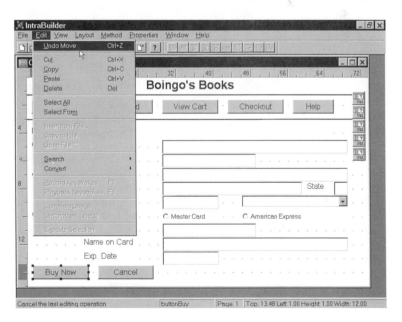

Using the Edit menu, you can cut and paste objects, search and replace text, record and play back keystrokes, and insert and save file fragments. You can even switch the case of selected text, jump to a given line number, and search for matching delimiters.

View Menu

By default, the View menu lists items that affect the appearance of the IntraBuilder development environment overall. Using the View menu, you can determine the types of icons viewed and how they're sorted, as well as what toolbar and palettes are visible. Figure 1.31 shows the options on the View menu.

Figure 1.31.

Changing the icon sort through the View menu.

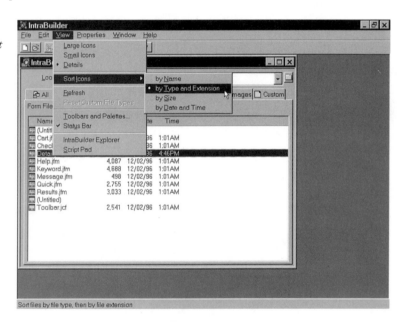

As with the other menus, the View menu changes to accommodate IntraBuilder's current state. Figure 1.32 shows its appearance during form design.

Window Menu

IntraBuilder's default Window menu is about what you would expect from any Windows application. You can tile and cascade windows, make a different window the current window, and generally navigate the currently opened windows on the desktop. Figure 1.33 shows what the Window menu looks like during form design.

Figure 1.32.

The View menu as it appears during form design.

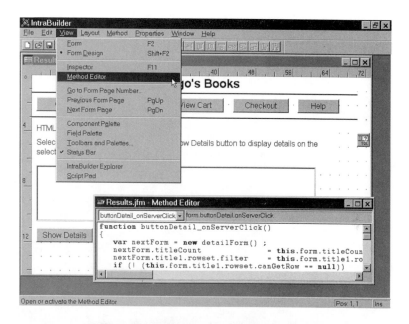

Figure 1.33.

The Window menu as it appears while a form is being designed.

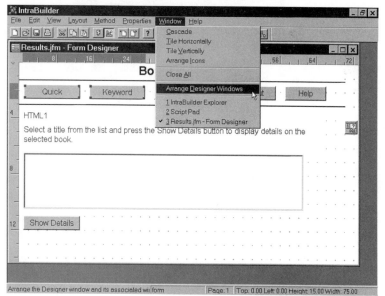

Help Menu

The one menu that doesn't change based on IntraBuilder's current state is the Help menu. From the Help menu, you can view both general and context-sensitive help, as well as language and keyboard help. Figure 1.34 shows the IntraBuilder Help menu.

Figure 1.34.

You can access a variety of different kinds of help from the IntraBuilder Help menu.

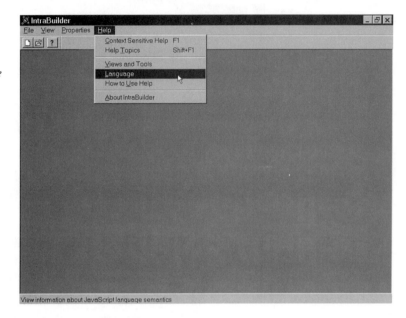

In addition to the six base menus, four additional menus show up when objects are being designed. These are the Layout, Method, Structure, and Script menus. I'll cover each of them separately.

Layout Menu

The Layout menu is displayed when either a form or report is being designed. It includes options for sizing and aligning components as well as applying an overall interface scheme to the form or report. Figure 1.35 shows the Layout options for adjusting the space between controls.

Method Menu

Like the Layout menu, the Method menu is displayed when a form or report is being designed. It includes options for creating and modifying method definitions, as well as editing and linking events. Figure 1.36 shows IntraBuilder's Method menu.

Figure 1.35.
You can adjust horizontal and vertical spacing using the Layout menu.

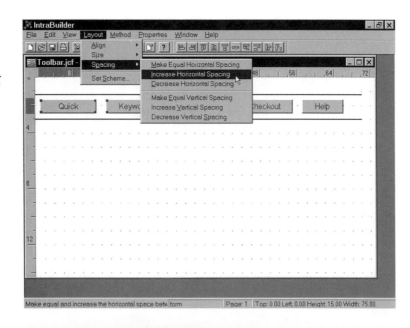

Figure 1.36.
You use the Method menu to manipulate methods and events.

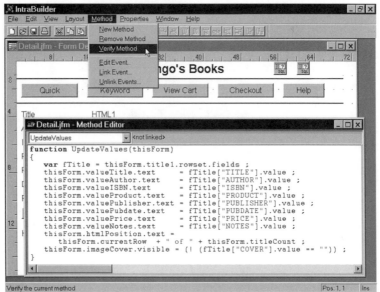

Structure Menu

IntraBuilder's Structure menu appears when a table object is being designed. It allows fields to be added, inserted and deleted from the table, as well as index creation and management. Figure 1.37 shows the Structure menu.

Figure 1.37.

IntraBuilder's Structure menu has options for defining fields and indexes.

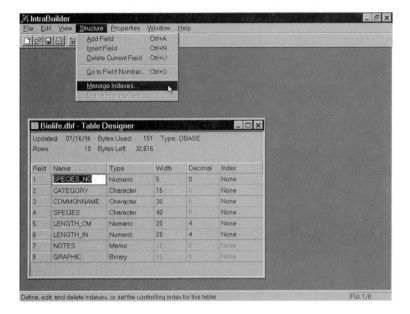

Script Menu

The Script menu appears when a script is being edited in the Script Editor. It includes options for running and compiling the script, as illustrated in Figure 1.38.

Figure 1.38.

Use the Script menu to edit and compile the current script.

Toolbars and Palettes

In addition to IntraBuilder's menu system, the program also provides a number of toolbars and palettes (floating toolbars). The availability and makeup of these toolbars varies based on what is currently going on in IntraBuilder. To find out what a particular toolbar button does, rest the mouse pointer over it momentarily. A pop-up hint window should display and describe the button's function. Figure 1.39 shows the Standard toolbar.

Figure 1.39.
The Standard toolbar.

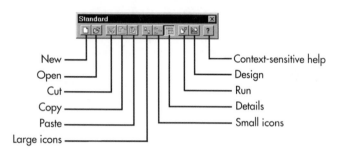

When a form or report is being designed, an Alignment toolbar opens with a number of new buttons. (See Figure 1.40.)

Figure 1.40.
The Alignment toolbar.

As you might expect, you can click the buttons on the toolbar to carry out their corresponding functions. For example, to open a form in the Form Designer, select it in the IntraBuilder Explorer, and then click the Design button. To run the form, click the Run button.

To activate the alignment buttons, select multiple objects on a form or report. You can then align the objects on their left, right, top, or bottom edges using the alignment buttons on the toolbar.

NOTE

Note that objects aligned this way will be lined up with the object that is outermost in the direction you're aligning. For example, if you align several objects on their left edges, they'll all be aligned with the leftmost object in the group.

When you're editing a table's data using IntraBuilder's default table viewer, a set of VCR-style buttons appears on the default toolbar. You can use these buttons to move around in the table.

Note the inclusion of the Previous and Next Form Page icons on the toolbar during design mode. These buttons enable you to move forward and backward through the pages in a multipage form or report.

The Component Palette

When designing forms or reports, IntraBuilder also displays the Component Palette by default. Figure 1.41 shows this palette.

Figure 1.41.

The IntraBuilder Component Palette.

The Component Palette contains a number of user-interface and data-access controls. When a report is being designed, the palette also contains several report-specific components, as Figure 1.42 illustrates.

Figure 1.42.

The IntraBuilder Component Palette as it appears during report design.

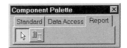

Unlike the buttons on the standard toolbar, the items in IntraBuilder's Component Palette are designed to be dropped onto other objects. To add a new button control to a form, for example, click the button control in the Component Palette and then click the place on the form where you would like to position the button.

The Field Palette

As Figure 1.43 illustrates, the Field Palette contains the fields currently available to a given form or report. If multiple tables have been added to the form or report, the Field Palette will have a separate page tab for each.

You can drop a new field onto a form or report by clicking it in the Field Palette and then clicking the form or report where you would like the field placed. If you drop the field onto a form, IntraBuilder will automatically drop a data-linked text control to service the field. If you drop it onto the detail band of a report, a new column will be added to the report containing the field's values from its host table.

Figure 1.43.

You can place table fields using IntraBuilder's Field Palette.

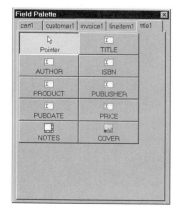

The Inspector

The Inspector is the last stop on our tour of the IntraBuilder development environment. In design mode, the IntraBuilder Inspector enables you to configure the characteristics of individual items via the Properties tab. You can bring up the Inspector either by pressing F11 while an item is selected or by selecting the Inspector option from the item's shortcut menu.

You can use the Inspector to set the attributes of a component, field, form, or report. As Figure 1.44 illustrates, the item's properties, events, and methods can be accessed via the IntraBuilder Inspector. Note that the Methods page is read-only. Use the Method menu to create or modify methods.

Figure 1.44.

The Inspector lets you configure items on forms and reports.

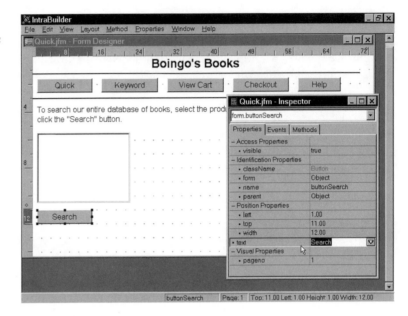

Summary

In this chapter, you learned to set up IntraBuilder database connections, you got acquainted with ODBC and SQL Links, and you learned to navigate the IntraBuilder Explorer. You also took a tour of the IntraBuilder development environment and learned about IntraBuilder's underlying architecture.

Q&A

Q What part of IntraBuilder is responsible for providing my Web pages with data from my database server?

A IntraBuilder brokers function as the "conduit" between your Web server and your database server. They communicate with your Web server using one of the three supported APIs—WINCGI, NSAPI, or ISAPI—and with your database server using the Borland Database Engine.

Q Besides an HTML 2.0 compatible browser, what other software or drivers will users need to access data-aware Web pages that I build using IntraBuilder?

A None.

Workshop

The Workshop section provides questions and exercises to help you get a better feel for the material you learned today. Try to answer the questions and at least think about the exercises before moving on to tomorrow's lesson. You'll find the answers to the questions in Appendix A, "Answers to Quiz Questions."

Quiz

1. What facility in IntraBuilder is used to edit forms?
2. What part of IntraBuilder allows you to navigate the various types of objects that IntraBuilder uses and produces?
3. What types of client/server DBMSs does IntraBuilder Professional support via SQL Links?
4. What types of client/server DBMSs does IntraBuilder Client/Server support via SQL Links?
5. How do you utilize Access databases in IntraBuilder applications?

Exercises

1. Create a new ODBC data source that references a database server or format that you would like to access from IntraBuilder.
2. Create a BDE alias that references either a local database or a database that lives on a database server; then open a table from the database in the IntraBuilder Table Designer.
3. Review the SERVER.HLP file that ships with IntraBuilder for specific information on setting up IntraBuilder to work with your particular Web server.

Day 2

The Sample and Pre-Built Solution Applications

by Ken Henderson

Today we'll explore the Samples and Solutions that ship with IntraBuilder. Samples are individual programs and data, such as forms and tables, included as examples with IntraBuilder. The Pre-built Solutions, on the other hand, are complete applications—some consisting of many individual forms and tables— that you can use just as they are or you can customize to fit your needs.

Finding the Samples

By default, IntraBuilder's Samples are located in the C:\ProgramFiles\ Borland\IntraBuilder\Samples folder. If you haven't already done so, fire up

IntraBuilder and click on the folder button to the right of the Look In drop-down list box. After the folder list is displayed, select the Samples folder under your IntraBuilder folder, as demonstrated by Figure 2.1.

Figure 2.1.

You can find the sample objects in IntraBuilder's Samples folder.

If you click the All tab, you'll see all the objects in the Samples folder. If you click one of the individual object type tabs, you'll see the objects that match the type you select. You can double-click an object to run it, or double-right-click it to open it in design mode. Figure 2.2 shows the Biolife.jfm sample form opened in design mode.

Figure 2.2.

Double-right-click a form to open it in the IntraBuilder Designer.

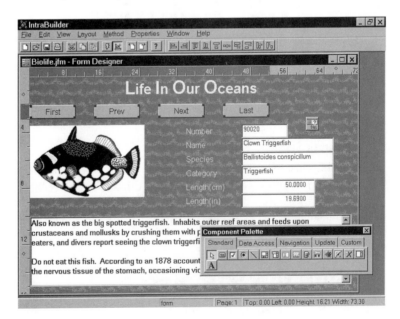

Running the Pre-Built Solutions

As with the Sample forms, the forms, reports, and other objects that make up IntraBuilder's Pre-built Solution applications can be opened by simply double-clicking them from the IntraBuilder Explorer. By default, the Solution applications are located in the `C:\Program Files\Borland\IntraBuilder\APPS` folder. Click the folder button to the right of the Look In drop-down list box, and then click the APPS folder. At this point, you should see a number of folders within the APPS folder. IntraBuilder comes with five Pre-built Solution applications: a guest book application, a contacts manager, an employee phone book, a security system, and a knowledge base. Click the guestbk folder within the APPS folder and then click OK.

As you can see, there are a number of individual objects within the guest book application. It consists of six forms, one report, and five images. The application tables reside in a separate folder.

NOTE

> IntraBuilder Professional and IntraBuilder Client/Server come with additional solution applications, including some Web utilities and an InterBase version of the Knowledge Base.

Opening Forms and Reports from the IDE

As mentioned earlier, you can run the forms and other objects that make up Solution applications by opening them in the IntraBuilder IDE (Integrated Development Environment). You can also open them via a JavaScript-enabled Web browser. Let's start with running them from the IDE.

Forms in the IDE

Double-click the `Guest.jfm` form to open it now. IntraBuilder runs the form, and you can access it just as you did the Sample forms earlier. Figure 2.3 illustrates what you should see.

Figure 2.3.

The Guest.jfm *form opened in run mode.*

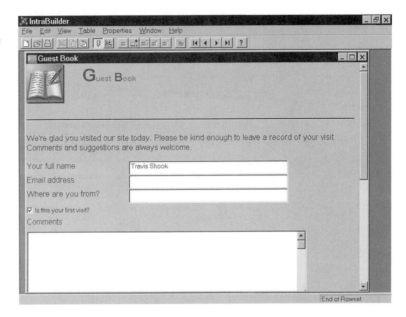

Reports in the IDE

You can also run and design the reports that are included with the Solution applications from within IntraBuilder. Close the Guest.jfm form and double-click the Entries.jrp report to run it. Figure 2.4 illustrates what you should see.

Figure 2.4.

You can open reports from the IntraBuilder IDE.

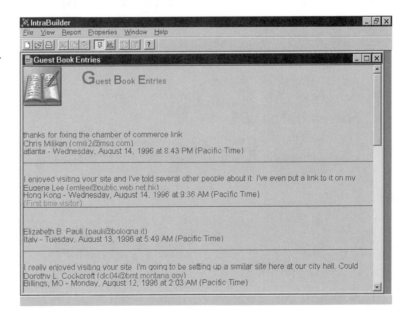

Switching from Run Mode to Design Mode

After an object has been executed from the IDE, you can easily switch to design mode by clicking the Design mode button on the IntraBuilder toolbar. This button is immediately to the right of the lightning bolt Run button on the toolbar. You can also press Shift+F2 to switch to design mode or select the object Design option on the IntraBuilder View menu.

Viewing IntraBuilder Forms and Reports in a Browser

There's a bit of setup that has to occur before you can open the Solution applications from your Web browser. Normally, this setup is done automatically when you install IntraBuilder. However, if you later install a new Web server, you'll have to configure it manually. Check this section if you have problems viewing your IntraBuilder forms and reports from a Web browser.

To begin with, you'll need to tell your Web server where it can find your IntraBuilder Server and the Solution INDEX.HTM file (the opening page of the Solution applications). To do this, follow these steps:

1. Make a note of the full path name to the IntraBuilder APPS folder. By default this is in

   C:\Program Files\Borland\Intrabuilder\APPS

2. Consult the IntraBuilder Server Help file for information on properly configuring your Web server and the IntraBuilder Server.

3. Typically, your Web server will limit folder access to those under its document root directory, but it can be configured to access other folders as well. Create a document alias called ibapps that your Web server can use to locate files in the IntraBuilder APPS folder by following these steps (for your particular Web server):

   a. Right-click the WebSite server icon and select WebSite server properties from the context menu. You can also double-click the WebSite Server Properties icon in the WebSite folder.

   b. When you are in the properties editor, click the Mapping tab.

   c. Type /ibapps/ in the Document URL Root field.

   d. Type C:\Program Files\Borland\IntraBuilder\APPS\ in the Directory field. (Obviously, you'll need to type a different path if you changed IntraBuilder's default installation folder.)

   e. Click the Add button, and then click OK.

   To Configure Netscape FastTrack 2.0, use the following steps:

   a. Execute the Administer Netscape Servers program.

   b. Click your server's link.

    c. Click the top frame's Content Mgmt button.

    d. Click the left frame's Additional Documents link.

    e. Type `ibapps` in the URL Prefix field.

    f. Type `C:\Program Files\Borland\IntraBuilder\APPS` in the Map to Directory field. (You'll need to type a different path if you changed IntraBuilder's default installation folder.)

    g. Click OK, and then click the Save and Apply button.

    h. Click OK on the confirmation message that appears momentarily.

Configure Microsoft Internet Information Server with these steps:

    a. Double-click the Internet Service Manager icon in the Microsoft Internet Server folder (or group if you're running under Program Manager). You should see the Microsoft Internet Service Manager window.

    b. Double-click your Web server's icon. Click OK if you're asked whether to start the server. You should then see the Service Properties dialog.

    c. Click the Directories tab and then click the Add button.

    d. Type `C:\Program Files\Borland\IntraBuilder\APPS` in the Directory field. (You'll need to type a different path if you changed IntraBuilder's default installation folder.)

    e. Type `/ibapps` in the Alias field.

    f. Click the Execute checkbox.

    g. Click OK, and then click the Apply button.

    h. Click Add once more and type `C:\Program Files\Borland\IntraBuilder\Server\` into the Directory field. (You'll need to type a different path if you changed IntraBuilder's default installation folder.)

    i. Type `/svr` into the Alias field, and then click the Execute checkbox.

    j. Click OK, and click the Apply button.

    k. Click OK again to exit the Service Properties dialog.

    l. Right-click your Web server's icon in the administration window and choose Stop from the context menu.

    m. Double-click the IntraBuilder Server icon. You should see a minimized IntraBuilder icon appear for the broker. In Windows NT 4.0, this icon will appear on the taskbar; under Windows NT 3.51, it will appear as a simple minimized icon on the Program Manager desktop.

    n. Right-click your Web server's icon in the administration window and choose Start from the context menu.

2

Forms in a Browser

After your Web server is properly configured, accessing forms via your browser is fairly straightforward. You'll begin by opening the INDEX.HTM file. To do this, type the URL of your Web server, followed by your ibapps alias and the filename INDEX.HTM, into your browser's URL entry field (it's labeled "Location" in Netscape Navigator and "Address" in Microsoft Internet Explorer) like so:

```
http://serveripaddress/ibapps/index.htm
```

In this syntax, serveripaddress is either the IP address of your server, or its name as specified on your DNS server or in your HOSTS file. If you've changed your Web server's port number (the default is 80), you'll need to specify it as well, like so:

```
http://serveripaddress:nn/ibapps/index.htm
```

In this syntax, nn is the port number you selected. If your server and browser are running on the same machine, you can use the localhost designation in place of the server's IP address, like so:

```
http://localhost/ibapps/index.htm
```

Figure 2.5 shows the INDEX.HTM page as it should appear in your browser.

Figure 2.5.

The Solution index page as it appears in Netscape Navigator.

After INDEX.HTM is opened, you can click any of the links to the Solution applications to view their forms and reports. Click the Guest Book link now to view the Guest.jfm form. Figure 2.6 shows what you should see.

Figure 2.6.

Guest.jfm *as it appears in Netscape Navigator.*

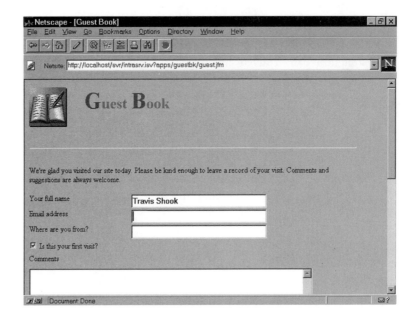

 TIP

You don't have to go through the INDEX.HTM page in order to access the Solution applications. You can go directly to a form or report page by simply keying in its full URL, like this:

`http://localhost/svr/intrasrv.isv?apps/guestbk/guest.jfm`

Perhaps this is a good time to explain what the ? is for. Users often get confused and try to use an alias such as /ibapps/ as part of the path to the .JFM after the ?. Web server aliases are only used before the ? (/svr/) or when accessing an HTML document (/ibapps/). The ? specifies that a parameter is being passed to intrasrv.isv.

Reports in a Browser

In addition to forms, you can also access IntraBuilder reports via your browser. To check this out, click the View Current Guest Book Entries link toward the bottom of Guest.jfm to run the Entries.jrp report. Figure 2.7 shows what you should see.

Figure 2.7.

Entries.jrp *as it appears in Netscape Navigator.*

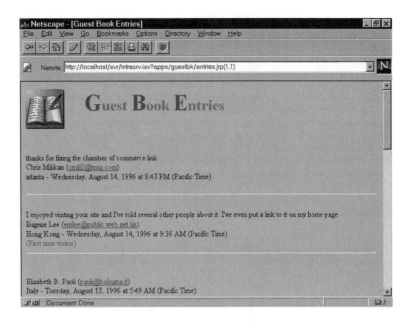

You can now return to the Solutions index page by clicking the Return to Home Page link at the bottom of the report page.

Now that you've seen how easy it is to access the Solution applications from your Web browser, you can tour each one of them separately. Let's begin with the Employee Phone Book app.

The Employee Phone Book

You can use the Phone Book application to easily access basic employee information, such as an employee's full name, phone extension, or department. This information is centralized on your Web server and can be accessed by anyone within your company or department with a browser. You can view the phone book sorted alphabetically by employee name or by department. Click the Phone List By Employee link on the IntraBuilder home index page to view it by employee name, as shown in Figure 2.8.

Figure 2.8.

Opening the Phone List By Employee report page lists employees alphabetically by name.

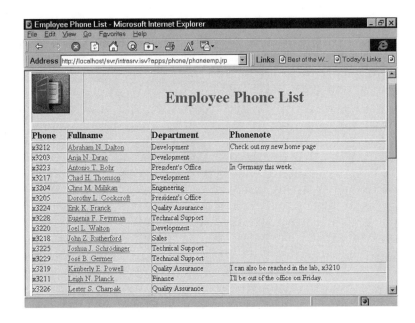

Now return to the home index page and click the Phone List By Department link. Figure 2.9 shows what you should see.

Figure 2.9.

The Phone List By Department report as it appears in Internet Explorer.

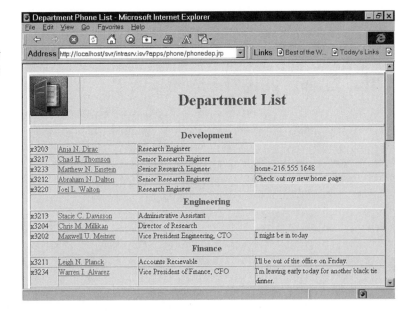

To view additional information about a given employee, click one of the employee name links on the report. Figure 2.10 illustrates what you should see.

Figure 2.10.

You can view information for a specific employee by clicking his or her link.

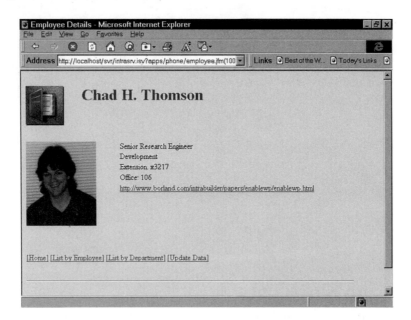

The name link references a document specific to the employee and includes a photo as well as other information.

The phone list reports consist of two different IntraBuilder reports, Phoneemp.jrp and Phonedep.jrp. You can open these reports in IntraBuilder to see how they're actually constructed.

If you inspect the lower portion of either report, you'll notice an Update link. This link enables you to update a given employee's phone book information. Click the update link to log in as illustrated by Figure 2.11. The login is part of the Solution application's security system. See Day 16, "Debugging and Error Handling," to learn how to integrate the security system into your own applications.

NOTE

To see how Update link works, you must run the phone list reports from a Web browser. The links are inactive within the IntraBuilder Designer.

Figure 2.11.

*Using the Login form
to get to the employee
Update form.*

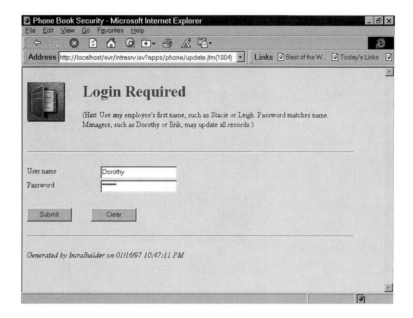

The Knowledge Base

Using the Knowledge Base application, you can build a "knowledge" database and then search it using a form. A knowledge database is simply a collection of facts or documents deemed important by an organization. These need not be related to one another in any particular fashion and tend to be rather freeform. You use the Knowledge Base app's search form to locate entries in the knowledge database and its update form to add, change, and delete those entries.

From the index page, click on the Document Administration link to open the Knowledge Base Update form. After you log in, the form will appear as shown in Figure 2.12. You can enter Mark as the name and password to complete the login.

After you've opened the Update form, you can enter a title, product, category, and set of keywords for knowledge base entries. Selecting the All option for either the product or category fields causes the document to show up only in searches looking specifically for All. You put the actual text of the entry in the TextArea box.

Figure 2.12.

The Knowledge Base Updates form lets you modify records in the knowledge base table.

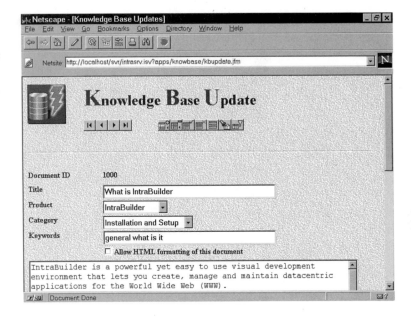

 NOTE

If you search the knowledge database using a keyword search, IntraBuilder will search both the title and keywords entries, so you need not list words from a document's title in its keywords field.

Checking the "Allow HTML formatting of this document" checkbox causes the knowledge base entry to be streamed directly to the client browser as normal text. Extra spaces and hard returns will be removed from the text as it's sent. Because the document is sent as HTML text, you can include HTML tags in it. Leaving this box unchecked will cause the document text to be sent as preformatted text. Of course, if you don't allow your document to be treated as HTML text, you'll need to be sure to format it yourself, placing hard returns as needed.

Note the database navigation and manipulation buttons at the top of the form. You can move to the first or last record in the database, and add, update, or delete individual records. If you make changes to an entry in the database, be sure to click either the Save or Abandon button when you finish.

You can use the New Filter button (which is the rightmost of the buttons at the top of the form) to restrict the documents that can be viewed. When you click New Filter, you're prompted for filter criteria. These criteria are similar to query-by-example criteria in that specifying them will restrict the rows you can access in the knowledge database. Figure 2.13 shows the New Filter criteria form.

Figure 2.13.

Enter criteria into the New Filter form to limit the entries you can see in the database.

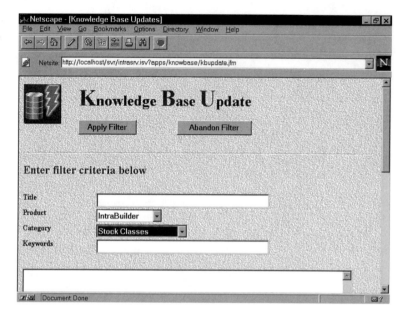

NOTE

The default Knowledge Base contains information for IntraBuilder only. Searching for information on other products will result in an empty result set. You can submit a blank search to restore the unfiltered view.

After you've specified your filter criteria, click the Apply Filter button to activate it. If you wish to cancel a filter (either the one you've just specified or a previous one), click the Abandon Filter button. Note that the filter you specify is not case-sensitive and will match field values from the left of each field (but you can't search for the middle or right of a given field).

You can use the New Query button to locate the next entry that matches a specified set of criteria. Unlike the filter facility, the query facility is designed to locate records, not restrict your view of them. After you specify your query criteria and apply them, you're positioned at the next record that meets the criteria.

Beyond updating the entries in your knowledge database, you also might need to make changes to the tables used to build the category and product lists shown on various knowledge base forms. Because no forms are provided in the Knowledge Base app for doing this, you'll have to edit these tables in the IntraBuilder designer itself. The names of the product and categories tables are Kbprod.db and Kbcat.db, respectively. You can simply double-click these tables (which are found on the All and Tables tabs in the IntraBuilder Explorer) to open them in IntraBuilder.

WARNING

The Pre-built Solution applications might cease to work properly if you make changes to the table structures. Be careful that you don't break the applications with changes to their underlying data.

You can search the knowledge database by clicking the Knowledge Base Search link on the home index page. Figure 2.14 shows what the search form should look like.

Figure 2.14.

The Knowledge Base Search form in Netscape Navigator.

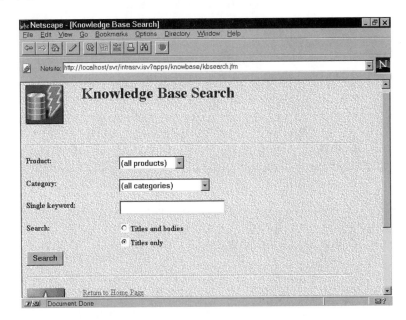

By using the search form, you can search using a particular category, product, or set of keywords. You could, for example, search for knowledge database entries that contain "IntraBuilder" in the product field and "How do I..." in the category field, as illustrated in Figure 2.15.

Figure 2.15.

*You can specify
individual products
and categories as
search criteria.*

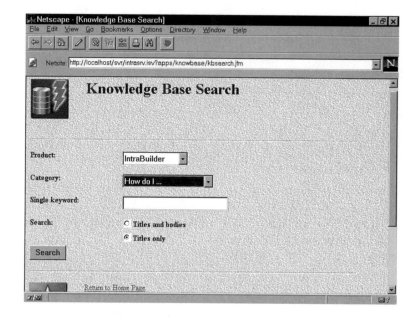

Beyond products and categories, you can also search the database using document keywords. As with the filter and query facilities on the Knowledge Base Update form, keyword searches scan document titles as well. In addition to document titles, you can tell IntraBuilder to search the document's text itself. Although the keyword search is case-insensitive when searching keyword lists and document titles, it *is case-sensitive* when searching the actual document text.

You can click the Search button to search the database for entries that match your specified search criteria. The search itself is performed by the Kbsearch.jfm form. Basically, Kbsearch creates an SQL SELECT statement, which is then passed to the Kbresult.jrp report for processing. After the SELECT statement is executed, Kbresult returns the rows from the knowledge database that match your criteria. Figure 2.16 shows what this output looks like.

The title of each document listed is a link to the document itself. You can click it to quickly jump to the related document, as illustrated by Figure 2.17.

Click the Return to Home Page link to return to the Solutions index page.

2

Figure 2.16.

The Kbresult.jrp *report lists the results of your Knowledge Base search.*

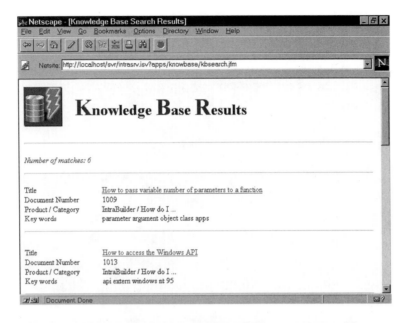

Figure 2.17.

You can access Knowledge Base articles from the Kbresults.jrp *report.*

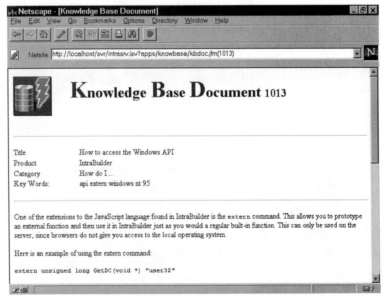

The Guest Book

The Guest Book application is used to enable visitors to log records of their visits to your Web site. Visitors can view other users' comments along with their own. Like a real guest book, the Guest Book application can provide valuable information regarding who's accessing your server.

Click the Guest Book link on the home index page to open the Guest.jfm form file. Figure 2.18 illustrates what it should look like.

Figure 2.18.

The Guest Book form in Netscape Navigator.

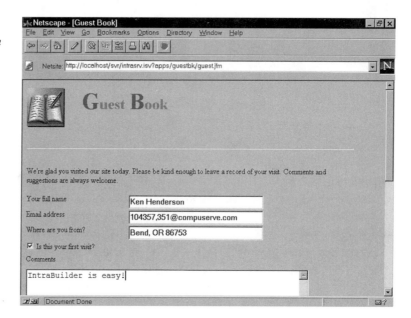

At this point, you can either enter your own guest book information or click the View Current Guest Book entries link to view a report form listing the entries on file. On the Guest.jfm form itself, you can specify your name and e-mail address, as well as your location. You can also specify whether this is your first visit to the site. After you've entered your basic information, you can key comments regarding your visit in the Comments box. When your entry is complete, click the Submit button to send it to the server.

Note that if you opt to make your own guest book entry before viewing the others, viewing the list of guest book records will show your entry along with the others, as shown in Figure 2.19.

Figure 2.19.

The current Guest Book entries in Netscape Navigator.

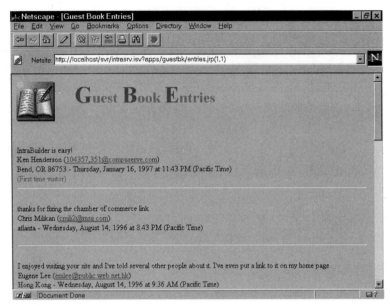

The report itself is contained in the file Entries.jrp, which you visited briefly earlier. You can open it in the IntraBuilder designer to see how it's actually constructed.

The entries in the report are listed in descending order based on the date and time of the visit. This means that the most recent visits will be listed first. If you have an entry in the guest book, it should be at the top of the list.

Each entry in the list of guest book records contains a mail link to the person who posted the entry. This means that you can click the mail link and send the person a message using an Internet mail program. After you finish exploring the Guest Book application, click the Return to Home Page link.

Summary

In this chapter, you learned how to locate and open the Sample forms and reports, and how to locate and open the pre-packaged Solution applications. You saw how to access applications both through IntraBuilder and via a browser. You also learned the specifics of the Employee Phone Book, Knowledge Base, and Guest Book Solution applications.

Q&A

Q Can I use the Solution applications included with IntraBuilder as they are? Do I owe Borland anything for using them?

A Yes, you can use the Solution applications just as they are—that's one of the reasons they're included with IntraBuilder. And, no, you do not have to pay Borland royalties for making use of them.

Q What types of database tables are in the Solution applications?

A Most of the Solution applications use Paradox tables. The contact manager uses an Access database. IntraBuilder Professional and IntraBuilder Client/Server come with an InterBase application and a Microsoft SQL Server sample form. Other sample forms work with dBASE tables.

Q Do the tables that service the Solution applications have to reside on my Web server?

A No, they do not. You can modify the forms and reports that make up the Solution applications to point to tables on an SQL server or to local tables located across a network.

Q What types of information can go into the Knowledge Base databases?

A You can use any type you like. Because you can edit both the products and the categories tables (Kbprod.db and Kbcat.db, respectively), you can customize the Knowledge Base app to meet your needs.

Workshop

The Workshop section provides questions and exercises to help you get a better feel for the material you learned today. Try to answer the questions and at least think about the exercises before moving on to tomorrow's lesson. You'll find the answers to the questions in Appendix A, "Answers to Quiz Questions."

Quiz

1. What key(s) do you press to open the currently selected form or report?
2. What Solution applications ship with IntraBuilder?
3. What's the full path to your IntraBuilder Solutions home page?
4. When searching the full text of knowledge database entries, is the search case-sensitive or case-insensitive?

5. What's the default Web server port number?

6. What's the name of the alias that you create so that your Web server can locate files outside its document root directory?

7. What's the difference between the Samples and Pre-built Solution applications?

Exercises

1. Open the Knowledge Base search form, Kbsearch.jfm, in the IntraBuilder Designer and also in your Web browser and compare the differences. What differences do you notice when opening the form in IntraBuilder versus opening it in your browser?

2. Run the Guest Book Entries report (Entries.jrp) using your browser, and then view the HTML source that IntraBuilder created for the report. (It's the Document Source option on the View menu in Netscape Navigator.) Note the HTML generated by IntraBuilder to produce the report.

2

Day 3

Forms, Part 1

by Ken Henderson

Today you'll learn two distinct methods for creating new forms. First, you'll create a simple form using the IntraBuilder Form Expert, and then you'll create one from scratch using IntraBuilder's Form Designer.

Going down both paths should give you a nice initiation into the mechanics of IntraBuilder form design. The method you choose when developing real applications will depend largely on the type of form you're building at any given time. Issues, such as the complexity of the form and whether it's database-related, will affect whether you use the Form Expert or build the form from the ground up. You even might use a combination of the two approaches. Keep in mind that forms built using the Form Expert can still be customized in the Form Designer.

The Form Expert

Let's begin by creating a form using the IntraBuilder Form Expert. Click the New button on the IntraBuilder toolbar, and then select Form from the pop-up menu, as illustrated by Figure 3.1.

Figure 3.1.

Click the New toolbar button to start a new form.

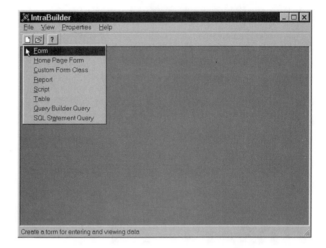

After you've selected Form, a dialog box appears asking you to choose whether to create the new form using the Form Expert or the Form Designer, as shown in Figure 3.2. Click the Form Expert button.

Figure 3.2.

You can create forms using the Form Expert.

There are six steps involved in creating a form using the IntraBuilder Form Expert. The first one is to select a table or query on which to base the form.

Creating a Simple BIOLIFE Edit/Entry Form

After you've clicked the Form Expert button, you'll be presented with a dialog box in which you can specify your new form's base table or query. By default, Paradox and dBASE tables are listed, along with any query files (those having .SQL or .QRY extensions) presently in the Look In directory. Click the folder icon to the right of the Look In drop-down list box and select the Samples subdirectory under your IntraBuilder base directory (which will probably be C:\Program Files\Borland\IntraBuilder\SAMPLES).

You should then see a list of tables and queries located in this directory. Select the biolife.dbf table and then click Next. Figure 3.3 shows the Look In list box.

Figure 3.3.

Select the BIOLIFE table as the basis of your new form.

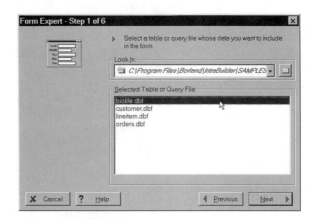

After you've selected your base table, the next step is to select which of its columns you'd like included in the new form. A dialog box like the one shown in Figure 3.4 is displayed, and you can choose which of the table's fields you want on the form. You can click the single right-arrow (>) to add individual fields, or you can click the double right-arrow (>>) to add all the fields to the form. Click the doubleright-arrow now to add all of BIOLIFE's columns to your new form, and then click Next.

After you've selected which columns to include, you're then asked to select a basic layout for the new form, as shown in Figure 3.5. You've got two choices: Columnar and Form Layout. Selecting Columnar Layout vertically aligns the table columns on the form. Selecting Form Layout places them next to each other in a multiple-row, horizontal format. Click Next to accept the default Columnar Layout for your new form.

Figure 3.4.

The Step 2 dialog as it appears when all fields have been selected.

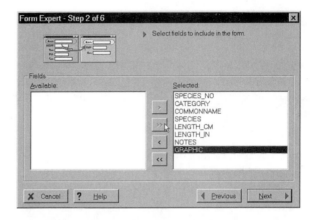

Figure 3.5.

Select the way you'd like your new form laid out.

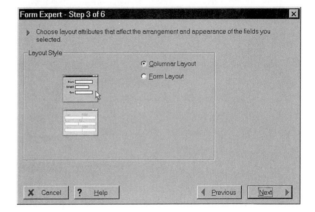

Using Color and Font Schemes

Now that the database underpinnings of the new form are in place, you're ready to specify some of its more visual aspects. You specify display attributes for the various items on the form in the fourth step of the six-step Form Expert process.

IntraBuilder groups font and color attributes into sets called "schemes." These are not unlike the color and font schemes available in Windows itself. IntraBuilder includes a number of ready-to-use schemes that you can make use of either directly or as the basis for new schemes of your own.

 An IntraBuilder *scheme* is a collection of font, color, and bitmap settings that you can apply as a set. They save you the trouble of having to set item attributes individually and help your apps adhere to a specific motif.

Each element of a form's basic appearance can be customized from the Step 4 dialog box. You can control the color and font of a form's title and labels. You can also specify a form's background bitmap and its base color. As you modify a form's display settings, the Sample area in the upper-left corner of the dialog box changes to reflect your selections.

Changing Colors

To adjust the color of a particular display element, either select a new color from the element's Color drop-down list or click the adjust button (the wrench) to the right of the list. Figure 3.6 illustrates the Choose Color dialog box that appears.

Figure 3.6.

Adjust colors using the palette in the Choose Color dialog box.

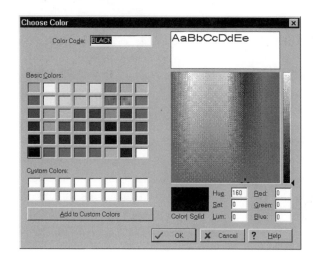

Changing Fonts

If you want to change the font specification for the title or labels placed on the form by the Form Expert, click either the Title or the Labels tab, and then click the adjust button (the wrench) to the right of the Font box. Figure 3.7 illustrates the Font dialog box.

You can set the form's background color and bitmap by clicking the dialog box's Form tab and then clicking either the Color or Background Image drop-down lists.

After you've finished customizing the new form to your satisfaction, you can save the selections you made as a custom scheme. If you click the Save As Scheme button, you'll be asked to name your new scheme for insertion into the IntraBuilder scheme list. Figure 3.8 shows the Scheme Name dialog box.

Figure 3.7.

Use the Font dialog box to change the display font.

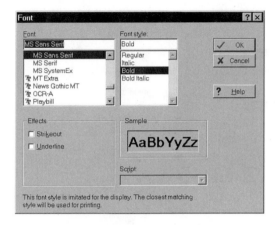

Figure 3.8.

You can add custom color and font schemes to those included with IntraBuilder.

For now, select one of the built-in schemes and click Next to continue. Figure 3.9 shows how IntraBuilder displays the chosen scheme in a window.

Figure 3.9.

IntraBuilder comes with a number of built-in schemes that you can use, or you can create your own.

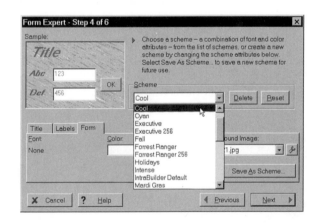

Row Operations

The fifth step in the Form Expert process consists of configuring the types of database operations that the new form is expected to support. These are referred to as "Row Operations" by the dialog box. There are three basic types of row operations:

- ☐ Navigation operations
- ☐ Update operations
- ☐ Search (or limit) operations

Navigation consists of moving backward and forward through the rows in a datasource. For example, you can include buttons that enable users to move to a table's first row, its previous row, its next row, and its last row.

Update operations consist of making changes to data in a table's or query's rows. You can include buttons that permit rows to be added, edited, or deleted. You also can include Save and Abandon buttons to allow the user to specify whether to save data changes permanently or to discard them.

Search or limit operations facilitate either locating a given row using a query expression or restricting the row view to a subset matching a set of criteria. Selecting the Query by Form option causes a New Query button to be added to the form. This enables the user to locate a given record by specifying search criteria on the form. Selecting the Filter by Form option includes a New Filter button on the form. This permits the user to restrict the rows displayed to just those matching a set of criteria. These criteria are specified by the user using the form itself.

Let's say, for example, that a user wants to find rows containing the species *Ginglymostoma cirratum*. She can click the form's New Query button, type Ginglymostoma cirratum into the SPECIES field, and then click the Run Query button. The form will then display the next row containing the species she specified. Likewise, if she wants to limit the rows visible on the form to just those of the category "Shark," she can click the New Filter button and key Shark into the CATEGORY field, and then click the Run Filter button. This will restrict the rows displayed to just those whose CATEGORY column contains "Shark".

Click the All button in the Row Operations panel to include all possible buttons on the form. If you select Buttons in the Control Type radio button group, you'll get buttons with text labels on your new form. If you select Images, you'll get buttons with graphic labels instead. The Location on Form drop-down list determines where the buttons actually appear on the form.

Linking Forms and Reports

The lower portion of the Step 5 dialog box includes entry fields for specifying other objects that you want to link to the new form. The Form Expert creates links to the objects you specify when it creates your new form. If you opt to create button controls on the form (in the Control Type radio button group), you'll get buttons labeled Run Form or Run Report. If you select image controls, you'll get an icon for each linked object instead.

Figure 3.10 shows the completed dialog box from Step 5. Click Next to proceed to the final Form Expert dialog box.

Figure 3.10.

In Step 5 of the Form Expert, specify which buttons to include.

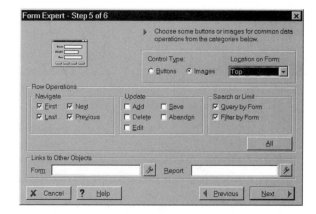

Now that you've given the Form Expert all the information it needs to create your new form, you can either run the new form or open it in the IntraBuilder Form Designer. Click the Run Form button (as illustrated in Figure 3.11) to run your new form.

Figure 3.11.

After the Form Expert has built a new form, you can either run it or open it in the Form Designer.

When you elect to run a newly created form, IntraBuilder requires that you save the form to disk first. Key in a name for your new form and click Save, as Figure 3.12 shows.

NOTE

The forms you create in IntraBuilder have the extension .JFM by default. This stands for JavaScript Form (in case you've forgotten, JavaScript is IntraBuilder's native language). Likewise, reports use the .JRP extension by default. This stands for JavaScript Report.

Figure 3.12.
IntraBuilder requires you to save new forms before running them.

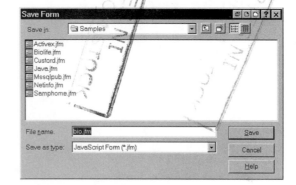

After you've saved the file to disk, IntraBuilder runs it. Figure 3.13 shows what your new form might look like at runtime. Note that I've maximized it here so that all its buttons are visible.

Figure 3.13.
Your new form as it might appear when run.

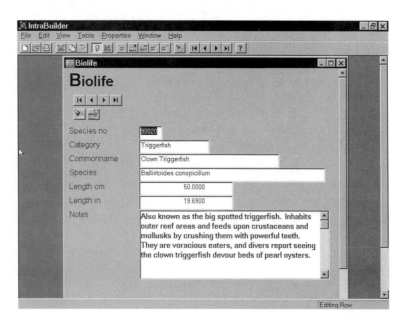

The Form Designer

As mentioned previously, the second major task you'll undertake today is the building of a new form from scratch. To do this, you'll work in IntraBuilder's Form Designer instead of its Form Expert. Before you start, make sure you are in the Samples folder. Begin by clicking New on the IntraBuilder toolbar and then selecting Form from the pop-up menu. When the dialog box appears asking whether to start the Form Expert or Designer, click the Designer button. Figure 3.14 shows what your new form should look like.

Figure 3.14.

A new form as it initially appears in the Form Designer.

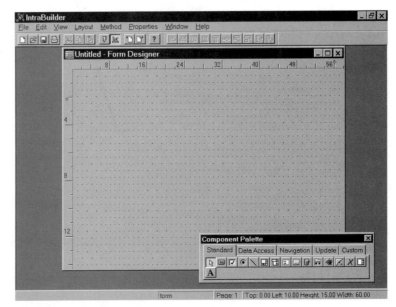

Selecting a Datasource

As when building a form via the Form Expert, the first order of business is to choose a datasource on which to base your new form. You'll set this up using the IntraBuilder Query component, regardless of whether you wish to base your form on an entire table or use a custom SQL query.

Click the Query component now on the Component Palette (it should be the third component from the right of the palette if the toolbar is docked at the top of the screen) and then click your form to drop the component onto it. The actual location of the Query component on the form is unimportant because it will not display at runtime.

After you've done this, either press F11 or right-click the Query component and select Inspector from the content menu to bring up the IntraBuilder Inspector. You use the Inspector to set an object's individual attributes. In this case, you'll need to set only two properties of the Query component. First, click the Query's `sql` property and set it to `select * from "BIOLIFE.DBF"`. This causes all the columns in the Biolife table to be returned when the query is executed. Next, click the Query component's `active` property and set it to `true`. This actually executes the query and causes its result set to be available to your form. Figure 3.15 shows what the form should look like thus far.

Figure 3.15.

Your new form as it appears with the Query component in place.

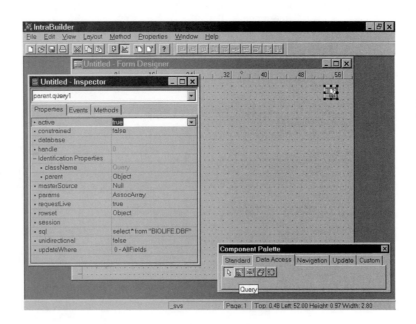

Now that your Query component is in place, click the Save button on the IntraBuilder toolbar to save your work before going further. Name the new form `bio2`.

TIP

An easier way to add queries to a form is to drag them from the IntraBuilder Explorer and drop them on the Form Designer. When you drop a table on a form, IntraBuilder sets the `sql` and `active` properties for you. The drag-and-drop approach also creates more intuitive query names such as `biolife1`, instead of `query1`. The first table you drop on a form is set to the form's rowset.

Dropping Fields onto the Form

The next step you'll take is to drop the fields returned by your Query component onto your new form. If the Field Palette isn't visible already, click the View|Field Palette option to make the palette visible. After the Field Palette is on-screen, drag each of the fields it lists onto the form, positioning them toward the horizontal center of the form, each one below its predecessor. Align the fields along their left edges and size the NOTES and GRAPHIC fields so that they look sensible. Note that you may need to widen your form to achieve the desired effect. Notice that each field already displays data. This is because you set the Query component's active property to TRUE earlier. Because the Query is active (open), its result set is available and displayed by the IntraBuilder Designer.

After you've added some fields, close the Field Palette. Figure 3.16 shows what the form should look like after adding some fields.

Figure 3.16.

Your new form with its fields in place.

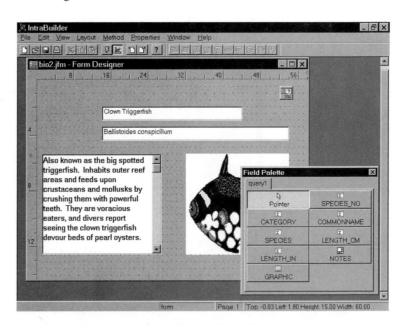

<table>
<tr><td>**NOTE**</td><td>The IntraBuilder Designer automatically sizes fields you drag from the Field Palette onto a form or report. Sizes are based on the field's length in its host table. This saves you the trouble of having to size controls individually and ensures that there is sufficient editing room in each field.</td></tr>
</table>

Setting Up Your Labels

Now that the fields are in place, the next step is to set up field labels. In IntraBuilder, you set up labels and other types of static form text using the HTML control. Locate the HTML component in the IntraBuilder Component Palette and drop one to the left of each of your field components. Bring up the Inspector for each HTML control and set its text property to the name of the field to its right. Don't worry about specifying fonts or colors right now—you'll do that later. Figure 3.17 illustrates what you should see thus far.

Figure 3.17.

Setting up field labels using the HTML component.

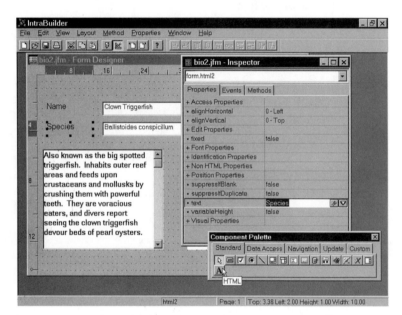

TIP

A great way to know which labels go with which field components is to open the field components' host Query from the Designer. (You did this earlier by setting its active property to true.) This will cause data from the underlying database to be displayed in your field components, which will help you decide what to label them.

Establishing a Form Rowset

Before you begin dropping Button components onto the form, you'll want to set the form's rowset property. The rowset property defines the form's base datasource. By establishing a form-wide rowset, you can reference your Query component indirectly and more flexibly from other components, such as the Button components you'll be setting up soon. If you later change the form's datasource to a different component, you'll have to change only one reference to it—the form's rowset property—as opposed to modifying every data-related component on the form.

Click anywhere on the background of the form, and then bring up the Inspector and set the form's rowset property to parent.query1.rowset, as shown in Figure 3.18.

Figure 3.18.

Specify a form-wide rowset for maximum flexibility.

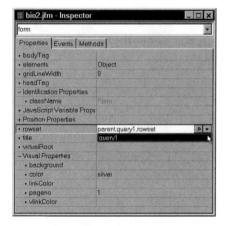

Setting Up the Form's Buttons

The next step in building your new form is to set up its buttons. These buttons enable the Biolife table to be navigated and searched.

All told, you'll need six buttons to provide access to all the data facilities your form will support. You'll need to set each button's caption via its text property in the Inspector. You'll also need to set each button's onServerClick event using the Inspector. The onServerClick event specifies what the button should do when clicked. To set it, you'll click the onServerClick event on the Inspector's Events page, and then key in a simple code block that will execute when the button is clicked. Table 3.1 summarizes the buttons you need to drop and their required property settings.

3

Table 3.1. The 10 button components and their settings.

Text	Code for onServerClick
First	`{;form.rowset.first()}`
Previous	`{;if (!form.rowset.next(-1)) form.rowset.next();}`
Next	`{;if (!form.rowset.next()) form.rowset.next(-1);}`
Last	`{;form.rowset.last()}`
New Query	`{;with(this) {if (form.rowset.state==5)`
	`{text="New Query";form.rowset.applyLocate();} else`
	`{text="Run Query";form.rowset.beginLocate();}}}`
New Filter	`{;with(this) {if (form.rowset.state==4)`
	`{text="New Filter";form.rowset.applyFilter();} else`
	`{text="Run Filter";form.rowset.beginFilter();}}}`

TIP

Instead of building buttons from scratch, you can use preprogrammed custom controls. A complete set of rowset navigation and modification controls are in the EXPERT.CC custom control library that comes with IntraBuilder. These controls provide buttons and images for all the options shown in Table 3.1.

Figure 3.19 shows what the form looks like with its buttons in place.

WARNING

Remember that, unlike most scripting languages, JavaScript (IntraBuilder's scripting language) is case-sensitive. Be sure to enter the code blocks above exactly as they are listed, or you'll have problems.

Figure 3.19.

Your new form as it appears after you've added navigational and search buttons.

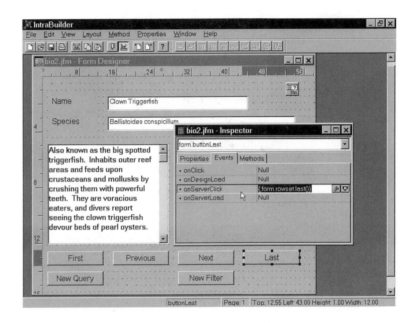

Before moving further, I should probably regress for a moment and discuss the code blocks listed in the preceding paragraphs in more detail. Understanding them more fully will give you a greater insight into how things work in IntraBuilder.

Take, for example, the code block associated with the Previous button, `{;if (!form.rowset.next(-1)) form.rowset.next();}`. The rowset object's next method is called and passed a parameter of -1. This has the net effect of moving the current row pointer backward one row in the datasource. That said, why do you then need the if logic? The reason you must test the return value of the next(-1) call is that it might fail, and, if so, it will leave the row pointer at the beginning of the rowset, prior to the first record. That's why the next() method is called (without the -1) to move the row pointer back to the first row if the attempt to move to the previous row fails. You'll see this technique employed in the code block for the Next button, as well.

Note the code blocks associated with the New Query and New Filter buttons. Look, for example, at the code associated with the New Query button:

```
{;with(this) {if (form.rowset.state==5) {text="New
&Query";form.rowset.applyLocate();} else {text="Run
&Query";form.rowset.beginLocate();}}}
```

What does the this in the code block refer to? It references the object that initiated the event. In this case, that's the New Query button. with this permits the references to the button's text property to be *unqualified*—that is, not to require direct references to their host objects. Instead of saying button1.text=, you can just say text=.

Notice the way that the code block switches the text and function of the button based on the current state. If the button is clicked and a query is not already being entered, the button's text changes to Run &Query, and the beginLocate() method is called. This puts the form in a special state that enables query values to be entered into field components. If the button is clicked while the form is in this special state, the applyLocate() method is called (which causes the query to be processed) and the button's text is set back to New &Query. This technique essentially enables one button to perform two different functions. It keeps the user interface simple and intuitive.

NOTE

> Notice that the New Query button's accelerator key is the same regardless of whether its caption is New Query or Run Query.
> This is a good idea if you opt to provide this type of dual-function button in your own apps. It alleviates the confusion that might be caused by alternating accelerators.

Setting the Form's Visual Elements

Now that your form's buttons are set up, you're ready to move on to some of the less critical aspects of the form. In this section, you'll establish a title for the form, the colors and fonts used for the form's labels, and a background bitmap for the form itself.

Begin by clicking the form's background and then selecting its title property in the Inspector. Set the form's title property to Biolife2. Next, drop an HTML component onto the form and position it in the upper-left corner. Size the control so that it forms a vertical rectangle to the left of your label components. Set its name property to TITLE. Next, set its text property to the following string:

```
<H2><Font Size="+2">B</Font>iolife2</H2>.
```

NOTE

> IntraBuilder includes many properties on HTML controls that are not currently supported in Netscape Navigator or Internet Explorer. For example, the rotate property allows you to rotate text. The rotation only takes effect when running with the IntraBuilder Designer.

Specifying the title component's text property using an HTML H2 tag (rather than keying in literal text) gives you more control over the appearance of the label. In this case, you have increased the size of the first character of the Biolife2 label by two points in order to make it stand out. Figure 3.20 illustrates what your form should look like thus far.

Figure 3.20.

Your form as it appears with an HTML title.

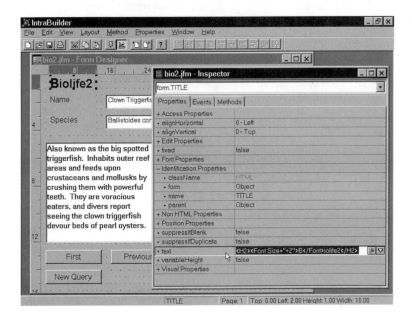

Now that your form's title component is established, you're ready to set the color and font scheme that you want the form to use. Select Layout|Set Scheme. Just as when you constructed a new form using the Form Expert, you're able to set the colors and fonts of the items on the form, as well as the background bitmap of the form itself, in one easy step. After the Set Scheme dialog box appears, select one of the built-in schemes, then click Apply, followed by OK. Figure 3.21 shows what your new form might look like if you apply the Oceanographer scheme.

NOTE

The background bitmap that you select here is a small JPEG file that is automatically replicated to fill the height and width of the displayed form. Your forms will load faster because backgrounds are synthesized at the client rather than downloaded as large graphics.

3

Figure 3.21.

Applying a color and font scheme to the form.

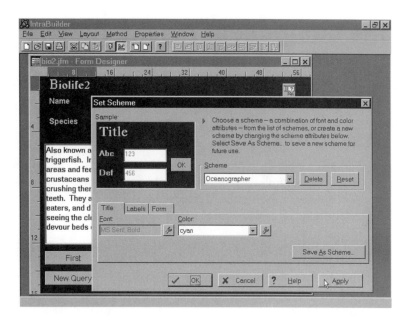

Running the Completed Form

Your new form is now complete. Click the Save button on IntraBuilder's standard toolbar to save your work before proceeding. After your work is saved to disk, click Run on the toolbar to run your new form. Figure 3.22 approximates what you might see.

Figure 3.22.

After you've completed a new form, you can run it by clicking the Run button.

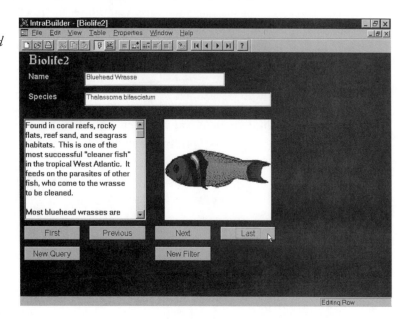

The Component Palette

Now that you've learned the "ins and outs" of dropping components to create IntraBuilder forms, let's explore IntraBuilder's Component Palette to see what controls are actually available to you.

Standard Controls

Although some components are available only under certain circumstances, there are a number of controls that are always available when you're designing forms. You'll find these components on the IntraBuilder standard toolbar. The next few sections list the components on the standard toolbar and the purpose of each one.

Button

Button components enable you to set up specific actions to occur when an area of the form is clicked. You can set the label (or bitmap) that is displayed on the button's face, and you can set the action that is to occur when the button is clicked.

CheckBox

CheckBox components enable you to provide the user with the ability to select True or False type values. They can also be used to select multiple items from a list of choices. For example, you might use CheckBox components to enable a user to select what items (from a small list of fixed choices) he or she wants to order. You can set the label that is to appear on the CheckBox as well as the action that is to occur when it's clicked. You can also set the component's `datalink` property to specify the table field the component will display/modify.

Radio

Radio components enable you to prompt the user for a single choice from a list of alternatives. Just like the pushbuttons on old car radios (thus the name), selecting one button deselects all others. You can set the label that appears on the control as well as its underlying data field.

Rule

The Rule component is used to display a horizontal line on a form. It usually serves to break a form visually into smaller segments. You can adjust the thickness of the line via the component's `size` property.

TextArea

TextArea components enable you to display/edit text of virtually any size in a scrollable window. You can configure a TextArea component's underlying data field via its `datalink` property, and you can set the text it displays via its `value` property.

Select

The Select component is analogous to the standard Windows combo box control. It enables you to make a selection from a list of items by clicking a list to display it and then clicking an item on the list. You can set its underlying field via its `datalink` property, and you can specify the items that it lists via its `options` property. For example, if you want to create a simple three-item list, you might specify the following value for the `option` property: `array {"one", "two", "three"}`. This would cause the entries `one`, `two`, and `three` to appear in the list displayed by the component.

Text

The Text component enables textual data to be entered and displayed. When you dropped field components from the Field Palette onto the new form you built in today's lesson, IntraBuilder actually placed Text components onto the form and linked them to the fields in your Field Palette. That is, you didn't actually drop separate field components onto the new form, even though IntraBuilder gave the illusion of that happening. Instead, IntraBuilder created Text components configured so that they referenced your fields.

Image

You use the Image component to place graphics on your Web page forms. These can either be static graphics that you set up at design time, or can be dynamically linked to graphics fields in database tables. You can also set up Image controls that perform special functions when clicked—as an alternative to standard text and button controls. IntraBuilder supports a number of different graphics formats. Table 3.2 lists the supported formats.

Table 3.2. IntraBuilder supported graphics formats.

Abbreviation/Extension	Description
BMP	Bitmap
EMF	Enhanced Windows Metafile
EPS	Encapsulated PostScript
GIF	Graphics Interchange Format
JPEG, JPG	Joint Photographic Experts Group
PCX	PC Paintbrush
TIF, TIFF	Tag Image File Format
WMF	Windows Metafile
XMP	X-Bitmap

Note that IntraBuilder converts graphics formats that are not typically supported by Web browsers (BMPs, for example) to the GIF format (the most popular Web graphic format) before sending them to the browser.

Reset

The Reset component is used to clear a Web page form of user input. By including a Reset button on a form, you provide a way for a user to clear the entries he's made and start over.

Password

You use the Password component to enable the entry of hidden text. This component is usually used with passwords and login-type information. It's virtually identical to the standard Text control with the exception that, when characters are typed, it displays asterisks rather than the characters themselves. Note that, as with Text components, you can link Password components to table fields.

JavaApplet

A JavaApplet component consists of a resizable area on a form (similar to a graphic) in which a Java applet can be implemented. Java applets are programs written in Java, Sun Microsystem's object-oriented, platform-independent programming language. When a Java-compatible browser jumps to a Web page containing a Java applet, the applet's code is downloaded from its location on the Internet to the browser and executed. This enables Web pages to break out of the page orientation of the World Wide Web, to an extent, and behave more like "real" applications.

3

Follow these steps to add a JavaApplet component to a form:

1. Drop a JavaApplet component onto your form and size it to the approximate size the applet requires.

2. Set the component's width and height properties to match the applet code. (You can determine the area required by the applet by inspecting its code.)

3. Enter an absolute or relative URL to the Java applet into the component's codeBase property. For example, you might use

   ```
   http://java.sun.com/java.sun.com/applets/JackhammerDuke
   ```

4. Enter the name of the Java applet's access function into the component's code property in the Inspector. For example, you might enter

   ```
   JackhammerDuke.class
   ```

Hidden

You use the Hidden component to store a value in a Web page's header and return it to the server. This value can consist of just about anything and is not seen by the user. It travels to the Web server when the form is submitted.

ActiveX

The ActiveX object is a container for Microsoft's multilanguage scripting technology and is very similar to Java applets. Though ActiveX is touted as being language independent, Web pages that use ActiveX controls will run only under Microsoft's Internet Explorer and its Windows 95 and Windows NT operating systems. So, though it may be language independent, it's still very much platform dependent.

Follow these steps to add an ActiveX object to a form:

1. Drop an ActiveX component onto your form and size it to the approximate size the applet requires.

2. Set the component's width and height properties to that of the applet code.

3. Enter an absolute or relative URL to the ActiveX control or application into the component's codeBase property in the Inspector.

4. Enter the name of the ActiveX applet's access function into the component's code property.

SelectList (a.k.a. the ListBox)

The SelectList component is similar to the standard Windows listbox control. It enables you to make a selection from a fixed list of items. You can set its underlying field via its datalink property, and you can specify the items that it lists via its options property. You can configure whether the control enables multiple items to be selected via its multiple property, and you can access the component's selected item(s) via its selected array property.

HTML

The HTML object is used to place text on a Web page form. Full HTML tag functionality is included, as are support for font and color settings and links to other pages.

Data Access Objects

The next set of components to examine are those having to do with databases. You use Data Access objects to include data on your forms and configure the form's interaction with its underlying database objects.

Query

The Query component is your chief means of linking database tables with IntraBuilder forms. Using its sql property, you specify the tables and columns you want available to your form. Then, after you've opened the Query (by setting its active property to true), you can drag the fields returned by your Query from the Field Palette onto a form.

You have three options for setting up the sql property. First, you can key your SQL code right into the property in the Inspector. Second, you can load an SQL script file (.SQL) from disk. Third, you can load a Query Builder file (.QRY) from disk (or use the Query Builder to create a new one on-the-fly).

If you elect to use a Database component on a form, you can reference it via the Query component's database property. Click the database property's drop-down list to select from the list of available Database components.

Database

Though it's optional, by making use of the Database component in your applications, you have greater control and more flexibility with your forms' database access. Because Query components can't reference remote databases directly (such as Sybase, Oracle, and so on), you'll have to include a Database component if you wish to access them. Also, including a Database component enables you to use several advanced database features such as cached updates, index creation, and table duplication.

Session

The Session object is also optional, but making use of it in your forms enables you to place each user of your page on a separate thread. This is useful for ensuring that record locking works properly. After you've set up a Session object, you reference it from a Database component. The Database object, in turn, is referenced by a Query component. The net result is that each user's entire chain of database access occurs on its own thread.

Summary

Today you learned to create forms automatically by using the Form Expert, and manually by using the Form Designer. You learned about the relationships between the various objects, as well as how they interact on live data forms. You also took a brief tour of the IntraBuilder Component Palette.

Q&A

Q Can forms that have been generated via the Form Expert be modified in the Form Designer?

A Yes, forms built using the Form Expert are normal forms, just like the ones you build from scratch.

Q How do I make a Query component a form's default datasource?

A Set the form's rowset property to reference the Query component's rowset property.

Q Is it necessary to include a Database component in order to access databases?

A Only client/server and ODBC-based databases require that you include a Database component on your forms. Local files (Paradox and dBASE tables) can be accessed directly from the Query component.

Q What if I want to simply key in a few HTML tags? What component should I use?

A Use the HTML component. Rather than keying straight text into its text property, type your HTML tags instead.

Q Can IntraBuilder use graphics file formats not supported by Web browsers?

A Yes, all formats not traditionally supported by Web browsers are converted to the Graphics Interchange Format (GIF) before being sent to the browser.

Workshop

The Workshop section provides questions and exercises to help you get a better feel for the material you learned today. Try to answer the questions and at least think about the exercises before moving on to tomorrow's lesson. You'll find the answers to the questions in Appendix A, "Answers to Quiz Questions."

Quiz

1. What property do you use to set up the items displayed by the Select and SelectList objects?
2. Where do you set a form's background bitmap?
3. Where is the record pointer left if you call the next() function at the end of a rowset?
4. What component provides a Query component with access to SQL DBMSs?
5. What property of the Text component is used to link the component to a field in a table?

Exercises

Add some additional objects to the forms you designed today. For example, you might add a Rule control to the Biolife2 form to separate your data entry fields from the form's buttons. Another fun thing to try might be to add a Java applet to your new page. You can find several of these at http://java.sun.com/java.sun.com/applets.

Day 4

Forms, Part 2

by Ken Henderson

Today, you'll delve more deeply into the task of constructing IntraBuilder forms. You'll build on the knowledge you acquired in Day 3, "Forms, Part 1," regarding form construction and the ways that components interact with one another, including the following:

- ☐ Sizing and aligning a form's objects
- ☐ Setting up multi-page forms
- ☐ Moving objects between pages
- ☐ Creating custom form classes
- ☐ Creating and using your own custom components

Layout Tools

The Layout menu is visible only when you're designing a form or report. It includes options for changing the appearance of the form or report currently open in the Designer. Using the Layout menu, you can align controls with one another, size controls relative to each other, change the spacing between controls, and apply font and color schemes.

Aligning Controls

Essentially, there are two ways to align controls in IntraBuilder. The first way is through the use of the Align control buttons on the standard toolbar. The second way is through the use of the Align option on the Layout menu. In either case, you begin by selecting the controls you want to align.

 NOTE

> You can select multiple controls in the Designer by dragging a rectangle around them or by clicking the first one and Shift-clicking any additional controls.

After you select a group of controls, you have a variety of alignment options. You can choose any of the following alignments:

- ☐ Align controls on their left edges.
- ☐ Align controls on their right edges.
- ☐ Align controls on their bottom edges.
- ☐ Align controls on their top edges.
- ☐ Position controls at a form's horizontal center.
- ☐ Position controls at a form's vertical center.
- ☐ Position controls at the horizontal center of the selected group of controls.
- ☐ Position controls at the vertical center of the selected group of controls.

To see how this works, reload the Bio2 form you created yesterday and select some of the Text controls. After you've selected them, click the Right alignment button on the standard toolbar (it's the button with the vertical bar on the right). You should see the selected controls realigned so that they all share the same right margin, as illustrated by Figure 4.1.

Figure 4.1.

Align buttons on their left, right, top, or bottom edges.

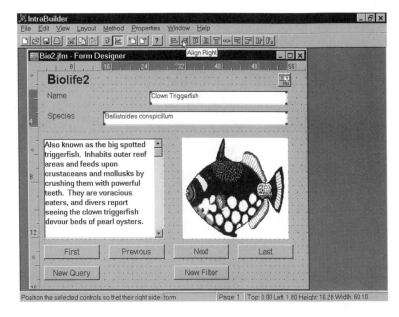

Now, while the Text controls are still selected, click the Layout|Align|Align Left option in the IntraBuilder menu system to return them to their former positions. (Your Text controls should have been left-aligned initially if you constructed the Bio2 form as shown on Day 3.) Figure 4.2 shows what the form should again look like.

Figure 4.2.

Realigning controls to the left after experimenting with alignment.

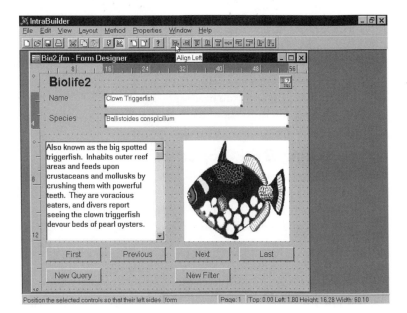

Sizing Groups of Controls

Sizing a group of controls works much the same way as aligning them. Select the controls you want to resize and select Layout|Size. You have the following four options when sizing a group of controls using the Layout menu:

☐ Size their widths to that of the widest component in the group.

☐ Size their heights to that of the tallest component in the group.

☐ Shrink their widths to that of the narrowest component in the group.

☐ Shrink their heights to that of the shortest component in the group.

There are two easy ways to size a group of controls. One is the way just mentioned: the Layout|Size menu selection. The other way is to change the width property of the controls in the Inspector. You can do this by first selecting the group and then pressing F11 to call up the Inspector. In the Inspector, change the value of the width property to adjust the widths of the selected controls. Changing the width of all the controls at once might or might not result in what you want, but at least it's easy to do.

Placing Controls Using the Grid

IntraBuilder provides a nifty grid facility for helping you align controls. When you have the Snap to Grid option turned on in the Form Designer, moving a component causes it to jump (or, *snap*) to the nearest horizontal or vertical grid.

When to Use the Grid

Obviously, when you are dropping onto a form a number of controls that you want to be aligned in an intuitive and systematic fashion, a grid can be quite helpful. However, grids can get in the way of making minor adjustments to controls. If you want to move a control only slightly, having it jump to a nearby grid line can be annoying. In these cases, you should turn off the Snap to Grid option (on the Properties|Form Designer Properties menu).

Changing Grid Properties

To change the way that grids behave, use Properties|Form Designer Properties on the IntraBuilder menu. You can configure whether or not a grid is displayed, whether or not items snap to it, and how fine or granular the lines on the grid are (that is, how close the grid's horizontal and vertical lines are). Figure 4.3 shows the various grid options you can specify.

Figure 4.3.

*Set grid options with
the Form Designer
Properties dialog box.*

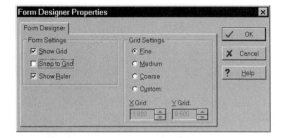

Working with Pages

IntraBuilder enables you to build multi-page forms. These translate into multi-page Web pages when accessed with a browser. Adding a new page to an existing form is simple: Just click the Next Form Page button on the IntraBuilder toolbar. Every time you do this from a form's last page, a new page is added.

Switching Pages Through the Form Designer

You can move backward to previously created pages by clicking the Previous Form Page button also on the toolbar. You also can set the current page number by using the pageno property of the base form class. Setting the pageno property in the Inspector changes the current form page.

The Global Page

Note that page zero has a special meaning among the pages in a multi-page form. It's known as a *global* page because any component whose pageno property is set to zero shows up on *every* page in a multi-page set. Page zero also shows the contents of all the other pages, layered one on top of the other. Of course, this could look pretty bizarre if you didn't already know that this is how things work. By displaying all the controls on all pages at once, you can more easily align controls between pages. You can ensure that they don't overlap controls on the other pages.

Moving a Control to Another Page

There are a couple of ways you can move a control or set of controls from one page to another. You can do this either using the Inspector or via the Windows Clipboard. I'll explain each technique in the next sections.

Moving Controls Using the Inspector

Moving a control or group of controls using the Inspector is as simple as changing any other property in the Inspector. Select the controls you want to move, and then bring up the Inspector (by pressing F11) and set the pageno property to the target page. Figure 4.4 shows how to make the buttons appear on all pages by moving them to page zero.

Figure 4.4.

Set the pageno *property in the Inspector to move between pages.*

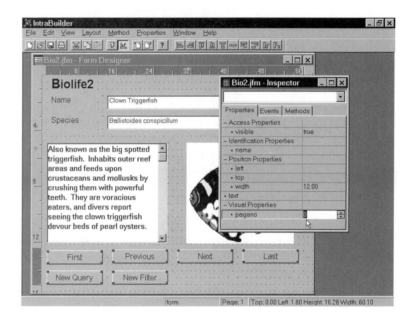

Using Cut and Paste

You can also move controls from page to page using the Windows Clipboard and these steps:

1. Select the controls you want to move (by dragging a rectangle around them or Shift-clicking the ones you want to select).

2. Cut the selected controls to the Clipboard (by pressing Ctrl+X or selecting Edit|Cut).

3. Switch to the target page and paste the controls from the Clipboard to the new page (by pressing Ctrl+V or selecting Edit|Paste).

Using Code Blocks to Select Pages

You might find that you want to change a form's current page while the form is running (while a user is browsing it). The easiest way to change pages at runtime is with a code block. To do this, follow these steps:

1. Drop two buttons onto your form.

2. Set the label of the first button to something such as Page Up and the label of the second to Page Down.

3. Set the pageno property of both buttons to zero.

4. Set the onServerClick event of the first button to

   ```
   { ; form.pageno -= 1 }
   ```

5. Set the onServerClick event of the second button to

   ```
   { ; form.pageno += 1 }
   ```

Figure 4.5 shows the form with page navigation buttons.

Figure 4.5.

You can switch pages at runtime using code blocks.

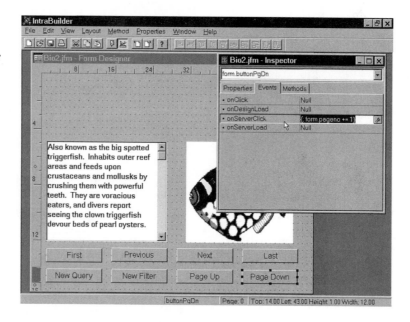

WARNING

IntraBuilder remembers the current page in a multi-page form when you save the form to disk. If you then make the form available on your Web server, users will be presented with the page that was current when you last saved the form. This could be somewhat confusing, especially if page zero is the page they see. For this reason, be sure to set a form's current page to page one before saving it. (Do this by setting the form's pageno property to 1.)

Custom Components

IntraBuilder enables you to create custom components and add them to the Component Palette for use in forms and reports. You base a custom component on an existing component, giving it property values, event handlers, and methods that you want to reuse. You might, for example, configure a set of buttons for navigating a form's rowset and then save them to the Component Palette for use on other forms. When you later drop them onto a form, the text property and onServerClick event of each button would already be set—so you wouldn't have to reset it.

Setting Up Custom Components

To set up a new custom component, follow these steps:

1. Select the control or controls on which you want to base your new component(s).

2. Select File|Save As Custom and supply a class name and a filename for your new component. The file should have the extension .CC.

3. If you want to add the component to the Component Palette, make sure the Place in Component Palette checkbox is checked. Figure 4.6 shows the Save as Custom dialog box.

Figure 4.6.

Use the Save as Custom dialog box to create new custom components.

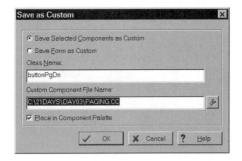

Using Custom Components

After you add a custom component to the Component Palette, you can use it like any other component. You'll notice that the properties, event handlers, and methods that you established for a custom component before saving it already are in place when you drop the component onto a form. This saves you from having to reset commonly used settings for a number of similar controls.

Custom Form Classes

You can create custom forms to provide consistency between the forms within an application and between applications. You might, for example, configure a special background bitmap that all of your forms share. You would begin by creating a custom form class and then using it with your forms as you build them.

Creating a Custom Form Class

You can take any of these three basic approaches to create a custom form class:

☐ Use File|Save as Custom to save the current form as a custom form class.

☐ Use the Custom Form Class Designer to create a custom form class. You access this expert either by clicking the New button and selecting the Custom Form Class option or by double-clicking the second (from the left) blank form component on the IntraBuilder Explorer's Forms page.

☐ Code the custom form class definition manually in JavaScript.

Custom form files have an extension of .JCF. When you get ready to save a custom form class, you'll need to supply a class name for the new class definition, as well as a base filename for the file in which it is to be saved to disk. Figure 4.7 illustrates the process of saving a custom form class.

Figure 4.7.

You can create custom form classes on which to base other forms.

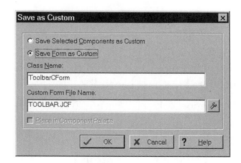

Using a Custom Form Class

You can set the custom form class on which to base a new form by selecting File|Set Custom Form Class. As you can see in Figure 4.8, you're required to specify the name of the file containing the custom class definition. From this, IntraBuilder extracts the name of the custom form class. After you've set up a custom form class as the basis for a new form, the new form inherits the properties of the custom form class.

Figure 4.8.

Base one form on another by specifying a custom form class.

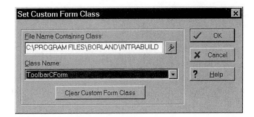

Clearing a Custom Form Class

You can clear a form's custom form definition by using the Set Custom Form Class dialog box. Select File|Set Custom Form Class and click the Clear Custom Form Class button in the ensuing dialog box. See Day 9, "Creating a Common Look and Feel," for more information about custom form classes.

Summary

In this chapter you learned how to construct more sophisticated forms and how controls interact with one another. Specifically, you discovered how to align controls with one another and how to size a form's controls. You also saw the usefulness of the Form Designer's grid and how to configure it. You finished up by learning how to set up and traverse multi-page forms and how to create and use custom components and forms.

Q&A

Q When I attempt to align two controls along their left edges, which control is considered the base control?

A The leftmost control. This is also true when aligning controls on their other edges. The control that is farthest in the direction you are aligning will serve as the base control; the other controls will line up with it.

Q When I align a set of controls to the "relative" horizontal center of a form, where are the controls actually aligned?

A They are aligned with the horizontal center of the selected controls.

Q What is the difference between a control and a component?

A Controls are components that the IntraBuilder Server renders as visible HTML controls in a browser. Other types of components include data access objects and report objects.

Q Can multiple custom components be added to the Component Palette in a single step?

A Yes; simply select them before clicking File|Save as Custom.

Workshop

The Workshop section provides questions and exercises to help you get a better feel for the material you learned today. Try to answer the questions and at least think about the exercises before moving on to tomorrow's lesson. You'll find the answers to the questions in Appendix A, "Answers to Quiz Questions."

Quiz

1. What sorts of things can be embedded in custom components for reuse on other forms?
2. What are the three methods of creating a custom form class?
3. What are the two methods for selecting a group of controls?
4. What should you always do prior to saving a multi-page form?
5. What is the purpose of page zero of a multi-page form?
6. What sorts of things does a new form inherit from a custom form class?
7. What's the easiest way to add a custom component to the Component Palette?
8. What happens to components you drop onto page zero of a multi-page form?
9. What's the name of the form class property that you change to switch to a different page in a multi-page form?
10. What are some potential uses of custom form classes?
11. What components show up when you're viewing page zero in a multi-page form?

4

Exercises

1. Construct a form hierarchy using custom form classes.

2. Lay out a set of buttons that perform the navigational, update, and search functions of the Bio and Bio2 forms that you built earlier this week; then save these buttons as custom components and build a new form using them.

3. Set up a multi-page form and add controls to several of its pages. Then drop onto the form the buttons that enable the current page to be switched at runtime. Save and run your new form and experiment with moving from page to page while the form is running.

4. Change the Bio2 form you built in Day 3 to be oriented horizontally rather than vertically. Use the Align and Size options on the Layout menu to organize your components on the form.

5. Set up a custom form class for a new form and clear the custom form class reference from the new form.

Day 5

Reports

by Ken Henderson

Today you'll explore the details of building reports with IntraBuilder. As we did with forms, we'll approach report building from two different directions. First you'll learn to build reports the "easy" way, using the Report Expert. Then, you'll learn to construct them from scratch, using the Report Designer. Learning to use both methods should provide you with valuable experience in the details of IntraBuilder report design. The approach you take when building real-world reports will vary based on your needs.

Today's tasks consist of

☐ Creating reports using the Report Expert

☐ Creating reports from scratch

☐ Grouping reports

☐ Setting up report aggregate fields

☐ Formatting reports to give them a more polished look

The Report Expert

If you haven't already done so, start IntraBuilder now and click the Reports tab in the IntraBuilder Explorer. After the Reports page is visible, click the New button on the IntraBuilder toolbar and select Report from the shortcut menu. You'll then be asked whether to create the new report using the Report Designer or the Report Expert. Click the Expert button to begin the seven-step process of building a new report using the Report Expert.

Selecting a Rowset

As illustrated by Figure 5.1, the first order of business is to select a table or query for your new report. This can be a table, SQL script, or query generated by Query Builder. You can tell the Expert where to locate these objects by selecting a directory folder in the Look In drop-down list. For our purposes, make sure that the Look In list points to the SAMPLES directory under your main IntraBuilder directory and double-click the BIOLIFE.DBF table to select it.

Figure 5.1.

Begin a report by adding a table or query.

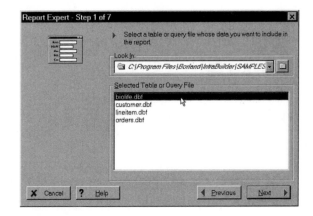

Selecting a Report Type

After you've selected a table or query, you're ready to choose which type of report you'd like to build. You have two choices. You can build a report that includes detail-level information or one that includes summary information only. Click Next to accept the default and include detail rows on the report. Figure 5.2 shows the second step of the Report Expert.

Figure 5.2.

You can create either detail-level or summary reports.

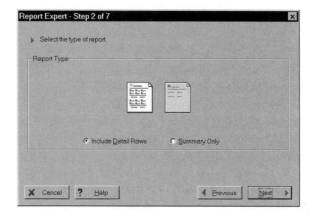

Selecting the Fields to Include

Now that you've specified both your base table and what type of report to create, you're ready to choose the fields you want to include on the report. Step 3 presents a dialog box in which you can select which fields you want on the new report. Select the CATEGORY, COMMONNAME, SPECIES, and GRAPHIC fields. Figure 5.3 shows the Report Expert's Step 3 dialog.

Figure 5.3.

You can specify which fields to include on the report.

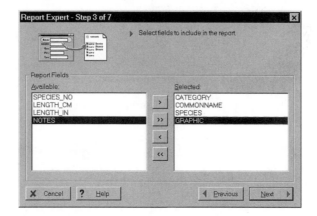

TIP

You can double-click a field to move it from the Available to the Selected list or vice versa.

Selecting Group Fields

After you've identified the fields that are to appear on the report, you're ready to select the report's grouping fields. Click Next to proceed to Step 4.

The dialog box presented in Step 4 is very similar to the one shown in Step 3. A list of fields is displayed, from which you can select grouping fields for the report. Selecting a field for grouping causes the report to be sorted on the field. First and foremost, this means that the rows displayed on the report will be ordered using its grouping fields. In addition, you can link the report's subtotals to specific grouping fields so that they return totals based on them. For example, suppose you have a CUSTOMER table that you want to list in a report. You might group the report by its State field. Your customer list would then be ordered alphabetically by state, and subtotals and summary fields could be rendered for each state.

Notice that BIOLIFE's GRAPHIC field is missing from the list. This is due to the fact that it's very difficult to derive a value for BLOB data types such as graphics and free-form text. This makes them unsuitable for grouping and summarization on reports. Note, however, that this limitation doesn't prevent you from including BLOB fields in report detail.

Double-click the CATEGORY field now to select it as a grouping, as illustrated by Figure 5.4. After you've done this, click the Next button.

NOTE

> Notice that you can choose to order each grouping in either ascending or descending order. To specify the ordering for a particular grouping, click it in the Selected list and click the Ascending or Descending radio button in the lower-right of the dialog. Each grouping can have its own ordering designation, so feel free to order each group individually.

Figure 5.4.

Selecting a field for a group band.

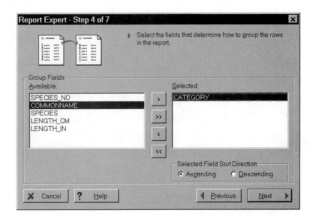

Setting Up Summary Fields

Beyond merely ordering the report, you can use groups to summarize and aggregate your report's detail data. The Report Expert's Step 5 is where you do this.

 An *aggregate* is a summary field—a subtotal or other summation of your data. If you total, count, or otherwise summarize a field on a report, you aggregate it.

You need to do three things to set up a summary field:

1. Select the field that you want to summarize or aggregate.
2. Select the aggregate operation that you want to perform on it.
3. Select the grouping level for the new summary field.

 NOTE The aggregate operations available to you vary based on the type of field you're summarizing. For non-numeric data, you're limited to calculating the minimum or maximum value in a set or to simply counting them. For numeric data, you can also total the values in a set of values or determine its variance or standard deviation.

Click the CATEGORY field (if it isn't already selected) and select the Count operation in the Aggregate Operation drop-down list. Next, ensure that the CATEGORY field is selected in the Selected Group list and click the right arrow (>) to add your summary definition to the Select Summary list. Figure 5.5 shows what the completed dialog box should look like.

Figure 5.5.

You create report summary fields in Step 5 of the Report Expert.

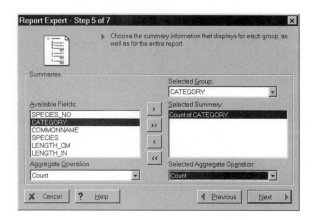

After you've defined the Count of the CATEGORY summary field, click Next to continue.

Specifying a Layout

Though the Report Expert consists of seven steps, Step 6 is actually the last one where you configure what the report will look like. Step 7 is reserved for deciding whether to run the report or load it in the Report Designer; you don't actually make any changes to the report.

In Step 6, you specify a number of details regarding the final appearance of the report. For example, you can decide whether to include the current date and the page number on the report. You can specify whether to arrange the report in a tabular or columnar fashion. You also can specify a report title, and you can decide whether to print one row per page or print them one after another in a continuous fashion. All these details dramatically affect the report definition you end up with, so it's important to understand what they do.

The best way to understand the impact of the various settings is to try them out. Let's make a few changes to the defaults presented in the Step 6 dialog. The first thing you'll change is the report's title. The default title should be Biolife. Convert it to uppercase by changing it to BIOLIFE. Next, change the report from its default tabular layout to the columnar layout. Figure 5.6 shows the dialog box for the sixth step.

Figure 5.6.

You can specify a number of report attributes in Step 6 of the Report Expert.

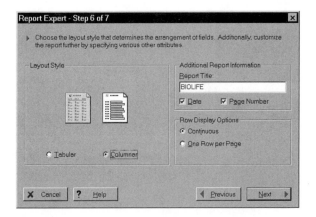

After you've completed Step 6, click Next to proceed to Step 7 and click the Run Report button to run your new report. As with the Form Expert, you'll be asked to supply a name for the new report before it's executed so that it can be saved to disk. Name the report BIOLIFE and click Save. Figure 5.7 shows what your new report will look like.

Figure 5.7.

The Report Expert allows you to build complete reports with minimal effort.

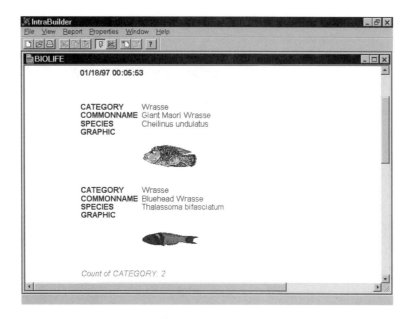

After the report is on-screen, you can use the page buttons on the IntraBuilder toolbar to move around in the report. You can either move forward to the next page or backward to the first page of the report. Note that IntraBuilder supports moving backward only to the *first* page of the report; you can't, for example, move backward from page three to page two.

If you want to print the report, click Print on the IntraBuilder toolbar. You can print just the current page or opt to print all pages. Close the report when you're done viewing it and return to the IntraBuilder Explorer.

The Report Designer

Having quickly whipped out a report using the Report Expert, you're now ready to build one from the ground up. Begin by clicking the New button on the IntraBuilder toolbar and selecting Report. This time, click the Designer button in the ensuing dialog box to start the IntraBuilder Report Designer. As illustrated by Figure 5.8, you're immediately presented with a blank report form. The blank report is visually divided into two areas—the header/footer area and the detail area. The detail area is a StreamFrame object and is the inner of the two rectangular areas that you see on the blank form. A StreamFrame object is simply a container for streams—report data—on your reports. Dropping items into the header/footer area will cause them to be printed in the report's page header or footer. Dropping them into the detail StreamFrame will cause them to be printed as part of the report's detail data.

Figure 5.8.

*A blank report form
showing the group
pane.*

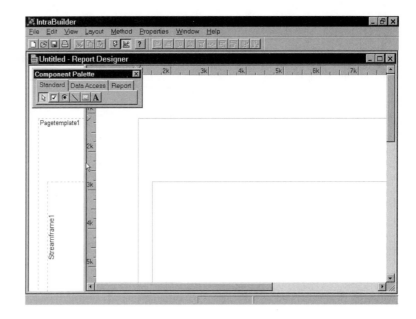

 TIP   You can get a better view of the report bands by opening the group
             pane. By default, this pane is closed. Open it by moving the divider
             from the left edge of the Report Designer.

Setting Up a Query

Begin by dropping a Query object onto the report surface. The actual location of the
component is unimportant, because it won't be visible when the report is run. Next, right-
click the Query component and choose the Inspector option on the shortcut menu. Select
the Query's sql property and set it to

```
select * from 'BIOLIFE.DBF' order by CATEGORY
```

 WARNING   You need to create the report in the folder that contains the BIOLIFE
                    table. You will not be able to activate the query if the Explorer Look In
                    folder is not set to the Samples folder.

Next, click the object's `active` property and set it to `true`. This will open the table and make its fields available for placement on the report. You can now close the Inspector and return to the Report Designer.

The `order by CATEGORY` clause lets you set up the report to be grouped by the `CATEGORY` field. This will cause a group break each time the `CATEGORY` field changes in the rowset. If the rows returned from the `BIOLIFE.DBF` table aren't ordered by the `CATEGORY` field, you'll get nonsensical group breaks and inaccurate group aggregates on your report.

If the table had an index on the `CATEGORY` field, you could leave out the `ORDER BY` clause and set the rowset `indexName` property. Setting the `indexName` is faster than using an `ORDER BY` clause when using dBASE and Paradox tables. The BIOLIFE table does not come with any predefined indexes.

TIP

> You can also add the query by dragging the BIOLIFE table from the IntraBuilder Explorer. This will set the `sql` and `active` properties for you. If you use the drag-and-drop method, you will need to deactivate the query to edit the SQL command and add the `ORDER BY` clause.

Placing Fields on the Report

The next step is to open the Field Palette so that you can place fields on the report. Right-click the report surface and select Field Palette on the shortcut menu. You should then see a palette containing the fields in the `BIOLIFE.DBF` table. Drag the `CATEGORY`, `COMMONNAME`, and `SPECIES` fields onto the detail `StreamFrame`. Orient them horizontally, in a side-by-side fashion. You might want to widen the resulting Text controls to prevent the field values from wrapping. Figure 5.9 shows the result of adding three fields from the Field Palette.

NOTE

> You can move a column and its heading by moving just the column. When you do this, the column's heading will automatically move with it. If, on the other hand, you move the column's heading first, the column itself will stay put.

5

Figure 5.9.

*Adding fields from
the Field Palette.*

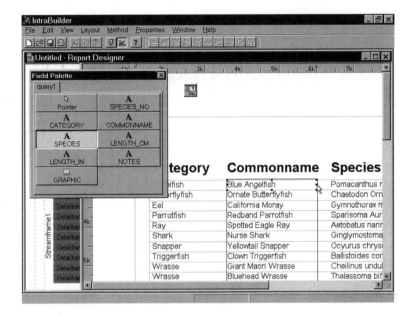

Grouping the Report

You add groups to reports by using the Group object. Click the Group object now in the IntraBuilder toolbar and drop it within the page template.

You should immediately notice that dropping the Group object onto the report has had the effect of also creating a header object and a footer object, which correspond to the group. Click the HTML control that serves as the label for the header (it should contain the text Header Text for Group1) and delete the control. This will keep your group from having a label in the header, which is what you want.

Next, bring up the Inspector and select form.StreamSource1.Group1 from the drop-down list. Set the groupBy property to the CATEGORY field. As I mentioned when we first began building it, the report will be grouped by the CATEGORY field. You establish this by setting your Group object's groupBy property. When you're finished, close the Inspector.

The Layout menu also has an option for adding groups. When you add groups through the Layout menu, IntraBuilder sets the groupBy property for you.

> **TIP**
>
> Deleting a Group object is not as obvious as it could be. Follow these steps to delete a Group object:
>
> 1. Right-click the report form surface and select Inspector from the shortcut menu.
> 2. Select the Group object that you want to delete in the Inspector's drop-down list.
> 3. Either press the Delete key or select Edit|Delete from the menu.

Setting Up a Group Aggregate

Now that you have a Group object in place, you can add an aggregate that depends on the Group. In this example, you add a count aggregate that renders a count of the rows in each group. Think of this group aggregate as a subtotal—a calculation, which corresponds directly to a particular report group.

You can add group and summary components to existing reports the same way you add them in the Report Expert. To add a summary, select Layout|Add Groups and Summaries from the menu. Select the Summaries tab and add a count of the CATEGORY fields for the CATEGORY group. Figure 5.10 shows the completed dialog. For information on how to create summaries from HTML controls, see Day 14, "Checking Out."

Figure 5.10.

Adding a group count through the Layout menu.

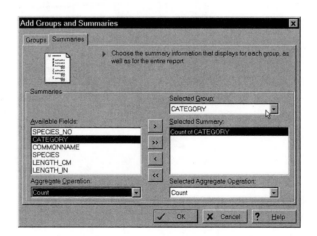

Constructing Page Headings

After you've finished the real work of building your report, you'll want to give the report a more professional appearance by adding a few items to its page heading. In this section, you'll add a report title, a control that displays the current date and time, and one that prints the current page number.

To set up your report title, follow these steps:

1. Drop an HTML control at the top of the page template. Make the control as wide as your page template and leave some room between the control and the column titles.

2. Bring up the Inspector and set the HTML control's text property to `<H1>BIOLIFE2</H1>`.

3. Set its alignHorizontal property to 1 - Center.

Figure 5.11 shows the report with a title.

Figure 5.11.

You add items, such as report titles, using the HTML control.

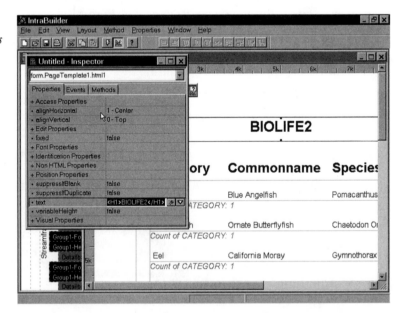

Next on the list is the addition of a field that lists the current date and time. Placing the date and time on your reports allows users to easily determine when the report was printed. To set up your date/time control, follow these steps:

1. Drop an HTML control between the report title and the first column title.
2. Bring up the Inspector and set the new control's `text` property to

   `{ ¦¦ new Date() }`
3. Set the `text` property's type to `CodeBlock`.
4. Make the control wide enough to show the time.

Figure 5.12 illustrates what your new control should look like.

Figure 5.12.

You can set up basic report elements using HTML controls and CodeBlocks.

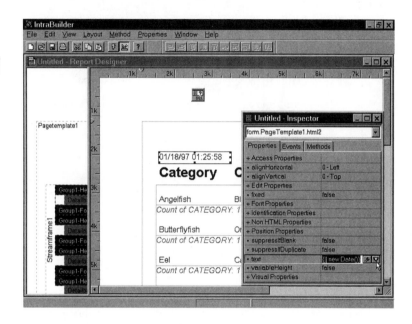

 TIP   You can left align the date/time control with the first column title by selecting both and clicking the Left Align toolbar button. You can also use the Layout menu to align controls.

Now that you've successfully set up the report title and date/time fields, you're ready to add the page number control to the report's page footer. To do this, follow these steps:

1. Scroll down in the Report Designer so that the bottom of the detail `StreamFrame` rectangle displays.
2. Drop an HTML component beneath the bottom of the detail `StreamFrame`, on the report `PageTemplate` object itself.

3. Bring up the Inspector and set the control's `text` property to

   `{ || 'Page: ' + this.parent.parent.reportPage }`

4. Change the `text` property's type to `CodeBlock` and exit the Inspector.

Figure 5.13 demonstrates what your new page number control should look like.

Figure 5.13.

Adding fixed report elements, such as page number controls, is easy using HTML objects.

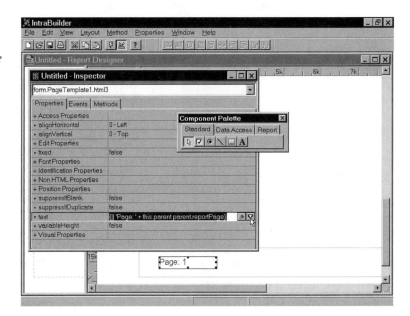

Now that your page number control is in place, let's add one more enhancement to the report before running it. Let's add a Rule control to the report's header to separate column headings from column data. To add the Rule control, follow these steps:

1. Drop a Rule line onto the report form between the column headings and their corresponding data fields.

2. Position the control so that its left edge is aligned with the left edge of the report.

3. Stretch the line so that it spans the entire horizontal width of the report.

Figure 5.14 shows what your new Rule control might look like.

Figure 5.14.

You can use Rule lines to break a report into different sections.

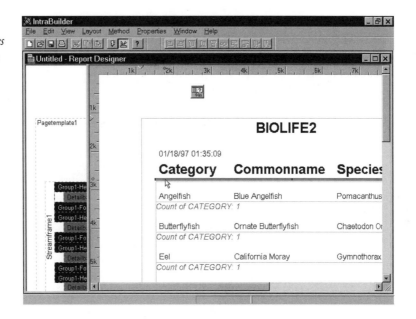

 TIP

When creating reports for browsers, it is a good idea to make the margins smaller and set the form.PageTemplate1.gridLineWidth to 0. The default margins work well for laser printers but are not necessary if you are only targeting a browser. The default gridLineWidth is 1.

Testing the Finished Report

Now that you've finished setting up the report's header and footer, you're ready to test the report itself. Click Run on the IntraBuilder toolbar to execute the report. As with the Report Expert, you'll be asked to save the report before it runs. Name the report BIOLIFE2 and click Save. Figure 5.15 shows what the finished product looks like after setting the page template margins to 520 and the gridLineWidth to 0.

Figure 5.15.

The BIOLIFE2 report running in Netscape Communicator.

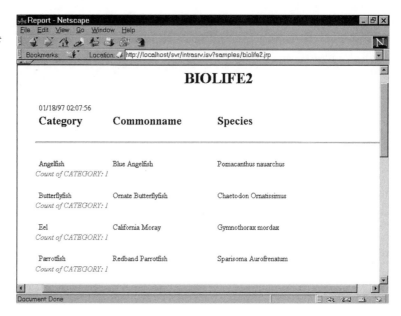

NOTE

When running a report in the IntraBuilder Designer, you can select the Save Snapshot as Static HTML option from the shortcut menu. This lets you create an HTML file that you can publish on Web servers that are not running IntraBuilder Server.

Summary Reports

You've now learned to create detailed reports using two different approaches. You've quickly cranked out a report using the Report Expert, and you've created one from scratch using the Report Designer. Now that you know how to put together detailed reports, let's build a summary report just for completeness.

Click New on the IntraBuilder toolbar and select Report from the shortcut menu. We'll begin by creating the report using the Report Expert, and then customize it later in the Report Designer. Click Expert to proceed.

Adding a Query

To begin, you'll be asked what table or query to reference in the report's Query object. Double-click the BIOLIFE.DBF table to proceed to Step 2 of the Report Expert.

Choosing a Report Type

Next, you're asked to select what type of report to build. Click the Summary Only radio button and click Next to proceed to Step 3. As with other Expert dialogs, you can select options by clicking the images as well as the radio buttons. Figure 5.16 shows the second step dialog box.

Figure 5.16.

Click Summary Only to build a summary report.

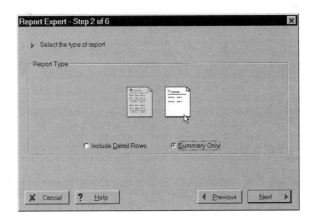

Grouping the Report

Because this is a summary report, you won't be asked which fields to include on the report, as you were the first time you went through the Report Expert. This time, you proceed directly to specifying grouping fields for the report. As you did the first time, select the CATEGORY field as the report's grouping field and proceed to the Expert's next step.

Establishing Group Aggregates

Unlike the first report you built, you won't count merely the items in each group in this new report. Instead, you'll list the average length (in inches) of the fish in each group. You'll also include an average length computation for the entire BIOLIFE table. To do this, follow these steps:

☐ Click the LENGTH_IN field in the Available Fields list.

☐ Click Average in the Aggregate Operation list.

☐ Click the right arrow (>) to create a report-wide aggregation.

Figure 5.17 shows the fourth step's dialog box.

Figure 5.17.

Begin by creating an average length calculation for the entire BIOLIFE table.

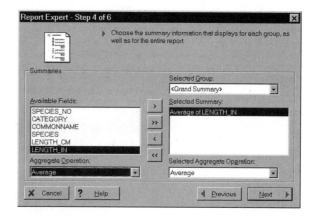

Now that you have your grand summary calculation in place, setting up the group-based computation is easy. Simply click the CATEGORY field in the Selected Group drop-down list box and click the right arrow to add the new calculation. Figure 5.18 shows the highlighted selections.

Figure 5.18.

Your new report includes an average length summary for the CATEGORY group and for the entire table.

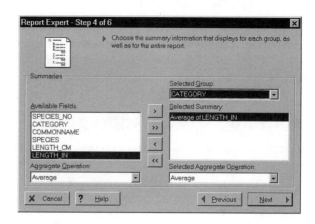

Completing the Report Definition

Click Next to proceed to the Report Expert's Step 5. Now that you've defined your grouping fields and aggregations, you're ready to finish the report definition by specifying a few additional details. The only alteration you'll make to the Step 5 dialog box is to change the report name from Biolife to BIOLIFE SUMMARY. Make that change now and click Next.

Running the New Report

Now that the report definition is complete, click Run Report to execute it. You'll then be prompted for a name for your new report. Name the new report BIOSUM and click the Save button. Figure 5.19 shows what your new report should look like.

Figure 5.19.

Your new summary report as it appears at runtime.

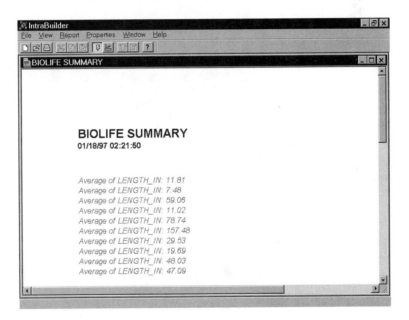

Customizing the New Report

Your new summary report lists the data you asked it to list, but there's one problem: Each group aggregate fails to list its corresponding CATEGORY value. For this reason, the items listed on the report are virtually useless. You need to know the actual name of the CATEGORY to which each average computation corresponds. You'll therefore need to customize the report so that each group footer lists the necessary information. To accomplish this, follow these steps:

1. Click the Design button on the toolbar to start the Report Designer.
2. Open the Field Palette and drop the CATEGORY field on top of the group averages. This will move the group averages to the right and insert the CATEGORY field to the left.
3. Select the average in the report footer and move it to the right to align it with the group averages.
4. Your reports should now resemble the one in Figure 5.20. Save the report and rerun it.

Figure 5.20.

Adding the CATEGORY field to the BIOSUM report.

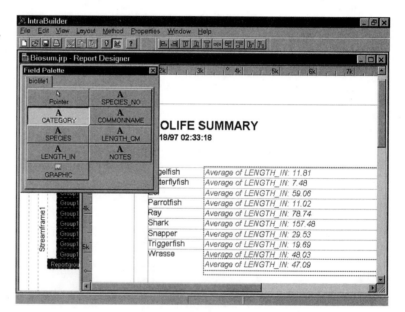

Summary

In this chapter, you learned how to create three different types of reports using the IntraBuilder Report Expert and Report Designer and how to add fields onto reports. You customized header and footer information and worked with groups and group aggregates. You also learned how to create summary fields and how to customize the report definitions created for you by the Report Expert.

5

Q&A

Q What types of files can you use with a Query component?

A Tables, SQL queries, and Query Builder queries.

Q What's the best way to visually separate the parts of a report from each other?

A Place a Rule line between the report's various sections for a neater appearance.

Q Is it possible to navigate backward from the last page of a report to a previous page using the IntraBuilder page buttons?

A This will work only if the report is no longer than two pages. IntraBuilder supports moving backward to the report's *first* page; you cannot arbitrarily move backward.

Q What's the name of the object that's used as a container for the report's detail data?

A That's the `StreamFrame` object.

Workshop

The Workshop section provides questions and exercises to help you get a better feel for the material you learned today. Try to answer the questions and at least think about the exercises before moving on to tomorrow's lesson. You'll find the answers to the questions in Appendix A, "Answers to Quiz Questions."

Quiz

1. What are two types of reports you can build using the IntraBuilder Report Expert?

2. What are the two layout choices available to you when building reports using the IntraBuilder Report Expert?

3. Where do you place heading information that you want to appear on every page of a report?

4. When you're modifying a report that was generated using the Report Expert, moving a report column left or right will cause what to happen to its heading?

Exercises

1. Modify the first report you created using the Report Expert to list each CATEGORY value in its group footer.

2. Alter the last report you built so that the page number control is relocated from the report's footer to the far right of its header and right-aligned.

3. Create a report that's based on two or more tables joined together in a single SQL statement.

4. Link the reports you've built today to the forms you built earlier this week.

Day **6**

Scripts, Events, and Methods

by Ken Henderson

Today, you'll learn to create and enhance IntraBuilder scripts, methods, and events. These are the specific tasks you'll cover today:

- ☐ Using the IntraBuilder Script Editor to edit forms and reports as scripts
- ☐ Constructing handlers for IntraBuilder events
- ☐ Editing and linking methods using the Method Editor
- ☐ Learning about the _sys object and discovering the many ways that you can use it
- ☐ Using the Script Pad to enter simple JavaScript expressions
- ☐ Becoming familiar with the advantages and disadvantages of client- and server-side JavaScript

The Script Editor

The IntraBuilder Script Editor enables you to edit forms and reports as JavaScript code. (JavaScript is IntraBuilder's native language.) It also enables you to write your own JavaScript methods and event handler code. You can think of the Script Editor as a behind-the-scenes view of the IntraBuilder development environment.

You can invoke the Script Editor by right-clicking a form or report in the IntraBuilder Explorer and selecting Edit as Script from the shortcut menu, as illustrated by Figure 6.1.

Figure 6.1.

Edit forms and reports using the Script Editor.

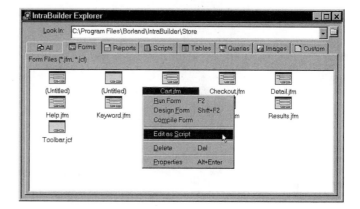

JavaScript

Editing forms and reports as scripts is a good way to learn IntraBuilder's underlying language, JavaScript. JavaScript was designed by Netscape as an object-oriented, platform-independent programming language. All a user needs to access IntraBuilder apps written in JavaScript is a browser that supports HTML 2.0. Regardless of whether the user is a UNIX, Mac, or PC user, JavaScript-based IntraBuilder apps will run just fine in any HTML 2.0 compatible browser.

Unlike most scripting languages, JavaScript is case-sensitive, so you'll have to be careful when keying scripts manually. In structure, JavaScript is reminiscent of C++, but it is easier and safer than either C++ or JavaScript's big brother, Java. It also includes a number of advanced features such as a dynamic object model and support for automatic type conversion. IntraBuilder builds on the JavaScript language definition and has enhanced it to support literal arrays, exception handling, and code blocks.

Customizing the Script Editor

Note the syntax highlighting and other programmer's editor amenities of the IntraBuilder Script Editor. The editor supports two base keyboard layouts: the IntraBuilder set and the Brief set. It also supports a number of user-configurable features such as indent/outdent, editor font attributes, smart tabs, and undo. You can configure these settings by using the Editor Properties dialog box. To bring up the dialog, right-click the Editor and select Editor Properties from the shortcut menu. Figure 6.2 shows some of the settings you can configure.

Figure 6.2.

Use the Editor Properties dialog box to customize the Script Editor.

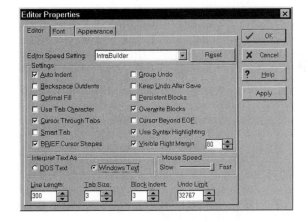

 NOTE

One of the niftier features of the Script Editor is its support for dragging and dropping text. Drag-and-drop support enables you to drag a selected area of text to another location within a file. Think of it as an automated cut and paste operation. The text is moved from its original location to wherever you decide to drop it.

You also might have noticed that the Script Editor defaults to a monotype (fixed pitch) font. Monotype fonts lend themselves more readily than variable pitch fonts when working with source code. Symbols and numbers also are generally easier read when all characters are the same size.

Running Scripts from the Editor

If you want to run a script from the Script Editor, you can use any one of these three methods:

- ☐ Click the Run button on the IntraBuilder toolbar
- ☐ Select the Script|Run menu option
- ☐ Press Ctrl+D

Any of these methods will run the report or form just as though you'd double-clicked it in the IntraBuilder Explorer.

Click the Close button now to return to the IntraBuilder Explorer.

The Script Pad

IntraBuilder also includes a handy script entry pad for testing JavaScript expressions, inspecting the environment, and generally giving you a behind-the-scenes look at what's going on in IntraBuilder. It's similar to the JavaScript typein prompt that appears when you enter javascript: in Netscape Navigator's Location entry box. You can access IntraBuilder system variables, display JavaScript expression results, and execute JavaScript commands.

Testing Expressions

Bring up the Script Pad now by selecting View|Script Pad. You should see a double-paned dialog box. By default, the top pane is the input pane and the bottom pane is the results pane, as shown in Figure 6.3.

Let's try a couple of expressions to see how the Script Pad works. Type the following statements into the Script Pad's top pane:

```
_sys.scriptOut.clear() ;
_sys.scriptOut.writeln("Hello World!") ;
```

Your output should resemble that shown in Figure 6.4.

6

Figure 6.3.

Activate the IntraBuilder Script Pad by using the View|Script Pad menu option.

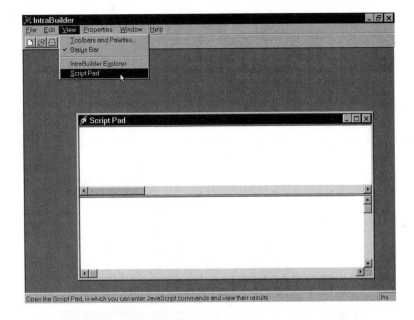

Figure 6.4.

Use the Script Pad to execute JavaScript code.

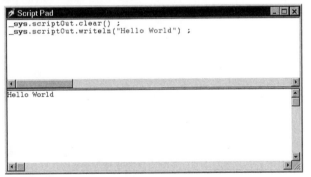

Now, let's change the expression a bit to show off JavaScript's automatic type conversion. Enter the following statements:

```
_sys.scriptOut.clear() ;
_sys.scriptOut.writeln( "2 + 2 = " + 4 ) ;
```

Figure 6.5 shows what you should see.

Figure 6.5.

Check JavaScript's implicit type conversion in your Script Pad expressions.

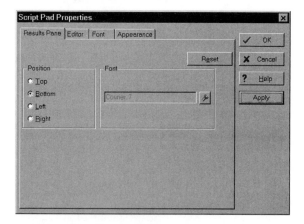

```
_sys.scriptOut.clear() ;
_sys.scriptOut.writeln("Hello World") ;
_sys.scriptOut.clear() ;
_sys.scriptOut.writeln( "2 + 2 = " + 4 ) ;
```

```
2 + 2 = 4
```

You can change the appearance of the Script Pad by using its Properties dialog box. As with the other facilities in IntraBuilder, the Script Pad Properties dialog can be accessed by using its shortcut menu. Right-click the Script Pad to pop up the shortcut menu. From the shortcut menu, you can either bring up the Script Pad property sheet or clear the results window. Figure 6.6 shows the Script Pad property sheet.

Figure 6.6.

Customizing the Script Pad by using its Properties dialog.

The Script Pad as an X-Ray Machine

In addition to keying in your own JavaScript, you also can use the Script Pad to watch what's going on in the rest of IntraBuilder. Actions you take in the IntraBuilder Explorer are echoed to the Script Pad as JavaScript statements. To see how this works, arrange your screen so that the Script Pad and the IntraBuilder Explorer are both visible and double-click a report or form in the IntraBuilder Explorer to run it. You should see the appropriate JavaScript run method called in the Script Pad, as shown in Figure 6.7.

Figure 6.7.

Use the Script Pad to learn JavaScript statements.

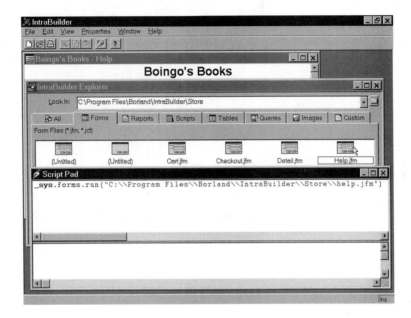

The _sys Object

If you look closely at the JavaScript statement that appears in the Script Pad when you open a form, you can see that a method of the _sys object executes. Any time you navigate or execute commands within the IntraBuilder IDE, you're actually calling methods of the _sys object. Beyond merely acting as the basis for IntraBuilder IDE, the _sys object also can be used in JavaScript functions that you write. I'll show you how in the sections that follow.

The _sys object is a global object that represents the current instance of the IntraBuilder Designer or IntraBuilder Agent. It's created automatically when IntraBuilder starts. You can access it and its methods and properties from the Script Pad and from within JavaScript functions. For example, when you wrote JavaScript earlier that sent text to the Script Pad, you referenced the _sys object when you called the _sys.scriptOut.writeln() method. To check out what's available to you in the _sys object, type this into the Script Pad:

```
inspect(_sys)
```

Figure 6.8 shows what you should see.

Figure 6.8.

The properties and methods of the _sys object appear in the Inspector.

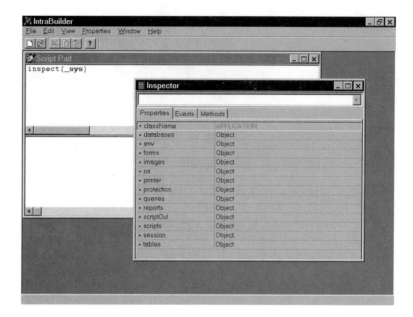

Debugging and the Script Pad

Because you can access the _sys object's properties and methods from within JavaScript code, use them to help debug scripts. For example, you could use the Script Pad to see when a given form or report is loaded, or what the value of a particular variable is at runtime. In this sense, the Script Pad functions similarly to the "watch window" you often see in debuggers. Figure 6.9 illustrates the use of the _sys object's `writeln()` method, which sends output to the Script Pad while an application is running.

 TIP

In either the Script Pad or your JavaScript code, you can use the ? in place of the `_sys.scriptOut.write()` method. In the Script Pad, ? places its output on a new line just like `_sys.scriptOut.writeln()`. You can also use `clear` in place of `_sys.scriptOut.clear()`.

Figure 6.9.

Tracking events by sending messages to the Script Pad.

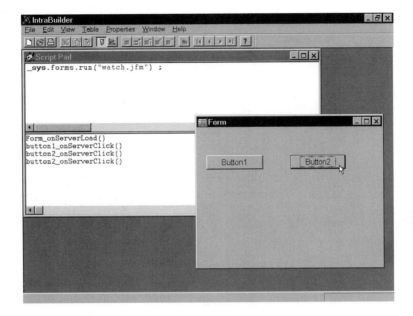

Listing 6.1 shows a form with writeln() methods embedded to show when events fire.

INPUT **Listing 6.1. The WATCH form.**

```
 1: // {End Header} Do not remove this comment//
 2: // Generated on 01/20/97
 3: //
 4: var f = new watchForm();
 5: f.open();
 6: class watchForm extends Form {
 7:    with (this) {
 8:       onServerLoad = class::Form_onServerLoad;
 9:       height = 10;
10:       left = 0;
11:       top = 0;
12:       width = 40;
13:    }
14:
15:    with (this.button1 = new Button(this)){
16:       onServerClick = class::button1_onServerClick;
17:       left = 2;
18:       top = 2;
19:       width = 12;
20:       text = "Button1";
21:    }
22:
```

6

continues

Listing 6.1. continued

```
23:    with (this.button2 = new Button(this)){
24:        onServerClick = class::button2_onServerClick;
25:        left = 20;
26:        top = 2;
27:        width = 12;
28:        text = "Button2";
29:    }
30:
31:    function button1_onServerClick()
32:    {
33:        _sys.scriptOut.writeln("button1_onServerClick()") ;
34:    }
35:
36:    function button2_onServerClick()
37:    {
38:        _sys.scriptOut.writeln("button2_onServerClick()") ;
39:    }
40:
41:    function Form_onServerLoad()
42:    {
43:        _sys.scriptOut.clear() ;
44:        _sys.scriptOut.writeln("Form_onServerLoad()") ;
45:    }
46:
47: }
```

ANALYSIS The WATCH form is a simple form with two buttons and three event handlers. Lines 8, 16, and 24 assign methods to events. When you run the form, the first event to fire is the form's onServerLoad event. Lines 41 through 45 define a method that clears the results pane and prints the function name.

After the form opens, you can click the buttons to fire onServerClick events. Lines 31 through 34 define a method for the first button's onServerClick event. Line 33 prints the method name in the results pane. A similar method is defined on lines 36 through 39 for the second button.

The Method Editor

You use the Method Editor to write code that responds to events in IntraBuilder applications. These events can be server-side or client-side events. Server-side events (and their associated method code) are processed entirely on the server. Client-side events require the user to have a browser that supports JavaScript. Both Netscape Navigator and Microsoft Internet Explorer support JavaScript. Microsoft refers to its implementation of JavaScript as JScript. Table 6.1 summarizes some of IntraBuilder's events.

6

Table 6.1. Popular IntraBuilder events.

Object	Event	Server-Side/Client-Side
Button	onClick	Client
Button	onServerClick	Server
JavaApplet	onServerLoad	Server
Text	onBlur	Client
Rowset	(all events)	Server

Usually, you create a new method by clicking the tool button to the right of an event on the Events page of the Inspector. You can, however, open the Method Editor without creating a new method by using either of the following methods:

- ☐ Click the View|Method Editor menu option.
- ☐ Select the Method Editor option from a form's shortcut menu (open the shortcut menu by right-clicking the form).

If you open the Method Editor this way and the form already has methods attached to it, the first method will be displayed. If the form has no methods attached to it, the form Header section opens. Figure 6.10 shows an onServerClick method loaded into the Method Editor. See Day 20, "Mastering Object-Oriented Programming," for more information on the Header section.

Figure 6.10.

Edit and link methods using the Method Editor.

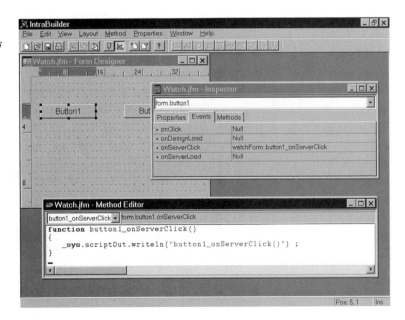

6

If you want to open the Method Editor and create a new method, follow these steps:

1. Open the Inspector.
2. Click the Events page.
3. Click the tool button to the right of the event for which you wish to define the new method.

Following these steps creates a new method and links it to the selected event. The Method Editor is then opened (or made active), and you can key in your new method.

Note that you don't have to write every method from scratch. To link a method that already exists to an event, follow these steps:

1. Load the Method Editor to edit the event's method, as described in the previous list of steps.
2. Click the drop-down list at the top of the Method Editor and select the method that you would like to link to the event.
3. Right-click the method in the Method Editor and select Link Event from the shortcut menu. (Figure 6.11 shows the Method Editor's shortcut menu.)
4. Click the object that you want to link to in the Link Event dialog box's left pane.
5. Click the event to which you want to associate the method in the Link Event dialog box's right pane.
6. Click OK. (Figure 6.12 shows the Link Event dialog.)

Figure 6.11.

Choose the Link Event menu option to link existing methods to events.

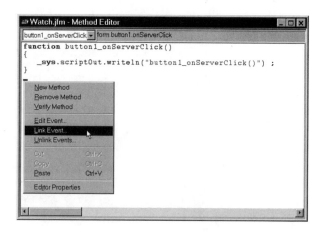

Figure 6.12.
Click the object and event to link in the Link Event dialog box.

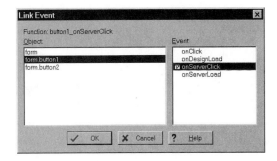

The top line of the Method Editor dialog box displays the events to which a method is linked. When a method is linked to multiple events, the Method Editor displays them one after another, separated by commas.

The Method Menu

You'll find the facilities provided by the Method menu helpful when working with methods. You can use the options on this menu to create a new method or remove or verify an existing one. Verifying a method simply compiles it so that you can detect any errors before you attempt to run its host form or report. The Method menu also offers commands related to linking methods with events. As an alternative to the steps listed earlier today, use Method|Event options to link and unlink events and methods. These commands function the same regardless of whether you access them by using the Method menu or by using the Method Editor's shortcut menu.

New Method

Selecting the Method|New Method option creates a JavaScript definition for a new method in the Method Editor like this:

```
function Method()
{
// {Export} This comment causes this function body to be sent to the client

}
```

Remove Method

Clicking the Remove Method option removes the selected method and all references to it from the current script.

6

Verify Method

Choosing Verify Method compiles the method, instantly revealing any syntax errors. Figure 6.13 shows the Compilation Status dialog box, which displays when you verify a method.

Figure 6.13.

Verifying a method causes it to be compiled and immediately shows any syntax errors.

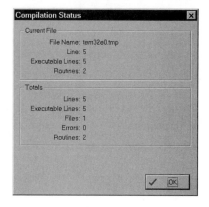

Edit Event

If you select the Edit Event option for the Method Editor shortcut menu, the Edit Event dialog box enables you to modify events in the right pane associated with objects in the left pane. The event you select is loaded into the Method Editor so that you can edit it.

Link Event

The Link Event option displays a dialog box that enables you to link the current method with an object from the left pane and one of its events in the right pane. As I mentioned earlier today, after you link a method to an event, the event is listed next to the method name at the top of the Method Editor dialog box.

Unlink Events

The Unlink Events menu option enables you to view the events linked to a particular method and unlink any or all of them. When you unlink an event from a method, the link is removed from the list of links to the right of the method name at the top of the Method Editor. Figure 6.14 shows the Unlink Events dialog box.

Figure 6.14.
*The Unlink Events
dialog box enables you
to manage a method's
linked events easily.*

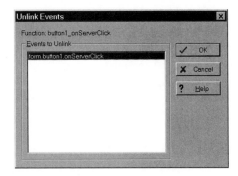

Client-Side Versus Server-Side Event Handling

As you might guess, server-side events and methods are run on IntraBuilder Agents. Applications that are completely server-based require only that users have browsers that support HTML 2.0. Client-side events, on the other hand, require browsers that support JavaScript, such as Netscape Navigator, Netscape Communicator, and Microsoft Internet Explorer.

In order to ensure that your IntraBuilder applications are accessible to the broadest number of users, your applications should be primarily server-based. You should then supplement your server-side logic with client-based code where necessary. This helps achieve a nice balance between the various tiers that make up your applications. It also helps ensure that your applications are as compatible with as many browsers as possible and as functional on the client-side as possible.

The trade-off you have to consider is this: Even though locating events on the server makes your applications more accessible, they are somewhat less functional than apps that include client-side event processing. Nowhere is this more evident than in data validation events. Server-side data validation does not occur until a form is submitted to the server. Client-side validation, by contrast, can happen on a field-by-field basis. This way, users can be made aware of data validation errors as they occur.

Though it might seem otherwise, the answer here is not to pick one approach over the other. Rather, you should place as much of your code as possible on your Web server and augment it with client-side JavaScript where necessary. With data validation events, this means validating your data in both places—the idea being that the server-based validation will act as a safety net for those client browsers that do not support JavaScript. For those browsers that do support JavaScript, the validation will be handled at the client and will be more functional and more user-friendly.

6

Embedding JavaScript in an HTML Document

Browsers support JavaScript through HTML tags. These tags consist of the `<script>` and `</script>` identifiers. Although browsers default to using JavaScript, the `script` tag allows for other scripting languages such as VBScript. Scripts are embedded between the two tags like so:

```
<script language = "JavaScript">

   function button1_onClick()
   {
      history.back() ;
   }

</script>
```

Your JavaScript functions are placed between the two tags. Because browsers that don't support JavaScript will display the functions as plain text (ignoring the `<script>` tags), it's a good idea to embed JavaScript inside HTML comments. When you link methods to client-side events, IntraBuilder automatically streams out the appropriate tags and comments as shown here:

```
<script language = "JavaScript">

<!--

   function button1_onClick()
   {
      history.back() ;
   }

//-->

</script>
```

Summary

In this chapter you learned to edit IntraBuilder scripts and event code using the Script Editor and Script Pad. You learned how to inspect IntraBuilder's internals in detail and to tweak IntraBuilder applications using JavaScript. Specifically, you learned how to use the Script Editor to edit JavaScript code, how to use the Script Pad to see exactly how the IntraBuilder Explorer behaves, and how to use the Method Editor to edit and link methods and events. You discovered the purpose of the _sys object and ways that you can utilize it, and you examined the difference between client- and server-side JavaScript and the advantages of each, as well as how to embed client-side JavaScript without worrying about browsers that don't support it.

Q&A

Q How do I write client-side functions that are not directly linked to client-side events?

A IntraBuilder exports any functions that contain the following comment line. Exported functions appear in the HTML pages that the IntraBuilder Server sends out to a browser.

```
// {Export} This comment causes this function body to be sent
```

Q How do I send messages to the Script Pad from within my JavaScript code?

A You can use _sys.scriptOut.writeln() to send messages to the Script Pad from within JavaScript code.

Q How do I link a given method to more than one event?

A With the method loaded in the Method Editor, right-click the method and select Link Event from the menu. In the ensuing dialog box, choose the object and event to which you want to link the method and click OK.

Workshop

The Workshop section provides questions and exercises to help you get a better feel for the material you learned today. Try to answer the questions and at least think about the exercises before moving on to tomorrow's lesson. You'll find the answers to the questions in Appendix A, "Answers to Quiz Questions."

Quiz

1. What's the difference between client-side JavaScript and server-side JavaScript and what are some of the advantages and disadvantages of each?

2. What object is actually being used as you perform tasks in the IntraBuilder Explorer and represents the current instance of the IntraBuilder Designer?

3. What tool enables you to evaluate JavaScript expressions and execute JavaScript code?

4. What tool enables you to edit forms and reports as JavaScript code?

5. What tool enables you to edit and link JavaScript methods?

Exercises

1. Edit one of the forms you created earlier this week as a script and add calls to the
   `_sys.scriptOut.writeln()` method so that you can watch what's going on inside
   the form or report as it's running.

2. Try various JavaScript expressions in the Script Pad and watch the results of each.

3. Construct a new method that you then link to multiple events.

4. Create a form that calls the JavaScript `alert()` function from a server-side event
   and a client-side event. Try running the form in the IntraBuilder Designer and
   through a browser that supports JavaScript.

Day 7

Tables, Queries, and Database Administration

by Ken Henderson

Today you'll become quite acquainted with tables and queries. Here's what you can expect to learn today:

- [ ] You'll learn about the different types of tables you can create and the advantages and disadvantages of each.

- [ ] You'll learn to create both Paradox and dBASE tables, and you'll learn to create indexes over them.

- [ ] You'll explore database access by using SQL Link drivers and through ODBC.

- [ ] You'll learn about IntraBuilder's support for database administration and how you can use it to manage your databases.

- [ ] Basically, you'll understand everything you need to know to wire your IntraBuilder applications for database access.

Tables

Though IntraBuilder doesn't have a separate table object (tables are accessed by using Query objects), you can still readily access tables from a variety of Database Management System (DBMS) platforms. For example, you can access dBASE and Paradox tables because the Borland Database Engine (BDE) supports them natively. You can also access DBMSs for which you have BDE SQL Links drivers. SQL Links drivers are included with the Professional and Client/Server versions of IntraBuilder. IntraBuilder Professional includes SQL Links drivers for Microsoft SQL Server and Borland InterBase. IntraBuilder Client/Server includes these two plus drivers for Oracle, Sybase, DB2, and Informix.

IntraBuilder Client/Server also includes support for ODBC drivers. Thanks to the ubiquity of ODBC, this means that you can access virtually any type of DBMS. ODBC drivers are available for everything from flat text files to IBM AS/400 databases. You can get to Microsoft's Excel workbooks, as well as Microsoft's own DBMS, Access. There are very few popular DBMSs for which you can't get an ODBC driver. After you have the appropriate driver, all you need is IntraBuilder Client/Server to access your data.

WARNING

Remember that IntraBuilder works only with 32-bit ODBC drivers. You can't use 16-bit drivers (which are readily available) with IntraBuilder because it's a 32-bit tool. Make sure you have 32-bit ODBC drivers before attempting to access databases by using ODBC from IntraBuilder.

Choosing a Table Type

Even if you eventually intend to place the tables an IntraBuilder application references on an SQL Server, you might want to start off developing the application using local tables. This is simpler, quicker, and easier to manage from a development standpoint. Whether you intend to merely use local tables as precursors to remote ones or you plan to actually build applications around local tables, it's important to know what the different local DBMS formats offer you and what their strengths and weaknesses are.

dBASE Tables

dBASE tables have the extension .DBF. dBASE is by far the most popular local DBMS format, having engendered an entire cottage industry of products seeking to copy and enhance it. It is the native table format for Borland Visual dBASE, Microsoft Visual FoxPro, and Computer Associates Clipper. The dBASE format initially gained widespread use through the popularity of dBASE III Plus in the early 1980s and has continued to evolve through the many incarnations that dBASE has taken since then. IntraBuilder supports level 3, 4, and 5 dBASE tables. Table 7.1 summarizes the support for dBASE tables by level. Level 6 tables are in development and may include some of the data integrity options currently available for Paradox tables.

Table 7.1. dBASE table levels.

Level	Base Product	IntraBuilder Support
1	Vulcan	None. Not a publicly released format.
2	dBASE II	None. Not supported by BDE.
3	dBASE III Plus	DBF table and DBT memo files. NDX index files are not supported.
4	dBASE IV	Full support for DBF table, DBT memo and production MDX index tags. Non-production MDX index tags are not supported.
5	Visual dBASE	Full support for DBF table, DBT memo, and production MDX index tags. Automatic conversion for OLE and binary fields.

Benefits

Some of the many advantages of using the dBASE table format are described in the next few sections. Despite the technical differences between dBASE and other local DBMS formats, the decision is largely a personal one. What do you feel most comfortable using? Is it dBASE? Paradox? Maybe Access? People tend to get a little testy when you try to swap DBMSs on them. Choose what works for you and stick with it. All of the major players provide sufficient features, speed, and reliability to make excellent candidates for most local DBMS tasks.

7

Fastest Native Format

Of the two formats native to the BDE—dBASE and Paradox—dBASE is the faster of the two. To an extent, this is due to the fact that dBASE is also less capable than Paradox, but nevertheless, if speed is all you care about, the nod has to go to dBASE. See Day 10, "Querying for the Quickest Searches," for more information on table performance.

Extremely Portable

Because it's been around so long and been supported on so many platforms, dBASE tables are extremely portable. Many third-party utilities will work directly with dBASE tables. Consider, for example, Microsoft Excel. It includes drivers that let you edit dBASE .DBF files as though they were Excel worksheets. If you intend to access your databases from a number of third-party packages (especially non-Borland ones), the dBASE format is the best choice.

Expression Indexes

 Expression indexes are indexes whose keys consist of expressions, not just field references. These expressions are then evaluated and processed at runtime, giving the BDE interpreter-like characteristics.

The dBASE format is also the only local format to support expression-based indexes. You can do all sorts of interesting things using this expression support, including things that have nothing to do with building or searching indexes. The following columns list the dBASE functions and logical operators that the BDE supports in expression indexes:

ABS()	ACOS()	ALIAS()	.AND.
ANSI()	ASC()	ASIN()	AT()
ATAN()	ATN2()	BITAND()	BITLSHIFT()
BITOR()	BITRSHIFT()	BITSET()	BITXOR()
CEILING()	CENTER()	CHR()	COS()
CTOD()	DATABASE()	DATE()	DAY()
DBF()	DELETED()	DIFFERENCE()	DOW()
DTOC()	DTOR()	DTOS()	ELAPSED()
EMPTY()	EXP()	FCOUNT()	FIELD()
FIXED()	FLDCOUNT()	FLOAT()	FLOOR()
FV()	HTOI()	ID()	IIF()
INT()	ISALPHA()	ISBLANK()	ISLOWER()
ISUPPER()	ITOH()	LEFT()	LEN()
LENNUM()	LIKE()	LOG()	LOG10()
LOWER()	LTRIM()	MAX()	MEMLINES()
MIN()	MLINE()	MOD()	MONTH()
.NOT.	OEM()	.OR.	OS()
PAYMENT()	PI()	PROPER()	PV()
RANDOM()	RAT()	RECNO()	RECSIZE()

REPLICATE()	RIGHT()	ROUND()	RTOD()
RTRIM()	SECONDS()	SIGN()	SIN()
SOUNDEX()	SPACE()	SQRT()	STR()
STUFF()	SUBSTR()	TAN()	TIME()
TRIM()	UPPER()	VAL()	VERSION()
YEAR()			

Robust Security System

The dBASE table format supports a full-featured security system. If you want to set up complex or extensive permission levels for tables accessed by your IntraBuilder apps, dBASE tables are your best choice.

dBASE tables support table and field level security. Table level security is implemented by using data encryption. With protected systems, data is encrypted so that it cannot be read until it's decrypted. Encrypted tables contain data that has been scrambled to the extent that it's unreadable. IntraBuilder automatically encrypts/decrypts tables, indexes, and memo files after the required password information is entered.

Beyond table-level access, dBASE tables also allow you to specify which fields a user can access. You can define the level of access—read, read/write, or full. Again, if you have need of a robust security system for local tables, the dBASE format is the way to go.

Drawbacks

As you might expect, there are drawbacks that go right along with the benefits of using dBASE tables. Again, the local format you choose is very much a judgment call.

No Data Dictionary

The biggest drawback to using dBASE tables is that there is no data dictionary. You can't set up a validation mask at the database engine level. Many of the field attributes that users have come to expect from SQL databases are missing from the dBASE format.

Without a data dictionary, database integrity becomes the responsibility of the application developer. IntraBuilder provides a robust set of database classes that a programmer can use to ensure data validation and relational integrity.

Limited Field Types

Another limitation results from the types of fields you can create in dBASE tables. IntraBuilder supports the eight dBASE field types available for level 5 dBASE tables. Paradox, Access, and most SQL tables offer a wider selection of field types. Figure 7.1 shows the field types supported by dBASE tables. The IntraBuilder Server automatically converts images stored in dBASE binary and OLE fields to Web-compatible formats.

Figure 7.1.

Selecting a dBASE field type in the Table Designer.

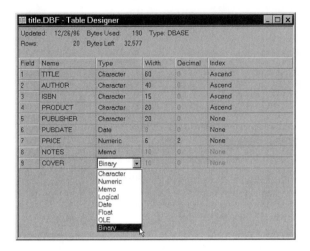

Paradox Tables

Paradox has many advanced features such as referential integrity, lookup fields, and a wide selection of field types. Because of its support for these advanced features, porting Paradox tables to a SQL database can be easier than porting from dBASE tables.

Benefits

Paradox has a number of strengths that make it a good choice for small projects and for prototyping large ones. In the next few sections, I've listed a few of its features that stand out more than others, but, again, selecting a local table type is largely a matter of personal choice.

Column Constraints

Paradox tables support column validation constraints. You can define default values for each field. Some field types allow you to set maximum and minimum constraints. All the Paradox field types support the required constraint. The database engine will not commit required fields that contain a null value.

WARNING

IntraBuilder ignores column constraints that are not enforced by the database engine. For example, the picture attribute has no effect on data entry within IntraBuilder. The picture field mask is only enforced when editing data within Paradox for Windows. Unsupported constraints do not appear in the Table Designer's Field Inspector.

Relational Integrity

Paradox tables also support referential integrity relationships. For example, you can specify that values entered into TableA must be contained in TableB. You can also specify which of a table's fields are its primary key and which ones must be unique. This support for referential and entity integrity makes it easy to migrate data to a client/server database.

Rich Set of Field Types

As illustrated by Figure 7.2, Paradox tables support a wide array of field types. The list of supported types compares quite well with supported field types in SQL databases.

Figure 7.2.

Paradox tables support a wide variety of field types.

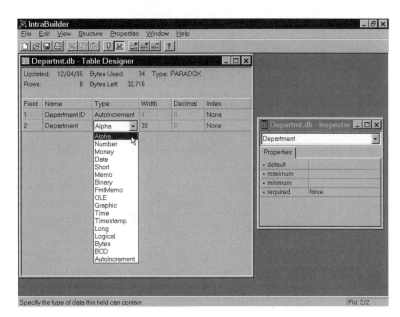

Drawbacks

All the benefits of the Paradox format don't come without a price. Usually, more features means more complexity. The question you have to answer is, "What are my needs?" If you need referential integrity at the database engine level, Paradox is the obvious choice. On the other hand, if you need in-depth security support, dBASE would be better.

Configuring the NET DIR

The biggest hassle with Paradox tables is the management of the NET DIR parameter and its associated PDOXUSRS.NET network control file. To access a Paradox table that's located on a network drive, the NET DIR parameter must be set and must point to a network drive. It cannot point to a local drive.

Even though the current NET DIR setting is stored in the PARADOX driver section of the BDE configuration file, it can also be found in a number of other places. You might find one in the system Registry or in a 16-bit BDE Configuration file. The variety of locations in which you might find NET DIR settings is due to the evolution of the BDE and of Paradox over the years. Progress, at least in this case, has its price.

Although you might find NET DIR settings in several different places, the one in the BDE Configuration Utility's PARADOX driver section has precedence. When NET DIR has been set in the BDE Configuration Utility's PARADOX driver section, settings found in other locations have no effect. This can make properly configuring the Paradox NET DIR confusing, especially for the uninitiated.

Limited Security System

Unlike dBASE, Paradox lacks a sophisticated access control system. Paradox doesn't support internal users or user groups; those are left to the domain of the network. You can control table-level access with network access rights, but there's no provision for field-level access control in IntraBuilder. If you need security features beyond the most basic, the Paradox table format is not your best choice.

Vulnerable VAL Files

The extra field validation and masking that you can apply to a Paradox table is stored in a separate file with an extension of .VAL. There are two problems with this approach. First, the .VAL file can be deleted, effectively removing all validity checking for the fields in the table. Second, the file can be viewed, and possibly manipulated, outside your apps. The design employed here by the Paradox database format makes your field-level constraints vulnerable to possible tampering or deletion.

SQL Links

The Borland SQL Link drivers are special DLLs that allow the BDE to access SQL databases. There are SQL Links drivers for Sybase, InterBase, Oracle, Informix, DB2, and Microsoft SQL Server. As I mentioned earlier today, you get SQL Links drivers only with the Professional and Client/Server versions of IntraBuilder; none come with the Standard version. The InterBase and Microsoft SQL Server drivers come with IntraBuilder Professional. IntraBuilder Client/Server includes these two, plus drivers for Sybase, Oracle, DB2, and Informix. SQL Links drivers are highly tuned for their respective back-ends and are usually more fully featured and faster than their ODBC counterparts.

Benefits

Of course, moving to a client/server DBMS brings with it many of the benefits typically touted by client/server aficionados. You should get better performance when working with large sets of data. Also, you should see greater reliability and recoverability after errors. You should see improved transaction management, and so forth. Naturally, these benefits are passed on to your apps from your SQL Link drivers. Though (when compared with local DBMS drivers) the SQL Links drivers perform a relatively small portion of the work, you have to pretend they do more for the sake of comparison with local drivers. That is, when you're trying to make a decision on whether to go with dBASE tables or InterBase tables, you have to look at the big picture. You have to weigh everything from the database drivers themselves to the format, speed, and integrity of the underlying DBMSs. These elements amount to a sum-total of the reasons you should or shouldn't choose a particular platform.

The bottom line is that a comparison between the BDE's native formats (dBASE and Paradox) and SQL Links drivers must include not only a discussion of the client-side features of a given driver, but also of the server-side features of its back-end DBMS. The comparison isn't so much one of local drivers versus SQL Links drivers as it is the dBASE and Paradox table formats versus client/server DBMSs.

Best Security

Because objects can reside on an entirely different computer or set of computers, client/server DBMSs definitely have the upper hand as far as security is concerned. In contrast to dBASE and Paradox tables, it is often virtually impossible to modify SQL Server-based objects except through the server program itself. Client/server DBMSs typically support their own logins and passwords and force access to be explicitly granted to user accounts.

Best Integrity

Because they normally support complex transaction logs and log management functions, SQL DBMSs are usually more reliable than local table-based systems. It's easy enough to corrupt dBASE indexes by turning off your machine while building them. However, SQL databases provide a number of recovery processes and checks against data corruption. They also support advanced features such as replication, backup servers, and clustered servers, so usually you can rely more heavily on them than you can on local formats such as dBASE and Paradox.

Drawbacks

The benefits of using the client/server DBMSs to which the SQL Links drivers provide access are not without their costs. To begin with, having your databases on a separate computer or computers adds a level of complexity in itself. Other drawbacks include the configuration

7

headaches that can occur with client/server DBMSs and their reliance on networks and network bandwidth.

Complex Configuration

Because you're locating database objects on a separate database server, you automatically double your machine administrative overhead. Not only do you have the client machine to consider, now you have to think about a server as well. If you upgrade the OS on one, maybe you should look at upgrading it on the other. If you come up with a backup solution for one, you've got a second backup solution to think about, as well. Of course, this increase in overhead isn't exponential. It applies only when you first add your database server. As you add additional clients to your server, you won't see repeated doubling of your administrative overhead.

In addition to server machine complexities, client/server DBMSs also bring with them client machine complications. Fortunately, IntraBuilder's server-based approach to database access alleviates the need to make a number of changes to client machines simply to run database apps. Your database access happens on the server; all a client needs is a compatible browser. On the other hand, it's not as though you'll access only client/server DBMSs with IntraBuilder apps, even if the purpose of the server is to support IntraBuilder apps exclusively. This is because you'll need to manage the server itself. It will have to be backed up. It will have to be administrated. You'll probably do at least some of this from machines other than the server. If this is the case, your client machines will have to have the proper database and network libraries and drivers installed on them. This adds a level of complexity that is a constant source of headaches for database administrators.

A final area that is more complicated with SQL databases than with local ones is that of network access. Many client/server DBMSs place unusual demands on their host networks. A client/server DBMS might, for example, insist on using a given protocol on the network. It might require TCP/IP and refuse to use IPX. It might require support of Out of Bound Data (OOBD) or multiple connections between the server and its clients. A good client/server database administrator usually ends up receiving a thorough, if not painful, introduction to network management. You have to weigh these additional complexities when deciding whether a given client/server platform is for you.

ODBC

Microsoft's Open Database Connectivity (ODBC) specification is by far the most popular of the database access middleware specs in existence. There are ODBC drivers available for just about everything. The drivers you can't get from DBMS vendors themselves can usually be acquired from a third-party such as Intersolv. To an extent, ODBC suffers from the "jack of all trades, master of none" syndrome, but things are improving. Gradually, the spec has been enhanced to support increasingly more advanced features, and vendors continue to enhance their own drivers to support proprietary innovations.

Benefits

ODBC's most significant benefit is its ubiquity. It seems that you find a new ODBC driver under every rock these days. PC software and mainframe vendors alike have adopted the standard and include ODBC drivers with their products. Beyond that, about the only other real benefit to using ODBC is that Microsoft backs it. Due to Microsoft's huge market presence, the fact that it backs a technology is reason in itself to consider using the technology. You can probably count on the technology, whether it's ODBC or something else, being around for awhile.

Connecting to Microsoft Access Databases

If you're a Microsoft Access user, you'll have to use ODBC to make use of your tables within IntraBuilder. Microsoft hasn't published the internal specifications of the Access database format. If using Access is important to you, you'll definitely need ODBC.

NOTE

> If you've installed Microsoft Office Professional, you might already have an ODBC driver for Access databases. You can install the driver when installing any of the Microsoft Office products.

Access to Other DBMSs

As I've mentioned, not only does ODBC provide access to Microsoft products, it's also supported by most other vendors. You can usually find an ODBC driver for just about any popular DBMS or file format. ODBC provides a generic, vendor-independent interface to databases and files of all kinds. By providing support for ODBC, the Borland Database Engine has ensured that it is as compatible with as many platforms as possible.

Drawbacks

The Borland SQL Links drivers that come with the Professional and Client/Server versions of IntraBuilder are faster and generally more feature-rich than their ODBC counterparts. Because full support for ODBC is provided only by the Client/Server version of IntraBuilder, you should resort to ODBC only if you don't already have an SQL Links driver for your particular DBMS. That is, if you buy IntraBuilder Client/Server, you automatically receive SQL Links drivers for Sybase, Oracle, InterBase, DB2, Informix, and Microsoft SQL Server. As a rule, don't bother with ODBC drivers if you're using one of these platforms. Likewise, you can get by just fine without ODBC support if you're using either InterBase or Microsoft SQL Server because IntraBuilder Professional includes SQL Links drivers for both of them.

7

NOTE

Every rule has an exception, and so does my recommendation regarding not using ODBC when an equivalent SQL Links driver is available. I've had a variety of problems with the Microsoft SQL Server SQL Links driver. Of particular concern was a recurrent problem with one connection from my application blocking another. Performance was also a major problem with the SQL Links driver. It appeared painfully slow at times. Switching to the ODBC driver cured these ills every time. If you run into a similar situation with the Microsoft SQL Server SQL Links driver, you might give the ODBC driver (which is included with the server software) a try.

Performance

One disadvantage of using ODBC in comparison with SQL Links drivers is the lack of performance. You'll often see a perceptible speed degradation with ODBC drivers. This isn't always the case. There are, in fact, some rather speedy ODBC drivers available. However, the general consensus is that ODBC drivers are not highly tuned for speed. The one-size-fits-all approach that ODBC takes to database access prevents it from taking advantage of some vendor-specific performance enhancements. SQL Links drivers, on the other hand, usually provide complete access to their back-end DBMSs. They even provide the API calls and data structures necessary to make vendor-specific client library calls. This results in better performance and a richer feature set than similar ODBC drivers.

Complex Configuration

Like their SQL Links counterparts, ODBC drivers also involve configuration issues that are outside the Borland Database Engine. You have vendor-supplied client libraries that might need to be installed (if you're accessing a remote SQL database), you have network issues to consider, and you have the additional machine management issues that I mentioned earlier in the "Choosing a Table Type" section. In a sense, ODBC gives you the worst of both worlds: You get the complexities of SQL Links drivers, but slower performance and a least-common-denominator feature set not unlike local tables. This isn't to say that you'll have problems configuring or using ODBC drivers. Most people don't have serious problems using ODBC in their apps. Just keep in mind that many of the same complexities that you face with SQL Links drivers apply equally well to ODBC drivers.

7

Accessing Tables from IntraBuilder

Now that you've learned a little about the background and feature set of the various table formats and database drivers, the next task is learning how to access them from IntraBuilder. I'll take you first through the process of creating tables and then through referencing them from IntraBuilder. We'll finish up today by exploring IntraBuilder's database administration facilities.

The Table Expert

As with forms and reports, IntraBuilder includes a wizard facility for creating tables. To invoke it, click the New button on the IntraBuilder toolbar and select Table from the pop-up menu. After the New Table dialog box appears on-screen, click the Expert button.

As illustrated by Figure 7.3, the first step in the two-step Table Expert process is to select fields from a list of sample tables that you want to include in your new table. You can include fields from several different sample tables in the table you're building. Clicking a table in the samples list causes the fields it contains to be listed in the From Sample Table list. Click the arrow buttons to add fields from the sample tables to your new table definition. Select a variety of fields so that you have a wide range of field types in your new table.

Figure 7.3.
IntraBuilder provides a number of sample tables that you can use when building new tables.

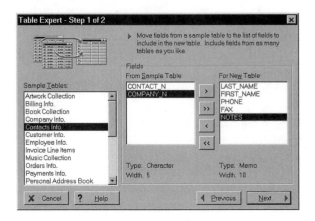

After you've selected the fields you want in your new table, click the Next button to proceed.

7

TIP   Don't fret if you can't find a needed field definition in one of the
           sample tables using the Table Expert. Go ahead and create the
           new table anyway. After the Table Expert has created the table, you
           can modify it using the Table Designer and add any missing field
           definitions.

The next, and final, step of the Table Expert is to select the table type you want to create and
either "run" the table (open it), or modify it in the Table Designer. For now, choose the
Paradox table type. Figure 7.4 shows the Table Expert.

Figure 7.4.

*You choose the type of
table to create in the
Table Expert's final
dialog box.*

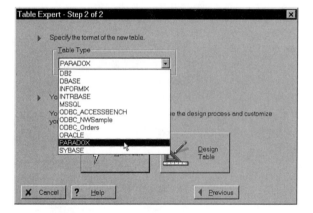

Now that you've selected a table type, click the Run Table button to open your new table.
Before the table actually runs, you'll be asked to save the new table. Supply a name for the
new table and click the Save button. Figure 7.5 shows what your new table might look like
at runtime.

NOTE   When you run a table, IntraBuilder provides buttons to add, delete,
           search, and navigate the table's rows. You don't need to build a special
           form to do these things; you can perform most basic data navigation
           and modification tasks by simply running the table.

Figure 7.5.

You can open new tables in a simple form that IntraBuilder creates for you.

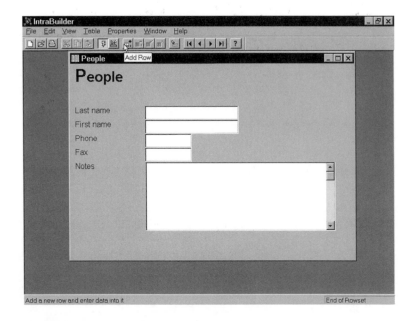

The Table Designer

Now that you've created and run your new table, it's easy enough to modify the table by using the Table Designer. With your new table still running, click the Table Design button on the IntraBuilder toolbar. Figure 7.6 shows what you should see.

Figure 7.6.

The new table as it might appear in the Table Designer.

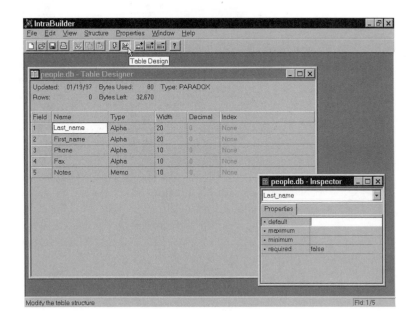

TIP You can rearrange the columns represented in the Table Designer by simply dragging them to new locations. To do this, position the mouse pointer over the heading of the column you want to move (the pointer should change to a hand), and drag it to a new location. A rectangle should appear around the column as you drag it.

Adding/Inserting Fields

You can add a field to the end of your table definition by clicking just below the last field or by clicking the Add Field button on the IntraBuilder toolbar. Add a Number field now to the end of those already listed. Figure 7.7 illustrates adding a field in the Table Designer.

Figure 7.7.

Adding a field to your new table is easy in the Table Designer.

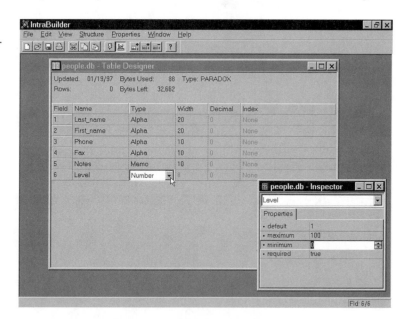

TIP As an alternative to clicking the buttons on the IntraBuilder toolbar, you can right-click the header area of the Table Designer (not the field list) and select the Add Field, Insert Field, or Delete Current Field options from the shortcut menu.

You might have noticed that a Field Inspector automatically appeared when you began editing your table in the Table Designer. The Field Inspector enables you to define a default, maximum, and minimum value for each field. It also enables you to flag whether a field is required. Table 7.2 shows you the properties you should enter for the new field you just created.

NOTE

You'll only see the Field Inspector when working with Paradox tables. Level 5 dBASE tables do not support declared default, maximum, or minimum values, so you won't see a Field Inspector when working with them.

Table 7.2. Properties for the new field.

Property	Value
default	1
maximum	100
minimum	0
required	true

You can establish these same four properties for every field in the table, if you like. (Provided they apply, of course; you can't, for example, define value properties for BLOB or OLE fields.) These field properties are built into the Paradox database format.

Now that you've fully set up the new field, click the Run button on the toolbar to run the table again. You'll then be prompted to save the changes you've made to the table. Click the Yes button. You should then see your new field in the running table. If you click the Add Row button, the default value you defined for the new field should appear in it, as shown in Figure 7.8.

TIP

You can rearrange the order of a table's field definitions by simply dragging them to new locations. To do this, position the mouse pointer over the field number of the definition you want to move (the mouse pointer should change to a hand) and drag the field definition to a new location. You should see a rectangle around the definition as you drag it.

7

Figure 7.8.

Adding a new row with the new field.

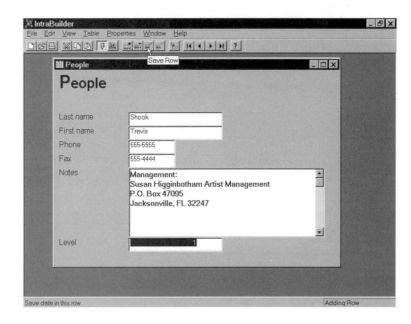

Deleting a Field

Deleting a field from a table definition is equally simple. With your new table still running, click the Table Design button on the toolbar. Next, select one of the fields in your table and click the Delete Current Field button on the toolbar. Figure 7.9 shows how to delete a field using the toolbar.

Figure 7.9.

Deleting fields is as easy as selecting a field definition and clicking the Delete Current Field button.

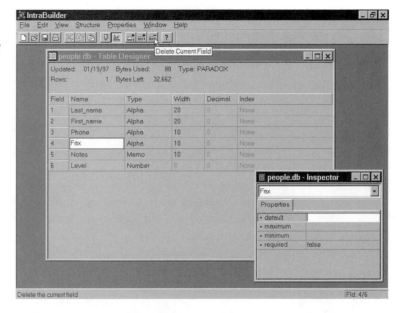

NOTE

In addition to the buttons on the toolbar, you can also manipulate field definitions by using the options on the Structure menu.

Inserting a Field

There might be times that you want to add a new field definition somewhere besides the tail end of your existing table structure. If you'd rather insert the new field into the middle of your field list somewhere, click or highlight a field, and then click the Insert Field button. The new field will be inserted *before* the highlighted field. Figure 7.10 illustrates inserting a new field.

Figure 7.10.

You can use the Insert Field button to insert new field definitions.

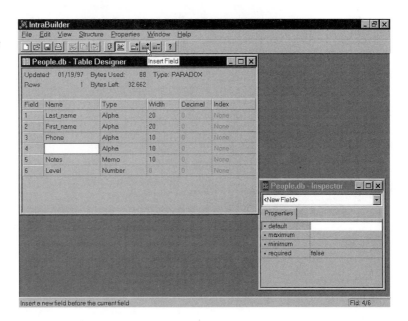

After you've clicked the Insert Field button, the field on which you were positioned should be shifted down and a blank field definition should appear in its place. You can then key in your new field's name, length, and other attributes, as shown in Figure 7.11.

7

Figure 7.11.
After clicking the
Insert Field button,
key in your new field's
attributes.

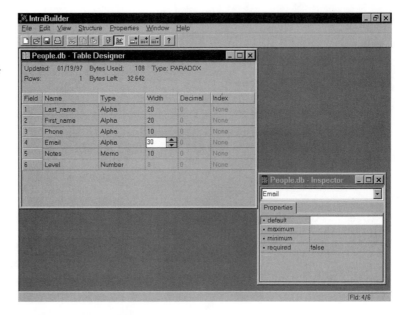

After you're finished editing your table definition, click the Save button to save your table structure to disk.

 TIP

IntraBuilder provides keyboard shortcuts for a number of operations, including several that are available in the Table Designer. Table 7.3 lists some that help with editing table definitions.

Table 7.3. Table Designer keyboard shortcuts.

Keys	Operation
Ctrl+A	Add Field
Ctrl+N	Insert Field
Ctrl+U	Delete Field
Ctrl+G	Goto Field

Defining a Primary Key

A *primary key* is the field or set of fields in a table that can be used to uniquely identify individual records. Examples of primary keys include customer number fields from customer tables, invoice number fields from invoice tables, and so on. A table can only have one primary key, although it can have more than one set of unique fields.

Now that you've learned to add, insert, or delete fields, let's define the table's primary key. Selecting a primary key ensures that each row in a table is uniquely identified. It also allows the table to participate in foreign key references from other tables. You set up primary keys by selecting Structure|Define Primary Key. Click it now.

After the Define Primary Key dialog box is displayed, select a field or two as your table's primary key and click OK. The fields you select must be consecutive beginning with the first field in the table (the Paradox table format imposes this restriction). Figure 7.12 shows a primary key definition.

NOTE

As with other extended column attributes, you can't define primary keys for level 5 dBASE tables. If you want to experiment with primary key definitions, be sure you're using Paradox tables or some other format that supports primary keys.

Figure 7.12.

Use the Define Primary Key dialog box to select your table's primary key fields.

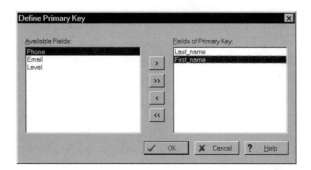

TIP

You can configure the appearance of the Table Designer. Right-click its header area and select Table Designer Properties from the shortcut menu. The Table Designer Properties dialog box allows you to configure whether horizontal and/or vertical lines are displayed between rows and columns in the Table Designer.

After you've finished defining your new table's primary key, resave your table definition. You can do this either by clicking the Save button on the IntraBuilder toolbar, by pressing Ctrl+S, or by selecting File|Save.

Defining Indexes

Now that your table has a primary key, you're ready to define additional indexes for it. Secondary indexes can help speed access to your table's data. Suppose you have a table with the following fields: Last_name, First_name, Phone, Email, and Level. The table's primary key might be the Last_name and First_name fields. However, you might often need to search the table using the Level field as well. The table's Level field, then, would be a good candidate as the key field for a secondary index. If you create an index for the Level field, searches against the table using the field could be sped up by the index—meaning that they could make use of it. In terms of searching for data, secondary indexes can dramatically improve access time.

With this in mind, it might seem reasonable to create secondary indexes over every remaining field in a table after the primary key is defined. This brings up the one downside to creating additional indexes: They cause additional overhead when inserting or updating data. As you add rows to a table, its indexes must be updated to reflect the key values introduced by the new rows. Indexes also must be updated when you delete rows from a table or modify the fields that make up their keys. In short, indexes speed data access, but slow data modification.

The trick with wise index selection is in indexing enough fields to give you the query performance you need without losing the data insertion/update performance you require. Knowing what to index and what not to index is a balancing act between speed when accessing data and speed when inserting or updating it. Often, this varies from application to application and can be determined only by trial and error.

Keep in mind that index searches work left to right in a composite index key. This means that you might not need as many indexes as you think. For example, if you have an index whose key fields are the Last_name and First_name fields from a table, you don't need an index on Last_name alone in order to search using only the Last_name field; your composite key will service any queries against Last_name just fine.

 A *composite index key* is an index key that consists of multiple fields. You can use multiple fields in both a table's primary key and in its secondary index keys.

Define a secondary index by selecting Structure|Manage Indexes. Click it now. Immediately, you should see the index created by your primary key definition listed. Figure 7.13 shows what you should see.

Figure 7.13.

*The Manage Indexes
dialog box lists index
definitions, including
those associated with
primary keys.*

Let's add a new index definition to your table. Click the dialog box's New button to display
the Define Index dialog box. Click the arrow buttons to select a field or two as the key field(s)
for your new index. If you selected multiple fields as your index key, supply a name for the
index as well. After you're done, click OK. Figure 7.14 illustrates the addition of an index.

Figure 7.14.

*Create new indexes
using the Define
Index dialog box.*

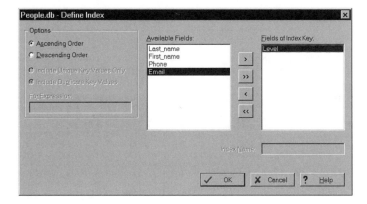

TIP

You can also double-click fields to move them between the Available
Fields and Fields of Index Key lists.

After you return to the Manage Indexes dialog box, you should see your new index listed.
IntraBuilder names single field indexes after their key fields. Composite key index names are
blank by default, though you can (and should) name them. Figure 7.15 shows what your
Manage Indexes dialog box might look like now.

7

Figure 7.15.

Your new index is listed in the Manage Indexes dialog box.

WARNING

Even though IntraBuilder doesn't force you to, be sure to name composite key indexes. If you fail to, IntraBuilder will not provide a default name for them. Unnamed indexes cannot be immediately deleted or edited using the Manage Indexes dialog box. You'll have to exit and re-enter the dialog box in order to edit or delete them.

Click OK to leave the Manage Indexes dialog box and save your revised table definition to disk. After you've saved your table definition to disk, close the Table Designer.

Database Administration

Because we're currently dealing with Paradox tables, I'll begin discussing IntraBuilder's database administration as it applies to Paradox tables. Later, we'll cover database administration with dBASE tables, as well.

As far as IntraBuilder is concerned, there are two areas of database administration— referential integrity constraint definition and table security. Defining referential integrity constraints amounts to defining relationships between tables. Setting up table security consists of defining a password that's required to access a given table. There are no provisions in the Paradox file format for users, groups, user or group rights, and so on. You might say that Paradox's administration facilities are a bit weak.

NEW TERM *Referential integrity* ensures that references between tables are valid. That is, if TableA references a row in TableB, referential integrity constraints help ensure that this relationship is respected. Referential integrity prevents the row in TableB from being deleted as long as TableA references it. Likewise, it forces new entries in TableA to have corresponding entries in TableB. In this sense, the referential integrity constraint is bidirectional; it restricts, or constrains, both tables involved in a table-to-table relationship.

You set up both of these items by selecting File|Database Administration. Change the Table Type to Paradox. Figure 7.16 shows the Database Administration dialog box.

Figure 7.16.

Using IntraBuilder's Database Administration facility to set up referential integrity and table security.

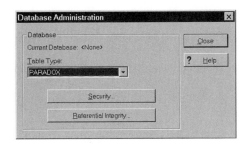

Referential Integrity

Click the Referential Integrity button to bring up the Referential Integrity Rules dialog box. Here you can define relationships between tables. Click the New button to begin defining a new referential integrity rule. Figure 7.17 shows the dialog box you should see.

Figure 7.17.

Define table relation-ships in the New Referential Integrity Rule dialog box.

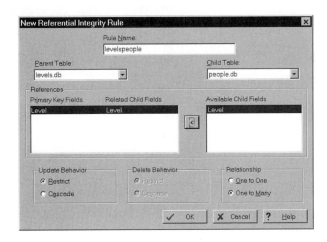

You can use tables from the CD-ROM Day 7 folder to set up a relationship between the Levels table and the People table. To set up a referential integrity relationship between two tables, load the New Referential Integrity Rule dialog box and follow these steps:

1. Select the master or parent table from the Parent Table list. (This should be the table containing values that the other table needs.)

2. Select the slave or child table from the Child Table list. (This should be the table that needs to access data contained in the first table.)

3. Select the field in the child table that is to reference the primary key in the parent table. (Referential integrity relationships require that the parent table have a primary key and that foreign keys referencing the table reference it.) Click the left arrow button to link the field in the child table to the one in the parent table.

4. Select what you want to occur when an update is attempted on the parent table's key field and there are dependent rows in a child table. You can choose either to allow the update and apply it to the child table's rows as well, or you can choose to prohibit (restrict) the update.

5. Select the type of relationship you want established between the two tables. You have two choices: one to one and one to many.

NEW TERM A one to one relationship is one in which there's a maximum of one row in the child table for each row in the parent table. A one to many relationship is one in which one or more rows exist in the child table for each row in the parent. Referential relationships are usually one to many in nature.

Figure 7.18 shows the newly defined relation. You can modify relations from this dialog.

Figure 7.18.

A sample referential integrity rule definition as it might look when completed.

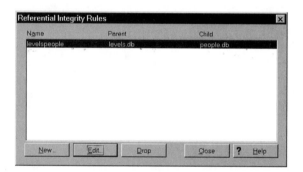

You can click Cancel now to exit the rule definition dialog box. Next, click Close to exit the Referential Integrity Rules dialog box.

Table Security

You should again see the Database Administration dialog box. This time, click Security. You should then see the Security dialog box. Select the new table you created earlier and click Edit Table as shown in Figure 7.19.

Figure 7.19.

*Use the Security
dialog box to specify
passwords for Paradox
tables.*

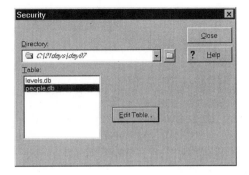

You should next see the Master Password dialog box. Enter the password you want users to enter to access the table and then enter it a second time for confirmation. Asterisks will be displayed in place of the characters you type in order to keep them from being visible. After you've typed the password twice, click Set to set the password. Figure 7.20 shows the Master Password dialog.

Figure 7.20.

*Enter Paradox table
passwords in the
Master Password
dialog box.*

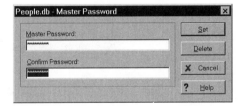

After you're back in the Security dialog box, click Close to return to the Database Administration dialog box.

WARNING

After you set a table access password, you'll have to supply it in order to access the table. This includes changing the password by using the Security dialog box. You'll have to supply the old password to change or delete it. It's a good idea to record in a safe place passwords you use.

Working with Encrypted Paradox Tables

You have a couple of options available to you for providing access to Paradox tables that require passwords. The first is simply to let IntraBuilder display a default login form, which prompts the user for the required password. You don't need to do anything to utilize this facility—it's automatic. If a form attempts to open a password-protected table, the built-in password form is displayed automatically. For Paradox tables, this form is PASS_PDX.JFM. It's located by default in the C:\Program Files\Borland\IntraBuilder\Bin folder.

The second option available to you is to hard-wire passwords by supplying them with JavaScript code. Passwords for Paradox tables are handled by using Session objects and are supplied with the addPassword method. The following is some sample JavaScript code to supply a Paradox table password:

```
_sys.databases[0].session.addPassword("MyPassword");
```

NOTE

Referring to _sys in JavaScript code isn't the preferred method of adding Paradox passwords. Instead, call the query component's addPassword method from its canOpen event. This fires before PASS_PDX.jfm. For example, here is the query's canOpen:

```
function myquery1_canOpen()
{
    this.parent.session1.addPassword("MyPassword") ;
    return true ;
}
```

You could place code like this strategically so that it preempts the automatic password form. This way, users are not bothered with repeatedly typing a minimal access level password.

The dBASE Security System

As I mentioned previously, dBASE supports a much richer security system than Paradox does. dBASE tables support user-level access, group-level access, table-level access, and field-level access. I'll give you a brief tour of the dBASE security system and how to set it up.

The Administrator

Each time you click the Security button in the Database Administration dialog box when you're working with dBASE tables, you'll be prompted for the Administrator account's password. The first time you do this, you'll actually set up the password. You'll be prompted to enter it a second time for confirmation, and whatever you type will be displayed as asterisks. Be sure to record the password in a safe place, because you'll need it to access the dBASE security system in the future.

The second time, and all subsequent times, you enter the security system, you'll be required to type the Administrator password before proceeding. After you're in, you'll be able to define users and groups and their access rights.

Defining Users and Groups

If you haven't done so already, change the Database Administration dialog box's Table Type to DBASE and click Security. Key in the Administrator password as necessary and proceed to the next dialog box. Figure 7.21 shows what you should see.

Figure 7.21.

The dBASE Security dialog box is where you define users and groups.

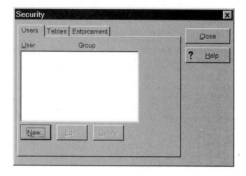

The first order of business is to define your groups. After the groups are set up, you'll add users to them. Each table in your database(s) can belong to only one group, so it's important to plan ahead. You'll probably want to organize groups similarly to your organization. For example, you might organize them by department or by sales area. Click New to begin simultaneously defining a new user and group.

For our purposes, you can come up with your own user and group name. You can leave the Access Level entry box at its default of 1. Click OK when you're finished. Figure 7.22 shows an example of the completed New User dialog box.

Figure 7.22.

You add new users and groups by using the New User dialog box.

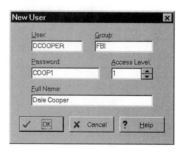

NOTE Though a user can belong to more than one group, a user must be logged into each group separately.

7

You might be wondering what the function of the Access Level setting is. Access levels range from 1 to 8. Lower numbers provide greater access; higher numbers provide lesser access. Establishing access levels within groups enables you to give different users different rights to tables and their fields. Apart from the rights they provide, access levels themselves are conceptual in nature; they have no actual value or meaning.

Typically, you assign the more powerful levels (such as 1-3) to fewer users than you do the less powerful levels. If you want to secure your system, assign only small numbers of users access levels with greater rights. Keep in mind that you can assign as many users as you want to each access level. Note that there's no reason to alter a user's default access level if you don't intend to modify the access levels of the tables belonging to his or her group. User access levels and table/field access levels work hand-in-hand; you don't need one without the other.

Table-Level Security

Now that your user and group are defined, click the Tables tab in the Security dialog box. Select a dBASE table from the list and click Edit Table. Figure 7.23 shows the Edit Table Privileges dialog box.

Figure 7.23.

You use the Edit Table Privileges to set up dBASE table and field security.

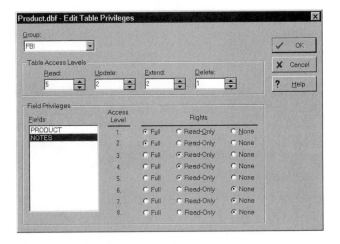

Table access can be divided into four distinct categories: read, update, extend (append), and delete. By default, users with an access of eight (that is, anybody) can perform all these tasks. You can limit who can perform a given task by changing the access level associated with the task. Users with an access level higher than that associated with a given task will not be able to perform the task. For example, if you set the Delete access level to 5, users with access levels between 1 and 5 will be able to delete records; however, those with levels of 6 or higher will not.

Field-Level Security

Field level security works very similarly. Each access level has three privileges that it can have associated with it: Full, Read-Only, and None. So, for each field, you can control which tasks each access level can perform. You might, for example, decide that you want only users of access level 2 or higher to be able to update the Notes field in the Product table and that users below level 5 shouldn't even see the field. In this scenario, you'd click the Notes field and set the privileges of access levels 3, 4, and 5 to Read-Only and levels 6 through 8 to None. Click Cancel when you're done experimenting with dBASE table and field security.

Working with Encrypted dBASE Tables

You have two choices for providing access to encrypted dBASE tables. The first is to allow IntraBuilder to automatically display the default dBASE login form, which prompts the user for the required information. If a form attempts to open an encrypted dBASE table, the built-in password form is displayed automatically. For dBASE tables, this form is PASS_DBF.JFM. It's located by default in the C:\Program Files\Borland\IntraBuilder\Bin folder.

The second option is to hard-wire passwords with JavaScript code. Login information for dBASE tables is set up using the Session object's login method. The following is some sample JavaScript code to supply dBASE login parameters:

```
_sys.databases[0].session.login("FBI", "DCOOPER", "COOP1") ;
```

WARNING

When working with encrypted dBASE tables, a file called dbsystem.db is created (which is not a Paradox table). This file holds all encryption keys. If this file is deleted or damaged to the point of being inaccessible, all encrypted files will no longer be accessible.

If you are no longer working with encrypted tables, you can erase the dbsystem.db and forget your master password. If the dbsystem.db file is not found, IntraBuilder will not prompt you to log in during startup.

You could strategically place code like this so that it preempts the automatic login form. You might, for example, encrypt all tables on your Web server in order to protect them from intruders and hard-code a read-only access user account to provide access to the general public with your IntraBuilder apps. User accounts with greater privileges could be defined for staff members and others who need additional rights.

You can now exit completely out of the Database Administration dialog box.

Working with SQL Tables

As with SQL and Paradox tables, you have two choices for providing access to SQL tables. The first is to allow IntraBuilder to automatically display the default SQL login form, which prompts the user for the required information. If a form attempts to open an SQL table, the built-in password form is displayed automatically. For SQL tables, this form is PASS_SQL.JFM. It's located by default in the C:\Program Files\Borland\IntraBuilder\Bin folder.

Alternatively, you can hard-wire passwords with JavaScript code. Login information for SQL tables is set up using the Database object's loginString property. You can set this property using the Inspector while editing your forms in the Form Designer. The property takes the form *user/password*, like so:

DCOOPER/COOP1

NOTE

Sharing a Database object among multiple forms can create more problems than it solves. Until you feel comfortable with the IntraBuilder dynamic object model, set up your forms so that each one has its own Database object. Each Database object should then have the appropriate loginString property value for its particular form.

Queries

Tables are accessed in IntraBuilder through Query objects. Query objects are driven by SQL SELECT statements, which reference the tables you want to include on a given form. For example, you might build an SQL SELECT statement like

SELECT * FROM "PRODUCT.DBF"

to include the PRODUCT.DBF table on a form. Conversely, you might construct a much more complicated SQL statement to join multiple tables together or restrict the rows returned using a complex WHERE or HAVING clause.

The Easy Way

The quickest way to add a table (and thereby a Query object) to a form is simply to drag the table from the Tables page of the IntraBuilder Explorer and drop it onto a form or report. IntraBuilder will automatically set up and open a corresponding Query component. If you drag a table from a BDE alias (Sybase, Oracle, and so on), the database object is also created.

The Hard Way

If you need something a little more sophisticated than a simple SELECT * against a single table, you might want to drop a Query component onto your form or report "manually." You'll then need to set its sql property to the SQL code that you want to execute and set its active property to true.

Building SQL Using the Visual Query Builder

As an alternative to keying in your SQL "by hand," you can use IntraBuilder's Visual Query Builder to create the code for you. To do this, follow these steps:

1. Drop a Query component onto your form or report.
2. Right-click the Query component to bring up the Inspector.
3. Click the Tool button to the right of the sql property.
4. Click the Query Builder File radio button.
5. Click the New button to the right of the Query Builder File radio button.
6. After the Visual Query Builder appears on-screen, use it to construct your query visually.

You can use the SQL button (which appears as a pair of spectacles) on the Visual Query Builder toolbar to view the SQL being built for you. Figure 7.24 shows an example of what a query might look like in the Visual Query Builder.

Figure 7.24.

*You can build
complex SQL queries
using the Visual
Query Builder.*

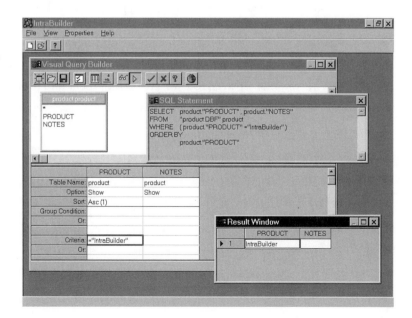

> **NOTE**
>
> When you furnish SQL to the Query object's sql property using either SQL script files or Query Builder .QRY files, IntraBuilder places the name of the external file itself in the sql property, prefixed with the @ character.

Summary

In this chapter you learned the advantages and disadvantages of the Paradox and dBASE table formats and the advantages and disadvantages of using SQL Links and ODBC drivers. You learned how to create tables, to build indexes, and to modify table definitions. You also saw how to define primary keys and establish referential integrity relationships. You finished the day by learning how to set up Paradox table passwords, how to set up the dBASE security system, and how to build queries using SQL and the Visual Query Builder.

Q&A

Q If I'm wanting to prototype applications with local tables that I eventually plan to move to a client/server DBMS, what's the best local table format for me?

A I would pick Paradox because of its support for declarative referential integrity and its rich palette of supported field types.

Q What's the best local table type in terms of security?

A That would definitely be the dBASE table type.

Q What options are available for prompting users for encrypted table passwords?

A You can let the automatic password form display or force passwords yourself using either JavaScript and the Session object, or the Database object and its loginString property.

Q Which is better—ODBC or SQL Links?

A That's a difficult question, and the answer could be a book unto itself. The short answer is that I prefer SQL Links. The long answer is, it depends on your needs, and keep in mind that they aren't mutually exclusive. You can use ODBC drivers with the Borland Database Engine in the same apps where you're using SQL Links drivers.

Workshop

The Workshop section provides questions and exercises to help you get a better feel for the material you learned today. Try to answer the questions and at least think about the exercises before moving on to tomorrow's lesson. You'll find the answers to the questions in Appendix A, "Answers to Quiz Questions."

Quiz

1. Which local table format supports users and user groups?
2. What IntraBuilder object is used to provide access to database tables?
3. What happens when you "run" a table?
4. Where do you define Paradox table passwords?
5. What's an alternative to keying SQL directly into IntraBuilder?

Exercises

1. Create a couple of dBASE tables and create users and groups that have varying levels of access to them.
2. Create a couple of Paradox tables and relate them using referential integrity.
3. Create an ODBC alias in the BDE Configuration program (for example, you might create one for the Northwind Access sample database) and build an IntraBuilder form that references it.
4. Create a table on an SQL server for which you have an SQL Links driver and open it in IntraBuilder.

7

In Review

Week 1 introduced you to the many tools that comprise IntraBuilder and make it easy to build dynamic Web pages. The first chapter helped you connect to existing data sources through BDE, ODBC, and SQL-Links. The second chapter provided a tour of the solution applications and tips on configuring a Web server to work with the IntraBuilder Server. The Form Designer was the focus of Days 3 and 4. Reports took center stage for Day 5. On Day 6, you learned about the various tools that IntraBuilder provides for application partitioning with client-side and server-side JavaScript. The week ended with a comparison of dBASE, Paradox, ODBC, and SQL-Link data sources and a guide to table creation.

1

2

3

4

5

6

7

Week 2

2

At a Glance

During Week 2, you create one of the most common applications found on the Web—a shopping cart application. It consists of one custom form class, eight JavaScript forms, one JavaScript report, six dBASE tables, two images, and a header file. You learn a lot about JavaScript, performance, and getting forms to look good in a browser.

The week starts off with a day of investigation, design, and setup. During Day 8, you don't do much with IntraBuilder itself. Instead, you examine several Web stores and break down the functionality into components that you will tackle in the following days. Day 8 also includes an introduction to the Navigator Gold HTML editor.

You really start building the application on Day 9. Here you create a custom form class that establishes the look and feel for all other forms. The first standard form is the Help form. The major JavaScript concept of the day is exception handling.

The primary and most complex function of the shopping cart application is giving shoppers the ability to search for items quickly and easily. On Day 10, you take time out of the application development to examine some of the built-in capabilities such as query by form. The day's lesson also includes an extensive series of benchmarks that show the effects of using indexes and changing table types.

Day 11 brings together some of the performance features uncovered during the previous day to create a quick search form. While creating the quick search form, you learn techniques for sharing information between forms. Day 11's lesson also shows how to create a read-only form for viewing the results of a query.

The focus of Day 12 is the creation of a multiple row grid control. Although neither IntraBuilder nor HTML provides a built-in control for working with an array of values, JavaScript makes it easy to create your own dynamic grid.

On Day 13, you return to the subject of searching and learn how to create complex searches. IntraBuilder allows for simple searches through SQL expressions and complex searches through database events. The quick search form relies on SQL expressions. The form you create on Day 13 takes advantage of database events.

The week ends with the development of the only form in the application to use standard datalinks that directly update a table. The final form also takes advantage of form pages for data validation on mimicking modal behavior. The last task on the last day is the creation of a report that uses events to calculate totals.

You are encouraged to go through each day and build up to the complete application, but you can also jump to any day using the example files provided. You can find day-by-day iterations of forms, reports, scripts, images, and header files in separate example folders. All the days require the same set of tables. The tables are in a separate tables folder. To get the examples for any day, copy all the files for that day and all the files from the tables folder to your working folder.

Day 8

Designing the Shopping Cart Application

by Paul Mahar

Today is the only day this week where you won't be immersed in JavaScript. This is the day to prepare the groundwork for an Internet shopping cart application. Today's tasks include the following:

☐ Checking out some existing shopping cart applications.

☐ Seeing what components make up such an application.

☐ Getting a set of tables ready.

☐ Creating an HTML doorway to launch the application.

IntraBuilder's Web applications can run within the corporate firewall as intranet systems or on public Web sites as Internet applications. Most of the prebuilt solutions that come with IntraBuilder are geared toward intranets. This chapter covers the design of a public Internet shopping cart application and preparing the tables that go with it. Although the IntraBuilder Server does not distinguish between intranet applications and Internet applications, there are a few things to keep in mind when designing an application for public use.

Shopping cart sites are one of the most common Web applications you'll run into while surfing the Net. You can use them to search for and purchase books, compact discs, software, and thousands of other items. A typical shopping cart application lets you search for items in a vendor's catalog, select items for purchase, review your order, and supply billing information. If you haven't purchased something on the Web lately, you might want to warm up your browser and cruise through a few Web stores. Visiting some Web stores helps you see what is expected of a merchant that sets up shop on the information superhighway.

TIP

> If you want as many people to use your site as possible, you need to take a least common denominator approach when developing your site. This is critically important if you want to support low bandwidth connections. As you work through the shopping cart application, keep the following guidelines in mind:
>
> ☐   Avoid a heavy reliance on images.
>
> ☐   Do not require frames, Java, ActiveX controls, or client-side JavaScript.

On Being a Virtual Mall Rat

In the physical world, a mall rat is a teenager whose primary after-school activity consists of hanging out at the local mall. Mall rats don't go to the mall to buy anything, but rather to socialize and check out cool stuff. As commerce moves from the physical to the virtual realm, the original mall rat heads for extension. The new breed is the virtual mall rat who hangs out in chat rooms and checks out cool Web sites, including those with shopping cart applications. Like the old style mall rat, the new virtual mall rat does little in the way of actual purchasing. To get a good sense of how to build a shopping cart application, one must become a virtual mall rat.

If you haven't already, hide your credit card, start up your browser, and head out to the shops. This list provides some sites to visit.

☐   http://www.cdnow.com/   CDNOW is an online CD and video store. It has a button bar at the top of each page to move between areas of the store. The primary pages are for locating items, setting up a shipping account, and getting help. Try to find a CD or video and add it to your shopping cart. From the shopping cart page, remove the item from your cart.

☐ `http://www.egghead.com/` This address takes you to the Web version of the Egghead software store. Here again, you will find buttons to search for products, view your shopping cart, and get help. Try adding something to your shopping cart, jumping back to a URL of `www.egghead.com`, and using refresh or reload. After jumping back to Egghead's home page, your shopping cart will be empty.

When you jump directly to a specific URL and bypass the internal links, most shopping cart applications lose track of the user and assume you are starting a new shopping spree. Some Web sites avoid this by creating accounts for users and requiring user names and passwords to access the site. You should consider the password approach if your site is expecting frequent repeat customers.

☐ `http://www.clbooks.com/` The Computer Literacy Bookshop is the first of two online bookstores to visit. Bookstores deserve a little extra attention because that is exactly the type of shopping cart application that you are about to create.

As with the other applications, you can use a keyword search with various categories. If the search finds some matching titles, you can drill down to see detailed information on any of the resulting books.

☐ `http://www.mcp.com/bookstore/` Macmillan Publishing's Information SuperLibrary bookstore is the model for the bookstore you will create. Macmillan Publishing USA houses several publishers including Sams, Que, New Riders, and Adobe Press.

Although you will not implement every feature on this site in the next week, you will re-create the most important pages. Pay particular attention to the keyword search, the more general category search, the shopping bag (also known as cart), and the checkout page. The custom search option takes you to the page shown in Figure 8.1.

NOTE

> The books referenced throughout the building of this application are available through Macmillan's bookstore. This is also the place to download all the source code, images, and tables used in the shopping cart application. If you haven't downloaded the tables already, click the Software Library link.

Although each of the shopping cart applications uses different images and styles to embellish its site, the underlying functionality is almost identical. Now that you've seen how the pros do it, it's your turn, and you have less than seven days to get your site up and running. Don't worry; all will go smoothly after you get a solid understanding of what the application entails.

Figure 8.1.

Using a keyword search.

Dissecting a Shopping Cart Site

Let's look at the individual components that make up a shopping cart application. The easiest components to identify are different pages you see while perusing a store. Other portions of the application are hidden from the end user. Here are the components you can see through a browser:

☐ The storefront is the home page or starting point for the Web site. The storefront can tie directly into the shopping cart system as in the Egghead site, or it can offer many other items. The starting point for the Macmillan site is www.mcp.com, and it contains dozens of links in addition to the bookstore.

☐ Help components, like storefronts, vary in scope. Simpler sites rely on prompts to guide users through the pages, while most sites have one or two dedicated help pages that describe common buttons and actions relevant to the site.

☐ Common links are page jumps available from any page. Common links keep the user from getting lost by providing an overview of the site and a quick way to jump to the main pages. Common links can be implemented through HTML links, buttons, or images. Most sites use image links across the top of the page to form a toolbar of common links.

☐ A quick search gives shoppers a fast way to locate items through predefined categories. An example of a quick search is the subject search on the Macmillan site. Other quick searches can include selections of best sellers and new releases. In addition to being easy on the user, a quick search is the fastest type of search for a Web server. Predefined sets can use indexes and simple expressions to extract data.

☐ A keyword search provides advanced lookups based on one or more fields. Users can search for one or more words contained anywhere in a field. Some of the more advanced search pages let users specify how to handle multiple word searches.

☐ A results list gives shoppers an overview of items found in a search. Some sites enable users to purchase items directly from the results list, while others require the user to descend to a detailed view before adding an item to the shopping cart.

☐ A Detail View describes a particular item and often includes an image of the item. The Detail View enables shoppers to continue browsing or place the item in their shopping cart.

☐ The shopping cart lets you review items selected for purchase. Most shopping carts also enable the user to adjust the quantity ordered and remove items from the cart.

☐ The checkout stand is where the buyer supplies shipping and billing information. Some online systems establish permanent accounts, and others require the user to enter all relevant information during each shopping trip. The checkout stand is where Internet security comes into play. Most online vendors ask for credit card information at this point.

The more popular online stores use a secure server to encrypt credit card information that is passed between the browser and the Web server. You can quickly identify a secure site by an address that begins with `https:` instead of `http:`. The CDNOW store uses a secured server.

☐ The receipt is the page of a shopping cart application that is least likely to be seen by a virtual mall rat because you actually have to purchase something to ever see it. The receipt provides a confirmation of your purchase and usually includes an invoice or tracking number. It may also show additional charges such as shipping and taxes.

Most of these components are dynamic Web pages that you can create as JavaScript forms. Other components include the static store front, the common links that appear on various forms, and the receipt. The receipt is dynamic in its data but does not offer any interactive features. You can create a receipt using a JavaScript Report. Table 8.1 lists the JavaScript forms required for the shopping cart application.

Table 8.1. JavaScript forms for the shopping cart application.

Filename	Description
cart.jfm	Shows the contents of the shopping cart.
checkout.jfm	Lets shoppers purchase items in their cart.
detail.jfm	Shows a detailed description of an item.
help.jfm	Help for other forms.
keyword.jfm	Enables shoppers to perform complex searches.
message.jfm	Displays status information to the shopper.
quick.jfm	Provides a fast and simple search.
results.jfm	Lists all items found in a search.

What you can't see through the browser are table structures, administrative tools, and what happens after you get your receipt. Before you start developing any JavaScript forms, you need to create and populate the tables. After you have tables, you can design a storefront and the help page. The rest of this chapter takes you through these tasks. Today you will go over the structure of each table used in the shopping cart application.

Stores have to sell something, and it is also really helpful if they have a name. For this exercise we'll be selling books. Why books? They are easy to sell on the Web, and Sams has a lot of book type data and owns the rights to images that are going to prove useful for this application. Not only that, but because you've got one in your hands right now, you're already familiar with the merchandise. The name, "Boingo's Books," seems pretty catchy and makes for an easy to create double-B logo. (Well, that, and I was trying to think of the book store name while listening to an Oingo Boingo song.)

Setting Up the Tables

The easiest way to set up an application in IntraBuilder is to place all related files in a single folder under the IntraBuilder folder. Follow these steps to create a new Store folder and select it as the active IntraBuilder folder:

1. Create a new Store folder using the Windows Explorer. If you installed IntraBuilder in the default location, the complete path for the new folder will be

   C:\Program Files\Borland\IntraBuilder\Store

2. Open the IntraBuilder Explorer and use the folder button to select the new folder as the Look In box.

The application requires six tables: Cart, Customer, Invoice, Lineitem, Product, and Title. The table structures are simple, and you can create them using any of the supported IntraBuilder table types. If you are using the standard version of IntraBuilder, your choices are limited to dBASE, Paradox, and Access table formats.

TIP

> Although this section walks you through the table design and population process, you should still consider downloading fully populated tables from the Macmillan Web site.

IntraBuilder uses native BDE calls to work with dBASE and Paradox tables and external ODBC drivers to connect to Access tables. To get the most functionality and performance, we'll skip the Access format and get our choices down to dBASE and Paradox. Paradox has a lot more field types, including the ever handy auto-increment type. However, I'm a diehard performance enthusiast, and the Borland Database Engine works a little faster with the simpler dBASE table type. Now that we have a table type selected, let's look at how to create the tables and their structure in detail.

The Cart Table

The Cart table is the basis for what will appear on the shopping cart page. It contains one row for each book a user selects for purchase. The Cart table contains four fields: CARTUSER, CARTDATE, ISBN, and QTY. Listing 8.1 shows the structure for the Cart table.

INPUT   **Listing 8.1. The structure for table CART.DBF.**

```
Table type: Visual dBASE
-----------------------------------------------------------------
Field   Field Name          Type          Length  Dec   Index
    1   CARTUSER            CHARACTER         20           Y
    2   CARTDATE            DATE               8           Y
    3   ISBN                CHARACTER         15           Y
    4   QTY                 NUMERIC            5           N
-----------------------------------------------------------------
** Total **                                  49
```

NEW TERM   A *row* is a unique set of fields within a table or view. For most queries, each row corresponds to a single physical record in a table. Rows are distinct from records when they contain calculated values or values from more than one table.

Although you could also name the first two fields USER and DATE, you should avoid doing so. USER and DATE are SQL reserved words that can cause unexpected errors when using table utilities such as the Calculate Aggregates dialog. Figure 8.2 shows the database engine error that occurs when attempting to calculate the minimum of a field named DATE.

TIP

> The IntraBuilder help file contains a complete list of SQL reserved words for dBASE and Paradox tables. You can locate the list by looking up Reserved words in the help index. Consult your server documentation for field naming conventions when working with tables through ODBC or SQL-Links.

Figure 8.2.

Error caused by using SQL reserved words as field names.

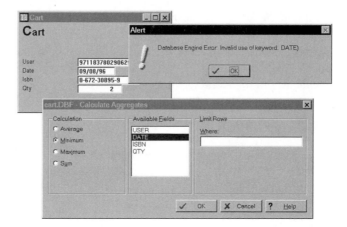

The first field, CARTUSER, contains a randomly generated number that identifies a shopper during a single session. Each time a shopper jumps to the help form from outside the application, the form generates a new user number. The application maintains the user number until the shopper jumps to a Web page outside the shopping cart application. When a shopper adds a book to the cart, the user number is used to identify the books of any single shopper. Although the data stored in the field is all numeric, the field is a character type. The database engines floating point system loses precision after 16 digits. Character expressions do not have any such limits.

The CARTDATE field contains the date that a row is added to the table. None of the JavaScript forms that a shopper sees will use this field. Database administrators can use the CARTDATE field to purge old rows from the Cart table. The dBASE date type internally stores four digits for the year, two for the month, and two for the day. Within a JavaScript event, date values appear as JavaScript date objects.

The ISBN and QTY fields display when a shopper views the shopping cart page. The ISBN number relates to an identically named field in the Title table. The QTY field lets shoppers order more than one of each book title. If a shopper tries to set the QTY field to zero, the record is deleted.

Indexes help the database engine speed up queries against the table. This table indexes all fields that the application uses to locate and filter rows.

The Customer Table

The Customer table contains customer, shipping, and billing information. The customer number is generated when a shopper commits an order through the Checkout page. The shopper enters information for the rest of the fields when checking out. The Customer table has a one-to-many relation with the Invoice table. Listing 8.2 shows the structure for the Customer table. The CARDDATE field is of type character to accommodate entry of expiration dates that do not include the day of the month.

INPUT   **Listing 8.2. The structure for table CUSTOMER.DBF.**

```
Table type: Visual dBASE
- - - - - - - - - - - - - - - - - - - - - - - - - - - - - - - - - - - - - - - - -
Field  Field Name          Type          Length  Dec  Index
    1  CUSTOMER            NUMERIC           10            Y
    2  NAME                CHARACTER         40            N
    3  PHONE               CHARACTER         20            N
    4  STREET              CHARACTER         40            N
    5  CITY                CHARACTER         30            N
    6  STATE               CHARACTER          2            N
    7  POSTALCODE          CHARACTER         10            N
    8  COUNTRY             CHARACTER         30            N
    9  CARD                CHARACTER         10            N
   10  CARDNUMBER          CHARACTER         20            N
   11  CARDDATE            CHARACTER          8            N
   12  CARDNAME            CHARACTER         40            N
- - - - - - - - - - - - - - - - - - - - - - - - - - - - - - - - - - - - - - - - -
** Total **                                261
```

The Invoice Table

The Checkout form adds a row to the Invoice table when a shopper commits an order. The Receipt page contains the invoice number, customer number, and order date.

A "real-world" Invoice table would likely include other fields, such as date filled. Although the Invoice table is one of the final destinations of the shopping cart applications, it is the beginning of the order processing system. An application written with C++ Builder or Visual dBASE could use BDE to work with the same tables and fulfill customer orders. The Invoice table has a one-to-many relation to the Lineitem table. Listing 8.3 shows the structure for the Invoice table.

INPUT   **Listing 8.3. The structure for table INVOICE.DBF.**

```
Table type: Visual dBASE
---------------------------------------------------------------------
Field  Field Name           Type          Length  Dec  Index
    1   INVOICE              NUMERIC           10          Y
    2   CUSTOMER             NUMERIC           10          Y
    3   ORDERDATE            DATE               8          Y
---------------------------------------------------------------------
** Total **                                   29
```

The Lineitem Table

Like the Invoice table, the Lineitem table is an end result of the shopping cart application. When a shopper commits an order, the Checkout form moves records from the Cart table to the Lineitem table. The Invoice field relates to a matching Invoice key in the Invoice table. Listing 8.4 shows the structure for the Lineitem table.

INPUT   **Listing 8.4. The structure for table LINEITEM.DBF.**

```
Table type: Visual dBASE
---------------------------------------------------------------------
Field  Field Name           Type          Length  Dec  Index
    1   INVOICE              NUMERIC           10          Y
    2   ISBN                 CHARACTER         15          Y
    3   QTY                  NUMERIC           10          N
---------------------------------------------------------------------
** Total **                                   36
```

The Product Table

The Product table is a look-up table for a quick search. Boingo's Books only carries books on Borland products. The Product table is a list of Borland's current software catalog. The shopping cart application can use the Product table to create a quick search. Shoppers can use a product quick search to locate all books related to a single product. The Notes field is a memo field that Boingo personnel can use to keep notes about a given product. Although the IntraBuilder table designer reports a width of 10 for a dBASE memo field, this is only the length of the pointer to the actual data. The memo data is stored in a separate file with a .DBT extension. Memo fields are variable-length text fields that provide an efficient method of storing unstructured text such as comments. Listing 8.5 shows the structure for the Product table.

INPUT   **Listing 8.5. The structure for table PRODUCT.DBF.**

```
Table type: Visual dBASE
-----------------------------------------------------------------
Field  Field Name            Type         Length  Dec  Index
    1  PRODUCT               CHARACTER        20          Y
    2  NOTES                 MEMO             10          N
-----------------------------------------------------------------
** Total **                                  31
```

The Title Table

The Title table lists all the book titles in the Boingo's book inventory. The shopping cart application never writes to the Title table. You need to ensure valid data exists in the Product and Title tables before you begin to create the application.

Shoppers can locate books by looking for values in any of the first four fields: Title, Author, ISBN, and Product. Each of the search fields has an index allowing for the ordering of results. The Title, Author, and ISBN field searches are complex keyword look-ups in which the index does not benefit the look-up. The Product field is a quick search that will run faster with an index. The Product field also relates to the Product field in the Product table. Listing 8.6 shows the structure for the Title table.

INPUT   **Listing 8.6. The structure for table TITLE.DBF.**

```
Table type: Visual dBASE
-----------------------------------------------------------------
Field  Field Name            Type         Length  Dec  Index
    1  TITLE                 CHARACTER        60          Y
    2  AUTHOR                CHARACTER        40          Y
    3  ISBN                  CHARACTER        15          Y
    4  PRODUCT               CHARACTER        20          Y
    5  PUBLISHER             CHARACTER        20          N
    6  PUBDATE               DATE              8          N
    7  PRICE                 NUMERIC           6    2     N
    8  NOTES                 MEMO             10          N
    9  COVER                 BINARY           10          N
-----------------------------------------------------------------
** Total **                                 192
```

The Price field has a width of six, which includes a fixed decimal place. This means books can have prices up to $999.99. Fortunately for the buying public, most books require a Price field with a width of only five.

WARNING

> If you attempt to store a number too large to fit into a field, IntraBuilder will fill the field with asterisks. IntraBuilder does not throw any errors for this situation, nor does it when you attempt to use the value from an asterisk-filled numeric field in a calculation. Such calculations will result in unpredictable values.

The Title table's Notes field has the same format as the Product table's Notes field. The text from the Notes field contains a description of the book. The text should not contain any formatting such as hard carriage returns. When the memo appears in a JavaScript form, the browser will control the word wrap.

The Cover field contains GIF images of the book covers. You can import a wide variety of image types into a field when viewing a table in the IntraBuilder Designer. The dBASE DBF structure uses a ten-digit pointer to a variable length binary image in a DBT file. DBT files contain all dBASE variable-length types including memo, binary, and OLE fields. Follow these steps to create the Title table from the Script Pad and import a GIF file into a new row:

1. From the menu, choose View|Script Pad.

2. Enter the following JavaScript statement to open the table designer and name the new table TITLE.DBF. Remember that JavaScript is case sensitive.

   ```
   _sys.tables.design("TITLE.DBF")
   ```

3. For the first field, enter TITLE, leave the type as CHARACTER, change the width to 60, and select Ascend for the Ascending index.

4. After completing the first field, tab down to a new row and continue entering the structure as shown in Listing 8.6. Where the listing shows an index, select Ascend; otherwise, leave the Index column at None.

5. After the structure looks the same as in Figure 8.3, choose File|Close and save your changes.

6. To add a new row, run the table from the Script Pad. Enter the following JavaScript statement:

   ```
   _sys.tables.run("TITLE.DBF")
   ```

8

7. From the menu, choose Table|Add Row and enter information in each field. When you first open an empty table, the row pointer is at endOfSet and you cannot save any changes. Selecting Add Row opens a row buffer but does not actually add a row.

Figure 8.3.

Designing the Title table.

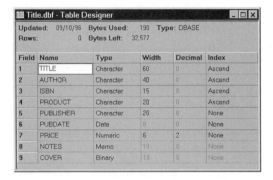

New Term Whenever a row is not available for the current query or table, the object is at *endOfSet*. An endOfSet condition can occur when you try to move before the first row or past the last row of a table. An empty table or view is always at endOfSet.

8. When you get to the Cover field, right-click the field to open a shortcut menu, and select Import Image, as shown in Figure 8.4.

Figure 8.4.

Importing an image into the Cover field.

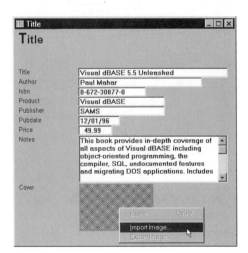

9. Select an image and save the new row. From the Choose Image dialog, you can select any image and navigate to other folders. To commit the new data, choose Table|Save Row. If you do not explicitly save the row, all the data in the new row will be lost.

WARNING

Changing folders from the Choose Image dialog or any other IntraBuilder dialog changes the default folder for all IntraBuilder dialogs.

The IntraBuilder Table Run window contains several basic table utilities in addition to data entry and navigation options. The Table Run window provides options to query, sort, and perform simple calculations. These tools can help you with many data administration tasks.

When you open a table, IntraBuilder creates and opens a temporary form using the same columnar layout that you can get from the Form Expert. This temporary form includes all fields and enables you to perform row operations through the IntraBuilder toolbar and menu. IntraBuilder deletes the temporary form when you close the window.

TIP

You can use the Visual Query Builder's result window to view more than one row at a time. When you have a query defined, click the Query Builder's run button to open a result window. This window is read only.

Although IntraBuilder has some convenient database administration features, you should consider using another product such as a desktop database to assist you in routine table management. If you're using Access tables, you probably already have the best tool for managing Access tables, MS-Access. If you are creating new dBASE or Paradox tables, you can use any other BDE-based product to assist you.

Taking Advantage of Other BDE-Based Products

The Borland Database Engine (BDE) is a shared technology that provides native dBASE and Paradox support for IntraBuilder, Visual dBASE, Delphi, Borland C++, and Paradox. The same query engine retrieves SQL results, regardless of which BDE front-end product you're

using. Microsoft uses a similar architecture to share the Access Jet engine with MS-Access and Visual Basic. If you are using dBASE or Paradox tables with IntraBuilder, you can enhance your data management functionality with other BDE products. Developers will find Visual dBASE and Delphi to be the most complimentary products to use with IntraBuilder.

WARNING

> Set the BDE LOCALSHARE system setting to TRUE if you are sharing tables between 16-bit and 32-bit versions of BDE products. LOCALSHARE enables record locking between the two platforms.

Visual dBASE

Anyone who has learned his or her way around the IntraBuilder development environment will experience a sense of déjá vú when first exploring Visual dBASE. In place of the IntraBuilder Explorer, Navigator provides the same function. There is even a Command window that works like the Script Pad. The Two-Way Tools also function in a similar manner. Of particular interest to the IntraBuilder developer is the Table Records window and the dBASE soft delete system.

The Table Records Window

When you open a table in Visual dBASE, it comes up in a window similar to the IntraBuilder Table Run window. Both windows have a single, records-columnar view. The dBASE window contains two additional views: a Form view and a Browse view. The Form view is similar to a Form Layout generated by IntraBuilder Form Expert. The Form view displays a single record with fields going both across and down. The Browse view is a grid with full update functionality. You can add, edit, and delete records within the grid.

The Table menu in the dBASE Table Records window has several options that either are not surfaced in the IntraBuilder development environment or are not otherwise available in the IntraBuilder Table Run window. Figure 8.5 shows some of the additional table utilities that you can use in dBASE. These include managing indexes, generating test data, and working with deleted records.

In dBASE you can create, modify, and set indexes while viewing the grid. IntraBuilder has a similar index manager in the table designer. To set the row order in IntraBuilder, you must first create a query file or set the indexName property of a rowset object.

Figure 8.5.

Using the Visual dBASE Table Records window.

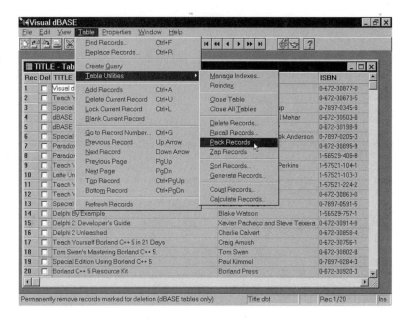

NEW TERM A *rowset* is comprised of all the rows of a query. The rowset object is a property of a query. All table navigation and searching is done through the rowset object.

Finding Those Long Lost Deletions

The dBASE table soft deletion system is unlike the more common and irreversible deletes used with Paradox, Access, and SQL tables. The first byte in each row of a dBASE table contains an asterisk or a null value. This byte is the deletion byte and the default value is null. If the deletion byte contains an asterisk, the database engine hides the row from the application. This occurs in Visual dBASE by default and in IntraBuilder always. In Visual dBASE, you also have the option of viewing and recalling deleted rows. Recalling a row sets the deletion byte back to a null value.

IntraBuilder treats all table types the same. There is no way to undelete a row from other table types because most automatically reuse the spaces occupied by deleted rows when inserting new rows. This means you cannot recall a deleted row from a dBASE table with IntraBuilder. However, if you have a copy of Visual dBASE handy, you can still get your data back by following these steps.

1. Open Visual dBASE and turn off the option to hide deleted rows. You can do this by unchecking the Deleted option on the Table tab of the Desktop Properties dialog.

2. Open your table and locate the deleted row.

3. From the menu, choose Table|Recall Current Record.

Optimizing dBASE Tables

You can pack a dBASE table to reclaim the space occupied by deleted rows. From within IntraBuilder, you can use a method of the database class called packTable(). You can use the following line to call the method through the default database object.

```
_sys.databases[0].packTable("table.dbf") ;
```

If you have a copy of Visual dBASE, you can open the table and choose Table|Table Utilities|Pack Table to accomplish the same thing.

The Database Desktop

The Database Desktop is an abbreviated version of Paradox that was first developed as an add-in to Quattro Pro. Today, a 32-bit version is bundled with C++ Builder and Delphi. The Database Desktop has the following features:

☐ A table editor that provides add, update, and deletion of rows through a flexible grid window.

☐ SQL and QBE query editors. These queries are not compatible with the IntraBuilder query system.

☐ Table utilities for copying, emptying, and restructuring tables. A pack option is available through the Restructure dialog.

When you first open a table in the Database Desktop, it is read only. Press F9 to place the table into an edit mode. Figure 8.6 shows the Title table as it appears in the Database Desktop.

Figure 8.6.

Using the Database Desktop.

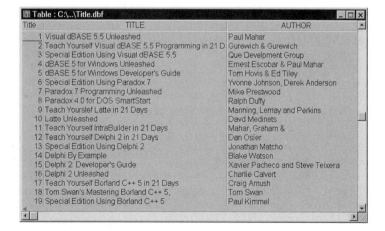

Building a Storefront

The last step for the day is preparing an HTML index page. This will be the default Web page for the bookstore. For this task, you will not be using IntraBuilder because it does not contain a static HTML page designer. Instead, you'll use Netscape's Navigator Gold, which is bundled with all versions of IntraBuilder. This section also describes how to set up custom mappings for the Borland Web Server, WebSite, and FastTrack.

 NOTE
> At this point, you should have all six tables and couple images in the store folder. The images are available with the source code and are `logo.gif` and `vcr.gif`.

The HTML index page for the storefront is very simple. It needs to contain only a single link to call the IntraBuilder Agent with a JavaScript form. To make the storefront a little nicer, it includes an image link in addition to a text link. To make bookstore hopping easy, you can add an extra link to the Macmillan Web site.

 NOTE
> If you're a Microsoft Internet Explorer user and don't want to try out Navigator Gold, you can use Microsoft's FrontPage to create this simple form.

Designing the Storefront with Navigator Gold

Navigator Gold's HTML editor works like a word processor. You can enhance text using a toolbar to adjust font size, bold, and italics. The editor's toolbar also contains HTML-specific tool buttons for creating links and publishing pages directly to remote Web sites. If you have Navigator Gold, follow these steps to create Boingo's index page:

1. Start Netscape and select File|New Document|Blank.
2. To make a heading, enter `Welcome to Boingo's Books`. Select the text and pick Heading1 from the style drop-down list that appears on the bottom toolbar. This applies HTML codes to give the text a larger font. With the text still selected, click the centering toolbar button.
3. From the menu, select Insert|Image. This prompts you to save the file. Save it as `index.htm` in the store folder (by default `C:\Program Files\Borland\IntraBuilder\Store`).

8

 TIP Navigator Gold recognizes only GIF and JPEG files as valid images, whereas most Windows tools work with BMP files. You can use IntraBuilder to solve this dilemma by translating images between these types. As an example, I created a logo as a BMP using the Windows 95 Paint accessory, opened the logo in IntraBuilder, and exported it to GIF. This allows the logo to work with Navigator Gold.

4. With the file saved, enter LOGO.GIF as the Image filename for the store logo and click the Link tab. Enter the following link and close the Properties dialog box:

   `http://localhost/svr/intrasrv.isv?store/help.jfm`

   Let's take a closer look at this URL:

   - ☐ `localhost` refers to a locally running Web server that is using the default port of 80. You can use `localhost` when developing an application on a single machine. If you have the luxury of having separate machines as your development Web server and workstation, enter the host's true name instead.

   - ☐ `svr` is a Web server mapping to the location of the IntraBuilder Server DLL files. It is shorthand for `C:\Program Files\Borland\IntraBuilder\Server`.

   - ☐ `intrasrv.isv` is the IntraBuilder Agent that can run an instance of a JavaScript form.

   - ☐ `?` is a delimiter that indicates that what follows is a parameter.

   - ☐ `store/` is an alias mapping that refers to the folder that contains the tables and JavaScript forms for the bookstore application. The last section of this chapter describes how to create an alias mapping.

   - ☐ `help.jfm` is the parameter passed to the IntraBuilder Agent. This is a JavaScript form that you will create in Day 9.

5. To make the image blend with the form, set the background color to white. From the menu, select Properties|Document. Select the Appearance tab and click the Background button. This lets you pick a color. Select a white background. While you're in the Document Properties dialog, give your form a title. Click the General tab and enter a title of `Boingo's Books - The Store Front`.

6. Click the left-align button and enter the company slogan, "The best Web source for books on Borland database and development tools."

7. On the next line, insert a text link to the same JavaScript form that opens for the logo. From the menu, select Insert|Link. Enter the same link information and some descriptive text as shown in Figure 8.7.

Figure 8.7.

Creating a text link in Navigator Gold.

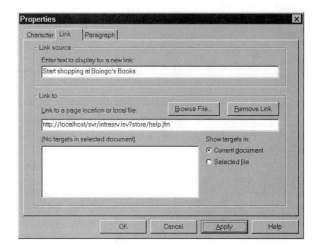

8. Click the View in Browser button to run your HTML form. This is similar to switching from design to run mode in the IntraBuilder Form Designer.

That's all you need for your index form. If you are having fun with Netscape Gold, go ahead and add some more descriptive text and some more links. You might also want to emphasize text links by making the font larger. Listing 8.7 shows the complete HTML source for an index page as generated by Netscape Gold.

INPUT   **Listing 8.7. HTML source for `index.htm`.**

```
 1: <!DOCTYPE HTML PUBLIC "-//W3C//DTD HTML 3.2//EN">
 2: <HTML>
 3: <HEAD>
 4:    <TITLE>Boingo's Books - Store Front</TITLE>
 5:    <META NAME="Author" CONTENT="">
 6:    <META NAME="GENERATOR" CONTENT="Mozilla/3.0Gold (Win95; I) [Netscape]">
 7: </HEAD>
 8: <BODY TEXT="#000000" BGCOLOR="#FFFFFF">
 9:
10: <H1 ALIGN=CENTER>Welcome To Boingo's Books</H1>
11:
12: <CENTER><P><A HREF="http://localhost/svr/intrasrv.isv?store/help.jfm">
13: <IMG SRC="logo.gif" HEIGHT=100 WIDTH=126></A></P></CENTER>
14:
15: <P><FONT SIZE=+1>The best web source for books on Borland database and
16: development tools.</FONT></P>
17:
18: <P><FONT SIZE=+2><A HREF="http://localhost/svr/intrasrv.isv?store/help.jfm">
19: Start Shopping at Boingo's Books</A> </FONT></P>
20:
21: <P><FONT SIZE=+1>Boingo's Books contains more than a dozen books about
```

```
22: Borland software. OK that is not really that many books, but descriptions
23: of all books are included, many include a book cover image.</FONT></P>
24:
25: <P><FONT SIZE=+1>There are many different ways to search for titles, so
26: the book you're looking for is never more than a few mouse clicks away.
27: </FONT></P>
28:
29: <P><FONT SIZE=+2><A HREF="http://www.mcp.com/bookstore">
30: Go to a real bookstore</A></FONT></P>
31:
32: </BODY>
33: </HTML>.
```

ANALYSIS You can view the HTML source by selecting View|Source Document from within Navigator. The important lines in index.htm are lines 12 and 18. The URL in each line uses localhost to look for a Web server running on the same machine that is running the browser.

TIP

Netscape Navigator Gold contains an interactive JavaScript prompt that enables you to test JavaScript expressions. The JavaScript prompt is similar to the IntraBuilder Script Pad. To open the prompt, enter JAVASCRIPT: as a location. When the prompt is active, the Navigator window splits into upper and lower panes. The lower pane contains the prompt. If you enter an expression such as navigator.appVersion, the value appears in the top pane. Microsoft Internet Explorer does not contain a similar feature.

Mapping Out the Storefront

The index page doesn't do much good if your Web server doesn't have a mapping to it. Web server mappings make it easy to locate groups of documents. This section covers how to create mappings for WebSite, the Borland Web Server, and FastTrack. If you are running Microsoft Internet Information Server, NT Workstation Peer Server, or another server, the general rules will still apply, although the specific implementations vary.

NEW TERM *Mapping* in a Web server is similar to mapping a Netware server drive to a local drive. A map provides a logical shortcut name for a physical location. For a Netware drive you might map \\NWSERVER\PUBLIC as F:. There are two main differences between Web server mappings and Netware mappings. Mappings for Web servers are defined on the server, and they map to logical names rather than drive letters.

WebSite is a great server to use with IntraBuilder during the development cycle. It is compact and contains a wealth of easy-to-set options. The Borland Web Server also is compact and well suited for single system development. The Borland Web Server lacks some of the configuration options that are available with WebSite. Both servers are also dependable for small intranet applications.

The Borland Web Server contains an API that is a reduced set of the Netscape Server API. This API makes the Borland Web Server faster than WebSite, which relies on Windows CGI. The Windows CGI protocol uses files to communicate between Web servers and applications such as IntraBuilder. The Web server API systems that come with Netscape FastTrack, Microsoft Internet Information Server, and the Borland Web Server handle all communication through in-memory function calls.

WARNING

Windows CGI does not support the IntraBuilder Server `Timeout` registry setting. When using the Windows CGI, all forms that are not explicitly released are left in memory until the `MaxSessions` threshold is reached. For this reason, you should not use the Windows CGI interface for anything other than development.

When you deploy an application, consider scaling up to a more robust server such as Netscape FastTrack for NT. For secure transactions, you can use Netscape Enterprise Server or Microsoft Internet Information Server. Place the Web server on Windows NT 4.0 if you have a process that can tie up a single agent for several minutes. Windows 95 and NT 3.51 are not as adept at multitasking the agents. During development, keep your Web server simple and avoid the overhead associated with these higher end servers.

For the shopping cart application, create a mapping called `store` that points to `C:\Program Files\Borland\IntraBuilder\Store`. This lets you quickly open the storefront by entering `http://localhost/store`.

Making a Map for WebSite

Here is a step-by-step guide to creating the store mapping for WebSite version 1.1. If you have a newer version, the procedure might be slightly different.

1. Open WebSite and choose Properties|Control to open the WebSite property sheet.
2. Open the Mappings tab and select the Documents radio button.
3. Enter `/store/` for the Document URL Path.
4. Enter `C:\Program Files\Borland\IntraBuilder\Store` for the full directory path (see Figure 8.8).

Figure 8.8.

*Creating a document
mapping in WebSite.*

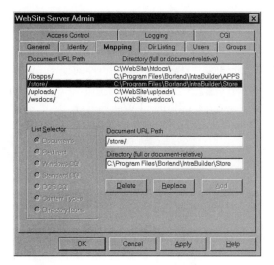

5. Click Add and Apply to save and activate the new mapping.

6. Close the WebSite property sheet.

You can now try out the new mapping inside your browser. With WebSite running on the same machine, enter http://localhost/store into a browser. You should see the index page that you recently created with Netscape Gold. If it comes up okay, save it to your bookmark or favorites list.

Rigging the Registry for the Borland Web Server

If you are running the Borland Web Server, things are not quite as simple as they are with WebSite. To create a mapping for the Borland Web Server, you need to edit the Windows registry directly. The following steps show how it works:

1. If it is running, shut down the Borland Web Server. The registry settings are read only once during startup.

2. Open the Windows Registry Editor. Run REGEDIT.EXE (REGEDT32.EXE for Windows NT 3.51).

3. Locate and open the following key:

    HKEY_LOCAL_MACHINE\SOFTWARE\Borland\Web Server\1.0\Alias Manager\Map

4. With the Map branch selected, choose Edit|New|String Value.

5. Enter STORE as the branch value. After creating the name, choose Edit|Modify to enter the directory path. The path you enter in the registry must end with \ to work correctly. Enter the following path:

```
C:\Program Files\Borland\IntraBuilder\Store\
```

6. When you have the registry set up as shown in Figure 8.9, close the Registry Editor and restart the Borland Web Server.

Figure 8.9.

Editing the registry for the Borland Web Server.

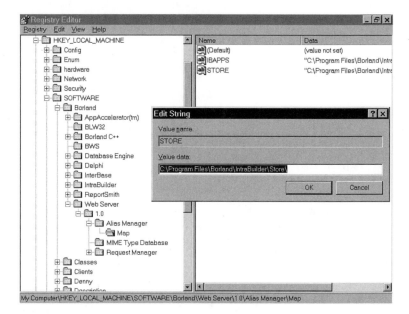

You can now try opening the index.htm with your browser. Enter http://localhost/store/ index.htm. The Borland Web Server will substitute the full path to the index file in place of store.

NOTE

Unlike most Web servers, the Borland Web Server does not use index.htm as a default document name. When creating links or bookmarks, you must include the index.htm with the server name. If you do not specify the document name, the Borland Web Server returns an error.

8

If all was successful, your browser displays the Store Front page for Boingo's Books as shown in Figure 8.10. If you get an error, try restarting your computer to clear out the Borland Web Server buffer.

Figure 8.10.

Viewing the Store Front through Navigator.

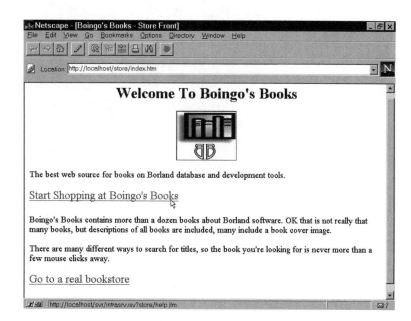

Creating a Document Directory for FastTrack

If you have IntraBuilder Professional or IntraBuilder Client/Server, you also have Netscape FastTrack for Windows NT. You can download FastTrack for Windows 95 from Netscape. FastTrack is a robust server that you can also use during development and deployment. All Netscape servers use the same Netscape Server Administrator for customizing server configurations. The Administrator is built with JavaScript and runs from within Netscape Navigator. The following are the steps for using the Netscape Server Administrator to create a mapping to the Store folder:

1. Open the Netscape Server Administrator.

2. Select the FastTrack server you want to use with IntraBuilder.

3. Load the configuration file as needed. This is required after installing IntraBuilder.

4. From the Content Management page, select Additional Document Directories.

5. Under Add Document Directories, enter a prefix and map as shown. Do not end the directory mapping with a slash.

   URL prefix: `/store`

   Map to directory: `C:/Program Files/Borland/IntraBuilder/STORE`

You can use either a forward slash or a backslash to separate folder names. However you enter them, FastTrack will save the mapping as shown in Figure 8.11.

Figure 8.11.

Creating a mapping for FastTrack.

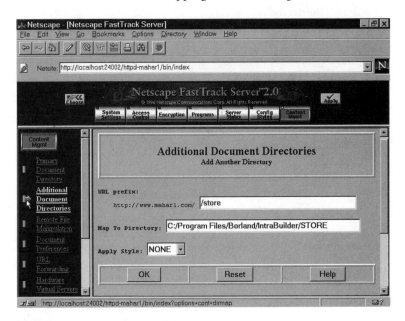

6. After entering the new document directory, click OK and then Save and Apply to begin using the new mapping.

You can also create mappings for FastTrack through the obj.conf file. This text file works like a Windows INI file for Netscape Servers. When you use the Netscape Server Administrator, you are actually editing the obj.conf file.

Summary

You have done just about everything you can do to create an IntraBuilder-driven application without really using IntraBuilder. The chapter started with an overview of shopping cart applications. All the major components of the Boingo's Books Web store have been identified. All the tables are in place and a storefront is up and running.

Tomorrow's chapter builds up the store with a JavaScript form. At the end of Day 9, shoppers can go through the storefront and launch a JavaScript form with a toolbar and help. On Day 9, you will create a custom form class containing the toolbar, which serves as a set of common links for all the other pages. The help page will explain what the common links do and show how many items are in the shopping cart.

Q&A

Q I noticed that most of the online shopping cart applications use images that look like buttons. Why don't they just use buttons?

A HTML does not provide many of the button formatting features that Windows users have grown accustomed to seeing. For example, HTML buttons cannot be disabled, and they cannot contain bitmaps. If you use images, you can create what looks like a disabled button.

Q If I'm expecting a lot of usage, is it better to keep my data in a server such as SQL Server or a native BDE format such as dBASE tables?

A It depends on what your application does. SQL Server and InterBase will outperform BDE in complex queries; however, the simpler tables are faster for low volume transactions. This speed is not so much from the database engine but from a more direct path between the data and the application.

Q I have an old copy of dBASE for DOS. Can I use it to work with dBASE tables created in IntraBuilder?

A IntraBuilder creates level 5 tables with support for field types such as binary and OLE. These field types are not supported by dBASE for DOS.

Q I tried to find a trial copy of WebSite at `http://www.website.com/`, but all I found was an advertising agency. Where can I get a trial copy of WebSite?

A You can find complete information about WebSite, including trial versions, at the O'Reilly & Associates site, `http://website.ora.com/`. The site at `www.website.com` is not affiliated with O'Reilly or the WebSite product line.

Workshop

The Workshop section provides questions and exercises to help you get a better feel for the material you learned today. Try to answer the questions and at least think about the exercises before moving on to tomorrow's lesson. You'll find the answers to the questions in Appendix A, "Answers to Quiz Questions."

Quiz

1. How can you identify whether a page you are working with has a secured server?
2. What do the *m* and the *p* stand for in the `mcp` part of `http://www.mcp.com`?
3. For what types of searches do indexes help performance?
4. What sets the Gold version of Navigator apart from its non-Gold sibling?

5. What types of images does the Navigator Gold editor support?

6. How can you open a Script Pad in Navigator?

Exercises

1. Try using Navigator Gold as a Two-Way Tool. Edit the `index.htm` file and add another image or some text. After making changes by hand, open the HTML document in the Netscape editor and resave it. View the source and see how it alters the code you handwrote.

2. The setup program for IntraBuilder creates an IBAPPS mapping for the prebuilt solutions applications. It does not create one for the Sample files. Create your own mapping to the Samples folder and use it to run the Biolife JavaScript sample form through a browser.

Day 9

Creating a Common Look and Feel

by Paul Mahar

Today's chapter guides you through the design of a custom form class that will set the look and feel for the application. You will use the custom form class to create the store's first JavaScript form. Along with setting a standard color and heading for each form, the custom form class will contain a toolbar with buttons to take the shopper to each major area of the Web bookstore application you started on Day 8. The JavaScript form is the Help form referenced by the index HTML file from Day 8. The following are the major tasks for the day:

- ☐ Finding common links that you can use for toolbar buttons.
- ☐ Designing a custom form class with a standard banner.
- ☐ Adding toolbar buttons to the custom form class.
- ☐ Writing a JavaScript method for each toolbar button.
- ☐ Designing the Help form.

☐ Creating a user key value to track users.

☐ Creating a JavaScript preprocessor file to link all the form source files together.

You will learn how to write methods for both the Help form and the toolbar custom form class. Most of the methods are simple functions that open other forms. The most advanced method in this chapter tells the shopper how many books are in the shopping cart. You'll also get a brief introduction to the JavaScript preprocessor.

Making a Common Look and Feel with a Custom Form Class

For the bookstore application, Boingo (the boss) insists all forms include a banner with the store name and a common set of navigation buttons. Here are several basic approaches to giving Boingo what he wants:

☐ Add standard buttons and methods to each form. You could use the Form Designer's Clipboard support to copy buttons from one form to another. This would make the task a little less tedious, but still not a delight.

☐ Create custom components for each button. This lets you add the common buttons directly from the component palette. You have to write the methods only once. Using custom components does take advantage of reusable objects but you still have to add and position five or six components for each form. There must be an easier way.

☐ Use a custom form class complete with the banner, buttons, and events. Controls from a custom form class require no repositioning and make it easy to add multiple components to multiple forms.

One of the most powerful benefits of object orientation is the ability to create reusable classes. A custom form class lets you create a standard template for a set of JavaScript forms. Custom form classes can add properties, components, and methods to standard JavaScript forms.

A custom form class also streamlines application maintenance. If you decide you want to add a new button to the toolbar for all forms or change the way one of the buttons works, you need to change only the custom form class. All derived forms will inherit your changes automatically.

Figuring Out Which Forms Can Be Common Links

Not all forms can be common links. From the dissecting done on Day 8, you determined that your application requires eight forms. The shopper needs the ability to jump to some of the forms at any point. Other forms can open only at certain points. To make a sensible toolbar with common links, start by taking a closer look at each form.

As shoppers move around from form to form, the application needs to keep track of them. This can be done by creating a user key value when the user first enters the application. Each form can then pass the key value along to the next form. As long as the shopper stays within the application, it can keep track of the shopping cart contents.

☐ The Cart form shows the shopper what is in the shopping cart. This form requires a user identification key so that it can filter out rows from the Cart table that belong to other shoppers.

☐ The Checkout form enables the user to enter billing information and commit an order. Like the Cart form, the Checkout form requires a user identification key so that it can locate the correct rows in the Cart table.

☐ The Detail form shows information for a single book. Shoppers can add books to the shopping cart from this form. The user key is required to add books to the cart. The Detail form requires query and row positioning information from the Results form. The Detail form is not a common link because it can open only from the Results form.

☐ The Help form displays information about each of the common links. This is the only form that does not require a user key to open. If the Help form opens without a user value, it generates a new user key. This is the only form that a shopper can open through a URL. All the other forms open in response to a request to an IntraBuilder server.

☐ The Keyword form performs a complex search for books in the Titles table. It requires only the user key to pass on to other forms. The Keyword form can open the Results form.

☐ The Message form opens when no rows are available for another form. It requires the user key to pass on to other forms. The toolbar does not need a common link to this form.

☐ The Quick form has simple search capabilities. Like the Keyword form, it opens the Results form and passes on query information and the user key. It requires only the user key to open.

☐ The Results form presents a list of rows matching either a keyword or quick search. It requires query information from a search form and is not a common link.

The only forms that work as common links are the Cart form, the Checkout form, the Help form, the Keyword form, and the Quick form. All the others require more information than the user key.

Designing the Toolbar

So far this application is only an idea. You have yet to develop any forms, but that won't stop you from charging ahead and creating a set of toolbar buttons that can link the applications forms together. This section describes how to create a custom form class with five buttons, each linked to an event that can open another form. The custom form class will also contain a banner and a ruler. Here are the steps for creating the Toolbar custom form class:

1. Open the IntraBuilder Explorer with the Look In box set to the Store folder.

2. Select the Forms tab and double-click the (untitled) Custom Form Class icon. This is the second icon in the group. It contains less detail than the standard Form icon. If you are prompted for an Expert, you'll know you clicked on the wrong icon.

3. Clear any current custom form class by selecting File|Set Custom Form Class. Use the Clear Custom Form Class button to force the designer to derive your new class from the base Form class (refer to Figure 9.1).

Figure 9.1.

Creating a new custom form class from the base class of Form.

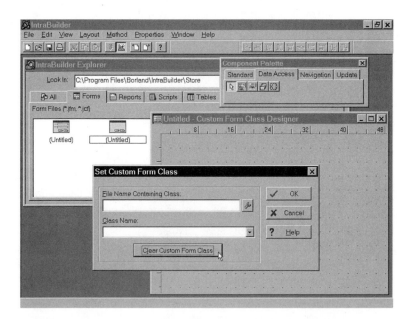

4. Drop an HTML component on the form to use as a banner. Place the component near the top of the form and make it large enough to hold "Boingo's Books" in a large font.

5. Open the Inspector and change the HTML component's name property to htmlBanner. The name property is one of the identification properties.

All component names must be unique to a form. Be sure to change the default name property of each component you place in a custom form class. Leaving the default names increases the likelihood of conflicts with components on forms derived from a custom form class.

6. Locate the text property and open the Text Property Builder by clicking on the tool (also known as the *wrench*, or *spanner*) button.

7. Enter Boingo's Books into the Text without Tags box. Select the text and apply the Header 2 tag. You can select the Header 2 tag from the Custom Tags drop-down list. Click Add to place HTML tags around the selected text as shown in Figure 9.2.

Figure 9.2.

Adding HTML header tags with the Text Property Builder.

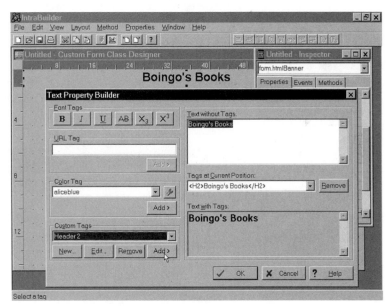

TIP

Use standard HTML tags to control the emphasis of text items. Although IntraBuilder does support selecting specific fonts, not all browsers support font name tags. All Web browsers support HTML tags for header levels.

8. The last property to change for htmlBanner is alignHorizontal. Set this to
   1 - Center.

9. Add five buttons and set the names and text properties as shown in Table 9.1.
   For all buttons, set the top to 1.6 and the width to 12.

Table 9.1. The toolbar button properties.

Name	Text	Left
buttonQuick	Quick	1
buttonKeyword	Keyword	15
buttonCart	View Cart	29
buttonCheckout	Checkout	43
buttonHelp	Help	57

TIP Many position values given throughout the text do not conform to the default grid. If you have not already done so, uncheck the Snap to Grid option. You can set this and other Form Designer properties by selecting Properties|Form Designer Properties.

10. The last property to alter before saving this custom form class is the form's color property. Use the Color Property Builder or enter white into the Inspector for form.color. Your custom form class should now appear similar to the one in Figure 9.3.

11. Save your form and close the Custom Form Class Designer. From the menu, select File|Close and save the file as Toolbar.JCF.

The custom form class file is actually a library that can hold many different custom form classes. When you save a custom form class to a new file, the first class is given the name of the file plus CForm. This makes the new toolbar class ToolbarCForm. If you save additional forms to this file as custom form classes, you are prompted for a class name.

9

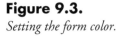

Figure 9.3.
Setting the form color.

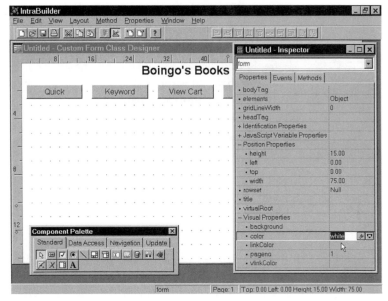

Creating a Simple Help Form

Currently, the buttons in the custom form class do nothing at all. They do not even show up in any forms that you run. To remedy this situation, this section works through the development of a simple Help form. The Help form, like all the other forms in the application, derives the toolbar buttons from the custom form class.

The first rendition of the Help form will contain only some HTML text in addition to the components inherited from the custom form class. The new HTML text is a list with brief instructions on what each of the common link buttons do. After creating the Help form, you can try opening it through the index.htm file. After the Help form is up and running through a browser, JavaScript methods need to be added to both the custom form class and the Help form to make them actually do something dynamic. After all, dynamic forms are what IntraBuilder is all about! These steps show how to make the initial static Help form.

1. Open the Form Designer. Double-click the standard (untitled) forms icon to create a new form. When prompted, click Designer to avoid the way of wizards, warlocks, and experts.

2. Set the custom form class to the Toolbar class. From the menu, select File|Set Custom Form Class. Use the tool button to open the Toolbar.jcf file. This file has only one class, so you can leave the class name set to ToolbarCForm.

When you click OK to close the Set Custom Form Class dialog, the Form Designer shows what appears to be your custom form class. If you select one of the buttons, you'll notice a difference in the nibs.

NEW TERM   *Nibs* are the dots that appear on a component to indicate selection. The nibs for components that exist within a class appear black. Nibs on inherited components, such as the toolbar buttons, appear white.

3. Add five HTML controls and set their respective name and text properties as shown in Table 9.2. It is easier to enter long text properties from within the Text Property Builder.

   To make each item appear as an HTML bullet, start each text with <UL><LI> and place </LI></UL> at the end. The LI tag specifies that the text is part of a list. The default list type is a numbered list. The UL tag makes a list item into an unnumbered list item.

Table 9.2. The HTML bullet properties for the Help form.

Name	Text
bulletQuick	<UL><LI>Quick - Search for books by product covered.</LI></UL>
bulletKeyword	<UL><LI>Keyword - Start up a search engine to help find the book you want directly. A keyword search looks at title, author, or ISBN. </LI></UL>
bulletCart	<UL><LI>View Cart - Show books currently selected for purchase. You can edit quantities and remove books while viewing the shopping cart. </LI></UL>
bulletCheckout	<UL><LI>Checkout - Verify purchase and enter name, address and billing information. </LI></UL>
bulletHelp	<UL><LI>Help - Show this page. </LI></UL>

4. Position the bullets in a vertical list and leave enough space between the toolbar buttons and the first bullet to add a rule and another line of text. Position the bullets with a left property of 0.

5. When you have the form looking like Figure 9.4, press F2 to save and run it as help.jfm.

Figure 9.4.

Laying out a bulleted list.

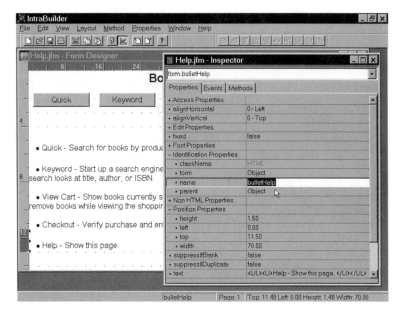

Checking Your Work

After you design a form in IntraBuilder, it is a good idea to view it through Navigator and Internet Explorer. What looks okay in the IntraBuilder Designer and Navigator might look surprisingly bad in Internet Explorer. The opposite can be true, too. So, now is a good time to try out that link in index.htm.

Close the IntraBuilder Designer and start a Web server and an IntraBuilder Server. When your server environment is running, open the index.htm file created on Day 8. If you're running the Borland Web Server on the same machine that your browser runs on, the URL will be http:\\localhost\store\index.htm. Other servers will let you get away with http:\\localhost\store.

WARNING

Close the IntraBuilder Designer before starting an IntraBuilder Server. The IntraBuilder Server uses some of the same underlying data structures and can conflict with Designer sessions.

Try loading the Help form with both the text and image links on the index page. You can also start the Help form directly with a URL of `http://localhost/svr/intrasrv.isv?store/help.jfm`. Figure 9.5 shows the form as it looks in Navigator. It looks pretty good.

Figure 9.5.

Running the Help form through Netscape Navigator.

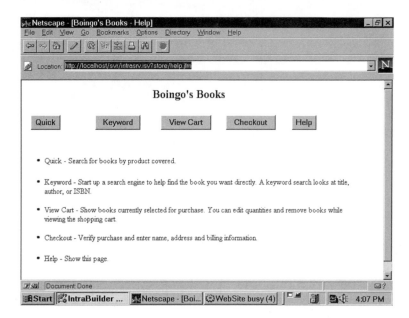

If you run the same form in Internet Explorer, things look even better. From Figure 9.6, you can see that toolbar buttons maintain a consistent width. In Navigator the button width is determined by the text within the button.

If you view the source HTML, you will see that IntraBuilder uses HTML tables to control positioning. IntraBuilder 1.0 uses HTML tables to create a grid where components are placed in relative positions. Version 1.01 goes beyond relative positioning to enable pixel level placement of controls. The pixel positioning is accurate for the top and left properties. The width and height can be altered by other factors. For instance, the width of a select control is determined by the widest option value.

WARNING

When positioning buttons and select controls, leave ample room so that the controls will not overlap in Navigator. If you place a row of buttons too close together, Navigator keeps the top and left positions while expanding the width. Internet Explorer prevents overlapping controls by repositioning controls as needed.

Figure 9.6.

Running the Help form through Microsoft Internet Explorer.

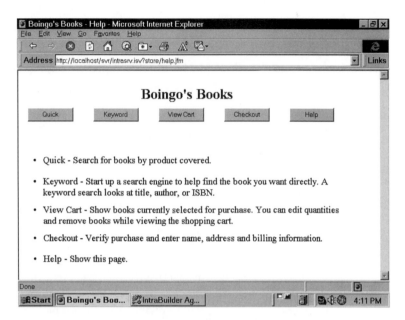

One of the objectives of the original HTML specification was to avoid any type of true formatting. As a document language, not an application language, the emphasis was on describing how ideas interrelated. As a result, you have things such as <H2> for a heading. With HTML, you can identify text by content. Instead of specifying that an HTML object appears in an Arial bold font with a point size of 20, you make it a heading, and let the browser pick the font. As the browser vendors engage in feature wars, they continue to extend HTML with more positioning and physical appearance tags. This does defeat the total platform-independent nature of the original Web creators, but it also gives us application developers the control we so desire.

Creating the User Key

Now that you have verified that you can run your new JavaScript form successfully, it's time to complete it and add some dynamic HTML. To complete the Help form, you will add two methods. The first generates a unique value for the user key. The second method shows how many items are currently in the shopper's cart. Because there really isn't any way to add items to the cart, this number should come up as zero. This first set of steps shows you how to add the user property and provides a glimpse at the exception handler.

NEW TERM An *exception* is a runtime error that you can trap within a JavaScript function. Exception is also the class name of the standard error information object.

Before you start, close down the IntraBuilder Server by closing the Web server and all the IntraBuilder Agents. Then follow the next steps to start some real JavaScripting.

> **TIP** If you're running Windows NT 3.51, the quickest way to shut down the IntraBuilder Agents is through the Windows task list.

1. Open the Help form in the Form Designer. A quick way to do this is to double-click the Help.jfm file in the IntraBuilder Explorer.

2. Open the Inspector and locate the onServerLoad event for the form. This is a server-side event that fires when the form opens.

   The client-side equivalent is onLoad. The onLoad event runs within the browser and requires a JavaScript-compatible browser. All client-side events are ignored if a browser user sets the option to disable ActiveScript or JavaScript.

3. Click the tool button for the onServerLoad event to create an empty method, open the method editor, and link the new method to the onServerLoad event.

   A method is a function that resides inside a class. Methods and functions can optionally receive and return values. The method you're about to write does neither.

4. Enter the method from Listing 9.1 and then try to run your form.

INPUT ### Listing 9.1. Using an exception to see whether the user property exists.

```
1: function Form_onServerLoad()
2: {
3:     // first pass
4:     try
5:     {
6:        var x = this.user ;   // Is user key undefined?
7:     }
8:     catch (Exception error)
9:     {
10:        var errorLog = new File() ;
11:        if (errorLog.exists("errorlog.txt"))
12:        {
13:            errorLog.open("errorlog.txt","RW") ;
14:        }
15:        else
16:        {
```

```
17:            errorLog.create("errorlog.txt") ;
18:        }
19:        errorLog.puts("") ;
20:        errorLog.puts("Unexpected exception in Help.jfm");
21:        errorLog.puts("Date:     " + (new Date())) ;
22:        errorLog.puts("Code:     " + error.code) ;
23:        errorLog.puts("Message: " + error.message) ;
24:        errorLog.close() ;
25:    }
26: }
```

ANALYSIS Shoppers can open Help from the store front (index.htm) or from any other JavaScript form in the application. This means that during the onServerLoad, the user property may or may not exist. The Form_onServerLoad method uses exception handling to see if the user property is already defined.

Exception handling works with try and catch blocks. A try block contains the code that you want to try to run. If anything goes wrong when trying to run the try block, the error is caught by the catch block. The catch block can determine what went wrong and decide what to do next.

The try block in the Form_onServerLoad contains only the statement on line 6. It tries to assign form.user to a new variable. This works—as long as the user property exists. If it does, the catch block is ignored and the function ends. If the user property does not exist, the catch block writes out the error to a log file.

When an error is caught on line 8, the method creates an Exception object. This object contains a text message and a numeric code to indicate what went wrong. The catch routine takes this code and writes it to a file using two other objects. The File class contains methods to work directly with files. The errorLog is an instance of the File class that is used to check whether a log already exists. If the log file exists, it is opened, and the new error is written out. Otherwise, the catch block creates a new error log before writing out the error information.

If you run the form now, it creates an errorlog.txt file. You can open the text file from the Custom tab on the IntraBuilder Explorer. To see the newly created files in the IntraBuilder Explorer, use View|Refresh. The file will contain something like this:

OUTPUT
```
Unexpected exception in Help.jfm
Date:    09/13/96 01:30:19 AM
Code:    167
Message: Error:  Variable is not defined:  user
```

From this file, you can see that the code for an undefined variable is 167. You can update the Form_onServerLoad method to generate a new user property in the catch block if a code of 167 is caught. If an existing shopper runs the form, the user property will already exist, and the method does not need to do anything else. To complete the event, open the form in the Script Editor, locate the Form_onServerLoad method, and modify it to match Listing 9.2.

INPUT
Listing 9.2. The complete `Form_onServerLoad` method for the Help form.

```
 1: function Form_onServerLoad()
 2: {
 3:    // complete
 4:    try
 5:    {
 6:       var x = this.user ;   // Is user key undefined?
 7:    }
 8:    catch (Exception error)
 9:    {
10:       if (error.code == 167) //  not defined
11:       {
12:          if ( (new NetInfo()).sessionID == -1 )
13:          {
14:             var cUser = new StringEx("" + Math.int(Math.random(-1)
15:                      * Math.pow(10,20))) ;
16:             this.user = cUser.left(20) ;
17:          }
18:          else
19:          {
20:             this.user = "" + (new NetInfo()).sessionID
21:          }
22:       }
23:       else
24:       {
25:          var errorLog = new File() ;
26:          if (errorLog.exists("errorlog.txt"))
27:          {
28:             errorLog.open("errorlog.txt","RW") ;
29:          }
30:          else
31:          {
32:             errorLog.create("errorlog.txt") ;
33:          }
34:          errorLog.puts("") ;
35:          errorLog.puts("Unexpected exception in Help.jfm");
36:          errorLog.puts("Date:    " + (new Date())) ;
37:          errorLog.puts("Code:    " + error.code) ;
38:          errorLog.puts("Message: " + error.message) ;
39:          errorLog.close() ;
40:       }
41:    }
42: }
```

ANALYSIS The complete version of the Help form's `Form_onServerLoad` adds two more sets of `if` and `else` blocks. If the error code that is caught is 167, then a new user key is generated. Otherwise, the error is written to the error log file.

When the form is run through a browser, the IntraBuilder Server creates a unique identifier for the session. The session ID is a property of the `NetInfo` class. When run in the Designer, the session ID is always -1. Line 12 checks whether the session ID can be used as the user key. To let the application also run correctly in the Designer, an alternate key can be generated using a random string.

NOTE

The NetInfo class is not available in version 1.0. If you encounter a class not loaded error when trying to use NetInfo, check what version you are running. A free patch from 1.0 to 1.01 is available from the IntraBuilder Web site.

Two new classes are used to create the alternate user key on lines 18 through 20. The first is the Math class. It has many methods to help out in complex calculations. The Math class is one of the few classes that enables static use. To create a random number, you could use something like this:

```
m = new Math()
x = m.random( -1 )
```

It works just as well to use this:

```
x = Math.random( -1 )
```

NEW TERM

Static use refers to using methods of the class without creating an instance of it. For example, you can use methods of the Math and Date classes without creating a new object.

The random() method returns a value between 0 and 1. To make this number a little more unique as a whole number, it is multiplied by 10 to the power of 20. You end up with a 20-digit random value. The random() method does not return a truly random number. It actually returns a fixed set of numbers in a fixed order. You can pass it a parameter to mix up the order. Passing a negative value to the random() method bases the return value on the system clock. This ensures more uniqueness than the system time itself.

The function converts the 20-digit number to a string. Strings are completely accurate in query operations, while numbers lose precision after 16 digits. Making a simple string in JavaScript is easy. Just add quotation marks ("") to the start of a number, and it becomes a string. All strings are string objects with a small set of methods for string manipulation. More advanced string manipulation methods are available with the StringEx class.

To create a more perfect user key, line 20 removes trailing decimal points from the string. There isn't an easy way to do this through the standard String class. StringEx contains a left() method that will do the trick. Passing a string to StringEx creates a string of the same value with additional methods. The left() method returns the leftmost digits of a string.

Passing 20 to the left() method truncates anything past the 20th position. This removes the decimal points and completes the user key.

Counting Items in the Cart

Now that the Help form has a user key, let's make use of it. In the next series of steps, you'll create an HTML object that defines its own message with another onServerLoad event. This also involves the application's first query.

1. Open the Help form in the Designer and add another HTML component directly above the bullets.

2. Change the name to htmlCount. You can leave the text property as is.

WARNING

> Always press Enter to commit changes when editing property values in the Inspector. If you do not press Enter, shifting focus to another window can cause the property to revert to the previous value.

3. Add a Query object for the Cart table. The easiest way to do this is to open the IntraBuilder Explorer, select the Tables tab and drag the Cart table to the Form Designer as shown in Figure 9.7. When you drop the table on the form, it creates a query with a reference of cart1.

Figure 9.7.

Using drag-and-drop to add the Cart table to the Help form.

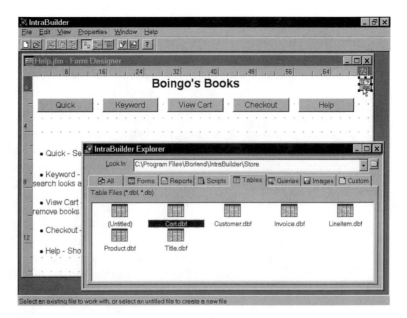

NOTE

Unlike standard controls, the data access components do not have a name property. To change the reference name for a query, you must edit the JavaScript source code. When you use drag-and-drop to add a query, the Form Designer creates a name based on the query. Adding a query from the component palettes leaves the less desirable name of query1. This naming convention starts to get confusing when you have more than one query.

4. Whenever you add a table from the current folder, you should edit the sql property to remove the full path. Select the query, open the Inspector, and locate the sql property. The default statement will be

```
SELECT * FROM "C:\Program Files\Borland\IntraBuilder\Store\cart.DBF"
```

Change this to the following:

```
SELECT * FROM "cart.DBF"
```

Now you can deploy the application to another drive or folder without any problems. If you need to work with tables in a directory other than where the JavaScript forms are located, consider using a BDE alias. When you work with a BDE alias, the folder name is defined in a BDE configuration file rather than in the application's source files.

5. Inspect the htmlCount object and create a new method linked to the htmlCount onServerLoad event. The onServerLoad event for a component fires after the onServerLoad event of the form.

6. Enter the method in Listing 9.3. When you're done, run the form to see the message saying that you have no items in your shopping cart.

INPUT **Listing 9.3. The htmlCount_onServerLoad() method.**

```
 1: function htmlCount_onServerLoad()
 2: {
 3:     var nCount = 0 ;
 4:     this.form.cart1.rowset.filter =
 5:         "CARTUSER = '" + this.form.user + "'" ;
 6:     this.form.cart1.rowset.first() ;
 7:     while ( ! this.form.cart1.rowset.endOfSet )
 8:     {
 9:        nCount+=this.form.cart1.rowset.fields["QTY"].value ;
10:        this.form.cart1.rowset.next() ;
11:     }
12:     nCount = Math.int(nCount) ;
13:     if ( nCount == 0 )
14:     {
```

continues

Listing 9.3. continued

```
15:        this.text = "Your shopping cart is empty." ;
16:    }
17:    else
18:    {
19:        this.text = "Your shopping cart contains " + nCount +
20:            ( (nCount==1) ? " item." : " items." ) ;
21:    }
22: }
```

ANALYSIS   This function introduces many new concepts, so let's go through it in detail. The basic idea is to filter the query to just those rows that belong to the current user. The QTY field is summed up. If the total is zero, the message says the cart is empty; otherwise, it displays the total.

```
function htmlCount_onServerLoad()
```

The function statement on line 1 names the function and sets the parameter list. In this case, there are no parameters. If there were, the parameters would be listed between the parentheses after the function name.

```
var nCount = 0 ;
```

The var statement on line 3 creates a local variable. If you leave off the var, the variable becomes public and has a higher chance of conflicting with other functions. Here, a local variable is assigned and initialized to zero:

```
this.form.cart1.rowset.filter =
    "CARTUSER = '" + this.form.user + "'" ;
this.form.cart1.rowset.first() ;
```

Lines 4 and 5 set a filter property on a query. Notice that the query is referenced through the form. Each standard control has a form property that points to the container form. The form property of a control is equal to its parent property.

The filter is a property of the rowset class. All query objects contain a rowset object. When you use a simple SQL select statement that queries a single table, the query refers to the table as a whole, while the rowset refers to individual records. The filter property determines what records you can navigate to. You can set the filter property to a SQL expression.

The SQL expression is much more limited than a JavaScript expression. For example, the SQL expression cannot include references to objects. The expression is a string that IntraBuilder passes to the Borland Database Engine. If the user property is equal to 100, the resulting filter would become "CARTUSER = '100'". Notice that the filter property requires nested quotes to work with literal strings. Although this.form.user does not start as a literal string, its value transforms into one before being passed to BDE.

The first() method simply moves the row pointer to the first row that matches the filter. If no rows match, the rowset is at endOfSet.

```
while ( ! this.form.cart1.rowset.endOfSet )
{
   nCount+=this.form.cart1.rowset.fields["QTY"].value ;
   this.form.cart1.rowset.next() ;
}
```

The while loop starting at line 7 moves through all rows that match the filter. The loop uses nCount to sum up values from the QTY field. The += operator is used as shorthand. The summation line could also be written as

```
nCount = nCount + this.form.cart1.rowset.fields["QTY"].value ;
```

The next() method moves the row pointer ahead one row. It optionally takes a parameter to specify direction and how many rows to move. Passing next a negative value moves the pointer backward. In other words, a negative next is a previous.

```
nCount = Math.int(nCount) ;
```

Line 12 removes the decimal places and makes the nCount variable an integer. This is done to make the sum display as a whole number.

```
if ( nCount == 0 )
{
   this.text = "Your shopping cart is empty." ;
}
```

Here the text property of the htmlCount object is set to "Your shopping cart is empty", if the nCount is equal to zero. Notice that the JavaScript equality operator is a double equal sign; however, the equality operator used in the filter is a single equal sign. In the assignment, this refers to the object that owns the current event. The function is linked to the onServerLoad event of htmlCount. That makes this equal to htmlCount. The same statement also could be written as

```
this.form.htmlCount.text = "Your shopping cart is empty."
```

One benefit of using a this reference is that you can change the name of the control, and the function still works. An explicit reference is more difficult to maintain.

```
else
{
   this.text = "Your shopping cart contains " + nCount +
      ( (nCount==1) ? " item." : " items." ) ;
}
```

The else on line 17 takes effect when the if fails. This block actually contains a second set of if and else conditions on lines 19 and 20. The question mark is a shorthand way to use a condition. The same block could also be written as follows:

```
else
{
   if (nCount==1)
   {
      this.text = "Your shopping cart contains " + nCount +" item." ;
   }
   else
   {
      this.text = "Your shopping cart contains " + nCount +" items." ;
   }
}
```

Making a Footer of a Header

To finish up the Help form, you need to fix the bullets so they show up better in Internet Explorer and provide a way to locate code for other forms. The first part can be done with a few mouse clicks. The second requires a new file and some imagination. To begin, you'll need to create a header file that is really more of a footer file.

Open the Script Editor to create a new file. Double-click the (untitled) icon on the Script tab of the IntraBuilder Explorer. Enter the preprocessor statements from Listing 9.4. Save the file as store.h. If you refresh the IntraBuilder Explorer window, the header file will appear on the Custom tab.

INPUT   **Listing 9.4. The shell for the `store.h` file.**

```
 1: #define DEBUG  // for development only
 2: #ifndef STORE
 3:    #define STORE
 4:    #ifdef DEBUG
 5:       // Load scripts
 6:       // _sys.script.load statements go here.
 7:    #elseif
 8:       // Include scripts
 9:       return null
10:       // #include statements go here
11:    #endif
12: #endif
```

ANALYSIS   The header file actually gets included at the bottom of the Help form's source code. The header gives you a central location to specify additional source files for the store application. This is the only file, outside of index.htm, that will reference physical JavaScript source filenames.

The header file is primarily composed of JavaScript preprocessor statements. These statements follow the same conventions found in the C++ Builder and Visual dBASE preprocessors.

To avoid duplicate definitions from accidental multiple inclusions, the file checks to see if the constant STORE exists in line 2. If it does, nothing else happens. If it does not already exist, STORE gets defined.

NEW TERM A *constant* is a value defined within the preprocessor that cannot be altered through a JavaScript assignment. The value of a constant is set prior to compilation. One of the most common uses of constants is to create more meaningful names for API parameter values. Programmers usually separate constant definitions from other source files by placing them in a header file. IntraBuilder comes with several header files that contain constants for working with the Windows API. You will find these files in the IntraBuilder include folder.

The second condition checks to see whether the constant DEBUG exists. If so, additional scripts are loaded through _sys.scripts.load(). This method requires slightly more overhead than direct inclusion, but it makes debugging much easier. If a file has a runtime error during development, the IntraBuilder error dialog can take you directly to the line where the error occurred. This is a great debugging feature that you don't want to be without until final deployment. The first line of the header creates the DEBUG constant.

When the application is done, you can use #include statements to consolidate all the source code into one compiled object file. This reduces the system's use of file handles. When you include JavaScript form files at the end of other JavaScript form files, you must be sure to add an extra return statement on line 9. Without the return null, the first included JavaScript form would open in addition to the Help form.

Therefore, if you can imagine having other JavaScript forms to include, then you can imagine this header being useful. For now it is just a placeholder that lets you finish work on the Help form.

Finishing Touches

With the store.h include file in place, you are set for the last modifications to the Help form. To complete the form, you can give it a proper title and make sure controls have proper spacing. The following steps show you how:

1. Open the Help form in the Form Designer.
2. Click the htmlCount object and Shift-click all the bullets to select them.
3. From the menu, choose Layout|Spacing|Make Equal Vertical Spacing. You can also left align the controls as shown in Figure 9.8.

Figure 9.8.

Left aligning the bullets and the htmlCount *control.*

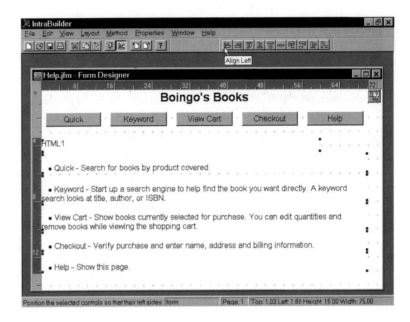

4. Open the Method Editor. From the menu, select View|Method Editor. It will open showing the Form_onServerLoad method.

5. Switch to the general section of the source file. From the drop-down list, select (general). This is the footer of the JavaScript form file. Here you can create functions that reside outside the class definition.

6. Enter the following line as shown in Figure 9.9:

    ```
    #include <store.h>
    ```

7. Change the title of the form to Boingo's Books - Help. The title appears in the title bar of the browser. That's it—you're done with the Help form. Save your changes and close the Designer.

As when you make any modifications to a form, it is a good idea to run it through a browser to see if the changes look okay. From Figure 9.10, you can see the new form title in Internet Explorer's title bar.

If you need to make any more minor position adjustments, you might want to do so with the Script Editor. Sometimes, it can be quicker to change a top property through source code than through the Designer. This is especially true of shorter forms. If you open the Help form as JavaScript, it should resemble Listing 9.5.

9

Figure 9.9.

Placing the #include outside the class definition.

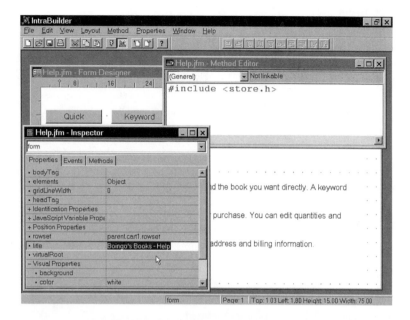

Figure 9.10.

The revised Help form in Internet Explorer.

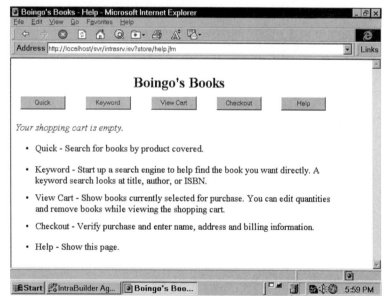

```
 1: // {End Header} Do not remove this comment//
 2: // Generated on 11/02/96
 3: //
 4: var f = new helpForm();
 5: f.open();
 6: class helpForm extends ToolbarCForm from "TOOLBAR.JCF" {
 7:    with (this) {
 8:       height = 15;
 9:       left   = 0;
10:       top    = 0;
11:       width  = 75;
12:       title  = "Boingo's Books - Help";
13:       onServerLoad = class::Form_onServerLoad;
14:    }
15:
16:    with (this.cart1 = new Query()){
17:       left   = 72;
18:       top    = 0;
19:       sql    = 'SELECT * FROM "cart.DBF"';
20:       active = true;
21:    }
22:
23:    with (this.cart1.rowset) {
24:    }
25:
26:    with (this.htmlCount = new HTML(this)){
27:       height = 1;
28:       top    = 3.5;
29:       width  = 70;
30:       color  = "black";
31:       text   = "HTML1";
32:       onServerLoad = class::htmlCount_onServerLoad;
33:    }
34:
35:    with (this.bulletQuick = new HTML(this)){
36:       height = 1.5;
37:       top    = 4.5;
38:       width  = 70;
39:       color  = "black";
40:       text   = "<UL><LI>Quick - Search for books by product " +
41:                "covered.</LI></UL>";
42:    }
43:
44:    with (this.bulletKeyword = new HTML(this)){
45:       height = 2;
46:       top    = 6;
47:       width  = 70;
48:       color  = "black";
49:       text   = "<UL><LI>Keyword - Start up a search " +
50:                "engine to help find the book you want " +
51:                "directly. A keyword search looks at title, " +
52:                "author, or ISBN. </LI></UL>";
53:    }
54:
```

```
55:     with (this.bulletCart = new HTML(this)){
56:         height = 2;
57:         top    = 8;
58:         width  = 70;
59:         color  = "black";
60:         text = "<UL><LI>View Cart - Show books currently " +
61:                 "selected for purchase. You can edit " +
62:                 "quantities and remove books while viewing " +
63:                 "the shopping cart. </LI></UL>";
64:     }
65:
66:     with (this.bulletCheckout = new HTML(this)){
67:         height = 1.5;
68:         top    = 10;
69:         width  = 70;
70:         color  = "black";
71:         text = "<UL><LI>Checkout - Verify purchase and enter " +
72:                 "name, address and billing information. </LI></UL>";
73:     }
74:
75:     with (this.bulletHelp = new HTML(this)){
76:         height = 1.5;
77:         top    = 11.5;
78:         width  = 70;
79:         color  = "black";
80:         text = "<UL><LI>Help - Show this page. </LI></UL>";
81:     }
82:
83:     this.rowset = this.cart1.rowset;
84:
85:     function Form_onServerLoad()
86:     {
87:         // complete
88:         try
89:         {
90:             var x = this.user ;   // Is user key undefined?
91:         }
92:         catch (Exception error)
93:         {
94:             if (error.code == 167) //  not defined
95:             {
96:                 if ( (new NetInfo()).sessionID == -1 )
97:                 {
98:                     var cUser = new StringEx("" + Math.int(Math.random(-1)
99:                             * Math.pow(10,20))) ;
100:                    this.user = cUser.left(20) ;
101:                }
102:                else
103:                {
104:                    this.user = "" + (new NetInfo()).sessionID
105:                }
106:            }
107:            else
108:            {
```

continues

Listing 9.5. continued

```
109:                    var errorLog = new File() ;
110:                    if (errorLog.exists("errorlog.txt"))
111:                    {
112:                        errorLog.open("errorlog.txt","RW") ;
113:                    }
114:                    else
115:                    {
116:                        errorLog.create("errorlog.txt") ;
117:                    }
118:                    errorLog.puts("") ;
119:                    errorLog.puts("Unexpected exception in Help.jfm");
120:                    errorLog.puts("Date:    " + (new Date())) ;
121:                    errorLog.puts("Code:    " + error.code) ;
122:                    errorLog.puts("Message: " + error.message) ;
123:                    errorLog.close() ;
124:                }
125:            }
126:        }
127:
128:    function htmlCount_onServerLoad()
129:    {
130:        var nCount = 0 ;
131:        this.form.cart1.rowset.filter =
132:            "CARTUSER = '" + this.form.user + "'" ;
133:        this.form.cart1.rowset.first() ;
134:        while ( ! this.form.cart1.rowset.endOfSet )
135:        {
136:            nCount+=this.form.cart1.rowset.fields["QTY"].value ;
137:            this.form.cart1.rowset.next() ;
138:        }
139:        nCount = Math.int(nCount) ;
140:        if ( nCount == 0 )
141:        {
142:            this.text = "Your shopping cart is empty." ;
143:        }
144:        else
145:        {
146:            this.text = "Your shopping cart contains " + nCount +
147:                ( (nCount==1) ? " item." : " items." ) ;
148:        }
149:    }
150:
151: }
152: #include <store.h>
```

You've seen the fuctions before, so let's look at some of the other code. The code starts out with some functional comments. Although most comments do nothing, others contain special identifiers such as {Export} and {End Header}. IntraBuilder uses these comments to identify sections of code. The {End Header} comment in line 1 separates any header code you enter from the standard form open code that the Form Designer adds to every form.

```
// {End Header} Do not remove this comment//
// Generated on 11/02/96
//
var f = new helpForm();
f.open();
```

Line 4 contains a var statement, which creates a new instance of the helpForm. The form then opens. For the Help form, the application relies on these lines to open the form. All the other forms in the application use custom opening code rather than what is included at the top of the JavaScript form file.

```
class helpForm extends ToolbarCForm from "TOOLBAR.JCF" {
```

The class statement starts the class definition on line 6. This class is named helpForm and is derived from a class called ToolbarCForm. If you're not using a custom form class, forms are derived from the standard Form class. The last part of the class statement tells IntraBuilder where to find the source code for the ToolbarCForm. The TOOLBAR.JFM file opens without the need for an explicit _sys.scripts.load().

```
with (this) {
   height = 15;
   left   = 0;
   top    = 0;
   width  = 75;
   title  = "Boingo's Books - Help";
   onServerLoad = class::Form_onServerLoad;
}
```

The with statement makes it easier to set a group of properties for a single object. The same code could also be written like this:

```
this.height = 15;
this.left   = 0;
this.top    = 0;
this.width  = 75;
this.title  = "Boingo's Books - Help";
this.onServerLoad = class::Form_onServerLoad;
```

Anywhere in the class constructor, this refers to the form. So the height of the form is set to 15. The position properties for the form are relevant only when running within the Designer. When run through a browser, the form sizes to the current browser window or active frame.

The onServerLoad assignment links a method in the current class to the form's onServerLoad event. Although the default name of the method matches the event and object, it is arbitrary. You could link the onServerLoad event to a method called bob with the following line:

```
this.onServerLoad = class::bob;
```

The class:: specifies that the method belongs to the current class using the scope resolution operator. The class specifies the scope or location to use. You can also give a specific class name, including the class name of the current class. In that case, the same assignment could be written as

```
this.onServerLoad = helpForm::Form_onServerLoad;
```

 The *scope resolution operator* is the double colon that you place between a class name and a method name. Use this operator instead of the dot operator when working with a class definition rather than a specific instance of a class.

Specifying a different class name is rarely done. A more common option is to call methods from a parent or superclass. Because this form is derived from ToolbarCForm, it can call any methods defined within ToolbarCForm using the super:: operator. This is handy when the current class overrides a method defined in its parent class. For example, both the ToolbarCForm and helpForm classes could contain a Form_onServerLoad event. The following code will call a method in the parent class called Form_onServerLoad as the first line of the current class's Form_onServerLoad method. This makes it easy to extend the behavior of a method.

```
Function Form_onServerLoad;
{
   super::Form_onServerLoad;
   var nCount = 0 ;
   // do some other stuff.
}
```

The rest of the code simply creates each component and sets values for each property. Notice that the last line is the #include statement that was added to the general section of the form.

Giving Life to the Toolbar Buttons

Well, you sure have a nice Help form, but it still doesn't do anything. If you click any of the buttons, the browser refreshes with the same form. In this section, you make the buttons do something different. Instead of doing nothing, they will cause an error. Is an error really better than nothing? In this case, yes, because the errors will go away as other forms are created and added to store.h.

Each button needs its own `onServerClick` method to open the next form and release the current form. The code for each method is essentially the same. The only difference is the class name of the next form. The Help button can also be optimized not to reopen the Help form if the current form is already the Help form. Other buttons do not need this optimization because they will be disabled when inappropriate.

The custom form class could also use some rule lines for beautification. To continue, open `Toolbar.jfm` in the Custom Form Class Designer and follow these steps:

1. Make sure you are in the Custom Form Class Designer rather than the regular Form Designer. You can tell from the form's title bar. The run toolbar button is also disabled when in the Custom Form Class Designer.

2. Select the Quick button, open the Inspector, and locate the Quick button's `onServerClick` event. Use the tool button to open the Method Editor and link to the current event.

3. Enter the following code as shown in Figure 9.11. Select the code and copy it to the Clipboard.

```
function buttonQuick_onServerClick()
{
      var nextForm = new quickForm() ;
      nextForm.user = form.user ;
      nextForm.open() ;
      form.release() ;
}
```

Figure 9.11.

Copying a new method to the Clipboard.

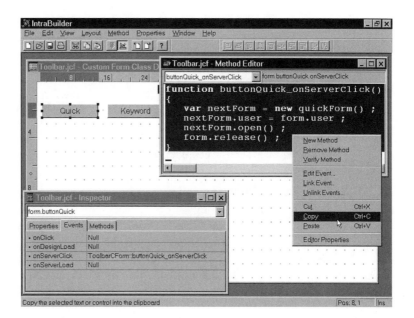

4. From the Method Editor's right-click shortcut menu select New Method.

5. Paste the method in the Clipboard over the default method template that the editor provides. Edit the method name and the new form line to match the following:

```
function buttonKeyword_onServerClick()
{
      var nextForm = new keywordForm() ;
      nextForm.user = form.user ;
      nextForm.open() ;
      form.release() ;
}
```

6. Link the new buttonKeyword_onServerClick() method to the buttonKeyword component's onServerClick event. From the shortcut menu, select Link Event. In the Link Event dialog, select form.buttonKeyword from the Object list and onServerClick from the event list. Click OK to confirm the link as shown in Figure 9.12.

Figure 9.12.

Linking methods through the Link Event dialog.

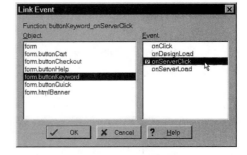

7. Repeat this process to create a new buttonCart_onServerClick() and link it to the buttonCart component. The only differences in the function definitions are the name and variable assignment lines. They should look like this:

```
function buttonCart_onServerClick()
{
      var nextForm = new cartForm() ;
      nextForm.user = form.user ;
      nextForm.open() ;
      form.release() ;
}
```

8. Three down, two to go. Repeat the process again for the onServerClick event of buttonCheckout. Again, the only differences are the function name and the assignment statements.

9

```
function buttonCheckout_onServerClick()
{
     var nextForm = new checkoutForm() ;
     nextForm.user = form.user ;
     nextForm.open() ;
     form.release() ;
}
```

9. You might have become used to a pattern here, but it is about to change in a subtle way for the Help button. Here, you need to enclose the new form code within a conditional block. The method needs to open the Help form only if the current form is not the Help form. The last method looks like this:

```
function buttonHelp_onServerClick()
{
   if (this.form.title.indexOf("Help") == -1)
   {
     var nextForm = new helpForm() ;
     nextForm.user = form.user ;
     nextForm.open() ;
     form.release() ;
   }
}
```

10. The methods are done; the last change to make is purely cosmetic. Add rules over and under the toolbar buttons. This keeps the first item on the derived form from squishing up against the toolbar buttons. When you're done, save and run the form within the Designer.

As you add more and more controls to a form, the difference between the way the form appears in the Designer and the way it appears in the browser *increases*. Keep in mind that the way the form runs in the Designer is of secondary importance. Figure 9.13 shows that I did not make the second rule line wide enough for the Help button. I set the `right` property to `60` instead of `70`.

Although the finished product looks sloppy in the Designer, it looks better in both Netscape and Internet Explorer. When running through a browser, the rules are closer to the same length, as shown in Figure 9.14. To get a perfect match, both rule lines should have the `right` property set to `70`. Rule lines also have more vertical space around them when running in a browser. The more rule lines a form has, the more it stretches out when streamed to HTML.

You might find another surprise lurking for you when you view your form through a browser. If your buttons are too close together, the buttons can overlap in Navigator. Figure 9.15 shows the Help form with each button set to a width of `9` and no space left between the buttons. The same form looks all right in the designer and in Internet Explorer.

Figure 9.13.

Running the Help form with a short rule line in the IntraBuilder Designer.

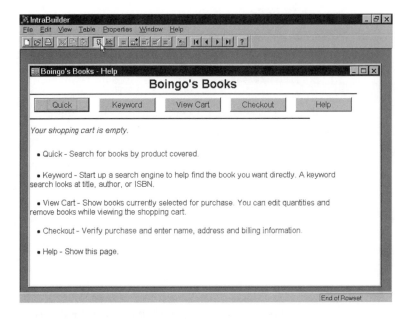

Figure 9.14.

Running the Help form with the short rule line through Netscape Navigator.

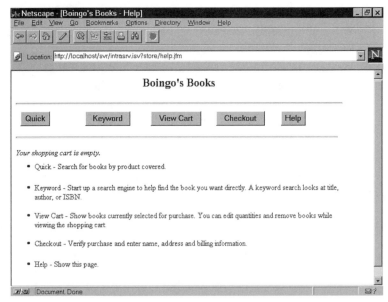

Figure 9.15.
Overlapping buttons in Netscape Navigator.

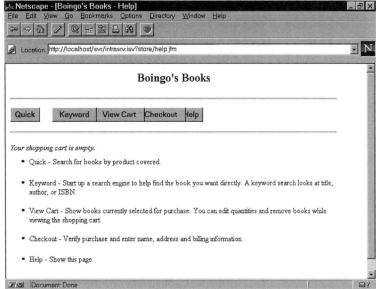

The complete source for the toolbar custom form class with the good looking rules is in Listing 9.6. You will use this toolbar custom form class for all the forms in the shopping cart application.

Listing 9.6. The complete code for the toolbar custom form class.

```
1: class ToolbarCForm extends Form custom {
2:     with (this) {
3:         color = "white";
4:         height = 15;
5:         left = 0;
6:         top = 0;
7:         width = 75;
8:         title = "";
9:     }
10:
11:     with (this.rule1 = new Rule(this)){
12:         top = 1.25;
13:         size = 2;
14:         right = 70;
15:     }
16:
17:     with (this.rule2 = new Rule(this)){
18:         top = 3;
```

continues

Listing 9.6. continued

```
19:        size = 2;
20:        right = 70;
21:    }
22:
23:    with (this.htmlBanner = new HTML(this)){
24:        height = 1.2;
25:        width = 70;
26:        color = "black";
27:        alignHorizontal = 1;
28:        text = "<H2>Boingo's Books</H2>";
29:    }
30:
31:    with (this.buttonQuick = new Button(this)){
32:        left = 1;
33:        top = 1.6;
34:        width = 12;
35:        text = "Quick";
36:        onServerClick = class::buttonQuick_onServerClick;
37:    }
38:
39:    with (this.buttonKeyword = new Button(this)){
40:        left = 15;
46:        top = 1.6;
42:        width = 12;
43:        text = "Keyword";
44:        onServerClick = class::buttonKeyword_onServerClick;
45:    }
46:
47:    with (this.buttonCart = new Button(this)){
48:        left = 29;
49:        top = 1.6;
50:        width = 12;
51:        text = "View Cart";
52:        onServerClick = class::buttonCart_onServerClick;
53:    }
54:
55:    with (this.buttonCheckout = new Button(this)){
56:        left = 43;
57:        top = 1.6;
58:        width = 12;
59:        text = "Checkout";
60:        onServerClick = class::buttonCheckout_onServerClick;
61:    }
62:
63:    with (this.buttonHelp = new Button(this)){
64:        left = 57;
65:        top = 1.6;
66:        width = 12;
67:        text = "Help";
68:        onServerClick = class::buttonHelp_onServerClick;
69:    }
70:
71:    function buttonQuick_onServerClick()
72:    {
```

```
73:        var nextForm = new quickForm() ;
74:        nextForm.user = form.user ;
75:        nextForm.open() ;
76:        form.release() ;
77:    }
78:
79:    function buttonKeyword_onServerClick()
80:    {
81:        var nextForm = new keywordForm() ;
82:        nextForm.user = form.user ;
83:        nextForm.open() ;
84:        form.release() ;
85:    }
86:
87:    function buttonCart_onServerClick()
88:    {
89:      var nextForm = new cartForm() ;
90:      nextForm.user = form.user ;
91:      nextForm.open() ;
92:      form.release() ;
93:    }
94:
95:    function buttonCheckout_onServerClick()
96:    {
97:        var nextForm = new checkoutForm() ;
98:        nextForm.user = form.user ;
99:        nextForm.open() ;
100:        form.release() ;
101:    }
102:
103:    function buttonHelp_onServerClick()
104:    {
105:      if (this.form.title.indexOf("Help") == -1)
106:      {
107:        var nextForm = new helpForm() ;
108:        nextForm.user = form.user ;
109:        nextForm.open() ;
110:        form.release() ;
111:      }
112:    }
113:
114: }
```

ANALYSIS The source code for a custom form class looks a lot like the source code for a standard form class. Let's look at the differences. First, there is no code to create an instance of the class at the top. This is why you cannot run a custom form class file.

Line 1 of the class definition ends with the custom option. You can inherit from any class; there is no need to have the custom option if you are writing your own JavaScript outside of the designers. The Form Designer uses the custom option when writing JavaScript out to a JFM file. Properties that are inherited from a class that has the custom option do not stream into a JFM.

If you remove the custom option and resave the Help form, the banner, buttons, and rules will save into the Help form. That sort of defeats the purpose of inheritance to always leave the custom option on your custom form classes.

Encountering Uncaught Errors

So now the buttons do something: they cause runtime errors. Runtime errors are one of three major categories of errors. The other two are compile-time errors and logic errors.

Compile-time errors occur when you try to run a JavaScript file after making a change. Whenever you make a change to a source file, IntraBuilder compiles the source into a new object file. Syntax errors are the primary cause of compile-time errors. These happen when you leave out a closing brace or misplace some other symbol.

Runtime errors occur in files that compile successfully. Trying to open a file that does not exist or referencing an undefined variable will generate a runtime error. When you're running in the Designer, IntraBuilder prompts you to fix the errors as they occur.

If you run the Help form and click the Quick button, the method tries to create an instance of the quickForm class. Figure 9.16 shows the error dialog that appears in the Designer. The three choices you get are to Cancel, Fix, or Ignore. The best thing to do here is to cancel, which stops executing the method, but keeps the form running. If you select Fix, the Script Editor opens at the line of the error. This is handy if you are fixing a misspelling, but doesn't do you much good in this case. To really fix the problem, you need to design the Quick form, and you don't have time to do that today. If you select Ignore, IntraBuilder skips the line of the error and tries to execute the next line. However, the line that follows requires that the current line must work. If you select the Ignore option, you will encounter another runtime error.

Figure 9.16.

Encountering a
runtime error in the
Designer.

IntraBuilder Alert
Error: Class not loaded into memory: quickForm::quickForm
File: TOOLBAR.JCF
Routine: ToolbarCForm.buttonQuick_onServerClick
Line: 82
✗ Cancel   Fix   Ignore   ? Help

NOTE

IntraBuilder cannot locate the line or an error if it comes from a file compiled through an #include statement. When an error occurs within source code from an included file, the Fix option simply takes you to the #include statement.

The error trapping system is much simpler when running through a browser. There are no choices—the browser just gets back a message about the error. No links are provided. Figure 9.17 shows the same error message it appears in Navigator.

Figure 9.17.

Encountering a runtime error through Navigator.

IntraBuilder cannot detect a logic error. This type of error happens when the JavaScript compiles okay and runs without any problems except that it does not do what you really wanted it to do. A logic error would occur if you forgot to link one of the toolbar button methods to an event. The code would compile, and the button would not cause any errors. The only problem would be that the button would not do anything.

Summary

Today you created a set of toolbar buttons in a custom form class. You will reuse the toolbar as you design new forms during the next few days. The toolbar provides a common look and feel for all the shopping cart application forms. The toolbar is also a set of common links between some of the application's main forms.

The other big activity of the day was the creating of the Help form. This is the first JavaScript form shoppers will see when entering the Web store. The Help form serves three major functions. First, it has a bulleted list that explains what each toolbar button does. Second, it tells the user how many items are currently in the shopping cart. Last, it creates a user key to track the current shopper. The generation of the user key is transparent to the shopper.

Day 10 adds two new forms to the application and provides in-depth information on creating queries with different table types. The new forms, the Quick form and the Results form, provide a framework for shoppers to search for books. You will also find a benchmark that you can modify for your own data sources to determine the fastest data access methods.

Q&A

Q **Wouldn't it have been easier to define the toolbar buttons within the Help form?**

A It would have made things easier today, when there was only one form that used the toolbar, but it would make things much more difficult in the days to come as you create many more forms that use the toolbar custom form class.

Q **Can I use images to create a toolbar?**

A Yes, you will even find applicable GIF files in the following folder:

```
C:\Program Files\Borland\IntraBuilder\Clipart\Business
```

In the folder you can find a shopping cart image (`shopca11.gif`), a checkout image (`cashrg21.gif`), and a search image (`search42.gif`).

Q **Why are all the methods used so far linked to server-side events?**

A Everything done so far requires a class or file that is not available to the client browser. For example, the method that counts how many items are in the cart uses a `Query` class to open the Cart table. Client-side JavaScript does not contain any database classes or the ability to open tables located on a Web server.

Q **My screen gets very cluttered when I design forms. What is the best way to arrange windows in the Designer?**

A The best thing is to have a 21-inch monitor. The second best thing is to use the Window|Arrange Designer Windows menu option to close all unrelated windows. You will also have more room if you drag the component palette off the main toolbar and use it as a floating palette. This way, you can close the palette when you don't need it and get more vertical design space.

Workshop

The Workshop section provides questions and exercises to help you get a better feel for the material you learned today. Try to answer the questions and at least think about the exercises before moving on to tomorrow's lesson. You'll find the answers to the questions in Appendix A, "Answers to Quiz Questions."

9

Quiz

1. What is the HTML tag for a list item?
2. How do you rename a query object?
3. What should you do after dropping a table onto a form?
4. `Filter` is a property of what class?
5. What is the difference between an object and a class?
6. What symbol makes up the scope resolution operator?

Exercises

1. The query on the Help form is used only to count values. There is no need to have the ability to update the table. Locate the property that determines whether a query requests a rowset that you can update. Set that property to `false`. Hint: If you can update the rowset, the query is said to be live.

2. If the Cart table is empty, you cannot verify that the filter on the query is actually working. Try adding a few records to the Cart table and running the Help form. It should still say that there are no items in the cart.

Day 10

Querying for the Quickest Searches

by Paul Mahar

Today you'll learn the ins and outs of query building and data manipulation. Like most data-driven Web applications, the basis of the shopping cart application is a query system. Four of the eight forms in the application are dedicated to searching the Title table. The cornerstone of any query system is performance. To make each of the shopping cart query forms as fast as possible, you need a solid understanding of the database classes and how BDE interacts with different table types. The following tasks of the day will provide you with the knowledge you need to make efficient and effective queries.

☐ **Experimenting with query by form.**

Query by form is available through the Table Run window, the Form Expert, and the database classes. The first task of the day is to investigate this easy-to-use search system and see how it works from the user and programmer perspectives.

☐ **Comparing query performance with different table types and property values.**

With IntraBuilder, you can create search systems from almost infinite combinations of table types and properties. The resulting performance can also be wide ranging.

This chapter includes an extensive benchmark script for testing query speeds with different property settings and different table types. You can customize the benchmark for your own environment.

Go through the benchmark code not only to see how to get great query performance, but to learn how to create complex data manipulation routines using the IntraBuilder database classes. You can learn many of the idiosyncrasies of dBASE, Paradox, and Access tables from the benchmark table creation script.

☐ **Creating a Quick search form.**

The day ends by starting to apply some of the knowledge gained through the preceding two tasks. You will create a form that enable shoppers to search for books and get a count of how many books match the search. In the process, you will add two new forms to the application: the Quick form and the Results form. The Quick form lets shoppers select a Borland Product and search for related books. The Results form will eventually list books found in a search. Today it will display only a count of how many books it should list.

This chapter introduces many new methods and properties for working with databases, tables, and rows. You will learn about methods to create, copy, and delete tables. The information about working with rows includes methods and properties to order, append, filter, locate, and modify rows. You also will learn about some of the undocumented classes that the benchmark script employs to create indexes.

Using Query by Form

The database classes in IntraBuilder have properties that make searching tables easy. With very little code, you can add query by form and filter by form capabilities to a JavaScript data entry form. The Form Expert can also generate forms that include query by form and filter by form.

You can test drive query by form and filter by form without creating any forms or scripts. When you open or run a table, IntraBuilder adds both search options to the menu. Give them a try to find books about Delphi by following these steps:

1. Double-click `Titles.dbf` from the tables tab of the IntraBuilder Explorer.

2. From the menu, select Table|Begin Query by Form.

3. Tab down to the `Product` field and enter `Delphi` as shown in Figure 10.1.

Figure 10.1.

Looking for Delphi books with query by form.

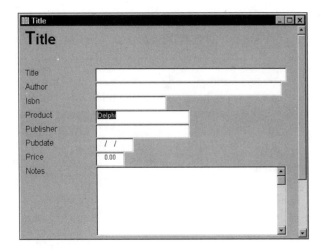

4. From the menu, select Table|Apply Query by Form.

IntraBuilder will look for the first row that contains "Delphi" in the Product field. If the table does not contain any books on Delphi, an alert message informs you that the value was not found, and the window shows the last row in the table.

Query by form tries to locate rows without restricting the rowset. If a matching value is found, the row pointer moves to show that row, but the user can still navigate to non-matching rows. Filter by form does restrict the available rowset.

NOTE

> The Apply Query By Form menu option sets the last row as the current row when the query does not match any rows in the table. This behavior is unlike the Rowset::applyLocate() method, which moves the row pointer beyond the last row to endOfSet.

If you repeat the preceding exercise, substituting filter by form for query by form, the available rowset becomes much smaller. After a filter is in place, you can use queries to move around within the filtered rowset. Filters are not accumulative. If you apply another filter by form, IntraBuilder reverts to using the entire table before using the new filter.

If you know exactly what you are looking for, query by form and filter by form work great. When you are not as familiar with the data, these searches quickly lose their appeal. When you enter the search criteria in the Table Run window, you must enter exact values that match in length and case. If you look for DELPHI instead of Delphi, you will find no books. Similarly, if you enter Visual to look for books on Visual dBASE, the search comes up empty.

The Table Run window works around this limitation with a Find Rows dialog. The dialog, shown in Figure 10.2, defaults to search for rows with partial matches that ignore case.

Figure 10.2.

Using a partial case-insensitive search to find books on Visual dBASE.

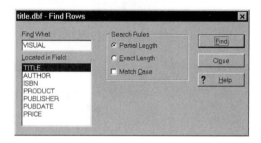

TIP

You can remove a filter by form condition by selecting Table|Clear Filter by Form. This menu option is only enabled after creating a filter through Table|Apply Filter by Form.

What the Form Expert Has to Offer

The IntraBuilder Form Expert can generate JavaScript forms that use query by form and filter by form. Things get a little more flexible when the query by form and filter by form operations take place in a JavaScript form. With this flexibility also comes a slight loss of intuitiveness. To see how it works, follow these steps to create a simple form that works with the Title table:

1. Open the Form Expert. Select File|New|Form and pick Expert when prompted.
2. Select the Title.dbf table and click Next.
3. Select the first four fields: TITLE, AUTHOR, ISBN, and PRODUCT.
4. Click Next a few times to get to step 5 of the Form Expert.
5. From step 5 of the Form Expert, check the Query by Form and Filter by Form options as shown in Figure 10.3.

Figure 10.3.

Generating search buttons through the Form Expert.

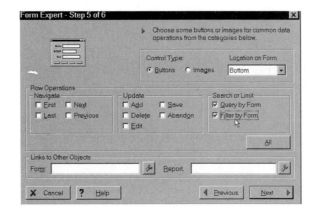

6. Click Next, Run, and name the form expert1.JFM.

Try out the new form. Like the Table Run window, Expert-generated forms are case sensitive and require a complete match. Unlike the Table Run window, generated forms display no alert dialog when rows are not found. Instead the query is placed at endOfRowset, a place beyond the last row.

The Rowset class contains two properties to control case sensitivity and partial matches. The filterOptions property works with filter by form, and the locateOptions property works with query by form. Table 10.1 shows the options you can use with each property.

Table 10.1. Values available for filterOptions and locateOptions.

Value	Meaning
0	Match length and case (the default)
1	Match partial length, case sensitive
2	Ignore case, match length
3	Match partial length and ignore case

These values for filterOptions and locateOptions correspond to all possible combinations of the Table Run window's Find Rows dialog. These values have no effect on numeric or date values. Exact matches are required for all non-string searches.

There isn't an option to search for values contained within a field. For example, you cannot look for Visual dBASE books by searching for dBASE if all the values start with Visual rather than with dBASE. Such a search is possible through events, and you'll get to that later this week when you create the Keyword form.

> **NOTE**
> Properties that deal with query by form use the term *locate* instead of query. In the database class system, all tables are opened through a query. You cannot query a query, but you can apply a filter to a query or locate a row in a query. The filter terms in the user interface do match the underlying property names.

You can set the rowset locateOptions and filterOptions properties of an Expert-generated form to 3. Changing the properties to 3 lets the end user relax about matching exact length or case. You can make this change through the Form Designer's Inspector. Another change to consider making is the removal of the full path for the query's sql property. As when you drop a table on a form, the Form Expert creates query objects with a full path in the sql property. Follow these steps to make these minor improvements:

1. Open expert1.JFM in the Form Designer.
2. Click the query object and open the Inspector.
3. Edit the sql property from

   ```
   SELECT * FROM "C:\Program Files\Borland\IntraBuilder\Store\title.dbf"
   ```

   to this line:

   ```
   SELECT * FROM "title.dbf"
   ```

4. Locate the rowset property and click the tool button to descend into the rowset object.
5. Use the drop-down lists to change filterOptions and locateOptions to 3 as shown in Figure 10.4.
6. Press F2 to run the form and try locating books in the *Teach Yourself* series. Click the New Filter button, enter TEACH in all uppercase, and click Run Filter.

The form will restrict the rowset to show several books from the *Teach Yourself* series. These are easy to find because each one starts with the word "Teach." Locating books in the *Unleashed* series is not so easy. The titles of books in the *Unleashed* series start with product names and cannot be filtered into a group with this form. You'll learn how to deal with this type of search tomorrow.

Figure 10.4.

Setting the `locateOptions` *property to 3.*

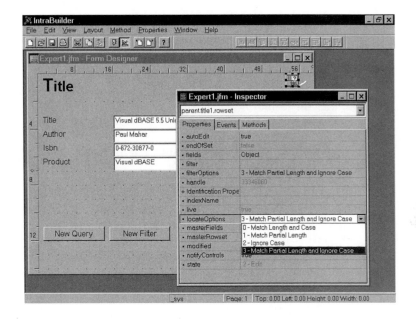

10

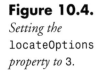 **TIP** To remove a filter from an Expert-generated form, click New Filter and Run Filter without entering any values. The filter goes away, and the row pointer moves to `endOfSet`. Press Ctrl+PgUp to move back to the top of the rowset.

Inside the Expert Code

The Form Expert generates a JavaScript form class with button events set to code blocks. As a rule of thumb, you should not use code blocks for anything but simple routines that contain fewer than five statements. Explicit functions are also necessary for routines that you plan to call from more than one event.

 A *code block* is an unnamed or anonymous function. Code blocks are handy for writing short routines and attaching statements directly to an event.

Unfortunately, the Form Expert ignores the rule and creates code blocks containing logical blocks that extend beyond five statements. Listing 10.1 shows a more readable but less executable version of the search code blocks. In this listing, each statement of the code block appears on a separate line. The logic and sequence are the same as is generated. Only the line breaks are different. This version of the code does not compile, because code blocks can reside only on a single line.

INPUT   **Listing 10.1. The Expert1 form with expanded code blocks.**

```
 1: // {End Header} Do not remove this comment//
 2: // Generated on 11/02/96
 3: //
 4: var f = new expert1Form();
 5: f.open();
 6: class expert1Form extends Form {
 7:    with (this) {
 8:       height = 15;
 9:       left = 10;
10:       top = 0;
11:       width = 61;
12:       title = "Title";
13:    }
14:
15:    with (this.title1 = new Query()){
16:       left = 53;
17:       top = 0;
18:       sql = 'SELECT * FROM "title.dbf"';
19:       active = true;
20:    }
21:
22:    with (this.title1.rowset) {
23:       filterOptions = 3;
24:       locateOptions = 3;
25:    }
26:
27:    with (this.html1 = new HTML(this)){
28:       height = 1;
29:       left = 1;
30:       top = 3;
31:       width = 14;
32:       color = "black";
33:       text = "Title";
34:    }
35:
36:    with (this.text1 = new Text(this)){
37:       left = 16;
38:       top = 3;
39:       width = 41;
40:       dataLink = parent.title1.rowset.fields["TITLE"];
41:    }
42:
```

10

```
43:    with (this.html2 = new HTML(this)){
44:        height = 1;
45:        left = 1;
46:        top = 4;
47:        width = 14;
48:        color = "black";
49:        text = "Author";
50:    }
51:
52:    with (this.text2 = new Text(this)){
53:        left = 16;
54:        top = 4;
55:        width = 40;
56:        dataLink = parent.title1.rowset.fields["AUTHOR"];
57:    }
58:
59:    with (this.html3 = new HTML(this)){
60:        height = 1;
61:        left = 1;
62:        top = 5;
63:        width = 14;
64:        color = "black";
65:        text = "Isbn";
66:    }
67:
68:    with (this.text3 = new Text(this)){
69:        left = 16;
70:        top = 5;
71:        width = 15;
72:        dataLink = parent.title1.rowset.fields["ISBN"];
73:    }
74:
75:    with (this.html4 = new HTML(this)){
76:        height = 1;
77:        left = 1;
78:        top = 6;
79:        width = 14;
80:        color = "black";
81:        text = "Product";
82:    }
83:
84:    with (this.text4 = new Text(this)){
85:        left = 16;
86:        top = 6;
87:        width = 20;
88:        dataLink = parent.title1.rowset.fields["PRODUCT"];
89:    }
90:
91:    with (this.button1 = new Button(this)){
92:        left = 1;
93:        top = 11;
94:        width = 13;
```

continues

Listing 10.1. continued

```
 95:          text = "New Query";
 96:          onServerClick = {; with(this)
 97:                          {
 98:                              if (form.rowset.state==5)
 99:                              {
100:                                  text="New Query";
101:                                  form.rowset.applyLocate();
102:                              }
103:                              else
104:                              {
105:                                  text="Run Query";
106:                                  form.rowset.beginLocate();
107:                              }
108:                          }
109:                      };
110:      }
111:
112:      with (this.button2 = new Button(this)){
113:          left = 15;
114:          top = 11;
115:          width = 13;
116:          text = "New Filter";
117:          onServerClick = {; with(this)
118:                          {
119:                              if (form.rowset.state==4)
120:                              {
121:                                  text="New Filter";
122:                                  form.rowset.applyFilter();
123:                              }
124:                              else
125:                              {
126:                                  text="Run Filter";
127:                                  form.rowset.beginFilter();
128:                              }
129:                          }
130:                      };
131:      }
132:
133:      with (this.TITLE = new HTML(this)){
134:          height = 2;
135:          left = 1;
136:          width = 51;
137:          color = "black";
138:          fontBold = true;
139:          text = '<H1><Font Size="+4">T</Font>itle</H1>';
140:      }
141:
142:      this.rowset = this.title1.rowset;
143:
144: }
```

ANALYSIS Most of the form defines the HTML and text components that show the field names and values. The default component names are composed of the class name and a number. It is a good idea to change the default names to more specific names if you plan to add methods that refer to these components. One popular naming convention is to replace the number with the field name. For example, change `text3` to `textISBN`. This makes it easily identifiable as a text component that is linked to the `ISBN` field. If you're not going to add any methods, keep the default names.

The following two `with` blocks define the `query` and `rowset` objects. The first, on line 16, creates both the `query` and the `rowset`. The `Rowset` class is one of several that exist only within the context of another class. You cannot use `new Rowset()` to create an independent `rowset`. The same is true with the field classes, which exist only within the context of a `Rowset` or `TableDef` class.

The `with` block on line 22 does not contain a new operator. The `rowset` object was created along with the `query` object on line 15. Most `with` blocks in a form class definition create objects in addition to setting property values.

```
with (this.title1 = new Query()){
     sql = 'SELECT * FROM "title.dbf"';
     active = true;
}
with (this.title1.rowset) {
     filterOptions = 3;
     locateOptions = 3;
}
```

Like the other controls, the buttons are given very generic names. The first button is defined on line 91. It controls the query and contains the following as a code block of the `onServerClick`. This code executes on the IntraBuilder server when someone clicks the button and submits the form through a browser. Standard IntraBuilder buttons are submit type buttons in HTML.

```
with(this)
{
   if (form.rowset.state==5)
   {
      text="New Query";
      form.rowset.applyLocate();
   }
   else
   {
      text="Run Query";
      form.rowset.beginLocate();
   }
}
```

The query code block is enclosed in a with block to avoid including a this reference prior to the text and form property references. The code block relies on the rowset's state property to determine whether the user wants to enter a locate condition or has already entered values and wants to start looking for values. Table 10.2 shows the possible values for the state property.

Table 10.2. Rowset state values.

State	Meaning	Query	DataLinks	Position
0	Closed	Inactive	None	EndOfSet
1	Browse	Active	Read only	True row
2	Edit	Active	Modifiable	True row
3	Append	Active	Modifiable	Buffer
4	Filter	Active	Inactive	Buffer
5	Locate	Active	Inactive	Buffer

Prior to setting the active property to true, a query is closed. When you drop a table on a form or use the Form Expert, the query defaults to an edit state. When a query is in an edit state, changes to dataLinks are saved if the query is live. The dataLinks are fields tied to controls through the dataLink property. Not all controls have a dataLink property. The most common dataLink happens through a text control.

NOTE

An edit state is not synonymous with a live query. You can create queries against SQL tables where the requestLive property is false and the state property is 2. Such a query appears to be in an edit state although the data remains read-only. Do not assume all dataLink updates can be saved when in an edit state.

The browse state occurs when the autoEdit property is set to false, which is not the default. In a browse state, dataLinks are read-only and an explicit call to the Rowset::beginEdit() method is required to switch to an edit state. When autoEdit is true, IntraBuilder works like Visual dBASE, where any modifications made to live rows get saved. Setting autoEdit to false makes IntraBuilder work more like Paradox or the Database Desktop, where a conscious effort is required to change from a read-only view to enable data editing.

Calling the Rowset::beginAppend() method sets the rowset into an append state. This causes IntraBuilder to create an empty row buffer that you can update through dataLinks or through

10

the value properties of a field object. The Rowset::abandon() and Rowset::save() methods switch the rowset from an append state to the previous state.

The filter and locate states apply only to queries used within forms with dataLinks. The other four states can exist without a form or on forms without dataLinks. The Rowset::beginFilter() and Rowset::beginLocate() methods invoke these very similar states. In either state, all dataLinks go blank, and the user can enter sample values. The Rowset::applyLocate() and Rowset::applyFilter() methods change the state back to either edit or browse depending on autoEdit.

The two code blocks use the state property to figure out whether it is time to prepare or run a search. Prior to switching states, each code block also sets the text properties of the current button to an appropriate string value.

Creating Lightning-Quick Queries

IntraBuilder enables you to create queries for many data sources. With any given data source, an IntraBuilder query has a wealth of properties for controlling how the query works. Minor modifications to a query can have a major impact on performance. Although an application may dictate using a particular table type or setting certain properties, you are likely to still have some leeway in how you set up your queries.

The best way to understand query performance is to try out a wide array of configurations and get times on each. This type of speed test is often called a *benchmark*. In the previous section you learned how filters and locate operations work. In this section you will learn how to make them work fast, and then you can get back to the shopping cart application armed with an in-depth understanding of queries.

The first step in doing a benchmark is figuring out what to test. Perhaps the biggest factor in query speeds is the table type. IntraBuilder uses BDE for dBASE and Paradox tables, and ODBC for Access tables. The professional edition can also connect to Microsoft SQL Server and InterBase through SQL-Links. The Client/Server edition adds SQL-Links for Sybase, Oracle, DB2, and Informix.

When you work with dBASE, Paradox, and Access tables, the data processing happens on the same PC that runs IntraBuilder. Some client/server configurations run database servers on the same machine as IntraBuilder; however, it is more common to run the database server on another dedicated server. The database servers also provide many configuration options that affect query speeds and are beyond the scope of this book. As a result, the benchmark presented here deals only with dBASE, Paradox and Access tables. You can run it with any version of IntraBuilder. If you are working with a client/server system, consider modifying the benchmark to work with your server. Most of the code shown for Access tables will work with SQL-based systems. See Day 7, "Tables, Queries, and Database Administration," for more information on setting up connections through SQL-Links.

To make a benchmark realistic, it should mimic what happens in common applications. The shopping cart application requires searches through a table of books based on products covered. Shoppers will frequently look for all the books about Delphi. Because this is a public Internet application, many shoppers may perform similar searches in a very short period of time. To emulate this, the benchmark will perform 25 consecutive searches through a table looking for Delphi books.

NOTE

> Searching the current Title table will not reveal much because it only contains 20 rows. To make a more realistic data set, the table needs to expand to 10,000 rows. This has proven to be enough records to detect differences between table types. Increasing the row count to 100,000 gives unreliable results due to disk caching. A 10,000-row table can immediately load into the cache of a machine with 32MB of memory. Running with much larger tables makes consecutive queries against the same table increase in speed because the table gradually loads into the cache over the course of the benchmark.

Generating the Benchmark Tables

The sample Title table is a dBASE table with 20 rows. The benchmark requires dBASE, Paradox, and Access tables with 10,000 rows each. The Bench0 JavaScript in Listing 10.2 creates the tables for you.

An ODBC driver is required to create the Access table. If you do not have an Access ODBC driver, comment out the call to makeAccess() before running the script. If you do want to create Access tables, you must first create an empty MDB file along with a matching BDE alias. Use the following steps. If you do not have the 32-bit ODBC driver for Access, skip ahead to Listing 10.2.

1. Open the Windows Control Panel and locate the 32-bit ODBC icon. If this icon is not present, you do not have 32-bit ODBC drivers installed. You can install them with any 32-bit Microsoft Office product. These drivers do not ship with IntraBuilder.

2. Double-click the 32-bit ODBC icon to open the administration utility. Click Add to define a new data source and select the Microsoft Access Driver as shown in Figure 10.5.

Figure 10.5.

Adding a new ODBC data source.

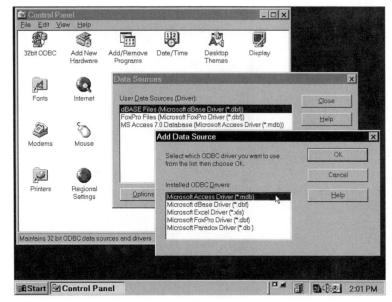

3. Enter ACCESSBENCH for the data source name and add any description.
4. To create an empty MDB, click Create, pick a folder, and enter bench.mdb as the new database name. Create the new MDB file in any folder that uses a short filename. See Figure 10.6.

   Although you can create new Access tables within IntraBuilder, you must place them in an existing Access database. IntraBuilder does not provide a facility to create an Access database.

WARNING

The ODBC Access driver does not surface indexes for MDB files stored in folders that use long filenames. If you place the bench.mdb file in C:\Program Files\Borland\IntraBuilder\Store, you will be able to create but not use indexes on the Access tables. This problem also arises when working with the Solution application Contacts database. The setup program installs the MDB to a lone filename folder by default.

Figure 10.6.

Creating a new Access database.

5. Close the ODBC administration utility and open the BDE Configuration utility. Redefine the ODBC data source as a BDE alias that IntraBuilder can use.

6. Click New ODBC Driver and select the Microsoft Access Driver as the default ODBC driver. After picking the ODBC driver, you can select ACCESSBENCH as the default data source and enter ACCESSBENCH to make the new SQL Link driver name ODBC_ACCESSBENCH, as shown in Figure 10.7.

7. Believe it or not, you must define the data source one more time. This time, you'll be creating a new BDE alias. Click the Alias tab of the BDE Configuration utility.

8. Click the New Alias button, enter ACCESSBENCH as the new alias name, and pick ODBC_ACCESSBENCH as the alias type, as shown in Figure 10.8.

You can now open the empty database from the IntraBuilder Explorer. Try it out to see whether the connections are working. If you click the Table tab, the alias will appear in the Look In drop-down list.

10

Figure 10.7.
Defining a BDE driver for the Access database.

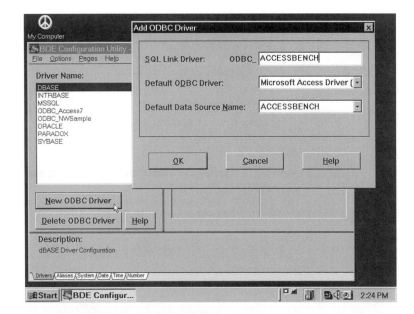

Figure 10.8.
Defining a BDE alias for the Access database.

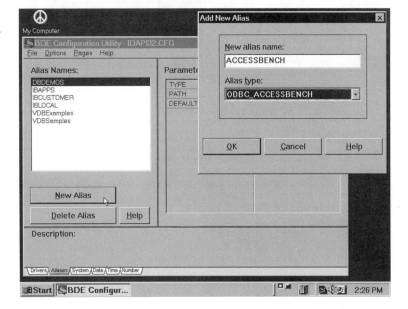

WARNING

> Always close all IntraBuilder Agents and instances of the Intra-
> Builder Designer before making changes to the BDE configuration.
> IntraBuilder loads BDE definitions at startup. Attempting to use an
> alias created during the current IntraBuilder session can lead to
> unexpected results.

INPUT   **Listing 10.2. Bench0—The benchmark table generation script.**

```
 1: //
 2: //  Script:        bench0.JS
 3: //
 4: //  Author:        Paul Mahar
 5: //
 6: //  Date:          11/02/96
 7: //
 8: //  Version:       IntraBuilder 1.01
 9: //
10: //  Description:   Create dBASE, Paradox and Access tables for benchmark.
11: //                 Access table create requires an installed ODBC driver
12: //                 with an alias of ACCESSBENCH pointing to an empty MDB.
13: //
14: //  Parameters:    None
15: //
16: //  Tables:        Titles.DBF - 20 row dBASE sample table
17: //
18: //  Usage:         _sys.scripts.run("bench0.JS")
19: //
20: //  Reference:     Chapter 10
21: //
22: //
23:
24: makeBench("title.dbf") ;
25: makeParadox() ;
26: makeAccess() ;  // Comment out if ODBC driver not available.
27:
28: function makeBench(cTable)
29: {
30:    make1000(cTable) ;
31:    dittoBench(9) ;
32: }
33:
34: function make1000(cTable)
35: {
36:    var q = new Query() ;
37:    q.sql = "select * from " + cTable ;
38:    q.active = true ;
39:    var nCount = q.rowset.count() ;
40:    q.active = false ;
41:    _sys.databases[0].copyTable("title.dbf","bench.dbf") ;
```

```
42:     generate("bench.dbf",1000 - nCount) ;
43: }
44:
45:
46: function generate(cTable, nCount)
47: {
48:     var q       = new Query(),
49:         status  = new Form(),
50:         fObj    = new Object() ;
51:     status.top    = 1 ;
52:     status.left   = 1 ;
53:     status.height = 1 ;
54:     status.open() ;
55:     q.sql = "select * from " + cTable ;
56:     q.active = true ;
57:     for (var i = 0 ; i < nCount ; i++ )
58:     {
59:         status.title = "Creating record: " + (i+1) +
60:                        " of " + nCount ;
61:         q.rowset.beginAppend() ;
62:         for (var nf = 0 ; nf < q.rowset.fields.length ; nf++)
63:         {
64:             fObj = q.rowset.fields[nf] ;
65:             if (fObj.type == "CHARACTER" )
66:             {
67:                 fObj.value =  randomString(fObj.length) ;
68:             }
69:             if (fObj.type == "NUMERIC" )
70:             {
71:                 if (fObj.decimalLength > 0)
72:                 {
73:                     fObj.value = Math.random() * Math.pow(10,
74:                         (fObj.length - (1 + fObj.decimalLength))) ;
75:                 }
76:                 else
77:                 {
78:                     fObj.value = Math.random() *
79:                                  Math.pow(10,fObj.length) ;
80:                 }
81:             }
82:         }
83:         q.rowset.save() ;
84:     }
85:     status.close() ;
86:     status.release() ;
87: }
88:
89: function randomString(nLength)
90: {
91:     var cReturn = "",
92:         sX      = new StringEx() ;
93:     for (var i = 0 ; i < nLength ; i++)
94:     {
```

continues

Listing 10.2. continued

```
 95:        cReturn += sX.chr( 65 + ( Math.random() * 57 ) ) ;
 96:     }
 97:     return ( cReturn ) ;
 98: }
 99:
100: function dittoBench(nCount)
101: {
102:    var q       = new Query(),
103:        u       = new UpdateSet(),
104:        status = new Form() ;
105:    status.top    = 1 ;
106:    status.left   = 1 ;
107:    status.height = 1 ;
108:    status.title  = "Copying the source table" ;
109:    status.open()   ;
110:    _sys.databases[0].copyTable("bench.dbf","temp1.dbf") ;
111:    q.sql = "select * from temp2" ;
112:    u.source = "temp2.dbf" ;
113:    u.destination = "bench.dbf" ;
114:    for (var i = 0 ; i < nCount ; i++ )
115:    {
116:        _sys.databases[0].copyTable("temp1.dbf","temp2.dbf");
117:        q.active = true ;
118:        while (! q.rowset.endOfSet )
119:        {
120:            q.rowset.fields[0].value = "" + i + "-" +
121:                            q.rowset.fields[0].value ;
122:            q.rowset.save() ;
123:            q.rowset.next() ;
124:        }
125:        q.active = false ;
126:        status.title = "Expanding table - pass " +
127:                        (i+1) + " of " + nCount ;
128:        u.append() ;
129:    }
130:    _sys.databases[0].dropTable("temp1.dbf");
131:    _sys.databases[0].dropTable("temp2.dbf");
132:    status.close() ;
133:    status.release() ;
134: }
135:
136: function makeParadox()
137: {
138:    var u       = new UpdateSet(),
139:        q       = new Query(),
140:        d       = _sys.databases[0],
141:        cSQL    = "";
142:        status = new Form();

143:
144:    status.title = "Creating Paradox bench table" ;
145:    status.top    = 1 ;
146:    status.left   = 1 ;
147:    status.height = 1 ;
```

10

```
148:     status.open() ;
149:     u.source      = "bench.dbf";
150:     u.destination = "temp1.db";
151:     u.copy();
152:
153:     q.sql = "select * from 'temp1.db'" ;
154:     q.active = true ;
155:     cSQL = getCreateStatement(q.rowset.fields,"bench.db",false);
156:     q.active = false ;
157:     if (d.tableExists("bench.db"))
158:     {
159:         d.executeSQL("DROP TABLE 'bench.db'");
160:     }
161:     d.executeSQL(cSQL);
162:     u.source = "temp1.db";
163:     u.destination = "bench.db";
164:     u.append() ;
165:     d.executeSQL("DROP TABLE 'temp1.db'");
166:     status.close() ;
167:     status.release() ;
168: }
169:
170: function getCreateStatement(feildObject, cTable, lODBC )
171: {
172:     var cStatement = "CREATE TABLE "
173:     if (lODBC)
174:     {
175:         cStatement += cTable + " (" ;
176:     }
177:     else
178:     {
179:         cStatement += "'" + cTable + "' (" ;
180:     }
181:     cStatement += q.rowset.fields[0].fieldName + " " +
182:         typeSQL( q.rowset.fields[0], lODBC ) ;
183:     for (var i = 1; i < q.rowset.fields.length ; i++)
184:     {
185:         cStatement += ", " + q.rowset.fields[i].fieldName + " " +
186:                     typeSQL( q.rowset.fields[i], lODBC ) ;
187:     }
188:     if ( ! lODBC )
189:     {
190:         cStatement += ", PRIMARY KEY(" +
191:                     q.rowset.fields[0].fieldName + "))" ;
192:     }
193:     else
194:     {
195:         cStatement += ")" ;
196:     }
197:     return ( cStatement ) ;
198: }
199:
200: function typeSQL( dbField, lODBC )
201: {
202:     DBTypes = new AssocArray();
```

10

continues

Listing 10.2. continued

```
203:     DBTypes["ALPHA"]           = "CHAR(" + dbField.length + ")" ;
204:     DBTypes["AUTOINCREMENT"] = "AUTOINC" ;
205:     DBTypes["BCD"]             = "DECIMAL(20,0)" ;
206:     DBTypes["BINARY"]          = (lODBC ? "BINARY" : "BLOB(0,2)") ;
207:     DBTypes["LOGICAL"]         = "BOOLEAN" ;
208:     DBTypes["BYTES"]           = "BYTES(0)" ;
209:     DBTypes["DATE"]            = "DATE" ;
210:     DBTypes["FMTMEMO"]         = (lODBC ? "BINARY" : "BLOB(10,3)") ;
211:     DBTypes["GRAPHIC"]         = (lODBC ? "BINARY" : "BLOB(10,5)") ;
212:     DBTypes["LONG"]            = "INTEGER" ;
213:     DBTypes["MEMO"]            = (lODBC ? "BINARY" : "BLOB(10,1)") ;
214:     DBTypes["MONEY"]           = "MONEY" ;
215      DBTypes["NUMBER"]          = "NUMERIC" + ( lODBC ? "" : "(20,0)") ;
216:     DBTypes["OLE"]             = "BLOB(10,4)" ;
217:     DBTypes["SHORT"]           = "SMALLINT" ;
218:     DBTypes["TIME"]            = "TIME" ;
219:     DBTypes["TIMESTAMP"]       = "TIMESTAMP" ;
220:     return ( DBTypes[ dbField.type ] ) ;
221: }
222:
223: function makeAccess()
224: {
225:     try
226:     {
227:         var d = new Database("ACCESSBENCH") ;
228:         var q   = new Query(),
229:             u   = new UpdateSet(),
230:             cSQL = "",
231:             status = new Form() ;
232:         status.title = "Creating Access bench table" ;
233:         status.top    = 1 ;
234:         status.left   = 1 ;
235:         status.height = 1 ;
236:         status.open() ;
237:         q.sql    = "select * from 'bench.db'" ;
238:         q.active = true ;
239:         cSQL     = getCreateStatement(q.rowset.fields,"bench",true) ;
240:         q.active = false ;
241:         if (d.tableExists("bench"))
242:         {
243:             d.executeSQL("DROP TABLE bench") ;
244:         }
245:         d.executeSQL(cSQL) ;
246:         q.database = d ;
247:         q.sql = "select * from bench" ;
248:         q.active = true ;
249:         u.destination = q.rowset ;
250:         u.source = "bench.db" ;
251:         u.append() ;
252:         u.null = false ;
253:         status.title = "Indexing Access bench table" ;
254:         indexAccess(d,q) ;
255:         status.close() ;
256:         status.release() ;
```

```
257:    }
258:    catch (DBException e)
259:    {
260:        alert(e.message) ;
261:    }
262: }
263:
264: function indexAccess(d,q)
265: {
266:    var idx = new Index() ;
267:    for (var i = 0 ; i < 4 ; i++ )
268:    {
269:        idx.indexName = q.rowset.fields[i].fieldName ;
270:        idx.fields    = q.rowset.fields[i].fieldName ;
271:        d.createIndex("bench",idx) ;
272:    }
273: }
```

ANALYSIS The Bench0 script is an example of a script that you should run only in the designer. It uses a procedural rather than an event-driven approach. When you run a JavaScript form, the only procedural statements are the lines that create and open a form instance. Everything else is invoked through an event such as onServerLoad. In Bench0, the functions fire in sequence without event triggers.

A default or unnamed function consists of three function calls on lines 24 through 26. This code runs when the script is called through _sys.scripts.run(). IntraBuilder considers all statements that appear outside function and class declarations as part of the default function. The script would run the same if you were to move lines 24 through 26 to the bottom of the file.

The makeBench() function creates a 10,000-row dBASE table. The makeParadox() function duplicates the dBASE table as a Paradox table, and makeAccess() creates an Access table from the Paradox table. Comment out the call to makeAccess() if you do not have the 32-bit Access driver installed.

Line 28 calls make1000() to create the Bench table as a 1,000-row copy of the Title table. Then dittoBench() expands the Bench table to 10,000 rows.

```
function makeBench(cTable)
{
   make1000(cTable) ;
   dittoBench(9) ;
}
```

The make1000() function on line 34 starts by creating a query for the base table and then uses Rowset::count() to figure out how many rows exist. For the Title table, the count will be 20. After deactivating the query, it uses the default database object to copy the table. The default database object is _sys.databases[0]. It points to an active database that works with dBASE and Paradox tables. You cannot deactivate the default database.

> The `Database::copyTable()` method copies tables of the same type. If you try to copy a dBASE table to a Paradox table with `Database::copyTable()`, you will end up with a dBASE table with a `.DB` extension. To copy a table from one table type to another, use `UpdateSet::Copy()`.

After the Bench dBASE table is created, line 42 calls `generate()` with two parameters. The first parameter is the table to add rows to and the second is how many rows to add. In this case, 980 rows will be added to the Bench table.

```
function make1000(cTable)
{
   var q = new Query() ;
   q.sql = "select * from " + cTable ;
   q.active = true ;
   var nCount = q.rowset.count() ;
   q.active = false ;
   _sys.databases[0].copyTable("title.dbf","bench.dbf") ;
   generate("bench.dbf",1000 - nCount) ;
}
```

The `generate()` function provides status information while it runs. The status is shown in the title bar of a status form. Lines 59 and 60 update the `title` property once for each append. The title bar of the form dynamically updates while the function is running.

The function contains one loop nested inside another. The outer loop executes once for each appended row. The inner loop goes through the fields. For the Bench table, the outer loop executes 980 times while the inner loop executes nine times per outer loop. The inner loop executes a total of 8,820 times.

```
function generate(cTable, nCount)
{
   var q         = new Query(),
       status    = new Form(),
       fObj      = new Object() ;
   status.top    = 1 ;
   status.left   = 1 ;
   status.height = 1 ;
   status.open() ;
   q.sql = "select * from " + cTable ;
   q.active = true ;
   for (var i = 0 ; i < nCount ; i++ )
   {
       status.title = "Creating record: " + (i+1) +
                      " of " + nCount ;
```

On line 61, `Rowset::beginAppend()` creates a row buffer to fill with random data. Fields are referenced through the `fields` property of the rowset. The `fields` property is a zero-based array. The inner loop uses the `length` property of the fields object to determine how many loops to go through.

```
q.rowset.beginAppend() ;
for (var nf = 0 ; nf < q.rowset.fields.length ; nf++)
{
```

Line 64 sets up `fObj` as a shortcut reference to the current field. The reference is used to assign random data to character and numeric fields. The generation of random string data is handled by `randomString()`. Random numeric values are adjusted to the field size, taking into account that a decimal place requires a single space.

```
   fObj = q.rowset.fields[nf] ;
   if (fObj.type == "CHARACTER" )
   {
      fObj.value =  randomString(fObj.length) ;
   }
   if (fObj.type == "NUMERIC" )
   {
      if (fObj.decimalLength > 0)
      {
         fObj.value = Math.random() * Math.pow(10,
            (fObj.length - (1 + fObj.decimalLength))) ;
      }
      else
      {
         fObj.value = Math.random() *
                     Math.pow(10,fObj.length) ;
      }
   }
}
```

NOTE
The `DbfField` class property `decimalLength` was changed from `decimalsLength` in Version 1.0 to `decimalLength` in Version 1.01.

Line 83 uses `Rowset::save()` to commit the new row. After all the rows have been added, the status form is closed and released. Closing a form removes it from view without removing it from memory. IntraBuilder automatically removes forms from memory if they have no references. The system adds one reference to a form while it is open. You can use `Form::release()` to remove a form from memory without destroying the reference variable. Releasing an open form also closes it. An error occurs if you attempt to close a form after releasing it.

```
      q.rowset.save() ;
   }
   status.close() ;
   status.release() ;
}
```

The randomString() function uses Math::random() and StringEx::chr() to generate random
string values. The ASCII values from 65 to 122 contain uppercase and lowercase letters and
the following six symbols: [, \,], ^, _, and `. The formula 65 + (Math.random() * 57 returns
values from 65 to 122, and passing this to the StringEx::chr() gives you a random character.
Line 93 sets up a for loop to grow the random string one character at a time.

```
function randomString(nLength)
{
    var cReturn = "",
        sX      = new StringEx() ;
    for (var i = 0 ; i < nLength ; i++)
    {
        cReturn += sX.chr( 65 + ( Math.random() * 57 ) ) ;
    }
    return ( cReturn ) ;
}
```

After make1000(), the table contains 1,000 rows of unique data. The first 20 rows contain the
five original rows with Delphi books. This set is followed by 980 rows of randomness. To
grow the table again, this set is copied back to itself nine times to make 10,000 rows. When
copying the rows out and back, you need to maintain unique values in the first field. The
Paradox table type requires the first field to have unique values for a single field primary key.
A primary key must exist before adding secondary indexes.

The dittoBench() function maintains unique values by including the current ditto pass
number as part of the field value. The pass number increments each time the table is appended
back to the original Bench table. It starts by declaring local variables on line 102. The function
works with two temporary tables. Temp1 is an image of the original 1,000-row Bench table.
Temp2 is the same image modified with the ditto pass number.

```
function dittoBench(nCount)
{
    var q      = new Query(),
        u      = new UpdateSet(),
        status = new Form() ;
    status.top    = 1 ;
    status.left   = 1 ;
    status.height = 1 ;
    status.title  = "Copying the source table" ;
    status.open()  ;
    _sys.databases[0].copyTable("bench.dbf","temp1.dbf") ;
```

A query is used to update the Temp2 table. The UpdateSet object works with two tables. The
source property points to the table containing values used to update the destination table.

```
q.sql = "select * from temp2" ;
u.source = "temp2.dbf" ;
u.destination = "bench.dbf" ;
```

The for loop starts by creating a fresh image of the original 1,000-row table called Temp2. A loop works through the Temp2 to update the first field of each row. After updating Temp, Line 125 deactivates the query. If the query has been left active, the next iteration of the loop would run into a problem when trying to overwrite the Temp2 table. The UpdateSet::append() method appends rows from the Temp2 table to the Bench table.

```
for (var i = 0 ; i < nCount ; i++ )
{
   _sys.databases[0].copyTable("temp1.dbf","temp2.dbf");
   q.active = true ;
   while (! q.rowset.endOfSet )
   {
       q.rowset.fields[0].value = "" + i + "-" +
                          q.rowset.fields[0].value ;
       q.rowset.save() ;
       q.rowset.next() ;
   }
   q.active = false ;
   status.title = "Expanding table - pass " +
                   (i+1) + " of " + nCount ;
   u.append() ;
}
```

Along with the standard status shutdown, the function ends by deleting the two temporary tables. At this point, the dBASE table is done. The data in the dBASE table will be carried forward through the Paradox and Access tables.

```
   _sys.databases[0].dropTable("temp1.dbf");
   _sys.databases[0].dropTable("temp2.dbf");
   status.close() ;
   status.release() ;
}
```

The idea of copying the dBASE Bench table over to a Paradox table sounds pretty easy, and UpdateSet::Copy() seems like the perfect solution. Unfortunately, UpdateSet::copy() does not copy indexes when copying the table, and it does not create tables that have a primary key.

You can make secondary indexes using Database::createIndex() with an index object or Database::exectuteSQL() with the SQL CREATE INDEX command. Creating a primary key on a Paradox table is done by creating a new table with Database::executeSQL(). The makeParadox() function jumps through several hoops to create a Paradox Bench table with a primary key. It starts by declaring some string and object variables on line 138. It then shows status information and creates a Paradox version of the Bench table called Temp1.

```
function makeParadox()
{
   var u        = new UpdateSet(),
       q        = new Query(),
```

```
d       = _sys.databases[0],
cSQL    = "";
status = new Form();

status.title = "Creating Paradox bench table" ;
status.top    = 1 ;
status.left   = 1 ;
status.height = 1 ;
status.open() ;
u.source       = "bench.dbf";
u.destination = "temp1.db";
u.copy();
```

The Database::executeSQL() method enables you to get access to database operations that are unavailable through other methods. One common use of Database::executeSQL() is to create a new table. The database classes do not contain a method specifically designed for creating a new table.

Line 155 calls getCreateStatement() with three parameters to construct the SQL CREATE TABLE command. The first parameter is a reference to a field object. The second parameter is the table name to be created. The third parameter is a SQL dialect flag for BDE and ODBC. Although SQL is a standard language, most vendors extend it with new field types and options. The extended field types for BDE and ODBC differ. The getCreateStatement() function can construct SQL statements for both BDE and SQL.

```
q.sql = "select * from 'temp1.db'" ;
q.active = true ;
cSQL = getCreateStatement(q.rowset.fields,"bench.db",false);
q.active = false ;
```

If a Paradox Bench table already exists, line 159 will delete it. You could substitute Database::dropTable() for the DROP TABLE command on line 159. With the path clear and the CREATE TABLE command in hand, the Paradox Bench table is created through Database::executeSQL(). Line 164 uses UpdateSet::append() to copy data from the Temp1 table.

```
if (d.tableExists("bench.db"))
{
    d.executeSQL("DROP TABLE 'bench.db'");
}
d.executeSQL(cSQL);
u.source = "temp1.db";
u.destination = "bench.db";
u.append() ;
```

Like the dittoBench() function, the cleanup code drops a table and releases the status form. Notice that, once again, a DROP TABLE is used in place of Database::dropTable().

```
    d.executeSQL("DROP TABLE 'temp1.db'");
    status.close() ;
    status.release() ;
}
```

The `getCreateStatement()` function reveals some differences between BDE and ODBC SQL. BDE SQL supports table names that include folder names and file extensions. The table name for a BDE `CREATE TABLE` command is specified in quotes and the extension determines the table type. The ODBC Access driver does not support quoted table names. Line 175 starts the ODBC SQL with `CREATE TABLE bench (`. The BDE version starts with `CREATE TABLE 'bench.db' (`.

```
function getCreateStatement(fieldObject, cTable, lODBC )
{
   var cStatement = "CREATE TABLE "
   if (lODBC)
   {
      cStatement += cTable + " (" ;
   }
   else
   {
      cStatement += "'" + cTable + "' (" ;
   }
```

The function builds up a comma-delimited field list. Each field is followed by SQL type information. The function places a comma between each field by creating the first field without a comma. All subsequent fields are preceded by a comma and created within a `for` loop. Note that because the field array is zero based, starting the loop at one skips past the first field.

```
cStatement += q.rowset.fields[0].fieldName + " " +
    typeSQL( q.rowset.fields[0], lODBC ) ;
for (var i = 1; i < q.rowset.fields.length ; i++)
{
    cStatement += ", " + q.rowset.fields[i].fieldName + " " +
               typeSQL( q.rowset.fields[i], lODBC ) ;
}
```

The ending of the SQL command is also dialect dependent. BDE supports creating a primary key through the `CREATE TABLE` statement. The Access ODBC driver does not support the same syntax.

```
   if ( ! lODBC )
   {
      cStatement += ", PRIMARY KEY(" +
                    q.rowset.fields[0].fieldName + "))" ;
   }
   else
   {
      cStatement += ")" ;
   }
   return ( cStatement ) ;
}
```

Lines 200 through 221 define the `typeSQL()` function. This function translates Paradox field types into SQL field types for BDE and ODBC. Rather than having an extensive set of `if` logic, the function uses an associate array to determine the return value. The major difference between associative arrays and standard arrays is that the index of an associative array is a character string instead of a number. Like standard arrays, an associative array is an object created with the new operator. You cannot pass anything to the constructor of an associative array.

```
function typeSQL( dbField, lODBC )
{
    DBTypes = new AssocArray();
```

To add an element to an associative array, assign a value using an index that you have never used before. Lines 203 through 219 create elements for 17 field types. Some field types differ for ODBC and BDE. The numeric type for an ODBC field does not require any length or precision information, and the BDE numeric definition requires both.

```
DBTypes["ALPHA"]         = "CHAR(" + dbField.length + ")" ;
DBTypes["AUTOINCREMENT"] = "AUTOINC" ;
DBTypes["BCD"]           = "DECIMAL(20,0)" ;
DBTypes["BINARY"]        = (lODBC ? "BINARY" : "BLOB(0,2)") ;
DBTypes["LOGICAL"]       = "BOOLEAN" ;
DBTypes["BYTES"]         = "BYTES(0)" ;
DBTypes["DATE"]          = "DATE" ;
DBTypes["FMTMEMO"]       = (lODBC ? "BINARY" : "BLOB(10,3)") ;
DBTypes["GRAPHIC"]       = (lODBC ? "BINARY" : "BLOB(10,5)") ;
DBTypes["LONG"]          = "INTEGER" ;
DBTypes["MEMO"]          = (lODBC ? "BINARY" : "BLOB(10,1)") ;
DBTypes["MONEY"]         = "MONEY" ;
DBTypes["NUMBER"]        = "NUMERIC" + ( lODBC ? "" : "(20,0)") ;
DBTypes["OLE"]           = "BLOB(10,4)" ;
DBTypes["SHORT"]         = "SMALLINT" ;
DBTypes["TIME"]          = "TIME" ;
DBTypes["TIMESTAMP"]     = "TIMESTAMP" ;
```

Line 220 is a return with all the logic needed to select the appropriate return string. It uses the type property of the field object as an index to the associative array.

```
    return ( DBTypes[ dbField.type ] ) ;
}
```

The getCreateStatement() function completes by passing back a CREATE TABLE command for a Paradox or Access table. Here are the final results for the two table types.

BDE Paradox:

```
CREATE TABLE 'bench.db' (TITLE CHAR(60), AUTHOR CHAR(40),
     ISBN CHAR(15), PRODUCT CHAR(20), PUBLISHER CHAR(20),
     PUBDATE DATE, PRICE NUMERIC(20,0), NOTES BLOB(10,1),
     COVER BLOB(10,5), PRIMARY KEY(TITLE))
```

ODBC Access:

```
CREATE TABLE bench (TITLE CHAR(60), AUTHOR CHAR(40), ISBN CHAR(15),
     PRODUCT CHAR(20), PUBLISHER CHAR(20), PUBDATE DATE,
     PRICE NUMERIC, NOTES BINARY, COVER BINARY)
```

The last two functions create and index the Access table. The makeAccess() function is similar to the makeParadox() function. The main difference is the catch for the DBException error on line 258. A DBException is a runtime error for a database operation. It provides more information than the standard Exception class.

```
function makeAccess()
{
   try
   {
      var d = new Database("ACCESSBENCH") ;
```

Passing a BDE alias to the constructor of a Database object is a shortcut to assigning the database name and activating the database. Line 227 could also be written as this:

```
var d = new Database() ;
d.databaseName = "ACCESSBENCH" ;
d.active = true ;
```

If a database error occurs, an alert displays showing the error. Otherwise, the connection to the MDB is established, and normal initialization code begins on line 228.

```
var q     = new Query(),
    u     = new UpdateSet(),
    cSQL = "",
    status = new Form() ;
status.title = "Creating Access bench table" ;
status.top    = 1 ;
status.left   = 1 ;
status.height = 1 ;
status.open() ;
```

This function uses both the default database and one pointing to the ACCESSBENCH BDE alias. The same query reference is used against both. Line 239 passes the query to getCreateStatement() using the Paradox version of the Bench table.

```
q.sql    = "select * from 'bench.db'" ;
q.active = true ;
cSQL     = getCreateStatement(q.rowset.fields,"bench",true) ;
q.active = false ;
```

In makeParadox(), Database::tableExists() checks for the existence of a file in the current folder. This time the method is linked to an Access database that uses logical tables rather than physical files. With an Access database, all the table, indexes, views, and even source code are stored within a single MDB file. Line 245 passes the CREATE TABLE command to the ODBC driver.

```
if (d.tableExists("bench"))
{
   d.executeSQL("DROP TABLE bench") ;
}
d.executeSQL(cSQL) ;
```

10

Queries have a database property that you can set to work with non-default databases. After the database property is set, IntraBuilder looks to the specified database for tables referenced in a SQL command. Line 246 sets the database property to the Access database. When working with BDE files, you can set the source and destination properties to strings containing filenames. Line 246 shows how to substitute a query reference for a physical filename.

```
q.database = d ;
q.sql = "select * from bench" ;
q.active = true ;
u.destination = q.rowset ;
u.source = "bench.db" ;
u.append() ;
u.null = false ;
```

The remainder of the function calls a function to create indexes on the new table and has standard cleanup code. The statements for the catch start on line 258.

```
        status.title = "Indexing Access bench table" ;
        indexAccess(d,q) ;
        status.close() ;
        status.release() ;
    }
    catch (DBException e)
    {
        alert(e.message) ;
    }
}
```

Lines 264 through 273 define the indexAccess() function. This function creates indexes for the first four fields of the Access version of the Bench table. It uses parameters to select the table and database.

```
function indexAccess(d,q)
{
    var idx = new Index() ;
    for (var i = 0 ; i < 4 ; i++ )
    {
        idx.indexName = q.rowset.fields[i].fieldName ;
        idx.fields    = q.rowset.fields[i].fieldName ;
        d.createIndex("bench",idx) ;
    }
}
```

Run the script, after you feel familiar with what it does. Because it does many things, you should set up to 30 minutes aside for the script to complete. Figure 10.9 shows how the title bar of the status form keeps you informed of the script's progress.

Figure 10.9.

Creating the bench-mark tables.

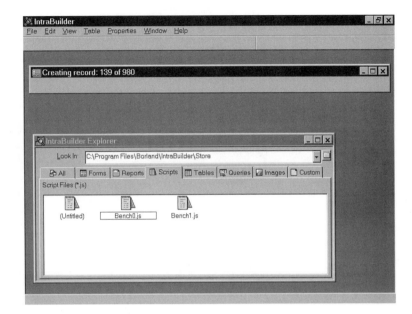

WARNING

Close all non-essential programs before running the Bench0 scripts. These scripts are resource intensive and may fail if virtual memory is already consumed by a large application such as Microsoft Word or Excel.

When the script completes, open each of the Bench tables to examine the different table types. If the IntraBuilder Explorer is not showing file extensions, you will not be able to visually differentiate between the dBASE and Paradox versions of the Bench table. You can check the option to show extensions from the IntraBuilder Explorer Properties dialog.

Opening the dBASE Bench table reveals that the first 20 rows are the original rows from the Title table. The dBASE table defaults to the physical order in which the rows were generated. The Paradox table opens in logical order. Figure 10.10 shows all three open at once. Notice that the PUBDATE is a date-time field in Access. The first row of the Paradox table contains a Title field prefixed with a zero and a dash. If you select Table|Row Count for any of the tables, the dialog returns 10,000.

Figure 10.10.

Viewing the dBASE, Paradox, and Access versions of the Bench table.

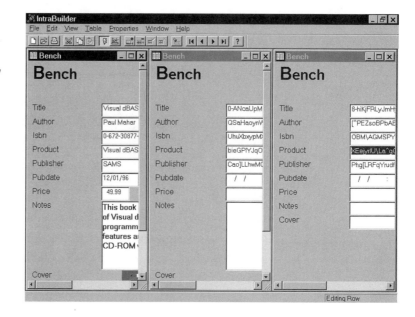

The Benchmark

Having three different table types makes it easy to decide that at least one of the variables to check is table type. Here are the others:

☐ **Search Keys** are indexes for the field being searched. The benchmark will search using the Product field. Any index on the Product field is a search key. Search keys have three states: ascending keys, descending keys, and not existing. Each affects performance and will be incorporated into the benchmark.

☐ **indexName** is a property controlling the current row order. By default, the indexName is blank, and the table appears in natural or primary key order. Natural order is the physical order of row creation.

☐ **filterOptions** is the property that controls whether exact case and length matching is required. As you learned with the query by form, the default behavior is to require both exact case and length.

NOTE

If you modify the benchmark to work with remote SQL-Linked tables, add requestLive to the list of properties to test. The requestLive property determines whether rows can be edited. It can have a dramatic effect on SQL-Link operations while having no effect on the local table performance.

The script contains four declared functions. Like the Bench0 script, the Bench1 script starts with function calls corresponding to each of the table types. Listing 10.3 shows the complete script with comments.

INPUT **Listing 10.3. Bench1—The main benchmark script.**

```
 1: //
 2: // Script:        bench1.JS
 3: //
 4: // Author:        Paul Mahar
 5: //
 6: // Date:          11/02/96
 7: //
 8: // Version:       IntraBuilder 1.01
 9: //
10: // Description:   Benchmark for comparing Query performance against
11: //                dBASE, Paradox and Access tables.
12: //
13: //                Access table create requires an installed ODBC driver
14: //                with an alias of ACCESSBENCH pointing to an MDB
15: //                containing an indexed Bench table.
16: //
17: // Parameters:    None
18: //
19: // Tables:        Bench.DBF, Bench.DB and Bench.MDB
20: //
21: // Usage:         _sys.scripts.run("bench1.JS")
22: //
23: // Reference:     Chapter 10
24: //
25: //
26: #DEFINE TABLENAME "bench"
27:
28: _sys.os.delete("bench.txt") ;
29: keyGroups("DBF") ;
30: keyGroups("DB") ;
31: keyGroups("Access") ;  // Comment out if not using Access
32:
33: function keyGroups(cType)
34: {
35:    if (cType == "Access")
36:    {
37:       // Keys already exist for MDB
38:       d = new Database("ACCESSBENCH") ;
39:       benchGroup(d,cType,"Ascend","PRODUCT") ;
40:       d.active = false ;
41:       d = null ;
42:    }
43:    else
44:    {
45:       d = _sys.databases[0]
46:       idx = ( cType == "DBF" ? new DbfIndex() : new Index() ) ;
```

continues

Listing 10.3. continued

```
47:         idx.indexName   = "ISBN" ;
48:         idx.expression  = "ISBN" ;
49:         idx.fields      = "ISBN" ;

50:         d.createIndex( TABLENAME + "." + cType,idx) ;
51:
52:         idx.indexName   = "PRODUCT" ;
53:         idx.fields      = "PRODUCT" ;
54:         idx.expression  = "PRODUCT" ;
55:         d.createIndex( TABLENAME + "." + cType,idx) ;
56:         benchGroup(d, cType,"Ascend","PRODUCT") ;
57:
58:         d.dropIndex( TABLENAME + "." + cType, "PRODUCT") ;
59:         benchGroup(d, cType,"","") ;
60:
61:         if (cType == "DBF")
62:         {
63:            idx.descending = true ;
64:            d.createIndex( TABLENAME + "." + cType,idx) ;
65:            benchGroup(d, cType,"Descend","PRODUCT") ;
66:         }
67:     }
68: }
69:
70: function benchGroup(d, cType, cKey, cKeyIdx)
71: {
72:     if (cKeyIdx.length > 0)
73:     {
74:         benchTimer( d, cType, cKey, 0, "") ;
75:     }
76:     benchTimer( d, cType, cKey, 0, cKeyIdx) ;
77:     benchTimer( d, cType, cKey, 0, "ISBN") ;
78:     benchTimer( d, cType, cKey, 3, "ISBN") ;
79: }
80:
81: function benchTimer( d, cType, cKey, nFO, cIndex )
82: {
83:     var status      = new Form(),
84:         q           = new Query(),
85:         start       = new Date(),
86:         nCount      = 0 ;
87:     status.top      = 1 ;
88:     status.left     = 1 ;
89:     status.height   = 1 ;
90:     status.title    = cType + " " + cKey + " " + nFO + " " + cIndex
91:     status.open() ;
92:     start = new Date() ;
93:     for (var x = 0;x < 5;x++)
94:     {
95:         q = new Query() ;
96:         q.database = d ;
```

```
 97:        q.sql      = "select * from " + TABLENAME +
 98:                       ( cType == "Access" ? "" :   "." + cType ) ;
 99:        q.active      = true ;
100:        q.rowset.filterOptions = nFO ;
101:        q.rowset.indexName      = cIndex ;
102:        q.rowset.filter      = "PRODUCT = 'Delphi'" ;
103:        for (var y = 0 ; y < 5; y++)
104:        {
105:           q.rowset.first() ;
106:           while (! q.rowset.endOfSet)
107:           {
108:              nCount++ ;
109:              q.rowset.next() ;
110:           }
111:        }
112:        q.active = false ;
113:        q = null ;
114:     }
115:     writeTime(cType, cKey, nFO, cIndex, nCount, start, (new Date())) ;
116:     status.close() ;
117:     status.release() ;
118: }
119:
120: function writeTime(cType, cKey, nFO, cIndex, nCount, start, end)
121: {
122:     var fOut     = new File(),
123:         elapsed = 0 ;
124:     elapsed = ((end.getHours()   * 3600) +
125:                 (end.getMinutes()* 60)   +
126:                  end.getSeconds() )
127:              -((start.getHours()   * 3600) +
128:                 (start.getMinutes()* 60)   +
129:                 start.getSeconds()) ;
130:     if ( fOut.exists("bench.txt") )
131:     {
132:        fOut.open("bench.txt","rw") ;
133:        fOut.seek(0,2) ; // go to end of file.
134:     }
135:     else
136:     {
137:        fOut.create("bench.txt") ;
138:     }
139:     fOut.puts("***") ;
140:     fOut.puts("Table type:    " + cType) ;
141:     fOut.puts("Search key:    " + cKey) ;
142:     fOut.puts("filterOptions: " + nFO) ;
143:     fOut.puts("indexName:     " + cIndex) ;
144:     fOut.puts("Count:         " + nCount ) ;
145:     fOut.puts("Seconds:       " + elapsed ) ;
146:     fOut.close() ;
147: }
```

10

Line 26 defines the benchmark table name. You can change this line to run the benchmark against the original Title table. If you want to see what happens with the Title table, change "bench" to "title" on line 26 and comment out lines 30 and 31.

```
#DEFINE TABLENAME "title"

_sys.os.delete("bench.txt") ;
keyGroups("DBF") ;
// keyGroups("DB") ;
// keyGroups("Access") ;   // Comment out if not using Access
```

The keyGroups() function controls what combinations of properties are used with each table type. Not all combinations are possible to script. For example, the IntraBuilder 1.01 does not support scripting the creation of descending indexes on Paradox tables. The function runs all applicable queries for each table type. Lines 39, 56, 59, and 65 call benchGroup() with four parameters as shown in Table 10.3.

Table 10.3. Parameters passed to benchGroup().

Sample Value	Meaning	Possible Values
d	Database handle	n/a
cType	Table type	Access, DB, or DBF.
"Ascend"	Search key	Ascend, Descend, or blank
"PRODUCT"	Search key name	PRODUCT or blank

After timing the Access table, the function deactivates the database. Line 41 releases the database object. Although you cannot release a variable, you can assign null to the variable to release the referenced object.

```
function keyGroups(cType)
{
   if (cType == "Access")
   {
      // Keys already exist for MDB
      d = new Database("ACCESSBENCH") ;
      benchGroup(d,cType,"Ascend","PRODUCT") ;
      d.active = false ;
      d = null ;
   }
}
```

For dBASE and Paradox tables, the function creates appropriate indexes before calling benchGroup(). The first group of benchmarks requires indexes on the ISBN and Product fields. The second group requires the absence of an index on the Product field. If the table type is dBASE, an additional benchmark is applied with a descending index.

10

NOTE

> The DbfIndex and Index classes are undocumented in IntraBuilder 1.01. See Appendix B, "The Undocumented IntraBuilder," for more information about using these and other undocumented classes.

The DbfIndex and Index classes have slightly different property sets. DbfIndex uses the expression property to determine the index key values. This enables you to use a simple field name or a complex dBASE expression. The Index class uses a fields property in place of an expression property. The fields property accepts a list of one or more fields as the index key. Lines 46 through 49 assign values to both expression and fields.

```
else
{
    d = _sys.databases[0]
    idx = ( cType == "DBF" ? new DbfIndex() : new Index() ) ;
    idx.indexName  = "ISBN" ;
    idx.expression = "ISBN" ;
    idx.fields     = "ISBN" ;
    d.createIndex( TABLENAME + "." + cType,idx) ;

    idx.indexName  = "PRODUCT" ;
    idx.fields     = "PRODUCT" ;
    idx.expression = "PRODUCT" ;
    d.createIndex( TABLENAME + "." + cType,idx) ;
    benchGroup(d, cType,"Ascend","PRODUCT") ;

    d.dropIndex( TABLENAME + "." + cType, "PRODUCT") ;
    benchGroup(d, cType,"","") ;
    if (cType == "DBF")
    {
        idx.descending = true ;
        d.createIndex( TABLENAME + "." + cType,idx) ;
        benchGroup(d, cType,"Descend","PRODUCT") ;
    }
}
}
```

The benchGroup() function passes on the first three parameters it gets to benchTimer() and adds two new options. This function starts the benchmark with different filterOptions and indexName values. Table 10.4 shows the four possible configurations used by benchGroup().

Table 10.4. Configurations defined in the benchGroup() function.

filterOptions	indexName
0	(blank)
0	(same as search key)
0	ISBN
3	ISBN

Line 72 adds a conditional optimization. If the current search key is blank, it does not run the same set of options twice.

```
function benchGroup(d, cType, cKey, cKeyIdx)
{
   if (cKeyIdx.length > 0)
   {
      benchTimer( d, cType, cKey, 0, "") ;
   }
   benchTimer( d, cType, cKey, 0, cKeyIdx) ;
   benchTimer( d, cType, cKey, 0, "ISBN") ;
   benchTimer( d, cType, cKey, 3, "ISBN") ;
}
```

The benchTimer() function contains the query loops along with code to capture the start and end times of each benchmark. It starts out by opening a status form on line 91.

```
function benchTimer( d, cType, cKey, nFO, cIndex )
{
   var status      = new Form(),
       q           = new Query(),
       start       = new Date(),
       nCount      = 0 ;
   status.top    = 1 ;
   status.left   = 1 ;
   status.height = 1 ;
   status.title  = cType + " " + cKey + " " + nFO + " " + cIndex
   status.open() ;
```

Line 92 recaptures the start time to avoid timing any delay caused by the status form. Two nested loops control the query iterations. The outer loop creates a new query based on all the parameters passed to the function. It uses a filter to search for Delphi books.

```
start = new Date() ;
for (var x = 0;x < 5;x++)
{
   q = new Query() ;
   q.database = d ;
   q.sql       = "select * from " + TABLENAME +
                 ( cType == "Access" ? "" :  "." + cType ) ;
   q.active    = true ;
   q.rowset.filterOptions = nFO ;
   q.rowset.indexName    = cIndex ;
   q.rowset.filter       = "PRODUCT = 'Delphi'" ;
```

The inner loop passes through the current query five times without resetting any properties. It counts how many books are found as a check sum. Each pass through the query locates 50 books out of the 10,000 rows. This is based on the original five Delphi books from the Title table. After going through the table 25 times for the inner and outer loops, the book count completes at 1,250 successful finds.

```
for (var y = 0 ; y < 5; y++)
{
   q.rowset.first() ;
```

```
while (! q.rowset.endOfSet)
{
   nCount++ ;
   q.rowset.next() ;
}
}
```

Line 113 deactivates and releases the query to prepare for the next pass. At this point, the variable q still exists but the query is cleared from memory.

```
q.active = false ;
q = null ;
}
```

Line 115 calls another function to write the elapsed time to a file. The end time is passed as the expression (new Date())).

```
writeTime(cType, cKey, nFO, cIndex, nCount, start, (new Date())) ;
status.close() ;
status.release() ;
}
```

The writeTime() function records the benchmark results into a text file. The elapsed time is calculated from the start and end date objects. A date object contains both the time and the date. To make calculations on the time, the function converts the time values to seconds using Date::getHours(), Date::getMinutes(), and Date::getSeconds().

```
function writeTime(cType, cKey, nFO, cIndex, nCount, start, end)
{
   var fOut    = new File(),
       elapsed = 0 ;
   elapsed = ((end.getHours()   * 3600) +
              (end.getMinutes()* 60)    +
               end.getSeconds() )
           -((start.getHours()   * 3600) +
             (start.getMinutes()* 60)    +
              start.getSeconds()) ;
```

NOTE   The formula to calculate elapsed time does not account for running the benchmark into a new day. If you plan to run the benchmark near midnight, you might want to add a call to Date::getDate().

The rest of the function opens or creates the text file and writes out the results. Line 28 erases the bench text file making results accumulative only to the current run.

```
if ( fOut.exists("bench.txt") )
{
   fOut.open("bench.txt","rw") ;
   fOut.seek(0,2) ; // go to end of file.
}
```

```
        else
        {
           fOut.create("bench.txt") ;
        }
        fOut.puts("***") ;
        fOut.puts("Table type:    " + cType) ;
        fOut.puts("Search key:    " + cKey) ;
        fOut.puts("filterOptions: " + nFO) ;
        fOut.puts("indexName:     " + cIndex) ;
        fOut.puts("Count:         " + nCount ) ;
        fOut.puts("Seconds:       " + elapsed ) ;
        fOut.close() ;
}
```

That does it for Bench1. If you haven't already done so, run the script now. Like the Bench0 script, this can take up to 30 minutes to run. It will provide the most accurate results when all other processes are closed prior to running the script. Avoid task switching during the run.

The Results

The benchmark results reveal some key aspects to the IntraBuilder query system. The numbers given here are from my home PC and are only for reference. I encourage you to run the benchmark in your own environment to get a better picture of how performance tradeoffs are likely to affect your applications. Also be sure to get the latest ODBC, BDE, and IntraBuilder patches before running. Microsoft and Borland are continually improving their software, and some enhancements that were unavailable as of this writing may have a significant impact.

The benchmark machine used here was a 60Mhz Dell OmniPlex with 48MB RAM. All times were run under Windows 95. Although this system is adequate for development, I recommend that you deploy applications under Windows NT using a machine of at least 90Mhz.

After running the Bench1 script, you can open the resulting text file from the IntraBuilder Explorer. It appears on the Custom tab after selecting View|Refresh. It contains a long list of results. A portion of the bench.txt file is shown in the following code. The count is provided to double-check the query accuracy. All counts should appear as 1,250.

OUTPUT
```
Table type:     DBF
filterOptions:  0
indexName:
Search key:     Ascend
Count:          1250
Seconds:        1
***
Table type:     DBF
filterOptions:  0
indexName:      PRODUCT
Search key:     Ascend
```

```
Count:          1250
Seconds:        7
***
Table type:     DBF
filterOptions:  0
indexName:      ISBN
Search key:     Ascend
Count:          1250
Seconds:        8
```

A quick glance through the file is enough to show that the dBASE table type is faster than a Paradox table, and a Paradox table is faster than an Access table. For a more complete picture, you can rearrange the numbers as shown in Table 10.5.

Table 10.5. Configurations defined in the `BenchGroup()` function.

filterOptions	indexName	Search Key	dBASE	Paradox	Access
0	(blank)	Ascend	1	23	122
0	PRODUCT	Ascend	7	92	111
0	ISBN	Ascend	8	90	101
3	ISBN	Ascend	27	92	175
0	(blank)	(none)	3	23	
0	ISBN	(none)	24	90	
3	ISBN	(none)	27	93	
0	(blank)	Descend	4		
0	PRODUCT	Descend	29		
0	ISBN	Descend	25		
3	ISBN	Descend	27		

The table reveals that, without question, IntraBuilder performs much faster with dBASE tables than with the other two desktop formats. It also shows how unordered queries work faster than when using an index, even when the search key is the current index.

All the differences can be traced back to the database engine. Whenever BDE searches for values, it looks to see whether an index is available for the field being searched. If one is found, the engine reads the index rather than the table. If the search is unordered, the engine can rely exclusively on the index to find rows. When the set is ordered, the engine must bounce between two indexes to perform the search.

10

The advantage of a dBASE table is also its weakness. The dBASE format uses fixed length fields. All variable length information is stored in a separate DBT file. The fixed length format allows the engine to use simple offsets to navigate through the table. The level 5 dBASE table also contains no data integrity information.

Both the Paradox and Access formats are much more complex. The structures provide for storing template, relation, and other validation information as part of the table definition. The price of this integrity is speed.

Figure 10.11 shows another view of the results. This graph was created by placing the data from Table 10.5 into Excel. Again, the results show significant differences. The conclusion of this benchmark is to remember that the F in DBF is for "Fast."

Figure 10.11.
Graphing the results where shorter bars mean better performance.

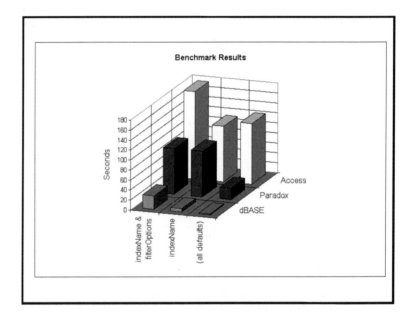

Creating a Prototype for the Quick Form

Let's get back to the shopping cart application and put some of the performance tricks into practice. To create a Quick search form, you can use the fastest combination of properties and table type. This form needs to list all the products about which the store has books. The product list is in a Product table. One of the main tasks for this form is getting the product list from the table and placing it in a list box.

The list box control does not have a property to populate the control directly from a table. Instead, it has an options property that you can assign to an array or a file list. The Quick form will use the array feature after filling an array with field values. This is a case where you will have to employ the use of JavaScript rather than a property builder.

The form also needs a button that lets shoppers move from the Quick form to the Results form. The Quick form needs to configure a query on the Results form before calling it. Today's version of the Results form is a simple stub form that shows only the count of how many books are available for a given product.

NEW TERM A *stub* form is a placeholder for an undeveloped form. Stubs are used to test dependencies between forms before all forms are complete.

Populating a Select List

Start developing the Quick form by creating a form that ties a select list to the Product table. Like the Help form, this form will use the toolbar custom form class. Follow these steps to create the new Quick form:

1. Create a new form with the designer. From the menu, select File|New|Form and pick the designer option.

2. See that the new form is derived from the toolbar custom form class. If the untitled form appears with the toolbar buttons and the bookstore name, you can skip to the next step. If not, select File|Set Custom Form Class. Open the toolbar.jcf file and select the ToolbarCForm class.

3. Drop a select list onto the form. Position it at the left edge of the form so that it is aligned under the Quick Search button.

NOTE

The component palette shows the list box as a select list. Also, the default name for a list box is select1. The discrepancy comes from the different ways that HTML and Windows work. In Windows, the control is a list box and it is independent from a combo box. In an HTML form, both controls are variations of a select control.

4. From the IntraBuilder Explorer, drop the Product table onto the form. This creates a query with no indexName set and with filterOptions defaulting to 0. From the benchmark, you know this to be the most efficient query configuration.

5. Remove the path from the `sql` property of the `product1` query. The command should read as follows:

```
SELECT * FROM "product.dbf"
```

6. Inspect the select list and change the name from `select1` to `selectProducts`.

7. Switch over to the Inspector's events tab and click the tool button for the `onServerLoad` event. This opens a newly linked method where you can enter code to tie the query to the select list.

8. Enter the following for the `onServerLoad` event. An array is created as a property of the select list. The method passes once through the table, adding an array element for each row. The method ends by sorting the array and assigning it to the select list `option` property. By sorting the array, you can get a nicely sorted select list without slowing down the query.

```
function selectProducts_onServerLoad()
{
   var rProduct = this.parent.product1.rowset ;
   this.productArray = new Array() ;
   while ( ! ( rProduct.endOfSet ))
   {
     this.productArray.add( rProduct.fields["product"].value) ;
     rProduct.next();
   }
   this.productArray.sort() ;
   this.options =  "Array this.productArray"
}
```

9. Press F2 to save and run the form. Name the form `quick.jfm`. When running in the designer, the form should now resemble the one in Figure 10.12.

Figure 10.12.

Running the Quick form in the designer.

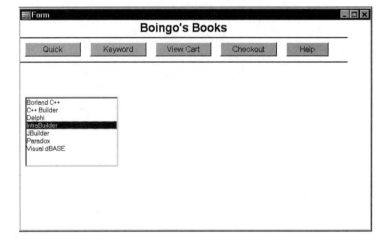

10

Creating a Stub Form for Results

Before adding the Search button to the Quick form, you'll need to create a stub form for the Results form. A stub form allows another form to work with the least amount of effort on your part. That sounds pretty good at the end of a long day of running benchmarks. The stub form eventually will evolve into the Results form. For now, all it needs to include is a query, an HTML object, and one method. Use the following steps:

1. Create a new form. Leave the custom form class set to the toolbar class.

2. From the IntraBuilder Explorer, drop the Title table onto the new form.

3. Drop an HTML component below the toolbar and make it stretch out to be about the same length as the rule lines. A width of 65 works well. Change the name from `html1` to `htmlCount`.

4. Switch to the Event tab of the Inspector and click the tool button to create a new method for `htmlCount`'s `onServerLoad` event.

5. Enter the following for the new method:

```
function htmlCount_onServerLoad()
{
    this.text = "Number of matches found: " + this.form.titleCount ;
}
```

6. Close the Form Designer and save the form as `results.jfm`.

NOTE

The capitalization you enter when saving a new JavaScript form is used for the class definition. If you save the form as `RESULTS.JFM`, the class name becomes `RESULTSForm`.

The shopping cart application assumes that JavaScript forms are always created with lowercase filenames. Future references to the Results form class name will be `resultsForm`.

You may change the case of an existing JavaScript form by opening the file in the Script Editor and modifying two lines near the top of the script. The first line is the one that creates an instance and contains `var f = new <class name>()`. The other line to change is the first line of the class definition. It begins with `class <class name> extends`.

You just created a form that doesn't work. If you run the form, it calls the `htmlCount_onServerLoad()` function. That function references a non-existent property called titleCount. There is no need to fix the error within this form, because shoppers will not be able to run this form without running the Quick form or Keyword form first. Both search forms will create the titleCount property before opening the Results form.

Adding the Search Button

It is now time to go back to the Quick form and add the Search button that opens the Results form. All that you need to do in this part is add one button and a linked onServerClick with these steps:

1. Open the Quick form in the Form Designer and drop a new button under the select list.

2. Change the button name property from button1 to buttonSearch and change the text property to Search.

3. Add the following method to the button's onServerClick event. This method is similar to the onServerClick events for the toolbar buttons in that it creates a reference to a new form, opens the new form, and closes the current form.

   The major difference is that it modifies existing properties of the next form using values from the current form. The filter property is defined from the value currently selected in the list box.

   The this.form.selectProducts.value contains the value currently highlighted in the select list. If nothing is selected, the value is an empty string. The searchProduct property of the next form is created so that it can exist while the filter is active and the current form is no longer in memory.

```
function buttonSearch_onServerClick()
{
_sys.scripts.load("results.jfm") ; // debug code
    var nextForm = new resultsForm() ;
    nextForm.searchProduct = this.form.selectProducts.value ;
    nextForm.title1.rowset.filter =
        "PRODUCT = '" + nextForm.searchProduct + "'" ;
    nextForm.titleCount = nextForm.title1.rowset.count() ;
//  nextForm.user = this.form.user
    nextForm.open() ;
    form.close() ;
}
```

 NOTE

This rendition of the buttonSearch_onServerClick() method contains some items that you will modify on Day 11. The first is the _sys.scripts.load() statement. This is included so that you can call the Results form directly from the Quick form without going through the Help form.

4. Save the form when you have the button configured and the method entered as shown in Figure 10.13.

Figure 10.13.

Adding a method to the Quick form.

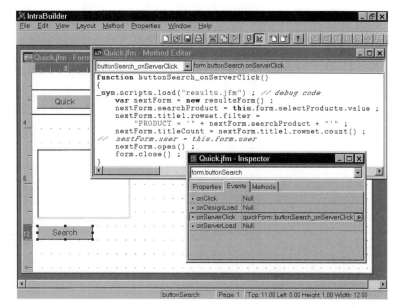

You can now run the Quick form without running the Help form. This makes it a little easier to debug and see the interaction between the Quick form and the Results form. If you pick Delphi from the select list and click search, the Results form opens to show you that five books have been found. These are the same five books that the benchmark found 27,500 times if you ran against all three table types.

In its current state the Quick form provides a one-way street to the Results form. After the Results form opens, it is the only open script and every toolbar button returns an error. Figure 10.14 shows the search results along with the error that occurs if you click the Quick toolbar button.

Figure 10.14.

Viewing results and a
runtime error.

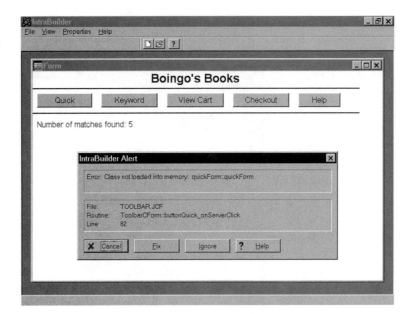

Summary

Today's topics were all focused on queries. The day began by learning about query by form and filter by form. The Table Run window and Form Expert give you fast access to both query by form and filter by form. You learned the strengths and weaknesses of both form searching techniques.

After looking at some of the code behind the query by form and filter by form, you delved into an extensive set of benchmarks. The investigation into query performance started with a detailed analysis of a JavaScript script that generates 10,000 row tables for dBASE, Paradox, and Access tables. The generation script revealed many differences between the table types and how the database classes interact with them.

The table generation process consumed more than half the day, but you finally reached the benchmark script. The analysis of the benchmark script focused more on the properties that impact query performance than on differences between table types. Both scripts showed how IntraBuilder can work as a procedural data-processing engine in addition to an event-driven Web form server.

The results from the benchmark showed some extreme differences between table types and property settings. The fastest query beat the slowest by a factor of 170. Although table type had the biggest impact on performance, the `indexName` and `filterOption` values were also shown to be significant.

The end of the day brought you back to the shopping cart application. You started to develop the Quick form and Results form. You learned how to populate a list box and how to use a selection from the list box as part of a query filter. The day concluded with a working prototype of the Quick form and a stub for the results form. That is where you will start tomorrow when you finish up these forms and tie them into the Help form.

Q&A

Q **If I use an Oracle server, can I get better performance than is possible with dBASE tables?**

A It depends on what you're doing. The dBASE tables are likely to out-perform Oracle when the data sets are small and the searches are simple. SQL servers, such as Microsoft SQL Server, Oracle, Sybase, and InterBase, have the performance edge when it comes to extremely large data sets and complex queries. They also have the advantage of running on machines other than the one running the IntraBuilder Server. Unlike client/server connections, the BDE and ODBC processes must share CPU time with IntraBuilder.

Q **I tried to run the benchmark, but I ran into many problems when trying to create the Access table. What is going wrong?**

A IntraBuilder is certified only with specific versions of the Access ODBC driver. Please check the `readme.txt` file that comes with IntraBuilder for a list of supported driver versions.

Q **I checked in the `readme.txt` file and found the supported ODBC driver versions, but I still can't tell if I'm using the right ones. How do I get the driver version from an ODBC driver?**

A From the Windows Control Panel, open the 32-bit ODBC administration tool. Click the Drivers button, select the Access driver, and click About. The About box lists the driver filename, date, and version information.

Q **Is the search key optimization done in IntraBuilder similar to FoxPro's Rushmore technology?**

A The BDE equivalent to Rushmore is SpeedFilters. Part of the technology involves using indexes for searches in addition to the more traditional use of table ordering. SQL servers also use this technique in addition to other optimizations. Other parts of the Rushmore and SpeedFilter technologies involve Xbase expression optimization and are not applicable to IntraBuilder.

10

Workshop

The Workshop section provides questions and exercises to help you get a better feel for the material you learned today. Try to answer the questions and at least think about the exercises before moving on to tomorrow's lesson. You'll find the answers to the questions in Appendix A, "Answers to Quiz Questions."

Quiz

1. What `filterOptions` setting makes it easier for the user to work with query by form and filter by form?

2. What `filterOptions` setting is most likely to slow down a query?

3. What method can create a primary key on a Paradox table?

4. What is the difference between query by form and filter by form?

5. What three expression types can you use in an IntraBuilder application?

6. List the three table types that you can use with the standard edition of IntraBuilder in order from fastest to slowest.

Exercises

1. Although the benchmark does compare different table types and other options, it uses only a single character field to filter the table. Change the benchmark script to filter on a numeric field or a date field, and chart the results.

2. During the course of the day, this chapter never asked you to try anything through a browser, which is the main purpose of the product. If you miss running your browser, try running the Expert1 form through your browser.

Week 2

Day 11

Delivering the Details

by Paul Mahar

Today you will work with more forms than on any other day. By the end of the day, you will have designed and modified six of the eight forms that make up the shopping cart application. Day 11 begins with the creation of a new form and continues into tying up some loose ends left from yesterday's JavaScript adventure. These are the tasks of the day:

- [ ] **Design a Message form:** The Message form is a general-purpose form that you can use to provide simple feedback to the shopper. In this chapter, you'll use the Message form to inform the shopper when no books are found for a particular product.

- [ ] **Finish up the Quick form:** The version of the Quick form from Day 10 leaves something to be desired. Today, you will enhance the form with help text, add a proper title, and modify the JavaScript to pass on more information to the Results form.

☐ **Update the Help form:** After enhancing the Quick form, it will be time to integrate it with the Help form and give it the browser test. On this form, you will work with a JavaScript header file and learn more about the compiler.

☐ **Finish up the Results form:** Once again, you will need to complete a form that was left over from yesterday. The Results form is currently a stub form that needs a little more work to finish than the Quick form. You will be adding a select list to show query results and a link to the Details form.

☐ **Design a Details form:** Perhaps the biggest challenge of the day is the creation of the Details form. Here you will go from a Form Expert prototype to a highly customized form in one day. Getting the Details form right requires some trial and error using both the Netscape and Explorer browsers.

☐ **Start up the Cart form:** The last task is in preparation for tomorrow. Today you will create a simple stub form that can be called from the toolbar and the Details form. In Day 12, you will evolve this form into the most complex form of the application.

At the end of today's lesson, shoppers will be able to enter the store through the Help form and do a quick search for books. The Results form will show shoppers a list of all found books and let shoppers descend to the Details form to get more information on any listed book.

Putting the Finishing Touches on the Quick Form

So what does the Quick form need to be complete? On the surface, it needs only a better title and one more HTML component to tell the shopper what the form does. Under the covers, the `buttonSearch_onServerClick()` method needs revising to pass on the user key to the Results form. The Quick form also needs a better way to handle searches that find no books and searches initiated without a selected product.

The new search handlers require a new generic form that you can use to provide simple feedback to the shopper. The Message form is the generic feedback form, and it contains only one component in addition to what it inherits from the toolbar custom form class. The new component is an HTML control containing the message that you want to send back to the shopper.

Making a Message Form

The Message form is the simplest form in the shopping application. It takes only a few minutes to create. Use these steps:

1. Open the Form Designer with a new form. To bypass the expert prompt and pre-name your form, select View|Script Pad and enter the following:

   ```
   _sys.forms.design("message.jfm")
   ```

NOTE You can call _sys.forms.design() with or without a filename. If you do not pass a filename, the Designer opens with a new untitled form. Passing an existing name opens that form in Design mode. If you pass a non-existent filename, the Designer opens with a new, titled, yet unsaved form. Naming a new file at the start of the design session eliminates the new filename prompt when you close the Designer.

2. Drop an HTML component on the form and give it the following position properties: height 2, left 1, top 3.5, width 65.

3. Rename the component from html1 to htmlMessage.

4. Change the form.title property to Boingo's Books - Message.

5. Press Ctrl+F4 to close the Designer and save the new form.

That's all you need for the Message form. If you run the form, the default text, "HTML1", appears as the message text. When the form is incorporated into the shopping cart application, the text property is set dynamically to an appropriate value prior to opening the form. Listing 11.1 shows the JavaScript generated by the Form Designer.

INPUT **Listing 11.1. The Message form.**

```
 1: // {End Header} Do not remove this comment//
 2: // Generated on 11/02/96
 3: //
 4: var f = new messageForm();
 5: f.open();
 6: class messageForm extends ToolbarCForm from "TOOLBAR.JCF" {
 7:     with (this) {
 8:         height = 15;
 9:         left   = 0;
10:         top    = 0;
11:         width  = 75;
12:         title  = "Boingo's Books - Message";
13:     }
14:     with (this.htmlMessage = new HTML(this)){
15:         height = 2;
16:         left   = 1;
17:         top    = 3.5;
18:         width  = 65;
19:         color  = "black";
20:         text   = "HTML1";
21:     }
22: }
```

ANALYSIS Such a simple form might appear too basic for any analysis. Actually, it is the form's simplicity that makes it a good candidate to demonstrate how the IntraBuilder dynamic object model works. The best place to see this is in the Script Pad. Open the Script Pad and enter the following JavaScript statements:

```
_sys.scripts.load("message.jfm") ;
f = new messageForm() ;
f.htmlMessage.text = "Hello World" ;
f.open() ;
```

The Script Pad lets you experiment with setting properties dynamically without the need to create or compile a JavaScript script. Assigning the `text` property in the Script Pad overrides the original value set on line 20. Figure 11.1 shows the form and Script Pad interacting.

Figure 11.1.

Using the Script Pad to test the Message form.

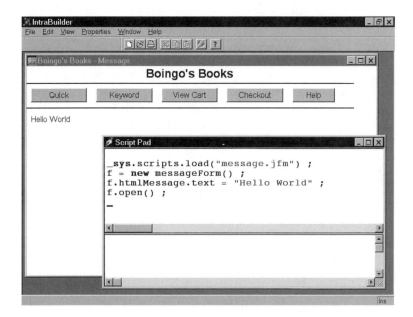

NEW TERM A *dynamic object model* is an implementation of object classes that enables the creation of properties outside the class definition. The ability to create properties at runtime allows for truly data-driven applications where the desired property set is unknowable at compile time.

To take this experiment a step further, you can create an instance of a message form directly from the toolbar custom form class. First close the Message form but leave the Script Pad open. Enter the following JavaScript statements to open the custom form class and create a new Message form.

```
_sys.scripts.load('toolbar.jcf') ;
f = new ToolbarCForm() ;
f.htmlMessage = new HTML(f) ;
f.htmlMessage.top = 3.5 ;
f.htmlMessage.text = "Hello World" ;
f.open() ;
```

This time you are not only setting a property on-the-fly, but you are creating a new component outside of a form class. The new form looks almost identical to the one defined in the message.jfm file. The only difference is in the title bar that is set in line 12. You can fix this while the form is open. Enter the following assignment statement into the Script Pad to change the title of the open form:

```
f.title = "Boingo's Books - Message" ;
```

You can also delete components and inspect properties of an open form. Try deleting htmlMessage and open the Inspector to check out the form's properties. Enter the following statements:

```
f.htmlMessage.release() ;
inspect(f) ;
```

The ability to create and release components of a running form is key to creating dynamic forms that adjust to the current data set and user requirements. In this application, the dynamic object model will prove vital to the implementation of the shopping cart form.

A Slight Redesign

At this point, the Quick form can run independently of the Help form, but it does not keep track of the user key. Once you complete the Quick form, neither will be true. Keeping track of the user key is dependent upon starting with the Help form. The benefit of ignoring the user key issue up to now was that you could test the link between the Quick form and the Results form.

Being confident that the link works okay, it is time to finish the Quick form. Follow these steps to add another HTML object and make a few other modifications:

1. Open the Quick form in the Form Designer. Use the IntraBuilder Explorer or enter the following in the Script Pad:

    ```
    _sys.forms.design("quick.jfm") ;
    ```

2. Drop an HTML control from the component palette. Place it between the toolbar and list box. Move the list box down if necessary. For the new HTML control, set the position properties to height 2, left 1, top 3.5, width 65.

3. Change the name from html1 to htmlHelp.

4. Click the tool button for the text property to open the Text Property Builder.

5. In the Text without Tags box enter this text: To search our entire database of books, select the product you are interested in, then click the "Search" button.

6. Use the drop-down list at the top of the Inspector to switch focus from form.htmlHelp to form.

7. Drop the Title table from the IntraBuilder Explorer onto the Form Designer. As with any dropped table, take the explicit path out of the sql property.

8. Change the form.title property to Boingo's Books - Quick Search. Your form should now look similar to the one in Figure 11.2.

Figure 11.2.

Redesigning the Quick form.

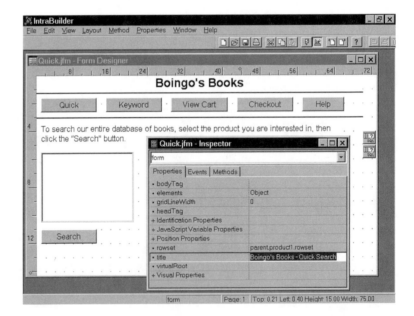

9. Switch over to the Events tab in the Inspector and enter the following code block for the form's onServerLoad event. Remember to press Enter after typing in the code block.

```
this.form.buttonQuick.visible = false
```

When you press Enter, the Form Designer changes the code block to the following:

```
{ ; this.form.buttonQuick.visible = false }
```

10. Open the Method Editor for the `buttonSearch_onServerClick` function. Select View|Method Editor and pick the function name from the editor window's drop-down list.

11. Edit the function to match the following:

```
function buttonSearch_onServerClick()
{
    if ( this.form.selectProducts.value.length > 0 )
    {
        this.form.searchProduct = this.form.selectProducts.value ;
        this.form.title1.rowset.filter =
            "PRODUCT = '" + this.form.searchProduct + "'" ;
    }
    var nCount = this.form.title1.rowset.count() ;
    if (nCount == 0)
    {
        var nextForm = new messageForm() ;
        nextForm.htmlMessage.text = "<H3>No titles found for: " +
            this.form.selectProducts.value + "</H3>" ;
    }
    else
    {
        var nextForm = new resultsForm() ;
        nextForm.titleCount = nCount ;
        nextForm.title1.rowset.filter = this.form.title1.rowset.filter ;
    }
    nextForm.user = this.form.user ;
    nextForm.open() ;
    form.release() ;
}
```

The revised function is more flexible and informative than the previous version. With this one, shoppers can view all book titles by not selecting a product. When no titles are found for a product, the Message form appears in place of the Results form.

12. Switch to Run mode to save the form and see the Quick toolbar button disappear.

If you try any of the buttons, you will get a runtime error. To prevent these errors, you will need to modify the store.h file and recompile the Help form. Before doing that, take a closer look at the Quick form in Listing 11.2.

INPUT   **Listing 11.2. The Quick form.**

```
1: // {End Header} Do not remove this comment//
2: // Generated on 11/02/96
3: //
4: var f = new quickForm();
5: f.open();
```

continues

Listing 11.2. continued

```
6:  class quickForm extends ToolbarCForm from "TOOLBAR.JCF" {
7:      with (this) {
8:          height = 15;
9:          left = 0;
10:         top = 0;
11:         width = 75;
12:         title = "Boingo's Books - Quick Search";
13:         onServerLoad = {;this.buttonQuick.visible = false};
14:     }
15:
16:     with (this.product1 = new Query()){
17:         left = 70;
18:         top = 4;
19:         sql = 'SELECT * FROM "product.dbf"';
20:         active = true;
21:     }
22:
23:     with (this.product1.rowset) {
24:     }
25:
26:     with (this.title1 = new Query()){
27:         left = 70;
28:         top = 5;
29:         sql = 'SELECT * FROM "title.dbf"';
30:         active = true;
31:     }
32:
33:     with (this.title1.rowset) {
34:     }
35:
36:     with (this.selectProducts = new ListBox(this)){
37:         height = 5;
38:         left = 1;
39:         top = 5.5;
40:         width = 20;
41:         onServerLoad = class::selectProducts_onServerLoad;
42:     }
43:
44:     with (this.buttonSearch = new Button(this)){
45:         left = 1 ;
46:         top = 11;
47:         width = 12;
48:         text = "Search";
49:         onServerClick = class::buttonSearch_onServerClick;
```

```
 50:     }
 51:

 52:     with (this.htmlHelp = new HTML(this)){
 53:         height = 2;
 54          left = 1;
 55:         top = 3.5;
 56:         width = 65;
 57:         color = "black";
 58:         text = 'To search our entire database of books, select ' +
 59:                   'the product you are interested in, then click ' +
 60:                   'the "Search" button.';
 61:     }
 62:
 63:     this.rowset = this.product1.rowset;
 64:
 65:     function selectProducts_onServerLoad()
 66:     {
 67:         var rProduct = this.parent.product1.rowset ;
 68:         this.productArray = new Array() ;
 69:         while ( ! ( rProduct.endOfSet ))
 70:         {
 71:             this.productArray.add( rProduct.fields["product"].value) ;
 72:             rProduct.next();
 73:         }
 74:         this.productArray.sort() ;
 75:         this.options =  "Array this.productArray"
 76:     }
 77:
 78:     function buttonSearch_onServerClick()
 79:     {
 80:         if ( this.form.selectProducts.value.length > 0 )
 81:         {
 82:             this.form.searchProduct = this.form.selectProducts.value ;
 83:             this.form.title1.rowset.filter =
 84:                 "PRODUCT = '" + this.form.searchProduct + "'" ;
 85:         }
 86:         var nCount = this.form.title1.rowset.count() ;
 87:         if (nCount == 0)
 88:         {
 89:             var nextForm = new messageForm() ;
 90:             nextForm.htmlMessage.text = "<H3>No titles found for: " +
 91:                 this.form.selectProducts.value + "</H3>" ;
 92:         }
 93:         else
 94:         {
 95:             var nextForm = new resultsForm() ;
 96:             nextForm.titleCount = nCount ;
 97:             nextForm.title1.rowset.filter = this.form.title1.rowset.filter ;
 98:         }
 99:         nextForm.user = this.form.user ;
100:         nextForm.open() ;
101:         this.form.release() ;
102:     }
103: }
```

ANALYSIS The first thing the form does when it loads is to execute the code block on line 13. The code block hides the Quick button. When you run the form in the Designer, the Quick button is visible for a split second before the `visible` property is set to `false`. At first this might seem like something needs fixing, but it is not so. When the form runs in a browser, the Quick button is never visible.

Similarly, the list box opens as an empty box before getting filled through the `onServerLoad` event linked on line 41. When the list fills up in the Designer, it causes a noticeable flicker. Think of the Designer's Run mode as a dress rehearsal. When you run something in the Designer, function is more important than style. The same select list makes a perfectly clean debut when appearing in a browser.

When a shopper does not select a product, the `value` property of the select list is an *empty string*. Otherwise, it is the selected value. An empty string has a length of zero. The button search method checks for this on line 80 and applies a filter only if a product is selected.

NEW TERM An *empty string* is a string with a length of zero. An empty string is not equal to a null value. An expression that includes an empty string can result in a non-empty string. Expressions containing a null value always yield a null value.

```
if ( this.form.selectProducts.value.length > 0 )
{
   this.form.searchProduct = this.form.selectProducts.value ;
   this.form.title1.rowset.filter =
      "PRODUCT = '" + this.form.searchProduct + "'" ;
}
var nCount = this.form.title1.rowset.count() ;
```

Line 86 figures the title count for both the Quick form and the Results form. After the filter is set, the count does not change. All three forms could recount the rows as needed, but this would slow down the application. To keep counting to a minimum, the count is made once and passed on to the Results form. The Results form displays the count and passes it on to the Details form.

NOTE The `Rowset::count()` method does not move the row pointer, but setting the `filter` property does. If you set a `filter` property, the current row changes unless the current row matches the filter condition. The `Rowset::count()` method counts rows using an independent row cursor that can ignore the index order for faster counts.

The Quick form uses the count to determine whether any rows match the current filter. Another way to check whether rows exist for a filter is to evaluate the `endOfSet` property. When the count is zero, `endOfSet` is `true`.

The next form to open depends on whether any rows have been found. If the count is zero, line 89 creates an instance of the Message form. The text for the message includes HTML heading tags to make the message appear with a bolder font.

```
if (nCount == 0)
{
   var nextForm = new messageForm() ;
   nextForm.htmlMessage.text = "<H3>No titles found for: " +
      this.form.selectProducts.value + "</H3>" ;
}
```

If books have been found, line 95 creates an instance of the Results form and passes on the row count and title filter. For the filter to pass from one form to another, both forms should contain query objects with identical `sql` properties.

```
else
{
   var nextForm = new resultsForm() ;
   nextForm.titleCount = nCount ;
   nextForm.title1.rowset.filter = this.form.title1.rowset.filter ;
}
```

The same `nextForm` reference is used for both the Message form and the Results form. This allows both to share the same user key assignment and form open statements on lines 99 and 100.

```
nextForm.user = this.form.user ;
nextForm.open() ;
this.form.release() ;
```

Letting the Help Form in on the Changes

Remember that `store.h` file created back on Day 9? Now that the application has grown from one Help form to four forms (Help, Quick, Message, and Results), the time for `store.h` has come. This file will open all the JavaScript form files needed to run the application. With all the scripts loaded into memory, any server-side event will be able to create an instance of any form.

To add a form to the `store.h` file, you will add a call to `_sys.scripts.load()` and an `#include` preprocessor directive. During development, the application will rely on the slightly more resource-intensive, script loading system. You are not likely to see the difference between the two techniques, but it never hurts to end up with the most efficient systems possible.

When you call `_sys.scripts.load()`, IntraBuilder first looks for a compiled version of the script. If it finds the compiled version, that version loads into memory. If only a source file is found, IntraBuilder automatically calls the `_sys.scripts.compile()` method to create a new compiled object file. An error occurs if neither a source script nor a compiled object is found.

JavaScript object files use a simple naming convention. The last letter of the extension of the source file is replaced with the letter o to designate the object file. If you are familiar with Visual dBASE, you recognize this naming convention.

NOTE

> JavaScript compiles to object files that use the instruction set of the IntraBuilder virtual machine rather than the instruction set of a physical CPU. The advantage of using a virtual machine is platform independence.
>
> The Java language also uses the virtual machine's model to run on a wide variety of operating systems. Although the IntraBuilder virtual machine is currently available only for Windows platforms, it is designed for portability.

IntraBuilder can run compiled object files without the accompanying source file. If you are a developer who is selling applications systems, you can use this feature to protect your source code. You might distribute object files to clients or customers. Your applications require no changes to take advantage of this technique. Calls to source files such as _sys.scripts.run("myscript.js") work when the myscript.jo exists without myscript.js.

To update the store.h file, move to the IntraBuilder Explorer's Custom tab and double-click the header file. This opens the header file in the Script Editor. Edit the file to match Listing 11.3.

Listing 11.3. Loading the Help, Message, Quick, and Results forms.

INPUT

```
 1: #define DEBUG  // for development only
 2: #ifndef STORE
 3:    #define STORE
 4:    #ifdef DEBUG
 5:       // Load scripts
 6:       // _sys.script.load statements go here.
 7:       _sys.scripts.load("help.jfm") ;
 8:       _sys.scripts.load("message.jfm") ;
 9:       _sys.scripts.load("quick.jfm") ;
10:       _sys.scripts.load("results.jfm") ;
11:    #elseif
12:       // Include scripts
13:       return null
14:       // #include statements go here
15:       #include <help.jfm>
16:       #include <message.jfm>
```

```
17:        #include <quick.jfm>
18:        #include <results.jfm>
19:    #endif
20: #endif
```

ANALYSIS Lines 7 through 10 open the four forms that you have created already. These lines correspond to lines 15 through 18. As long as you're continuing to modify forms, leave in line 1 so that all the forms are loaded at runtime. The `#include` statements should be used only when you are ready to deploy the application.

To make the new header take effect, you must explicitly recompile the Help form. You can recompile quickly any JavaScript file using the shortcut menu from the IntraBuilder Explorer, shown in Figure 11.3. If you do not recompile the file, the changes to `store.h` will not take effect until you make some other changes to the Help form file. IntraBuilder forces a compile when you modify a form with the Form Designer or the Script Editor. When you make changes to `store.h`, the Help form is not modified directly so IntraBuilder doesn't know to force a recompile.

Figure 11.3.

Recompiling the Help form to incorporate changes in the store.h *file.*

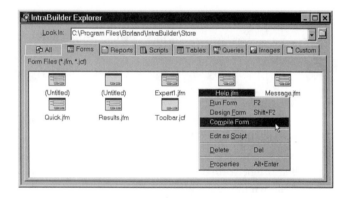

After you recompile the Help form, it's time to take the browser test. The last time you ran the application through a browser, you could go from the static HTML index to the Help JavaScript form, and that was it. The number of possible links has gone up from one to 10 as shown in Table 11.1.

Table 11.1. Form link matrix.

From	To Index	To Help	To Quick	To Results	To Message
Index	X	X			
Help		X	X		
Quick		X		X	X

continues

Table 11.1. continued

From	To Index	To Help	To Quick	To Results	To Message
Results		X	X		
Message		X	X		

Table 11.1 shows how shoppers can jump to the Help from any other JavaScript form. This contrasts greatly from the HTML index page. None of the JavaScript forms provide a link to the index page. The reasoning is that if a shopper jumps to an external page such as the HTML index, the user key value is lost.

Except for the Quick form itself, any JavaScript form can jump to the Quick form. All forms that have an associated toolbar button work like this. The Results and Message forms are accessible only through the Quick form. Use the following steps to try the various jumps:

1. Close the IntraBuilder Designer.
2. Start a local Web server, such as the Borland Web Server or WebSite.

 Tip   For faster performance when using the Borland Web Server as a local host, uncheck the Enable Client Name Lookup from the server property sheet. You will find this property on the Status tab.

3. Start one Agent through the IntraBuilder Server icon. When you install IntraBuilder, the default number of agents is three. During development when you are the only one using the IntraBuilder Server, reducing the agent count to one can increase performance. You can change the agent count through the Registry Editor, as shown in Figure 11.4.

   Leaving the agent count at one can hamper performance when an application is placed into a production environment with many users. The number of agents is equal to the number of simultaneous requests that IntraBuilder can handle. This is not to say that a single agent can service only one user. If all the requests are quick, a single agent can handle many requests from different users. It is long requests, such as complex reports, that can tie up a single agent for several minutes. If one agent is processing a long request when another request comes in, the new request is sent to an available agent.

Figure 11.4.

Setting the registry to load only one agent.

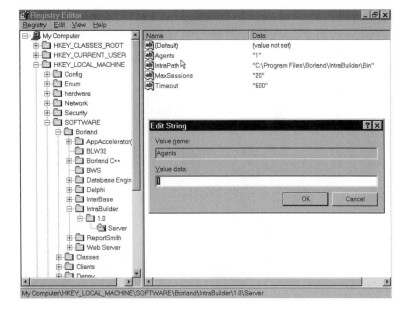

NOTE

The IntraBuilder Server reads the registry settings at initiation only. If you modify any registry settings, close down all agents and restart the IntraBuilder Server to see them take effect.

4. Open your browser and point it to the index URL, like this:

   `http://localhost/store/index.htm`

5. Click the logo that links to the Help form. If the Help form does not appear, check that the Web server and IntraBuilder agents are running.

6. Click the Quick tool button to open the Quick form. The browser window should appear similar to the one in Figure 11.5.

7. Select C++ Builder from the list and click Search. Because there are no books in the Title table for C++ Builder, the count is zero, and the Message form opens.

8. From the Message form, use the Quick toolbar button to return to the Quick form and try again, as shown in Figure 11.6.

Figure 11.5.

Viewing the Quick form with Internet Explorer.

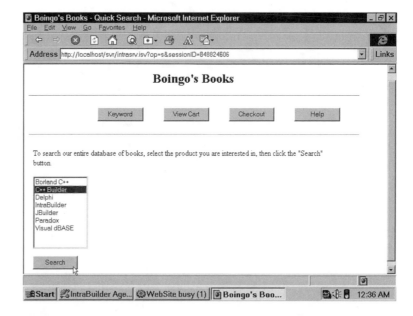

Figure 11.6.

Viewing the Message form with Internet Explorer.

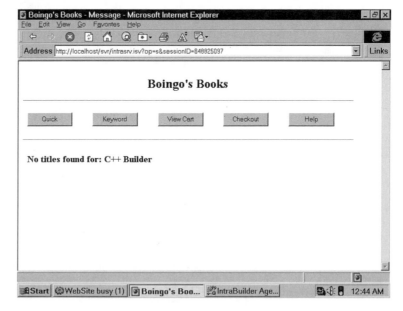

9. This time, pick any other product to get to the Results form.

10. Try the Help toolbar button to reload the Help form and continue exercising each jump to see whether any forms need any adjustments.

> The Keyword, View Cart, and Checkout toolbar buttons call form classes that do not yet exist. This sends an IntraBuilder Alert back to the browser without any links back to the application.

As you test your forms, make sure they look acceptable in both Netscape Navigator and Microsoft Internet Explorer. This will cover almost every person ever destined to visit your site. You will find that many of the less popular browsers do not support all of the HTML layout tags that IntraBuilder streams out. If the application does not use Java applets, ActiveX controls, or client-side JavaScript, it will function properly on older browsers. The only problems are cosmetic, as demonstrated by Figure 11.7. This figure shows how the toolbar gets a vertical orientation within an older version of SPRY Mosaic. This is the version that CompuServe bundled with WinCim 2.

Figure 11.7.

Viewing the Results form with SPRY Mosaic.

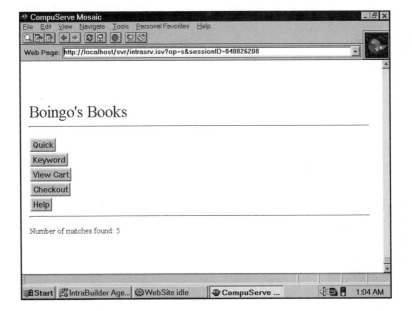

Resolving the Results

Currently, the Results form contains a query on the Title table and an HTML control showing the book count. To complete the form, you can add a select list showing book titles, a button to get details on a selected book, and some help text. The finished Results form is similar to the Quick form in that the select list shows the values of field objects and the button acts on what the user selects from the list.

The Quick form modifies the Results form in two ways before opening it. First, it adds the titleCount property, which the Results form uses to display the book count. Second, the Quick form modifies the filter property for the title1 query. This relieves the Results form of any responsibility in figuring out what rows to show, which is set up already. Now the only thing the Results form needs to do is show the rows and pass the filter and count on to the Details form.

1. Open the Results form in the Form Designer.

2. Add a select list to the form using the following position properties: height 4, left 1, top 6.5, width 60.

   The select list will show the Title field from the Title table, which has a field width of 60. The browser will determine the width of the select control at runtime based on the widest item in the option list.

3. Change the select list name from select1 to selectTitle.

4. Switch over to the Events tab and click the tool button for the select list's onServerLoad event. Enter the following function:

```
function selectTitle_onServerLoad()
{
    var rTitle = this.parent.title1.rowset,
        i = 0 ;
    this.dataSource = new Array( this.parent.titleCount ) ;
    rTitle.first() ;
    while ( ! ( rTitle.endOfSet ))
    {
        this.dataSource[i] = rTitle.fields["TITLE"].value ;
        rTitle.next() ;
        i++ ;
    }
    this.dataSource.sort() ;
    this.options =  "Array this.dataSource"
}
```

NOTE

The selectTitle_onServerLoad() function is similar to the function in the Quick form that fills the product select list. The main difference is in how items are added to the array. In the Quick form, the array starts

> empty, and the Array::add() method creates a new element for each pass through the while loop. Dynamically adding array elements works well when the final size is unknown. The extra time consumed by calling the Array::add() method is offset by not having to add an extra call to Rowset::count().
>
> The Results form is different in that it already has a property containing the required row count. Having this number up front makes the method in the Results form more efficient than the predecessor in the Quick form. By passing the size to the array constructor, IntraBuilder can allocate a block of memory for the array elements in one pass.

5. Drop a new HTML control above the select list and set the position properties to the following: height 2, left 1, top 4.5, width 65.

6. Change the HTML name from html1 to htmlHelp.

7. Open the Text Property Builder and enter the following:
   ```
   Select a title from the list and press the Show Detail button to display
   details on the selected book.
   ```

8. Drop a new button below the select list and set the position properties to the following: left 1, top 11, width 12. As with the select control, the runtime width of the button is set by the browser.

NOTE

> Unlike most controls, buttons do not have height or font properties. When you run a form through a browser, buttons conform to the default font of the browser, and the height is matched to the same font.

9. Change the button name to buttonDetail and the button text to Show Details. Your form should now resemble the one in Figure 11.8.

10. From the Events tab of the Inspector, create the following function for the new button's onServerClick event:
    ```
    function buttonDetail_onServerClick()
    {
       var nextForm = new detailForm() ;
       nextForm.user = this.form.user ;
       nextForm.open() ;
       this.form.release() ;
    }
    ```

Figure 11.8.

Redesigning the
Results form.

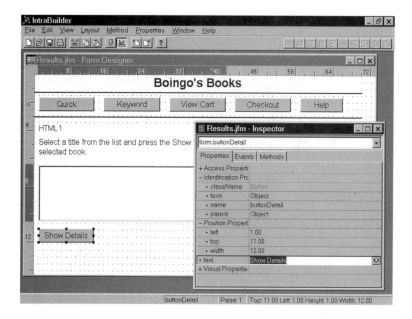

Save the form and try it out. The `buttonDetail_onServerClick` event is a stub function to call a new form. You need to add to this function to pass several new properties down to the Details form.

You can run the form through the Designer or through a browser to test the new select list. Remember that like other forms, the Results form is dependent on the user key and cannot run as a standalone form. If you run the Help form, click Quick, select Visual dBASE, and choose Search, the Results form lists five books, as shown in Figure 11.9.

Figure 11.9.

Running the Results
form in the Designer.

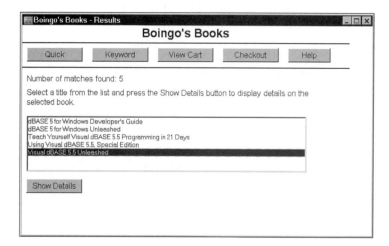

Designing the Details

The Details form needs to show all the fields from the Titles table. It also must enable shoppers to navigate through titles. To complete the form, you also need another button that adds the current book to the shopping cart. You can easily accomplish the first two objectives through the Form Expert.

Creating a form through the Form Expert enables you to try the connection from the Results form to the Details form. It also gives you a jump start on the new form. As you go through the development of the Details form, you will replace much of the original Expert code. In fact, so much of the original code ends up on the cutting room floor that you might wonder whether it would have been better to start from scratch.

Starting a data entry form from scratch can be quicker after you are thoroughly familiar with the Designer and query manipulation concepts. For now, the Expert code provides a solid framework for data entry form design.

One of the enhancements to make to the default data entry form is a way to inform shoppers of where they are in a table. Desktop database managers, such as Access and Visual dBASE, show the current row number in a status bar at the bottom of a window. The position is usually presented as Row X of Y, where X is the current and Y is the total number of rows in the current view. You can add an HTML object that displays similar information to a JavaScript data entry form.

Currently, the Results form opens the Details form without passing any filter or position information. Before adding position information, the Results form needs some modifications.

Prototyping with the Expert

On Day 10, you used the Form Expert to create a form for the Title table. That form contained a few fields, a query-by-form button, and a filter-by-form button. The new prototype needs to have all the fields from the Title table and some navigation buttons. This time, you leave off the search buttons. Use the following steps for creating the Details form prototype:

1. Start up the Form Expert. To avoid the first prompt, you can launch the Expert from the Script Pad. Select View|Script Pad and enter the following:

    ```
    _sys.forms.expert("detail.jfm")
    ```

2. Select the Title table and click Next.

3. Select all the fields from the Title table and click Next.

11

4. Select the Columnar Layout and click Next.

5. Leave the default scheme and click Next.

6. Check the First, Last, Next, and Previous navigation options and select the Images for the control type. Change the Location on Form option to be Top as shown in Figure 11.10.

Figure 11.10.

Creating a VCR navigation control through the Form Expert.

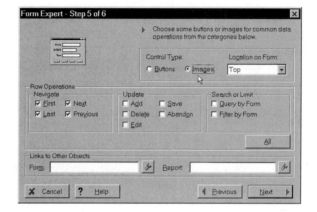

7. Choose the Design Form option to open the new form in the Form Designer. If you started the Expert from the Script Pad, it already has a name. If you started the Expert through the menu or IntraBuilder Explorer, save the form as `detail.jfm`.

8. The first thing to change in the Expert-generated form is the path on the `sql` property of the `Query` object. Inspect the `title1` query and remove the path from the `sql` property so that it appears as follows:

```
SELECT * FROM "title.dbf"
```

9. Delete the large title, which appears at the top, to make room for the toolbar buttons.

10. Set the custom form class to the toolbar custom form class. Select File|Set Custom Form Class and pick the `ToolbarCForm` class from the `toolbar.jfm` file.

11. Adjust the size of the form so that all five toolbar buttons are visible.

12. When the form resembles the one in Figure 11.11, close the Form Designer, and save all the changes.

Each time the Form Expert creates a unique navigation image, it adds a GIF file to the current folder. Depending on your choices, the Form Expert can create a single image that handles multiple operations or separate images for each action.

Figure 11.11.

Using the toolbar custom control class with an Expert-generated form.

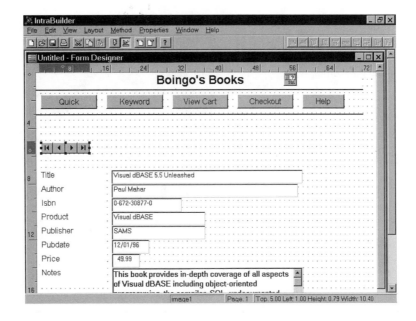

When you select all the navigation options, the Form Expert creates a single GIF called `expinavh.gif`. You can use the IntraBuilder Explorer to rename it to something a little more intuitive. The image looks like the buttons on a VCR. Follow these steps to rename the image to `vcr.gif` and change the form reference:

1. Select the Images tab of the IntraBuilder Explorer.

2. Double-click `expinavh.gif` to open the Image Viewer window.

3. Right-click in the window to open the shortcut menu and select Export Image.

4. Export the image to `vcr.gif`.

5. Close and delete the original image.

6. Try running the Details form. The error box shown in Figure 11.12 appears when a JavaScript statement references the previous image filename.

7. Choose the Fix button to open the Script Editor at the line where the error occurred.

8. Modify the following statement:

```
dataSource = "filename EXPINAVH.GIF";
```

Change the assignment to refer to `vcr.gif` as shown:

```
dataSource = "filename VCR.GIF";
```

Figure 11.12.

*Attempting to run a
form that references a
non-existent image.*

When you close the Script Editor, the form opens in the Designer's Run mode. Try the
navigation buttons on the form. The new image provides the same look and function as the
navigation buttons built into the IntraBuilder Designer's own toolbar.

 NOTE

> Unlike JavaScript variable names, the filenames are not case sensitive.
> Table names might be case sensitive depending on the data source.
> dBASE, Paradox, and Access table names are never case sensitive. Some
> SQL servers enable optional case sensitivity.

Descending from the Results to the Details

To test the Details form with the rest of the application, you need to update the store.h file.
Open the header file in the Script Editor and add load and include lines for the detail.jfm
file, as shown in Listing 11.4.

INPUT **Listing 11.4. Adding support for the Details form.**

```
 1: #define DEBUG  // for development only
 2: #ifndef STORE
 3:    #define STORE
 4:    #ifdef DEBUG
 5:       // Load scripts
 6:       // _sys.script.load statements go here.
 7:       _sys.scripts.load("detail") ;
 8:       _sys.scripts.load("help.jfm") ;
 9:       _sys.scripts.load("message.jfm") ;
10:       _sys.scripts.load("quick.jfm") ;
11:       _sys.scripts.load("results.jfm") ;
12:    #elseif
13:       // Include scripts
14:       return null
15:       // #include statements go here
16:       #include <detail.jfm>
```

11

```
17:        #include <help.jfm>
18:        #include <message.jfm>
19:        #include <quick.jfm>
20:        #include <results.jfm>
21:    #endif
22: #endif
```

 Except for lines 11 and 20, this version of the header file is exactly like its predecessor. Keep in mind that, at this point, line 20 is ignored by the compiler. If you are curious about how the preprocessor works, check out the SET PREKEEP section of Appendix B, "The Undocumented IntraBuilder."

After updating the header file, recompile the Help form. You can force a compile from the IntraBuilder Explorer shortcut menu, from the Script Editor menu, or by using the _sys.scripts.compile() method. You must recompile the help.jfm file before any changes in store.h take effect.

WARNING

If you have run the Help form since you last started the IntraBuilder Designer, you need to exit and restart the application to load the new compilation. The Help form loads itself into memory, and the version in memory is the only version you can run until you exit and restart the application.

This architecture also manifests itself if you try to modify a form in an IntraBuilder Designer while an IntraBuilder Agent is currently running the same form. An agent can continue using the previous version until you exit and restart the IntraBuilder Server.

When you run the application, you can open the Details form by clicking on the Show Details button in the Results form. The only problem is that the Details form always shows the first row of the Title table, rather than the selected title. To remedy the situation, the buttonDetail_onServerClick() method needs enhancements.

Try using the Script Editor rather than the Form Designer when all the changes you are making to a form are non-visual. In this case, you do not need to make any changes to the look of the Results form. Follow these steps to take advantage of IntraBuilder's Two-Way-Tools:

1. Select the results.jfm file in the IntraBuilder Explorer.
2. Right-click to open the shortcut menu and select Edit as Script.
3. Right-click once more and select Find Text from the Script Editor shortcut menu.

4. Enter `function buttonDetail` and click Find to locate the method as shown in Figure 11.13. If you search only for `buttonDetail`, you will encounter a reference in the class constructor prior to the actual function definition.

Figure 11.13.

Searching for the `buttonDetail_` `onServerClick()` *method.*

5. Modify the script to match the script in Listing 11.5. The most likely change you will need to make is to the `buttonDetail_onServerClick()` method.

Do not concern yourself with matching every position property to the last digit. If your form looks okay through a browser, the positions are close enough. If not, you can review this listing later.

Listing 11.5. The Results form with the new `buttonDetail_onServerClick()` **method.**

INPUT

```
 1: // {End Header} Do not remove this comment//
 2: // Generated on 11/02/96
 3: //
 4: var f = new resultsForm();
 5: f.open();
 6: class resultsForm extends ToolbarCForm from "TOOLBAR.JCF" {
 7:     with (this) {
 8:         height = 15 ;
 9:         left = 0 ;
10:         top = 0 ;
11:         width = 75 ;
12:         title = "Boingo's Books - Results" ;
13:     }

14:
15:     with (this.title1 = new Query()){
16:         left = 70 ;
17:         top = 4 ;
18:         sql = 'SELECT * FROM "title.dbf"' ;
19:         active = true ;
20:     }
21:
22:     with (this.title1.rowset) {
23:     }
24:
25:     with (this.htmlCount = new HTML(this)){
26:         onServerLoad = class::htmlCount_onServerLoad;
27:         height = 1;
28:         left = 1;
```

11

```
29:         top = 3.5;
30:         width = 65;
31:         color = "black";
32:         text = "HTML1";
33:     }
34:
35:     with (this.selectTitle = new ListBox(this)){
36:         onServerLoad = class::selectTitle_onServerLoad;
37:         height = 4;
38:         left = 1;
39:         top = 6.5;
40:         width = 60;
41:     }
42:
43:     with (this.buttonDetail = new Button(this)){
44:         onServerClick = class::buttonDetail_onServerClick;
45:         left = 1;
46:         top = 11;
47:         width = 12;
48:         text = "Show Details";
49:     }
50:
51:     with (this.htmlHelp = new HTML(this)){
52:         height = 2 ;
53:         top = 4.5 ;
54:         width = 65 ;
55:         color = "black" ;
56:         text = "Select a title from the list and press " +
57:                 "the Show Details button to display details " +
58:                 "on the selected book." ;
59:     }
60:
61:     this.rowset = this.title1.rowset ;
62:
63:     function htmlCount_onServerLoad()
64:     {
65:         this.text = "Number of matches found: " +
66:                     this.form.titleCount ;
67:     }
68:
69:     function selectTitle_onServerLoad()
70:     {
71:         var rTitle = this.parent.title1.rowset,
72:             i = 0 ;
73:         this.dataSource = new Array( this.parent.titleCount ) ;
74:         rTitle.first() ;
75:         while ( ! ( rTitle.endOfSet ))
76:         {
77:             this.dataSource[i] = rTitle.fields["TITLE"].value ;
78:             rTitle.next() ;
79:             i++ ;
80:         }
81:         this.dataSource.sort() ;
82:         this.options =  "Array this.dataSource" ;
83:     }
84:
```

continues

Listing 11.5. continued

```
85:     function buttonDetail_onServerClick()
86:     {
87:        var nextForm = new detailForm() ;
88:        nextForm.titleCount            = this.form.titleCount ;
89:        nextForm.title1.rowset.filter   = this.form.title1.rowset.filter ;
90:        if (! (this.form.title1.rowset.canGetRow == null))
91:        {
92:           nextForm.scopeAll = this.form.scopeAll ;
93:           nextForm.keyfield = this.form.keyfield ;
94:           nextform.keywords = this.form.keywords ;
95:           nextForm.title1.rowset.canGetRow = KeywordCanGetRow ;
96:        }
97:        nextForm.title1.rowset.first() ;
98:        nextForm.currentRow = 1 ;
99:        if ( ! ( this.form.selectTitle.value == "" ) )
100:       {
101:          while ( ! (nextForm.title1.rowset.fields["TITLE"].value ==
102:                 this.form.selectTitle.value ) )
103:          {
104:             nextForm.title1.rowset.next() ;
105:             nextForm.currentRow++ ;
106:          }
107:       }
108:       nextForm.user = this.form.user ;
109:       nextForm.open() ;
110:       this.form.release() ;
111:    }
112:
113: }
```

ANALYSIS The Results form is like a transfer station, a short stop along the way rather than a destination. It takes information from one of two search forms, makes some enhancements, and passes a little more information to the Details form. The two search forms are the Quick form and currently "vaporware" Keyword form.

Opening the Results form fires the htmlCount_onServerLoad() method, which is linked to an event on line 26. This method uses a titleCount property to display the number of titles appearing in the list. The titleCount property is not created in the class constructor. It must be added by an external routine prior to the form opening. The responsibility for adding the titleCount property falls to the search forms. Because line 66 references the titleCount when the form opens, its absence will cause an immediate error.

```
function htmlCount_onServerLoad()
{
   this.text = "Number of matches found: " +
             this.form.titleCount ;
}
```

The following partial function also shows how the `titleCount` property becomes an integral part of building the array for the select list. Notice that line 73 references `titleCount` through `this.parent.titleCount` instead of `this.form.titleCount`. For controls, the references are identical. Events on a query object require that the container be referenced through `parent` instead of `form`.

```
function selectTitle_onServerLoad()
{
   var rTitle = this.parent.title1.rowset,
       i = 0 ;
   this.dataSource = new Array( this.parent.titleCount ) ;
```

The most complex method in the class begins on line 85. A good portion of the `buttonDetail_onServerClick()` method involves assigning property values. Some assignments modify existing properties of the Details form, whereas others create new custom properties.

```
function buttonDetail_onServerClick()
   {
       var nextForm = new detailForm() ;
```

The count and filter properties are passed as identical properties of the Details form. Remember that both of these properties also have been passed to the Results form. The values are passed unmodified to the Details form.

```
nextForm.titleCount             = this.form.titleCount ;
nextForm.title1.rowset.filter   = this.form.title1.rowset.filter ;
```

The following block works with the Keyword form. You will learn more about each of these properties during the design of the Keyword form. For now, keep in mind that the `scopeAll`, `keyfield`, and `keywords` properties are passed in the same way the `titleCount` property was previously. These three properties are passed to the Results form from the Keyword form and are passed from there to the Details form.

Line 95 assigns the `KeywordCanGetRow()` function to the `canGetRow` event. This JavaScript function resides outside any class definitions and is therefore not a method. The `canGetRow` event enables complex searches that cannot be expressed in SQL.

```
if (! (this.form.title1.rowset.canGetRow == null))
{
   nextForm.scopeAll = this.form.scopeAll ;
   nextForm.keyfield = this.form.keyfield ;
   nextform.keywords = this.form.keywords ;
   nextForm.title1.rowset.canGetRow = KeywordCanGetRow ;
}
```

After setting up the same search criteria for the Details form as exist for the current Results form, the function calculates the current row position. Unlike records in Visual dBASE,

IntraBuilder rows have no number. Here, a `currentRow` property simulates a row number. Line 98 sets `currentRow` to 1 for the first row.

```
nextForm.title1.rowset.first() ;
nextForm.currentRow = 1 ;
```

As in the Quick form, this form also checks to see whether the user did not select an item. This is optional validation for a condition that occurs only when running in the IntraBuilder Designer. The HTML select list always forces at least one selection on lists that do not support multiple selection.

```
if ( ! ( this.form.selectTitle.value == "" ) )
{
```

To calculate the current row, a `while` loop moves through the table until it finds the row that matches the item highlighted in the select list. Line 105 increments the `currentRow` property each time the correct row is not found.

```
while ( ! (nextForm.title1.rowset.fields["TITLE"].value ==
            this.form.selectTitle.value ) )
{
   nextForm.title1.rowset.next() ;
   nextForm.currentRow++ ;
}
```

The function finishes out with the standard call statements to open the next form. The user property is assigned outside the `with` block to remain consistent with all the other `nextForm` open routines.

```
   }
   nextForm.user = this.form.user ;
   nextForm.open() ;
   this.form.release() ;
}
```

NOTE

> At first glance, the `buttonDetail_onServerClick()` method looks like a good place to use a `with` block. However, a `with` block helps only when assigning values to existing properties. A complete reference is required to add a new property to an object.

As when you make any major changes, it is a good idea to first run the application through the IntraBuilder Designer and then through a browser. Minor errors such as misspellings or mismatched capitalization are easy to fix in the Designer. After you know the application is free of runtime errors, you need to verify the look and feel from the browser perspective.

At this point, close the IntraBuilder Designer and load the IntraBuilder Server. Start a browser and open the Quick form from the Help form. Pick a product that has titles and continue to the Results form. Make sure the positions of the select list, text, and buttons look okay on the Results form. Highlight a title and see whether the correct title opens in the Details form. Figure 11.14 shows a shopper selecting the Borland C++ 5 Resource Kit.

Figure 11.14.

Viewing the Quick form's select list in Internet Explorer.

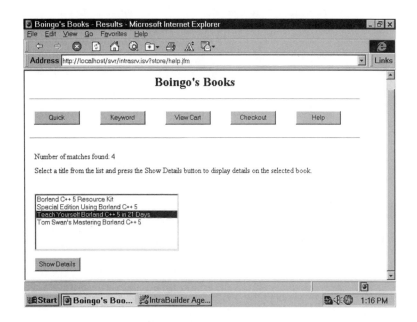

HTML Versus Text and TextArea

After you get to the Details form, a major flaw in the form's current implementation becomes apparent. *Shoppers can modify the data and the form commits all the changes to the table.* In this case, the concept of live data is going a bit too far. IntraBuilder provides several ways to cope with the situation. For this form, HTML controls would be more appropriate than Text or TextArea controls. Users will never mistake an HTML control as something that they can edit. Text and TextArea controls will always appear editable even in a read-only form. You can use any of the following techniques to create a read-only, data-entry form.

☐ Set `Query.requestLive` to `false`.

Advantages

Setting `requestLive` to `false` is the easiest way to make form data read-only. If you modify the Details form's `title1` query so `requestLive` is false, the query opens as a read-only view. IntraBuilder ignores any changes a user makes to a dataLink value.

Disadvantages

This technique has two major disadvantages. First, the property is a permanent setting. You cannot change the value of requestLive after the query is active. The other disadvantage is that data looks like you can edit it.

☐ Set Rowset.autoEdit to false.

Advantages

This is the best technique to use when you want to allow the same controls to work both ways. The initial state of a form with autoEdit false is the same as a form where requestLive is false. Usually, if a form has a rowset with autoEdit false, it also has buttons that enable the user to move between read-only and editing states.

Disadvantages

As with requestLive, when autoEdit is false, users can modify data in a browser, only to have those changes ignored.

☐ Use HTML in place of Text controls.

Advantages

HTML is read-only text in a browser. Using HTML eliminates any confusion over whether a user can modify data. It is the best technique to use when the data is always in a read-only state and the presentation of the data does not rely on radio or checkbox controls.

Disadvantages

The Form Expert does not generate code to update HTML controls automatically with data from the current row. HTML controls do not have a dataLink property. You must update the text property when the form loads and when any row navigation occurs. Another disadvantage is that HTML controls cannot represent read-only radio buttons or checkboxes.

For the shopping cart application, the Details form contains no values that you can allow a shopper to update. It would not work out very well if a shopper decided to change the titles or lower the prices to 50 cents per book. There are also no radio buttons or checkboxes required. As a result, the technique of replacing each Text control with an HTML control works best.

Viewing the Details form through a browser reveals another potentially confusing item. The Title table does not contain cover images for all books. When a book does not have a cover image, the IntraBuilder Server sends a default image that says "IntraBuilder," as shown in Figure 11.15. If the example application had been a shopping cart for organic potatoes, this image would not have caused confusion. However, in a store that has books on IntraBuilder, a cover image saying "IntraBuilder" for a C++ book just doesn't look appropriate.

11

NOTE

Image controls do not show the default IntraBuilder image when run within the IntraBuilder Designer. Instead, the images are transparent, and the form background appears where the image typically would be.

Figure 11.15.

An image with an empty dataSource.

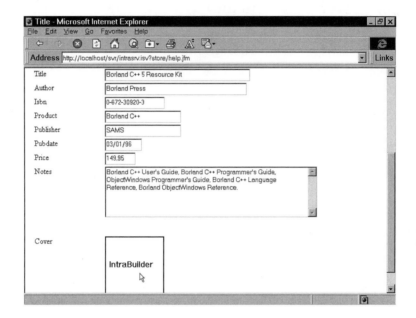

The first task in morphing the current Details form into something better suited for a Web shopper is to replace the Text controls with HTML controls and add a new method to update the text properties.

NEW TERM *Morphing* means to change one thing into another. The term usually is associated with a graphics technique used in science fiction movies, such as *Terminator 2*, where one actor is transformed into another. You will find the term used throughout the IntraBuilder help system where it describes techniques to transform coded field values into descriptive text.

In the first pass, the controls will only show data from the first row. After this is working, you can go back and call the method as needed. So, let's start the renovation.

1. Open the Details form in the Form Designer.
2. Delete all the Text controls and the TextArea for the Notes field.
3. Change the generic HTML label names, as shown in Table 11.2. Delete the labels for the Notes field and the cover image. Update the text properties for the ISBN and Pubdate fields.

Table 11.2. New name and text values for the field labels.

Old name	New name	Old text	New text
html1	labelTitle	Title	Title
html2	labelAuthor	Author	Author
html3	labelISBN	isbn	ISBN
html4	labelProduct	Product	Product
html5	labelPublisher	Publisher	Publisher
html6	labelPubdate	Pubdate	Date
html7	labelPrice	Price	Price
html8	(delete)	Notes	
html9	(delete)	Cover	

4. To maximize the available screen real estate, move the VCR image below the labels and move the labels up closer to the toolbar. First, select the VCR image and set the top property to 14.

   After moving the VCR image, select all seven labels along with the VCR image. You can use the mouse pointer to lasso the group or hold down the Shift key and click each item. Use the Up Arrow key to move the group up so that the first label has a top position of 3.5. When done, your form should resemble the one shown in Figure 11.16.

Figure 11.16.

Arranging the HTML label controls.

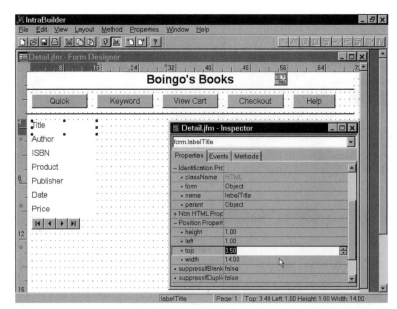

5. Add HTML controls for each field. Name and position them as shown in Table 11.3. Setting the height to more than 1 is all you need to do to allow the text to wrap for the Notes field.

Table 11.3. Position properties for the HTML field value controls.

Name	Height	Top	Left	Width
valueTitle	1	3.5	16	55
valueAuthor	1	4.5	16	55
valueISNB	1	5.5	16	20
valueProduct	1	6.5	16	20
valuePublisher	1	7.5	16	20
valuePubdate	1	8.5	16	20
valuePrice	1	9.5	16	20
valueNotes	4	11.5	1	70

6. Bring the cover image into view by moving it above the Notes field. Select the Cover image and set the position properties as follows: height 5, top 6.5, left 43, width 12. Set the alignment property to 3, if it is not already set.

7. Rename the control from image1 to imageCover. At this point, the form should resemble the one shown in Figure 11.17.

Figure 11.17.

Arranging the HTML value controls.

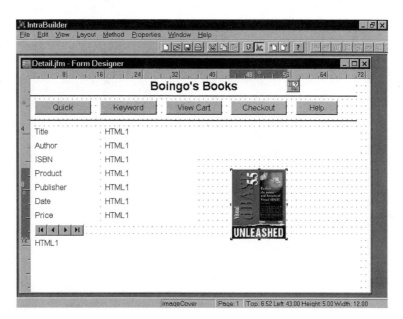

8. Create a new method to breathe some life into the field value controls. Unlike most of the methods you have created so far, this one is not directly linked to any specific event. To make an unlinked method, select Method|New Method. The Method Editor creates a blank method for exporting as client-side JavaScript.

```
function Method()
{
// {Export} This comment causes this function body to be sent...

}
```

9. Remove the // {Export} comment line and rename the method to UpdateValues(). Add a parameter to the function statement. The parameter list should be placed between the parentheses after the function name.

```
function UpdateValues(thisForm)
{

}
```

10. Add assignment statements to update the text properties of the various HTML controls with the value properties of the fields. Save the method after it matches the following:

```
function UpdateValues(thisForm)
{
    var fTitle = thisForm.title1.rowset.fields ;
    thisForm.valueTitle.text      = fTitle["TITLE"].value ;
    thisForm.valueAuthor.text     = fTitle["AUTHOR"].value ;
    thisForm.valueISBN.text       = fTitle["ISBN"].value ;
    thisForm.valueProduct.text    = fTitle["PRODUCT"].value ;
    thisForm.valuePublisher.text  = fTitle["PUBLISHER"].value ;
    thisForm.valuePubdate.text    = fTitle["PUBDATE"].value ;
    thisForm.valuePrice.text      = fTitle["PRICE"].value ;
    thisForm.valueNotes.text      = fTitle["NOTES"].value ;
}
```

11. Add a code block to call UpdateValues() when the form opens. Inspect the form and locate the onServerLoad event. Instead of creating a linked method, enter class::UpdateValues(this) directly into the Inspector. When you press Enter, the Inspector adds braces and a prefixing semicolon, as shown in Figure 11.18.

After adding the code block, save and run the form. In the Designer, all HTML value controls display HTML1. When you run the form, the HTML text shows values from the current record. If you navigate through rows with the VCR buttons, the text remains static and only the cover image reflects the row navigation.

The next task is to enhance the navigation operation so the HTML value controls refresh as necessary. This also is an appropriate time to add a row position indicator to the form. To accomplish the task, you will need to revamp the navigation code that occurs for the onServerImageClick event.

Figure 11.18.
*Creating a code block
to call*
`UpdateValues()`.

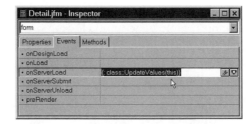

Tapping into the Magic Behind the Image

Images fall into three basic categories within an IntraBuilder application: static images, dynamic images, and action images. The simplest type is the static image that always shows the same picture and does nothing when clicked. Static images can be logos or pictures that beautify a Web page, without adding any links or processing. Dynamic images change as events take place. The book cover in the Detail form is a dynamic image that needs to refresh with different covers during row navigation. An action image does something when clicked. Web pages often use action images for links to other Web pages. The index.htm page for the store has an action image with a link to the Help form. Action images can also replace buttons as the VCR image does. Although not as common as the three basic image types, a dynamic image can also be an action image.

Some action images, such as the index page link, have a single purpose. No matter where you click the index link image, the same action always takes place. Other action images perform different tasks depending on where you click. The VCR image is a multiple action image. It functions as though it is four separate buttons. If you click the far right, you move to the last row. Clicking on the far left moves you to the first row. IntraBuilder supports image mapping by passing the mouse click coordinates to the `onImageServerClick` event.

NEW TERM *Image mapping* is the act of dividing an image into separate action regions. Image mapping enables you to use a single image for multiple actions.

The four regions of the VCR image are represented by the symbols <<, <, >, and >>. Each region requires separate logic. The Form Expert uses `if` blocks to separate the logic for each region. As with any Form Expert event, the entire sequence is inside of a single code block, which is difficult to read.

```
{¦nLeft, nTop¦;if (nLeft >= 26*0 && nLeft < 26*1){form.rowset.first()}
➤else if (nLeft >= 26*1 && nLeft < 26*2){if (!form.rowset.next
➤(-1)) form.rowset.next();}else if (nLeft >= 26*2 && nLeft < 26*3)
➤{if (!form.rowset.next()) form.rowset.next(-1);}else
➤{form.rowset.last()}}
```

The first and last regions use simple logic with no position validation. The middle two regions are a little more complex. Each must check to see whether the row pointer has gone past the edge of the view to create a state known as being at endOfSet. The regions break down as follows:

|<   Move to the first row.

<   Move to the previous row. If moving to the previous row places the row pointer outside the rowset, move back to the original row.

>   Move to the next row. If moving to the next row places the row pointer past the last row, move back to the original row.

>| Move to the last row.

The coordinates returned to the onImageServerClick are in pixels rather than the much larger scale used to lay out controls in the Form Designer. There are many applications that you can use to assist you in mapping out an image. Most create map files for CGI programs. Although IntraBuilder does not have direct support for map files, you can use the coordinates from a generated map file to set up the logic of an onImageServerClick.

If you do not have a mapping utility, you can create a simple JavaScript form to show coordinate values interactively. The Imap form in Listing 11.6 updates an HTML control with the left and top coordinates each time you click the GIF file. The coordinates return the same values when run in the IntraBuilder Designer as when run through a browser.

INPUT   **Listing 11.6. IMAP.JFM, a simple interactive map form.**

```
 1: // {End Header} Do not remove this comment//
 2: // Generated on 11/02/96
 3: //
 4: var f = new imapForm();
 5: f.open();
 6: class imapForm extends Form {
 7:    with (this.image1 = new Image(this)){
 8:       dataSource = "filename VCR.GIF";
 9:       alignment = 4;
10:       onImageServerClick = class::image1_onImageServerClick;
11:    }
12:
13:    with (this.html1 = new HTML(this)){
14:       top = 3;
15:       width = 50;
16:    }
17:
18:    function image1_onImageServerClick(nLeft, nTop)
19:    {
20:       this.form.html1.text = "Left: " + nLeft + " Top: " + nTop
21:    }
22: }
```

ANALYSIS The image is linked to the `image1_onImageServerClick()` method on line 10. Although the method name and the event match in this case, the form doesn't have to run. You could rename the method to any valid function name as long as the names on lines 10 and 18 match.

The event automatically passes the coordinates to the linked method as parameters. Line 20 displays the parameter values by assigning them to the text property of an HTML object. This assignment uses the JavaScript automatic type conversion to combine string values with the numeric parameter values.

The relevant coordinates for the VCR file appear in Table 11.4. The coordinates are zero-based. The VCR image is broken into four square regions that are each 26 pixels wide and 23 pixels high. Only the left value is needed to determine what region has been clicked.

Table 11.4. Mapping for the VCR GIF file.

Symbol	Left
|<	0-25
<	26-51
>	52-77
>|	78-103

For the Details form, the VCR `onImageServerClick` needs both a regional specific enhancement and an added function call for all regions. Keeping track of the current row number is regional-specific. The HTML values need to be refreshed for all regions. The following are the steps to enhance the VCR image:

1. Open the Details form in the Form Designer.
2. Add a new HTML control above the image. Set the position properties to `height 1`, `left 43`, `top 5.5`, `width 12`. Name the new control `htmlPosition`.
3. Add the following statement to the end of the `UpdateValues()` function.
   ```
   thisForm.htmlPosition.text =
       thisForm.currentRow  + " of " + thisForm.titleCount ;
   ```
4. Inspect the VCR image and change the name from `image1` to `imageVCR`.
5. Locate the code block for the VCR image `onImageServerClick` and click the tool button to open the Method Editor. This action brings up the warning dialog shown in Figure 11.19.

11

Figure 11.19.

Overwriting the Expert-generated code block.

6. When prompted whether you want to overwrite the code block, select Yes.

7. Enter the function as shown in Listing 11.7. Save the changes and try the application. Start with the Help form so that all the correct properties are sent to the Details form.

INPUT **Listing 11.7. Keeping track of the current row.**

```
 1: function imageVCR_onImageServerClick(nLeft, nTop)
 2: {
 3:    var lRefresh = true ;
 4:    if (nLeft >= 26*0 && nLeft < 26*1)
 5:    {
 6:        this.form.rowset.first() ;
 7:        this.form.currentRow = 1 ;
 8:    }
 9:    else if (nLeft >= 26*1 && nLeft < 26*2)
10:    {
11:        if (! this.form.rowset.next(-1))
12:        {
13:            this.form.rowset.next() ;
14:            lRefresh = false ;
15:        }
16:        else
17:        {
18:            this.form.currentRow-- ;
19:        }
20:    }
21:    else if (nLeft >= 26*2 && nLeft < 26*3)
22:    {
23:        if (! this.form.rowset.next())
24:        {
25:            this.form.rowset.next(-1) ;
26:            lRefresh = false ;
27:        }
28:        else
29:        {
30:            this.form.currentRow++ ;
31:        }
32:    }
33:    else
34:    {
35:        this.form.rowset.last() ;
36:        this.form.currentRow = this.form.titleCount ;
37:    }
```

```
38:    if (lRefresh)
39:    {
40:        class::UpdateValues(this.form) ;
41:    }
42: }
```

ANALYSIS This function contains two optimizations. Both deal with how often the UpdateValues() method is called. The first optimization deals with how the UpdateValues() method is called. An onNavigate event is a more instinctive place to call the UpdateValues() method. However, invoking the UpdateValues() method in the onNavigate event leads to unnecessary processing.

Before the Details form opens, many navigation events take place as the Results form determines the currentRow value. If a shopper picks the fifth book from the Results form, the onNavigate event fires five times before the Details form opens.

The second optimization avoids extra calls to UpdateValues() through a lRefresh flag. Line 3 defaults the flag to true. It is set to false on lines 14 and 26 when a navigation operation fails.

```
function imageVCR_onImageServerClick(nLeft, nTop)
{
    var lRefresh = true ;
```

Each if block corresponds to an image region. The first if block spans from lines 4 to 8 and handles the first region that ranges from 0 to 25 pixels. Each if block relies on the region width being 26 pixels. The logic might look a little complicated because (nLeft <26) has the same result as (nLeft >= 26*0 && nLeft < 26*1). The advantage of the more complex expression is that it is really a formula for all the regions—the formula being (nLeft >26*<(region - 1)> && 26*<region>). The formula repeats for the second and third regions.

```
if (nLeft >= 26*0 && nLeft < 26*1)
{
    this.form.rowset.first() ;
    this.form.currentRow = 1 ;
}
```

NOTE The Form Designer automatically makes the default the rowset for the first table you drop onto a form rowset for the form. You can use this.form.rowset to reference the default rowset. When you run a form within the IntraBuilder Designer, the default rowset works with options on the Table menu.

The second region is handled by lines 9 through 20. The `Rowset::next()` method returns `true` if the navigation has been a success and `false` if it moved the row pointer to `endOfSet`. The nested `if` checks to see whether the navigation fails and moves the row pointer back to the previous row if it went to `endOfSet`. In this case, the row pointer appears to have never moved, and there is no need to refresh the HTML field value controls.

```
else if (nLeft >= 26*1 && nLeft < 26*2)
{
    if (! this.form.rowset.next(-1))
    {
        this.form.rowset.next() ;
        lRefresh = false ;
    }
    else
    {
        this.form.currentRow-- ;
    }
}
```

The third region is a mirror image of the second. If the navigation is successful, the counter increments. Otherwise, line 26 sets the refresh flag to `false`.

```
else if (nLeft >= 26*2 && nLeft < 26*3)
{
    if (! this.form.rowset.next())
    {
        this.form.rowset.next(-1) ;
        lRefresh = false ;
    }
    else
    {
        this.form.currentRow++ ;
    }
}
```

The last region is the default region. If the value of `nLeft` falls outside all the other regions, it must be valid for the last region which, appropriately enough, goes to the last row. No error trapping is done here. Line 35 calls `Rowset::last()` to move the row pointer to the last row. The only way this would fail is if the view has no rows, and in that case there is no valid row to recover to. When you're at the last row, the position is the same as the total number of rows in the set.

```
else
{
    this.form.rowset.last() ;
    this.form.currentRow = this.form.titleCount ;
}
```

The last section depends on whether the navigation has been successful rather than what the current region is. If a refresh is necessary, line 40 calls `UpdateValues()` with a reference to the current form. By accepting the form reference as a parameter, the `UpdateValues()` method is callable from events that use different properties to reference the form. For instance, the `onServerLoad` event uses this instead of `this.form` to reference the form. A query event uses `this.parent` instead of `this.form`.

```
if (lRefresh)
{
    class::UpdateValues(this.form) ;
}
}
```

Making a Buy

The Details form is almost done. Shoppers can navigate through selected titles and all the HTML value controls refresh. If you've followed all the recommended positioning, the form will configure the controls appropriately in both Navigator and Internet Explorer. Figure 11.20 shows the Details form with position information in Internet Explorer.

Figure 11.20.

Checking the current row position in the Details form.

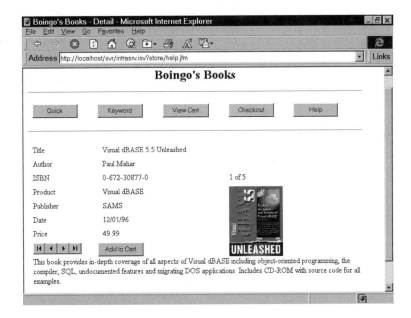

The last task is to provide a button that lets shoppers place the current title into the shopping cart. This requires a new button, a new `onServerClick` method, and a new query. The new query is for the Cart table, and it will be the first that is updated directly from the application. Here now is the last set of steps for the Details form.

1. Open the Details form in the Form Designer.
2. Change the title property of the form from `Title` to `Boingo's Books - Detail`.

3. Drop the Cart table from the IntraBuilder Explorer onto the Form Designer.

4. Remove the full path from the new query's `sql` property. The stripped version should appear like this:

```
SELECT * FROM "cart.DBF"
```

5. To suppress the default IntraBuilder image when no cover image is available, add the following line to the end of the `UpdateValues()` method.

```
thisForm.imageCover.visible = (! (fTitle["COVER"].value == "")) ;
```

6. Add a new button with property settings as listed in Table 11.5. This places the new button next to the VCR image.

Table 11.5. Properties for the Add to Cart button.

Property	Value
name	buttonAdd
text	Add to Cart
left	15
top	10.5
width	12

7. Create a new method linked to the `onServerClick` event of `buttonAdd`.

8. Enter the `buttonAdd_onServerClick()` method from Listing 11.8. After the function is done, so is the Details form. Save it and move on to the source code analysis.

INPUT **Listing 11.8. The Details form with `buttonAdd_onServerclick()`.**

```
 1: // {End Header} Do not remove this comment//
 2: // Generated on 11/02/96
 3: //
 4: var f = new detailForm();
 5: f.open();
 6: class detailForm extends ToolbarCForm from "TOOLBAR.JCF" {
 7:     with (this) {
 8:         onServerLoad = {; class::UpdateValues(this)};
 9:         height = 16;
10:         left = 0;
11:         top = 0;
12:         width = 75;
13:         title = "Boingo's Books - Detail";
14:     }
15:
16:     with (this.title1 = new Query()){
17:         left = 60;
```

11

```
18:        top = 0;
19:        sql = 'SELECT * FROM "title.dbf"';
20:        active = true;
21:     }

22:
23:     with (this.title1.rowset) {
24:     }
25:
26:     with (this.cart1 = new Query()){
27:        left = 55;
28:        top = 0;
29:        sql = 'SELECT * FROM "cart.DBF"';
30:        active = true;
31:     }

32:
33:     with (this.cart1.rowset) {

34:     }

35:
36:     with (this.imageVCR = new Image(this)){
37:        onImageServerClick = class::imageVCR_onImageServerClick;
38:        height = 0.8;
39:        left = 1;
40:        top = 10.5;
41:        width = 10.5;
42:        dataSource = "filename VCR.GIF";
43:        alignment = 4;
44:     }

45:
46:     with (this.labelTitle = new HTML(this)){
47:        height = 1;
48:        left = 1;
49:        top = 3.5;
50:        width = 14;
51:        color = "black";
52:        text = "Title";
53:     }

54:
55:     with (this.labelAuthor = new HTML(this)){
56:        height = 1;
57:         left = 1;
58:        top = 4.5;
59:        width = 14;
60:        color = "black";
61:        text = "Author";
62:     }
63:
64:
65:     with (this.labelISBN = new HTML(this)){
66:        height = 1;
```

continues

Listing 11.8. continued

```
 67:        left = 1;
 68:        top = 5.5;
 69:        width = 14;
 70:        color = "black";
 71:        text = "ISBN";
 72:    }
 73:
 74:
 75:    with (this.labelProduct = new HTML(this)){
 76:        height = 1;
 77:        left = 1;
 78:        top = 6.5;
 79:        width = 14;
 80:        color = "black";
 81:        text = "Product";
 82:    }
 83:
 84:    with (this.labelPublisher = new HTML(this)){
 85:        height = 1;
 86:        left = 1;
 87:        top = 7.5;
 88:        width = 14;
 89:        color = "black";
 90:        text = "Publisher ";
 91:    }
 92:
 93:    with (this.labelPubdate = new HTML(this)){
 94:        height = 1;
 95:         left = 1;
 96:        top = 8.5;
 97:        width = 14;
 98:        color = "black";
 99:        text = "Date";
100:    }
101:
102:    with (this.labelPrice = new HTML(this)){
103:        height = 1;
104:        left = 1;
105:        top = 9.5;
106:        width = 14;
107:        color = "black";
108:        text = "Price";
109:    }
110:
111:    with (this.imageCover = new Image(this)){
112:        height = 5;
113:        left = 43;
114:        top = 6.5;
115:        width = 12;
```

```
116:        dataSource = parent.title1.rowset.fields["COVER"];
117:        alignment = 3;
118:    }
119:

120:    with (this.valueTitle = new HTML(this)){
121:        height = 1;
122:        left = 16;
123:        top = 3.5;
124:        width = 55;
125:        color = "black";
126:        text = "HTML1";
127:    }

128:
129:    with (this.valueAuthor = new HTML(this)){
130:        height = 1;
131:        left = 16;
132:        top = 4.5;
133:        width = 55;
134:        color = "black";
135:        text = "HTML1";
136:    }

137:
138:    with (this.valueISBN = new HTML(this)){
139:        height = 1;
140:        left = 16;
141:        top = 5.5;
142:        width = 20;
143:        color = "black";
144:        text = "HTML1";
145:    }

146:
147:    with (this.valueProduct = new HTML(this)){
148:        height = 1;
149:        left = 16;
150:        top = 6.5;
151:        width = 20;
152:        color = "black";
153:        text = "HTML1";
154:    }

155:
156:    with (this.valuePublisher = new HTML(this)){
157:        height = 1;
158:        left = 16;
159:        top = 7.5;
160:        width = 20;
161:        color = "black";
162:        text = "HTML1";
163:    }

164:
```

11

continues

Listing 11.8. continued

```
165:    with (this.valuePubdate = new HTML(this)){
166:        height = 1;
167:        left = 16;
168:        top = 8.5;
169:        width = 20;
170:        color = "black";
171:        text = "HTML1";
172:    }

173:
174:    with (this.valuePrice = new HTML(this)){
175:        height = 1;
176:        left = 16;
177:        top = 9.5;
178:        width = 20;
179:        color = "black";
180:        text = "HTML1";
181:    }

182:
183:    with (this.valueNotes = new HTML(this)){
184:        height = 4;
185:        left = 1;
186:        top = 11.5;
187:        width = 70;
188:        color = "black";
189:        text = "HTML1";
190:    }

191:
192:    with (this.htmlPosition = new HTML(this)){
193:        height = 1;
194:        left = 43;
195:        top = 5.5;
196:        width = 12;
197:        color = "black";
198:        text = "HTML1";
199:    }

200:
201:    with (this.buttonAdd = new Button(this)){
202:        onServerClick = class::buttonAdd_onServerClick;
203:        left = 15;
204:        top = 10.5;
205:        width = 12;
206:        text = "Add to Cart";
207:    }
208:
209:    this.rowset = this.title1.rowset;
210:
211:    function UpdateValues(thisForm)
212:    {
213:        var fTitle = thisForm.title1.rowset.fields ;
```

11

```
214:        thisForm.valueTitle.text      = fTitle["TITLE"].value ;
215:        thisForm.valueAuthor.text     = fTitle["AUTHOR"].value ;
216:        thisForm.valueISBN.text       = fTitle["ISBN"].value ;
217:        thisForm.valueProduct.text    = fTitle["PRODUCT"].value ;
218:        thisForm.valuePublisher.text  = fTitle["PUBLISHER"].value ;
219:        thisForm.valuePubdate.text    = fTitle["PUBDATE"].value ;
220:        thisForm.valuePrice.text      = fTitle["PRICE"].value ;
221:        thisForm.valueNotes.text      = fTitle["NOTES"].value ;
222:        thisForm.htmlPosition.text  =
223:            thisForm.currentRow  + " of " + thisForm.titleCount ;
224:        thisForm.imageCover.visible = (! (fTitle["COVER"].value == "")) ;
225:    }
226:
227:    function imageVCR_onImageServerClick(nLeft, nTop)
228:    {
229:        var lRefresh = true ;
230:        if (nLeft >= 26*0 && nLeft < 26*1)
231:        {
232:            this.form.rowset.first() ;
233:            this.form.currentRow = 1 ;
234:        }
235:        else if (nLeft >= 26*1 && nLeft < 26*2)
236:        {
237:            if (! this.form.rowset.next(-1))
238:            {
239:                this.form.rowset.next() ;
240:                lRefresh = false ;
241:            }
242:            else
243:            {
244:                this.form.currentRow-- ;
245:            }
246:        }
247:        else if (nLeft >= 26*2 && nLeft < 26*3)
248:        {
249:            if (! this.form.rowset.next())
250:            {
251:                this.form.rowset.next(-1) ;
252:                lRefresh = false ;
253:            }
254:            else
255:            {
256:                this.form.currentRow++ ;
257:            }
258:        }
259:        else
260:        {
261:            this.form.rowset.last() ;
262:            this.form.currentRow = this.form.titleCount ;
263:        }
264:        if (lRefresh)
265:        {
266:            class::UpdateValues(this.form) ;
267:        }
268:    }
269:
```

continues

Listing 11.8. continued

```
270:    function buttonAdd_onServerClick()
271:    {
272:       var rCart  = this.form.cart1.rowset,
273:           rTitle = this.form.title1.rowset ;
274:       rCart.applyLocate(
275:          "ISBN = " + "'" + rTitle.fields["ISBN"].value + "'"
276:          + "AND CARTUSER = " + "'" + this.form.user + "'" ) ;
277:       if ( rCart.endOfSet )
278:       {
279:          rCart.beginAppend() ;
280:          rCart.fields["ISBN"].value = rTitle.fields["ISBN"].value ;
281:          rCart.fields["CARTUSER"].value = this.form.user ;
282:          rCart.fields["CARTDATE"].value = new Date() ;
283:       }
284:       rCart.fields["QTY"].value++ ;
285:       rCart.save() ;
286:       rCart.active = false ;
287:       nextForm = new cartForm() ;
288:       nextForm.user = this.form.user ;
289:       nextForm.open() ;
290:       this.form.release() ;

291:    }
292:
293: }
```

ANALYSIS The detailForm class starts by assigning a code block to the onServerLoad on line 8. The code block contains a single call to the UpdateValues() method. This is almost the same as directly linking the onServerLoad event to UpdateValues(). The difference is that a direct link does not enable you to pass custom parameters. Links pass either no parameters or a predefined set of parameters. Most events, including onServerLoad, pass no parameters. The onImageServerClick is an example of an event with predefined parameters.

```
class detailForm extends ToolbarCForm from "TOOLBAR.JCF" {
   with (this) {
      onServerLoad = {; class::UpdateValues(this)};
      height = 16;
      left = 0;
      top = 0;
      width = 75;
      title = "Boingo's Books - Detail";
   }
```

The definitions for the HTML value controls have no links or code blocks to set up the initial text value. All the value definitions end by setting the text property to "HTML1". You can remove lines 126, 135, 144, 153, 162, 171, 180, 189, and 198 without affecting the form.

```
with (this.valueTitle = new HTML(this)){
   height = 1;
   left = 16;
```

```
        top = 3.5;
        width = 55;
        color = "black";
        text = "HTML1";
}
```

The `onServerLoad` fires the `UpdateValues()` method to assign the `text` properties on lines 214 through 223. Code blocks offer another way to accomplish the same thing. The following `with` block shows a technique that works without anything happening in the `onServerLoad`. When you use a code block in this manner, the code block executes only when the HTML control is rendered. Unlike a datalink, code blocks do not reevaluate when the row navigation occurs in the IntraBuilder Designer.

```
with (this.valueTitle = new HTML(this)){
        height = 1;
        left = 16;
        top = 3.5;
        width = 55;
        color = "black";
        text = {¦¦this.form.title1.rowset.fields["TITLE"].value};
}
```

NOTE When you are working with HTML controls in a report, code blocks do work more like a data link. As a report runs, navigation occurs and new HTML controls display the new data. The difference between the form and the report is that a form reuses the same HTML control for different rows. Reports create new HTML controls for each row.

The `UpdateValues()` method assigns new values to the text properties of HTML controls. It uses the parameter `thisForm` to refer to the current form. Keep in mind that `thisForm` is a local variable unlike the native `this` and `this.form` references. The `thisForm` parameter enables the method to work with both the `onServerLoad` event of the form and the `onServerImageClick` event of the VCR image.

Line 213 creates the `fTitle` variable as a temporary shortcut reference to the `fields` object of the `title1` query. You could substitute the entire reference wherever `fTitle` appears.

```
function UpdateValues(thisForm)
{
    var fTitle = thisForm.title1.rowset.fields ;
    thisForm.valueTitle.text     = fTitle["TITLE"].value ;
    thisForm.valueAuthor.text    = fTitle["AUTHOR"].value ;
    thisForm.valueISBN.text      = fTitle["ISBN"].value ;
    thisForm.valueProduct.text   = fTitle["PRODUCT"].value ;
    thisForm.valuePublisher.text = fTitle["PUBLISHER"].value ;
    thisForm.valuePubdate.text   = fTitle["PUBDATE"].value ;
    thisForm.valuePrice.text     = fTitle["PRICE"].value ;
```

```
    thisForm.valueNotes.text     = fTitle["NOTES"].value ;
    thisForm.htmlPosition.text =
        thisForm.currentRow  + " of " + thisForm.titleCount ;
    thisForm.imageCover.visible = (! (fTitle["COVER"].value == "")) ;
}
```

Line 224 checks to see whether the binary field is blank. The value property of a binary field contains the entire bit stream for the field as a string. You can compare a binary value to a string, but you cannot use string methods to manipulate it.

The buttonAdd_onServerClick() method adds information from the current Title row to the shopping cart table. The process starts by looking to see whether the current title already is in the shopping cart for the current shopper. This is done through an alternate form of Rowset.applyLocate(). On Day 10, you learned how query by form uses an interactive form of Rowset::applyLocate(). With query by form, dataLinks control the search criteria. Lines 274 through 276 pass the search criteria to Rowset::applyLocate() as a SQL expression.

```
function buttonAdd_onServerClick()
{
    var rCart  = this.form.cart1.rowset,
        rTitle = this.form.title1.rowset ;
    rCart.applyLocate(
        "ISBN = " + "'" + rTitle.fields["ISBN"].value + "'"
        + "AND CARTUSER = " + "'" + this.form.user + "'" ) ;
```

WARNING

You must escape any single quotes in look-up strings that you pass to Rowset.applyLocate() or the filter property. For example, if you want to locate *Tom Swan's Mastering Borland C++ 5*, the apostrophe after Swan must be prefixed with a triple backslash.

The following code contains a handy sqlString() function. Using this function, it's possible that a look-up string could contain the single quote symbol.

```
// file: sqlquote.js
clear ;
var cLookFor = "Tom Swan's Mastering Borland C++ 5" ;
var q = new Query("select * from title") ;
// q.rowset.applyLocate("TITLE = '" + cLookFor + "'" ) ;     //
error
? q.rowset.applyLocate("TITLE = " + sqlString(cLookFor)) ; //
OK

function sqlString(cString)
{
  var nIndex = cString.indexOf("'") ;
  while ( nIndex > -1 )
  {
     cString = cString.substring(0,nIndex) +
      "\\\'" + cString.substring(nIndex + 1, cString.length) ;
     nIndex = cString.indexOf("'",nIndex + 2) ;
```

```
    }
    return ("'" + cString + "'") ;
}
```

The triple backslash provides two levels of evaluation protection.
IntraBuilder evaluates the string once before it is passed to the
`Rowset::applyLocate()` method. The first evaluation removes the first
and third backslash. The resulting string, `Tom Swan\'s Mastering`
`Borland C++ 5`, is passed to the BDE SQL processor.

If the shopper already added the same book to the cart, the rowset will not be at `endOfSet`.
Otherwise, line 279 creates a new row buffer and lines 280 through 282 fill the buffer with
the ISBN, user key, and current date.

```
if ( rCart.endOfSet )
{
   rCart.beginAppend() ;
   rCart.fields["ISBN"].value = rTitle.fields["ISBN"].value ;
   rCart.fields["CARTUSER"].value = this.form.user ;
   rCart.fields["CARTDATE"].value = new Date() ;
}
```

The QTY field defaults to zero when new rows are added to the table. The field is incremented
by one each time the user tries to add a book to the cart. If the book is already found, QTY
increases by one. If it is a new book, the same logic makes QTY equal to one. After setting the
quantity to the appropriate value, `Rowset::save()` commits the row buffer to the table and
line 286 deactivates the query.

```
rCart.fields["QTY"].value++ ;
rCart.save() ;
rCart.active = false ;
```

The remainder of the function is very much like the end of `buttonDetails_onServerClick()`.
It opens the `cartForm` after adding the user key property.

```
    nextForm = new cartForm() ;
    nextForm.user = this.form.user ;
    nextForm.open() ;
    this.form.release() ;
}
```

Adding the Cart Form

Before you can test the new Add button, you need to create a stub form for the shopping cart
and tie it into the Help form. For now, the Cart form needs only the components inherited
from the toolbar class. The first steps to building the Cart form are as follows:

1. Open the Form Designer to create a new form named `cart.jfm`. You can avoid the Expert and filename prompts by entering a _sys method in the Script Pad.

   ```
   _sys.forms.design("cart.jfm") ;
   ```

2. If the Form Designer comes up without the toolbar buttons, set the custom form class to `ToolbarCForm`.

3. Press Ctrl+S to save the new form and then close the Designer.

NOTE

> When creating stub forms, which contain nothing other than default or inherited properties, you must explicitly save the form before closing it.

4. Add `_sys.scripts.load()` and `#include` statements for the Cart form into the `store.h` file, as shown in the following lines. For more information on the `store.h` file, see the Analysis for Listing 11.3.

INPUT

```
#define DEBUG   // for development only
#ifndef STORE
    #define STORE
  #ifdef DEBUG
     // Load scripts
     // _sys.script.load statements go here.
     _sys.scripts.load("cart.jfm") ;
     _sys.scripts.load("detail.jfm") ;
     _sys.scripts.load("help.jfm") ;
     _sys.scripts.load("message.jfm") ;
     _sys.scripts.load("quick.jfm") ;
     _sys.scripts.load("results.jfm") ;
  #elseif
     // Include scripts
     return null
     // #include statements go here
     #include <cart.jfm>
     #include <detail.jfm>
     #include <help.jfm>
     #include <message.jfm>
     #include <quick.jfm>
     #include <results.jfm>
  #endif
#endif
```

5. Exit and restart the IntraBuilder Designer to clear out all scripts from memory.

6. Recompile the Help form to include all changes from the `store.h` file.

Now you can try the Add to Cart button from the Details form and the View Cart toolbar button. When you click either the Add to Cart button or the View Cart toolbar button, a form containing only the toolbar opens.

11

Summary

Today, the shopping cart application really started to take shape. The following five forms are complete: the Help form, the Quick form, the Message form, the Results form, and the Details form. The day started with a very simple Message form that had only an HTML control and an inherited set of toolbar buttons. The simplicity of the Message form made it easy to demonstrate how you can experiment with the dynamic object model without creating any JavaScript files.

The Quick form and the Results form that you started on Day 10 got their finishing touches. You added an extensive routine to the Results form so that it could provide the Details form with enough information.

The major task of the day was the development of the Details form. This started as a prototype from the Form Expert. Starting with the Expert generated code, the form evolved to become a dynamic read-only form with simulated dataLinks. You learned some of the behind-the-scenes workings of images that perform actions. In replacing the Expert-generated navigation code block, you learned how to track the current row position and display it to the shopper.

The day ended with a foreshadowing of tomorrow. The last enhancement to the Details form was a call to the shopping cart form. You also created an empty Cart form to test the Add button. In Day 12, you'll develop the Cart form and learn how to simulate both the read-only datalinks and read-write datalinks. Of course, the whole purpose of simulating the read-only datalinks is to make them truly read-only. If you're wondering why on earth you would ever want to simulate a read-write datalink, be sure to tune in tomorrow and find out.

Q&A

Q **I updated the `store.h` file, recompiled the Help form, and even restarted the IntraBuilder Designer—but whatever I do, I always encounter the error `Class not loaded into memory: detailForm::detailForm`. How can I fix this?**

A Make sure the capitalization of the class name in the `detail.jfm` file matches the class name in the function that is attempting to create a new instance of the Details form.

Q **When I run the Details form through Netscape Navigator, there is no space between one of the field labels and its value. It looks okay in the Designer and in Internet Explorer. How can I insert a space between the label and the value?**

A You can force spaces between two columns of HTML controls by adding trailing spaces to values of the first column. For instance, if the `Product` field label is

11

running into the `Product` field value, you can add two spaces to the end of the text string, as shown here:

```
with (this.labelProduct = new HTML(this)){
     height = 1;
     left = 1;
     top = 6.5;
     width = 14;
     color = "black";
     text = "Product   ";
}
```

Q **I'm having trouble whenever I run the shopping cart forms. I was able to design them without any problems, but when I run the forms through the browser, the controls shift around. If I run within the IntraBuilder Designer, the system becomes unstable as soon as I try to move from one form to another. What is going wrong?**

A Make sure you are not running IntraBuilder version 1.0. Some of the techniques shown throughout this book are not compatible with the initial release. For instance, `this.form.release()` can crash IntraBuilder 1.0. You can replace each instance of `this.form.release()` with `this.form.close()` to get forms to run. Also, the positions of many controls will need adjusting to work with the relative coordinate system that was replaced in version 1.01.

Q **When I create a form with the Form Expert, it sometimes creates new images in my current folder. Where do these image files come from?**

A The Form Expert copies image files from a `Designer` files folder. By default the folder is located at

```
c:\Program Files\Borland\IntraBuilder\Designer\Form
```

You can copy images directly from this folder for your own use. You can also modify the images to customize the look of a Form Expert generated form.

Workshop

The Workshop section provides questions and exercises to help you get a better feel for the material you learned today. Try to answer the questions and at least think about the exercises before moving on to tomorrow's lesson. You'll find the answers to the questions in Appendix A, "Answers to Quiz Questions."

Quiz

1. What character in a SQL look-up value must you prefix with a triple backslash?
2. The `onImageServerClick` event is passed to parameters. What are they and how can you use them?

3. What displays in a browser for an image if the dataSource is an empty `binary` field?

4. How can you tell if a `binary` field is empty?

5. What is meant by `this.form.title1.rowset.next(-1)`?

6. What is an advantage of using the `autoEdit` property to make a form read-only?

Exercises

1. The VCR image is missing the fast forward and fast rewind buttons that are often found on a real VCR. Try expanding the image to include regions to move five rows at a time.

2. Currently, the order of the Results list does not match the order books appear on the Details form. Although it is faster to leave it as is, you might want to alter the `title1` query to set the `indexName` to `TITLE`.

Day 12

Creating a Dynamic Grid for the Cart Form

by Paul Mahar

Today you will take the Cart form from Day 11 and expand it into a form that allows dynamic updates of multiple rows of the Cart table. The challenge of the day is to create a grid that displays and allows updates to more than the current row. IntraBuilder does not have any multiple row controls, such as the Delphi DBGrid or the Visual dBASE Browse control. For the Cart form, you will need to create a "roll your own" grid.

Creating your first dynamic live data grid can be a daunting task. To make it easy, you can break the process into the following tasks:

☐ Create a single row grid or, in other words, a few controls that are top aligned. You can use the Form Designer to lay out the controls that make up the first row of the grid.

☐ Take the single row grid and convert it to a grid that can display no rows, one row, or many rows. The second incarnation of the Cart form moves you beyond the realm of the Form Designer. To create a data-driven grid, the elements of the grid must be defined after the constructor. The Form Designer allows layout of only the controls that appear within the constructor.

☐ Modify some of the controls to be live rather than read-only. The last task is to add the ability to edit table data. This is where you will be simulating a datalink for a Text control. Real datalinks allow only a single row of data to appear for any given query. The simulated datalink allows read and write capabilities to as many rows as will fit comfortably in your form.

By the end of the day, you will know how to dynamically generate and manipulate controls from JavaScript methods. The ability to create controls at runtime lets you build data-driven forms that are difficult or impossible to represent through the visual tools of the Form Designer.

TIP   The three tasks are represented by three incarnations of the Cart form on the CD-ROM. They are available with the Day 12 source files as `cart1.jfm`, `cart2.jfm`, and `cart3.jfm`. You can use these files to skip over any of the tasks or as reference points if you get lost along the way.

The Single Item Starter Cart

The arrangement of the Cart form is similar to an order form. The main portion of the Cart form is a grid or table consisting of five columns. Two columns show values from the Cart table. Another two show values from the Title table. The last column is a calculated expression. The five columns contain the following values:

☐ *ISBN* is the first of two fields that come from the Cart table. This is the key value, which links the Cart table to the Title table.

☐ *QTY* is the quantity of a single title that a shopper wants to buy. The default is always one. This field value comes from the Cart table. This column is a Text control and is the only column that shoppers can modify.

☐ *Title* is the book title. For a more generic shopping cart, you could rename this column to Description. The value for the Title is in the Title table. You must relate queries for the Cart table and Title table to retrieve the correct Title value.

- *Price*, like Title, comes from the Title table. Neither the title nor price is stored into the Cart table.
- *Total* is calculated by multiplying the QTY field value by the Price field value. The result is not stored to a table.

> **NOTE**
>
> To see an order form example that uses the same basic layout as the Cart form, turn to the back of this book. In the pages following the index, Macmillan includes an order form for books with topics similar to the one you're reading.

In addition to the columns, the Cart form contains several other new controls. When you move from the single item cart to using a grid, all the column controls move from visible controls in the Form Designer to JavaScript statements. The other controls are more static than the grid controls. The non-grid controls will display only once; however, grid controls can display more than once. The following controls will remain visible in the Form Designer throughout the three incarnations of the Cart form:

- *Column Headings* are HTML labels for the top of the grid. There are five headings: ISBN, QTY, Title, Price, and Total.
- *Grand Total* is an HTML control, which displays the sum of the grid totals. The value is calculated and not stored to either the Cart or Title table.
- *Grand Total Label* is an HTML label for the Grand Total HTML control.
- *Help Text* is a multiple line HTML control with instructions on how the Cart form works.
- *The Update Button* is a standard button with an onServerClick event to commit changes in the grid to the Cart table. Shoppers can use this button to update the QTY column and remove items from a cart.
- *The Reset Button* works like the undo feature in a browser. You do not have to add any methods or code blocks to make a Reset button work. It also has no effect when running within the Designer.

The Grand Total, Help Text, and buttons have positions relative to the size of the grid. They all appear under the grid. The more rows that go into the grid, the lower each of the other controls moves down. The column headings are the only controls you will be adding with a fixed position.

12

Finding the Best Way to Relate Tables

The IntraBuilder database classes provide four ways to relate tables. Each relation technique relies on different properties. You can mix and match each option as required. The four relation-forming properties are `sql`, `masterRowset`, `masterSource`, and `beforeGetValue`.

☐ `sql`: Relating tables through the `sql` property is the simplest technique for anyone familiar with the SQL language. This technique also helps reduce the number of query components you'll need.

☐ `masterRowset`: The Inspector can assist you when you're relating queries in the Form Designer. You will find drop-down lists for the `masterRowset` and `masterFields` properties. The relation does not take place until both the `masterRowset` and `masterFields` properties are set. The `masterRowset` property is optimized for row-oriented navigation and works best with dBASE and Paradox tables.

☐ `masterSource`: You can relate two set-oriented queries by including the related field value as a parameter of the SQL command. The `masterSource` property creates the parameter for the join. Use this technique when working with ODBC or SQL-Link drivers.

☐ `beforeGetValue`: The last technique is the most complex. It involves setting the `beforeGetValue` event to a function that looks up related values. This allows a great deal of flexibility by not creating a conventional relation.

Let's take a closer look at each relation technique so that we can find the approach that works best for the Cart form. To create a meaningful relation, the Cart table needs to have at least two rows. You can use the Add to Cart button on the Detail form to add rows, or you can add them manually. If you do add them manually, make sure the ISBN numbers are valid. For this exercise, the user, data, and quantity field values are irrelevant. Figure 12.1 shows the five Cart rows used for this text.

Figure 12.1.

Viewing the Cart table in Delphi's Database Desktop.

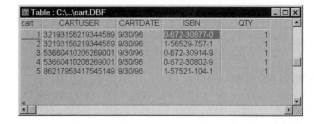

The sql property lets you join more than one table in a single query. You can create the query, assign the sql property, and activate the query in a single statement. Listing 12.1 shows an example of using the sql property to relate tables. The script is included on the CD-ROM as relate1.js.

INPUT

Listing 12.1. Relate1.js—Using the sql property to relate tables.

```
1: q = new Query('SELECT cart.isbn, title.title ' +
2:                 'FROM "cart.dbf" cart, "title.dbf" title ' +
3:                 'WHERE cart.isbn = title.isbn') ;
4: _sys.scriptOut.clear() ;
5: while (! q.rowset.endOfSet)
6: {
7:   _sys.scriptOut.writeln("ISBN: " + q.rowset.fields[0].value +
8:                        " TITLE: "+ q.rowset.fields[1].value) ;
9:   q.rowset.next() ;
10: }
```

ANALYSIS   Lines 1 through 3 create an instance of the Query class. The SQL command is passed as a string to the Query constructor. This automatically sets the sql property and activates the query. The SQL command creates alias names for the dBASE tables. In this case, the alias names match the root of the filename. However, you can also use an alias to shorten the SQL command. For example, the following SQL command does the same thing using t and c in place of title and cart.

```
SELECT c.isbn, t.title FROM "cart.dbf" c, "title.dbf" t WHERE c.isbn = t.isbn
```

The remainder of the script prints out values to the Script Pad. Line 4 clears the contents of the results pane.

```
_sys.scriptOut.clear() ;
```

The while loop goes through each row of the view and prints the values of the ISBN and TITLE fields. You can check the Script Pad to see whether the relation is working properly.

```
while (! q.rowset.endOfSet)
{
  _sys.scriptOut.writeln("ISBN: " + q.rowset.fields[0].value +
                       " TITLE: "+ q.rowset.fields[1].value) ;
  q.rowset.next() ;
}
```

Before running the Relate1 JavaScript, open the Script Pad. Figure 12.2 shows the results for a Cart table containing five rows. Listings 12.2, 12.3, and 12.4 contain slightly modified versions of the output routine.

12

Figure 12.2.

Verifying results with the Script Pad.

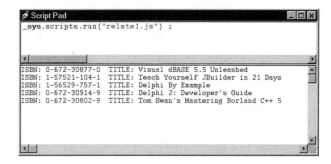

The next script, shown in Listing 12.2, increases in JavaScript complexity while using much simpler SQL commands. The script is more representative of dropping two tables onto a form and using the Inspector to relate them. Relating queries involves two properties: `masterRowset` and `masterFields`. The `masterRowset` property points from the child query to the parent query. The parent is the controlling query. When the row pointer moves in the parent, the pointer also moves in the child. However, the child row pointer can move without affecting the parent row pointer. This enables you to move among multiple child rows for a single parent.

NEW TERM A *parent and child table relation* exists when a row in one table corresponds to no row, one row, or more rows in another table. If the child table can contain more than one related row, the relation is a one-to-many relation. A common example is between a customer table and an invoice table. If you navigate to a different customer, the invoice number must also be different. A customer can have multiple invoices, so that you can navigate through different invoices without changing customers.

INPUT **Listing 12.2.** `Relate2.js`—**Using** `masterRowset` **to relate queries.**

```
 1: q1 = new Query('SELECT * FROM "cart.dbf"') ;
 2: with ( q2 = new Query('SELECT * FROM "title.dbf"') )
 3: {
 4:   rowset.masterRowset = q1.rowset ;
 5:   rowset.masterFields = "ISBN" ;
 6: }
 7: _sys.scriptOut.clear() ;
 8: while (! q1.rowset.endOfSet)
 9: {
10:   _sys.scriptOut.writeln("ISBN: " + q1.rowset.fields["ISBN"].value +
11:                     " TITLE: "+ q2.rowset.fields["TITLE"].value) ;
12:   q1.rowset.next() ;
13: }
```

ANALYSIS The relate2.js script starts by creating two simple queries and relating them. Line 1 creates the q1 query that points to the Cart table. The child query is defined as q2 on lines 2 through 6. The with block assigns two properties of the child query to form the relation. In this case, the with block might actually complicate the script. You could substitute the following three statements for lines 2 through 6:

```
q2 = new Query('SELECT * FROM "title.dbf"')
q2.rowset.masterRowset = q1.rowset ;
q2.rowset.masterFields = "ISBN" ;
```

The masterFields property must match an existing index in the Title table. When you set masterFields, IntraBuilder looks for a matching field in the parent table and a matching index in the child table. If an index is not found for an identically named field in the child table, a runtime error occurs, as shown in Figure 12.3.

Figure 12.3.

An error when re-lating tables without an index.

If the field names of the parent and child tables do not match, you can force the index of the child. For example, if the Title table used ISBNUMBER as the ISBN field name and index name, it could still relate to the Cart table. The trick is to explicitly set the indexName before setting the masterFields property, like this:

```
q2 = new Query('SELECT * FROM "title.dbf"')
q2.rowset.indexName = "ISBNUMBER"
q2.rowset.masterRowset = q1.rowset ;
q2.rowset.masterFields = "ISBN" ;
```

The relation between the Cart table and Title table is a one-to-one relation and not the one-to-many that typically occurs between parent and child. So does it matter which table is the master? Absolutely. If you were to reverse the relation as shown in the next code segment, the first part of the script would have no complaints.

```
q1 = new Query('SELECT * FROM "title.dbf"') ;
with ( q2 = new Query('SELECT * FROM "cart.dbf"') )
{
 rowset.masterRowset = q1.rowset ;
 rowset.masterFields = "ISBN" ;
}
```

However, when the script reached the `while` loop, it would go through every row in the Title table. As soon as it found a book that no one had ordered, you would get an `endOfRowset` error.

If you modify the loop to travel through the child query, you would find it to be a short trip. The following code never goes beyond a single title. Although you can navigate around in the child rows, you can navigate only to other rows with the same parent. This would list a single title as many times as it has been ordered by different shoppers.

```
while (! q2.rowset.endOfSet)
{
 _sys.scriptOut.writeln("ISBN: " + q2.rowset.fields["ISBN"].value +
          " TITLE: "+ q1.rowset.fields["TITLE"].value) ;
 q2.rowset.next() ;
}
```

Then again, if you don't modify anything, there still would be something interesting to note. The resulting order of the SQL join differs from the `masterRow` join. The `masterRow` join moves through the Cart table in the physical or natural order of the dBASE table.

OUTPUT
```
ISBN: 0-672-30877-0 TITLE: Visual dBASE 5.5 Unleashed
ISBN: 1-56529-757-1 TITLE: Delphi By Example
ISBN: 0-672-30914-9 TITLE: Delphi 2: Developer's Guide
ISBN: 0-672-30802-9 TITLE: Tom Swan's Mastering Borland C++ 5
ISBN: 1-57521-104-1 TITLE: Teach Yourself JBuilder in 21 Days
```

The SQL results are based on the physical order of the Title table. In the Title table, the books are physically grouped by product in the following order: Visual dBASE, JBuilder, Delphi, Borland C++. The `relate2.js` script creates the join with the same groupings.

OUTPUT
```
ISBN: 0-672-30914-9 TITLE: Delphi 2: Developer's Guide
ISBN: 0-672-30877-0 TITLE: Visual dBASE 5.5 Unleashed
ISBN: 1-57521-104-1 TITLE: Teach Yourself JBuilder in 21 Days
ISBN: 1-56529-757-1 TITLE: Delphi By Example
ISBN: 0-672-30802-9 TITLE: Tom Swan's Mastering Borland C++ 5
```

INPUT

Listing 12.3. `Relate3.js`—Using `masterSource` to create a set-oriented relation.

```
1: q1 = new Query('SELECT * FROM "cart.dbf"') ;
2: with ( q2 = new Query())
3: {
4:   masterSource = q1.rowset ;
5:   sql = 'SELECT * FROM "title.dbf" WHERE ISBN = :ISBN';
6:   active = true ;
7: }
8:
9: _sys.scriptOut.clear() ;
10: while (! q1.rowset.endOfSet)
11: {
12:   _sys.scriptOut.writeln("ISBN: " + q1.rowset.fields["ISBN"].value +
13:                 " TITLE: "+ q2.rowset.fields["TITLE"].value) ;
14:   q1.rowset.next() ;
15: }
```

12

ANALYSIS The relate3.js script sets up a relation between two queries without specifying any rowset properties on the child query. Line 4 makes the ISBN parameter available to the SQL command on line 5. When using masterSource parameters, you cannot pass the SQL command to the query constructor because the parameters are undefined until masterSource is set. See Day 21 for more information on creating set-oriented relations.

The relation technique in Listing 12.4 is more complex and flexible than the previous three. It uses a beforeGetValue event, two queries, a calculated field, and a function. It does not rely on any predefined indexes or matching field names.

INPUT
Listing 12.4. Relate4.js—Using beforeGetValue to simulate a relation.

```
 1: q1 = new Query('SELECT * FROM "cart.dbf"') ;
 2: q2 = new Query('SELECT * FROM "title.dbf"') ;
 3: q1.rowset.fields.add(new CalcField("TITLE")) ;
 4: q1.rowset.fields["TITLE"].beforeGetValue = getTitle ;
 5:
 6: _sys.scriptOut.clear() ;
 7: while (! q1.rowset.endOfSet)
 8: {
 9:  _sys.scriptOut.writeln("ISBN: " + q1.rowset.fields["ISBN"].value +
10:           " TITLE: "+ q1.rowset.fields["TITLE"].value) ;
11:  q1.rowset.next() ;
12: }
13:
14: function getTitle()
15: {
16:   if (q2.rowset.applyLocate("ISBN = '"+this.parent["ISBN"].value+"'"))
17:   {
18:    return (q2.rowset.fields["TITLE"].value) ;
19:   }
20:   else
21:   {
22:    return ("") ;
23:   }
24: }
```

ANALYSIS The relate4.js script has three main parts. The first part sets up the queries on lines 1 through 4. The second part is output code on lines 6 through 12. The remaining lines define the function that executes during the beforeGetValue event.

After the two query objects are created, line 3 adds a new calculated field to the field list for q1. The fields property of a rowset is a special type of array. The fields property doesn't contain all the methods of a standard array, but it does include methods to add and delete elements. You can use the delete() method on any existing field from the fields array. The add() method allows only the addition of calculated fields.

```
q1.rowset.fields.add(new CalcField("TITLE")) ;
```

The `fields` property has a string index like an associative array and a numeric index like a standard array. The string index is the field name and the numeric index is the field position. Like a standard array, the field position is zero-based.

| NEW TERM | A *zero-based* array starts with element 0. If the array contains 10 elements, the valid index values for the array are `0` through `9`. JavaScript, Java, and C++ use zero-based arrays. Some other languages, such as dBASE and Basic, work with one-based arrays where the first element has an index of `1`.

Calculated fields are fields with values that exist only in memory. They have no connection to a physical table. The value of a physical field is determined by the `beforeGetValue` event. The name of a calculated field is set by passing a string to its constructor. When you add a calculated field to a fields array, the name of the calculated field becomes a new index to the fields array.

The default value of a calculated field is an empty string. The calculation of new values occurs when the `beforeGetValue` event calls the `getTitle()` function. The `beforeGetValue` event is triggered whenever a JavaScript statement references the field value through a datalink or in an expression. Line 4 assigns the `getTitle()` function to the `beforeGetValue` event. The return value of the `getTitle()` function acts as the field value.

```
q1.rowset.fields["TITLE"].beforeGetValue = getTitle ;
```

The `getTitle()` function performs a lookup in the Title table for the title value. The lookup uses the ISBN value from the Cart table. The value for the ISBN number is referenced through a `parent` property on line 16. This is possible because the `this` reference points to the calculated field. The `parent` of the calculated field is the array containing both it and the ISBN field.

The ISBN value is a character field and must be enclosed in single quotes. When `"ISBN = '"+this.parent["ISBN"].value+"'"` is passed down to the engine, it becomes `ISBN = '0-672-30877-0'` for the first book in the Cart table. If the `Rowset::applyLocate()` is successful, it returns `true`, and the current row contains the desired title. The title from the q2 is passed back as the value for the title field in q1.

```
function getTitle()
{
  if (q2.rowset.applyLocate("ISBN = '"+this.parent["ISBN"].value+"'"))
  {
   return (q2.rowset.fields["TITLE"].value) ;
  }
```

If `Rowset::applyLocate()` fails, q1 is left without a valid rowset. When the rowset is invalid, it is at `endOfSet`. A runtime error occurs if you try to reference a field value when a rowset is at `endOfSet`. To avoid the error, line 22 returns an empty string if the search fails.

```
else
{
 return ("") ;
 }
}
```

The resulting output from the `relate3.js` JavaScript is identical to the output using `masterFields` and `masterRowset`. So far, one of the first two methods appears to be the best way to go for the Cart form. Because you have existing indexes and matching field names, the `sql`, `masterFields`, and `masterSource` techniques are easier to set up than using `beforeGetValue`. Let performance be the tie breaker.

Comparing performance of various joins is much simpler than the benchmarks from Day 10. You already have four scripts that get the same results using different techniques. You can run them one at a time to try to determine which is faster. However, with such small data sets, you are not likely to notice any substantial differences. To compensate, you can use bigger data sets or make repetitive runs against the existing data sets. The repetitive run approach is quicker to set up. Listing 12.5 shows the `bench2.js` script that you can use to compare the join operations.

Listing 12.5. `Bench2.js`—Timing 100 runs of each table
INPUT relation script.

```
1: _sys.os.delete("bench2.txt") ;
2: run100("relate1.js") ;
3: run100("relate2.js") ;
4: run100("relate3.js") ;
5: run100("relate4.js") ;
6:
7: function run100(cScript)
8: {
9:   var start = new Date() ;
10:   for (var i = 0 ; i < 100 ; i++)
11:   {
12:       _sys.scripts.run(cScript) ;
13:   }
14:   writeTime2(cScript, start, new Date())
15: }
16:
17: function writeTime2(cScript, start, end)
18: {
```

continues

Listing 12.5. continued

```
19:    var fOut  = new File(),
20:        elapsed = 0 ;
21:    elapsed = ((end.getHours() * 3600) +
22:        (end.getMinutes()* 60)  +
23:         end.getSeconds() )
24:      -((start.getHours() * 3600) +
25:        (start.getMinutes()* 60)  +
26:        start.getSeconds()) ;
27:    if ( fOut.exists("bench2.txt") )
28:    {
29:       fOut.open("bench2.txt","rw") ;
30:       fOut.seek(0,2) ; // go to end of file.
31:    }
32:    else
33:    {
34:       fOut.create("bench2.txt") ;
35:    }
36:    fOut.puts("***") ;
37:    fOut.puts("Script:     " + cScript) ;
38:    fOut.puts("Seconds:    " + elapsed ) ;
39:    fOut.close() ;
40: }
```

ANALYSIS The bench2.js script simply calls the other four scripts 100 times each and records the results in a text file. Like the bench1.js script from Day 10, this one starts by deleting the last copy of the results file. Lines 2 through 5 call the run100() function with each version of the relation script.

```
_sys.os.delete("bench2.txt") ;
run100("relate1.js") ;
run100("relate2.js") ;
run100("relate3.js") ;
run100("relate4.js") ;
```

The run100() function is a simple loop to run a script 100 times. The start and end times are calculated the same way they were for the bench1 script. The writeTime2() function is a simplified version of the writeTime() function in the bench1.js script. For more information on the bench1.js script and writeTime(), refer to Day 10.

```
function run100(cScript)
{
  var start = new Date() ;
  for (var i = 0 ; i < 100 ; i++)
  {
     _sys.scripts.run(cScript) ;
  }
  writeTime2(cScript, start, new Date())
}
```

If I had to make a bet before running the test, I definitely would have placed the `sql` technique as faster than using `beforeGetValue`. Fortunately, no one took me up on the bet. The results are shown in Table 12.1. Even with all the overhead of the extra function call, using `beforeGetValue` was much faster than using `sql`. The fastest technique uses `masterFields` to create the join.

Table 12.1. The results from `bench2.txt`.

Script	Technique	Seconds
relate1.js	sql	29
relate2.js	masterFields	18
relate3.js	masterSource	79
relate4.js	beforeGetValue	22

The graph in Figure 12.4 shows a more visual representation of the results. Here again, you can see that `masterFields` is the best way to join dBASE tables in the Cart form.

Figure 12.4.

Graphing the second benchmark (shorter bars are faster).

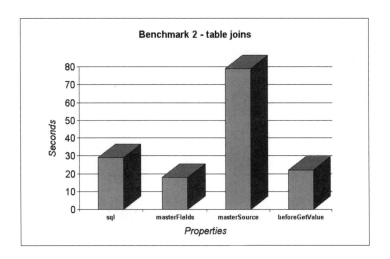

NOTE

The results shown in Table 12.1 and Figure 12.4 are not applicable to joins using ODBC or SQL-Link drivers. Although results vary from one database server to another, almost all will join tables fastest using the `sql` and `masterSource` properties.

The Visual Layout of the Cart Form

It is time to set up a framework for the Cart form by creating a layout with a few controls and two related queries. Here you will add the labels for the grid heading and a single row of the grid. Follow these steps:

1. Open the Cart form in the Form Designer. The current version is the stub form from Day 11.

2. This form needs a good deal of horizontal space. Set the width of the form to 75.

3. Drop the Title and Cart tables onto the form to create two query objects. Remove the full path from the sql property of both new queries.

4. From the Inspector drop-down list box, select parent.title1.rowset. You also can click on the rowset tool button when inspecting the title1 query to get to parent.title1.rowset.

5. Locate the masterRowset property and use the drop-down list box to select the cart1 query. After you set the masterRowset property, a drop-down list box becomes available for the masterFields property.

6. Use the drop-down list box to set the masterFields property to ISBN. As soon as you set the masterFields property, the indexName property changes to ISBN. (See Figure 12.5.)

Figure 12.5.

Relating queries with the Inspector.

7. Add five HTML controls for the grid column headings. Set the properties as listed in Table 12.2.

Table 12.2. The HTML field label controls.

Name	Text	Height	Left	Top	Width
labelISBN	<H4>ISBN</H4>	1	1	3.5	15
labelQty	<H4>Qty</H4>	1	17	3.5	5
labelTitle	<H4>Title</H4>	1	23	3.5	27
labelPrice	<H4>Price</H4>	1	51	3.5	9
labelTotal	<H4>Total</H4>	1	61	3.5	9

8. Add four more HTML controls that you will use to display values from the table. The QTY field is not included in this group. You can leave default values for the text properties. Use the values in Table 12.3 as a guide.

Table 12.3. The HTML field values controls.

Name	Height	Left	Top	Width
valueISBN	2	1	4.5	15
valueTitle	2	23	4.5	27
valuePrice	2	51	4.5	9
valueTotal	2	61	4.5	9

9. Add a Text control for the Qty field. Name the field textQty and position it at left 17, top 4.5, and width 4.

10. Set the template property to 999. You can enter a template directly or use the Template Property Builder as shown in Figure 12.6.

Figure 12.6.

Using a template for the textQty control.

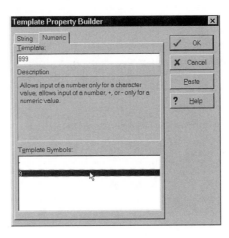

12

This is a good time to save the form and see how things are lining up for the browsers. The next group of controls have positions relative to the grid. If the grid does not look appropriate when viewed through a browser, the rest of the controls will also need adjustment. Figure 12.7 shows the Cart form in Netscape Navigator.

Figure 12.7.

Viewing an empty Cart form grid with Navigator.

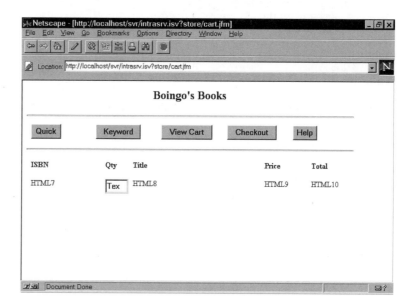

The values that appear in the first row are default control names such as HTML7 and Text1. These values vary depending on the order in which you placed and renamed each control. You will soon add code to overwrite each default value with a field value. At this point, there is no need to make any modifications to the value or text properties directly through the Form Designer.

The next step in the form's evolution is to add the methods required to show the row data. There are also a few more controls to drop on the form. Follow these steps to add some help text, an update button, a reset button, and some JavaScript:

1. Reopen the Cart form in the Form Designer. Remember to shut down all IntraBuilder Agents before returning to the design session.

2. Drop on another HTML control with the following properties: height 2, left 1, top 11, width 70.

3. Change the name to htmlHelp.

4. Open the Text Property Builder for htmlHelp and enter the following:
   ```
   To change the quantity, change the number in the Qty text box next for
   the book. To cancel a particular book, type a "0" in the text box.
   ```

5. Add a new button with the following position properties: left 1, top 13, width 12.

6. Change the button name to buttonUpdate and change the text to Update.

7. Add a Reset button next to the Update button. The Reset button has a switch icon on the Component Palette, but it looks like a regular button when dropped on the form. Use the following position properties: left 15, top 13, width 12. You can leave the Reset name and text properties as they are.

8. Add two more HTML controls for the Grand Total value. Use the property values shown in Table 12.4.

Table 12.4. The HTML Grand Total controls.

Name	Text	Height	Left	Top	Width
labelGrand	Grand Total	1	40	13	20
valueGrand	(default)	1	61	13	9

9. Right align the values within the following controls: labelPrice, labelTotal, valuePrice, valueTotal, and valueGrand. Aligning values within a control is not the same as aligning the control itself. To align values, set the alignment property. Use the value 2 to right-align.

At this point, the Cart form should resemble the one in Figure 12.8. That about does it for any visual design work for this form. The remainder of the Cart form development is centered on JavaScript methods.

Figure 12.8.

Using the Form Designer to lay out the Cart form.

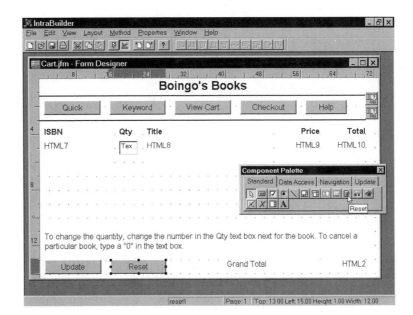

12

10. Create a code block for the form's `onServerLoad` event. Enter the following into the Inspector without creating a linked method:

```
{; class::ShowBooks(this)}
```

11. Before saving the form, add the following unlinked method. From the menu, select Methods|New Method. Remove the `{Export}` comment, rename the method to `ShowBooks`, and enter the JavaScript function shown in Listing 12.6.

INPUT

Listing 12.6. The single row version of the `ShowBooks()` method.

```
 1: function ShowBooks(thisForm)
 2: {
 3:    var titleRow = thisForm.title1.rowset,
 4:        cartRow = thisForm.cart1.rowset ;
 5:    with (thisForm)
 6:    {
 7:       valueISBN.text = titleRow.fields["ISBN"].value ;
 8:       textQty.value  = cartRow.fields["QTY"].value ;
 9:       valueTitle.text = titleRow.fields["TITLE"].value ;
10:       valuePrice.text = titleRow.fields["PRICE"].value ;
11:    }
12: }
```

ANALYSIS The `ShowBooks()` method contains three shorthand property references. Lines 3 and 4 create two temporary references for the query rowsets. Whenever a method references the same rowset more than three times, it is a good idea to make a shorthand reference. This can substantially reduce the length of assignment statements, making the script easier to read. If you do create shorthand references, be sure to include some indication of what type of class you are pointing to in the shorthand name. In this function, each shorthand reference ends with `Row` to indicate rowset. You could also begin each rowset reference with the letter `r`.

```
var titleRow = thisForm.title1.rowset,
    cartRow = thisForm.cart1.rowset ;
```

The third shortcut is through the `with` block on lines 5 through 11. The block assigns values to each grid control that relates directly to a field value. The three HTML controls derive values from the Title table. The Text control works with the `QTY` field in the Cart table.

Notice that the HTML and Text controls use different properties to determine what characters appear in the browser. With an HTML control, the critical property is `text`. HTML controls do not have a `dataLink` property. Controls that have a `dataLink` property also have a value property that you can use to set the display value. Text controls have the dataLink and value properties.

```
with (thisForm)
{
   valueISBN.text = titleRow.fields["ISBN"].value ;
   textQty.value  = cartRow.fields["QTY"].value ;
   valueTitle.text = titleRow.fields["TITLE"].value ;
   valuePrice.text = titleRow.fields["PRICE"].value ;
}
```

In this application, there always is a matching ISBN in both tables. The masterRowset relation forces the ISBN to be the same for both queries. Line 7 could also be written like this:

```
valueISBN.text = cartRow.fields["ISBN"].value ;
```

If you now run the application, the Cart form always displays the book contained in the first row of the Cart table. The Reset button already works. If you change the QTY field and click the Reset button, the value reverts back to the original QTY value. Figure 12.9 shows the first row of values through Internet Explorer.

Figure 12.9.

The Cart form showing values for the first row of the Cart table.

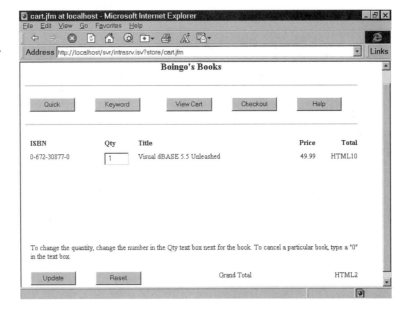

Calculating Totals

The Cart form currently displays default text values for the total and grand total values. The formula for the total is price multiplied by quantity. The grand total is the sum of all grid totals. With a single row grid the total is always equal to the grand total.

Two events require a calculation of both totals. The first calculation event is the onServerLoad. Currently, onServerLoad calls ShowBooks(). All calculation code belongs in the ShowBooks() method. The second calculation event is the Update button's onServerClick. If a shopper modifies a quantity, the totals need to reflect the change. This event can also call ShowBooks(), but first it must update the Cart table with the new QTY value.

The current version of the form has no direct links between methods and events. The only non-null event is for the form's onServerLoad. The completed form has two linked methods: Form_onServerLoad and buttonUpdate_onServerClick. You need to create both to create working totals. Although it is not really a visual task, creating linked events is easier in the Form Designer than in the Script Editor. Use the following steps to set a title and add three methods to the Cart form:

1. Open the Cart form in the Form Designer.
2. Change the form title to Boingo's Books - Shopping Cart.
3. Use the tool button to overwrite the form's onServerLoad code block with a new method. Enter the method as shown:

```
function Form_onServerLoad()
{
    this.buttonCart.visible = false ;
    class::ShowBooks(this) ;
}
```

4. Select the Update button and create the following new method for the onServerClick event:

```
function buttonUpdate_onServerClick()
{
    var cartRow = this.form.cart1.rowset ;
    cartRow.fields["QTY"].value = form.textQty.value ;
    cartRow.save() ;
    class::ShowBooks(this.form) ;
}
```

This method provides the write side of the datalink simulation. Notice that it is not enough to update the value. The rowset must be committed with Rowset::save().

After saving the new value, new totals can be calculated in the ShowBooks() method.

5. Open ShowBooks() from the Method Editor. Modify the method as shown in Listing 12.7. Save and run the form when you're done.

INPUT

Listing 12.7. ShowBooks() **with totaling statements shown in bold.**

```
 1: function ShowBooks(thisForm)
 2:   {
 3:   var titleRow = thisForm.title1.rowset,
 4:       cartRow = thisForm.cart1.rowset,
 5:       nTotal  = 0,
 6:       nGrand  = 0 ;
 7:   with (thisForm)
 8:   {
 9:       nTotal = cartRow.fields["QTY"].value *
10:           titleRow.fields["PRICE"].value ;
11:       nGrand += nTotal ;
12:       valueISBN.text = titleRow.fields["ISBN"].value ;
13:       textQty.value  = cartRow.fields["QTY"].value ;
14:       valueTitle.text = titleRow.fields["TITLE"].value ;
15:       valuePrice.text = titleRow.fields["PRICE"].value ;
16:       valueTotal.text = nTotal ;
17:   }
18:   thisForm.valueGrand.text = nGrand ;
19: }
```

ANALYSIS The ShowBooks() method now updates the total and grand total HTML controls. Line 11 sums the grand total using the += operator. In the method's current state, the = operator would work just as well. The += is typically used to sum values within a loop.

In the next incarnation of the Cart form, the entire with block will be in a loop. Line 18 could also be in the current with block. However, the grand total value is not part of the grid and must be summed outside the loop. To make it easier to add the grid loop, the grand total value is already outside the with block.

If you run the form now, you can modify the quantity and watch the totals update. Figure 12.10 shows the Cart form after updating the quantity to five. Your form should now match the Day 12 cart1.jfm file on the CD-ROM.

12

Figure 12.10.

The Cart form with working totals.

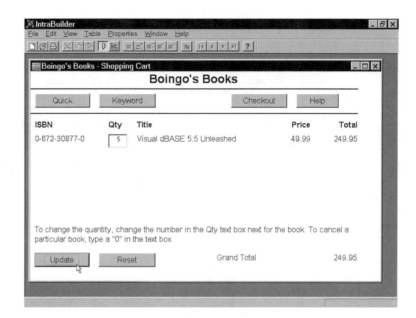

Making a Data-Driven Grid

The key to creating a data-driven grid is to use array elements as the control references. Arrays make it easy to modify sets of controls based on ever-changing data. Unfortunately, there is no visual way to do this through the Form Designer. The first row of grid controls, which you created this morning, must now be removed from the constructor. But don't open the Form Designer and start hitting the Delete key just yet. You can reuse the generated code inside your own method. With a few tweaks here and there, you can turn each control into an array of controls.

NEW TERM *Data-driven* describes highly flexible components and forms that adjust to best fit table values at runtime. A simple component such as a Text control with a dataLink property set to a field has minimal data-driven functionality. A grid that expands or contracts to match the current number of rows in a predefined table is moderately data-driven. A highly data-driven grid might generate columns to match any given table.

Before you start on the coding, reduce the number of rows in the Cart table to three. If you have less, it will be hard to tell if the grid is working. Any more than three, and you might need to scroll down to use the buttons.

Constructing the Grid

To make the modifications in this section, open the Cart form in the Script Editor. The File Open dialog that opens from the menu bar does not have an option to open a form in the Script Editor. However, such an option is available from a shortcut menu in the IntraBuilder Explorer. Another way to open the Cart form in the Script Editor is by entering the following in the Script Pad:

```
_sys.scripts.design("cart.jfm") ;
```

Create a new MakeGrid() method. To create a method in the Script Editor, press Ctrl+PgDn to move to the bottom of the script. Look for the closing bracket of the class definition. If you add function definitions below the bracket, they are not methods. Typically, methods also are indented three spaces; however, functions are not. Add the MakeGrid() method right above the closing bracket, as shown in bold in the following code. The notAMethod() function is shown for illustrative purposes only and is not required by the form.

```
   function buttonUpdate_onServerClick()
   {
    var cartRow = this.form.cart1.rowset ;
    cartRow.fields["QTY"].value = form.textQty.value ;
    cartRow.save() ;
    class::ShowBooks(this.form) ;
   }
   function MakeGrid()
   {
   }
}
function notAMethod()
{
   alert("Hi, I'm just a regular function") ;
}
```

The next step is to cut the grid control definitions from the constructor and paste them into the MakeGrid() method. If you scroll back toward the top of the script, you will find the definitions for each of the grid row controls. The following segment is the definition for the valueISBN control:

```
with (this.valueISBN = new HTML(this)){
   height = 2;
   left = 1;
   top = 4.5;
   width = 15;
   color = "black";
   text = "HTML7";
}
```

Move the definition code for valueISBN, textQty, valueTitle, valuePrice, and valueTotal into the MakeGrid() method. If you are lucky, all the definitions will be consecutive, and you can use a single cut and paste.

12

After they are all moved, you can tidy up the MakeGrid() method by indenting each control definition three spaces and removing unnecessary property assignments. Because black is the default HTML color, you can remove it from each HTML control with block. The text property of each HTML control is redundant, as is the value property for the Text control. The following rendition of the MakeGrid() method contains only the required property settings.

```
function MakeGrid()
{
   with (this.valueISBN = new HTML(this)){
      height = 2;
      left = 1;
      top = 4.5;
      width = 15;
   }

   with (this.textQty = new Text(this)){
      left = 17;
      top = 4.5;
      width = 4;
      template = "999";
   }

   with (this.valueTitle = new HTML(this)){
      height = 2;
      left = 23;
      top = 4.5;
      width = 27;
   }


   with (this.valuePrice = new HTML(this)){
      height = 2;
      left = 51;
      top = 4.5;
      width = 9;
      alignHorizontal = 2;
   }

   with (this.valueTotal = new HTML(this)){
      height = 2;
      left = 61;
      top = 4.5;
      width = 9;
      alignHorizontal = 2;
   }
}
```

If you run the form at this point, you get an error. The runtime error occurs when ShowBooks() tries to assign a value to one of the controls you just ripped out of the constructor. To remedy the situation, the new MakeGrid() method needs to run before ShowBooks().

From within the Script Editor, locate the `Form_onServerLoad()` method and add the `class::MakeGrid()` call, as shown in this segment:

```
function Form_onServerLoad()
{
  this.buttonCart.visible = false ;
  class::MakeGrid() ;
  class::ShowBooks(this) ;
}
```

Now the form will run as it did before. Try running it through the Designer to shake out any bugs that might have crept in so far. One common mistake is to accidentally use Copy instead of Cut when moving the controls. If you copy the lines, no runtime error occurs. The form simply creates an extra control that is released as soon as you make another control with the same name. It is not a critical error, but it does eat some extra resources and processing time.

After you have the form running as before, it is time to transform the value control references into arrays. From the Script Editor, you can complete the `MakeGrid()` method as shown in Listing 12.8.

INPUT **Listing 12.8. The complete `MakeGrid()` method.**

```
 1: function MakeGrid()
 2: {
 3:     var nCount = this.cart1.rowset.count() ;
 4:     this.valueISBN  = new Array(nCount) ;
 5:     this.textQty    = new Array(nCount) ;
 6:     this.valueTitle = new Array(nCount) ;
 7:     this.valuePrice = new Array(nCount) ;
 8:     this.valueTotal = new Array(nCount) ;
 9:
10:     for ( var i = 0 ; i < nCount ; i++ ) {
11:         with (this.valueISBN[i] = new HTML(this)){
12:             height = 2;
13              left = 1;
14:             top = 4.5 + ( i * 2 );
15:             width = 15;
16:         }
17:
18:         with (this.textQty[i] = new Text(this)){
19:             left = 17;
20:             top = 4.5 + ( i * 2 );
21:             width = 4;
22:             template = "999";
23:         }
24:
25:         with (this.valueTitle[i] = new HTML(this)){
26:             height = 2;
```

continues

12

Listing 12.8. continued

```
27:             left = 23;
28:             top = 4.5 + ( i * 2 );
29:             width = 27;
30:         }
31:
32:         with (this.valuePrice[i] = new HTML(this)){
33:             height = 2;
34:             left = 51;
35:             top = 4.5 + ( i * 2 );
36:             width = 9;
37:             alignHorizontal = 2;
38:         }
39:
40:         with (this.valueTotal[i] = new HTML(this)){
41:             height = 2;
42:             left = 61;
43:             top = 4.5 + ( i * 2 );
44:             width = 9;
45:             alignHorizontal = 2;
46:         }
47:     }
48: }
```

ANALYSIS The complete MakeGrid() method creates a new set of controls for each row in the Cart query. The only difference between one set of controls and the next is the value of the top property. No field values are assigned in MakeGrid().

Line 3 gets a count of the rows available to the Cart query. You can use the filter property to reduce the count. Lines 4 through 8 use the count to determine the array size for five new arrays. The array reference names match the names previously used for the grid controls.

```
var nCount = this.cart1.rowset.count() ;
this.valueISBN  = new Array(nCount) ;
this.textQty    = new Array(nCount) ;
this.valueTitle = new Array(nCount) ;
this.valuePrice = new Array(nCount) ;
this.valueTotal = new Array(nCount) ;
```

A for loop encloses the control definitions. Adding the array index after the control name allows the same reference name to work with a set of controls. Previously, this.valueISBN was the one and only ISBN value control. Now this.valueISBN is an array of controls, where this.valueISBN[1] is one of several ISBN value controls.

The top property also is relative to the value of i. Each set of controls appears slightly below the previous row. The first set is at 4.5, the second is at 6.5, and so on.

```
for ( var i = 0 ; i < nCount ; i++ ) {
   with (this.valueISBN[i] = new HTML(this)){
      height = 2;
```

```
    left = 1;
    top = 4.5 + ( i * 2 );
    width = 15;
  }
```

You can run the form to see how the grid displays. Because the ShowBooks() method is not in synch with the control arrays, the rows display default values in place of values from the queries. Figure 12.11 shows how the form looks when run in the Designer with three rows in the Cart table.

Figure 12.11.

The first visible signs of the grid.

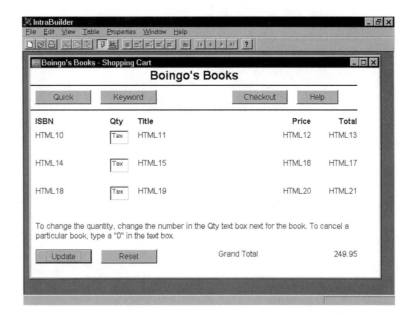

Check your running form against Figure 12.11 to verify that the MakeGrid() method is working correctly. If you have more than three rows in the table, the grid might overlap the help text, the update button, and the reset button.

Filling the Grid

The process of filling the grid is similar to creating it. In the MakeGrid() method, a for loop cycles through the control set once per row in the Cart table. ShowBooks() needs a similar while loop to assign field values. Reopen the Cart form in the Script Editor and locate the ShowBooks() method. Rewrite the method as shown in Listing 12.9.

INPUT **Listing 12.9. The complete** `ShowBooks()` **method.**

```
 1: function ShowBooks(thisForm)
 2: {
 3:    var titleRow = thisForm.title1.rowset,
 4:        cartRow = thisForm.cart1.rowset,
 5:        nTotal  = 0,
 6:        nGrand  = 0,
 7:        i       = 0 ;
 8:
 9:    cartRow.first() ;
10:    while ( ! cartRow.endOfSet ) {
11:        with (thisForm) {
12:            nTotal = cartRow.fields["QTY"].value *
13:                titleRow.fields["PRICE"].value ;
14:            nGrand += nTotal ;
15:            valueISBN[i].text = titleRow.fields["ISBN"].value ;
16:            textQty[i].value  = cartRow.fields["QTY"].value ;
17:            valueTitle[i].text = titleRow.fields["TITLE"].value ;
18:            valuePrice[i].text = titleRow.fields["PRICE"].value ;
19:            valueTotal[i].text = nTotal ;
20:        }
21:        i++
22:        cartRow.next() ;
23:    }
24:
25:    thisForm.valueGrand.text = nGrand ;
26:    thisForm.htmlHelp.top     = 4.5 + ( i * 2 ) ;
27:    thisForm.buttonUpdate.top = 7   + ( i * 2 ) ;
28:    thisForm.reset1.top       = 7   + ( i * 2 ) ;
29:    thisForm.labelGrand.top   = 7   + ( i * 2 ) ;
30:    thisForm.valueGrand.top   = 7   + ( i * 2 ) ;
31: }
```

ANALYSIS The revised `ShowBooks()` method is in synch with the control arrays. The major changes include the `while` loop on line 10 and control repositioning code on lines 26 through 30. Another change is on line 7, which creates a variable for the array index. `MakeGrid()` created and incremented the array index as part of the `for` loop. Because a `while` loop does not include incrementing as part of its structure, `ShowBooks()` must create and increment the index array apart from the loop.

```
var titleRow = thisForm.title1.rowset,
    cartRow = thisForm.cart1.rowset,
    nTotal  = 0,
    nGrand  = 0,
    i       = 0 ;
```

Line 9 calls `Rowset::first()` to reset the row pointer at the first row in the current view. By moving to the first row and then looping until `endOfSet`, the `while` loop is guaranteed to hit every available row. When `ShowBooks()` is called from the `onServerLoad` event, the row pointer is already at the first row. In that case, the call is unnecessary. It becomes important when the method is called from the Update button. After ShowBooks() runs once, the pointer is left at endOfSet. If you leave out the call to Rowset::first(), calling ShowBooks() a second time causes the while loop never to execute.

```
cartRow.first() ;
while ( ! cartRow.endOfSet ) {
```

The only change inside the with block is the addition of the array index after the control name. The logic to calculate totals is the same as before.

```
valueTotal[i].text = nTotal ;
```

Lines 26 through 30 reposition the help text, Update button, Reset button, grand total label, and grand total value. Each of these controls has a position under the grid. As the grid expands, it pushes these controls down. In the following segment, i is equal to the number of rows in the grid.

```
thisForm.htmlHelp.top      = 4.5 + ( i * 2 ) ;
thisForm.buttonUpdate.top  = 7   + ( i * 2 ) ;
thisForm.reset1.top        = 7   + ( i * 2 ) ;
thisForm.labelGrand.top    = 7   + ( i * 2 ) ;
thisForm.valueGrand.top    = 7   + ( i * 2 ) ;
```

With the completed ShowBooks() method, you can view data from more than one row at a time. Figure 12.12 shows the Cart form running in the Designer. The form would be complete if it were not for that Update button. The update stopped working when the grid went from simple controls to arrays of controls. You will correct that in the third and final part of the Cart form trilogy. The form should now match the Day 12 cart2.jfm file on CD-ROM.

Figure 12.12.

Viewing data for three books at once.

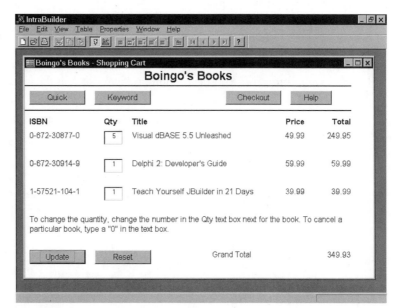

Adding Dynamic Updates

To handle dynamic updates, the Cart form needs to get a lot smarter about how it displays the grid. Right now it works great to display a fixed set of rows. However, dynamic updates require the grid to handle changes to the number of rows. The Cart form does not allow for new rows, but it does let the shopper remove an item by entering zero in the quantity field. When the shopper hits the Update button, any rows with a zero quantity should disappear from the grid.

If shoppers can delete a single row, they can delete all the rows. The Cart form has to handle having the grid go to zero rows. Remember that with the Quick form, this situation is handled with a Message form. If a query comes up empty, the Results form calls the Message form instead of the Results form. This is pretty easy, but it only works when the shopper is already moving to another form. The Update button on the Cart form is a self-contained process. Shoppers do not expect to move to a new form when they click the Update button. After the problem of an empty cart is solved, the update operation becomes a snap.

Dealing with an Empty Cart

Currently, the Update button and the Form_onServerLoad() method call on ShowBooks() to display the grid values. This works great when you know there are books to show. It does nothing if there are no rows left in the query. Because ShowBooks() is so good at what it does, you can keep it just the way it is. Instead of changing ShowBooks(), create three new methods that isolate ShowBooks() from the empty cart scenario. In this section, you will create the following three new methods:

- ☐ BlankGrid(): This first method goes through the grid and sets the visible properties to false for rows that no longer exist in the table.

- ☐ HideBooks(): The second method is a little more thorough than BlankGrid(). It sets visible properties to false for non-grid items such as the Update and Reset buttons.

- ☐ PaintForm(): This is the method to call from Form_onServerLoad() and the Update button. It figures out whether or not there are rows and calls either ShowBooks() or HideBooks(). In either case, it calls the BlankGrid() method to blank out any unnecessary rows.

It is time to open up the Cart form in the Script Editor and start coding away. Move to the bottom of the class definition and add the BlankGrid(), HideBooks(), and PaintForm() methods. Place them all before the closing bracket for the form class. Use Listings 12.10, 12.11, and 12.12 as your guides.

TIP After adding each function, select Script|Compile to check for syntax errors. If an error is found, note the line number from the Compile dialog and cancel the compile. Do not select Fix if you already have the Script Editor open. Selecting Fix opens another window with the same file. Things can get confusing when you have multiple copies of the script open.

INPUT **Listing 12.10. The complete `BlankGrid()` method.**

```
1: function BlankGrid(thisForm)
2: {
3:    for ( var i = thisForm.cart1.rowset.count() ;
4:        i < thisForm.valueISBN.length ;
5:        i++ ) {
6:        thisForm.valueISBN[i].visible  = false ;
7:        thisForm.textQty[i].visible    = false ;
8:        thisForm.valueTitle[i].visible = false ;
9:        thisForm.valuePrice[i].visible = false ;
10:       thisForm.valueTotal[i].visible = false ;
11:    }
12: }
```

ANALYSIS This method determines what rows to blank out in the `for` statement. All the arrays are the same length. The length of any array equals the number of rows existing in the view at the time the form opens. The `for` loop executes only if the current row count is less than the original count. Line 3 sets the initial array index to the current row count. Because arrays are zero-based and rows are not, the row count is one beyond the highest array index needed to contain all rows.

```
for ( var i = thisForm.cart1.rowset.count() ;
   i < thisForm.valueISBN.length ;
   i++ ) {
```

If the form opens with five rows, the length of the array is 5 and the valid array index values are from 0 to 4. If the user deletes two rows, the row count becomes 3 and the number of elements in the array stays at 5. With only three rows, the controls referenced by the array indexes of 3 and 4 need to be blanked. With literal values, the `for` statement becomes the following:

```
for ( var i = 3 ; i < 5 ; i++ ) {
```

After a control is invisible, it never returns to the visible grid. Because this routine is repeatedly called, the same controls will have their respective `visible` properties set to `false`. There is no harm done in hiding a control that is already hidden.

INPUT **Listing 12.11. The complete** `HideBooks()` **method.**

```
 1: function HideBooks(thisForm)
 2: {
 3:     with (thisForm) {
 4:         labelISBN.width = 50 ;
 5:         labelISBN.text = "<H3>Your shopping cart is empty.</H3>" ;
 6:         labelQty.visible     = false ;
 7:         labelTitle.visible   = false ;
 8:         labelPrice.visible   = false ;
 9:         labelTotal.visible   = false ;
10:         htmlHelp.visible     = false ;
11:         buttonUpdate.visible = false ;
12:         reset1.visible       = false ;
13:         labelGrand.visible   = false ;
14:         valueGrand.visible   = false ;
15:     }
16: }
```

ANALYSIS The `HideBooks()` method sets several `visible` properties to `false` and uses a `with` block to cut down on the required typing. The only interesting thing occurring here is that the ISBN column heading is transformed into a message line. Line 5 enhances the text with an HTML `<H3>` tag. This tag usually increases the font size by several point sizes.

After `HideBooks()` runs, the shopper can use only the Quick, Keyword, Checkout, and Help toolbar buttons to continue. This is one less choice than you have with the Message form.

WARNING Be very careful when spelling the `visible` property. More than one JavaScript programmer has wasted hours tracking down what turned out to be a misspelling. If you accidentally type the property as `visable`, you create a new property that does nothing.

INPUT **Listing 12.12. The complete** `PaintForm()` **method.**

```
 1: function PaintForm(thisForm)
 2: {
 3:     class::BlankGrid(thisForm) ;
 4:     thisForm.cart1.rowset.first() ;
 5:     if ( ! thisForm.cart1.rowset.endOfSet ) {
```

```
 6:          class::ShowBooks(thisForm) ;
 7:      }
 8:      else {
 9:          class::HideBooks(thisForm) ;
10:      }
11: }
```

ANALYSIS   The PaintForm() method is called from both the Form_onServerLoad (where the form reference is this) and the Update button's onServerClick, which has a this.form pointer to the form. The PaintForm() method uses a user-defined parameter, called thisForm, to reconcile the difference. The thisForm parameter is passed down to other methods.

Line 3 calls BlankGrid() to clear out any extra rows. It then checks to see whether the Cart query is empty. If so, line 9 calls HideBooks(), and the Cart form turns into a message form. If there are rows to show, line 6 calls ShowBooks() and the shopper is free to modify quantities and remove rows.

To try the three new functions, you will need to modify the Form_onServerLoad() method. Replace the call to ShowBooks() with a call to PaintForm(). If you run the Cart form with this change, the form appears exactly as it did before you did all this work.

```
function Form_onServerLoad()
{
  this.buttonCart.visible = false ;
  class::MakeGrid() ;
  class::PaintForm(this) ;
}
```

If you want to test the empty cart condition, add a filter assignment to Form_onServerLoad() or delete all the rows in the Cart table. To simulate an empty Cart table, add the filter before the call to MakeGrid(). Use a filter condition that does not match any rows in the current table. Figure 12.13 shows the Cart form with an empty rowset.

```
function Form_onServerLoad()
{
  this.buttonCart.visible = false ;
  this.cart1.rowset.filter = "CARTUSER = 'not likely'" ;
  class::MakeGrid() ;
  class::PaintForm(this) ;
}
```

12

Figure 12.13.

The Cart form after HideBooks() *has executed.*

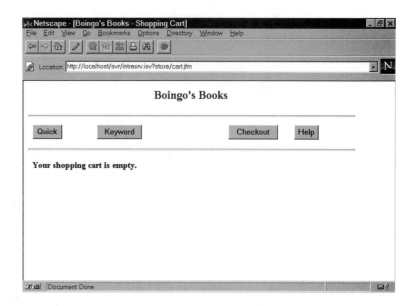

Synching Up Grid Values with Table Values

It is finally time to get back to the long-neglected Update button. In the first incarnation of the Cart form, the Update button could modify the quantity value for the first row in the Cart table. The method had a simple one-to-one relation between the controls and the first row of the table.

To complete the buttonUpdate_onServerClick() method, you need to make it work with any number of rows. Instead of updating the current row, the method must locate the appropriate rows while traversing an array of ISBN values.

The previous version also assumed that the quantity entered was valid. This time around, you will not give the benefit of the doubt to the shopper. Here are the four categories of values that a shopper can enter into the quantity field:

- [ ] 0: A valid value that triggers the deletion of a row.
- [ ] From 1 to 999: Valid values that can update a row.
- [ ] Below 0 or above 999: These numeric values are outside the acceptable range. When they are encountered, the previous valid value is restored.
- [ ] Alphabetic characters: Treat anything that is not a number as zero.

That's all there is for the design specifications of the Update button. To proceed, open the Cart form in the Script Editor and modify buttonUpdate_onServerClick(), as shown in Listing 12.13.

12

INPUT

Listing 12.13. The complete `buttonUpdate_onServerClick()` method.

```
 1: function buttonUpdate_onServerClick()
 2: {
 3:    var cartRow  = this.form.cart1.rowset ;
 4:    var nCount   = cartRow.count(),
 5:        nTrueQty = 0 ;
 6:
 7:    for ( var i = 0 ; i < nCount ; i++ ) {
 8:        this.form.textQty[i].template = null ;
 9:        nTrueQty = this.form.textQty[i].value ;
10:        this.form.textQty[i].template = "999" ;
11:        cartRow.applyLocate("ISBN='" + this.form.valueISBN[i].text + "'") ;
12:
13:        if ( ! cartRow.endOfSet ) {
14:            if ( nTrueQty == 0 ) {
15:                cartRow.delete() ;
16:            }
17:            else if ( ( nTrueQty > 999 ) ||
18:                      ( nTrueQty < 0  ) ) {
19:                // do nothing & the value will be restored in ShowBooks()
20:            }
21:            else {
22:                if ( ! ( cartRow.fields["QTY"].value == nTrueQty ) ) {
23:                    cartRow.fields["QTY"].value = nTrueQty ;
24:                    cartRow.save() ;
25:                }
26:            }
27:        }
28:
29:    }
30:
31:    class::PaintForm(this.form) ;
32: }
```

ANALYSIS Lines 3 and 4 start the method by making a shortcut reference to the Cart query rowset and by figuring out how many rows are visible in the grid. It does this by using two var statements. The statements are separated so that the second var statement can make use of the shortcut reference created in the first.

```
var cartRow = this.form.cart1.rowset ;
var nCount  = cartRow.count(),
   nTrueQty = 0 ;
```

The for loop creates an index into all visible grid controls. Line 7 uses the row count to determine when to exit the loop. If you replace nCount with an array length such as this.form.valueISBN.length, the loop processes invisible controls and updates the Cart table with improper values.

```
for ( var i = 0 ; i < nCount ; i++ ) {
```

12

Lines 8 through 10 extract the true value from the current text quantity. When a text control uses a template, only values that conform to the template are accessible through the `value` property. The `textQty` controls have a template of `999`, making the retrievable range `-99` to `999`. Any other number evaluates to zero.

The text object internally stores true values that are outside the template range. You can retrieve the true value by temporarily removing the template. Extracting the true value is essential if you want to treat invalid values differently from zero values. In this application, zero values cause a row deletion. It would be unfortunate to delete a row when the quantity field is out of the valid range.

```
this.form.textQty[i].template = null ;
nTrueQty = this.form.textQty[i].value ;
this.form.textQty[i].template = "999" ;
```

After establishing the `nTrueQty` value, the method looks for the row belonging to the current ISBN. Because this is the only routine that can delete a row, the ISBN should always be found. If, through some unforeseen circumstance, the row is not found, no further update processing takes place.

```
cartRow.applyLocate("ISBN='" + this.form.valueISBN[i].text + "'" ) ;
if ( ! cartRow.endOfSet ) {
```

Line 14 checks to see whether the shopper entered a zero. If so, the associated row is immediately deleted. The `Rowset::save()` method is not required to commit a deletion. `Rowset::delete()` removes the row from the current query rowset and the associated table. You cannot recall the row through IntraBuilder.

```
if ( nTrueQty == 0 ) {
    cartRow.delete() ;
}
```

NOTE	Unlike out-of-range numbers, a character string is not stored aside from the template. If the shopper enters FIVE into a quantity field, the value becomes 0. This can be prevented through client-side JavaScript.

When a shopper enters a quantity that is outside the valid range, you don't need to do anything. This is one of those problems that can take care of itself. All the grid values are overwritten by the `ShowBooks()` method. If you do not store any new values to the table, the previous values reappear. Line 31 calls `PaintForm()`, which in turn calls `ShowBooks()` when no updates take place.

```
else if ( ( nTrueQty > 999 ) ||
          ( nTrueQty < 0  ) ) {
    // do nothing & the value will be restored in ShowBooks()
}
```

TIP

Always include a comment for empty control blocks. For the most part, JavaScript is easy to read and requires little in the way of internal comments. However, it is a good idea to comment code that appears to be incomplete or in error. If you were reviewing a script with an empty `if` block, you might think the script was wrong and accidentally remove the empty block. Adding a comment makes the code appear more deliberate.

The update process is optimized by altering only rows where the shopper has modified the quantity. If a shopper clicks the Update button without making any changes to a quantity, the quantity is fine as it is. If the control value is not equal to the field value, the method assigns the new value to the field and commits the change by calling `Rowset::save()` on line 24.

```
else {
    if ( ! ( cartRow.fields["QTY"].value == nTrueQty ) ) {
        cartRow.fields["QTY"].value = nTrueQty ;
        cartRow.save() ;
    }
}
```

After performing any necessary updates, line 31 calls `PaintForm()`. Any changes to the row count and values are already committed by the time `PaintForm()` starts. `PaintForm()` and its related methods rework the grid to reflect any changes to the table.

```
class::PaintForm(this.form) ;
```

With the completed `buttonUpdate_onServerClick()`, you can test the dynamic updates through the Designer. Try changing some new quantity values, entering some invalid values, and deleting some rows.

12

If everything is working as expected, you can finally integrate the Cart form into the rest of the application. Up to this point, the Cart form has run from the Help form and ignored the user key value. It also has run directly from the IntraBuilder Explorer. Having the form independent makes development and debugging much easier. You can add one line into `Form_onServerLoad()` to finish the job. Add the following filter assignment as shown on line 164 of Listing 12.14:

```
this.cart1.rowset.filter = "CARTUSER = " + "'" + form.user + "'" ;
```

After you add this line, the cart will be empty each time you start the application from the Help form. As you add books, the cart fills up. Shoppers are in control of their own cart. Figure 12.14 shows the completed form after adding a few books and changing some quantities.

Figure 12.14.

Running the completed Cart form through Navigator.

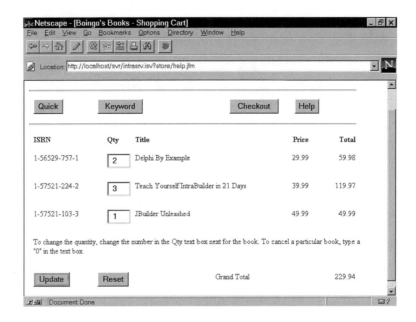

If things are not going as expected, review Listing 12.14, which shows the complete JavaScript source code for the Cart form. There is no analysis given here because every method has already been analyzed. This listing provides an overview, so that you can see how all the pieces fit together. The exact order of methods and controls is unimportant. The Day 12 cart3.jfm CD-ROM file is a copy of the Cart form in Listing 12.14.

Listing 12.14. Cart.jfm—**The final incarnation of the Cart form.**

```
 1: // {End Header} Do not remove this comment//
 2: // Generated on 01/02/97
 3: //
 4: var f = new cartForm();
 5: f.open();
 6: class cartForm extends ToolbarCForm from "TOOLBAR.JCF" {
 7:    with (this) {
 8:       onServerLoad = class::Form_onServerLoad;
 9:       height = 15;
10:       left = 0;
11:       top = 0;
12:       width = 75;
13:       title = "Boingo's Books - Shopping Cart";
14:    }
15:
16:    with (this.cart1 = new Query()){
17:       left = 70;
```

12

```
18:        top = 1;
19:        sql = 'SELECT * FROM "cart.DBF"';
20:        active = true;
21:    }
22:
23:    with (this.cart1.rowset) {
24:    }
25:
26:    with (this.title1 = new Query()){
27:        left = 70;
28:        top = 2;
29:        sql = 'SELECT * FROM "title.DBF"';
30:        active = true;
31:    }
32:
33:    with (this.title1.rowset) {
34:        indexName = "ISBN";
35:        masterRowset = parent.parent.cart1.rowset;
36:        masterFields = "ISBN";
37:    }
38:
39:    with (this.labelISBN = new HTML(this)){
40:        height = 1;
41:        left = 1;
42:        top = 3.5;
43:        width = 15;
44:        color = "black";
45:        text = "<H4>ISBN</H4>";
46:    }
47:
48:    with (this.labelQty = new HTML(this)){
49:        height = 1;
50:        left = 17;
51:        top = 3.5;
52:        width = 5;
53:        color = "black";
54:        text = "<H4>Qty</H4>";
55:    }
56:
57:    with (this.labelTitle = new HTML(this)){
58:        height = 1;
59:        left = 23;
60:        top = 3.5;
61:        width = 27;
62:        color = "black";
63:        text = "<H4>Title</H4>";
64:    }
65:
66:    with (this.labelPrice = new HTML(this)){
67:        height = 1;
68:        left = 51;
69:        top = 3.5;
70:        width = 9;
71:        color = "black";
72:        alignHorizontal = 2;
```

12

continues

Listing 12.14. continued

```
 73:        text = "<H4>Price</H4>";
 74:    }
 75:
 76:    with (this.labelTotal = new HTML(this)){
 77:        height = 1;
 78:        left = 61;
 79:        top = 3.5;
 80:        width = 9;
 81:        color = "black";
 82:        alignHorizontal = 2;
 83:        text = "<H4>Total</H4>";
 84:    }
 85:
 86:    with (this.htmlHelp = new HTML(this)){
 87:        height = 2;
 88:        left = 1;
 89:        top = 11;
 90:        width = 70;
 91:        color = "black";
 92:        text = 'To change the quantity, change the number in the ' +
 93:               'Qty text box next for the book. To cancel a ' +
 94:               'particular book, type a "0" in the text box.';
 95:    }
 96:
 97:    with (this.buttonUpdate = new Button(this)){
 98:        onServerClick = class::buttonUpdate_onServerClick;
 99:        left = 1;
100:        top = 13;
101:        width = 12;
102:        text = "Update";
103:    }
104:
105:    with (this.reset1 = new Reset(this)){
106:        left = 15;
107:        top = 13;
108:        width = 12;
109:        text = "Reset";
110:    }
111:
112:    with (this.labelGrand = new HTML(this)){
113:        height = 1;
114:        left = 40;
115:        top = 13;
116:        width = 20;
117:        color = "black";
118:        text = "Grand Total";
119:    }
120:
121:    with (this.valueGrand = new HTML(this)){
122:        height = 1;
123:        left = 61;
124:        top = 13;
125:        width = 9;
126:        color = "black";
```

```
127:        alignHorizontal = 2;
128:        text = "HTML2";
129:    }
130:
131:    function ShowBooks(thisForm)
132:    {
133:       var titleRow = thisForm.title1.rowset,
134:           cartRow  = thisForm.cart1.rowset,
135:           nTotal   = 0,
136:           nGrand   = 0,
137:           i        = 0 ;
138:       cartRow.first() ;
139:       while ( ! cartRow.endOfSet ) {
140:          with (thisForm) {
141:             nTotal = cartRow.fields["QTY"].value *
142:                      titleRow.fields["PRICE"].value ;
143:             nGrand += nTotal ;
144:             valueISBN[i].text  = titleRow.fields["ISBN"].value ;
145:             textQty[i].value   = cartRow.fields["QTY"].value ;
146:             valueTitle[i].text = titleRow.fields["TITLE"].value ;
147:             valuePrice[i].text = titleRow.fields["PRICE"].value ;
148:             valueTotal[i].text = nTotal ;
149:          }
150:          i++
151:          cartRow.next() ;
152:       }
153:       thisForm.valueGrand.text = nGrand ;
154:       thisForm.htmlHelp.top     = 4.5 + ( i * 2 ) ;
155:       thisForm.buttonUpdate.top = 7   + ( i * 2 ) ;
156:       thisForm.reset1.top       = 7   + ( i * 2 ) ;
157:       thisForm.labelGrand.top   = 7   + ( i * 2 ) ;
158:       thisForm.valueGrand.top   = 7   + ( i * 2 ) ;
159:    }
160:
161:    function Form_onServerLoad()
162:    {
163:       this.buttonCart.visible = false ;
164:       this.cart1.rowset.filter = "CARTUSER = " + "'" + form.user + "'" ;
165:       class::MakeGrid() ;
166:       class::PaintForm(this) ;
167:    }
168:
169:    function buttonUpdate_onServerClick()
170:    {
171:       var cartRow = this.form.cart1.rowset ;
172:       var nCount   = cartRow.count(),
173:           nTrueQty = 0 ;
174:       for ( var i = 0 ; i < nCount ; i++ ) {
175:          this.form.textQty[i].template = null ;
176:          nTrueQty = this.form.textQty[i].value ;
177:          this.form.textQty[i].template = "999" ;
178:          cartRow.applyLocate("ISBN='"+this.form.valueISBN[i].text+"'");
179:          if ( ! cartRow.endOfSet ) {
180:             if ( nTrueQty == 0 ) {
```

continues

Listing 12.14. continued

```
181:              cartRow.delete() ;
182:            }
183:          else if ( ( nTrueQty > 999 ) ||
184:                    ( nTrueQty < 0  ) ) {
185:            // do nothing & the value will be restored in ShowBooks
186:          }
187:          else {
188:            if (! ( cartRow.fields["QTY"].value == nTrueQty )){
189:                cartRow.fields["QTY"].value = nTrueQty ;
190:                cartRow.save() ;
191:            }
192:          }
193:        }
194:      }
195:      class::PaintForm(this.form) ;
196:  }
197:
198:  function MakeGrid()
199:  {
200:      var nCount = this.cart1.rowset.count() ;
201:      this.valueISBN  = new Array(nCount) ;
202:      this.textQty    = new Array(nCount) ;
203:      this.valueTitle = new Array(nCount) ;
204:      this.valuePrice = new Array(nCount) ;
205:      this.valueTotal = new Array(nCount) ;
206:      for ( var i = 0 ; i < nCount ; i++ ) {
207:          with (this.valueISBN[i] = new HTML(this)){
208:              height = 2;
209:              left = 1;
210:              top = 4.5 + ( i * 2 );
211:              width = 15;
212:          }
213:          with (this.textQty[i] = new Text(this)){
214:              left = 17;
215:              top = 4.5 + ( i * 2 );
216:              width = 4;
217:              template = "999";
218:          }
219:          with (this.valueTitle[i] = new HTML(this)){
220:              height = 2;
221:              left = 23;
222:              top = 4.5 + ( i * 2 );
223:              width = 27;
224:          }
225:          with (this.valuePrice[i] = new HTML(this)){
226:              height = 2;
227:              left = 51;
228:              top = 4.5 + ( i * 2 ) ;
229:              width = 9;
230:              alignHorizontal = 2;
231:          }
```

```
232:              with (this.valueTotal[i] = new HTML(this)){
233:                 height = 2;
234:                 left = 61;
235:                 top = 4.5 + ( i * 2 );
236:                 width = 9;
237:                 alignHorizontal = 2;
238:              }
239:          }
240:       }
241:
242:       function BlankGrid(thisForm)
243:       {
244:          for ( var i = thisForm.cart1.rowset.count() ;
245:             i < thisForm.valueISBN.length ;
246:             i++ ) {
247:             thisForm.valueISBN[i].visible  = false ;
248:             thisForm.textQty[i].visible    = false ;
249:             thisForm.valueTitle[i].visible = false ;
250:             thisForm.valuePrice[i].visible = false ;
251:             thisForm.valueTotal[i].visible = false ;
252:          }
253:       }
254:
255:       function HideBooks(thisForm)
256:       {
257:          with (thisForm) {
258:             labelISBN.width = 50 ;
259:             labelISBN.text = "<H3>Your shopping cart is empty.</H3>" ;
260:             labelQty.visible       = false ;
261:             labelTitle.visible     = false ;
262:             labelPrice.visible     = false ;
263:             labelTotal.visible     = false ;
264:             htmlHelp.visible       = false ;
265:             buttonUpdate.visible   = false ;
266:             reset1.visible         = false ;
267:             labelGrand.visible     = false ;
268:             valueGrand.visible     = false ;
269:          }
270:       }
271:
272:       function PaintForm(thisForm)
273:       {
274:          class::BlankGrid(thisForm) ;
275:          thisForm.cart1.rowset.first() ;
276:          if ( ! thisForm.cart1.rowset.endOfSet ) {
277:             class::ShowBooks(thisForm) ;
278:          }
279:          else {
280:             class::HideBooks(thisForm) ;
281:          }
282:       }
283:
284: }
```

12

Summary

Today you learned what can and can't be done in the Form Designer. You also discovered how JavaScript can overcome limitations to the visual design approach. Throughout the day, three distinct versions of the Cart form came into being.

The first was oriented around visual development. You added all the controls through the Form Designer to create a single row of the grid and other supporting controls. The first form provided a simple update capability and a simulated datalink.

The second incarnation of the Cart form moved you from visual-centric development to a JavaScript orientation. You leveraged the day's earlier work and morphed the single row of fixed position controls into dynamically sized arrays of controls. This version showed off the grid but lost the simulated datalink.

By the end of the day, you had added live data updating into the grid. It's interesting to note that the update portion was the simple part, and dealing with the possibility of a shrinking or disappearing rowset was the tougher nut to crack.

Now the shopping cart application has six fully functional forms: Help, Quick, Results, Message, Detail, and Cart. Although this is pretty good progress, two of the five toolbar buttons still lead to errors, and there are only two days left before the week of advanced topics. You should get a good night's rest, so that you are ready for tomorrow's JavaScript adventure: the Keyword form.

Q&A

Q If I run the final version of the Cart form in the Designer, I can switch from Run mode to Design mode. When that happens, all the grid elements disappear. Why don't the grid controls show up in the Form Designer?

A Switching to Design mode is really more like closing the current running form and reopening the form in the Designer. This protects the constructor code from any modifications that occur through events. Saving a form forces a regeneration of the constructor code. The Cart form would not run correctly if the grid elements suddenly moved back to the constructor.

Q After I fixed some errors in the Cart form, IntraBuilder kept running an unfixed version of the code. I had to exit and restart IntraBuilder before it recognized my changes. How can I avoid this situation?

A If you are fixing errors by selecting the Fix button, IntraBuilder opens a new Script Editor. This can lead to multiple Script Editors with the same script. Closing the current Script Editor does not save any changes if others are still open. Closing

IntraBuilder forces all Script Editors to close. Avoid opening a script in more than one window, and you will avoid many instances of this problem.

Q The QTY field value looks funny because it's over toward the left of the text control. The HTML properties had an `alignment` property that made the price and total look nicer. Is there any way to right-align the quantity value within the Text control?

A Although the Text control does not have an `alignment` property, you can use the `template` property to provide similar functionality for numbers. Numbers are right-justified within the template. Increasing the width of the template moves the number toward the right of the Text control.

Q The Cart form had an array of controls working with a single instance of each query. This rendered the `dataLink` property useless. Could I also create an array of queries so that each row in the grid has a related set of queries with which to datalink?

A Yes, you can create arrays of queries just as you can create arrays of controls. The advantage of this technique is that all the datalinks are automatic. The drawback is that creating an array of queries is more resource intensive than creating an array of controls. Creating arrays of both could lead to resource strain.

Workshop

The Workshop section provides questions and exercises to help you get a better feel for the material you learned today. Try to answer the questions and at least think about the exercises before moving on to tomorrow's lesson. You'll find the answers to the questions in Appendix A, "Answers to Quiz Questions."

Quiz

1. What properties does the Form Designer always stream out for HTML controls, and which one of them can you safely remove from the constructor?

2. Why is `myArray[myArray.length]` likely to cause a runtime error?

3. In a JavaScript form file, what is the difference between a function definition that occurs before the closing class bracket and one that occurs after the bracket?

4. What does the `value` property of a Text control return if the current value does not comply with the template?

Exercises

1. Currently, shoppers can enter alphabetic values into the quantity fields. JavaScript supports client-side validation through the onChange event of a text control. Modify the Cart form to take advantage of client-side JavaScript and prevent shoppers from entering non-numeric quantity values.

2. The Text control for the quantity value is wider than it needs to be, but the Title HTML control could use a little more room for long titles. Adjust the grid columns to better accommodate the data. Make sure the controls still align correctly in both Navigator and Internet Explorer.

Day **13**

Searching by Keywords

by Paul Mahar

Today's JavaScript journey is somewhat reminiscent of yesterday's. The objective is to create a form that lets shoppers search for books in much the same way you can search for Web sites using the Yahoo! and Excite search engines. As with the Cart form from Day 12, the Keyword form will evolve through three stages of functionality:

☐ The first version of the Keyword form contains all the visual elements and primitive search capabilities. It allows searching of a single word within a single field. You need to use the Form Designer only during the creation of the initial Keyword form.

☐ For the next stage, you expand the search to work with multiple fields and multiple keywords. With this version, shoppers can choose in which field to search. This search also looks for more than one keyword and returns books that match any of the keywords.

- [ ] The final alteration to the Keyword form enables shoppers to select the type of search to make. The first type is identical to what already works—that is, retrieving rows that include one of the keywords. The new search, dubbed the "best match" search, returns only rows that contain every keyword.

Creating the Keyword form doesn't take as long as creating the Cart form. At the end of the day, there will be some time left to prepare for Day 14, the final day of the shopping cart development cycle.

TIP

All three versions of the Keyword form are available on the CD-ROM with the Day 13 source files as keyword1.jfm, keyword2.jfm, and keyword3.jfm. You can use these files as a starting point if you want to skip over some of the exercises or as a reference point if you get lost along the way.

The Simple Search

All the controls in the Keyword form work through the Form Constructor. You can lay out every component with the Form Designer. So far, the controls used in any of the forms have been only HTML, text, image, button, and reset. This form also includes a checkbox and a set of radio buttons. Along with the inherited toolbar buttons, the Keyword form contains the following:

- [ ] htmlHelp: The first control is an HTML control with instructions on how to use the form. This is very similar to the htmlHelp control in the Quick form.
- [ ] textKeywords: The Text control is where shoppers enter one or more keywords for the search. This must be wide enough to accommodate four or five keywords.
- [ ] radioTitle, radioAuthor, and radioISBN: The set of radio buttons determines which field to use for the search. The default radio button is for the Title field. The first rendition of the Keyword form ignores the radio button set and always searches by title.
- [ ] checkAll: This checkbox enables users to select a search method. When the checkbox is checked, the search returns only rows containing all keywords. Otherwise, the search returns rows containing any keyword in the title. This checkbox will not be functional in the first two revisions of the Keyword form.
- [ ] buttonSearch: Like the button of the same name on the Quick form, this button starts the search. If rows are found, the Results form opens. Otherwise, the Message form opens.

13

☐ reset1: The last functional control is a default Reset button. It is identical to the Cart form's Reset button and works only when the form opens in a browser.

☐ rule3: The rule line helps offset the various control groups and makes for a better-looking form. Two other rule lines, rule1 and rule2, are inherited from the Toolbar custom form class.

Whenever you need to display a limited set of choices, you can use a select list, radio buttons, or a checkbox. The control you use corresponds to the number of choices in your list. If you have more than five choices, such as the product names in the Quick form, a select list is the way to go. Radio buttons are easier to use than a select list, but require more form real estate. Radio buttons are appropriate where there are less than five choices and your form has room. A checkbox is almost always the best choice when you have only two choices and one excludes the other.

There are a few places where radio buttons are preferable. In the Keyword form you could substitute two radio buttons for a checkbox labeled Match all keywords. A benefit of using two radio buttons instead of a checkbox is that the labels can be more descriptive. Consider having radio buttons labeled Require a match on all keywords and Find books with any keyword instead of the Match all keywords checkbox. Try not to substitute a checkbox for radio buttons where the unchecked condition is unclear or where it might appear judgmental. For instance, it is not a good idea to use only a checkbox labeled Male in place of radio buttons labeled Male and Female.

The Visual Layout of the Keyword Form

The steps in this section guide you through the user interface design of the Keyword form. There are three phases to the design. In the first set of steps, you create the form and add all necessary controls. You can then test the design by incorporating the Keyword form into the Help form's include file. The second series of steps takes care of cosmetic issues that appear when running the form. The last series of design steps includes adding a query to the form and setting up some JavaScript placeholders. The following is the first series of steps for creating the initial version of the Keyword form:

1. Open the Form Designer to start work on the new Keyword form. Use the Script Pad to provide a filename and bypass the Expert prompt.

   ```
   _sys.forms.design("keyword.jfm") ;
   ```

2. Make sure you are using the toolbar custom form class. If the new form does not contain toolbar buttons, select File|Set Custom Form Class and select ToolbarCForm from toolbar.jcf.

13

3. You can create a new `htmlHelp` control from scratch or get some reusability the old fashioned way, through cut and paste. Open the Quick form in the Form Designer while leaving the Keyword Form Designer window open. Copy the `htmlHelp` control from the Quick form to the new Keyword form as shown in Figure 13.1.

   When you paste a control from the Clipboard, the `name` property reverts to a default. Change the name from `HTML1` back to `htmlHelp`.

Figure 13.1.

Copying the htmlHelp control from the Quick form.

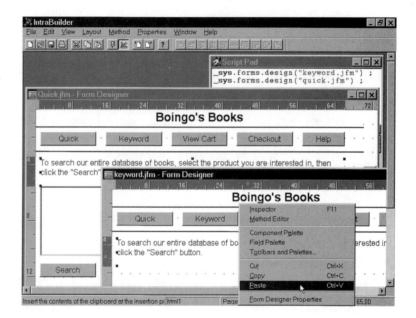

4. Use the `text` property tool button to open the Text Property Builder. Change the `text` property to the following lines:

   ```
   To search the book store, type keywords in the box below
   separated by a space, then click the "Search" button.
   ```

5. Add a Text control beneath the help text. Set the properties to the values listed in Table 13.1.

Table 13.1. Property values for `textKeywords`.

Property	Value
name	textKeywords
left	1
top	5.5
width	55

13

6. Add three radio buttons and set their properties to the values shown in Table 13.2. After adding the radio buttons, your form should resemble the one in Figure 13.2.

Table 13.2. Property values for the Keyword form radio buttons.

name	groupName	text	height	left	top	width
radioTitle	keyfield	Search by Title	1	1	6.5	20
radioAuthor	keyfield	Search by Author	1	1	7.5	20
radioISBN	keyfield	Search by ISBN	1	1	8.5	20

Figure 13.2.
Adding radio buttons to the Keyword form.

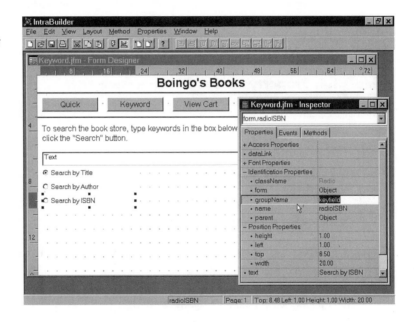

 TIP

When adding groups of radio buttons, add all the controls for a single group at one time. If you add two radio buttons and follow that by adding an HTML control before adding a third radio button, the Form Designer assumes the third radio button belongs to a new group.

7. Add a checkbox below the radio buttons. Use the property values listed in Table 13.3.

Table 13.3. Property values for `checkAll`**.**

Property	Value
name	checkAll
height	1
left	1
top	10.25
width	20
text	Match all keywords

8. Add the Search button below the checkbox. Use the property values listed in Table 13.4.

Table 13.4. Property values for `buttonSearch`**.**

Property	Value
name	buttonSearch
left	1
top	11.5
width	12
text	Search

9. Add the reset control to the left of the Search button. Set the position properties to top `11.5`, left `15`, and width `12`. You can leave the name and text properties as the default values.

10. Save the form when it resembles Figure 13.3.

All the required controls are now on the form. This is a good point to test the form in a browser. Before you can do that, you need to add `_sys.script.load()` and `#include` statements to the `store.h` file and force a recompile of the Help form. The application relies on the Help form to open all other forms. Any time you add or remove a form, you need to update the `store.h` file and recompile the Help form. You can force the recompile by deleting the `help.jfo` file or by using `_sys.scripts.compile("help.jfm")`. Listing 13.1 shows the new lines in bold. See Day 9 for an analysis of the `store.h` file.

13

Figure 13.3.

Adding a reset control to the Keyword form.

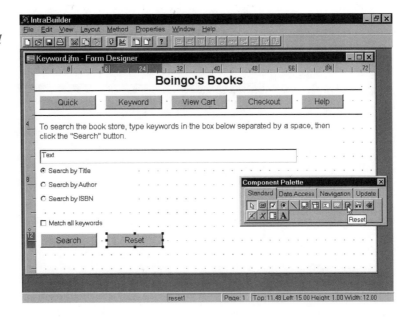

INPUT **Listing 13.1. Adding the Keyword form to** `store.h`.

```
 1: #define DEBUG // for development only
 2: #ifndef STORE
 3:  #define STORE
 4:  #ifdef DEBUG
 5:  // Load scripts
 6:  // _sys.script.load statements go here.
 7:  _sys.scripts.load("cart.jfm") ;
 8:  _sys.scripts.load("detail.jfm") ;
 9:  _sys.scripts.load("help.jfm") ;
10:  _sys.scripts.load("keyword.jfm") ;
11:  _sys.scripts.load("message.jfm") ;
12:  _sys.scripts.load("quick.jfm") ;
13:  _sys.scripts.load("results.jfm") ;
14:  #elseif
15:  // Include scripts
16:  return null
17:  // #include statements go here
18:  #include <cart.jfm>
19:   #include <detail.jfm>
20:  #include <help.jfm>
21:  #include <keyword.jfm>
22:   #include <message.jfm>
23:  #include <quick.jfm>
24:  #include <results.jfm>
25:  #endif
26: #endif
```

When you do run the form in a browser, the Keyword form becomes slightly taller. The browser adds some vertical space around each rule line. Figure 13.4 shows the Keyword form running in Internet Explorer.

Figure 13.4.

The Keyword form in a browser before adding a third rule line.

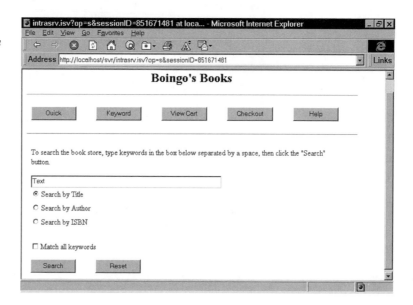

> **NOTE**
>
> Another way to add vertical spacing that only appears in a browser is to add line break tags. The HTML tag for a line break is `<BR>`.

There are a few minor cosmetic problems with the current form. The form has no title, the Keyword button is visible, and there is not much separation between the radio buttons and the checkbox. Follow these steps to add one more rule line and take care of the other loose ends:

1. Open the Keyword form in the Designer.
2. Inspect the form and change the `title` property to `Boingo's Books - Keyword Search` as shown in Figure 13.5.
3. Add a new rule line with the positions shown in Table 13.5.
4. Enter a code block to hide the Keyword toolbar button. Inspect `form` and enter the following code block in the form's `onServerLoad` event.

   ```
   this.buttonKeyword.visible = false ;
   ```

13

Figure 13.5.

Giving the Keyword form a proper title.

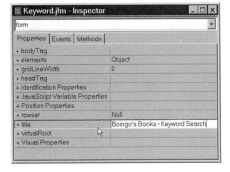

Table 13.5. Position properties for the third rule line.

Property	Value
name	rule3
left	0
top	10
right	70

5. Save the form when it looks like the one in Figure 13.6. After saving the form, close the Designer and run the form through a browser.

Figure 13.6.

Designing the Keyword form with rule lines.

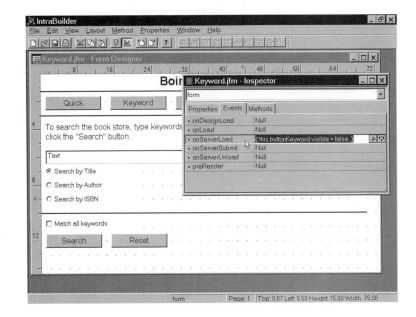

The revised Keyword form looks better in the area of the checkbox, but there is still a slight problem with the Text control. Figure 13.7 shows how the form opens with a default value of Text. It really should be blank.

Figure 13.7.

Running the Keyword form in Netscape Navigator.

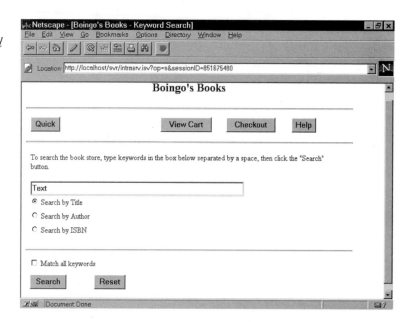

NOTE

Forms can appear with different color schemes when using Netscape Navigator. Users can override the colors in the HTML by checking the Always use my colors option in the Navigator Preferences dialog.

You can fix the default text problem and get ready for some JavaScript by creating a new method and a new function. You need to code only the following two routines for the Keyword search:

☐ buttonSearch_onServerClick(): The method linked to the onServerClick event of the search button gathers values from the form controls to configure the search. It creates a series of custom properties for use in the KeywordCanGetRow() function. Like a similar method in the Quick form, this method transfers control to either the Message form or the Results form.

13

☐ KeywordCanGetRow(): This is the only function in the application that is truly a function. All the others are methods related to a specific form class. This is a general function, which is used by the Keyword form, the Results form, and the Detail form.

The function acts as a complex filter expression. When attached to a canGetRow event, the function determines what rows appear in the rowset. This function must return a true value for a row to become part of the current rowset.

Before getting into the meat of these functions, create placeholders for both and take care of the other issues. This is the last time you need to use the Form Designer for developing the Keyword form. Here are the steps:

1. Open the Keyword form in the Form Designer.

2. Inspect form.textKeywords and blank out the value property.

3. Drag and drop the Title table from the IntraBuilder Explorer onto the Form Designer. Remove the full path from the sql property of the new query. After removing the path, the remaining SQL command should match the following:

```
SELECT * FROM "title.DBF"
```

4. Use the Inspector to create a new method linked to the onServerClick event of the Search button. For now, you can leave the method as an empty block.

```
function buttonSearch_onServerClick()
{
}
```

5. Select the Method Editor window. From the drop-down list at the top of the editor, select (General) as shown in Figure 13.8. Enter the following function:

```
function KeywordCanGetRow()
{
    return ( true )
}
```

Figure 13.8.

Selecting (General) *to add a function outside the class.*

6. Save your changes, close the Designer, and try the application in a browser.

NOTE

> There is no menu choice to generate a function definition outside the class. The Method|New Method option always places the code within the class.

Using the `canGetRow` Event

The form looks great. Now, let's make it do something. More specifically, let's make it find some rows and call the Results form for display. The Results form has some code already set up to handle keyword searches. There are four properties that the Results form passes on to the Detail form if the current search is a keyword search. To call the Results form correctly, the Keyword form must create all four expected properties. The four properties are as follows:

☐ `this.form.title1.rowset.canGetRow`: This property exists always as an event handler. The default value for any event handler is `null`. Because a `canGetRow` is always used with the keyword search, this property can serve as the search type indicator. If the value is `null`, the search is a quick search. Otherwise, the search is a keyword search.

☐ `this.form.scopeAll`: The `scopeAll` property is a custom logical property reflecting the state of the checkbox on the Keyword form. The property outlasts the checkbox by getting passed on to the Results form and then on to the Detail form. The default for `scopeAll` is `false`.

☐ `this.form.keyfield`: The `keyfield` property is based on the radio button that has been selected. It contains a character string, which corresponds to one of the three field names. The default `keyfield` value is `"TITLE"`.

☐ `this.form.keywords`: The keywords that a shopper enters into `textKeywords` are stored into the `keywords` property. The string is later spliced into array elements with one element for each word. The default is an empty string.

If you review the `buttonDetail_onServerClick()` in the Results form, you will find the following `if` block. This is where the four properties are passed from the Results form to the Detail form. In the Keyword form, similar assignments are made in the `buttonSearch_onServerClick()` method.

```
if (! (this.form.title1.rowset.canGetRow == null)) {
   nextForm.scopeAll = this.form.scopeAll ;
   nextForm.keyfield = this.form.keyfield ;
   nextForm.keywords = this.form.keywords ;
   nextForm.title1.rowset.canGetRow = KeywordCanGetRow ;
}
```

Open the Keyword form in the Script Editor and locate the `buttonSearch_onServerClick()` method. Because it's the only method, you will find it right after the default rowset

13

assignment. Update the method as shown in Listing 13.2. When you're done, try running the application.

INPUT **Listing 13.2. The initial `buttonSearch_onServerClick()` method.**

```
 1: function buttonSearch_onServerClick()
 2: {
 3:    var titleRow = this.form.title1.rowset,
 4:        nCount = 0 ;
 5:    this.form.scopeAll = false ;
 6:    this.form.keywords = this.form.textKeywords.value ;
 7:    this.form.keyfield = "TITLE" ;
 8:    titleRow.canGetRow = KeywordCanGetRow ;
 9:    nCount = titleRow.count() ;
10:    if (nCount == 0) {
11:       var nextForm = new messageForm() ;
12:       nextForm.htmlMessage.text = "<H1>No titles found for: " +
13:          this.form.textKeywords.value + "</H1>" ;
14:    }
15:    else {
16:       var nextForm = new resultsForm() ;
17:       nextForm.titleCount = nCount ;
18:       nextForm.scopeAll = this.form.scopeAll ;
19:       nextForm.keywords = this.form.keywords ;
20:       nextForm.keyfield = this.form.keyfield ;
21:       nextForm.title1.rowset.canGetRow = KeywordCanGetRow ;
22:    }
23:    nextForm.user = this.form.user ;
24:    nextForm.open() ;
25:    this.form.release() ;
26: }
```

ANALYSIS This first incarnation of `buttonSearch_onServerClick()` provides the property values necessary to get from the Keyword form to the Results form and from the Results form to the Detail form. The logic for selecting the next form to open is similar to that used in the Quick form.

Line 3 makes a shortcut reference to the Title query. This query is identical to those found in the Quick form, the Results form, and the Detail form.

```
var titleRow = this.form.title1.rowset,
    nCount = 0 ;
```

Lines 5 through 8 create the four keyword search properties on the current form. The properties must exist on any forms that contain a query using the `KeywordCanGetRow()` function. The `scopeAll`, `keywords`, and `keyfield` properties work like parameters for the `KeywordCanGetRow()` function.

```
this.form.scopeAll = false ;
this.form.keywords = this.form.textKeywords.value ;
```

13

```
this.form.keyfield = "TITLE" ;
titleRow.canGetRow = KeywordCanGetRow ;
```

The logic for opening the Message form is the same as it is in the Quick form. What might not be apparent is that when line 9 calls `Rowset::count()`, the `KeywordCanGetRow()` fires once for every row in the table. If the `KeywordCanGetRow()` function is simple, the performance is similar to having a filter on a field without an index. Performance degrades as the complexity of the function increases.

```
nCount = titleRow.count() ;
if (nCount == 0) {
   var nextForm = new messageForm() ;
   nextForm.htmlMessage.text = "<H1>No titles found for: " +
   this.form.textKeywords.value + "</H1>" ;
}
```

If `KeywordCanGetRow()` returns `true` for at least one row, the Results form is set up with the keyword properties. `KeywordCanGetRow()` is defined within the current script file. Because all scripts are loaded by or included in the Help form, the `KeywordCanGetRow()` function is available to any part of the application.

Lines 8 and 21 assign the `canGetRow` event to a function name without parentheses. This establishes a function pointer without calling the function. If you include the parentheses, IntraBuilder evaluates the function and assigns the return value to the event. A return value of `true` causes an error.

```
else {
   var nextForm = new resultsForm() ;
   nextForm.titleCount = nCount ;
   nextForm.scopeAll = this.form.scopeAll ;
   nextForm.keywords = this.form.keywords ;
   nextForm.keyfield = this.form.keyfield ;
   nextForm.title1.rowset.canGetRow = KeywordCanGetRow ;
}
```

The method ends with the standard "open the next form and release this form code." The end code works with both the Message form and the Results form.

```
nextForm.user = this.form.user ;
nextForm.open() ;
this.form.release() ;
```

Test the new method through a browser. From the Help form, you can click the Keyword toolbar button to open the Keyword form. The Search button on the Keyword form opens the Results form with every book in the Title table (see Figure 13.9). The Keyword form currently ignores any values you enter in the keyword Text control.

Figure 13.9.

*Getting all titles in
the results list.*

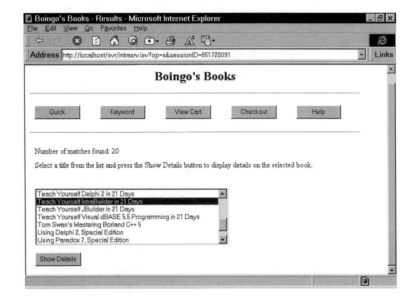

After verifying that you can navigate successfully from the Keyword form to the Results form,
reopen the Keyword form in the Script Editor. Replace the current all-too-positive
KeywordCanGetRow() function with the one from Listing 13.3. This version returns true if the
keyword string is found anywhere in the field value.

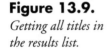 **Listing 13.3. The initial KeywordCanGetRow() function.**

```
 1: function KeywordCanGetRow()
 2: {
 3:    var lReturn = false,
 4:        thisForm = this.parent.parent ;
 5:    var sKeyValue = thisForm.title1.rowset.fields[thisForm.keyfield].value ;
 6:    if ( sKeyValue.indexOf( thisForm.keywords ) > -1 ) {
 7:       lReturn = true
 8:    }
 9:    return ( lReturn )
10: }
```

ANALYSIS The function starts with the assumption that the current row cannot be retrieved.
Line 4 creates a thisForm reference as a shortcut reference to the current form. The
canGetValue event belongs to a rowset. When you refer to this inside a rowset event, you are
referring to the rowset. The parent or container of a rowset is always a query. The parent of

a query is usually a form. When you drop a table onto a form, the query has a parent property pointing to the form. The standard relation between a rowset and a form is that the rowset is the grandchild of the form.

If you create your own instance of a query, it does not need any parent. In benchmarks from Day 10, you made extensive use of queries without parent forms.

```
var lReturn = false,
    thisForm = this.parent.parent ;
```

Using the new shortcut reference to the "grandpa" form, line 5 stores the relevant field value to a local variable. This is not creating a reference but creating a new variable, which stores a copy of the original field value.

```
var sKeyValue = thisForm.title1.rowset.fields[thisForm.keyfield].value ;
```

The String::indexOf() method determines whether sKeyValue contains the keyword string. String::indexOf() returns the position of one character string within another. Like arrays, string positions are zero based. When the keyword string is not found, String::indexOf() returns -1. Any greater value means the current row can be part of the rowset.

```
if ( sKeyValue.indexOf( thisForm.keywords ) > -1 ) {
    lReturn = true
}
```

If the condition has not been met, the default return value excludes the current row from the rowset. This moves the row pointer ahead one row, which fires the canGetRow event again. The process continues until an acceptable row is found or endOfSet is reached.

```
return ( lReturn )
```

With this function, you can create more sophisticated searches than are available through query by form. If you search for the word Visual, the result set shows books that contain the word Visual anywhere in the title. This retrieves three titles, as shown in Figure 13.10. Using query by form, only one of the three titles would be found. Your form should now match the Day 13 keyword1.jfm file from the CD-ROM.

NOTE

> You don't need to worry about shoppers entering keywords containing single quotes. Unlike SQL expressions, the String::indexOf() method is much more forgiving when non-standard string values are passed to it.

Figure 13.10.

The Results form after searching for the keyword Visual.

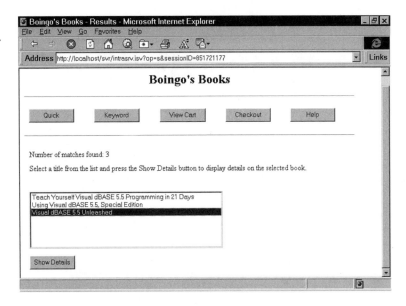

Searching with Multiple Fields and Multiple Keywords

To search for more than one non-consecutive keyword, you must be able to identify each keyword as a separate entity. The first version of the Keyword form stored the keywords in a single string variable. The primary difference between the first version and the one you are about to create is that the new version stores each keyword into a separate array element. Having each keyword as a separate array element lets you search for each keyword independently and without regard to the ordering of the keywords. If a shopper enters IntraBuilder Teach, the search needs to locate the title for Teach Yourself IntraBuilder in 21 Days.

While you're at it, you can make the Keyword form work with different fields. The multiple field issue is much simpler to solve than the multiple keyword issue. All you need to do to work with different fields is store the selected field name to the keyfield property. No modifications are needed in the KeywordCanGetRow() function to work with multiple fields.

13

This version on the Keyword form ignores the Match all keywords checkbox and operates as if it is not checked. Books will be included in the rowset if any keywords are found. The final Keyword form will allow shoppers to choose to see only books that contain either any listed keyword or every listed keyword.

Creating an Array of Keywords

The keyword array can use the same this.form.keywords reference that was used for the keyword string. The source for the array is this.form.textKeywords.value. Rewrite the buttonSearch_onServerClick() method in order to separate all the words in this.form.textKeywords.value. As in most English sentences, the single space serves as the delimiter between words. Use Listing 13.4 to modify the method with the Script Editor.

Listing 13.4. The multiple keyword
INPUT `buttonSearch_onServerClick()` **method.**

```
 1: function buttonSearch_onServerClick()
 2: {
 3:    var titleRow = this.form.title1.rowset,
 4:        nCount = 0,
 5:        nSpace = 0,
 6:        sWords = new StringEx() ;
 7:    // scopeAll
 8:    this.form.scopeAll = false ;
 9:    // keywords
10:    this.form.keywords = new Array() ;
11:    sWords.string = this.form.textKeywords.value ;
12:    while ( sWords.length > 0 ) {
13:       nSpace = sWords.indexOf(" ") ;
14:       if ( nSpace > -1 ) {
15:          this.form.keywords.add( sWords.left( nSpace++ ) ) ;
16:          sWords.string = sWords.right( sWords.length - nSpace ) ;
17:       }
18:       else {
19:          this.form.keywords.add( sWords.string ) ;
20:          sWords.string = null ;
21:       }
22:    }
23:    // keyfield
24:    if ( this.form.radioAuthor.value ) {
25:       this.form.keyfield = "AUTHOR" ;
26:    }
27:    else if ( this.form.radioISBN.value ) {
28:       this.form.keyfield = "ISBN" ;
29:    }
30:    else {
31:       this.form.keyfield = "TITLE" ;
32:    }
```

```
33:    // canGetRow
34:    titleRow.canGetRow = KeywordCanGetRow ;
35
36:    nCount = titleRow.count() ;
37:    if (nCount == 0) {
38:       var nextForm = new messageForm() ;
39:       nextForm.htmlMessage.text = "<H1>No titles found for: " +
40:          this.form.textKeywords.value + "</H1>" ;
41:    }
42:    else {
43:       var nextForm = new resultsForm() ;
44:       nextForm.titleCount = nCount ;
45:       nextForm.scopeAll = this.form.scopeAll ;
46:       nextForm.keywords = this.form.keywords ;
47:       nextForm.keyfield = this.form.keyfield ;
48:       nextForm.title1.rowset.canGetRow = KeywordCanGetRow ;
49:    }
50:    nextForm.user = this.form.user ;
51:    nextForm.open() ;
52:    this.form.release() ;
53: }
```

ANALYSIS   The basic structure of the buttonSearch_onServerClick() method does not change between versions. It starts by assigning the search properties to the current form. Then, the method counts to see how many rows exist. The last chore is to select the next form and open it. The only modifications take place on the lines that set up the search properties. In this version, the setup logic spans from line 7 to line 34. Each buttonSearch_onServerClick() method uses progressively more complex logic to set up properties.

The var statement initializes two new variables: nSpace and sWords. The nSpace variable keeps track of space delimiter position. The sWords variable acts as the scratch pad for dividing the string. As a StringEx object, it has all the normal functionality of a String object along with some additional methods, including StringEx::left() and StringEx::right().

```
var titleRow = this.form.title1.rowset,
    nCount = 0,
    nSpace = 0,
    sWords = new StringEx() ;
```

Line 10 creates the keywords property as an empty array. If no words are found in this.form.textKeywords.value, the array stays empty. If the method results in an empty array, the KeywordCanGetRow() function returns false for every row and no books are found.

```
// keywords
this.form.keywords = new Array() ;
```

The value of the Text control is itself a String object. That String object is assigned to the string property of sWords. Although standard String objects also have a string property, the property is relevant only to a StringEx object. When dealing with existing String objects, `myString = "Hello World"` is identical in function to `myString.string = "Hello World"`. The resulting `myString` is the same. If `myString` were a `StringEx` object, `myString = "Hello World"` would release the `StringEx` object and create a new standard `String` object in its place.

```
sWords.string = this.form.textKeywords.value ;
```

The `while` loop is used to work through `sWords`. The loop continues until `sWords` becomes `null` or an empty string. Using this kind of logic, something inside the loop must shrink down the size of `sWords` if you want to avoid an infinite loop. Line 13 looks for a space in `sWords` and stores the position to `nSpace`.

```
while ( sWords.length > 0 ) {
   nSpace = sWords.indexOf(" ") ;
```

If a space is found, the method divides `sWords` into two pieces. Any characters to the left of the space are considered a word. Line 15 creates a new element of the `keywords` array containing the current word. Line 16 takes everything to the right of the space and stores it to the `string` property of `sWords`.

```
if ( nSpace > -1 ) {
   this.form.keywords.add( sWords.left( nSpace++ ) ) ;
   sWords.string = sWords.right( sWords.length - nSpace ) ;
}
```

In the preceding code, the ++ increment operator adds one to `nSpace` after `StringEx::left()` executes and before the `StringEx::right()` executes. Without the ++ operator, the space would remain in the string and an infinite loop would result. Another way to accomplish the same task would be to prefix `nSpace` with ++ in the second assignment statement.

When ++ is a suffix, the incrementing does not take place until after all the other parts of the statement execute. This is why the `nSpace++` has no effect on the value passed to `StringEx::left()`. As a prefix, the opposite occurs. In the following code, the increment happens before `nSpace` is subtracted from `sWords.length`.

```
if ( nSpace > -1 ) {
   this.form.keywords.add( sWords.left( nSpace ) ) ;
   sWords.string = sWords.right( sWords.length - ++nSpace ) ;
}
```

The `StringEx::left()` and `StringEx::right()` methods are shorthand for a substring operation. If you want to use a `String` class for `sWords`, the same code could be written as follows. With `String::substring()`, you must pass two parameters instead of one.

```
 if ( nSpace > -1 ) {
   this.form.keywords.add( sWords.substring(0, nSpace++ ) ) ;
   sWords.string = sWords.substring( nSpace, sWords.length ) ;
}
```

If there are no more spaces in sWords, then sWords has the last word. After the last word is added as an array element, line 20 stores null to the string property. The length of the null string is zero, forcing the while loop to end.

```
else {
   this.form.keywords.add( sWords.string ) ;
   sWords.string = null ;
}
```

A series of if blocks sets the keyfield property. When a radio button is selected, the value property becomes true. The routine has a slight optimization in that it never checks to see whether the this.form.radioTitle value is true. If neither of the other two is selected, the title option must be selected.

```
// keyfield
if ( this.form.radioAuthor.value ) {
   this.form.keyfield = "AUTHOR" ;
}
else if ( this.form.radioISBN.value ) {
   this.form.keyfield = "ISBN" ;
}
else {
   this.form.keyfield = "TITLE" ;
}
```

NOTE   Unlike other controls, the value property of a radio button is not equal to the value of an associated dataLink. The value property of the radio button is a logical value; however, its dataLink can point only to a character string. The value of the dataLink is equal to the text of the radio button.

Searching Through an Array of Keywords

The Keyword form will not run correctly if buttonSearch_onServerClick() creates the keywords property as an array and KeywordCanGetRow() tries to use it as a character string. To remedy the situation, modify KeywordCanGetRow() as shown in Listing 13.5.

13

INPUT

Listing 13.5. The multiple keyword `KeywordCanGetRow()` function.

```
 1: function KeywordCanGetRow()
 2: {
 3:     var lReturn = false,
 4:         thisForm = this.parent.parent ;
 5:     var sKeyValue=thisForm.title1.rowset.fields[thisForm.keyfield].value;
 6:
 7:     for ( var i = 0 ; i < thisForm.keywords.length ; i++ ) {
 8:         if (sKeyValue.indexOf( thisForm.keywords[i] ) > -1 ) {
 9:             lReturn = true ;
10:             break ;
11:         }
12:     }
13:
14:     return ( lReturn )
15: }
```

ANALYSIS The variable declaration and return statements are identical to those found in the previous `KeywordCanGetRow()` function. The new statements are on lines 7 through 12 where a loop cycles through each element of the `keywords` array. Every array element is a keyword to seek in `sKeyValue`. Whenever the key is found, the return flag is set to `true`.

```
for ( var i = 0 ; i < thisForm.keywords.length ; i++ ) {
   if (sKeyValue.indexOf( thisForm.keywords[i] ) > -1 ) {
      lReturn = true ;
      break ;
   }
}
```

There is no need to continue the search after a keyword has been found. The `break` statement on line 10 exits the `for` loop as soon as the first keyword is found.

Your form should now match the Day 13 `keyword2.jfm` file from the CD-ROM. With this version complete, you can perform a wide range of searches. You could simultaneously look for all books on C++ and Delphi. Figure 13.11 shows the Keyword form set up to look for books listed with `Mahar` or `Swan` in the Author field. A keyword search with this criteria returns the following books:

OUTPUT
```
dBASE for Windows Unleashed
Teach Yourself IntraBuilder in 21 Days
Tom Swan's Mastering Borland C++ 5
Visual dBASE 5.5 Unleashed
```

Figure 13.11.

Searching for books by Mahar or Swan.

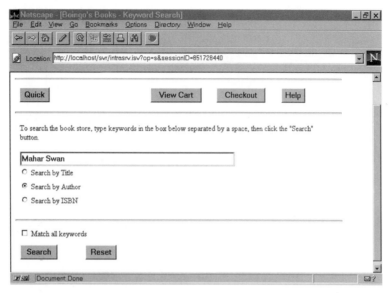

Adding Search Rule Options

The second version of the Keyword form is pretty good, but it has some bugs. If you enter more than one space between keywords, the extra space is treated as a keyword. This results in every book getting returned if the search is on the Title or Author fields.

Although it is not necessarily considered a bug, the searches are case sensitive. If shoppers enter Dbase, they get the message shown in Figure 13.12. To make it easy on shoppers, the system should be case insensitive. After all, how many shoppers will be able to remember whether dBASE is capitalized as Dbase, dbase, or DBASE?

Along with these bug fixes, the final version of the Keyword form will incorporate changes needed for the Match all keywords option. Fire up the Script Editor and modify buttonSearch_onServerClick() as shown in Listing 13.6 and KeywordCanGetRow() as shown in Listing 13.7.

13

Figure 13.12.

The results of searching for Dbase *with a case-sensitive search.*

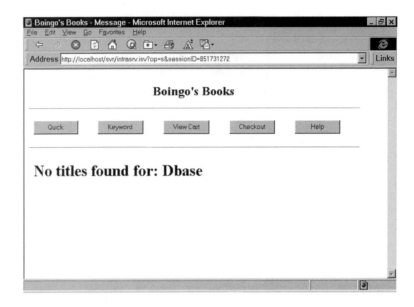

Listing 13.6. The final version of the

`buttonSearch_onServerClick()` **method.**

```
 1: function buttonSearch_onServerClick()
 2: {
 3:    var titleRow = this.form.title1.rowset,
 4:        nCount = 0,
 5:        nSpace = 0,
 6:        sWords = new StringEx() ;
 7:    // scopeAll
 8:    this.form.scopeAll = this.form.checkAll.checked ;
 9:    // keywords
10:    this.form.keywords = new Array() ;
11:    sWords.string = this.form.textKeywords.value ;
12:    sWords.string = sWords.toUpperCase() ;
13:    sWords.string = sWords.leftTrim() ;
14:    sWords.string = sWords.rightTrim() ;
15:    while ( sWords.length > 0 ) {
16:       nSpace = sWords.indexOf(" ") ;
17:       if ( nSpace > -1 ) {
18:          this.form.keywords.add( sWords.left( nSpace++ ) ) ;
19:          sWords.string = sWords.right( sWords.length - nSpace );
20:          sWords.string = sWords.leftTrim() ;
21:       }
22:       else {
23:          this.form.keywords.add( sWords.string ) ;
24:          sWords.string = null ;
25:       }
26:    }
27:    // keyfield
28:    if ( this.form.radioAuthor.value ) {
```

13

```
29:          this.form.keyfield = "AUTHOR" ;
30:       }
31:       else if ( this.form.radioISBN.value ) {
32:          this.form.keyfield = "ISBN" ;
33:       }
34:       else {
35:          this.form.keyfield = "TITLE" ;
36:       }
37:    // canGetRow
38:       titleRow.canGetRow = KeywordCanGetRow ;
39:
40:       nCount = titleRow.count() ;
41:       if (nCount == 0) {
42:          var nextForm = new messageForm() ;
43:          nextForm.htmlMessage.text = "<H1>No titles found for: "+
44:             this.form.textKeywords.value + "</H1>" ;
45:       }
46:       else {
47:          var nextForm = new resultsForm() ;
48:          nextForm.titleCount = nCount ;
49:          nextForm.scopeAll = this.form.scopeAll ;
50:          nextForm.keywords = this.form.keywords ;
51:          nextForm.keyfield = this.form.keyfield ;
52:          nextForm.title1.rowset.canGetRow = KeywordCanGetRow ;
53:       }
54:       nextForm.user = this.form.user ;
55:       nextForm.open() ;
56:       this.form.release() ;
57: }
```

ANALYSIS   The final changes to buttonSearch_onServerClick() are minor compared to the
final changes to KeywordCanGetRow(). Line 8 contains one change, and lines 12, 13,
14, and 22 are new. Line 8 now uses the checkbox value. If a shopper has checked the
checkbox, scopeAll becomes true, and all keywords must match in order for a row to be
accepted.

```
// scopeAll
this.form.scopeAll = this.form.checkAll.checked ;
```

NOTE   The checked property of a checkbox is similar to the value property of
a Text control. If a checkbox has a dataLink, the field value is equal to
the checked property. IntraBuilder can reflect changes to the dataLink
field value into the checked property.

Lines 12 through 14 use methods of sWords to modify its own string property. String
methods return new values without changing any properties of their related string. You can
assign the results of a string method to the string property to alter an existing String object.
String::toUpperCase() is available in the standard String class and the StringEx class. The
two trimming methods exist only in the StringEx class.

```
sWords.string = this.form.textKeywords.value ;
sWords.string = sWords.toUpperCase() ;
sWords.string = sWords.leftTrim() ;
sWords.string = sWords.rightTrim() ;
```

At this point all keywords are in uppercase, and excess spaces are trimmed from the ends of the keyword list. To take care of multiple spaces between words, line 22 calls `StringEx::leftTrim()` each time a new word is extracted from the string.

```
if ( nSpace > -1 ) {
   this.form.keywords.add( sWords.left( nSpace++ ) ) ;
   sWords.string = sWords.right( sWords.length - nSpace ) ;
   sWords.string = sWords.leftTrim() ;
}
```

These changes are all you need to do for `buttonSearch_onServerClick()`. Because the final version makes all the keywords uppercase, it will not work correctly with the previous version of `KeywordCanGetRow()`.

INPUT   **Listing 13.7. The third and final `KeywordCanGetRow()` function.**

```
 1: function KeywordCanGetRow()
 2: {
 3:     var thisForm = this.parent.parent,
 4:         nHits = 0 ;
 5:     var sKeyValue =
 6:     thisForm.title1.rowset.fields[thisForm.keyfield].value.toUpperCase();
 7:
 8:     for ( var i = 0 ; i < thisForm.keywords.length ; i++ ) {
 9:         if ( sKeyValue.indexOf( thisForm.keywords[i] ) > -1 ) {
10:             nHits++ ;
11:         }
12:     }
13:
14:     return thisForm.scopeAll ? nHits==thisForm.keywords.length : nHits>0;
15: }
```

ANALYSIS   This version of `KeywordCanGetRow()` is significantly different from the prior version. To start, the `lReturn` variable is gone, and line 4 creates a new `nHits` variable. The function uses `nHits` to track how many of the keywords can be found.

```
var thisForm = this.parent.parent,
    nHits = 0 ;
```

Lines 5 and 6 comprise a single statement that converts the key field value to uppercase and assigns the result to `sKeyValue`. The `value` property of a character field is also a `String` class. Having the field value and the keywords in uppercase removes all case sensitivity.

```
var sKeyValue =
  thisForm.title1.rowset.fields[thisForm.keyfield].value.toUpperCase() ;
```

13

The lReturn flag is replaced by the nHits counter when a keyword is found. Counting the number of hits is required for the scopeAll option.

```
if ( sKeyValue.indexOf( thisForm.keywords[i] ) > -1 ) {
   nHits++ ;
}
```

The break statement also has been removed. Although this does create some redundant processing when scopeAll is false, any alternative could slow down both types of searches. For instance, you could check the scopeAll property to see whether a break is possible as shown in the following code. This can speed up searches that match on any word and use more than three words. It slows down all other searches.

```
if ( sKeyValue.indexOf( thisForm.keywords[i] ) > -1 ) {
   nHits++ ;
   if ( ! thisForm.scopeAll ) {
      break ;
   }
}
```

The return statement on line 14 is fairly compressed. For most routines, a standard if block is preferable for readability. However, canGetRow event logic is close to being the definition of performance challenged. Using a single expression to calculate the return value makes for the fastest possible processing.

```
return thisForm.scopeAll ? nHits == thisForm.keywords.length : nHits > 0 ;
```

If the scopeAll property is true, the rowset is only included if the number of hits matches the number of keywords in the array. Because nHits can only increment once for each keyword, if nHits equals the array length, every keyword has been found. If scopeAll is false, the fact that there were any hits is good enough for a row to be in the rowset. Using a standard if block, the same logic would look like this:

```
if ( thisForm.scopeAll ) {
   return ( nHits == thisForm.keywords.length ) ;
}
else {
   return ( nHits > 0 ) ;
}
```

Rejoice, for the Keyword form is done. Shoppers now have an intuitive way to make complex searches. Try it and see how the form responds with different scopeAll settings. Figure 13.13 shows a search for titles that contain DELPHI and 2. If the Match all keywords option is checked, the result is four books about Delphi 2. When the Match all keywords option is not checked, the result has nine books, including a book on Delphi 1 and all the books in the *Teach Yourself in 21 Days* series.

If your form is not working as expected, compare it to Listing 13.8. The listing shows the complete source code for the final version of the Keyword form. This version is also available as the Day 13 keyword3.jfm file on the CD-ROM.

13

Figure 13.13.

Searching for books about Delphi 2.

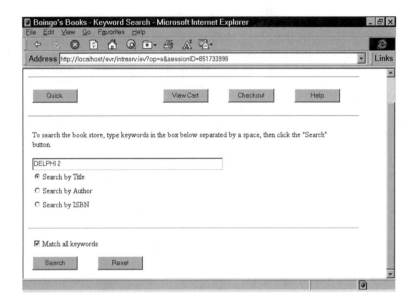

Listing 13.8. The complete source for the Keyword form.

```
 1: // {End Header} Do not remove this comment//
 2: // Generated on 01/02/97
 3: //
 4: var f = new keywordForm();
 5: f.open();
 6: class keywordForm extends ToolbarCForm from "TOOLBAR.JCF" {
 7:    with (this) {
 8:       onServerLoad = {;this.buttonKeyword.visible = false ;};
 9:       height = 15;
10:       left = 0;
11:       top = 0;
12:       width = 75;
13:       title = "Boingo's Books - Keyword Search";
14:    }
15:
16:    with (this.title1 = new Query()){
17:      left = 70;
18:      top = 2;
19:      sql = 'SELECT * FROM "title.DBF"';
20:      active = true;
21:    }
22:
23:    with (this.title1.rowset) {
24:    }
25:
26:    with (this.rule3 = new Rule(this)){
27:       top = 10;
28:       size = 2;
29:       right = 70;
```

```
30:    }
31:
32:    with (this.htmlHelp = new HTML(this)){
33:       height = 2;
34:      left = 1;
35:      top = 3.5;
36:      width = 65;
37:      color = "black";
38:      text = 'To search the book store, type keywords ' +
39:             'in the box below separated by a space, ' +
40:             'then click the "Search" button.';
41:    }
42:
43:    with (this.textKeywords = new Text(this)){
44:       left = 1;
45:       top = 5.5;
46:       width = 55;
47:       value = "";
48:     }
49:
50:    with (this.radioTitle = new Radio(this)){
51:       height = 1;
52:       left = 1;
53:       top = 6.5;
54:       width = 20;
55:       text = "Search by Title";
56:       value = true;
57:       groupName = "keyfield";
58:    }
59:
60:    with (this.radioAuthor = new Radio(this)){
61:       height = 1;
62:       left = 1;
63:       top = 7.5;
64:       width = 20;
65:       text = "Search by Author";
66:       value = false;
67:       groupName = "keyfield";
68:    }
69:
70:    with (this.radioISBN = new Radio(this)){
71:       height = 1;
72:       left = 1;
73:       top = 8.5;
74:       width = 20;
75:       text = "Search by ISBN";
76:       value = false;
77:       groupName = "keyfield";
78:    }
79:
80:    with (this.checkAll = new CheckBox(this)){
81:       height = 1;
82:       left = 1;
83:       top = 10.25;
84:       width = 20;
```

13

continues

Listing 13.8. continued

```
85:        text = "Match all keywords";
86:        checked = false;
87:    }
88:
89:    with (this.buttonSearch = new Button(this)){
90:        onServerClick = class::buttonSearch_onServerClick;
91:        left = 1;
92:        top = 11.5;
93:        width = 12;
94:        text = "Search";
95:    }
96:
97:    with (this.reset1 = new Reset(this)){
98:        left = 15;
99:        top = 11.5;
100:       width = 12;
101:       text = "Reset";
102:   }
103:
104:   this.rowset = this.title1.rowset;
105:
106:   function buttonSearch_onServerClick()
107:   {
108:       var titleRow = this.form.title1.rowset,
109:           nCount = 0,
110:           nSpace = 0,
111:           sWords = new StringEx() ;
112:       // scopeAll
113:       this.form.scopeAll = this.form.checkAll.checked ;
114:       // keywords
115:       this.form.keywords = new Array() ;
116:       sWords.string = this.form.textKeywords.value ;
117:       sWords.string = sWords.toUpperCase() ;
118:       sWords.string = sWords.leftTrim() ;
119:       sWords.string = sWords.rightTrim() ;
120:       while ( sWords.length > 0 ) {
121:           nSpace = sWords.indexOf(" ") ;
122:           if ( nSpace > -1 ) {
123:               this.form.keywords.add( sWords.left( nSpace++ ) ) ;
124:               sWords.string = sWords.right( sWords.length - nSpace );
125:               sWords.string = sWords.leftTrim() ;
126:           }
127:           else {
128:               this.form.keywords.add( sWords.string ) ;
129:               sWords.string = null ;
130:           }
131:       }
132:       // keyfield
133:       if ( this.form.radioAuthor.value ) {
134:           this.form.keyfield = "AUTHOR" ;
135:       }
136:       else if ( this.form.radioISBN.value ) {
137:           this.form.keyfield = "ISBN" ;
138:       }
139:       else {
140:           this.form.keyfield = "TITLE" ;
```

13

```
141:        }
142:        // canGetRow
143:        titleRow.canGetRow = KeywordCanGetRow ;
144:             nCount = titleRow.count() ;
145:        if (nCount == 0) {
146:            var nextForm = new messageForm() ;
147:            nextForm.htmlMessage.text = "<H1>No titles found for: "+
148:                 this.form.textKeywords.value + "</H1>" ;
149:        }
150:        else {
151:            var nextForm = new resultsForm() ;
152:            nextForm.titleCount = nCount ;
153:            nextForm.scopeAll = this.form.scopeAll ;
154:            nextForm.keywords = this.form.keywords ;
155:            nextForm.keyfield = this.form.keyfield ;
156:            nextForm.title1.rowset.canGetRow = KeywordCanGetRow ;
157:        }
158:        nextForm.user = this.form.user ;
159:        nextForm.open() ;
160:        this.form.release() ;
161:    }
162:
163: }
164:
165: function KeywordCanGetRow()
166: {
167:    var thisForm = this.parent.parent,
168:         nHits = 0 ;
169:    var sKeyValue =
170:  thisForm.title1.rowset.fields[thisForm.keyfield].value.toUpperCase();
171:
172:    for ( var i = 0 ; i < thisForm.keywords.length ; i++ ) {
173:       if ( sKeyValue.indexOf( thisForm.keywords[i] ) > -1 ) {
174:           nHits++ ;
175:       }
176:    }
177:
178:    return thisForm.scopeAll ? nHits==thisForm.keywords.length:nHits>0;
179: }
```

13

WARNING

Don't try to run the Keyword form by itself. The search routine requires that the user property be set on the Keyword form. The user property is set only when the application is started from the Help form.

Preparing to Check Out

To get ready for the final day of shopping cart application building, create a stub version of the Checkout form and add it to the store.h file. This will take care of the error that occurs when shoppers click on the Checkout toolbar button.

1. Open the Form Designer from the Script Pad. Use the following JavaScript statement:

   ```
   _sys.forms.design("checkout.jfm") ;
   ```

2. Make sure the toolbar custom form class is set as the active custom form class.

3. Change the form's `title` property to `Boingo's Books - Checkout`, as shown in Figure 13.14.

Figure 13.14.

Setting up a stub version of the Checkout form.

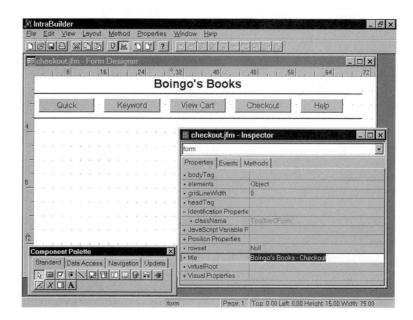

4. Save the form and close the Form Designer.

5. Open `store.h` in the Script Editor and add `load` and `include` statements for the Checkout form. When you have the form looking like Listing 13.9, save it and close IntraBuilder.

6. Reopen IntraBuilder and force a recompile of the Help form by selecting Compile from the IntraBuilder Explorer shortcut menu.

INPUT

Listing 13.9. The `store.h` file with support for the Checkout form.

```
1: #define DEBUG // for development only
2: #ifndef STORE
3:   #define STORE
```

```
 4:    #ifdef DEBUG
 5:        // Load scripts
 6:        // _sys.script.load statements go here.
 7:        _sys.scripts.load("cart.jfm") ;
 8:        _sys.scripts.load("checkout.jfm") ;
 9:        _sys.scripts.load("detail.jfm") ;
10:        _sys.scripts.load("help.jfm") ;
11:        _sys.scripts.load("keyword.jfm") ;
12:        _sys.scripts.load("message.jfm") ;
13:        _sys.scripts.load("quick.jfm") ;
14:        _sys.scripts.load("results.jfm") ;
15:    #elseif
16:        // Include scripts
17:        return null
18:        // #include statements go here
19:        #include <cart.jfm>
20:        #include <checkout.jfm>
21:        #include <detail.jfm>
22:        #include <help.jfm>
23:        #include <keyword.jfm>
24:        #include <message.jfm>
25:        #include <quick.jfm>
26:        #include <results.jfm>
27:    #endif
28: #endif
```

ANALYSIS The only changes are on lines 8 and 20 where the Checkout form is listed with the other application forms. Compiling in this header allows all the toolbar buttons to work without error. Each toolbar button opens a different form, and this header is the first one to include all the form filenames.

That is all for today. Tomorrow you can dive directly into the Checkout form development without having to worry about integrating the new form into the Help form initialization.

Summary

Today you learned about controlling a form's HTML layout and how to create a complex filter through the rowset canGetRow event. Throughout the day, you created three versions of the Keyword search form.

The day began with the visual layout of all the controls on the Keyword search form. After you had a professional-looking Keyword form, you gradually added more complex options to a function linked to a canGetRow event. The first version allowed searches for a single word on a single field. The second could search for multiple words on multiple fields. The final version was case insensitive and allowed the user to specify whether all or any of the search words are required.

13

After completing the Search form, you created a stub version of the Checkout form. Tomorrow, you will complete the Checkout form, and with that, you will complete the shopping cart application.

Q&A

Q **I am unable to enter some of the position property values as given. When I enter a top value of `10.25` into the Inspector, it changes to `10.23`. If I use the Script Editor and change the value to `10.25`, it is overwritten with `10.22` as soon as I make any new changes with the Form Designer. What is going on? Should I stress over this?**

A The Form Designer coordinate system is based on the system display font. If you change resolutions for system font size, the allowable values change slightly. There is no need to stress over the differences. The relative position of controls is much more critical than the actual position. Do not worry whether a control has a top position of `10.25` or `10.23`.

Q **When using the `filter` property or the `Rowset::applyLocate()` method, table type and indexing made a big difference. Are there similar factors to consider when using `canGetRow`?**

A The `filter` and `Rowset::applyLocate()` methods pass off the query processing details to the database engine. The table type you are using determines whether the query is run by BDE, ODBC, or a remote SQL server. The `canGetRow` shifts the query processing into IntraBuilder. The only thing the database engine does for `canGetRow` is the low overhead task of moving the row pointer. The best way to speed up a `canGetRow` event is to streamline your JavaScript and remove any excess processing.

Q **If I create a rule line through the Navigator Form wizard, I can select a wide range of line styles including some that have moving images. In the IntraBuilder Form Designer, the only option to change the rule style seems to be the `size` property. How can I create more exciting rule lines with IntraBuilder?**

A When you select an exotic rule line in the Navigator Form wizard, the generated HTML contains an image in place of the standard HTML rule tag. If you have an image file with the rule style you want to use, you can use the same approach with IntraBuilder. After you create a form with the Navigator Form wizard and store its associated GIF to a local folder, you can use the GIF with an IntraBuilder image control. The GIF files for rules have names like `rule07.gif`.

Q My boss says I always have to use object-oriented programming. Using `KeywordCanGetRow()` as a standard function that resides outside of a class seems as though it is breaking the rules. Is there any way to use `KeywordCanGetRow()` as a method instead of a function?

A Yes, you can use the scope resolution operator to call a method, which is defined within another class. If you move the `KeywordCanGetRow()` inside the `keywordForm` class, you only need to change three other lines to use it as a method. The following excerpt shows the changes.

In `keyword.jfm`, change:

```
titleRow.canGetRow = KeywordCanGetRow ;
```

To:

```
titleRow.canGetRow = keywordForm::KeywordCanGetRow ;
```

In both `keyword.jfm` and `results.jfm`, change:

```
nextForm.title1.rowset.canGetRow = KeywordCanGetRow ;
```

To:

```
nextForm.title1.rowset.canGetRow = keywordForm::KeywordCanGetRow
```

Workshop

The Workshop section provides questions and exercises to help you get a better feel for the material you learned today. Try to answer the questions and at least think about the exercises before moving on to tomorrow's lesson. You'll find the answers to the questions in Appendix A, "Answers to Quiz Questions."

Quiz

1. How do you reference a form from a `rowset` event?
2. What is the HTML tag for a line break?
3. How can you create more than one set of radio buttons in a single form?
4. What is the proper capitalization of Borland's DBF-oriented desktop database?
5. What class contains the `toUpperCase()` method?
6. How can you force any form to use a browser-defined color scheme in Navigator?

Exercises

1. Try replacing the checkAll checkbox in the Keyword form with two radio buttons. Remember that the groupName property of the new radio buttons must distinguish them from the form's existing radio buttons.

2. As presented here, the final Keyword form does not have very elegant handling of a blank keyword list. If the Match all keywords option is checked, every book comes back as found. If the option is not checked, no books are found. Add a routine to check for a blank keyword list in buttonSearch_onServerClick(). If the blank list is found, open the Message form with an appropriate message.

13

Day 14

Checking Out

by Paul Mahar

Today you will finish up the shopping cart application and learn how to validate data, work with form pages, and create a Receipt report. By the end of the day you will have a fully functional on-line order entry system. There are just two main tasks for the day:

☐ The first task is to design the Checkout form. The Checkout form is at the center of today's activities. It allows shoppers to place an order for the items in their shopping cart. After selecting one or more books, shoppers can place the order by entering address and credit card information. After the data is validated, the shopper gets an HTML receipt of the transaction.

This Checkout form is the first in the application to provide direct data entry through datalinks. It also is the first to take advantage of pages. The other shopping cart forms use a single page. The Checkout form uses three pages. When a shopper submits an order, the Checkout form updates the Customer, Invoice, and Lineitem tables. These tables provide the basis for the Receipt report.

☐ The last task of the day is to design the Receipt report. If `index.htm` is the virtual version of the bookstore's "In" door, the Receipt report is the "Out" door. The report contains three related tables, a calculated column, and grand total information. Like forms, reports contain programmable events. When creating the Receipt report, you will learn how to combine events and self-evaluating code blocks to calculate totals.

Both the Checkout form and the Receipt report demonstrate new ways to pass information between application objects. So far, the application has created custom properties, such as the `this.form.user`, to pass information from one form to the next. The Checkout form uses pages to combine the features of several forms into a single JavaScript form definition. This allows each page to appear as a separate form yet have access to the same set of properties and methods. The Receipt report receives information through a parameter list.

Designing the Checkout Form

The purpose of the Checkout form is to accept address and credit card information from shoppers when they want to make a purchase. To support this, the Checkout form needs some data entry controls with datalinks to the Customer table. To provide validation, the form needs to prevent two possible error conditions. First, the form needs to prevent any data entry when no items are in the cart. Second, it must validate the entered data when items are in the cart. To accomplish this, the Checkout form works like three forms in one, each functional form appearing on one of the following pages.

☐ The customer data entry page: Page one is comprised mostly of HTML field labels and Text controls. These correspond to fields in the Customer table. There also are a set of radio buttons and a select control. The radio buttons correspond to the three major credit cards. The select control contains country names for international orders.

☐ The "Empty Cart" message page: Page two is similar to the Message form. It displays if no rows are available in the Cart table. Shoppers cannot proceed with the Checkout form if they have not selected anything to buy.

☐ The data validation dialog box page: The third page works like an HTML version of an alert dialog box. It displays a message explaining why an order could not be filled. Clicking on the page's only button returns the shopper to the customer data entry page.

Although data from only one table ever appears on the Checkout form, it works with the following five tables. Two of the tables appear in many forms, but three are new to this form.

- ☐ The Cart table: Upon loading, the form must calculate the total price for items in the Cart and display a warning if the Cart contains no items. When a shopper makes a purchase, all rows associated with the current shopper move from the Cart table to the Lineitem table.

- ☐ The Customer table: A valid purchase causes the form to append a single new row to the Customer table. This is the only table with datalinks to controls on the form. The Customer table is not used by any other forms.

- ☐ The Title table: Calculating the total order price requires a link between the Title table and the Cart table. Book prices are stored only in the Title table.

- ☐ The Invoice table: This table relates the Customer table to the Lineitem table. Each purchasing action adds one new row to the Lineitem table. The Invoice table is new to this form.

- ☐ The Lineitem table: As shoppers move through the application, the Cart is a temporary storage area for items selected for purchase. At checkout time, the items move to the Lineitem table for permanent storage. Although the Lineitem table is a child of the Invoice table, no relation definition is required for the Checkout form. Like the Customer table and the Invoice table, the Lineitem table is not used in any other form.

Designing the Data Entry Page

The first and most complex page is for customer data entry. Page one contains controls for all but one field of the Customer table. The hidden field is the customer number field. The value for the customer number does not need to be calculated until all the other fields are validated.

Three field groupings exist in the Customer table. The first group consists of the customer name and phone number. The address group has all the common address fields and a country field for international orders. The last group contains fields for credit card information.

NOTE

> Many order systems allow for separate billing and shipping addresses. You could expand on the Customer table and Checkout form to contain both "bill to" and "ship to" fields. If you do, also add a checkbox to default them to being the same address.

14

Most of the fields are simple string values that work best as datalinks to Text controls. The exceptions are where you can limit the shopper to a list of valid choices. The bookstore can accept orders from a limited number of countries. Because the number of countries is greater than five, a select control is a good choice for the country field. Using a select control also makes it easy to expand the country list as the store expands. Boingo will accept only the three major credit cards. You can use a set of radio buttons to represent each type of credit card.

Along with all the controls for the Customer table, the customer data entry page can work with the standard toolbar buttons and two new buttons: one button to commit the purchase and another to cancel the Checkout process. Follow these steps to design the first page of the Checkout form.

1. Open the Checkout form in the Design mode.

2. Drop the following tables from the IntraBuilder Explorer onto the Checkout form: `Cart.dbf`, `Customer.dbf`, `Invoice.dbf`, `Lineitem.dbf`, and `Title.dbf`.

3. Remove the full path from the `sql` properties of the five new queries. Inspect each query and modify the SQL commands so that they match the following.

```
SELECT * FROM "customer.DBF"
SELECT * FROM "cart.DBF"
SELECT * FROM "lineitem.DBF"
SELECT * FROM "invoice.DBF"
SELECT * FROM "title.DBF"
```

4. Relate the `title1` query to the `cart1` query. Select the `title1` query and descend its `rowset` property. Use the drop-down list on `masterRowset` to select the `cart1` query. Use the drop-down list on `masterFields` to select `ISBN`. The `indexName` is automatically set to `ISBN`, as shown in Figure 14.1.

Figure 14.1.

Relating the Title query to the Cart query.

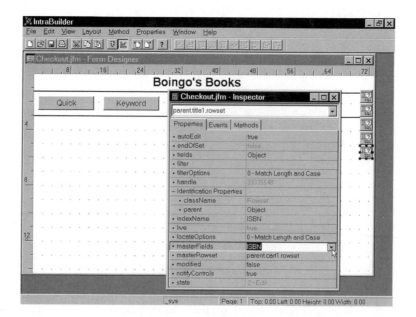

5. Add three HTML headings, as shown in Table 14.1. Each heading labels the group of fields that will appear to the right. As minor level-four headings, the <H4> font change might not be perceivable in the Designer.

Table 14.1. Minor headings for the field groups.

Name	Text	Height	Left	Top	Width
headCustomer	<H4>Customer</H4>	1	1	4.5	10
headAddress	<H4>Address</H4>	1	1	6.5	10
headCard	<H4>Credit Card</H4>	1	1	9.5	10

6. Add nine HTML field labels and configure them, as shown in Table 14.2. In this layout, each field group is horizontally separated by half a space. This division is more visible in the Designer than in a browser. All but the State label appears in the same column. The label layout leaves room for a set of radio button controls that you will later add above the card number. After you add the field labels, your form should resemble the one shown in Figure 14.2.

Table 14.2. Field labels for the Customer table.

Name	Text	Height	Left	Top	Width
labelName	Name	1	12	4.5	11.5
labelPhone	Phone	1	12	5.5	11.5
labelStreet	Street	1	12	6.5	11.5
labelCity	City	1	12	7.5	11.5
labelState	State	1	60	7.5	5
labelPostal	Postal Code	1	12	8.5	11.5
labelCNumber	Cart #	1	12	10.5	11.5
labelCName	Name on Card	1	12	11.5	11.5
labelCDate	Exp. Date	1	12	12.5	11.5

NOTE

Depending on the current display configuration, the entire text for labelCName might not be visible in the Designer. This does not affect how the HTML displays in a browser.

14

Figure 14.2.

Adding field labels to the Checkout form.

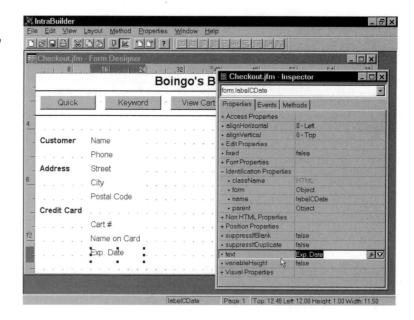

7. Open the Field Palette and add fields from the customer1 tab. When you drop controls from the Field Palette, the control names match the field names. Leave the given names and position the fields, as shown in Table 14.3.

Table 14.3. Datalinked controls from the Field Palette.

Name	Left	Top	Width
name	29	4.5	40
phone	29	5.5	20
street	29	6.5	40
city	29	7.5	30
state	66	7.5	3
postal	29	8.5	12
cardnumber	29	10.5	20
cardname	29	11.5	40
carddate	29	12.5	12

TIP

When you're working with large tables, the screen can quickly get cluttered by the Field Palette. You can shrink down the Field Palette by showing text only. This is an option in the Toolbars and Palettes dialog box.

8. Before adding any more controls, save the form and run it through both Navigator and Internet Explorer. If you need to make any adjustments, it is better to do that now rather than later. Figure 14.3 shows how the controls align in Navigator.

Figure 14.3.

Viewing the Text control layout in Netscape Navigator.

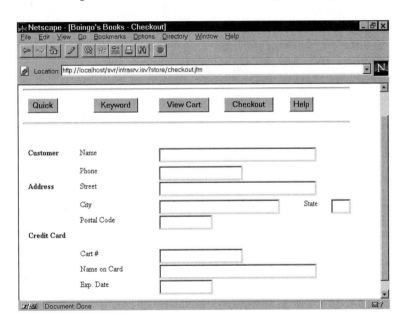

At this point, the Checkout form is void of logic and works without the rest of the shopping cart application. You can run it directly using the following URL:

```
http://localhost/svr/intrasrv.isv?store/checkout.jfm
```

The form still needs one more HTML control, two more buttons, three radio buttons, and a select control. The Checkout toolbar button also is inappropriate on the Checkout form. If you have the existing controls looking appropriate, continue on to finish up the layout of page one.

14

1. Reopen the Checkout form in the Form Designer.
2. Add an HTML control to display the total purchase price for items currently in the Cart. Use the properties listed in Table 14.4. You can leave the text property as a default. The form's onServerLoad event takes care of assigning the correct string to this control's text property.

Table 14.4. Properties for the `htmlTotal` control.

Property	Value
name	htmlTotal
height	1
left	1
top	3.5
width	65

3. Add three radio buttons, using the properties shown in Table 14.5. Note that the radio buttons might appear with a bold font when first added to a form. However, when you run or redesign the form, the radio buttons display with the correct font.

Table 14.5. Datalinked controls from the Field Palette.

name	groupName	text	height	left	top	width
radioVisa	card	Visa	1	12	9.5	11.5
radioMC	card	Master Card	1	29	9.5	12
radioAMEX	card	American Express	1	46	9.5	23

The radio buttons correspond to the Card field in the Customer table. Although you could create a direct datalink from the field to each radio button, the field length does not accommodate the current text properties. The field can store only up to 10 characters. Rather than storing the longer strings, the application will store VISA, MC, and AMEX to the field.

4. Add a select control with the properties shown in Table 14.6. This is the drop-down version, unlike the select list used in the Quick form and the Results form.

Table 14.6. Properties for the `selectCountry` control.

Property	Value
name	selectCountry
left	46

14

Property	Value
top	8.5
width	23

5. Datalink the `selectCountry` to the `Country` field in the Customer table. Use the visual property builder shown in Figure 14.4. Open the dialog box by clicking on the `dataLink` property tool button.

Figure 14.4.

DataLinking
`selectCountry` *to*
`parent.customer1.`
`rowset.fields`
`["COUNTRY"].`

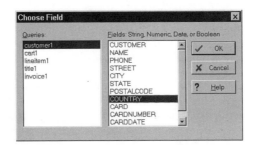

6. Attach an array to the Select control's `options` property. Click on the Options tool button to select `array` and click on the Array tool button to open the array builder.

7. Create the literal array by entering country names under String and adding them to the array. Use USA as the first element, so that it becomes the default. Add five or six more countries, as shown in Figure 14.5.

Figure 14.5.

Building an array for
the `options` *property.*

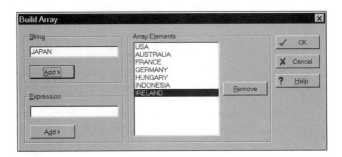

8. Add two buttons at the bottom of the form. Use the properties listed in Table 14.7.

Table 14.7. Datalinked controls from the Field Palette.

Name	Text	Left	Top	Width
buttonBuy	Buy Now	1	13.5	12
buttonCancel	Cancel	15	13.5	12

14

9. Before you can view the final appearance in a browser, you must hide the Checkout toolbar button. Inspect form and click the tool button for the onServerLoad event. Create a simple method as shown:

```
function Form_onServerLoad()
{
    this.buttonCheckout.visible = false ;
}
```

With all the visual design work done on page one, save the form and run it in the IntraBuilder Designer. Try using the select drop-down list and pay attention to the tab order. When you tab through the form in the Designer, the order matches the order in which you added controls in the Form Designer. The first controls are the toolbar buttons. The tab moves to the Text controls and then to the first radio button. Notice that the order does not flow from top to bottom. From the radio button, focus goes to the select list.

After you know the Checkout form runs okay in the Designer, try it in both Netscape Navigator and Internet Explorer. The tab order in both browsers goes from top to bottom. Internet Explorer treats the radio button group as a single tab stop and includes the URL field in the tab set of the form. Navigator treats each radio button as a separate tab and does not include the URL entry in the same tab set as form controls. Navigator has no default tab position.

Figure 14.6.

Using the Select control in Internet Explorer.

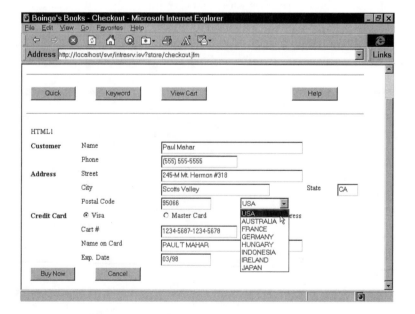

The Select control behavior is slightly different when run through a browser than when run through the Designer. In the Designer, the value of the control can differ from any elements in the list. Navigator and Internet Explorer render the Select control as a drop-down list box that forces all values to exist in the list. If a datalink value is not in the list, the value changes to the first item in the options array. This makes the Checkout form's select list appear blank in the Designer and default to USA in a browser.

Using Page Two for a Message

The checkout process works only if there are already items in the shopping cart. If the shopper attempts to open the Checkout form before adding items to the cart, the shopper needs to see an appropriate message. When no items have been found in a search, a separate Message form contains the message. When all items get deleted from the Cart form, the controls on the form morph into a message form. The Checkout form uses a third approach to messaging. Instead of using a separate form or changing the function of existing controls, this form uses a separate form page as a message form.

The Help form displays the Cart item count under the toolbar. It calculates the item count in an onServerLoad event. The Checkout form also displays summary information under the toolbar. In this case, the sum is the total price of all items rather than a simple item count.

You can create two methods to handle calculating the total price and handling an empty cart. The first method links to the form's onServerLoad event. The other moves the toolbar to page two. Here are the steps to create the two methods and add a message to page two.

1. Open checkout.jfm in the Form Designer.
2. Press the Page Down key to move to page two. The form will go blank because all controls currently reside on page one.
3. Add a single HTML control below where the toolbar would appear. Use the properties from Table 14.8.

Table 14.8. Properties for the htmlEmpty control.

Property	Value
name	htmlEmpty
height	2
left	1
top	3.5
width	65
text	<H3>Your shopping cart is empty.</H3>

14

The position of the htmlEmpty control shown in Figure 14.7 is identical to the htmlMessage control in the Message form. This provides a consistent look and feel between forms. After this page has the toolbar, it will look just like the standard Message form.

Figure 14.7.

Adding htmlEmpty *to page two.*

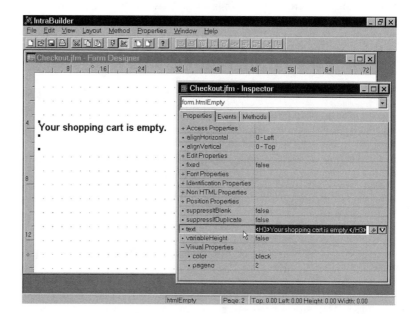

4. Create a new unlinked method to move the toolbar to page one. From the menu, select Method|New Method. Remove the {Export} comment, rename the method, and enter the following code.

```
function MoveToolbar( thisForm, nPage )
{
   // first 7 elements are the toolbar
   for (var i = 0 ; i < 8 ; i++ ) {
      thisForm.elements[i].pageno = nPage ;
   }
}
```

This method takes advantage of the elements array of a form. The elements array references all the controls contained in a form. It does not include database objects. You can use the elements array to modify controls without knowing the control names. In this case, the method uses elements to move the first seven controls to a given page.

5. Use the Method Editor to modify the Form_onServerLoad method. Enter the code shown in Listing 14.1. When you've finished, move back to page one and save the form.

14

Listing 14.1. The code for `checkout::Form_onServerLoad()`.

```
1: function Form_onServerLoad()2: {
2:     var cartRow = this.cart1.rowset,
3:         titleRow = this.title1.rowset,
4:         customerRow = this.customer1.rowset,
5:         nTotal = 0 ;
6:     this.buttonCheckout.visible = false ;
7:
8:     try {
9:        var x = this.user ;   // Is user key undefined?
10:     }
11:     catch (Exception error) {
12:        if (error.code == 167) {
13:            this.user = "" + (new NetInfo()).sessionID
14:        }
15:     }
16:
17:     cartRow.filter = "CARTUSER = " + "'" + this.user + "'" ;
18:     if ( cartRow.count() == 0 ) {
19:        this.pageno = 2 ;
20:        class::MoveToolbar( this, 2 ) ;
21:     }
22:     else {
23:        this.pageno = 1 ;
24:        cartRow.first() ;
25:        while ( ! cartRow.endOfSet ) {
26:            nTotal += ( cartRow.fields["QTY"].value *
27:                titleRow.fields["PRICE"].value ) ;
28:            cartRow.next() ;
29:        }
30:        this.htmlTotal.text = "<H4>Total Order $" + nTotal + "</H4>" ;
31:        customerRow.beginAppend() ;
32:     }
33: }
```

The `Form_onServerLoad()` method serves two functions. First it determines whether a shopper is ready to check out. If so, it creates a buffer in the Customer table. Otherwise, the function switches over to page two.

Like most methods that deal with queries, Listing 14.1 begins by creating shortcut references to the rowset objects. Lines 2 through 5 also create a temporary variable to use in calculating the total price.

```
function Form_onServerLoad()
{
   var cartRow = this.cart1.rowset,
       titleRow = this.title1.rowset,
       customerRow = this.customer1.rowset,
       nTotal = 0 ;
```

14

Lines 8 through 15 check to see whether the user property exists. This code is a shortened version of the user key generation routine in the Help form. This code lets you run the Checkout form directly from the IntraBuilder Explorer or a browser. If you are not running from a browser, line 13 creates the user property as an empty string.

```
try {
   var x = this.user ;   // Is user key undefined?
}
catch (Exception error) {
   if (error.code == 167) {
      this.user = "" + (new NetInfo()).sessionID
   }
}
```

The filter expression on line 17 is identical to the one in the Cart form and the Help form. You might want to comment out the filter assignment if you want to test run the Checkout form with all the data in the Cart table. If no rows are found, the form switches to page two, and the toolbar also moves.

Changing the pageno property of the form changes what page the user sees. Changing the pageno property of a control changes the control's page association. A control is not visible unless it is has a pageno equal to the form. The exception to this rule is if a control is on a pageno of zero. Controls on page zero appear on all pages. Normally, the form is set only to page zero at design-time.

```
cartRow.filter = "CARTUSER = " + "'" + this.user + "'" ;
if ( cartRow.count() == 0 ) {
   this.pageno = 2 ;
   class::MoveToolbar( this, 2 ) ;
}
```

If there are rows, line 23 sets the pageno to 1. Although 1 is normally the default, it is a good idea to explicitly set pageno in the onServerLoad whenever you are working with multiple page forms. By always setting the pageno property in the onServerLoad, the form will work, even if you forget to return to page one when you make changes in the Form Designer.

```
else {
   this.pageno = 1 ;
```

A while loop is used to calculate the total price of goods in the cart. Lines 26 and 27 comprise a single summation statement. The loop works only if the masterRowset property of the Title query points to the rowset of the Cart query. If the relation is not set correctly, no syntax error occurs, but the resulting nTotal value is incorrect.

```
cartRow.first() ;
while ( ! cartRow.endOfSet ) {
   nTotal += ( cartRow.fields["QTY"].value *
      titleRow.fields["PRICE"].value ) ;
   cartRow.next() ;
}
```

Line 30 displays the calculated field in a level-three heading, and line 31 creates an empty row buffer. The value in nTotal defaults to showing two decimal places, which is exactly what you need here. The Rowset::beginAppend() method creates an uncommitted buffer for a new row. Here, the new row is datalinked to several Text controls. All of them will appear blank and allow data entry. New rows cannot be committed without an explicit call to Rowset::Save().

```
this.htmlTotal.text = "<H4>Total Order $" + nTotal + "</H4>" ;
customerRow.beginAppend() ;
```

If you run the form in the Designer and have nothing in the cart, page one flashes on the screen before the message on page two. It doesn't look very good in the Designer, but this flash does not carry over into the browsers. Shoppers will see only the appropriate page with the toolbar, as shown in Figure 14.8.

Figure 14.8.

Viewing page two of the Checkout form in Navigator.

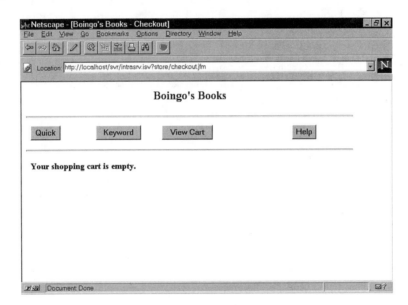

Validating Data with a Pseudo-Modal Dialog Box

Most Windows applications contain both modal and modeless windows. Common uses of *modal* dialog boxes are property sheets, error messages, and prompting for a filename. *Modeless* windows can be SDI (Single Document Interface) windows, such as Notepad, or MDI (Multiple Document Interface) windows, such as you find in Word, Excel, and IntraBuilder. Windows development environments make modal window creating easy through methods, such as Delphi's ShowModal() and Visual dBASE's ReadModal().

14

NEW TERM   *Modal dialogs* are windows that the user must respond to before continuing to work with an application. They usually contain buttons such as OK and Cancel that close the dialog. As a general rule, users cannot resize a modal dialog. HTML does not have any direct support for modal dialogs.

HTML forms are by nature non-modal. You can add some simple dialog boxes, such as `alert()` and `confirm()`, through client-side JavaScript. For server-side events, you can mimic the behavior of a modal dialog box by presenting an HTML form with limited links. These forms cannot prevent the user from jumping out of your application completely, but they can control the flow of forms within an application.

For the Checkout form, shoppers must fill in every field before the order can be processed. Although much more extensive validation is possible, including direct validation of credit card information with a credit card agency, this example checks only that fields are not blank. If one or more blank fields is found, the user needs notification and a way to correct the error. This is where the pseudo-modal form comes in. It can list any blank fields and provide a single button that returns the shopper to page one of the Checkout form. A good way to implement a pseudo-modal form is through form-paging. Follow these steps to set up page three as the pseudo-modal form.

1. Open the Checkout form in the Form Designer and switch to page three. You can press Page Up and Page Down to change pages. The current page number appears in the status line.

2. Add three HTML controls with the properties listed in Table 14.9. Notice that you are not leaving room for the toolbar. As a modal type form, this form will have only one point of departure rather than the array of options provided by the toolbar.

Table 14.9. Position properties for the error message controls.

name	height	left	top	width
errorPrompt	1	1	1	65
errorList	8	1	2.5	65
errorHelp	1	1	11	65

3. Change the text property for `errorPrompt` to the following:

   `Unable to process order. The following fields cannot be left blank:`

4. Leave the `errorList` with a default text property and change the text property for `errorHelp` to the following:

   `Press Continue to return to the Checkout form and correct the problem.`

5. Add a button with the properties shown in Table 14.10. This is the last form control for the shopping cart application.

Table 14.10. Properties for the `buttonContinue` control.

Property	Value
name	buttonContinue
left	1
top	13
width	12
text	Continue

6. Create and link a new method to the `onServerClick` event of the new button. Edit the `buttonContinue_onServerClick()` method as shown in the following code.

```
function buttonContinue_onServerClick()
{
    this.form.title = "Boingo's Books - Checkout" ;
    this.form.pageno = 1 ;
}
```

This button restores the title for page one and changes the page to page one. To the shopper, it will appear as though the Checkout form has reopened. The form maintains all previously entered data.

7. At this point, page three should resemble Figure 14.9. You are done with that page. Switch back to page one and select the Buy Now button.

Figure 14.9.

Designing page three of the Checkout form.

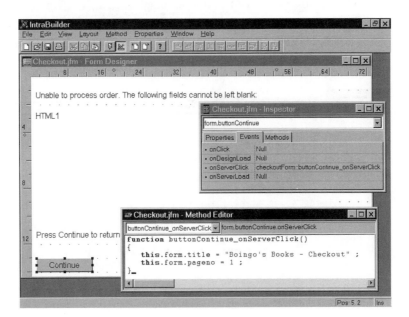

8. Create and link a new method to the Cancel button's `onServerClick` event. Enter the following method:

```
function buttonCancel_onServerClick()
{
    var nextForm = new messageForm() ;
    nextForm.htmlMessage.text = "Order canceled." ;
    nextForm.user = this.form.user ;
    nextForm.open() ;
    form.release() ;
}
```

Nothing really happens when a shopper cancels an order. The items remain in the cart, and the shopper moves to the Message form. Clicking any of the toolbar buttons has a similar effect. The Cancel button is simply a physiological aid for shoppers who expect to see a Cancel button.

9. Create and link a new method to the Buy Now button's `onServerClick` event. Enter the following method:

```
function buttonBuy_onServerClick()
{
    if ( class::Blanks( this.form ) ) {
        this.form.title = "Boingo's Books - Alert" ;
        this.form.pageno = 3 ;
    }
}
```

The `buttonBuy` is the counterpart of `buttonContinue`. If the `Blanks()` method returns `false`, the two buttons toggle the pages back and forth.

10. Create a new unlinked method. From the menu, select Method|New Method. Remove the {Export} comment and modify Listing 14.2. When you've finished, save the form and close the Designer.

INPUT **Listing 14.2. The `Blanks()` validation method.**

```
 1: function Blanks( thisForm )
 2: {
 3:     var lReturn = false,
 4:         textName = "",
 5:         fieldList = "" ;
 6:
 7:     for ( var i = 0 ; i < thisForm.elements.length ; i++ ) {
 8:         if ( thisForm.elements[i].className == "Text" ) {
 9:             if ( thisForm.elements[i].value.length == 0 ) {
10:                 lReturn = true ;
11:                 textName = thisForm.elements[i].name ;
12:                 fieldList += ("<LI>" + textName + "</LI>") ;
13:             }
14:         }
15:     }
16:
```

```
17:    thisForm.errorList.text = "<UL>" + fieldList + "</UL>" ;
18:    return ( lReturn ) ;
19: }
```

ANALYSIS This function checks to see whether any of the Text controls have a blank value. You could expand this function to include complex validation, such as checking whether the credit card expiration date has passed and that the postal code is formatted correctly for the selected country.

The method takes the `thisForm` parameter to allow calling from any event. In this case, the form will be called only from the button. You also could leave the parameter out and replace all instances of `thisForm` with `this.form`. Leaving in the parameter makes the method more flexible for future enhancements to the form. Lines 3 through 5 define three local variables with the var statement. The `lReturn` variable is a flag that is `true` if blanks are found. The function starts with the assumption that no blanks will be found. The other two variables are for building an HTML bulleted list of blank fields.

```
function Blanks( thisForm )
{
   var lReturn = false,
       textName = "",
       fieldList = ""
```

The `for` loop goes through all the controls on the form. The `if` on line 8 checks to see whether any of the controls are Text controls. No other control type requires validation.

```
for ( var i = 0 ; i < thisForm.elements.length ; i++ ) {
   if ( thisForm.elements[i].className == "Text" ) {
```

If a Text control is found, line 9 checks the length of the value to see whether the field is blank. The `value` property is always trimmed of trailing spaces. Any field that contains only spaces has a length of zero. Any blanks cause the `lReturn` flag to become `true`. If all you needed the method to do was find blanks, you could include a `break` statement to break out of the loop when the first blank was found.

The method does not break out of the loop, so it can build a bulleted list of all blank fields. The `<LI>` and `</LI>` HTML tags delimit the items in a list. These tags work for both numbered lists and bulleted lists.

```
if ( thisForm.elements[i].value.length == 0 ) {
   lReturn = true ;
   textName = thisForm.elements[i].name ;
   fieldList += ("<LI>" + textName + "</LI>") ;
}
```

14

Creating the field list is simple because each Text control name is identical to the datalink field name. If control names were not the same as the field names, you could substitute `dataLink.fieldName` for name when generating the list.

```
textName = thisForm.elements[i].dataLink.fieldName ;
```

Line 17 encloses the field list with HTML unnumbered list tags. An unnumbered list is a bulleted list. Figure 14.10 shows the bulleted field list as it appears in Netscape Navigator. An HTML bulleted list of the U.S. flag's colors would look like this:

```
<UL><LI>Red</LI><LI>White</LI><LI>Blue<LI></UL>
```

The tag for an automatically numbered list is <OL>. If you replace the <UL> tags with <OL> tags, the list becomes a numbered list instead of a bulleted list.

```
thisForm.errorList.text = "<UL>" + fieldList + "</UL>" ;
return ( lReturn ) ;
}
```

Figure 14.10.

Page three of the Checkout form in Navigator.

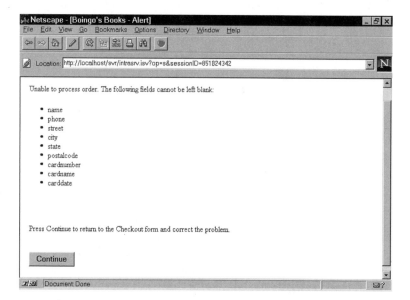

Populating the Customer, Invoice, and Lineitem Tables

Up to this point, the Invoice and Lineitem tables have been dormant. In this section, you will learn how to write the methods that populate these tables and commit a new row to the Customer table. It is okay to commit changes now that the form has checked for an empty Cart and blank customer fields.

You can make all the remaining changes to the Checkout form through the Script Editor. Open the Checkout form in the Script Editor and modify buttonBuy_onServerClick() to call three new methods, as shown in Listing 14.3. Also add the three methods from Listings 14.4, 14.5, and 14.6.

Listing 14.3. The `buttonBuy_onServerClick()` **method without a call to the Receipt report.**

```
1: function buttonBuy_onServerClick()
2: {
3:    if ( class::Blanks( this.form ) ) {
4:       this.form.title = "Boingo's Books - Alert" ;
5:       this.form.pageno = 3 ;
6:    }
7:    else {
8:       class::SaveCustomer( this.form ) ;
9:       class::SaveInvoice( this.form ) ;
10:      class::SaveLineitem( this.form ) ;
11:      this.form.release() ;
12:   }
13: }
```

The code to check for blanks remains the same. Lines 7 through 12 contain a new `else` block to call three methods and release the current form. Later, you can execute a report within this same block. However, to design the report, you first need some sample data. Running this block as it is will provide you with the data necessary to design the report.

```
else {
   class::SaveCustomer( this.form ) ;
   class::SaveInvoice( this.form ) ;
   class::SaveLineitem( this.form ) ;
   this.form.release() ;
}
```

This version of the `buttonBuy_onServerClick()` method is not designed to run in a browser. The form closes without creating new output for the browser. When run in a Designer, the form appears as an MDI window that closes normally. In a browser, the form occupies the browser display area without having its own window. A browser never expects a form to close without having something to take its place.

Listing 14.4. The `SaveCustomer()` **method.**

```
1: function SaveCustomer( thisForm )
2: {
3:    var customer2 = new Query("select * from customer") ;
4:    var customer1Row = thisForm.customer1.rowset,
5:        customer2Row = customer2.rowset ;
6:
```

14

continues

Listing 14.4. continued

```
 7:     if ( thisForm.radioVisa.value ) {
 8:         customer1Row.fields["CARD"].value = "VISA" ;
 9:     }
10:     else if( thisForm.radioMC.value ) {
11:         customer1Row.fields["CARD"].value = "MC" ;
12:     }
13:     else {
14:         customer1Row.fields["CARD"].value = "AMEX" ;
15:     }
16:
17:     customer2Row.indexName = "CUSTOMER" ;
18:     customer2Row.last() ;
19:     customer1Row.fields["CUSTOMER"].value =
20:      customer2Row.endOfSet ? 1 : customer2Row.fields["CUSTOMER"].value+1;
21:     customer1Row.save() ;
22:     customer2.active = false ;
23: }
```

ANALYSIS The SaveCustomer() method commits the datalinks in the row buffer along with the credit card type and a customer number. The credit card type is a simple code used in place of the longer descriptive text on the radio buttons. The codes VISA, MC, and AMEX translate to Visa, Master Card, and American Express, respectively. The customer number is a unique sequential number. To help in calculating the next available customer number, line 3 creates an additional query for the Customer table.

Line 3 passes the SQL command to the query constructor as a shortcut way to assign the sql property value and activate the query. Lines 4 and 5 contain a separate var statement that creates shortcut references to the rowset objects of the original and new customer queries.

```
var customer2 = new Query("select * from customer") ;
var customer1Row = thisForm.customer1.rowset,
    customer2Row = customer2.rowset ;
```

Lines 7 through 15 contain a series of if and else blocks to assign the correct credit card type based on the radio buttons. The value property of a radio button is true when the value is selected. Because all three have the same groupName property, only one can be selected at a time.

```
if ( thisForm.radioVisa.value ) {
    customer1Row.fields["CARD"].value = "VISA" ;
}
else if( thisForm.radioMC.value ) {
    customer1Row.fields["CARD"].value = "MC" ;
}
else {
    customer1Row.fields["CARD"].value = "AMEX" ;
}
```

An index helps quickly determine the highest customer number currently stored in the table. Line 18 moves the row pointer to the last row in the ascending index to locate the highest value. The next customer number is one higher than the current highest. If no rows are present in the table, the method uses one as the initial customer number.

```
customer2Row.indexName = "CUSTOMER" ;
customer2Row.last() ;
customer1Row.fields["CUSTOMER"].value =
  customer2Row.endOfSet ? 1 : customer2Row.fields["CUSTOMER"].value + 1 ;
```

You also could use a single query to perform the operation. Using two queries cuts down on the interval between the time the next highest value is calculated and the time the new row is committed. The longer the interval, the higher the probability that a conflict will occur when two shoppers fire the routine simultaneously on separate remote agents. If this happens, there is a possibility of both shoppers getting the same customer number.

If you are working with remote agents on a high-volume site, you can ensure unique key values by placing a lock on the last row. In that case, you will need to create another error-handling page similar to page three. The new page could inform the user to try again in a few seconds and use the same Continue button to return to page one.

```
customer2Row.indexName = "CUSTOMER" ;
customer2Row.last() ;
if ( customer2Row.lockRow() ) {
   customer1Row.fields["CUSTOMER"].value =
    customer2Row.endOfSet ? 1 : customer2Row.fields["CUSTOMER"].value + 1 ;
   customer1Row.save() ;
}
else {
   this.form.pageno = 4 ; // New page with "please wait" message.
}
```

Line 21 commits the new values and completes the append operation that began in the onServerLoad event. Line 21 deactivates the temporary query to recover resources no longer needed by the form.

```
customer1Row.save() ;
customer2.active = false ;
```

Another way to ensure unique customer numbers is to use Paradox tables in place of dBASE tables. Although Paradox tables are slower to work with, they do have an auto-increment field type that automatically does what this routine does for the customer number field.

INPUT **Listing 14.5. The SaveInvoice() method.**

```
1: function SaveInvoice( thisForm )
2: {
3:    var invoice2 = new Query("select * from invoice") ;
4:    var customerRow = thisForm.customer1.rowset
5:        invoice1Row = thisForm.invoice1.rowset,
```

continues

Listing 14.5. continued

```
 6:          invoice2Row = invoice2.rowset ;
 7:
 8:      invoice1Row.beginAppend() ;
 9:      invoice1Row.fields["CUSTOMER"].value =
10:          customerRow.fields["CUSTOMER"].value ;
11:      invoice1Row.fields["ORDERDATE"].value = (new Date()) ;
12:      invoice2Row.indexName = "INVOICE" ;
13:      invoice2Row.last() ;
14:      invoice1Row.fields["INVOICE"].value =
15:       invoice2Row.endOfSet ? 1 : invoice2Row.fields["INVOICE"].value+1;
16:
17:      invoice1Row.save() ;
18:      invoice2.active = false ;
19: }
```

ANALYSIS
The SaveInvoice() method uses the same logic as the SaveCustomer() method to increment the key value. It also places the incremental code right before the Rowset::save() to immediately commit the new key.

The new code starts on line 8 where a Rowset::beginAppend() creates a new row buffer. This was not necessary in the previous method because a buffer already existed on the Customer table. The customer number is set up as a foreign key that relates the Invoice table to the Customer table. Line 11 sets the ORDERDATE field value to a new Date object without creating a reference for the Date object. The (new Date()) expression creates a Date object that returns the current date and disappears.

```
invoice1Row.beginAppend() ;
invoice1Row.fields["CUSTOMER"].value =
    customerRow.fields["CUSTOMER"].value ;
invoice1Row.fields["ORDERDATE"].value = (new Date()) ;
```

The Results form uses a Date object in a similar manner when updating the Cart table. Each table type stores dates in a slightly different manner. IntraBuilder automatically translates the Date object into a format understood by the current table.

INPUT **Listing 14.6. The SaveLineitems() method.**

```
 1: function SaveLineitem( thisForm )
 2: {
 3:    var invoiceRow = thisForm.invoice1.rowset,
 4:        lineitemRow = thisForm.lineitem1.rowset,
 5:        cartRow = thisForm.cart1.rowset ;
 6:    cartRow.first() ;
 7:
 8:    while ( ! cartRow.endOfSet ) {
 9:        lineitemRow.beginAppend() ;
10:        lineitemRow.fields["INVOICE"].value =
11:            invoiceRow.fields["INVOICE"].value ;
```

14

```
12:        lineitemRow.fields["ISBN"].value = cartRow.fields["ISBN"].value;
13:        lineitemRow.fields["QTY"].value = cartRow.fields["QTY"].value;
14:        lineitemRow.save() ;
15:        cartRow.delete() ;
16:    }
17: }
```

ANALYSIS The Lineitem table does not contain an incremental key. The main key value of the Lineitem table is a foreign key linking it to the Invoice table. The SaveLineitem() method assigns that key to each new row that it moves from the Cart table to the Lineitem table.

Like the other save methods, this one starts by creating shortcut references to the rowsets. It does not create any temporary query objects. Line 7 calls Rowset::first() to make sure all rows in the Cart table get processed. Without this call, the method would do nothing because the row pointer was left at endOfSet after calculating the total price in the onServerLoad event.

```
var invoiceRow = thisForm.invoice1.rowset,
    lineitemRow = thisForm.lineitem1.rowset,
    cartRow = thisForm.cart1.rowset ;
cartRow.first() ;
```

The while loop moves through each row using Rowset::delete() in place of Rowset::next(). Line 15 deletes each row causing the row pointer to move to the same place as a Rowset::next() would. Typically, you would place a call to Rowset::next() at the bottom of a loop. For each row in the Cart table, a new row is created and committed into the Lineitem table.

```
while ( ! cartRow.endOfSet ) {
    lineitemRow.beginAppend() ;
    lineitemRow.fields["INVOICE"].value =
      invoiceRow.fields["INVOICE"].value ;
    lineitemRow.fields["ISBN"].value = cartRow.fields["ISBN"].value ;
    lineitemRow.fields["QTY"].value = cartRow.fields["QTY"].value ;
    lineitemRow.save() ;
    cartRow.delete() ;
}
```

The user key and cart date are not transferred into the Lineitem table. Equivalent values can be found in the related Customer and Invoice tables. The customer number in the Customer table replaces the functionality of the user key. The order date in the Lineitem table replaces the cart date.

After modifying the buttonBuy_onServerClick() and creating the three save methods, run the form in the Designer, add a few books into the cart, and make a purchase. This will set up some valid sample data for creating a Receipt report.

After you have some sample data, you can create an empty report and complete the Checkout form. Use the following steps to create an empty report and call it from the Checkout form.

14

1. Open the Script Pad and enter the following JavaScript statement:

   ```
   _sys.reports.design("receipt.jrp") ;
   ```

2. Press Ctrl+S to save the blank report. If you do not explicitly save the form, closing a blank report will abandon it without any prompting.

3. Close the Report Designer.

4. Open the Checkout form in the Script Editor and add the following JavaScript statement to the `buttonBuy_onServerClick()` method, as shown on lines 423 and 424 of Listing 14.7.

   ```
   _sys.scripts.run("RECEIPT.JRP", 1, -1,
       this.form.invoice1.rowset.fields["INVOICE"].value) ;
   ```

You can now try the Checkout form through a browser. However, the blank report translates into a blank HTML page. In the next section, you will learn how to design a receipt with the Report Designer. If things are not going as expected, refer to Listing 14.7, which shows the complete source code for the Checkout form.

INPUT   **Listing 14.7. The completed Checkout form.**

```
 1: // {End Header} Do not remove this comment//
 2: // Generated on 01/02/97
 3: //
 4: var f = new checkoutForm();
 5: f.open();
 6: class checkoutForm extends ToolbarCForm from "TOOLBAR.JCF" {
 7:     with (this) {
 8:         onServerLoad = class::Form_onServerLoad;
 9:         height = 15;
10:         left = 0;
11:         top = 0;
12:         width = 75;
13:         title = "Boingo's Books - Checkout";
14:     }
15:
16:     with (this.invoice1 = new Query()){
17:         left = 70;
18:         top = 2;
19:         sql = 'SELECT * FROM "invoice.DBF"';
20:         active = true;
21:     }
22:
23:     with (this.invoice1.rowset) {
24:     }
25:
26:     with (this.customer1 = new Query()){
27:         left = 70;
28:         top = 1;
29:         sql = 'SELECT * FROM "customer.DBF"';
30:         active = true;
```

```
31:     }
32:
33:     with (this.customer1.rowset) {
34:     }
35:
36:     with (this.lineitem1 = new Query()){
37:        left = 70;
38:        top = 3;
39:        sql = 'SELECT * FROM "lineitem.DBF"';
40:        active = true;
41:     }
42:
43:     with (this.lineitem1.rowset) {
44:     }
45:
46:     with (this.cart1 = new Query()){
47:        left = 70;
48:        top = 4;
49:        sql = 'SELECT * FROM "cart.DBF"';
50:        active = true;
51:     }
52:
53:     with (this.cart1.rowset) {
54:     }
55:
56:     with (this.title1 = new Query()){
57:        left = 70;
58:       top = 5;
56:        sql = 'SELECT * FROM "title.DBF"';
60:      active = true;
61:     }
62:
63:     with (this.title1.rowset) {
64:        indexName = "ISBN";
65:        masterRowset = parent.parent.cart1.rowset;
66:        masterFields = "ISBN";
67:     }
68:
69:     with (this.headCustomer = new HTML(this)){
70:        height = 1;
71:        left = 1;
72:        top = 4.5;
73:        width = 10;
74:        color = "black";
75:        text = "<H4>Customer</H4>";
76:     }
77:
78:     with (this.headAddress = new HTML(this)){
79:        height = 1;
80:        left = 1;
81:        top = 6.5;
82:        width = 10;
83:        color = "black";
84:        text = "<H4>Address</H4>";
85:     }
```

continues

14

Listing 14.7. continued

```
 86:
 87:    with (this.headCard = new HTML(this)){
 88:       height = 1;
 89:       left = 1;
 90:       top = 9.5;
 91:       width = 10;
 92:       color = "black";
 93:       text = "<H4>Credit Card</H4>";
 94:    }
 95:
 96:    with (this.labelName = new HTML(this)){
 97:       height = 1;
 98:       left = 12;
 99:       top = 4.5;
100:       width = 11.5;
101:      color = "black";
102:       text = "Name";
103:    }
104:
105:    with (this.labelPhone = new HTML(this)){
106:       height = 1;
107:       left = 12;
108:       top = 5.5;
109:       width = 11.5;
110:       color = "black";
111:       text = "Phone";
112:    }
113:
114:    with (this.labelStreet = new HTML(this)){
115:       height = 1;
116:       left = 12;
117:       top = 6.5;
118:       width = 11.5;
119:       color = "black";
120:       text = "Street";
121:    }
122:
123:    with (this.labelCity = new HTML(this)){
124:       height = 1;
125:       left = 12;
126:       top = 7.5;
127:       width = 11.5;
128:       color = "black";
129:       text = "City";
130:    }
131:
132:    with (this.labelState = new HTML(this)){
133:       height = 1;
134:       left = 60;
135:       top = 7.5;
136:       width = 5;
137:       color = "black";
138:       text = "State";
139:    }
140:
```

14

```
141:    with (this.labelPostal = new HTML(this)){
142:        height = 1;
143:        left = 12;
144:        top = 8.5;
145:        width = 11.5;
146:        color = "black";
147:        text = "Postal Code";
148:    }
149:
150:    with (this.labelCNumber = new HTML(this)){
151:        height = 1;
152:        left = 12;
153:        top = 10.5;
154:        width = 11.5;
155:        color = "black";
156:        text = "Cart #";
157:    }
158:
159:    with (this.labelCName = new HTML(this)){
160:        height = 1;
161:        left = 12;
162:        top = 11.5;
163:        width = 11.5;
164:        color = "black";
165:        text = "Name on Card";
166:    }
167:
168:    with (this.labelCDate = new HTML(this)){
169:        height = 1;
170:        left = 12;
171:        top = 12.5;
172:        width = 11.5;
173:        color = "black";
174:        text = "Exp. Date";
175:    }
176:
177:    with (this.name = new Text(this)){
178:        left = 29;
179:        top = 4.5;
180:        width = 40;
181:        dataLink = parent.customer1.rowset.fields["NAME"];
182:    }
183:
184:    with (this.phone = new Text(this)){
185:        left = 29;
186:        top = 5.5;
187:        width = 20;
188:        dataLink = parent.customer1.rowset.fields["PHONE"];
189:    }
190:
191:    with (this.street = new Text(this)){
192:        left = 29;
193:        top = 6.5;
194:        width = 40;
195:        dataLink = parent.customer1.rowset.fields["STREET"];
196:    }
```

14

continues

Listing 14.7. continued

```
197:
198:     with (this.city = new Text(this)){
199:         left = 29;
200:         top = 7.5;
201:         width = 30;
202:         dataLink = parent.customer1.rowset.fields["CITY"];
203:     }
204:
205:     with (this.state = new Text(this)){
206:         left = 66;
207:         top = 7.5;
208:         width = 3;
209:         dataLink = parent.customer1.rowset.fields["STATE"];
210:     }
211:
212:     with (this.postalcode = new Text(this)){
213:         left = 29;
214:         top = 8.5;
215:         width = 12;
216:         dataLink = parent.customer1.rowset.fields["POSTALCODE"];
217:     }
218:
219:     with (this.cardnumber = new Text(this)){
220:         left = 29;
221:         top = 10.5;
222:         width = 20;
223:         dataLink = parent.customer1.rowset.fields["CARDNUMBER"];
224:     }
225:
226:     with (this.cardname = new Text(this)){
227:         left = 29;
228:         top = 11.5;
229:         width = 40;
230:         dataLink = parent.customer1.rowset.fields["CARDNAME"];
231:     }
232:
233:     with (this.carddate = new Text(this)){
234:         left = 29;
235:         top = 12.5;
236:         width = 12;
237:         dataLink = parent.customer1.rowset.fields["CARDDATE"];
238:     }
239:
240:     with (this.htmlTotal = new HTML(this)){
241:         height = 1;
242:         left = 1;
243:         top = 3.5;
244:         width = 65;
245:         color = "black";
246:         text = "HTML1";
247:     }
248:
```

14

```
249:    with (this.radioVisa = new Radio(this)){
250:        height = 1;
251:        left = 12;
252:        top = 9.5;
253:        width = 11.5;
254:        text = "Visa";
255:        value = true;
256:        groupName = "card";
257:    }
258:
259:    with (this.radioMC = new Radio(this)){
260:        height = 1;
261:        left = 29;
262:        top = 9.5;
263:        width = 12;
264:        text = "Master Card";
265:        value = false;
266:        groupName = "card";
267:    }
268:
269:    with (this.radioAMEX = new Radio(this)){
270:        height = 1;
271:        left = 46;
272:        top = 9.5;
273:        width = 23;
274:        text = "American Express";
275:        value = false;
276:        groupName = "card";
277:    }
278:
279:    with (this.selectCountry = new Select(this)){
280:        left = 46;
281:        top = 8.5;
282:        width = 23;
283:        dataLink = parent.customer1.rowset.fields["COUNTRY"];
284:        options = 'array {"USA","AUSTRALIA","FRANCE","GERMANY",'+
285:                    '"HUNGARY","INDONESIA","IRELAND","JAPAN",""}';
286:    }
287:
288:    with (this.buttonBuy = new Button(this)){
289:        onServerClick = class::buttonBuy_onServerClick;
290:        left = 1;
291:        top = 13.5;
292:        width = 12;
293:        text = "Buy Now";
294:    }
295:
296:    with (this.buttonCancel = new Button(this)){
297:        onServerClick = class::buttonCancel_onServerClick;
298:        left = 15;
299:        top = 13.5;
300:        width = 12;
301:        text = "Cancel";
302:    }
```

14

continues

Listing 14.7. continued

```
303:
304:     with (this.htmlEmpty = new HTML(this)){
305:         height = 2;
306:         left = 1;
307:         top = 3.5;
308:         width = 65;
309:         color = "black";
310:         text = "<H3>Your shopping cart is empty.</H3>";
311:         pageno = 2;
312:     }
313:
314:     with (this.errorPrompt = new HTML(this)){
315:         height = 1;
316:         left = 1;
317:         top = 1;
318:         width = 65;
319:         color = "black";
320:         text = "Unable to process order. The following fields " +
321:                 "cannot be left blank:";
322:         pageno = 3;
323:     }
324:
325:     with (this.errorList = new HTML(this)){
326:         height = 8;
327:         left = 1;
328:         top = 2.5;
329:         width = 65;
330:         color = "black";
331:         text = "HTML1";
332:         pageno = 3;
333:     }
334:
335:     with (this.errorHelp = new HTML(this)){
336:         height = 1;
337:         left = 1;
338:         top = 11;
339:         width = 65;
340:         color = "black";
341:         text = "Press Continue to return to the Checkout "+
342:                 "form and correct the problem.";
343:         pageno = 3;
344:     }
345:
346:     with (this.buttonContinue = new Button(this)){
347:         onServerClick = class::buttonContinue_onServerClick;
348:         left = 1;
349:         top = 13;
350:         width = 12;
351:         text = "Continue";
352:         pageno = 3;
353:     }
354:
```

```
355:    function Form_onServerLoad()
356:    {
357:        var cartRow = this.cart1.rowset,
358:            titleRow = this.title1.rowset,
359:            customerRow = this.customer1.rowset,
360:            nTotal = 0 ;
361:        this.buttonCheckout.visible = false ;
362:
363:        try {
364:            var x = this.user ;   // Is user key undefined?
365:        }
366:        catch (Exception error) {
367:            if (error.code == 167) {
368:                this.user = "" + (new NetInfo()).sessionID
369:            }
370:        }
371:
372:        cartRow.filter = "CARTUSER = " + "'" + this.user + "'" ;
373:        if ( cartRow.count() == 0 ) {
374:            this.pageno = 2 ;
375:            class::MoveToolbar( this, 2 ) ;
376:        }
377:        else {
378:            this.pageno = 1 ;
379:            cartRow.first() ;
380:            while ( ! cartRow.endOfSet ) {
381:                nTotal += ( cartRow.fields["QTY"].value *
382:                    titleRow.fields["PRICE"].value ) ;
383:                cartRow.next() ;
384:            }
385:            this.htmlTotal.text = "<H4>Total Order $"+nTotal+"</H4>";
386:            customerRow.beginAppend() ;
387:        }
388:    }
389:
390:    function MoveToolbar( thisForm, nPage )
391:    {
392:        // first 7 elements are the toolbar
393:        for (var i = 0 ; i < 8 ; i++ ) {
394:            thisForm.elements[i].pageno = nPage ;
395:        }
396:    }
397:
398:    function buttonContinue_onServerClick()
399:    {
400:        this.form.title = "Boingo's Books - Checkout" ;
401:        this.form.pageno = 1 ;
402:    }
403:
404:    function buttonCancel_onServerClick()
405:    {
406:        var nextForm = new messageForm() ;
407:        nextForm.htmlMessage.text = "Order canceled." ;
408:        nextForm.user = this.form.user ;
```

continues

Listing 14.7. continued

```
409:         nextForm.open() ;
410:         form.release() ;
411:    }
412:
413:    function buttonBuy_onServerClick()
414:    {
415:       if ( class::Blanks( this.form ) ) {
416:          this.form.title = "Boingo's Books - Alert" ;
417:          this.form.pageno = 3 ;
418:       }
419:       else {
420:          class::SaveCustomer( this.form ) ;
421:          class::SaveInvoice( this.form ) ;
422:          class::SaveLineitem( this.form ) ;
423:          _sys.scripts.run("RECEIPT.JRP", 1, -1,
424:             this.form.invoice1.rowset.fields["INVOICE"].value);
425:          this.form.release() ;
426:       }
427:    }
428:
429:    function Blanks( thisForm )
430:    {
431:       var lReturn = false,
432:          textName = "",
433:          fieldList = "" ;
434:
435:       for ( var i = 0 ; i < thisForm.elements.length ; i++ ){
436:          if ( thisForm.elements[i].className == "Text" ) {
437:             if ( thisForm.elements[i].value.length == 0 ) {
438:                lReturn = true ;
439:                textName = thisForm.elements[i].name ;
440:                fieldList += ("<LI>" + textName + "</LI>") ;
441:             }
442:          }
443:       }
444:
445:       thisForm.errorList.text = "<UL>" + fieldList + "</UL>" ;
446:       return ( lReturn ) ;
447:    }
448:
449:    function SaveCustomer( thisForm )
450:    {
451:       var customer2 = new Query("select * from customer");
452:       var customer1Row = thisForm.customer1.rowset,
453:          customer2Row = customer2.rowset ;
454:
455:       if ( thisForm.radioVisa.value ) {
456:          customer1Row.fields["CARD"].value = "VISA" ;
457:       }
458:       else if( thisForm.radioMC.value ) {
459:          customer1Row.fields["CARD"].value = "MC" ;
460:       }
```

```
461:        else {
462:            customer1Row.fields["CARD"].value = "AMEX" ;
463:        }
464:
465:        customer2Row.indexName = "CUSTOMER" ;
466:        customer2Row.last() ;
467:        customer1Row.fields["CUSTOMER"].value =
468:    customer2Row.endOfSet ? 1 : customer2Row.fields["CUSTOMER"].value+1;
469:        customer1Row.save() ;
470:        customer2.active = false ;
471:    }
472:
473:    function SaveInvoice( thisForm )
474:    {
475:        var invoice2 = new Query("select * from invoice") ;
476:        var customerRow = thisForm.customer1.rowset
477:            invoice1Row = thisForm.invoice1.rowset,
478:            invoice2Row = invoice2.rowset ;
479:
480:        invoice1Row.beginAppend() ;
481:        invoice1Row.fields["CUSTOMER"].value =
482:            customerRow.fields["CUSTOMER"].value ;
483:        invoice1Row.fields["ORDERDATE"].value = (new Date()) ;
484:        invoice2Row.indexName = "INVOICE" ;
485:        invoice2Row.last() ;
486:        invoice1Row.fields["INVOICE"].value =
487:    invoice2Row.endOfSet ? 1 : invoice2Row.fields["INVOICE"].value+1;
488:
489:        invoice1Row.save() ;
490:        invoice2.active = false ;
491:    }
492:
493:    function SaveLineitem( thisForm )
494:    {
495:        var invoiceRow = thisForm.invoice1.rowset,
496:            lineitemRow = thisForm.lineitem1.rowset,
497:            cartRow = thisForm.cart1.rowset ;
498:        cartRow.first() ;
499:
500:        while ( ! cartRow.endOfSet ) {
501:            lineitemRow.beginAppend() ;
502:            lineitemRow.fields["INVOICE"].value =
503:                invoiceRow.fields["INVOICE"].value ;
504:            lineitemRow.fields["ISBN"].value=cartRow.fields["ISBN"].value;
505:            lineitemRow.fields["QTY"].value = cartRow.fields["QTY"].value;
506:            lineitemRow.save() ;
507:            cartRow.delete() ;
508:        }
509:    }
510:
511: }
```

14

The Receipt Report

The information to present on the Receipt report is a combination of some customer information and a listing of items purchased. Customer information goes into the page heading. The items go into the detail band and result in a table that is similar in layout to the Cart form. Fortunately, creating multiple rows is much easier in a report. You do not have to do anything beyond dropping fields in the detail band to have them replicated for each row in the table.

The receipt requires data from four tables: Customer, Invoice, Lineitem, and Title. The Customer and Invoice tables are for the page header only. The driving table for the report is the Lineitem table. This must be the first table added to the report. The Title table provides title and pricing information.

Three calculations are involved in the report. The total is calculated as quantity multiplied by price. Grand totals can be calculated for the quantity and total purchase.

Despite the fact that reports offer little in the way of user interaction, their design can be more challenging than designing a form. The IntraBuilder Report Designer is somewhat paradoxical. It provides incredibly precise layout control for printing reports from the Designer. However, you are likely to use it much more often for designing reports that display in a browser where HTML provides only crude control over the positioning.

 NOTE The unit of measure in a report is known as a *twip*. Twips are much smaller than a standard pixel. There are 1,440 twips in an inch.

To make the task easier, first design the report without any totals or calculations. After all the relations and basic positioning are set, you can go back and add in the JavaScript expressions required to perform totaling.

Receipt Relations

This section guides you through the initial report layout in two phases. The first phase is to lay out the detail bands. After that, you will tackle the header area. The design of the Receipt report does not involve the Report Expert. You will start by adding and relating the four tables. Unlike the Checkout form, all the query tables in the Receipt report have a specified relation. Use the following steps for setting up the detail band.

1. Open the blank Receipt report in the Report Designer.

   ```
   _sys.reports.design("receipt.jrp")
   ```

2. Drop the Lineitem table into the top-left corner of the report. Placing this table first establishes the Lineitem rowset as the driving rowset for the stream source.

   When the report runs, it shows a detail band for each row in the Lineitem table. If you add Customer first, the detail bands correspond to the customer. For a Receipt report, only one customer is ever printed.

   NEW TERM The *stream source* is the report object that determines what rowset has a one-to-one correspondence with the detail band. IntraBuilder is capable of running reports that contain more than one stream source. This allows for adjacent detail areas that come from independent views. The Report Designer does not have any visual tools for defining multiple stream sources.

3. Now add the Customer, Invoice, and Title tables. As you did when adding tables to forms, remove the full path from the `sql` property of each of the four queries.

4. Relate the Lineitem table to the Invoice table. Select the Lineitem query and inspect the rowset of the query. Use the `masterRowset` drop-down to select `invoice1`. After setting the `masterRowset`, you can use the `masterFields` drop-down to select the `INVOICE`. This automatically sets the `indexName` to `INVOICE`, as shown in Figure 14.11.

Figure 14.11.

Relating the Lineitem table to the Invoice table.

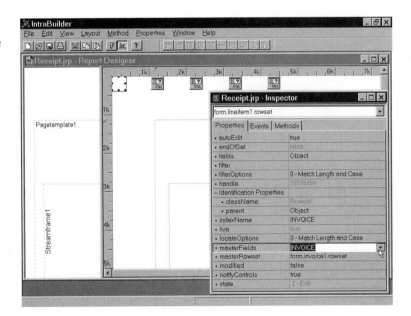

14

5. Select the customer1 query. The Customer table also relates to the Invoice table. Descend to the rowset object and again select invoice1 from the masterRowset drop-down. This time, the masterFields property needs to be set to CUSTOMER.

6. To create the third and last relation, inspect the rowset of the title1 query. The Title table relates to the Lineitem table on the ISBN field. Use the drop-down to select lineitem1 for the masterRowset. Set masterFields to ISBN.

7. Reduce the page margins. Inspect the page template by selecting form.PageTemplate1 from the Inspector's drop-down list box. This is the outermost of the two grid lines that appear in the report pane. It controls the report margins. Change all four margins from 1,080 to 360.

   This changes the margins from 0.75 inches to 0.25 inches. Large margins are not necessary when the output is targeted at a browser. Shrinking the margin gives you a larger work area in the Designer. If you plan to send the report to a laser printer, do not reduce the margin to less than 0.5 inches.

 TIP

Open up the group pane to see how the different bands of the report are laid out. By default, the group pane is closed. You can click and drag the window pane divider from the left edge to open the group pane.

8. Make room for the larger page header by altering the position properties of the stream frame. This is the innermost of the two grid lines. Select the stream frame and inspect form.PageTemplate1.StreamFrame1. Set the position properties, as shown in Table 14.11.

   These settings allow for 1.75 inches between the top margin and the start of the first detail band. The top of the stream frame is actually 2 inches from the top of the physical page.

Table 14.11. Position properties for form.PageTemplate1.StreamFrame1.

Property	Value	In Inches
height	10080	7
left	360	0.25
top	2520	1.75
width	8640	6

14

TIP

In the Report Designer, it is much easier to control positioning through the Inspector than by dragging items with the mouse. The lack of a snap-to-grid feature and the twip orientation can make attempts to reposition controls with the mouse almost unbearable. Save yourself the stress and use the Inspector.

9. Open the Field Palette and drop the ISBN field from the lineitem1 query into the stream frame. Position the ISBN field at the left edge of the stream frame. This automatically creates a detail band for each row in the lineitem1 query.

10. Add the Qty, Title, and Price fields into the detail band. Drop the Qty field from the lineitem1 query to the right of the ISBN field. Drop the Title field from the title1 query to the right of Qty. Drop the Price field to the right of the title.

As you add each field, the Designer adds two HTML controls. The first contains the field title and the second displays the actual value. The titles are given generic names such as titleIsbn, titleQty, and so on. The field value control names match the field names.

11. Adjust the title positions, as shown in Table 14.12. Also, change the text for ISBN to uppercase.

Table 14.12. Datalinked controls from the Field Palette.

name	text	height	left	top	width
titleIsbn	<H2>ISBN</H2>	396	360	2020	1440
titleQty	<H2>Qty</H2>	396	1980	2020	720
titleTitle	<H2>Title</H2>	396	2880	2020	2880
titlePrice	<H2>Price</H2>	396	5940	2020	1080

The positions allow for 1/8 inch or 180 twips between each column. Notice that the left property of the first field label matches the left property of the stream frame.

12. Bring the field values into alignment with the titles by using the positions shown in Table 14.13. Here, each left property is offset by 720 due to the stream frame margin. The widths are identical to the titles. You can quickly align and resize each column by selecting each title and field and using the sizing and alignment options of the Layout menu.

14

Table 14.13. Detail band field positions.

name	height	left	top	width
isbn	255	0	0	1440
qty	255	1620	0	720
title	255	2520	0	2880
price	255	5580	0	1080

At this point, the Receipt report should resemble the one shown in Figure 14.12. The detail area looks fairly acceptable, except for the Qty and Price figures appearing one line too low. This is caused by the fact that the default width of any numeric is wider than a half inch. For both values presented here, one half inch is more than enough space. You can use a template to override the default field width.

Figure 14.12.

Positioning fields in the detail band.

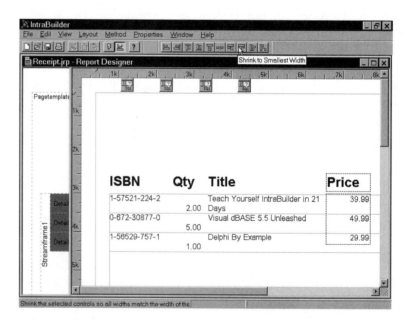

13. Because Boingo sells only whole books, you can set the template property of the Qty field to 999. Also set the template property of the Price field to 999.99. This will move the numeric fields back to the top line.

14

14. This is a good point to save the report and try running it through a browser. You can use the INTRASRV.ISV module to run reports the same way you run a form.

```
http://localhost/svr/intrasrv.isv?store\receipt.jrp
```

If you run the report through Navigator, you will see each field in a separate box. In Figure 14.13, you can see each cell of the table that defines the detail area. Viewing the cells can be handy in determining layout problems.

Figure 14.13.

Viewing the detail band layout through Navigator.

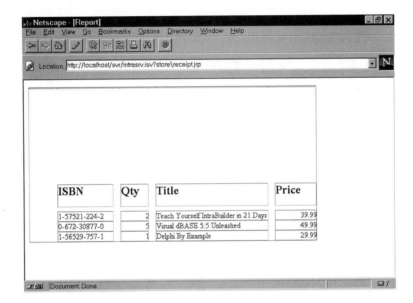

The browser shows how nicely the fields line up. Notice that the Title field does not wrap, which happens in the Designer. In the next phase of report design, you will be adding customer and invoice information into the header area.

1. Reopen the Receipt report in the Report Designer.

2. Before adding any new fields, right justify the titles for the Qty and Price fields. This will place the titles above the already right-aligned fields.

   HTML controls contain separate properties for horizontal and vertical alignment. To right align the titles, set the alignHorizontal properties to 2.

3. Add three HTML controls from the Component Palette to create three new titles in the page heading. When you add fields from the Field Palette into the page heading area, IntraBuilder does not include titles. Use the values from Table 14.14 to create each title.

14

Table 14.14. Titles for Invoice table fields.

name	text	height	left	top	width
titleInvoice	<H4>Invoice #</H4>	255	360	900	1440
titleCustomer	<H4>Customer #</H4>	255	360	1200	1440
titleDate	<H4>Order Date</H4>	255	360	1500	1440

These titles all align above the ISBN column. A heading level four makes the titles slightly larger than the field values but not as large as the column field titles.

4. Open the Field Palette and drop all three fields from the Invoice table next to the appropriate titles. You can fine-tune the position properties as listed in Table 14.15. To avoid a wrap-around of the numeric fields, add template values that match the defined field width of 10.

Table 14.15. Position properties for the Invoice table fields.

name	height	left	top	width	template
invoice	255	1980	900	1080	9999999999
customer	255	1980	1200	1080	9999999999
orderdate	255	1980	1500	1080	(blank)

5. Add the customer address fields from the Customer table. Use the positions listed in Table 14.16. These fields are self-explanatory and do not require any titles. Figure 14.14 shows how the fields align in the page heading.

Table 14.16. Position properties for the Customer table fields.

name	height	left	top	width
name	255	3600	900	2880
street	255	3600	1200	2880
city	255	3600	1500	2160
state	255	6120	1500	360
postalcode	255	6700	1500	720

6. Save and run the report in the Designer.

That is about all you can do for the Receipt report without getting your hands a little dirty. In the next section, you will add a calculated field and two grand totals.

Figure 14.14.
Positioning fields in the page heading.

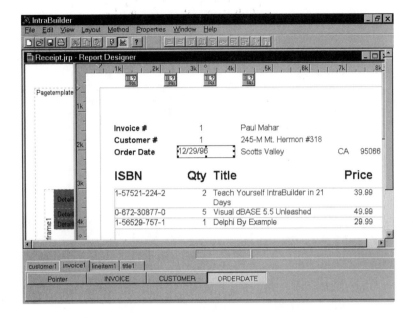

Using Events to Calculate and Summarize

To add summary information, you can take advantage of three events: onDesignLoad, preRender, and canRender. The onDesignLoad event fires when you open a report in the Report Designer. The preRender event fires before a report runs. It is very similar to the onServerLoad event of a form. Within a report, canRender fires before an HTML control is drawn. The canRender event also can prevent the control from being rendered or streamed into HTML. All three events are server-side events, as are all report-specific events.

Creating methods within a report is the same as creating a method for a form. The major difference is the added hierarchy levels that exist within a report. Most form events are events of a control. Controls are only one level removed from the container form. Within a report, there can be many levels between an HTML control and the report object.

NOTE

Methods linked to report events can use the shortcut reference form to refer to the report. There is not a shortcut reference called report. This allows you to share custom control methods between forms and reports.

There are two ways to add summary fields to a report: automatic and manual. The automatic way is to go through the Add Groups and Summaries dialog box. This dialog box contains

14

tabs that duplicate two steps from the Report Expert. The manual way is to use events and add your own code blocks. You also can modify the code blocks from generated summary fields. For the Receipt report summaries, you will use both automatic and manual summary creation.

Along with adding the total and grand total calculations, there are still a couple of HTML controls to add to the page heading. The following are the steps to complete the basic Receipt report.

1. Open the Receipt report in the Report Designer.
2. Add a large HTML control to the top-left of the form to thank shoppers for their purchases. Use the property values from Table 14.17 to create a heading that is centered across the entire report width.

Table 14.17. Property values for the "thank you" message.

Property	Value
name	htmlThanx
alignHorizontal	1-Center
height	400
left	0
top	0
width	9000
text	<H2>Boingo thanks you for your purchase!</H2>

3. Turn the "thank you" message into a link to the index page. Open the Text Property Builder and enter http://localhost/store/index.htm in the URL tag, as shown in Figure 14.15. You will need to change the localhost portion to the appropriate server name upon deployment. With the entire existing text selected, click Add to turn the text into a link.

TIP

> Avoid dead-end pages by always including at least one hyperlink in every report. Pages with no links can frustrate browser users.

4. Add another HTML control below the "thank you" message. This text is to remind people to create a hard copy of the receipt. Use the values shown in Table 14.18.

Figure 14.15.

Creating a link from the Receipt report back to the index.htm page.

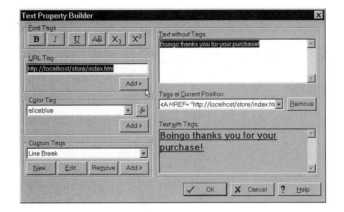

Table 14.18. Property values for the print message.

Property	Value
name	htmlPrint
alignHorizontal	1-Center
height	255
left	0
top	500
width	9000
text	Print this receipt for your records.

5. Add a sum for the QTY field using Expert assistance. From the menu, select Layout|Add Groups and Summaries. Click the Summaries tab, as shown in Figure 14.16. Select QTY from the Available Fields list and click OK.

Figure 14.16.

Adding a summary through the dialog box.

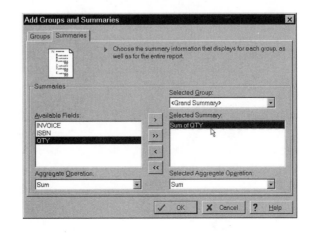

This creates a new, red, and italic HTML control with some descriptive text and a summary. The number is all you really want.

6. Select the new red control and adjust the property values as listed in Table 14.19. This places the total under the Qty column and leaves room for another summary on the same line.

Table 14.19. Adjusted properties for the Qty grand total.

Property	Value
name	grandQty
alignHorizontal	2-Right
template	99999
fontBold	true
fontItalic	false
height	255
left	1620
top	0
width	720
color	black

7. Remove the "Sum of Qty" from the text property code block. The resulting code block should read as follows:

```
{||this.parent.parent.agSum(
   {||this.parent.StreamSource1.rowset.fields["QTY"].value})}
```

You must edit the code block from within the Inspector. The Text Property Builder works only with literal strings. If you are having trouble with syntax, cut and paste the code block to a Script Editor window and copy it back after verifying the syntax.

8. From the Component Palette, drop an HTML control into the detail band to the right of the Price field. This creates an HTML control in the detail band and another in the page header.

9. Modify the name and positions of the two new controls. Use the values listed in Table 14.20. The title is contained in the page template object. The value control is within the detail band object.

14

Table 14.20. Properties for calculated total controls.

name	text	height	left	top	width
titleTotal	<H2>Total</H2>	396	7200	2020	1080
calcTotal	HTML1	255	6840	0	1080

10. Right-align both controls by setting the alignHorizontal property of labelTotal and calcTotal to 2. Also set the template property of calcTotal to 99999.99.

11. Add another HTML control to show the grand total of the Total field. Use the property values from Table 14.21 to set up the control to match the look of the Qty summary.

Table 14.21. Position properties for the grandTotal control.

Property	Value
name	grandTotal
alignHorizontal	2-Right
template	999999.99
fontBold	true
height	255
left	6840
top	0
width	1080

All the layout work is done. Your report should now resemble the one shown in Figure 14.17. The only thing left is to turn those HTML1 values into real totals.

12. Start with the report's preRender event. To select the report object, open the Inspector and choose form from the top of the drop-down list. Remember that form refers to the main container for both forms and reports. From the Events tab, click the preRender tool button to open the Method Editor. Enter the method as follows:

```
function Form_preRender()
{
   this.lineGrand = 0 ;
   this.lineTotal = 0 ;
   if (RECEIPT.arguments.length == 3) {
      this.invoice1.rowset.filter = "INVOICE = " + RECEIPT.arguments[2];
   }
}
```

14

Figure 14.17.

All controls before adding methods to calculate totals.

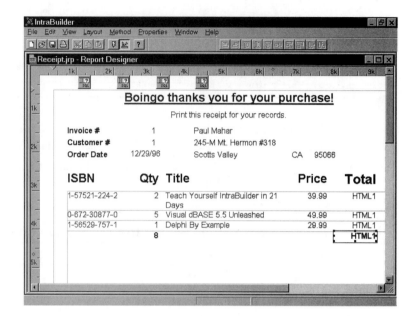

The method creates properties on the report object to store the values for the line-item total and grand total values. Additionally, it sets up a filter if three arguments are passed to the RECEIPT function. The RECEIPT function is the unnamed function that runs when you call the report with _sys.scripts.run(). This lets you run the report with no filter from the IntraBuilder Explorer. The filter selects the current invoice when called from the Checkout form.

13. Now create a method for the canRender event of the calcTotal field. Enter the following method:

```
function calcTotal_canRender()
{
   this.form.lineTotal =
      ( this.form.lineitem1.rowset.fields["QTY"].value *
        this.form.title1.rowset.fields["PRICE"].value ) ;
   this.form.lineGrand += this.form.lineTotal ;
   return ( true ) ;
}
```

This method does a simple quantity times price calculation to figure the total of any line item. It also adds the total into the grand total. The method must return true for the control to appear on the report.

If you try to save and run the report now, it will run just as before. However, you will encounter the error shown in Figure 14.18 if you try to reopen it in the Designer.

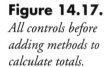

Figure 14.18.

*Error when designing
the Receipt report
without using*
`onDesignLoad.`

14. To avoid errors when redesigning, link the following method to the `report` object's
    `onDesignLoad` method. This method replicates the initialization code found in
    `Form_preRender()`.

```
function Form_onDesignLoad()
{
    this.lineGrand = 0 ;
    this.lineTotal = 0 ;
}
```

15. After adding the `Form_onDesignLoad()` method, you can move freely between Run
    and Design mode. Try the toggle now to make sure the methods work right and to
    initialize the `lineGrand` and `lineTotal` properties. Both properties need to exist
    before continuing with the report design.

16. Enter `{ ¦¦ this.form.lineTotal }` as a code block for the `text` property of
    `calcTotal`. Use the type drop-down list to change the property from a character
    string to a code block, as shown in Figure 14.19. If you don't change the type, the
    report prints the code block as literal text.

Figure 14.19.

*Setting up a self-
evaluating code block
for the line item total.*

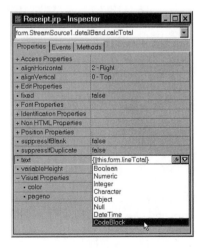

17. Enter `{ ¦¦ this.form.lineGrand }` as the code block for the grand total.

NOTE

> As you modify self-evaluating code blocks in the Designer, the canRender event continues to fire. This leads to incorrect grand total values when designing. There is no such adverse effect on the values when the report appears in Run mode.

18. Select form.PageTemplate1 in the Inspector and set the gridLineWidth property to 0. When you've finished, save the report and try it in Run mode.

You have completed the last step for the Receipt report and for the entire shopping cart application. If you run the report directly in the Designer, it will always show information for the first customer and invoice. Running the report from the Cart form shows the current customer and invoice. Figure 14.20 shows the totals as they appear in Internet Explorer.

Figure 14.20.

Running the report through Internet Explorer.

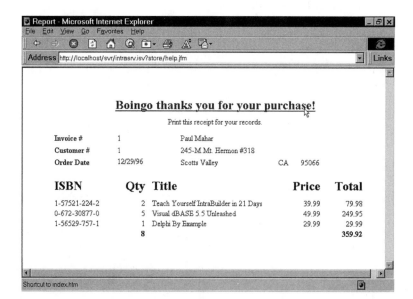

Summary

Today you completed a week-long journey into the land of shopping cart application development for the Web. Shoppers can now search for books, add books to the cart, modify the cart contents, and check out of the bookstore. The application has come full circle. The final destination is the Receipt report, which links back to the index.htm where the application begins.

14

During the last day of development, you worked with pages for the first time this week. You learned how pages appear as independent forms yet allow complete sharing of methods and values. Pages provide an easy way to mimic modal behavior within a browser.

In creating a report, you learned some of the difficulties of manual page design. By using the Inspector to set values, you could better align items and create even spacing between columns. The Receipt report also provided an example of using report events.

As the week ends, you should feel comfortable in creating simple applications that are based exclusively on client-side JavaScript events. You have learned all it takes to create applications that dynamically update and display data and are compatible with both Netscape Navigator and Internet Explorer. You are now ready for the advanced topics of week three.

Q&A

Q The Checkout form has some logic in the SaveCustomer() method to figure out the correct value for the Card field. Could this also be done through a field canChange event if the field were datalinked to the radio buttons?

A You can use the canChange event to directly update the field if you also link a method to Card field's beforeGetValue event. For an update form, this would be preferable. The method linked to canChange must translate the text of each datalinked radio button to the appropriate code. Here is a method you could use:

```
function Card_canChange(newValue)
{
    if ( newValue == "Visa" ) {
        this.value = "VISA" ;
    }
    else if ( newValue == "Master Card" ) {
        this.value = "MC" ;
    }
    else {
        this.value = "AMEX" ;
    }
    return false ;
}
```

With the Checkout form, there is never any existing data to worry about. The form appends only new rows. As such, the approach used is simpler. If you want to enhance the form to allow customers to modify their account information, you also will need to incorporate a beforeGetValue method similar to the following:

```
function Card_beforeGetValue()
{
    var cReturn = "American Express" ;
    if ( this.value == "VISA" ) {
        cReturn = "Visa" ;
    }
```

14

```
   else if ( this.value == "MC" ) {
      cReturn = "Master Card" ;
   }
   return cReturn ;
}
```

Q **The validation routine in the Checkout form checked only that the fields were not blank. Could this validation be done through client-side JavaScript?**

A Yes, simple validations can be made through client-side JavaScript. In fact, you could use the same logic because client-side JavaScript fully supports the elements array. If validation is not essential or you know that all users will have JavaScript-enabled browsers, it is a good way to offload some of the processing to the client. The danger in client-side validation is that some browsers do not support JavaScript and some users turn JavaScript off in browsers that do.

Q **The Customer table uses a character field for the card expiration date. Wouldn't it make more sense to use a Date field?**

A Most credit cards show the expiration date as only a month and a year. A character field is used so users can enter exactly what appears on the card. You could substitute a Date field if it did not have a direct datalink. A datalink to a Date field will reject any dates that do not contain the complete month, day, and year. You could write a routine to convert a given string into an appropriate date value. In this case, you could substitute 07/98 for 07/01/98.

Q **The elements array on a form is great for dealing with controls, but what if I need to work with an unknown set of other objects such as queries?**

A IntraBuilder provides an alternate form of the for loop to determine all the properties of any object. The interesting thing about using a for loop to go through properties is that the properties are returned as character strings rather than their actual values. You can use the eval() function to get a proper reference. The following method uses this technique to deactivate all queries in the current form.

```
function buttonDeactivate_onServerClick()
{
   var aProp = new Array() ;
   for ( var iProp in this.form ) {
     aProp.add( eval("this.form." + iProp) ) ;
   }
   for (var i = 0 ; i < aProp.length ; i++ ) {
      try {
         if ( aProp[i].className == "Query" ) {
            aProp[i].active = false ;
         }
      }
```

```
catch (Exception e) {
   if ( ! (e.code == 163) ) {
      _sys.scriptOut.writeln('Error: ' + e.message) ;
      _sys.scriptOut.writeln(' code: ' + e.code) ;
   }
 }
   }
 }
```

TIP

Extracting unknown property names is a good way to discover undocumented or hidden properties. A hidden property is one that does not show up in the Inspector. For more information on undocumented properties see Appendix B, "The Undocumented IntraBuilder."

Workshop

The Workshop section provides questions and exercises to help you get a better feel for the material you learned today. Try to answer the questions and at least think about the exercises before moving on to tomorrow's lesson. You'll find the answers to the questions in Appendix A, "Answers to Quiz Questions."

Quiz

1. What is the purpose of a form's page number zero?
2. What HTML tags are required to create a bulleted list?
3. What is the Paradox table field type that creates unique numeric key values for you?
4. How can you set the sql property and activate a new query with a single assignment statement?
5. What is the report equivalent of a form's onServerLoad event?
6. When creating a report, what method can you use to sum field values in a self-evaluating code block?

Exercises

1. The shopping cart application does not automatically delete rows from the Cart table if a shopper leaves the system without making a purchase. You can add automatic row deletion through the onServerUnload event of the Toolbar custom form class.

14

This event fires whenever a form is explicitly closed through Form::release() or when a form times out on an IntraBuilder Agent. In the shopping cart application, you want to delete rows from the Cart table only if a form times out or when the shopper makes a purchase. Explicit calls to Form::release() occur when a shopper moves from one form to another.

Add the following method to the Toolbar custom form class and add a custom timeout property to all forms in the application. Default the timeout property to true and set it to false prior to any call to Form::release().

```
function Form_onServerUnload()
{
   if ( this.timeout ) {
      var q = new Query('select * from "cart.dbf"') ;
      q.rowset.filter = " + "'" + form.user + "'" ;
      while (! endOfSet ) {
         q.rowset.delete() ;
      }
      q.active = false ;
   }
}
```

2. The current Checkout form requires shoppers to reenter address and credit card information for every purchase. The table structure has provisions for return customers. The Customer table contains a unique Customer number for all previous customers. As presented, the Checkout form creates a one-to-one corre-spondence between the Customer and Invoice tables. A business is more likely to succeed if the relation between Customer and Invoices is one-to-many.

   Change the Checkout form to accept an existing customer number for existing customers. You can do this by adding a new initial page with options for entering an existing Customer number or proceeding to the Customer data entry page.

3. When you have completed all modifications to all the application files, you can include rather than load the files. Try this out by commenting out the #define DEBUG line in the store.h file.

   If you check the file size of help.jfo before and after commenting #define DEBUG, you will see a substantial difference. The compile dialog box also will show the number of executable lines going up from less than 200 lines to over 1,500 lines. The newer object file will contain all source code except the report. Leave the receipt.jrp out of the store.h to avoid problems with parameter passing.

WEEK 2

8

9

10

11

12

13

14

In Review

The entire focus of Week 2 was the creation of a single application. Day 8 started the week with application design and preparation. On Day 9, you created a custom form class that provided all the other forms with a set of toolbar buttons to navigate between each major form. To determine the best way to add querying capabilities to the application, you spent most of Day 10 examining the built-in query by form capabilities and timing queries with different property settings and table types. The benchmarks revealed the dBASE table type to be far faster than Paradox or Access tables. Day 11 put the discoveries from Day 10 to practical use in a quick search form. You created a dynamic grid on Day 12. The grid lets shoppers view and update multiple rows in a table with a single submit. By Day 13, you had searches down pat, and you expanded from searches on SQL expressions to using the `canGetRow` event to perform complex filters. The week ended with the completion of the shopping cart application. On Day 14, you created a form with active datalinks and a report with summaries. That brought the saga of the shopping cart application to a close and prepared you for the advanced topics of Week 3.

WEEK

3

At a Glance

During the final week, you learn about advanced IntraBuilder features and how to get the most from JavaScript's dynamic object model. The topics for Week 3 give you a solid foundation for working with reusable components and extending your IntraBuilder applications.

Day 15 starts the week with an in-depth look at the IDE and how you can customize it to fit your development needs. You learn about exception handling and how it can help you create bug-free software on Day 16.

Whenever you build a new application, you should avoid reinventing the wheel by employing reusable components wherever possible. Days 17 through 19 focus on extending applications through pre-built components. Day 17 describes some of the ready-made solutions that come with the IntraBuilder business applications. Among the ready-made solutions is an extensible class library for handling sophisticated security schemes. On Day 18, you learn how to extend your forms with Java applets and ActiveX controls. These external controls take you beyond the bounds of the browser. Day 19 shows you how to take advantage of operating system calls through OLE automation and the Windows API.

Object orientation is the focus for Day 20. This lesson exposes the complete workings of the JavaScript dynamic object model. In taking a tour of OOP (object-oriented programming), you learn why this model has gained popularity as the most efficient way to build applications from reusable components.

The last day is geared toward developers working with IntraBuilder Client/Server or IntraBuilder Professional and a database server. Day 21 shows you how to optimize client/server applications by stepping through a migration of the shopping cart application. The day's lesson begins with the native dBASE system from Week 2 and concludes with the application using tables residing in an InterBase database. Although the exercises are specific to InterBase, the concepts discussed throughout the lesson apply to all SQL-Link connections including Oracle, Informix, DB2, Sybase, and Microsoft SQL Server.

Day 15

Customizing the IntraBuilder IDE

by Ken Henderson

You'll begin your third week using IntraBuilder by learning to customize the IntraBuilder Integrated Development Environment (IDE). Some of the changes you'll make involve cosmetic alterations to the environment itself—the types and layout of palettes, the general behavior of the IntraBuilder Explorer, and so on. Some involve the specific control of the form designer, and some involve other settings. IntraBuilder allows you to change your development environment to suit your needs in a number of useful ways. I'll cover each of them separately. Some of the things you'll learn to do today include the following:

- ☐ Configure the IntraBuilder start up folder and search path.
- ☐ Specify the types of files displayed in the IntraBuilder Explorer.
- ☐ Set up an external script editor.
- ☐ Suppress Expert prompting.

- [ ] Toggle between displaying object properties alphabetically or categorically in the Inspector.
- [ ] Enable or disable IntraBuilder's opening splash screen.
- [ ] Configure remote database access nuances.
- [ ] Set a variety of options that affect the behavior of the IntraBuilder Explorer.
- [ ] Configure custom controls using a custom control registration table.

Let's begin by selecting the Desktop Properties item on the Properties menu.

 NOTE

> Note that the configuration changes you'll make today affect only the IntraBuilder Designer, not the IntraBuilder Server. This chapter shows you how to customize your development environment; this chapter doesn't delve into customizing server software.

Desktop Properties

Desktop properties are broken into two categories: those relating to file manipulation and those relating to the IntraBuilder Designer application as a whole. By default, the Files tab is selected; this section discusses the options it allows you to configure. Figure 15.1 shows the Files tab of the Desktop Properties dialog.

Figure 15.1.

You specify file-related options on the Files tab of the Desktop Properties dialog.

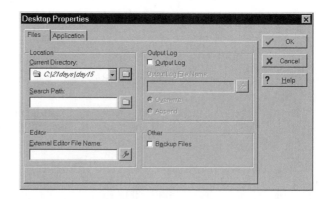

Current Directory

Setting the Current Directory option specifies the default folder for the IntraBuilder Explorer. When the IntraBuilder Explorer is started, it initially lists files from this folder. You can change the Explorer's current folder by selecting a different one in its Look In drop-down box.

Search Path

The Search Path option allows you to configure a search path for the IntraBuilder Explorer. The Explorer looks here as well as in its current folder when it needs to locate a file.

NOTE   You can specify multiple directories in the Search Path entry box by separating them with semicolons. If you enable the Use Supplemental Search Path option (in the IntraBuilder Explorer Properties dialog), the search path you specify will be displayed in the Explorer's Also Look In drop-down list.

External Editor File Name

Use the External Editor File Name option to set up an external script editor. Because JavaScript files are plain text, you can use virtually any ASCII text editor to edit them. You can use this entry box to specify your own, or simply leave it blank to use the built-in script editor.

Backup Files

You can check the Backup Files option to cause backup files to be displayed by the IntraBuilder Explorer. When you save changes you've made to a file, IntraBuilder saves a backup copy of it in its original folder. Enabling this option causes backup files that are created in this fashion to show up in the IntraBuilder Explorer. You can then open these files from the Explorer.

Output Log

When an output log is set, IntraBuilder writes anything that appears in the results pane to the output log file. You can use the output log and the _sys.scriptOut.writeln() method to help debug applications. The output log is a text file that you can edit after disabling the logging option. (See Figure 15.2.)

You can click the Application tab of the Desktop Properties dialog to configure the IntraBuilder application itself. These options aren't very different from those on the Files page, but Borland obviously felt they were different enough to belong on a separate page. Figure 15.3 shows the Application page.

Figure 15.2.

You can create an output log to capture output from sys. scriptOut.writeln().

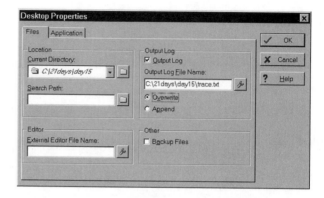

Figure 15.3.

You specify IntraBuilder application options on the Application page of the Desktop Properties dialog.

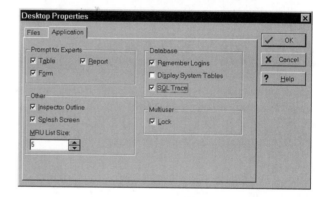

Prompt for Experts

You can use the checkboxes in the Prompt for Experts group to control when IntraBuilder asks whether you'd like to use an expert to create an object. Your choices are Form, Report, and Table. If you check one of these options and later attempt to create the corresponding file type, IntraBuilder presents a dialog asking whether you'd like to create the file using its associated designer or by stepping through a wizard. Experts are wizards that allow you to create objects by simply answering a set of questions. As you learned in Week 1, they do most of the work for you.

Remember Logins

Checking the Remember Logins checkbox tells IntraBuilder to keep use and password information when you attach to a remote DBMS (for example, an SQL database). This alleviates the need to constantly re-supply the login information that's required to access a particular remote database. The Remember Logins checkbox helps you avoid typing mistakes by retaining passwords to frequently used DBMSs.

15

15

Display System Tables

Because many SQL DBMSs include special tables that contain system-level information, IntraBuilder allows you to specify whether these tables should show up in the Explorer's table list. Normally, you won't reference these tables in the database applications you build, so there's usually no reason to include them. If you're building a special type of application that requires direct access to system tables, you can click this option to cause system tables to be displayed in the IntraBuilder Explorer.

SQL Trace

You can display calls made by SQL-Link drivers by checking the SQL Trace option. Use this option to troubleshoot and optimize routines that work with SQL data. SQL Trace has no effect when working with dBASE or Paradox tables. The output from SQL Trace appears in the results pane of the Script Pad. Because the output can be voluminous, you should use an output log when working with SQL Trace. See Day 21, "Building Client/Server Applications," for more information about SQL Trace.

Inspector Outline

By default, properties in the Inspector are displayed in an outline. They're organized into categories that you can double-click to display individual properties. You can uncheck this option to cause the Inspector to display properties alphabetically. You might find that this makes the properties displayed in the Inspector easier to navigate.

Splash Screen

As you might guess, the Splash Screen option configures whether the default splash screen is displayed when you start IntraBuilder. Obviously, IntraBuilder starts slightly more quickly when this option is disabled.

MRU List Size

IntraBuilder retains a list of files that you've recently opened so that you can easily reopen them. You can access this list via the File menu. The MRU (Most Recently Used) List Size option configures how many of these files are retained in the list. The default is five, but you can change it to suit your needs.

Lock

The Lock option enables you to specify whether IntraBuilder should lock database objects you're working on so that others cannot change them while you have them open. This option is checked by default, and you probably shouldn't change it. Allowing others to change objects you're currently working on could have catastrophic results.

Form Designer Properties

IntraBuilder also allows you to customize the behavior of the Form Designer. You can configure the Form Designer by selecting the Form Designer Properties option on the Properties menu. Figure 15.4 shows the Form Designer Properties dialog.

Figure 15.4.

You can configure the Form Designer via the Form Designer Properties dialog.

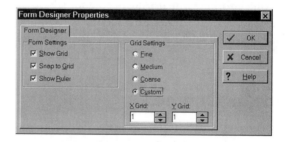

NOTE

The Form Designer Properties menu option is only present on the Properties menu while you are actually in the Form Designer itself.

Show Grid

The Show Grid option configures whether the Form Designer displays a grid across the background of forms you design. This grid helps you align and size controls on your forms. The grid is a design tool only; it won't be present when you run your form or when a user views it via a Web browser.

Snap to Grid

You use the Snap to Grid option to specify whether options you drop onto a form while designing it "snap" to its underlying grid. When this option is turned on, dropping an object near a grid line causes the object to move or snap to the line. This assists you with aligning controls because it alleviates the need to align them precisely by hand.

15

Show Ruler

The Show Ruler option toggles whether a ruler is displayed around the perimeter of forms in the Form Designer. Turning the ruler on can assist you with aligning controls and with positioning them on a form.

Grid Settings

In addition to displaying a grid while you design forms, you can also define the type of grid that you want to be displayed. Your options range from Fine to Custom; you can set them to suit your needs. You can specify the custom setting in order to fully configure the grid's granularity.

The View Menu

You can also configure IntraBuilder's development environment via the View menu. Several of the options on the menu affect the appearance and behavior of the development environment.

Toolbars and Palettes

You can click the Toolbars and Palettes option on the View menu to configure the appearance of toolbar buttons and palette tabs. Figure 15.5 shows the Toolbars and Palettes dialog.

Figure 15.5.

You can configure IntraBuilder's toolbars and component palettes via the Toolbars and Palettes dialog.

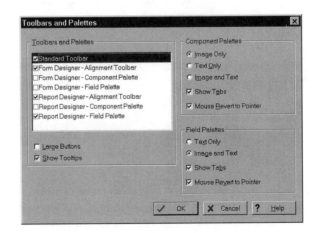

From this dialog you can specify which toolbars and palettes are to be displayed. You can also configure the types of buttons that are displayed and whether tooltips (fly-over hints) are displayed on your toolbars and palettes.

Customizing Custom Components

IntraBuilder includes a special facility for customizing the appearance of custom components. This facility works similarly to the Visual dBASE facility for configuring custom components and relies on a Component Registry table named IREG0009.DBF (the last four digits of which can vary, based on your Windows country setting).

You can use IREG0009.DBF to configure the placement and appearance of custom components you add to the Component Palette. Figure 15.6 illustrates the layout of the IREG0009.DBF table.

Figure 15.6.

You can supply bitmaps and other information for custom components using the IREG0009.DBF table.

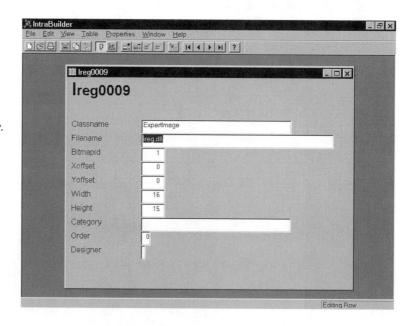

Each row in IREG0009 corresponds to a custom control. (You create custom controls via the Save as Custom option on the File menu.) CLASSNAME corresponds to the name of the custom control. IntraBuilder uses this name to look up the visual properties you've specified for a particular control, so be sure it's exactly right. FILENAME refers to the Dynamic Link Library (DLL) containing the bitmaps you want to utilize. This DLL should contain two bitmaps for each custom control—one for when the button is up, and one for when it's down.

15

The CATEGORY field specifies which tab the new control is to appear on. If you leave this field blank, your custom control appears on the Custom tab. The GROUP field specifies the group number for the control. Specifying the same number for a set of controls allows you to group them together. If you leave this field blank, controls within a given CATEGORY appear as a single group.

WARNING

Always exit and restart IntraBuilder after making changes to the Component Registry table. The product may become unstable if you attempt to open the Form Designer while editing the Component Registry table.

Summary

You've learned a number of useful ways for modifying and configuring the IntraBuilder development environment. Specifically, you've learned to configure the types of files displayed in the IntraBuilder Explorer, to establish an external script editor, and to specify the IntraBuilder startup folder and search path. You learned to list properties alphabetically in the Inspector and to turn off the opening splash screen. You learned to suppress Expert prompting and to configure IntraBuilder to retain remote database access passwords. You also learned to enable and disable the inclusion of system tables in the IntraBuilder table list and to control the appearance of custom controls using a custom control registration table.

Q&A

Q I'm accustomed to the Delphi development environment, particularly its Inspector. I find the hierarchical nature of the IntraBuilder Inspector to be confusing. How can I configure it to work like Delphi's Inspector?

A Follow these steps:

1. Select the Desktop Properties item on the Properties menu.

2. Click the Application tab in the Desktop Properties dialog.

3. Uncheck the Inspector Outline option. This causes the properties listed by the inspector to be listed alphabetically rather than categorically.

Q **I'm not seeing the Custom tab when I add a custom component to the Component Palette. In fact, I don't see any tabs at all. What could be causing this?**

A The Custom tab only appears when you set up custom components that do not specify their own tab in the Component Registry table. If you have set up a custom component, you need to check the Show Tabs option in the Toolbars and Palettes dialog on the View menu.

Workshop

The Workshop section provides questions and exercises to help you get a better feel for the material you learned today. Try to answer the questions and at least think about the exercises before moving on to tomorrow's lesson. You'll find the answers to the questions in Appendix A, "Answers to Quiz Questions."

Quiz

1. What's the name of the dBASE table in which you set up bitmaps for custom components?

2. In what IntraBuilder dialog do you specify an alternate script editor?

3. In IntraBuilder, where do you configure which toolbars and palettes are displayed?

4. How do you turn off IntraBuilder's Expert prompt for forms?

5. How can you prevent other users from changing the tables with which you're currently working?

6. How do you toggle the display of the status bar?

Exercises

1. Create a custom component, add it to the Component Palette, and then configure it to use a custom bitmap.

2. Toggle the Snap to Grid option and check out the effect this has on components you drop into place while designing a form.

3. Configure a search path, and then configure the IntraBuilder Explorer so that it displays your search path below the Look In drop-down list box.

4. Specify an external script editor, and then open a script for editing to test the execution of your editor.

15

Day 16

Debugging and Error Handling

by Ted Graham

One of the greatest benefits of visual design tools, such as IntraBuilder, is that large quantities of bug-free code are generated for you. This is code that you shouldn't have to debug later. However, as you begin to add code, invariably problems arise, some minor and some major. In fact there is probably more effort put into testing and debugging software than into the initial creation of it.

Problems come in several varieties, and some are easier to fix than others. For today's discussion, these problems fall into three categories: planning errors, coding errors, and unavoidable but predictable runtime problems.

Today you will learn about the following topics:

- [ ] How to plan before writing any script.
- [ ] How to debug JavaScript code.
- [ ] How to use exception handling to respond to runtime errors.

Planning Is A Good Thing

Analyzing the problem and creating a good plan are two essential steps before you start programming. Although few programmers enjoy "programming by committee," certainly many benefits can be gained from "designing by committee." It is vital to ask questions—even outrageous ones—about the problem and the necessary solution. Vital questions are

- [ ] What are the factors that have to be considered?
- [ ] What is the necessary input?
- [ ] What is the desired output?
- [ ] What conditions exist that are out of the ordinary?
- [ ] What should happen if...?

The more information that is gathered at the beginning, the easier it will be to avoid writing great code that does the wrong thing.

After getting a clear definition of the need, you need to carefully plan the solution to the problem. Although few programmers flowchart their programs like their professors wanted, some level of preparation is always helpful. Actually writing down the program logic flow will help you think through the logic before spending several hours coding, only to discover an easier way.

OOPS Is Not the Plural Form of OOP

Good preparation can prevent many of the logical errors, but only experience can prevent coding errors, especially in such a flexible product as IntraBuilder. Becoming proficient with the syntax of the language might take some time, and during that time you will inevitably use the wrong syntax on occasion. Many of these errors will be caught by the compiler, but others will slip through and only show up when the script produces an error or unexpected result. Programming errors are harder to catch, which is why the software industry keeps so many fine Quality Assurance specialists employed. Only careful coding and thorough testing will flush out these problems. But even if you are new to the JavaScript language, there are steps that you can take to reduce the number and magnitude of programming errors.

16

Expect the Unexpected

The third type of problem that you will see today is the expected but unusual problem that comes up as scripts run. The real world can present even perfect software with such problems as invalid data or full disk drives. Good software needs to anticipate these problems and prepare to handle them gracefully. This goes back to the planning phase, because part of good planning is to anticipate the unexpected and decide how to handle it.

Building the Perfect Function

To explore some of these problems and ways to solve them, you will write a couple of functions today. The first function will work around a particular oddity found in IntraBuilder's implementation of the JavaScript language. After identifying the problem and charting the course to the solution, you will go through the process of building, testing, and debugging some JavaScript code.

Identifying the Problem

There is an incompatibility between IntraBuilder's version of JavaScript and the implementations in Netscape Navigator and Microsoft Internet Explorer. This difference concerns the conversion of numbers to strings. All implementations of JavaScript allow you to concatenate disparate data types. The data is generally promoted to a string.

 The automatic conversion of one data type to another is called *promotion*. This is found in several programming languages, including C++, Java, and JavaScript.

Consider the following JavaScript assignment:

```
var x = "The answer is: " + 12.345;
alert(x);
```

The variable x should contain the string value "The answer is: 12.345", and does in most implementations of JavaScript. However, in IntraBuilder, floating point numbers are rounded to a fixed number of decimal places when converted to strings. By default, numbers are rounded to two decimal places. The actual number depends on the configuration of your Windows operating system. Because of this behavior in IntraBuilder, the preceding assignment stores the string "The answer is: 12.35" to x. This rounding occurs only when the number is converted to a string, so it will not affect any calculations; but it can be disconcerting to see the answer rounded like that.

TIP   To set the number of decimal places, select the Regional Settings icon in the Windows Control Panel. There is an option on the Number tab labeled "No. of digits after decimal." In Windows NT 3.51, you should select the International icon in Control Panel and then select the Change button in the Number Format box. This contains an option labeled "Decimal Digits."

Planning the Solution

Suppose that this conversion is the problem that you need to solve in IntraBuilder. So the planning begins. One important step in reducing errors and producing solid code is code reuse. Because you have to solve this problem now, solve it well and solve it in a way that enables you to reuse the solution later. So, rather than solve the problem in the particular form that is displaying the number, create a function that can be used any time that you need to convert a number to a string. As the planning phase continues, you come up with the criteria shown in Figure 16.1.

Figure 16.1.

*Functional require-
ments of the* str()
function.

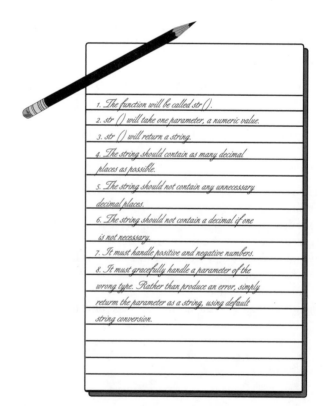

1. The function will be called str().
2. str() will take one parameter, a numeric value.
3. str() will return a string.
4. The string should contain as many decimal places as possible.
5. The string should not contain any unnecessary decimal places.
6. The string should not contain a decimal if one is not necessary.
7. It must handle positive and negative numbers.
8. It must gracefully handle a parameter of the wrong type. Rather than produce an error, simply return the parameter as a string, using default string conversion.

Up to this point, the planning has not taken into consideration the actual coding of the function, just the requirements of the function.

Coding the Solution

When you know what the function needs to do, you begin to think through how to code it. It is often easiest to start with a simple specific case and then get more generic. Consider the conversion that identified the problem. How would you produce the string `"The answer is: 12.345"`? Working through this helps when you are still learning the syntax of the language. The following code creates the desired result:

```
var num = 12.345;
var sNum = "" + (num * 1000);    // "12345"
sNum = sNum.substring(0,2) + "." + sNum.substring(2,5);
var string = "The answer is: " + sNum;
alert(string);
```

This code shows the basic approach that you need to solve the more generic problem. You multiply the number until all of the decimal places are to the left of the decimal place. Then when you convert it to a string, all of the significant digits remain visible. Then you insert the decimal place back into the string at the appropriate place.

But how can you tell when all the significant digits are to the left of the decimal place? Again, you can experiment with a small bit of code to find the answer. Try running this script to see what happens:

```
var num = 12.0000345;
for (var i = 1; i < 30; i++) {
    alert("" + num);
    num *= 10;
}
```

Two things become apparent from this little exercise. The first is that significant digits can be hidden. In the first couple of alerts, no significant digits are seen to the right of the decimal place. But as the number continues to be multiplied by 10, the other digits appear. The second thing to notice is that at some point the number is displayed in exponential notation. This is the key to finding all the significant digits. Find the largest number before exponential notation kicks in, and you will find the maximum number of significant digits.

Using this basic approach, you can create the generic `str()` function. Before coding, however, you'll want to diagram at least the basic script flow. Figure 16.2 shows a basic flowchart for this function.

Figure 16.2.

A flowchart for the
str() *function.*

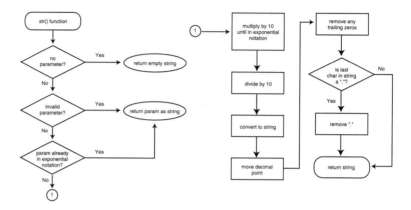

> **NOTE**
>
> There are many flow charting resources available on the Web these days. Use your favorite search engine to look for "flowchart." There are tutorials as well as shareware and evaluation copies of flowcharting software.

Based on this flowchart, you create the script shown in Listing 16.1. The listing contains a few test cases and the str() function. The output of the script is shown after the listing.

INPUT   **Listing 16.1. The JavaScript source for str1.js.**

```
 1: alert("The answer is: " + 12.345);
 2: alert("The answer is: " + str(12.345));
 3: alert("The answer is: " + str(-12.345));
 4: alert("The answer is: " + str(12));
 5: function str (num)
 6: {
 7:     var sNum = "",
 8:         pow  = 0,
 9:         tmp  = "";
10:     if (str.arguments.length == 0)
11:         return ("");
12:     if (num + 0 != num)
13:         return ("" + num);
14:     while (((""+(num*Math.pow(10,pow))).indexOf("E+") < 0)
15:         pow++;
```

16

```
16:     if (pow == 0)
17:         sNum = ("" + num);
18:     else {
19:         var tmp = "" + (num*Math.pow(10,pow-1));
20:         var dec = tmp.indexOf(".");
21:         pow--;
22:         sNum = tmp.substring(0,dec-pow) + "."
23:                     + tmp.substring(dec-pow, dec)
24:                     + tmp.substring(dec+1,tmp.length);
25:         while (sNum.substring(sNum.length-1,sNum.length) == "0")
26:             sNum.string = sNum.substring(0,sNum.length-1);
27:         if (sNum.indexOf(".") == sNum.length - 1)
28:             sNum.string = sNum.substring(0,sNum.length-1);
29:     }
30:     return (sNum);
31: }
```

ANALYSIS   This code follows the flowchart in Figure 16.2. Lines 10, 12, and 16 check for the exceptional cases and cause the parameter to be returned using default string conversion. Lines 19 to 28 perform the actual conversion of a numeric parameter to the string. Line 19 converts the number to a string with the maximum number of digits visible. Line 22 inserts the decimal into the string at the correct location, while lines 25 and 27 take care of any trailing zeros or decimal places.

Notice the use of the alert() function in the top of the script file (lines 1 to 4). This function is very useful while writing and testing your scripts, but it should be removed by the time the script is put into production.

 TIP   The script in Listing 16.1 assumes that the period is used as the decimal separator (see lines 25, 27, and 32). This might not always be the case. If the server machine has been configured to use different language or regional settings, you should make sure that this script (and others that parse numbers or dates) looks for the correct character.

The script shown in Listing 16.1 compiles fine and produces four alert boxes that show the expected results. Figure 16.3 shows the first of these alert boxes.

Figure 16.3.

The first alert dialog from the str() *function.*

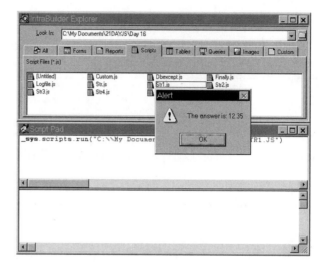

Debugging Techniques

Now that you are done, you hand the script off to the testers. As testers (and users for that matter) always do, they find several cases where the function returns the incorrect value. The three problems that they find are

```
alert("The answer is: " + str(.002));
alert("The answer is: " + str(-.002));
alert("The answer is: " + str(0));
```

In this case, the result shown in the first alert box is The answer is: .2. The second alert box shows the result The answer is: .-2. Neither of these is correct. The third alert seems to hang. Nothing happens. The script keeps running until you press the Esc key and cancel the script.

Now that you have some bugs to work on, the debugging begins. Although many development products come with integrated debuggers, IntraBuilder does not. This makes debugging a little more difficult, but it sure doesn't make it impossible. The real need during debugging (and which debuggers simply make easier) is to track script flow and the values of variables within the script.

Being an Alert Debugger

Because the str(0) problem seems a little more serious, start with that one. To begin debugging, you can again use the alert() function to monitor script flow and the values of variables. Because the script runs continuously, you know that one of the loops is stuck. So you might sprinkle a few alerts around the first while loop:

16

```
alert('before first while');
while ((""+(num*Math.pow(10,pow))).indexOf("E+") < 0) {
    alert(""+(num*Math.pow(10,pow)));
    alert("" + (""+(num*Math.pow(10,pow))).indexOf("E+"));
    pow++;
}
```

When you test `str(0)`, this time you see the following alerts:

- [ ] before first while
- [ ] 0
- [ ] -1
- [ ] 0
- [ ] -1

You will see more alerts than are shown in this list, because the last two alerts are repeated over and over again. Holding down the Esc key for a while breaks out of the loop. This tells you that the first `while` loop is in an endless loop, and a closer look at the test expression reveals why. Because num is zero, the calculation always results in zero. This is the standard fare in script debugging. After looking for a way to have the loop handle zero, you decide it's just easier to check for this case along with the parameter checking before the loop. You do this by adding the following lines between lines 13 and 14 in Listing 16.1:

```
if (num == 0)
        return ("0");
```

Reusing Debugging Code

Now that you have solved that problem, the alerts are no longer needed. You can delete them, or you can keep them around in case they are needed again in later testing. You can keep the debugging code in place, but not have it execute in the production version by using preprocessor directives.

NEW TERM If Borland's JavaScript is one of your first programming languages, you might not be familiar with the term *preprocessor*. The preprocessor evaluates the script before it is even compiled. It can substitute values in the script, and it can cause sections of script to be compiled under some circumstances but not others. There is more information about the preprocessor in tomorrow's chapter.

In this case the location alert might be worth keeping around, but the other two are pretty specific to the zero problem. The following listing shows the debug code surrounded with such directives:

```
#define DEBUG
#ifdef DEBUG
    alert('before first while');
```

```
#endif
    while ((""+(num*Math.pow(10,pow))).indexOf("E+") < 0)
        pow++;
```

The #define DEBUG shown in the preceding code is best placed at the very top of the script file, where it will be easy to find. When you are done testing this script, simply comment out the #define DEBUG command and the debugging code will no longer be compiled into the script.

NOTE

If you have beta tested software, you might have noticed that some beta versions are quite a bit larger than the actual shipping version. The reason is that debug code is often left in place until the product is ready to ship.

Using the Script Pad During Debugging

The next problem to look at is the case of the missing decimal places. If you remember, the tester discovered that str(.002) returns the string ".2", which is missing the leading zeros in the decimal value. Now, some programmer might already have noticed the problem, but like me, many others might initially be stumped by this result.

The alerts are a great help, but they interrupt script flow and can become cumbersome when there are too many of them. Another debugging technique is to output debugging information to the Script Pad window as the script is running.

NOTE

If the Script Pad is not open, you can open it by selecting the View|Script Pad menu option. The Script Pad can be used to test expressions, execute IntraBuilder commands, and view debugging output from scripts.

The Script Pad has an input pane and an output pane. You interact with the output pane by using the _sys.scriptOut object. To see what is in the object, type the following command in the Script Pad input pane:

```
_sys.inspect(_sys.scriptOut);
```

This opens the IntraBuilder Inspector so that you can see the properties and methods of the Script Pad output pane. You will probably be using the write(), writeln(), and clear()

methods pretty often during debugging, so you should become familiar with them. As an example, type the following commands in the Script Pad:

```
_sys.scriptOut.writeln("Mary had a little lamb,");
_sys.scriptOut.writeln("Whose fleece was white as snow.");
```

This should produce the results shown in Figure 16.4. Notice that the commands are collected in the top pane and the results are shown in the bottom pane. You can use the Script Pad to test command syntax. When you have the correct syntax, you can copy and paste the command to your script file.

Figure 16.4.

The `writeln()` *method generates output in the Script Pad window.*

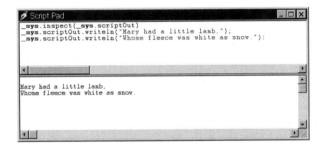

The method can be a little cumbersome to call, so you might want to use a shortcut technique that I picked up from a member of the IntraBuilder documentation team: Define a preprocessor macro to call the method. Using this technique, Listing 16.2 shows an updated version of the script that incorporates the fix for zero and some debugging information for the current problem. It also changes the `alert()` to a `writeln()` so that it becomes a little less intrusive.

INPUT **Listing 16.2. The JavaScript source for** `str2.js`**.**

```
 1: //alert("The answer is: " + 12.345);
 2: //alert("The answer is: " + str(12.345));
 3: //alert("The answer is: " + str(-12.345));
 4: //alert("The answer is: " + str(12));
 5: //alert("The answer is: " + str(0));
 6: alert("The answer is: " + str(.002));
 7: //alert("The answer is: " + str(-.002));
 8: #define DEBUG
 9: #define OUT(x) _sys.scriptOut.writeln(x)
10: function str (num)
11: {
12:     var sNum = "",
13:           pow   = 0,
14:           tmp   = "";
15:     if (str.arguments.length == 0)
16:          return ("");
```

continues

Listing 16.2. continued

```
17:       if (num + 0 != num)
18:           return ("" + num);
19:       if (num == 0)
20:           return ("0");
21: #ifdef DEBUG
22: OUT('before first while');
23: #endif
24:       while (((""+(num*Math.pow(10,pow))).indexOf("E+") < 0)
25:           pow++;
26: #ifdef DEBUG
27: OUT('pow is ' + pow);
28: #endif
29:       if (pow == 0)
30:           sNum = ("" + num);
31:       else {
32:           var tmp = "" + (num*Math.pow(10,pow-1));
33:           var dec = tmp.indexOf(".");
34:           pow--;
35: #ifdef DEBUG
36: OUT('tmp is ' + tmp + '\ndec is ' + dec + '\npow is ' + pow);
37: #endif
38:           sNum = tmp.substring(0,dec-pow) + "."
39:                     + tmp.substring(dec-pow, dec)
40:                     + tmp.substring(dec+1,tmp.length);
41:           while (sNum.substring(sNum.length-1,sNum.length) == "0")
42:               sNum.string = sNum.substring(0,sNum.length-1);
43:           if (sNum.indexOf(".") == sNum.length - 1)
44:               sNum.string = sNum.substring(0,sNum.length-1);
45:       }
46:       return (sNum);
47: }
```

ANALYSIS Line 8 defines the DEBUG preprocessor constant that causes the debugging code to be compiled into the script. Line 9 defines the preprocessor macro for writing information to the output pane.

Lines 19 and 20 show the fix for zero in its full context. The debugging code in lines 21 to 23 is compiled because of the #define on line 8. If line 8 is commented out, the debugging code is not compiled. The debugging code on lines 35 to 37 should provide the necessary information to solve the current bug. When this updated version of the script is executed, you should get a result like the one shown in Figure 16.5.

Notice the output displayed in the Script Pad window behind the alert box. In particular, notice that the final value of pow is larger than the value of dec. This causes the assignment on line 38 of Listing 16.2 to produce strange results. It seems that having the first significant digit to the right of the decimal throws the assignment off. This assignment can be rewritten to correctly handle the place-holding zeros.

16

```
if (dec <= pow)
    sNum = "0." + new StringEx().replicate("0",pow-dec);
else
    sNum = tmp.substring(0,dec-pow) + ".";
sNum += tmp.substring(dec-pow, dec)
            + tmp.substring(dec+1,tmp.length);
```

This change takes care of the problem with place-holding zeros. All of the test values now produce correct results except for this one:

```
alert("The answer is: " + str(-.002));
```

Figure 16.5.

Debugging information displayed in the Script Pad window.

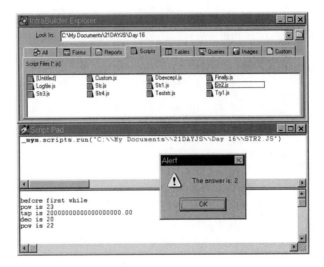

This one still puts the minus sign after the decimal place. Running this test case with the debugging information, you see that it is related to the last problem. The value of dec is less than the value of pow, so the string will start with "0" before adding the value in tmp (which has the minus sign). You could work another check into the part of the code that is building the sNum string to see whether the first character is a minus sign, but it might be easier to simply remove the minus sign before ever starting the conversion. This change has been applied to the code, whose final version is shown in Listing 16.3. Notice that the test code has been moved to a new file named TestStr.js, which is shown in Listing 16.4.

Listing 16.3. The JavaScript source for the final version

INPUT **of str.js.**

```
1: //#define DEBUG
2: #define OUT(x) _sys.scriptOut.writeln(x)
3: function str (num)
4: {
```

continues

Listing 16.3. continued

```
 5:        var sNum = "",        // string version of number
 6:             pow   = 0,         // keeps track of decimal places
 7:             tmp   = "",        // used while building sNum
 8:             neg   = false      // is num negative
 9:        if (str.arguments.length == 0) // no parameter
10:             return ("");
11:        if (("" + (num + 0)) != ("" + num))    // not a number
12:             return ("" + num);
13:        if (num == 0)
14:             return ("0");
15:        // if negative, set neg flag and make positive
16:        if (num < 0) {
17:             neg = true;
18:             num = -num;
19:        }
20: #ifdef DEBUG
21: OUT('before first while');
22: #endif
23:        // find out the largest number with these digits before
24:        // exponential notation kicks in.
25:        while (((""+(num*Math.pow(10,pow))).indexOf("E+") < 0)
26:             pow++;
27: #ifdef DEBUG
28: OUT('pow is ' + pow);
29: #endif
30:        // simply return the number if it is already in
31:        // exponential notation.
32:        if (pow == 0)
33:             sNum = ("" + num);        // this converts num to a string
34:        // otherwise, build a string with all the digits
35:        else {
36:             // decrement pow by one
37:             pow--;
38:             // create initial string
39:             var tmp = "" + (num*Math.pow(10,pow));
40:             // find current decimal
41:             var dec = tmp.indexOf(".");
42: #ifdef DEBUG
43: OUT('tmp is ' + tmp + '\ndec is ' + dec + '\npow is ' + pow);
44: #endif
45:             if (dec <= pow)
46:                  // build place holding zeros
47:                  sNum = "0." + new StringEx().replicate("0",pow-dec);
48:             else
49:                  // build whole number portion
50:                  sNum = tmp.substring(0,dec-pow) + ".";
51:             // now add the rest of the decimal places
52:             sNum += tmp.substring(dec-pow, dec)
53:                       + tmp.substring(dec+1,tmp.length);
54:             // remove trailing spaces
55:             while (sNum.substring(sNum.length-1,sNum.length) == "0")
56:                  sNum.string = sNum.substring(0,sNum.length-1);
57:             // remove trailing decimal if there are no decimal places
58:             if (sNum.indexOf(".") == sNum.length - 1)
59:                  sNum.string = sNum.substring(0,sNum.length-1);
```

16

```
60:     }
61:     return (neg ? "-" + sNum : sNum);
62: }
```

ANALYSIS For this production version of the script, the #define on line 1 has been commented out. The function no longer displays debugging information in the Script Pad window, and the function should run just a little faster. Also, the pseudo compiled file, str.jo, is a little smaller.

16

INPUT **Listing 16.4. The JavaScript source for** TestStr.js.

```
 1: // testing the str() function in Str.js
 2: _sys.scripts.load("str.js");
 3: //
 4: // test zero
 5: //
 6: if (str(0) != "0")
 7:     alert("0 Failed");
 8: //
 9: // test whole numbers
10: //
11: if (str(1) != "1")
12:     alert("1 Failed");
13: if (str(987654321) != "987654321")
14:     alert("987654321 Failed");
15: if (str(-1) != "-1")
16:     alert("-1 Failed");
17: if (str(-987654321) != "-987654321")
18:     alert("-987654321 Failed");
19: //
20: // test decimal values
21: //
22: if (str(.1) != "0.1")
23:     alert(".1 Failed");
24: if (str(.03) != "0.03")
25:     alert(".03 Failed");
26: if (str(12.345) != "12.345")
27:     alert("12.345 Failed");
28: if (str(-.1) != "-0.1")
29:     alert("-.1 Failed");
30: if (str(-.03) != "-0.03")
31:     alert("-.03 Failed");
32: if (str(-12.345) != "-12.345")
33:     alert("-12.345 Failed");
34: //
35: // test bad parameters
36: //
37: if (str("Hi Mom") != "Hi Mom")
38:     alert('"Hi Mom" Failed');
39: if (str(false) != "false")
40:     alert('false Failed');
```

ANALYSIS TestStr.js contains a more exhaustive collection of tests for the str() function. Line 2 loads the function into memory. The first test, on line 6, compares the return value from str() against the expected return value. If the values do not match, line 7 will produce an alert dialog to let you know which test failed. This same pattern is repeated for each of the other tests. Ideally, you should be able to run this test script with no alerts appearing.

Would You Care To Make a Comment?

Something else is different in Listings 16.3 and 16.4. You notice that these files finally have some comments in them. They were left out of the other listings just to save space. No one can ever say enough about the importance of commenting your code. While developing the code, the logic and flow will be obvious to you. After just a few months, however, the code will seem foreign even to you. The better you document the code, the easier it will be to maintain down the road.

Exception Handling

The information above is intended to help you reduce, find, and eliminate logical and coding errors. There is another type of problem that pops up in scripts that you can't eliminate. These problems can and should be prepared for. In object-oriented languages, such as Borland's object-oriented JavaScript, this type of problem is called an *exception*, and the art of managing the response to exceptions is called *exception handling*.

What Is an Exception?

The term *exception handling* seems a bit elusive and esoteric. It sounds like something that the truly geekie discuss at parties to weed out the true nerds from the "wannabes." In object-oriented languages, exceptions are simply objects. And they are very plain little objects at that.

NEW TERM An *exception* is an object that is created in response to an error condition. It contains properties that define the error that occurred.

To create and inspect one of these simple Exception objects, try running this script:

```
var x = new Exception();
_sys.inspect(x);
```

This lets you view the properties of an Exception object. As shown in Figure 16.6, the Exception object contains only three properties: classname, code, and message. The object is simply used to carry information about an error condition. This information can then be used by the IntraBuilder default exception handler or by script designed to handle the exception in some specific way.

16

Figure 16.6.

An Exception *object viewed in the Inspector.*

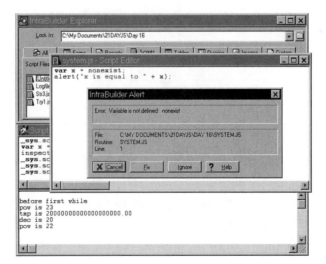

You can create an exception yourself, as shown in the previous code snippet. In addition, an exception is automatically created whenever a runtime error occurs. Try running the following script:

```
var x = nonexist;
alert("x is equal to " + x);
```

When this script is run, a runtime error occurs. The error is reported in the dialog box shown in Figure 16.7. In exception-handling terminology, an exception was *thrown* when the error occurred, and the default system handler *caught* the exception and handled it by displaying the dialog box.

Figure 16.7.

The dialog box produced by the system exception handler.

Throwing Exceptions

You can take control of any part of this exception-handling process. For example, you throw your own exceptions by using the throw command. In the following script, you generate and throw an exception:

```
var x = new Exception();
x.message = "An exception has been thrown";
x.code = 0;
throw x;
```

Just like before, the default IntraBuilder exception handler catches the exception. The dialog that the system displays is shown in Figure 16.8. Notice that it looks a little different for a custom exception than for a default, error-generated exception. IntraBuilder responds better to its own exceptions, providing the option to ignore or fix. However, when the default exception handler responds to your own exceptions, it only reports the message and terminates the script.

Figure 16.8.

The system handler responding to a custom exception.

Catching Exceptions

Not only can you take over the throwing of exceptions, but you can also take over the catching of them. The catching of exceptions is done through the use of a `try` statement and a `catch` statement. Each of these statements is followed by a block of code. The `try` statement is almost always followed by one or more `catch` statements. The use of multiple `catch` statements is described a little later. The system-generated exception you saw earlier is caught in the following code:

```
try {
    var x = nonexist;
}
catch (Exception e) {
    var x = 0;
}
alert("x is equal to " + x);
```

16

This code, like the code shown earlier, generates an exception when x is assigned the value of a nonexistent variable. The execution of the try block immediately terminates and script flow continues with the first command in the catch block. The catch block can report the error (using the alert() function or perhaps logging the error in a log file) or can attempt to recover from the error. In this simplistic example, the variable x is simply assigned another value. After the catch block executes and works around the error, script flow continues with the commands following the catch block.

The real power of exception handling is not in catching or throwing system-generated exceptions. The real benefits are derived by the strategic catching and throwing of your own exceptions. As demonstrated earlier, exception handling gives you a chance to recover from problems that can be anticipated.

And finally

As you have already seen, the try and catch statements generally come in sets. This team can be expanded with the inclusion of an optional finally statement, which is added after the last catch block. The finally block is executed after the try or catch block. If no exception is thrown in the try block, the finally block executes immediately after the final command in the try block. If an exception is thrown, the finally block executes immediately after the final command in the catch block that handles the exception.

The script shown in Listing 16.5 demonstrates the use of the finally statement. It also demonstrates the script flow associated with try, catch, and finally statements.

INPUT **Listing 16.5. The JavaScript source for finally.js.**

```
 1: var f=new File();
 2: try {
 3:     try {
 4:         f.open("test.txt","A");
 5:     }
 6:     catch (Exception e) {
 7:         var x = new Exception();
 8:         x.message = "Can not open test.txt";
 9:         x.code = 0;
10:         throw x;
11:     }
12:     f.writeln("Hi Mom");
13: }
14: catch (Exception e) {
15:     _sys.scriptOut.writeln("Exception: " + e.code);
16:     if (e.code != 0)
17:         throw e;
18: }
19: finally {
20:     f.close();
21: }
```

Analysis   This script is supposed to open a text file for output and then write the string `"Hi Mom"` to the file. The file is opened using the `File` object created on line 1. The first `try` block, lines 2 to 13, surrounds the code that opens (line 4) and writes to (line 12) the file. Any exceptions thrown in this block are caught by the `catch` block on lines 14 to 18. The `open()` method call on line 4 is also surrounded by a second `try` block. If the file cannot be opened, a system exception is thrown, which is caught by the `catch` block on lines 6 to 11. This then throws a custom exception to the outer catch block, essentially replacing the system exception with a custom one.

Assuming that `test.txt` exists (which it probably will not), no exceptions are likely and only four lines of code are executed: 1, 4, 12, and 20.

If the `test.txt` file does not exist, line 4 generates an exception, causing the lines of code in the inner `catch` block to execute. When line 10 executes, script flow passes to the outer `catch` block, so that line 12 is never executed. Line 15 writes a note about the exception to the Script Pad window. Then line 20 is executed.

Notice that the `finally` block is always executed. This makes sure that the file is closed, regardless of whether an error occurs. In the most likely scenario, the file is never opened; however, it is possible that the file could be opened, but then line 12 could fail. Any failure in writing to the file would be re-thrown by line 17. In this case, line 20 would be necessary to make sure that the file was not left open.

Subclassing Exceptions

So far, you have only thrown and caught objects of class `Exception`. Like all other IntraBuilder classes, you can create custom classes that are based on this base class. This is a common technique used to throw custom exceptions. Rather than create a standard exception with a specialized message and code, you can simply create a subclass of the `Exception` class. Then you can use multiple `catch` statements, each one catching a particular `Exception` class.

> **Tip**   When you have multiple `catch` statements after a `try` statement, each `catch` statement is checked in the same order in which it occurs in the code. The first `catch` statement that catches the thrown `Exception` class or any subclass of the thrown exception handles the exception. All other `catch` statements are ignored.

The script from Listing 16.5 has been rewritten in Listing 16.6 to use a custom exception class for the open error.

Listing 16.6. The JavaScript source for `finally2.js`.

```
 1: var f=new File();
 2: try {
 3:     try {
 4:             f.open("test.txt","A");
 5:     }
 6:     catch (Exception e) {
 7:             throw new FileOpenException();
 8:     }
 9:     f.writeln("Hi Mom");
10: }
11: catch (FileOpenException e) {
12:     _sys.scriptOut.writeln("Can not open file");
13: }
14: catch (Exception e) {
15:     throw e;
16: }
17: finally {
18:     f.close();
19: }
20: class FileOpenException extends Exception {}
```

ANALYSIS The custom exception class is defined on line 20 and is used on line 7. Notice how much more succinct line 7 is compared to lines 7 to 10 in Listing 16.5. Using custom exception classes really pays off when you will be catching and throwing many of your own exceptions.

Notice that this version of the script has two `catch` statements following the outer `try` statement. If the inner `catch` block throws a `FileOpenException`, the `catch` on line 11 handles it. If any other exception is thrown, the `catch` on line 14 handles it.

NOTE The `catch` block that starts on line 14 is there to demonstrate the principle. In this case, it could have been left out because the exception would have been passed on to the system handler anyway.

The `DbException` Class

In addition to the built-in `Exception` class, there is one custom exception class also built into IntraBuilder. The `DbException` class is thrown whenever an error is generated by the Borland Database Engine (BDE). In addition to the message and code properties, the `DbException` class contains a property named `errors`. This is an array of `DbError` objects. When a database error occurs, there could be one or more errors generated by the BDE. Each of these errors produces a `DbError` object that is stored as an element in the `errors` array.

The code in Listing 16.7 demonstrates catching DbException objects and then displaying each of the database errors.

Listing 16.7. The JavaScript source for dbexcept.js.

```
 1: try {
 2:     q=new Query();
 3:     q.sql = "select * from nonexist";
 4:     q.active = true;
 5: }
 6: catch (DbException e) {
 7:     for (var i = 0; i < e.errors.length; i++)
 8:         alert(e.errors[i].message + " (" +
 9:                     e.errors[i].context + ")");
10: }
11: catch (Exception e) {
12:     alert(e.message);
13: }
```

ANALYSIS The SQL statement on line 3 is very likely to cause an error (unless you happen to have a table named nonexist laying around). The actual error will occur when line 4 executes. This error causes a system exception to be thrown, which is caught by the catch on line 6. This catch block then displays an alert dialog for each of the database errors.

It is worth mentioning again that the order of multiple catch statements is significant. The catches are evaluated in the same order in which they appear in the script. Only one catch statement executes. A catch statement executes if it catches the thrown exception or any subclass of the thrown exception. If the two catch statements on lines 6 and 11 were reversed, the DbException one would never execute because the Exception one would catch every exception, due to the fact that all custom exceptions are subclassed from Exception.

Document the Exceptions

This final point about exceptions is very important. If you write a reusable component, such as a function or class, be sure to document any exceptions that might be thrown by the class. This allows those who use the class (which might be you in six months) to know what exceptions are thrown and to anticipate those exceptions.

You should document any system-generated exceptions that you anticipate being thrown from the component. For instance, if you create a component that accesses table data and you don't catch possible exceptions yourself, the calling script has to prepare for possible exceptions and try to handle any failure gracefully.

More importantly, you should document any custom exception classes that you throw from the component. For instance, consider a class that is used to generate log files. Such a class is shown in Listing 16.8. This script demonstrates many of the exception-handling principles that were covered today. In particular, it documents the exception classes that are thrown. These exception classes are defined right before the `LogFile` class itself.

Listing 16.8. The JavaScript source for `logfile.js.`

```
 1: // LogFile class helps keep activity logs
 2: //
 3: // NOTE: this class throws exceptions:
 4: //
 5: //    LfCanNotCreate - thrown from constructor if the log
 6: //                            file does not exist and cannot be
 7: //                            created. This exception is thrown
 8: //                            regardless of the throwExceptions
 9: //                            property value.
10: //    LfCanNotOpen    - thrown from methods if the log file
11: //                            cannot be opened. The log entry is
12: //                            cached and will be written the next
13: //                            time the file is opened.
14: //    LfInvalidLogName - thrown from methods if the log file
15: //                            name used to create the object was
16: //                            invalid. The constructor would also
17: //                            have thrown the LfCanNotCreate
18: //                            exception.
19: //
20: // Usage:
21: //
22: //     new LogFile(<logName>)
23: //
24: //     where <logName> is a valid file name. If the file does
25: //                            not exist, it will be created. Any
26: //                            directories in the path must already
27: //                            exist. If an existing file name is
28: //                            used, the new log entries will be
29: //                            appended to the end of the current file.
30: //
31: // Properties:
32: //
33: //    cacheSize - If a log entry cannot be written to the log
34: //                            file, it is cached. This is the maximum
35: //                            number of entries that can be cached. The
36: //                            next time the log is successfully opened, the
37: //                            cache is flushed.
38: //    retry      - The number of times that the object attempts
39: //                            to open the log file.
40: //    throwExceptions - Determines if internal exceptions are
41: //                            thrown out of the methods. If an
42: //                            exception is thrown during a method,
43: //                            the operation is simply aborted. To
44: //                            notify the calling script, set this
```

continues

Listing 16.8. continued

```
45: //                              property to true.
46: //
47: // Methods:
48: //
49: //      flush()          - Flushes the current contents of the
50: //                         cache, if any.
51: //      log(<entry>) - Writes the <entry> string to the log
52: //                         file. If the log file cannot be opened,
53: //                         up to cacheSize entries will be stored
54: //                         in memory. The contents of the cache are
55: //                         flushed the next time the log file is
56: //                         successfully opened (with a call to the
57: //                         flush() or log() method).
58: //
59: // Example:
60: //
61: //      try {
62: //          var log = new LogFile("test.log");
63: //          log.log("Start Operation");
64: //      }
65: //      catch (Exception e) { // just ignore any errors
66: //      }
67: //      var x = DoSomething();
68: //      try {
69: //          log.log("Results of DoSomething: " + x);
70: //          log.log("End Operation");
71: //      }
72: //      catch (Exception e) { // just ignore any errors
73: //      }
74: //
75: //
76: // Define the exception classes used by the LogFile class
77: //
78: class LfCanNotCreate    extends Exception {}
79: class LfCanNotOpen      extends Exception {}
80: class LfInvalidLogName extends Exception {}
81: //
82: // Define the LogFile class.
83: //
84: class LogFile(logName) extends File
85: {
86:     // set the property values
87:     this.cacheArray = new Array(); // cache unwritable entries
88:     this.cacheSize  = 10;                // size of cache
89:     this.logName    = logName;        // name of logfile
90:     this.retry      = 10;                  // open retry limit
91:     this.throwExceptions = false;    // throw exceptions out of
92:                                          // class methods
93:     //
94:     // This try block is used to surround code for
95:     // creating the log file. If any errors occur
96:     // the following catch will respond to them.
97:     //
98:     try {
```

```
 99:            // if the file does not exist, then create it
100:            if (!this.exists(this.logName)) {
101:                this.create(this.logName)
102:                this.writeln("Log File Created");
103:            }
104:        }
105:        //
106:        // Catch any errors that occur. If there is an error
107:        // override the open method (so the object doesn't
108:        // try to open a file that wasn't created) and then
109:        // throw an LfCanNotCreate exception to calling
110:        // script.
111:        //
112:        catch (Exception e) {
113:            this.open = {;throw new LfInvalidLogName()};
114:            throw new LfCanNotCreate();
115:        }
116:        //
117:        // The finally always happens. This is used to make
118:        // sure that the file is closed, even if an error
119:        // occurred.
120:        //
121:        finally {
122:            this.close();
123:        }
124:    function cache(logEntry)
125:    // This method stores an entry to the object's cache, if
126:    // the cache is not already full. After the cache is full,
127:    // new entries are lost.
128:    {
129:        if (this.cacheArray.length < this.cacheSize)
130:            this.cacheArray.add(logEntry);
131:    }
132:    function flush()
133:    // This method attempts to flush the cached entries to the
134:    // log file. The try block surrounds commands that may
135:    // produce exceptions. The catch then throws the exception
136:    // if the throwException property is true. The finally makes
137:    // sure that the file gets closed, whether or not an error
138:    // occurs.
139:    {
140:        try {
141:            this.open();
142:            this.flushCache();
143:        }
144:        catch (Exception e) {
145:            if (this.throwExceptions)
146:                throw e;
147:        }
148:        finally {
149:            this.close();
150:        }
151:    }
152:    function flushCache()
153:    // This method writes each cache entry to the open
154:    // log file. The open() method should be called before
```

continues

Listing 16.8. continued

```
155:       // calling the flushCache() method.
156:       {
157:            for (var i = 0; i < this.cacheArray.length; i++)
158:                this.writeln(this.cacheArray[i]);
159:            this.cacheArray = new Array();
160:       }
161:       function log(logEntry)
162:       // This method writes an entry to the log file. The entry
163:       // can be of any data type.
164:       {
165:            try {
166:                this.open();
167:                this.writeln("" + logEntry);
168:            }
169:            // The first catch block catches only the LfCanNotOpen
170:            // exceptions, which may be thrown by the open() method.
171:            // When this exception occurs, the entry is cached.
172:            catch (LfCanNotOpen e) {
173:                this.cache(logEntry);
174:                if (this.throwExceptions)
175:                    throw e;
176:            }
177:            // The second catch block catches any other exceptions
178:            // that may occur. This one simply throws the exception
179:            // to the calling script if throwExceptions is true.
180:            catch (Exception e) {
181:                if (this.throwExceptions)
182:                    throw e;
183:            }
184:            // The finally block makes sure that the log file is
185:            // closed, whether or not an error occurs.
186:            finally {
187:                this.close();
188:            }
189:       }
190:       function open()
191:       // This open() method overrides the built in open()
192:       // method of the file object. It makes multiple attempts
193:       // to open the log files, based on the retry property.
194:       // Once the log file is open, it flushes the cache.
195:       {
196:            var isOpen = false;
197:            var tries = 0;
198:            // make multiple attempts to open the file
199:            while (!isOpen && tries < this.retry) {
200:                // if the file cannot be opened, an exception is
201:                // thrown.
202:                try {
203:                    // notice the use of the scope resolution operator
204:                    // (::) to call the original open() method of the
205:                    // base class, File.
206:                    isOpen = File::open(this.logName,"A");
207:                }
208:                // any errors are simply ignored
```

16

```
209:                    catch (Exception e) {
210:                    }
211:                    tries++
212:            }
213:            // if the file was not opened, throw an LfCanNotOpen
214:            // exception. This passes control out of the method
215:            // before the call to flushCache can occur.
216:            if (!isOpen)
217:                throw new LfCanNotOpen();
218:            // flush the cache if necessary
219:            if (this.cacheArray.length > 0)
220:                this.flushCache();
221:            // if no exception was thrown, then everything must
222:            // have been successful, so return true.
223:            return (true);
224:        }
225:    function writeln(logEntry)
226:    // This method overrides the writeln method in the base
227:    // class. It writes the date and time before writing
228:    // the actual entry. Notice the use of File:: to refer
229:    // to the methods of the base class.
230:    {
231:        return File::write(new Date() + " ") +
232:                File::writeln(logEntry);
233:    }
234: }
```

ANALYSIS   This production script contains the necessary documentation on lines 3 to 18 so that users can prepare to catch the custom exception classes. These custom classes are defined on lines 78 to 80. The exceptions are thrown on lines 113, 114, and 217.

Take a minute to look at line 113. This line makes use of the dynamic object model by overriding the open() method if there were any errors creating the log file. If the log file could not be created, any calls to the open() method automatically throw an exception.

Summary

Today you learned about debugging scripts and handling runtime errors that can be anticipated. The most important step in eliminating logical and coding errors is thorough planning. After coding and testing, you can use alerts and output to the script pad or a log file to track program flow and the values of variables.

Iron-clad script also needs to anticipate problems that can occur at runtime. Exception handling allows you to catch these errors and gives you the opportunity to respond gracefully.

Q&A

Q **Can the planning period really prepare for all the possible problems that will arise during the development cycle?**

A Thorough planning can prepare you for many of the conditions and problems that may come up during development, but there might be situations that the planners don't anticipate. There are certainly trade-offs involved here. Planning time takes away from actual coding time and needs to be wrapped up at some point. If the planning period lasts too long, the benefits of the additional planning time might be outweighed by the lost coding and testing time. But too little planning or too little input from developers, testers, and users can end up crippling the development schedule as unforeseen problems are discovered, debugged, and fixed.

Q **Can you write to the Script Pad window in a production application?**

A You can write to the Script Pad window, but it does little good because the Script Pad window is not visible in the IntraBuilder Server. On the other hand, it does little harm, except causing the script to run a little slower. If you need to track information in a production application, consider writing it to a log file or storing information in a table.

Q **Is it better to throw an exception or to simply handle a problem right when it occurs?**

A In many cases, the place where you need to respond to an error condition is not the same place that the error actually occurs. In these cases, throwing an exception back to the calling script allows the error recovery to take the context into consideration.

Q **If an exception is thrown within a try block, does the `catch` statement that follows that try block have to handle the exception?**

A No. If none of the `catch` statements following that `try` statement catch that `Exception` class (or one of its base classes), then the exception will be thrown to any other `try`/`catch` block in the call stack. If there are no more `try`/`catch` blocks in the call stack, the system exception handler responds to the exception.

Workshop

The Workshop section provides questions and exercises to help you get a better feel for the material you learned today. Try to answer the questions and at least think about the exercises before moving on to tomorrow's lesson. You'll find the answers to the questions in Appendix A, "Answers to Quiz Questions."

Quiz

1. List three uses of the Script Pad window during script development.

2. When can you use an `alert()` function, and when should you not use it?

3. The following script seems to have a problem with the `sql` statement that is generated. How can `alert()` or `_sys.scriptOut.writeln()` be used to determine what the problem is? (To test this script, create the `.JS` file in the `IntraBuilder\Samples` directory.)

```
alert("Total orders for 1221: $" + totalOrder('1221'));
function totalOrder(custNum) {
    var sql = 'select sum(total) as totalOrder'
    sql += 'from orders.dbf o ' ;
    sql += 'where o."Customer_n" = '
    sql += ("'" + custNum + "'")
    q = new Query();
    q.sql = sql;
    q.active = true;
    return (q.rowset.fields["totalOrder"].value);
}
```

4. What is an exception?

5. Does a `try` statement always need a `catch` statement?

Exercises

1. Write a function, `DebugAlert()`, that takes a single parameter and then displays the parameter in an alert dialog. Use a preprocessor directive so that the alert only occurs when in debug mode.

2. Write a script that clears the Script Pad output pane and then displays your name and address in the output pane. The output should match the format that you commonly use when addressing an envelope.

3. There are at least two things wrong with the following code. What are they? Assume that the `DoSomething()` function is defined elsewhere in the same script and that it may or may not throw an exception.

```
try {
    var x = "tmp" + parseInt(Math.random()*10000);
    _sys.databases[0].copyTable("orders.dbf",x);
    DoSomething(x);
    _sys.databases[0].dropTable(x);
}
catch (Exception e) {
    _sys.scriptOut.writeln("An error occured.");
}
catch (DbException e) {
    _sys.scriptOut.writeln("A database error occured.");
}
```

4. Modify the script in exercise 3 to correct both of the problems that you found. Test with all three versions of DoSomething() shown in the following code:

```
function DoSomething(){
    throw new Exception();
}
function DoSomething(){
    throw new DbException();
}
function DoSomething(){
    return true;
}
```

Day 17

Reusable JavaScript Components

by Ted Graham

Over the last 16 days, you have learned how to use the IntraBuilder design tools, and you have built and deployed an IntraBuilder application. Even though you have the skills necessary to create Web-based applications, there is no need for you to build every part of these applications from scratch. So, today, you begin exploring the world of reusable components and how to integrate them into an IntraBuilder application.

Today you will learn about the following topics:

☐ What reusable components ship with IntraBuilder.

☐ How to reuse these components.

☐ How to use the collection of components that make up the application security system.

Types of Components

Several different items fall into the category of reusable JavaScript components. JavaScript components can be either visual components or non-visual components.

 Visual components are custom classes based on IntraBuilder's standard visual classes, such as Form, HTML, or Button.

 Non-visual components are custom functions or custom classes based on non-visual IntraBuilder classes, such as Object or Date.

Visual Components

In addition to the standard user interface components such as buttons and images, IntraBuilder ships with a wide variety of custom user interface components. Based on standard IntraBuilder components, these components are customized to meet specific needs.

Several custom component files ship with IntraBuilder. Two of them reside in the Custom folder. These are Expert.cc and ActiveX.cc. The third one, Controls.cc, resides in the Apps\Shared folder. The prebuilt business solutions use the Controls.cc file, and you can use it for your own applications as well. The last two files, Chart.cc and Counter.cc, reside in the Samples folder.

Loading Custom Components

Custom components are typically stored in a JavaScript source file with a .cc extension. After you load the classes defined in the .cc file into memory, they appear in the Custom tab of the Component Palette.

You can load a .cc file into memory in two different ways. The first way is to locate the file using the IntraBuilder Explorer. The .cc files appear in the Custom tab of the IntraBuilder Explorer, as shown in Figure 17.1. Double-clicking the .cc file loads the file into memory for the duration of the current IntraBuilder session.

Figure 17.1.

The Custom tab of the IntraBuilder Explorer showing custom component files.

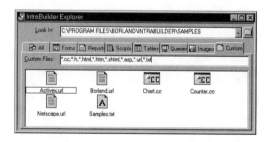

You can also configure IntraBuilder to load the .cc file every time the IntraBuilder Designer is loaded. In fact, the installation program has already configured the IntraBuilder Designer to load the Expert.cc file. You can add and delete .cc files from the process while in the Form Designer. To add a .cc file to the list of files, follow these steps:

1. Open the Form Designer.
2. Select File|Set Up Custom Components.
3. Press the Add button and select the custom component file.
4. Press OK to close the Set Up Custom Components dialog.

NOTE

Sometimes the components do not appear right away on the Component Palette. A quick way to get the palette to refresh is to right-click the palette and select the Toolbars and Palettes option. Then change the Component Palette's Show Tabs setting and press OK. This should update the palette, showing the new components. You can follow the same steps to change the tabs back if you want.

17

Expert.cc

The Expert.cc file contains classes that duplicate the image and button components generated by the Form Expert. As shown in Figure 17.2, the Form Expert can generate either buttons or images to perform many common table operations such as navigating, adding records, and performing searches.

Figure 17.2.

The Form Expert.

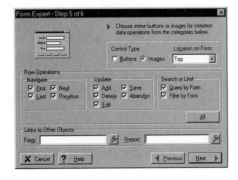

The same images and buttons can be added to your forms using the custom components in Expert.cc. The expert components appear on the Component Palette on two separate tabs: Update and Navigation. Figure 17.3 shows the Component Palette with some of the components from Expert.cc in the Update tab.

Figure 17.3.

Custom components in the Component Palette.

A few special notes should be made about these components. All of the components in Expert.cc require that the form's rowset property be set. This is the only way for the component to know what table to update or navigate. If you initially created the form using the Form Expert, the rowset property has already been set for you. If you create the form from scratch, you need to set the property yourself. You can do this by right-clicking on the form and then selecting the Inspector option on the shortcut menu. You then press the drop-down button next to the rowset property to open a list of all the open queries. Select the query that you want the components to manipulate. You can select only one of the available queries.

You should also be aware that the image components copy a small image file into the current folder when they are placed onto a form. This image file is copied from the Designer\Form folder. If the form is later moved to a new location, you should be sure to copy these image files as well.

Update Buttons

The components shown in Figure 17.3 are update buttons and update images. They are shown with pictures in the Component Palette to give you an idea what the components do. These components are also shown in Table 17.1 along with the class name that they represent and a brief description of what the buttons do.

Table 17.1. The update buttons in Expert.cc.

Icon	Text	Class Name	Description
	Add	AddButton	Begin appending a new record.
	Delete	DeleteButton	Delete the current record.
	Edit	EditButton	Begin editing the current record.

17

Icon	Text	Class Name	Description
	Save	SaveButton	Save changes to the current record.
	Abandon	AbandonButton	Abandon changes to the current record.
	New Query	SearchButton	Enter search mode/submit search.
	New Filter	FilterButton	Enter filter mode/submit filter.

You use these update buttons in the Form Designer just like you would use a standard IntraBuilder button. You just drag the button from the Component Palette to the form and place it wherever you choose. The benefit of using these custom components is that the JavaScript necessary to perform the action is already attached to the onServerClick event. However, you are free to modify any of the properties of the component, even the text or onServerClick.

The purpose of most of these buttons should be obvious, but a few might not be quite so obvious, such as the EditButton class. This button is unnecessary if the query's rowset.autoEdit property is left to its default value. When left to the default value of true, the rowset data displayed in the form can be updated automatically. However, when the value is false, attempts to update the data are ignored. Before you can update the data, you must call the rowset.beginEdit() method. After calling this method, you can update the data for the current record. The purpose of the EditButton class is to call this method to allow you to begin editing the current record.

The SearchButton and FilterButton classes are both two-state buttons. When you first press these buttons, they begin the search or filter operation. At this point, the text on the button changes to "Run Query" or "Run Filter." While it is in the second state, the button is used to apply the criteria that were entered during the search or filter mode and to change the text back to the original text.

Update Images

The remaining components shown in Figure 17.3 are all custom image components. They are shown with pictures in the palette to give you an idea of what the components do. These components are also shown in Table 17.2, along with the class name that they represent and a brief description of what the images do.

Table 17.2. The update images in Expert.cc.

Icon	Class Name	Image File	Description
	AddImage	UPDADD.GIF	Begin appending a new record.
	DeleteImage	UPDDEL.GIF	Delete the current record.
	EditImage	UPDEDIT.GIF	Begin editing the current record.
	SaveImage	UPDSAVE.GIF	Save changes to the current record.
	AbandonImage	UPDABAN.GIF	Abandon changes to the current record.
	SearchImage	SRCHQBF.GIF	Enter search mode/run search.
	FilterImage	FLTRFBF.GIF	Enter filter mode/run filter.
	UpdateHorizontal Image	EXPIROWH.GIF	All seven images aligned horizontally.
	UpdateVertical Image	EXPIROWV.GIF	All seven images aligned vertically.

The seven images corresponding to the update buttons perform the same function as their button counterparts. Likewise, the two composite images perform the same functions as the individual images. The only difference between the images and the buttons is the absence of any text. This has the potential to confuse users, particularly when switching between the two states of the SearchImage and FilterImage classes. You might want to include some other visual cues about the current state of the form when using the image components.

Navigation Components

In addition to the update components, Expert.cc also has navigation components. Like the update components shown in Figure 17.3, there are both navigation buttons and navigation images. Tables 17.3 and 17.4 show the palette icons, the text (only for the buttons), the class name, the image file (only for images), and the purpose of the navigation components.

17

Table 17.3. The navigation buttons in Expert.cc.

Icon	Text	Class Name	Description
	First	FirstButton	Move to first record.
	Previous	PreviousButton	Move to previous record.
	Next	NextButton	Move to next record.
	Last	LastButton	Move to last record.

Table 17.4. The navigation images in Expert.cc.

Icon	Class Name	Image File	Description
	FirstImage	NAVFIRST.GIF	Move to first record.
	PreviousImage	NAVPREV.GIF	Move to previous record.
	NextImage	NAVNEXT.GIF	Move to next record.
	LastImage	NAVLAST.GIF	Move to last record.
	NavigateHorizontal Image	EXPINAVH.GIF	All four images aligned horizontally.
	NavigateVertical Image	EXPINAVV.GIF	All four images aligned vertically.

The purpose for each of the navigation buttons and images should be quite clear. Each button has a corresponding image that performs the same action. The NavigateHorizontalImage and NavigateVerticalImage components are particularly useful because of the amount of capability that is packed into such a small amount of screen space.

ActiveX.cc

The ActiveX.cc file contains a collection of custom ActiveX components. This file is also located in the Custom folder; however, it is not automatically loaded when IntraBuilder begins.

The 12 custom components are used just like regular ActiveX components. You place the component on a form and then set the `params` property values to control the component's behavior.

These ActiveX components all ship with Microsoft Internet Explorer 3.0. Because they are all part of Internet Explorer, you do not have to set the `codeBase` property of the component. This makes these components very easy to use. Complete documentation for these components can be found on the Microsoft Web site. At the time of printing, this information was contained at the following address:

```
http://www.microsoft.com/intdev/controls/ctrlref.htm
```

The following components are contained in `ActiveX.cc`:

- [ ] `AnimatedButtonActiveX`
- [ ] `ChartActiveX`
- [ ] `GradientActiveX`
- [ ] `LabelActiveX`
- [ ] `MarqueeActiveX`
- [ ] `MenuActiveX`
- [ ] `PopupMenuActiveX`
- [ ] `PopupWindowActiveX`
- [ ] `PreloaderActiveX`
- [ ] `StockTickerActiveX`
- [ ] `TimerActiveX`
- [ ] `ViewTrackerActiveX`

Controls.cc

The `Controls.cc` file contains a variety of custom components. These were originally created for use in the prebuilt business solution applications that ship with IntraBuilder. This file is located in the Apps\Shared folder.

File Lists

There are two file list components. One is a custom `Select` component named `FileSelect`, and the other is a custom `ListBox` component named `FileListBox`. Both of these components are used in the same way.

Both Select and ListBox components take their options (the items that appear in the list) from an array. The Form Designer has an array builder tool for creating static arrays, but there are no visual tools to get the filenames from a folder into such an array. You would normally have to write some JavaScript code to read and store the filenames in an array.

The file list components are designed to do this work for you. The components have the same properties and methods of the standard components that they are based on. In addition, each component has one custom method.

To use the component, follow these steps:

1. Load Controls.cc as described earlier.

2. Place the FileSelect or FileListBox component on the form.

3. Right-click the component and select Inspector.

4. The options property currently contains

   ```
   array{"*.*"}
   ```

   Replace the *.* with the template for the files that you want shown in the list. For instance, to show a list of reports in the current folder, change the options property to read as follows:

   ```
   array{"*.jrp"}
   ```

   Figure 17.4 shows the Inspector after making this change.

Figure 17.4.

Inspecting the FileSelect *object.*

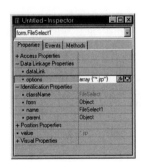

You can use the * wildcard character to represent any number of characters, and you can use the ? wildcard character to represent any single character. You can optionally include a path, such as this one:

```
array{"c:\\Borland\\IntraBuilder\\Apps\\*.gif"}
```

5. Set any additional properties or events for the component.

When the form is opened, the control automatically generates the list of options based on the file specification that you provided. This list is built only once, when the form is first opened. If you want to rebuild the list while the form is open, you call the custom `fillOptions()` method. This method regenerates the list based on the original file specification.

Field Lists

The two field list components are a custom `Select` component named `FieldSelect`, and a custom `ListBox` component named `FieldListBox`. Both of these components are used in the same way.

Like the file list components, the field list components are designed to create the options array for you. When you provide a table name and a field name, the field list component fills the options array with data from that field.

To use the component, follow these steps:

1. Load `Controls.cc` as described earlier in the "Loading Custom Components" section.

2. Place the `FieldSelect` or `FieldListBox` component on the form.

3. Right-click the component and select Inspector.

4. The options property currently contains

   `array{'table','field'}`

   Replace the word *table* with the name of any actual table. Likewise, replace the word *field* with the name of a field in that table. For instance, to fill a list with the names of products from a product table, you would set the options property as follows:

   `array{'product.db','Product Name'}`

5. Set any additional properties or events for the component.

NOTE

> The field list components only need the name of the table and the field. In order for the component to find this table, there must be a default query on the form, and the table must be in the same folder or database as the default query. If you use the Form Expert to create the form, then the expert created a default query. If you create the form from scratch, you need to add a query object yourself, and then set the form's `rowset` property to point to the query object.

17

When the form is opened, the control automatically generates the list of options based on the specification that you provided. This list is built only once, when the form is first opened. If you want to rebuild the list while the form is open, you call the custom fillOptions() method. This method regenerates the list based on the original specification.

The IntraBuilder Phone Book application uses a field list component in the Update form. View the source script for the Update form to see an example of using the fillOptions() method. The Phone Book application comes with IntraBuilder and can be found in the Apps\Phone folder.

Back Buttons

Two different buttons in Controls.cc can move you back a page. The first is the ClientBackButton component, and it uses client-side JavaScript. Clicking this button in a browser is the same as pressing the browser's own back button.

The second component is ServerBackButton. This component's action takes place on the server. This button closes the current form. IntraBuilder then re-renders the last form that was opened before the current form opened. This component acts as an *application back* more so than the *browser back*. For example, you use a browser to open a home page that was created with the IntraBuilder Home Page Expert. From that form, you select a second IntraBuilder form that contains customer data. You press the Next button a few times and then press the Back button. If the button performs a client-side back, you view the previous customer record (the last page viewed in the browser). If the back button performs a server-side action to close the customer form, you return immediately to the home page (the last IntraBuilder form that had focus).

| NEW TERM | An *application back* is a button or image that looks like a browser back button but submits the form to the IntraBuilder Server rather than retrieving the previous browser page from the browser cache. An application back button sends a new page to the browser that looks like the previous page but might have some updated information. A *browser back* button simply retrieves the previous page from a cache without making any modifications.

HTML **Components**

There are two HTML components in Controls.cc. The first is just like any standard HTML component except that the alignment properties have been set to center the text. This component is appropriately named CenterHTML.

The second HTML component is called GeneratedHTML. This component is used at the bottom of the prebuilt business solution application forms to indicate the date and time that IntraBuilder generated the HTML stream that is sent to the browser. Figure 17.5 shows a simple form with a GeneratedHTML component at the bottom.

Figure 17.5.

A browser showing the
GeneratedHTML
component.

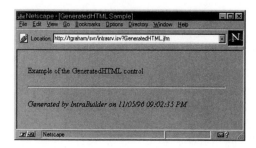

Chart.cc

The Chart.cc file resides in the Samples folder. It contains two charting components. These two components are used to display data from a table in the form of a chart. The two components are named as follows:

- ActiveXChartQuery
- JavaChartQuery

Both of these classes are used in the same way. After placing the components on the form, you need to set the form's onServerLoad() method to call the component's Init() method. You need to pass the Init() method three pieces of information that the component uses to build the chart. The first is the name of the field that is used to identify each piece of data. This field is used as the labels on the chart. The second is the name of the field that contains the data to be charted. The third is an object reference to the rowset object that contains the data.

The table used for the chart must already be open by the time you call the Init() method. The sql property for the Query object should take care of grouping the data and calculating the total for each group.

The sample files ActiveX.jfm and Java.jfm (also in the Samples folder) demonstrate the use of these two components. Listing 17.1 shows the contents of ActiveX.jfm, using the ActiveXChartQuery component.

INPUT   **Listing 17.1. The contents of ActiveX.jfm.**

```
1: // {End Header} Do not remove this comment//
2: // Generated on 02/14/97
3: //
4: var f = new activexForm();
5: f.open();
6: class activexForm extends Form {
7:   _sys.scripts.load("chart.cc")
8:    with (this) {
```

17

```
 9:        onServerLoad = class::form_onServerLoad;
10:        height = 14.6667;
11:        left = 0;
12:        top = 0;
13:        width = 76;
14:        title = "ActiveX Sample";
15:     }
16:     with (this.query1 = new Query()){
17:        left = 34;
18:        top = 8;
19:        sql = "select c.state_prov, sum(o.total) as sumTotal from " +
20:              "customer c, orders o where c.customer_n = o.customer_n " +
21:              "group by c.state_prov";
22:        active = true;
23:     }
24:     with (this.query1.rowset) {
25:     }
26:     with (this.ActiveXChartQuery1 = new ActiveXChartQuery(this)){
27:        height = 13;
28:        top = 1.5;
29:        width = 74;
30:        params["ChartType"] = "8";
31:     }
32:     with (this.html1 = new HTML(this)){
33:        height = 1.5;
34:        width = 74;
35:        color = "black";
36:        alignHorizontal = 1;
37:        text = "Total Sales by State (in U.S. Dollars)";
38:     }
39:     with (this.html2 = new HTML(this)){
40:        height = 1;
41:        top = 14.5;
42:        width = 74;
43:        color = "black";
44:        alignHorizontal = 1;
45:        text = "(Data computed from customer.dbf and orders.dbf.)";
46:     }
47:     with (this.button1 = new Button(this)){
48:        onClick = class::button1_onClick;
49:        left = 18;
50:        top = 16;
51:        width = 10.5;
52:        text = "Back";
53:     }
54:     with (this.switchViewButton = new Button(this)){
55:        onClick = class::switchViewButton_onClick;
56:        left = 42;
57:        top = 16;
58:        width = 16;
59:        text = "Switch View";
60:     }
61:     this.rowset = this.query1.rowset;
62:
63:     function form_onServerLoad()
64:     {
```

continues

Listing 17.1. continued

```
65:          this.ActiveXChartQuery1.Init( "state_prov", "sumTotal",
66:             this.query1.rowset ) ;
67:      }
68:
69:    function button1_onClick()
70:    {
71:        history.back();
72:    }
73:
74:    function switchViewButton_onClick()
75:    {
76:        var ChartType = document.forms[0].ActiveXChartQuery1.ChartType;
77:        if (ChartType == 5)
78:            ChartType = 8;
79:        else if (ChartType == 8)
80:            ChartType = 14;
81:        else
82:            ChartType = 5;
83:        document.forms[0].ActiveXChartQuery1.ChartType = ChartType;
84:    }
85: }
```

ANALYSIS Lines 16 to 23 define the query object, which contains the data to be charted. Lines 19 through 21 contain the SQL statement that retrieves the state names and the total sales for each state. This query's `rowset` is used later in the `form_onServerLoad()` method that begins on line 63.

Lines 26 to 31 define the chart component itself. The definition of the chart component is very simple. The actual initialization of the component is done in the `form_onServerLoad()` method. Line 65 calls the `Init()` method of the component.

Counter.cc

The `Counter.cc` file is also in the Samples folder. This contains a single custom component named `Counter`. This component is subclassed from the HTML component and has all the same properties and methods as a standard HTML component.

The `Counter` component is used to keep track of the number of times that an IntraBuilder Web page is visited, or *hit*. You place the component onto the form just like you would a normal HTML component. You can then set the visual properties, such as the color or font properties. You do not need to set any other properties at this time.

Here is an example from the `SampHome.jfm` file, which uses the `Counter` component:

```
with (this.Counter1 = new Counter(this)){
   height = 1.1667;
   top = 28;
   width = 70;
```

17

```
    color = "blue";
    fontBold = true;
}
```

Notice that the Counter component's definition is very simple. This is because the custom properties are set in the form's onServerLoad() event handler. Four custom properties need to be set. The following lines show each of these properties being set:

```
form.Counter1.cTableName= "COUNTERS"
form.Counter1.cCountName= "SAMPHOME"
form.Counter1.cFontSize = "5"
form.Counter1.cText      = "Number of visits to this page: "
```

Again, this code comes from the SampHome.jfm file. The cTableName property identifies a table that is used to keep track of the number of times this form is opened. If the table does not exist, it is created automatically. The same table can keep track of hits to more than one page. The cCountName property must uniquely identify this page within the table. The cText property is displayed to the left of the actual hit count, and the cFontSize property is the size of the count itself.

Non-visual Components

In addition to the many visual custom components that ship with IntraBuilder, there are also many non-visual custom components. These components take several forms, such as header files, functions, and classes that you can reuse in your own scripts.

Header Files

Several header files are in the Include folder. These header files can be included in your own script files to simplify your programming tasks. Two of these header files, Intra.h and Windef.h, are described here. The rest are used in conjunction with custom components.

Using Header Files

If you are already familiar with the use of header files and the #include preprocessor directive, you might want to go on to the next section. If you have not worked with header files before, this section describes what header files are and how to use them in your JavaScript source files.

In many programming languages, header files are used to store preprocessor directives, type declarations, function prototypes, and simple macros. A header file usually ends with a .h suffix, as in Intra.h. The header file is included in a source file by using the #include preprocessor directive. For instance, the following line includes file Intra.h in the current JavaScript file:

```
#include "intra.h"
```

The `#include` directive is handled by the preprocessor, which prepares the source code for compilation. Before compiling a JavaScript source file, the preprocessor goes through the source and executes any preprocessor commands. These commands are used to make changes to the source code "on the fly." The resulting source code is then sent to the compiler. You used preprocessor directives in yesterday's lesson when you included debug code in your scripts. Consider this script:

```
#define DEBUG
#define DEBUG_TEXT "In Debug Mode"
#ifdef DEBUG
alert( DEBUG_TEXT );
#endif
```

Before this script is executed, it must pass through the preprocessor and then the compiler. The preprocessor handles the lines beginning with the # symbols. After the preprocessor has processed the script, it simply looks like this:

```
alert( "In Debug Mode" );
```

This is the only command that is actually sent to the compiler. Notice that the `DEBUG_TEXT` identifier has been replaced by the string `"In Debug Mode"` and that the other preprocessor commands are no longer present.

This very brief explanation tries to get across the idea that the preprocessor generates a copy of the source file that has been reshaped based on the various preprocessor directives contained in the code.

The `#include` directive is used to instruct the preprocessor to insert the specified file into the source code at the current location. When the compiler gets the resulting file, it appears as a single source file. When the header file has been included in your source file, you can reference any of the identifiers that have been declared.

When you `#include` a file, the preprocessor looks for the included file in the current folder. If it is not found, the preprocessor looks in the Include folder for the file.

IntraBuilder Constants

IntraBuilder classes include many enumerated properties. For instance, the `rowset` class contains the `state` property, which contains a numeric value from zero to five. Each of these numeric values indicates that the `rowset` object is in a different state. For example, 3 indicates that the `rowset` is in append mode. The following code sets the text of an `HTML` component based on the rowset's state. It can be used in a form's `preRender` event.

```
if (this.rowset.state == 3)
    this.stateHTML.text = "Appending";
else
    this.stateHTML.text = "Editing";
```

It can be very difficult to remember what all the state values represent and even more difficult to remember what all the different enumerated property values mean. The Intra.h file helps to eliminate this problem by defining constants with more recognizable names for each of these cryptic numeric values. For example, the same code can be rewritten like this:

```
#include "intra.h"
if (this.rowset.state == STATE_APPEND)
   this.stateHTML.text = "Appending";
else
   this.stateHTML.text = "Editing";
```

This version of the code is much easier to understand when you go back to make changes later. Because it is much easier to remember descriptive identifiers such as STATE_APPEND than to remember numeric values, you might also find it much easier to write your scripts using this header file.

The constants defined in Intra.h follow the same basic naming convention. The constants start with the name of a property, such as STATE_, followed by a descriptive identifier, such as APPEND. The exceptions to this rule are the PRINTER_COLOR_ constants, which are used for the color property of Printer objects.

Windows API Data Types

Another header file in the Include folder is Windef.h. This header file defines preprocessor identifiers for the most common data types used by the Windows API. IntraBuilder allows you to use external functions (including Windows API functions) by use of the extern command. This command requires you to identify the data type used for each function parameter and the return value. Normally, you would identify the data type using one of the IntraBuilder type identifiers, such as int or char*.

The Windows API defines many custom data types, which are variations of the standard data types. The many API references available usually give the Windows data types while describing the prototype of the function. This requires you to convert from the Windows data type to the base data type in order to prototype the function in IntraBuilder. However, Windef.h makes this job easier by defining many of the Windows data types for you.

NOTE

To see an example of accessing the Windows API and of using the Windef.h header file, take a look at the Registry.js file in the Apps\Shared folder. This file contains the definition of a Registry class that is used by the solution applications that come with IntraBuilder.

The Registry Class

One of the most useful components that ships with IntraBuilder is the Registry class. This class reads and writes values to the Windows registry. This can be a very useful way of storing configuration information for a JavaScript application.

The Registry class is defined in the file Registry.js in the Apps\Shared folder. In order to use the Registry class, you must load this file into memory so that the class definition is available to IntraBuilder. In addition to loading this file into memory, you need to #include the file Winreg.h. This header file defines several constants that you need as you work with the Registry class.

Using the Registry Class

Using the Registry class, your scripts can read information directly from the system registry, as well as write data back to the registry. The following script demonstrates creating a Registry object:

```
#include "winreg.h"
_sys.scripts.load(_sys.env.home() + "apps\\shared\\registry.js");
var reg = new Registry(HKEY_LOCAL_MACHINE,"Software\\MyCompany");
```

The object that is created by new Registry contains a reference to a single key in the registry. That key is identified by the two parameters passed to the Registry class. The actual syntax for the registry class is as follows:

```
new Registry( <open key> , <sub-key> )
```

The <open key> parameter takes a Windows handle to an open registry key. The Winreg.h header file provides identifiers for the root keys, which are always open. You must use one of these identifiers, which are defined in Winreg.h:

- [ ] HKEY_CURRENT_USER
- [ ] HKEY_LOCAL_MACHINE
- [ ] HKEY_CLASSES_ROOT
- [ ] HKEY_USERS
- [ ] HKEY_PERFORMANCE_DATA
- [ ] HKEY_CURRENT_CONFIG
- [ ] HKEY_DYN_DATA

The <sub-key> is a character string identifying a subkey of the <open key>. This parameter is required, but it can be an empty string. In the previous code example, the Registry object references the HKEY_LOCAL_MACHINE\Software\MyCompany key.

Each `Registry` object can reference only a single key in the system registry. When you read from and write to multiple keys, you need to create multiple `Registry` objects.

Registry Properties and Methods

After you have created the `Registry` object, you can use any of the object's properties and methods. The object contains two properties—`newlyCreated` and `error`. When you create a new `Registry` object, the specified key is opened. If it does not already exist, it is created and then opened. If it was necessary to create the key, the `newlyCreated` property is set to `true`; otherwise, it is set to `false`. If any error occurs when trying to open or create the key, the `error` property is set. The `error` property contains the Windows error message that prevented the key from being opened or created. Each of the methods described in the following list can also set the `error` property. You might want to check its value after each call to one of the `Registry` methods.

The object also has five methods, which are shown in the following list along with their parameters:

- ☐ deleteValue(<name>)
- ☐ enumValue()
- ☐ queryKeyName()
- ☐ queryValue(<name>)
- ☐ setValue(<name> , <data> [, <type>])

The `deleteValue()` method deletes the named value. If <name> contains an empty string, the default value of the key is deleted. The method returns a Boolean value indicating whether or not the delete was successful.

The `enumValue()` method returns an array containing the name of each value contained in the current key.

The `queryKeyName()` method returns a string containing the name of the referenced registry key.

The `queryValue()` method takes a string that identifies a value contained in the current key. If <name> contains an empty string, the key's default value is returned. If <name> contains a string, the data associated with that named value is returned. The data type of the returned value depends on the data type of the value in the registry. Most registry entries are strings, including most of the numeric entries. However, some registry entries are actually identified as numbers. In such a case, the return value from `queryValue()` is actually an IntraBuilder numeric value.

The `setValue()` method takes three parameters. Only the third one is optional. The <name> property identifies the named value to set. This can contain an empty string to set the default value. The <data> parameter is generally a string value. This <data> is stored in the registry and identified by <name>. If the <type> parameter is omitted, the <data> is considered to be of a string type. To store the <data> in a different format, you must pass the <type> parameter as well. The Registry class currently supports only the two most common registry types—REG_SZ for strings, and REG_DWORD for four byte integer values. These data type identifiers are defined in Winreg.h.

WARNING

Be very careful when writing to the system registry. The operating system and many software packages keep their configuration information in the registry alone. If you inadvertently overwrite one of these configuration settings, the operating system or one of the software packages might stop working.

To see an example of using the Registry class, check out the file Server.jfm in the Server folder. (Note that this was in the Samples folder in the 1.0 release.) A portion of this file is shown in Listing 17.2.

INPUT   **Listing 17.2. Using the Registry class in Server.jfm.**

```
 1: #include "WINREG.H"
 2: #define SERVER_REG_KEY  "SOFTWARE\\Borland\\IntraBuilder\\1.0"
 3: function form_onServerLoad()
 4: {
 5:    // load the registry class library
 6:    _sys.scripts.load("registry.js");
 7:    // load the registry values
 8:    form.registry = new Registry(HKEY_LOCAL_MACHINE, SERVER_REG_KEY +
 9:       "\\Server" );
10:    form.remoteAgents = new Array();
11:    form.maxAgentID = -1;
12:    if (form.registry.error == 0) {
13:       form.pathText.value =
14:          form.resetPath = form.registry.queryValue("IntraPath");
15:       form.instancesText.value =
16:          form.resetInstances = form.registry.queryValue("Agents");
17:       form.sessionsText.value = form.resetSessions =
18:          form.registry.queryValue("MaxSessions");
19:       form.timeoutText.value = form.resetTimeout =
20:          form.registry.queryValue("Timeout");
21:       // load remote agent information
22:       form.readRemoteAgents(form);
23:    }
24:    else {
25:       form.pathText.value      = "Error reading system registry";
26:       form.instancesText.value = "Error";
27:       form.sessionsText.value  = "Error";
28:       form.timeoutText.value   = "Error";
```

17

```
29:            form.saveButton.visible  = false;
30:            // disable remote agent button
31:            this.remoteAgentsButton.visible = false;
32:        }
33: }
34: function readRemoteAgents(oForm)
35: {
36:     oForm.remoteAgents = new Array();
37:     oForm.maxAgentID = -1;
38:     var nAgentId = -1;
39:     var aValues = oForm.registry.enumValue();
40:     aValues.sort();
41:     for (var i = 0; i < aValues.length; i++)
42:         if (aValues[i].substring(0,6).toUpperCase() == 'REMOTE') {
43:             nAgentID = aValues[i].substring(6,aValues[i].length)
44:             oForm.remoteAgents.add(nAgentID + ", " +
45:                 oForm.registry.queryValue(aValues[i]));
46:             if (parseInt(nAgentID) > oForm.maxAgentID)
47:                 oForm.maxAgentID = parseInt(nAgentID);
48:         }
49:     oForm.remoteAgentsListBox.options = "array form.remoteAgents";
50:     if (oForm.remoteAgents.length == 0) {
51:         oForm.updateButton.visible = false;
52:         oForm.deleteButton.visible = false;
53:     }
54:     else {
55:         oForm.updateButton.visible = true;
56:         oForm.deleteButton.visible = true;
57:     }
58: }
59: function saveButton_onServerClick()
60: {
61:     this.form.registry.setValue("IntraPath",form.pathText.value);
62:     this.form.registry.setValue("Agents",form.instancesText.value);
63:     this.form.registry.setValue("MaxSessions",form.sessionsText.value);
64:     this.form.registry.setValue("Timeout",form.timeoutText.value);
65: }
66: function deleteButton_onServerClick()
67: {
68:     var agent = this.form.remoteAgentsListBox.value;
69:     if (agent.length > 0) {
70:         this.form.registry.deleteValue("Remote" +
71:             agent.substring(0,agent.indexOf(","))));
72:         this.form.readRemoteAgents(this.form);
73:     }
74: }
75: function saveAgentButton_onServerClick()
76: {
77:     this.form.registry.setValue("Remote" + this.form.agentIDText.value,
78:         this.form.userNameText.value + "@" + this.form.machineNameText.value);
79:     this.form.showAgentControls(this.form, false);
80:     this.form.readRemoteAgents(this.form);
81: }
```

17

ANALYSIS Line 1 uses the preprocessor to include the registry constants used by the script. Line 2 defines the base registry key name. This is used on line 8 to create the registry object.

> **TIP**
>
> The standard rule when writing application state information to the registry is to use the HKEY_LOCAL_MACHINE or the HKEY_CURRENT_USER key, depending on whether the setting is global to all users or specific to the current user. Then you should use the Software key. Under this key, you should use your company name, like Borland was used on line 2. Under this key, you should use your product name and then the version number. Under this version number key, you can create values for each piece of state information that you want to store.

Lines 13 to 20 use the queryValue() method to retrieve values from registry keys. These values are stored to the text objects on the form so that the user can view and edit the values. If the user edits the values and submits the form, the saveButton_onServerClick(), beginning on line 59, uses the setValue() method to write the new values back to the registry.

The readRemoteAgents() method begins on line 34. This method creates an array of values that are read from the registry. The remote agent values have names such as REMOTE0 and REMOTE2. There can be several values, which may or may not have sequential numeric values at the end. This method uses the enumValue() method on line 39 to create an array with all the values in the registry key. Lines 41 to 48 then check each value in the array to see whether it begins with the word 'REMOTE'. If it does, the method calls queryValue() and stores the result to a second array, which is then displayed to the user.

The deleteButton_onServerClick() method, which begins on line 66, uses the deleteValue() method to remove items from the registry.

Extended Date Class

A final class worth noting here is the DateEx class that is also found in the Apps\Shared folder. This class is contained in the Dateex.js file. The DateEx class is an extension to the standard Date class, like the StringEx class is an extension to the String class. In addition to the standard properties and methods of the Date class, the DateEx class adds several additional methods:

- ☐ getSDate()
- ☐ getSDay()
- ☐ getSMonth()

 17

☐ getSTime([<bSeconds> [,<bTwelveHour>]])

☐ getSTimezone()

These methods all return strings representing part of the date value.

NOTE

> Both the content and the exact structure of the strings that DateEx methods return are based on the configuration settings of Windows itself. The country settings in the Windows Control Panel determine how date and time information is displayed.

The getSDate() method returns the date as a character string. In the United States, this string would typically appear in the format "Saturday, December 30, 1995". The following example would typically store this string to the variable x:

```
var d = new DateEx(95,11,30,17,0,0);
x = d.getSDate();
```

The getSDay() method returns the day of the week, such as "Saturday" or "Tuesday". The actual string returned matches the language version of Windows as well as the country setting.

The getSMonth() method returns the name of the month, such as "December" or "August". Again, the actual names returned are dependent upon the country settings.

The getSTime() method returns the time portion of the DateEx value as a character string. The default formatting of the string depends upon the Windows settings. The optional Boolean <bSeconds> parameter determines whether the return string includes seconds. If you include this parameter, you might also specify the second optional Boolean parameter, <bTwelveHour>. This determines whether the return string uses a 12-hour clock (true) or a 24-hour clock (false).

The getSTimezone() method returns the name of the time zone to which the machine is set. The actual strings are hard coded into the Dateex.js file. Many of the time zone names are debatable and can be changed to match your preference. To change these names, edit the Dateex.js file.

The following script shows two functions taken from the Entries.jrp file in the Apps\Guestbk folder. These two functions make use of the DateEx class to format the date and time in the Guest Book Entries report:

```
function getVisitDate(frm) {
  var dateEx = new DateEx(""+frm.guest1.rowset.fields["VisitTime"].value);
  return (dateEx.getSDate());
}
function getVisitTime(frm) {
  var dateEx = new DateEx(""+frm.guest1.rowset.fields["VisitTime"].value);
  return (dateEx.getSTime(false,true) + " (" + dateEx.getSTimezone() + ")");
}
```

17

The `VisitTime` field already contains a Date type value. Notice the technique used to create a `DateEx` object from the existing `Date` object. The `Date` object is converted to a string by concatenating it with an empty string (`""`). The string is a valid parameter when creating a `Date` or `DateEx` object.

JavaScript Functions

In addition to the visual components and classes that ship with IntraBuilder, several useful functions are tucked away among the prebuilt business solutions. When these function library files have been loaded, the functions are used like standard functions such as `escape()` or `parseInt()`.

The `String.js` file in the Apps\Shared folder contains a handful of string manipulation functions. These are all rather simple; however, they do simplify your own coding and make for more readable code.

There are three functions for trimming strings:

- ☐ `ltrim( <expS> )`
- ☐ `rtrim( <expS> )`
- ☐ `alltrim( <expS> )`

All three of these take a single string parameter, `<expS>`. The `ltrim()` function removes spaces on the left side of the string, and `rtrim()` removes spaces on the right side of the string. The `alltrim()` function removes both leading (left) and trailing (right) spaces.

There is also a function for padding strings:

`pad( <expS>, <expN> )`

The `pad()` function takes a string parameter, `<expS>`, and a numeric parameter, `<expN>`. The string is padded with enough spaces to make the length `<expN>`. The returned string is exactly `<expN>` characters long. If `<expS>` has a length that is already greater than `<expN>`, the returned string is actually shorter than the original.

Another function in `String.js` converts numeric values to string values:

`str( <expN1> [,<expN2> [,<expN3>]] )`

The `str()` function takes at least one parameter, `<expN1>`, which is the number to be converted to a string. Optionally, a length can be passed, as well as the number of decimal places that should appear in the returned string. If no length is passed, the returned string is as long as necessary to hold the whole number portion of `<expN1>`. If a length is passed but not a decimal parameter, no decimals are included in the returned string.

Here are several examples of using the str() function. The values stored to x are shown in comments after the function:

```
x = str(1.23)     // "1"
x = str(1.23,4)   // "   1" (three spaces before 1)
x = str(1.23,4,2) // "1.23"
x = str(1,4,2)    // "1.00"
```

As you see from the last two examples in the preceding code, the str() function is very useful when trying to display numeric values with a consistent number of decimal places.

The last function in String.js is used to escape characters in a string. To *escape* a character simply means to identify it as a special character. You identify certain special characters by preceding them with a slash character. For example, the following command normally produces an error:

```
var x = 'Joe's Fender Shop'
```

The use of the apostrophe inside the quoted string produces too many apostrophes, and an error results. To correct this, you can escape the apostrophe:

```
var x = 'Joe\'s Fender Shop'
```

The escapeChar() function goes through a string and escapes all of a particular character. The syntax for the function is as follows:

```
escapeChar( <expS1>, <expS2> )
```

In this syntax, <expS1> is the original string and <expS2> is the character that needs to be escaped. The following example escapes a string before sending it to the rowset's applyLocate() method:

```
var x = escapeChar( this.form.text1.value, "'" );
this.form.applyLocate("name='" + x + "'");
```

Application Security Components

The application security components are some of the most powerful reusable components in IntraBuilder. Using these components, you can provide very powerful and very flexible application security. Application-level security allows you to control access by user or by group. You determine what parts of an application each user is given access to. Using this, you can establish security rules governing not only the parts of your application, but also your data, right down to the field level.

The security system is composed of several different parts, including the administrative tools, the security scripting API, reusable security form classes, and the security data files.

These components are used to manage users, groups, resources, and policies. Users represent a single person or process that needs access to secured resources. Groups allow you to identify logical collections of users that have shared access to resources. Resources are logical representations of any application, form, data file, or process to which you want to control access. You assign access to these resources to individual users or to groups. And policies are security rules that apply to all users, groups, and resources. As an example, one of the system policies determines whether or not passwords are case sensitive.

Security Administration Tools

The Security Administration tools enable you to view and update the entities described in the preceding section. These tools are located in the Apps\Security folder. The main form is called SmAdmin.jfm. You can run this form inside the IntraBuilder IDE, or you can run it over the Web.

In order to run this form, you must log into the security system as a user that is part of the ADMINISTRATORS group. The default administrator is named SYSDBA and has the password masterkey. Use this user to initially log into the Security Administrator.

The user name (as well as group, resources, and policy names) are never case sensitive. By default, passwords are not case sensitive either, but you can change this using the Policy Administration form.

WARNING

The SYSDBA user can be known to anyone who has used the application security system. At your earliest convenience, you should create a new user for yourself and add that user to the ADMINISTRATORS group. Then delete the SYSDBA user or change the password for this user.

After you have logged in, you can view each of the four types of entities (users, groups, resources, and policies). Figure 17.6 shows the Security Administration form running in the IntraBuilder IDE. Notice that you have options to add, copy, update, or delete entities.

The Add option creates a new entity. The Copy option creates a new entity that contains the same attributes as the currently selected entity. The Update option allows you to change the attributes of the currently selected entity. The Delete option removes the currently selected entity.

WARNING

You are not prompted to confirm deletes. Take extra care around that button.

Figure 17.6.

*The Security
Administrator.*

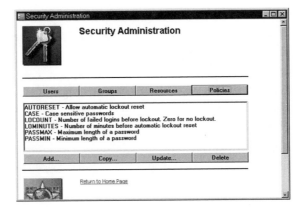

Entity Administration Forms

The User Administration form allows you to add, copy, or update a user entity. The user name cannot be changed while updating an existing user. The other pieces of information can be modified for both new and existing users. The description is optional. By default, users must have a password with a minimum length of four characters. This minimum length is controlled by a system policy that is described in the next section. As the system administrator, you can disable a user's account by checking the Account disabled check box. The Account locked out check box is used to unlock a user account after the security system has automatically disabled the account because of multiple login failures. The lockout behavior is turned off by default. The next section, "System Policies," describes the lockout feature.

The User Administration form also allows you to assign this user to groups and to grant access to resources. You use the Add Group and Remove Group buttons to move items between the list boxes. The list boxes to the left indicate which groups or resources this user is associated with.

The Group Administration form works very much like the User Administration form. After entering the group name and description, you can associate users with the group and grant the group access to resources. You might want to use many logical groups and then use these groups to control access to resources. This is generally much easier than trying to grant access to many individual users. Pay particular attention to the ADMINISTRATORS group. Any member of this group is able to run the Security Administration application. There is also one special restriction associated with this group. You are not allowed to remove the current user from the ADMINISTRATORS group. An administrator must be removed by a different administrator.

The Resource Administration form is very similar to the Group Administration form. Again, it has a place for the resource name and description and then two sets of list boxes for granting access to groups and users. You create resources that represent any application or part of an application. Using the scripting API described later in this chapter in the "Security Scripting APIs" section, you make sure that only authorized users access these resources.

The final entity administration form is used to configure policies. The Policy Administration form lets you set the policy name and description. Policies can contain either a Boolean or a numeric value. There is a check box for setting the Boolean value and a text component for entering the numeric value. There are also two radio components to determine the data type of the policy value.

The Policy Administration form lets you update system policies as well as create your own. The system policies are policies that control the operation of the security system itself.

NOTE

> You can change the description and value of these policies, but you cannot delete them or change their value type. You are free to create, modify, and delete your own policies.

Policies are rules that apply to all users. If you create your own policies, your scripts are responsible for checking these policy settings and responding accordingly.

System Policies

Six system policies have to do with passwords and lockout security. The PASSMIN and PASSMAX policies determine the minimum and maximum length of a password. The default values are 4 and 20, respectively. This is enforced when you create a new user or change the password of an existing user. Setting this policy does not affect existing passwords; however, the policy is enforced the next time the password changes. The CASE policy determines whether or not passwords are case sensitive.

The other three system policies control the lockout security feature. Lockout security disables a user's account if there are several failed login attempts in a short period of time. The LOCOUNT policy sets the number of failed logins that must occur before a lockout. If this is set to zero, lockout security is disabled. The LOMINUTES policy specifies the time frame in which these failed logins must occur. And AUTORESET determines whether the locked out account is reset after LOMINUTES have passed, or whether an administrator must manually unlock the account.

Security Scripting API

The security administration tools let you configure the entities in your security system. You make use of these entities in your application through the security scripting API. This API is implemented as two class libraries. You work exclusively with the SecurityManager class, unless you are writing your own security administration tools. A few notes about the SecurityManagerAdmin class are included at the end of this section.

The `SecurityManager` class is defined in the `Security.js` file in the Apps\Shared folder. Before using this class, you must load that script file. Then you can instantiate a `SecurityManager` object, which represents a single user entity. Although this object contains several methods, you will probably rely on `login()` and `hasAccessTo()` the most. The following example creates an object, logs in, and checks to see that the logged-in user can access a particular form:

```
_sys.scripts.load(_sys.env.home()+"apps\\shared\\security.js");
var user = new SecurityManager();
user.login("erik","erik")
if (user.hasAccessTo("PHONE UPDATE")) {
    // run the form
} else {
    // run an Access Denied form
}
```

This example actually logs into the system with a fixed user name and password. In your own applications, you should provide a login form where the user enters this information. A reusable login form is provided and is described in the next section.

The preceding example assumes that no errors are generated by the security system. This should never be assumed. The security system reports errors by throwing exceptions, as described in Day 16, "Debugging and Error Handling." Because the constructor and the methods can throw exceptions, surround these calls with a `try` block and catch the thrown exceptions with a `catch` block. The exceptions thrown are of a custom exception class `SmException`. Preprocessor constants are defined for the exception code values in the `Security.h` header file. This is demonstrated in Listing 17.3.

INPUT   **Listing 17.3. Using the `SecurityManager` class.**

```
 1: #include "security.h"
 2: _sys.scripts.load(SM_CLASS_LOCATION + "security.js");
 3: try {
 4:     var user = new SecurityManager();
 5:     user.login("erik","erik")
 7:     if (user.hasAccessTo("PHONE UPDATE")) {
 8:         // run the form
 9:     }
10:     else {
11:         // run an Access Denied form
12:     }
13: }
14: catch (SmException e) {
15:     switch (e.code) {
16:         case SM_ERROR_BDE_ALIAS_MISSING:
17:             alert("Security Data Not Available");
18:             break;
19:         case SM_ERROR_LOGIN_LOCKOUT:
20:             alert("Too many invalid login attempts");
21:             break;
```

continues

Listing 17.3. continued

```
22:        default:
23:            alert("Oops, something went wrong");
24:    }
25: }
```

 Line 1 includes the security header file. This file contains the SM_CLASS_LOCATION constant that is used on line 2, when the security classes are loaded into memory.

The try block on lines 3 to 13 contains the actual calls to the security class. The catch block on lines 14 to 25 handles any exception that the security class might throw.

The constructor for the SecurityManager class takes no parameters. It can throw an exception with a code value of SM_ERROR_BDE_ALIAS_MISSING if it cannot find the security data. By default, the data is found using the IBAPPS alias in the BDE. If you move the data to a new folder, you must create a BDE alias for that folder. Then edit the Security.h file. There is currently a line like this:

```
#define SM_DATABASE_ALIAS "ibapps"
```

Change this line to contain the new alias name.

SecurityManager **Methods**

The full list of methods for the SecurityManager class is covered in the following list, along with a brief description of each. The code values of exceptions that can be thrown from the method are also listed:

☐ **SecurityManager::changeDescription(<new description>)**

The changeDescription() provides a scripted way for you to change the description of the current user. The <new description> replaces the current description. A SM_ERROR_NOT_LOGGED_IN code is thrown if you call this method before a successful call to the login() method. A SM_ERROR_INVALID_USERNAME or SM_ERROR_LOGIN_DISABLED code is thrown in the unlikely event that the account has been deleted or disabled since this user logged in.

☐ **SecurityManager::changePassword(<old>, <new>)**

The changePassword() method allows users to change their own passwords. You pass the current password and the new password. It is recommended that the form that prompts the user for this information should confirm the new password before calling this method. A reusable change password form is available, which is described in the "Working with Security Base Forms" section of this chapter.

17

A SM_ERROR_NOT_LOGGED_IN code is thrown if you call this method before a successful call to the login() method. A SM_ERROR_INVALID_USERNAME or SM_ERROR_LOGIN_DISABLED code is thrown in the unlikely event that the account has been deleted or disabled since this user logged in. A SM_ERROR_INVALID_PASSWORD code is thrown if <old> does not match the current password setting. This can also be thrown if either <old> or <new> is null. If you want the user to have no password, you must set the PASSMIN policy to zero and pass an empty string ("") to this method. A SM_ERROR_PASSWORD_TOO_SHORT or SM_ERROR_PASSWORD_TOO_LONG code is thrown if the password violates either the PASSMIN or PASSMAX policy.

SecurityManager::getCreated()

The getCreated() method returns a date object specifying when the user was first created. It might throw a SM_ERROR_NOT_LOGGED_IN code if there has not been a successful login.

SecurityManager::getDescription()

The getDescription() method returns the description for the logged-in user. If there has not been a successful call to the login() method, a SM_ERROR_NOT_LOGGED_IN code is thrown.

SecurityManager::getGroups()

The getGroups() method returns an AssocArray object containing the names and descriptions of each group that the user is a member of. The names are used as the index, and the value associated with each index is the description. If there has not been a successful call to the login() method, a SM_ERROR_NOT_LOGGED_IN code is thrown.

SecurityManager::getLogin()

The getLogin() method returns a date object containing the date and time at which the current login was made. A SM_ERROR_NOT_LOGGED_IN code is thrown if you call this method before a successful call to the login() method.

SecurityManager::getPolicyValue(<policy name>)

The getPolicyValue() method allows you to query the value of any of the system or user-defined policies. You pass it the name of the policy (not case sensitive), and the value is returned. Note that the return value is Boolean or numeric depending on the nature of the policy. If there is no policy named <policy name>, a null value is returned. This method can be called at any time, even before a successful login. No SmException objects are thrown by this method.

SecurityManager::getResources()

The getResources() method returns an AssocArray object containing the names and descriptions of each resource to which the user has access. These resources can be available to the user because of a user-specific grant or because of membership in a group that has been granted access to the resource. The names are used as the index, and the value associated with each index is the description. If there has not been a successful call to the `login()` method, a `SM_ERROR_NOT_LOGGED_IN` code is thrown.

☐ **`SecurityManager::getUserName()`**

The `getUserName()` method returns the name of the currently logged-in user. If there has not been a successful call to the `login()` method, a `SM_ERROR_NOT_LOGGED_IN` code is thrown.

☐ **`SecurityManager::hasAccessTo( <resource name> )`**

The `hasAccessTo()` method returns a Boolean value indicating whether or not the user has access to the resource named `<resource name>`. If the user does have access, a `true` value is returned. If the user does not have access to that resource—regardless of whether it is a valid resource—a `false` is returned. A `SM_ERROR_NOT_LOGGED_IN` code is thrown if you call this method before a successful call to the `login()` method.

☐ **`SecurityManager::isMemberOf( <group name> )`**

The `isMemberOf()` method returns a Boolean value indicating whether or not the user is a member of the group named `<group name>`. If the user is a member, a `true` value is returned. If the user is not a member—regardless of whether it is a valid group—a `false` is returned. A `SM_ERROR_NOT_LOGGED_IN` code is thrown if you call this method before a successful call to the `login()` method.

☐ **`SecurityManager::login( <user name>, <password> )`**

The `login()` method must be called before you call any of the other methods (with the exception of `getPolicyValue()`). You must pass a user name and a password. If the user name and password are correct, a Boolean `true` is returned. If there are any problems, an `SmException` object is thrown. The code value is `SM_ERROR_INVALID_USERNAME` if `<user name>` is null or if the user name is not found in the security system. A `SM_ERROR_INVALID_PASSWORD` is thrown if `<password>` is null or if the password is not correct for this user. A `SM_ERROR_LOGIN_DISABLED` or `SM_ERROR_LOGIN_LOCKOUT` is thrown if the user's account has been disabled or has been locked out.

Administrative Scripting API

In addition to the `SecurityManager` class, you also have a `SecurityManagerAdmin` class. This class is also defined in `Security.js`. It is derived from the `SecurityManager` class, so it contains all the same methods as `SecurityManager`. In addition, it contains methods for creating, deleting, and updating the various security entities. There are also methods for relating the entities (adding users to groups, granting access to resources, and so on).

17

If you use the Security Administration forms to manage the security system, you might never need to use this class. However, if you want to manage the security information on the fly, use this class. For instance, you might allow new users to the site to enter a user name and password. You then use the `SecurityManagerAdmin` class to add them to the security system.

For more information about the `SecurityManagerAdmin` class, take a look at the `Security.js` file itself. In addition, you can look at the Security Administration forms to see how to use this class.

Reusable Form Classes

There are three reusable form classes in the Apps\Shared folder. These classes can be used as the basis of other forms that you create in the Form Designer. The base forms contain all of the necessary logic; all you have to do is apply appropriate user interface elements such as headings or colors, so that the form blends into the rest of your application. The three base form classes contain the logic necessary to perform the following tasks:

- ☐ Log into the security system (`security.jcf`).
- ☐ Display user profile information (`profile.jcf`).
- ☐ Change a user's password (`change.jcf`).

The base form classes are each contained in their own `.jcf` file. You can create a form derived from a base form class by following these steps:

1. Open a blank form in the Form Designer.
2. Select File|Set Custom Form Class from the menu.
3. Press the tool button and select the desired base form from the Apps\Shared folder.
4. Press the OK button to close the Set Custom Form Class dialog.

This causes the form to redraw with all of the components contained in the base form class. Then change the properties of the form or components, and add your own components so that the form follows the same look and feel as the rest of your application.

Working with Security Base Forms

All three reusable form classes require you to set custom properties before the forms are opened. The three forms take slightly different properties.

The `smLoginForm` class in `Security.jcf` requires two custom properties:

- ☐ `security`
- ☐ `nextForm`

The security property must be set to an existing `SecurityManager` object. The `nextForm` property is set to an object reference variable for a form that has already been created. The form is opened only if a valid user name and password are entered. It is up to the form itself to check that the valid user actually has access to the resource. Listing 17.4 shows the header section from the `Update.jfm` file in the Apps\Phone folder. This file uses the `smLoginForm` class and demonstrates the setting of the two custom properties.

INPUT **Listing 17.4. Using the `smLoginForm` class.**

```
 1: var f = new updateForm();
 2: f.argv = UPDATE.arguments;
 3: // then create a security object
 4: _sys.scripts.load(SM_CLASS_LOCATION + "security.js");
 5: f.security = new SecurityManager();
 6: // then create the login form
 7: _sys.scripts.load("emplogin.jfm");
 8: var login = new emploginForm();
 9: // the login form requires two custom properties be set
10: login.security = f.security;
11: login.nextForm = f;
12: // finally, open the login form
13: login.open();
14: return;
15: // {End Header} Do not remove this comment//
16: // Generated on 11/12/96
17: //
18: var f = new updateForm();
19: f.open();
```

ANALYSIS Line 1 creates a form object based on the `updateForm` class defined in the rest of the file. Normally this object is created and then immediately opened.

Line 4 loads the security classes into memory, and then line 5 creates a `SecurityManager` object. This object is created as a property of the update form.

Line 7 loads the Phone Book login form into memory. This form was derived from the `smLoginForm` class. Line 8 creates the form object for the login form.

Lines 10 and 11 assign the custom properties of the login form. The `security` property is set to the `SecurityManager` object that was created on line 5, and the `nextForm` property is set to the `Form` object created on line 1.

Normally, the header section of a form file opens the form that is defined in that file. In this case, the login form is opened instead (on line 13). The update form itself is opened by the login form after a successful login.

Notice that the header section ends with the `return` on line 14. This prevents the standard instantiation routine, on lines 18 and 19, from executing.

The `smProfileForm` class in `Profile.jcf` has four custom properties:

- [ ] `security`
- [ ] `callingForm`
- [ ] `changeForm`
- [ ] `changeFormClass`

The `security` property is assigned an existing security object. The `callingForm` property is assigned the form reference for the form that called the profile form. When the profile form is closed, focus is returned to the `callingForm` form.

The profile form contains a button that can be pressed to change the user's password. The name of the change password form and the name of the class defined in that `.jfm` file are assigned to the `changeForm` and `changeFormClass` properties, respectively.

The `smChangePasswordForm` defined in `Change.jcf` takes two custom properties:

- [ ] `security`
- [ ] `callingForm`

The `security` property is assigned an existing security object. The `callingForm` property is assigned the form reference for the form that called the change password form. When the change password form is closed, focus is returned to the `callingForm` form.

To see examples of these three forms, you can run the Phone Book Update form. From the main `Index.htm` page for the prebuilt solution applications, select the link for `"Phone List Administration"`. This opens up a login form based on the class in `Security.jcf`. When prompted for the user name and password, enter `ABRAHAM` for both. This opens the record for Abraham. There should be a button at the top labeled Security Profile. Pressing this button opens a form based on the class in `Profile.jcf`. Pressing the Change Password... button on that page opens a form based on the class in `Change.jcf`.

Data Files

The security data is stored in two files in the Apps\Data folder. These tables already contain security data for the prebuilt solution applications. If you want to start from scratch, you can use the copies of the tables in the Apps\Security folder. The two data files are called `smentity.db` and `smassign.db`.

Both of these files are password protected. You cannot open these files without knowing the password. The security scripting API uses the password to automatically open the table for its own use, so that the user never needs to have access to this password. This password is hard coded at the top of the application security API file (Apps\Shared\Security.js). The password (`masterkey`) is available to everyone who opens that file (or reads this sentence), so you might want to customize the password. To change the password in the data files themselves, follow these steps:

1. Change the working folder in the IntraBuilder Explorer to the folder containing the data files.
2. Select the File|Database Administration menu choice. This opens the Database Administration dialog shown in Figure 17.7.
3. Change the Table Type combo box to PARADOX and select the Security... button. This opens the Security dialog, which is also shown in Figure 17.7.
4. Select one of the two tables from the Table list box, and press the Edit Table... button. This opens the Password dialog, also shown in Figure 17.7.
5. Enter the current password, which is `masterkey` by default.
6. In the next dialog, you enter and confirm the new master password.
7. Repeat these steps for the other table.

Figure 17.7.

Changing the security table password.

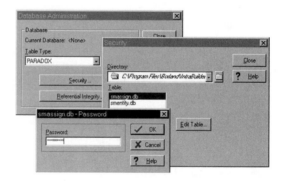

After you change the password for these two tables, you must also update the Apps\ Shared\Security.js file to match. The following line should appear at the very top of this file:

```
#define SM_PASSWORD "masterkey"
```

Simply change the text inside the quotation marks to match the new master password for the table. To ensure the integrity of this password after making this change, you can compile the script and remove the source file from the machine. You can compile the script by right-clicking on the `Security.js` file and selecting the Compile Script option. Then copy the `Security.js` file to a secure place and delete it from this machine. Be sure to delete only the `Security.js` file, leaving behind the `Security.jo` file. The .JO file must remain.

When you change the password on these tables and remove the source file that contains that password, you have a very secure security system in place. Please note that this security system keeps the data itself pretty secure, but you also need to take steps to ensure that unauthorized users cannot delete or replace the data files. And I qualify the security level as "pretty secure" because the system is as solid as JavaScript allows.

Summary

Today you went behind the scenes to discover the reusable components that exist in the prebuilt business solution applications and the samples that ship with IntraBuilder. These applications and samples provide many visual and non-visual components that you can use in your own applications.

The visual components consist of nearly 50 custom components that you can drop onto your forms. These components provide many different capabilities, reducing the amount of coding that you'll have to do in the long run.

The non-visual components are there to make your programming life just a little easier. The header files, functions, and classes allow you to leverage existing code.

The application security components combine visual and non-visual components to provide you with an application security system that can stand up to the demands of intranets and the Internet.

Q&A

Q **The reusable JavaScript components that come with IntraBuilder all seem to be server-side components. Are there any reusable client-side components?**

A There are many reusable client-side components available on the Web. A list of JavaScript resources can be found on the Borland Web site. At the time of printing, this list is found at

```
http://www.borland.com/intrabuilder/javasrc.html
```

Q **Are the sample files the same in version 1.0 and 1.01?**

A No. The sample files for 1.0 were created as the product itself was created. The samples were not able to use some features that came online late in the product cycle. The samples that shipped with the 1.01 release are more mature and feature-rich. The samples discussed in today's lesson are the ones that ship with 1.01.

Q **Where can I get more information about the Windows registry itself?**

A The Microsoft Developer Network provides a wealth of information about the Windows environment. There are also many books about Windows 95 and Windows NT on the market. You can find some great information on the Microsoft Web site; however, it takes a bit of searching. At the time of this writing, general information about the system registry can be found at

```
http://www.microsoft.com/win32dev/uiguide/uigui255.htm
```

17

Workshop

The Workshop section provides questions and exercises to help you get a better feel for the material you learned today. Try to answer the questions and at least think about the exercises before moving on to tomorrow's lesson. You'll find the answers to the questions in Appendix A, "Answers to Quiz Questions."

Quiz

1. How do you load a custom component file in the Form Designer?
2. Where do you find the `ActiveX.cc` custom component file?
3. What is output when the following script executes:

```
#include "intra.h"
#ifdef DEBUG
alert("Debugging");
#else
alert(OUTPUT_HTML);
#endif
```

4. What does the `DateEx` class do for you that the `Date` class does not?
5. What four entities are managed by the application security components?

Exercises

1. Use the expert to generate a form for the `orders.dbf` table in the Samples folder. Then replace the `Text` component for the customer number with a `FieldSelect` component. This component should display a list of customer numbers from the `customer.dbf` table.

2. Add a counter component to the form you created in the first exercise.

3. Write a script to write your name to the following registry key:

```
HKEY_CURRENT_USER\Software\Test\
```

   The value name should be `MyName`. After writing the value, have the script query the value and display it in an alert dialog. Then delete the value.

4. Write a function that takes a user name, password, and resource name. It should return a Boolean `true` if the user has access to the resource and a Boolean `false` if the user does not. Test with these two sets of parameters:

```
alert(check( "Erik", "Erik", "Phone Update" ));
alert(check( "Test", "Test", "Test" ));
```

   The first one should return `true` and the second should return `false`.

Day **18**

Using Java Applets and ActiveX Controls

by Paul Mahar

Java and related technologies are spreading across the computer industry like a wildfire on a dry and windy summer night. IntraBuilder itself is an outgrowth of the Java phenomenon. The most prevalent use of the Java language is for creating Java applets. An applet is a small application that breaks through the limitations of HTML while maintaining platform independence. ActiveX controls are Microsoft's recasting of Java applets into a Windows orientation. In this chapter you will learn how to extend your IntraBuilder applications with both Java applets and ActiveX controls. Here are the tasks for the day:

☐ Exploring Java and ActiveX resources on the Web: You will visit sites created by Sun and Microsoft to promote their competing strategies.

This chapter also describes Gamelan, the Grand Central Station for Java applets. As you travel through the various Web sites, you will see what is available for free and what has a fee. Along the way, you will also learn about the different security features provided with Java and ActiveX.

☐ Taking Tumbling Duke out for a spin: One of the first Java applets is Tumbling Duke. This is a little animation applet that shows the Java mascot doing some cartwheels. You will learn how to embed Tumbling Duke into an IntraBuilder application.

☐ Gluing IntraBuilder to a basic Java grid: A more serious use of Java is to create a data grid. The Sun folks have created a simple spreadsheet that you can use as a basic data grid. Doing so demonstrates how to pass information between the IntraBuilder Server and a Java applet.

☐ Popping off with an ActiveX popup: Microsoft has packaged all the native Windows controls into ActiveX controls. If you know your clients are going to be browsing through Windows NT or Windows 95, you can embellish your forms with native controls such as a Windows popup menu. In doing so, you will also learn how to use VBScript functions within an IntraBuilder application.

Keep in mind that the external controls presented here are some of the most primitive available. Advanced Java development environments such as Visual J++, Visual Café, and JBuilder are enabling a second generation of controls that allow tighter integration with database environments such as IntraBuilder.

The native IntraBuilder controls map to standard HTML controls such as text, select lists, buttons, and check boxes. Native controls are fully functional within the designer's run mode. You can also dynamically create instances of any native component with a simple call using the new operator. The widest array of clients—including those running older browsers under Windows 3.1, UNIX, or the Mac OS—can work with the native controls.

Using Java applets and ActiveX controls with IntraBuilder is similar to using a VBX control with the Windows 3.1 versions of Visual Basic, Visual dBASE, or PowerBuilder. You can set properties and call methods of an external control just as you do with native controls. The main difference for the developer is that an external control does not run within the design environment. The designer simply creates a placeholder for the external controls. To try out the control, you must run it through a browser.

Pouring on the Java Applets

So what makes Java so hot? Other than some great public relations on the part of Sun, there are at least three significant reasons for Java-mania.

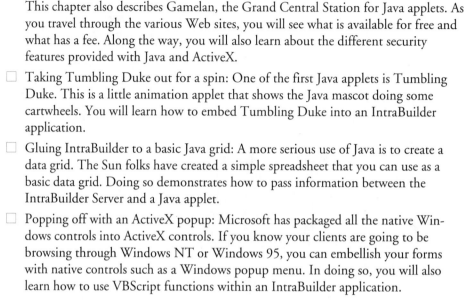

☐ Cross-platform compatibility: The same Java applet can run on any platform that contains the Java virtual machine or a Java just-in-time compiler. Today you can find Java support on all popular computing environments ranging from low-end Macintosh computers to large-scale, multiple-processor UNIX workstations. The industry-wide adoption of Java frees developers from a dependency on any one software vendor.

☐ Simple object orientation: Java combines the best object-oriented aspects of C++ with automatic memory management. The Java virtual machine recovers memory that is no longer required by an application. This is sometimes referred to as garbage collection. Java's object system supports all standard object constructs, such as encapsulation, inheritance, and polymorphism. These features are also found in IntraBuilder's extended JavaScript.

☐ Security: Java contains security levels that can restrict a program from making any direct operating system calls. This architecture makes it easy to prevent both intentional virus programs and the accidental memory overwrites that are so common to Windows developers.

NEW TERM A *virtual machine* is software implementation of a CPU that can translate generic low-level function calls into platform-specific calls. Java compiles to the same virtual machine instruction set regardless of platform. The virtual machine is the only portion of the Java architecture that requires a platform-specific implementation.

If you are already familiar with Java, you can skip past the next section and see how to make Duke tumble in a JavaScript form. If you are still not sold on Java, it is time to go surfing for a caffeine buzz.

Exploring Java Applets on the Web

There are two hot spots at which you can check out Java on the Web. They are JavaSoft and Gamelan. JavaSoft is the Java software division of Sun Microsystems, and it is the birthplace of Java. Gamelan, pronounced *gamma-lahn*, is the official directory for Java-related Web sites. You will find shortcuts for both sites in the Day 18 folder on the CD-ROM. Figure 18.1 shows the URL files as displayed in the custom tab of the IntraBuilder Explorer. You can load your browser and go to the selected site directly from the IntraBuilder Explorer.

The Applets shortcut takes you to the JavaSoft applet index. Here you will find the Java samples pages with complete source code that you can copy and modify. There are some simple games, graphics, and utility programs. The full URL for the applet index is

```
http://www.javasoft.com/applets/applets.html
```

Figure 18.1.

Viewing Web shortcuts in the IntraBuilder Explorer.

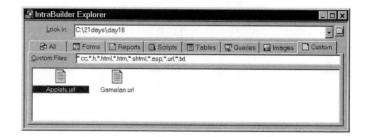

You can run any of the Java applets from both Netscape Navigator and Internet Explorer. As you run through the different Java applets, you might notice a slight delay as the Java applets download to your machine. Both browsers display an appropriate message in the status bar when loading a Java class. Like standard HTML pages, Java classes can also be retrieved from a browser cache for faster loading.

The source for each Java class is contained in a file with a `java` extension. When you run each example, the compiled versions of the files with a `class` extension are downloaded to your machine. The source file is not required to run a Java applet.

You can learn more about JavaSoft and the latest Java happenings from `www.javasoft.com`. The JavaSoft site also contains links to Gamelan. Visit the Gamelan site to see how commercial control builders are taking advantage of Java. Unlike the JavaSoft site, most of the controls found on Gamelan are not free to copy or distribute.

TIP

You can use the Netscape Java Console to help track down problems that occur when loading Java applets. From Netscape 3.0, you can load the Java console from the options menu.

While you're visiting Gamelan, be sure to check out the latest Java grid controls. Two promising controls are Vincent Engineering's JavaGRID and Philippe Thamié's Grid. Figure 18.2 shows the JavaGRID demo page. After trying the JavaSoft spreadsheet applet, you might want to try integrating JavaGRID with IntraBuilder.

Figure 18.2.

Vincent Engineering's JavaGRID control.

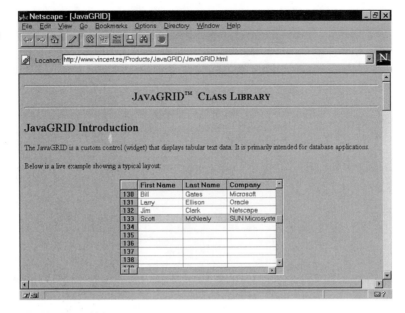

Tumbling Duke

If you got a chance to visit with Tumbling Duke on the JavaSoft site, you saw a silly triangular cartoon character doing cartwheels. In this section, you will learn how to embed Tumbling Duke into a JavaScript form and add a button that can start and stop the tumble action. The start and stop methods are common Java applet methods that start and stop the applet.

HTML includes an applets tag for embedding Java applets within a Web page. The applets tag has a few standard properties for identifying the Java class and setting the position of the applet. Custom java properties are set through a params property that points to a list of name-value pairs. The params property maps to an IntraBuilder associative array. You will find a Params Property Builder within the IntraBuilder Form Designer to help you set up the name-value pairs.

 A *name-value pair* is a property name and its associated value. For instance, top and 5 can be considered a name-value pair, where top is the name and 5 is the value. In the params associative array, the name portion of the pair serves as an array index.

How you determine valid name-value pairs depends on where you get the Java applet. For the JavaSoft applets, you can find them in the source files. Commercial control vendors are more likely to provide standard documentation in place of the source files. If you do have the Java source file, look to the init() method for calls to the Java getParameter() method. Listing 18.1 shows the init() method for the TumbleImage Java applet.

INPUT   **Listing 18.1. The `init()` method of `TumbleImage.java`.**

```
 1: /**
 2: * Initialize the applet. Get attributes.
 3: */
 4: public void init() {
 5:     String at = getParameter("img");
 6:     dir = (at != null) ? at : "images/tumble";
 7:     at = getParameter("pause");
 8:     pause = (at != null) ? Integer.valueOf(at).intValue() : 3900;
 9:     at = getParameter("offset");
10:     offset = (at != null) ? Integer.valueOf(at).intValue() : 0;
11:     at = getParameter("speed");
12:     speed = (at != null) ? (1000 / Integer.valueOf(at).intValue()) : 100;
13:     at = getParameter("nimgs");
14:     nimgs = (at != null) ? Integer.valueOf(at).intValue() : 16;
15:     at = getParameter("maxwidth");
16:     maxWidth = (at != null) ? Integer.valueOf(at).intValue() : 0;
17: }
```

ANALYSIS   The init() method is called whenever a new instance of the Java applet is created. The primary purpose of this init() method is to retrieve the parameter list and define defaults for any parameter not in the name-value pair list. The six calls to getParameter() on lines 5, 7, 9, 11, 13, and 15 show that the class can work with up to six name-value pairs, including img, pause, offset, speed, nimgs, and maxwidth.

All six parameters are optional. When a name-value pair is not found for a parameter, getParameter() returns null. If a null value is found, the init() method substitutes a valid default. For example, line 6 assigns "images/tumble" as the default for the img property.

The values for all name-value pairs are passed in as a string. The TumbleImage class needs all but the first parameter converted to an integer. In Java this is done through an Integer class instead of the parstInt() or eval() functions found in JavaScript.

In creating the Duke form, you will be assigning four of the name-value pairs. The form will need only two controls. The first is a button to start and stop the Java applet. The second is a placeholder for the applet. The placeholder defines the area in which the applet can paint, or in this case, tumble. Follow these steps to create the Duke form.

18

1. Load your browser and see that you can connect to the following URL. The form relies on images and Java class files at this location:

   `http://www.javasoft.com/applets/applets/TumblingDuke/`

2. Open the Form Designer to create a new form called `duke.jfm`. You can use the following JavaScript statement in the Script Pad to name the form and open the designer:

   `_sys.forms.design('duke.jfm') ;`

3. Add a button in the top-left corner. Change the button's `name` property to `buttonToggle` and the `text` property to `Stop`.

4. Add a Java applet control below the button. Set the position and name properties as shown in Table 18.1.

Table 18.1. Name and location properties for `javaDuke`.

Property	Value
name	javaDuke
height	5
left	0
top	5
width	40

5. Identify the Java class through the `code` and `codeBase` properties. The `code` property is where you enter the name of the compiled Java class. The `codeBase` is the URL that points to where the class resides. Table 18.2 shows the values required to access the Tumbling Duke class from the JavaSoft Web site.

Table 18.2. Source properties for `javaDuke`.

Property	Value
code	TumbleItem.class
codeBase	http://www.javasoft.com/applets/applets/TumblingDuke/

As you work with the Java applet, you will see a coffee cup image as a placeholder in the Form Designer. This image is replaced by the applet when you run the form through a browser. Figure 18.3 shows the coffee cup as it appears for the Duke form.

Figure 18.3.

Working with a Java applet in the Form Designer.

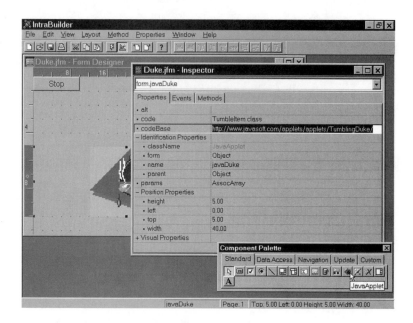

6. Open the Params Property Builder to set properties of the `javaDuke` object. So far, the properties you have been working with are part of the HTML applet tag. The `params` allow you to set properties that are associated directly with the current instance of the Java class.

    The Params Property Builder helps you create an associative array of name-value pairs. You can open the Params Property Builder by clicking on the Inspector's tool button for the `params` property.

7. The `TumbleItem` class can accept up to six name-value pairs. In this form, you will create only four and let the other two default to acceptable values. Add the first three name-value pairs, as listed in Table 18.3.

Table 18.3. Name-value pairs for `javaDuke`.

Name	Value
maxwidth	100
nimages	16
offset	0

To enter each value, fill in the name and value and click on Add. To modify an entry, click on Remove, change the value, and then click on Add again. The order of the name-value pairs does not affect the applet.

Note

You could also leave out the `nimages` and `offset` name-value pairs, because the values given in Table 18.3 are the default values. In this case, the name-value pairs serve as documentation and do not affect the resulting applet.

8. The last name-value pair has a short name and a wide value. The name is `img` and the value is the following URL. To enter the value, enter the URL in a text editor first. Then copy and paste the URL into the Params Property Builder, as shown in Figure 18.4. After adding the fourth name-value pair, close the Params Property Builder.

```
http://www.javasoft.com/applets/applets/TumblingDuke/images/tumble/
```

Figure 18.4.

Pasting in the `img` *URL value.*

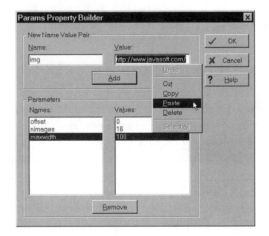

18

Warning

Do not forget to include the trailing slash on the URL values for the `codeBase` property and the `img` name-value pair. The browser will not be able to locate the files if you leave out the trailing slash.

9. Save the form and close the Form Designer. At this point, you can check the form links to the JavaSoft site. Shut down the IntraBuilder Designer and start up the IntraBuilder Server.

10. Open the Duke form through either Netscape Navigator or Internet Explorer. If you get a security error, check your connection to the JavaSoft site. If the applet

runs but does not present any animation, check the `img` name-value pair. Figure 18.5 shows the form running in Netscape Navigator.

Figure 18.5.

Running the Duke form in Netscape Navigator.

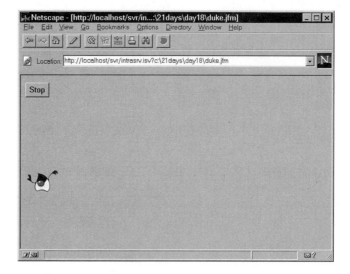

When you have the form running, you can add some logic to control the applet from client-side JavaScript. In this case, you want the applet to stop and start when you click the button. If you are running Internet Explorer, you might want to jump ahead to the next section. The capability for client-side JavaScript to call a Java method is currently only available with LiveConnect.

NEW TERM *LiveConnect* is a feature of Netscape Navigator. It allows JavaScript to interact with Java applets. LiveConnect is enabled if both Java and JavaScript are enabled.

You can use LiveConnect to call the start and stop methods from client-side JavaScript. To see how LiveConnect works, follow these steps to add a client-side `onClick` method to the Duke form:

1. Open up the Duke form in the Form Designer.
2. Inspect the `buttonToggle` control and use the tool button to create and link an `onClick` method.
3. Enter the method as shown in Listing 18.2. When you are done, save the form, close the IntraBuilder Designer, and run the form through Netscape Navigator.

Listing 18.2. A client-side method that works with LiveConnect.

INPUT

```
 1: function buttonToggle_onClick()
 2: {
 3:    if ( document.forms[0].buttonToggle.value == "Stop" ) {
 4:        document.forms[0].buttonToggle.value = "Start" ;
 5:        document.javaDuke.stop() ;
 6:    }
 7:    else {
 8:        document.forms[0].buttonToggle.value = "Stop" ;
 9:        document.javaDuke.start() ;
10:    }
11: }
```

ANALYSIS The purpose of the buttonToggle_onClick() method is to start and stop the applet and modify the button text to show the current option. This method shows some of the differences between client-side and server-side referencing.

Line 3 checks to see whether the button text is set to "Stop". This one line shows differences between client-side and server-side scripting. In client-side events, the current form is document.forms[0] instead of this.form. The other difference is the property that contains the text of the button. In a server-side event, the text property has the button text. In a client-side event, the value property contains the button text. If you want to do the same check as line 3 for a server-side event, the line would be as follows:

```
if ( this.form.buttonToggle.text == "Stop" ) {
```

Lines 4 and 8 toggle the button text from "Stop" to "Start". Here again, the client-side event substitutes the value property for the text property. Lines 5 and 9 call the Java applet methods as though they were native JavaScript methods.

The buttonToggle_onClick() event works correctly only when run through a Netscape browser. If you fire the event from within the IntraBuilder Designer, a runtime error occurs when the document object is not found on line 3. Running in a Microsoft browser without LiveConnect support causes an error on lines 5 and 9. Figure 18.6 shows the error that occurs when you click on the button in Internet Explorer. Notice that the Microsoft version of JavaScript is called JScript.

Within a Netscape browser, clicking on the Stop button causes Duke to stop in mid-tumble. This can catch the Duke in some funny postures. Although this example has much more entertainment value than practical functionality, it does demonstrate how to control a Java applet from both the server and client sides. The name-value pairs are all constructed on the server side, whereas the method calls come from the client side. The complete Duke form is shown in Listing 18.3.

Figure 18.6.

Trying to work with a Java applet in Internet Explorer.

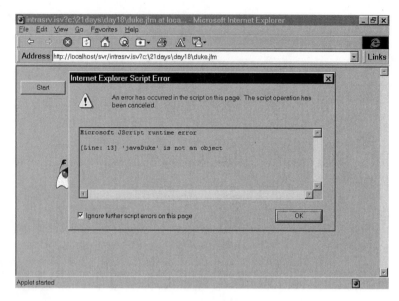

INPUT   **Listing 18.3. The `duke.jfm` JavaScript form file.**

```
 1: // {End Header} Do not remove this comment//
 2: // Generated on 01/02/97
 3: //
 4: var f = new dukeForm();
 5: f.open();
 6: class dukeForm extends Form {
 7:   with (this.buttonToggle = new Button(this)){
 8:     onClick = class::buttonToggle_onClick;
 9:     width = 10;
10:     text = "Stop";
11:   }
12:
13:   with (this.javaDuke = new JavaApplet(this)){
14:     height = 5;
15:     top = 5;
16:     width = 40;
17:     code = "TumbleItem.class";
18:     codeBase = "http://www.javasoft.com/applets/applets/TumblingDuke/";
19:     params["offset"] = "0";
20:     params["img"] =
21:   "http://www.javasoft.com/applets/applets/TumblingDuke/images/tumble/";
22:     params["maxwidth"] = "100";
23:     params["nimages"] = "16";
24:
25:   }
26:
27:   function buttonToggle_onClick()
28:   {
```

18

```
29:     if ( document.forms[0].buttonToggle.value == "Stop" ) {
30:        document.forms[0].buttonToggle.value = "Start" ;
31:        document.javaDuke.stop() ;
32:     }
33:     else {
34:        document.forms[0].buttonToggle.value = "Stop" ;
35:        document.javaDuke.start() ;
36:     }
37:   }
38:
39: }
```

ANALYSIS From the length of this form, you can see that it is pretty simple to integrate a Java applet into a JavaScript form. The most difficult part is figuring out the name-value pairs and callable methods for the applet. For the TumbleItem class, the source code is available for determining both.

The Java applet is defined on lines 13 through 23. Line 13 creates an instance of the IntraBuilder JavaApplet class. This class represents a placeholder for the actual Java class defined by the code property. The position properties are set up on lines 14, 15, and 16. There is no difference between setting up position properties for a native control or an external control. Lines 17 and 18 identify the Java class and where on the Web it can be found. The code property points to a compiled version of the applet. The source file is not required to create the applet. Lines 19 through 23 create four name-value pairs that serve as parameters for the applet. Each pair is an element of an associative array. The name is the index to the array. The order of name-value pairs is irrelevant. In fact, the order might change when you reopen the Params Property Builder.

WARNING

> LiveConnect sometimes fails in Navigator 3.0 after resizing the browser window. To prevent errors, reload the current form after you resize the browser window.

Using the JavaSoft Spreadsheet Applet as a Grid

Now that you've had some fun with Tumbling Duke, it is time to get down to some more practical business. In this section, you will use the JavaSoft Spreadsheet applet as a grid for the shopping cart application's Invoice table. Although the spreadsheet applet is not the ideal database grid, it does show you how to integrate server-side data with an applet.

Before you embark on creating a JavaScript form for the applet, visit the JavaSoft site and experiment with the example found there. Here is the complete URL for the JavaSoft example:

```
http://www.javasoft.com/applets/applets/SpreadSheet/example1.html
```

Try selecting the various cells. When you select a cell, the contents are displayed just below the grid caption. The JavaSoft example includes value cells and formula cells. The letter v is prefixed to each value cell. You can modify any value cell using numeric keys and the backspace. Pressing Enter commits the change and updates any related formulas. If you change the value in cell A1 from v10 to v15, the formula in cell C1 reflects the change. If you select a formula cell, the applet shows an f prefix. Figure 18.7 shows the initial values in the spreadsheet example.

Figure 18.7.

Running the JavaSoft spreadsheet example.

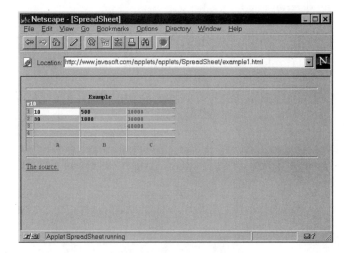

Although it is not shown in the example, the spreadsheet applet also supports an l cell prefix for labels and a u prefix for URL values. This is revealed by examining the setUnparsedValue() method in the applet source file. You can take advantage of the value, formula, and label cells to create a grid that displays information from the Invoice table and calculates the total cost for each line item.

WARNING

> Do not try to use the arrow keys to navigate around the spreadsheet. The applet interprets arrow keys as high ASCII values.

18

Before creating the Grid form, make sure the Lineitem table has several valid rows for invoice number 1. Vary the quantity amounts and make sure that each ISBN relates to a row in the Title table. See Day 8, "Designing the Shopping Cart Application," for more information about the table structures used in the shopping cart application. The following four rows provide an example of valid line item data.

```
Row#      INVOICE    ISBN             QTY
 1           1       0-7897-0591-5     2
 2           1       1-57521-103-3     1
 3           1       1-57521-104-1     4
 4           1       0-672-30877-0     1
```

The Grid form consists of two related queries—a Java applet and a server-side event for loading the data into the grid. This form works equally well in Netscape Navigator and Internet Explorer. The following steps guide you through the creating of the Grid form:

1. Open the Form Designer to create a new form called grid.jfm.

   ```
   _sys.forms.design("grid.jfm")
   ```

2. Drag the Lineitem and Title tables from the IntraBuilder Explorer onto the Form Designer.

> **TIP**
>
> You can make your forms more portable by removing the full path from the sql property. If the tables reside in the same folder as the form file, no path information is required by the database engine.

18

3. Limit the lineitem1 rowset to only the first invoice. Inspect the form.lineitem1.rowset. Locate the filter property and enter invoice = 1, as shown in Figure 18.8.

Figure 18.8.

Filtering line items for the first invoice.

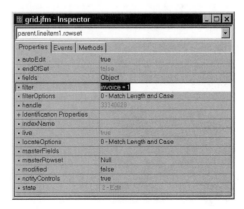

4. Relate the `Title` query to the `Lineitem` query. Inspect `form.title1.rowset`. Use the `masterRowset` property drop-down list to select `lineitem1`. After setting the `masterRowset`, you can use the `masterFields` drop-down list to select `ISBN` as the linking field. Setting the linking field also sets the `indexName` property.

5. Add a Java applet and set the position and name properties, as shown in Table 18.4.

Table 18.4. Name and location properties for `javaGrid`.

Property	Value
name	javaGrid
height	12
left	0
top	1
width	70

6. Identify the Java class and location through the `code` and `codeBase` properties. Use the values shown in Table 18.5 to point to the JavaSoft Web site.

Table 18.5. Source properties for `javaDuke`.

Property	Value
code	SpreadSheet.class
codeBase	http://java.sun.com/applets/applets/SpreadSheet/

7. Use the Inspector tool button to create and link a method to the Java applet's `onServerLoad` event. Enter the method as shown in Listing 18.4. After completing the method, save the form, close the designer, and try it through a browser.

INPUT   Listing 18.4. The `javaGrid_onServerLoad()` method.

```
 1: function javaGrid_onServerLoad()
 2: {
 3:    var i        = 2,
 4:        lineRow  = this.form.lineitem1.rowset,
 5:        titleRow = this.form.title1.rowset ;
 6:    this.params["title"] = "Line items" ;
 7:    this.params["columns"] = "5" ;
 8:    this.params["rows"]  = "" + ( lineRow.count() + 1 ) ;
 9:    this.params["a1"] = "lISBN" ;
10:    this.params["b1"] = "lQty" ;
11:    this.params["c1"] = "lTitle" ;
```

18

```
12:     this.params["d1"] = "lPrice" ;
13:     this.params["e1"] = "lTotal" ;
14:     lineRow.first() ;
15:     while (! lineRow.endOfSet ) {
16:        this.params["a" + i] = "l" + lineRow.fields["ISBN"].value ;
17:        this.params["b" + i] = "v" + lineRow.fields["QTY"].value ;
18:        this.params["c" + i] = "l" + titleRow.fields["TITLE"].value ;
19:        this.params["d" + i] = "v" + titleRow.fields["PRICE"].value ;
20:        this.params["e" + i] = "fB" + i + "*D" + i ;
21:        i++ ;
22:        lineRow.next() ;
23:     }
24: }
```

ANALYSIS The purpose of the javaGrid_onServerLoad() method is to create name-value pairs that correspond to the Lineitem table. In the Duke form, all the name-value pairs were known in advance and could be created as literal strings in the Params Property Builder. To populate the grid, you determine the name-value pairs at runtime. The onServerLoad event lets you do this.

On lines 3 through 5, the method defines the local variables. The first variable, i, is used to point to the current grid row. The grid coordinates are 1-based, and the first row is used for column headings. The second row of the grid will be the first to contain line item values. The other two variables are shortcut references for the query rowsets.

The next three statements set the grid caption and size. The grid caption is set through the title parameter on line 6. The number of columns is always 5 for the ISBN, Qty, Title, Price, and Total columns. Line 8 sets the number for rows to the current number in the lineitem1 rowset plus one for the column headings.

Lines 9 through 13 create column headings in row 1. The l prefix allows for literal character expressions. When the grid displays, the l is not visible in the cells.

The while loop on lines 15 through 23 populates the cells with values, labels, and formulas. Labels are used for the ISBN and Title character fields. To use the Qty and Price fields in a formula, they must be identified with the value prefix. Line 20 creates a formula for multiplying the Qty and Price columns.

If you run the Grid form through a browser, you can modify the Qty and Price fields and see the Total column automatically refresh. Figure 18.9 shows how the layout of the Grid resembles the Cart form of the shopping cart application.

The complete source for the Grid form is shown in Listing 18.5. Refer to this listing if your form is not acting as expected. The listing shows the queries with the full paths removed from the SQL statements.

Figure 18.9.

Viewing line items in the spreadsheet control.

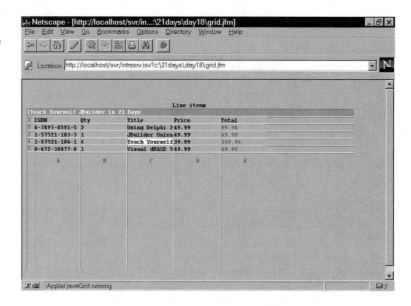

INPUT   **Listing 18.5. The `grid.jfm` JavaScript form file.**

```
 1: // {End Header} Do not remove this comment//
 2: // Generated on 01/02/97
 3: //
 4: var f = new gridForm();
 5: f.open();
 6: class gridForm extends Form {
 7:     with (this.lineitem1 = new Query()){
 8:         sql = 'SELECT * FROM "lineitem.DBF"';
 9:         active = true;
10:     }
11:
12:     with (this.lineitem1.rowset) {
13:         filter = "invoice = 1";
14:     }
15:
16:     with (this.title1 = new Query()){
17:         left = 4;
18:         sql = 'SELECT * FROM "title.DBF"';
19:         active = true;
20:     }
21:
22:     with (this.title1.rowset) {
23:         indexName = "ISBN";
24:         masterRowset = parent.parent.lineitem1.rowset;
25:         masterFields = "ISBN";
26:     }
27:
28:     with (this.javaGrid = new JavaApplet(this)){
29:         onServerLoad = class::javaGrid_onServerLoad;
```

18

```
30:        height = 12;
31:        top = 0;
32:        width = 70;
33:        code = "SpreadSheet.class";
34:        codeBase = "http://java.sun.com/applets/applets/SpreadSheet/";
35:    }
36:
37:    this.rowset = this.lineitem1.rowset;
38:
39:    function javaGrid_onServerLoad()
40:    {
41:       var i        = 2,
42:           lineRow  = this.form.lineitem1.rowset,
43:           titleRow = this.form.title1.rowset ;
44:       this.params["title"] = "Line items" ;
45:       this.params["columns"] = "5" ;
46:       this.params["rows"]   = "" + ( lineRow.count() + 1 ) ;
47:       this.params["a1"] = "lISBN" ;
48:       this.params["b1"] = "lQty" ;
49:       this.params["c1"] = "lTitle" ;
50:       this.params["d1"] = "lPrice" ;
51:       this.params["e1"] = "lTotal" ;
52:       lineRow.first() ;
53:       while (! lineRow.endOfSet ) {
54:           this.params["a" + i] = "l" + lineRow.fields["ISBN"].value;
55:           this.params["b" + i] = "v" + lineRow.fields["QTY"].value;
56:           this.params["c" + i] = "l" + titleRow.fields["TITLE"].value;
57:           this.params["d" + i] = "v" + titleRow.fields["PRICE"].value;
58:           this.params["e" + i] = "fB" + i + "*D" + i ;
59:           i++ ;
60:           lineRow.next() ;
61:       }
62:    }
63:
64: }
```

ANALYSIS   Two main tasks are occurring in the Grid form. The first is setting up the related queries, and the second is creating the name-value pairs. The analysis of Listing 18.4 already covered the second task that takes place in the `javaGrid_onServerLoad()` method. The query relations are set through the `masterRowset` and `masterFields` properties on lines 24 and 25. This technique of relating tables applies only to native dBASE and Paradox tables. If you are working with SQL Server, you need to use the `masterSource` property instead.

The `masterSource` property lets you relate queries without specifying an explicit index setting. This is critical when using SQL-Link drivers that do not allow setting an explicit index on a result set. You could replace lines 7 through 26 and achieve the same effect with the following. These lines also work with tables on remote servers such as Oracle or Microsoft SQL Server.

```
with (this.lineitem1 = new Query()){
   sql = 'SELECT * FROM lineitem WHERE invoice = 1';
   active = true;
}
```

```
with (this.title1 = new Query()){
   left = 4;
   sql = 'SELECT * FROM title WHERE ISBN=:ISBN';
   masterSource = parent.lineitem1.rowset;
   active = true;
}
```

> **NOTE** The masterSource property is not available in release 1.0. If you have release 1.0, install the 1.01 Trial edition to receive a free update.

Activating ActiveX Controls

ActiveX is a conglomeration of technologies that Microsoft is using to create a tight integration between the Web applications and Windows. The core of the ActiveX architecture comes from the Microsoft OLE technologies. OLE started life as a way to embed Excel data into a Word document. It was later expanded to include OLE automation and replace Visual Basic VBX controls with OCX controls. The OCX controls were then further morphed to work with Internet Explorer. At this point, the OCX controls were christened ActiveX controls.

More recently the ActiveX moniker was placed on services of the Internet Information Server. These services execute server-side VBScript in much the same way that Netscape LiveWire can execute server-side JavaScript.

 OLE automation allows the scripting language of one application to control another application. For example, OLE automation lets a Word Basic script control Excel. OLE automation is available to IntraBuilder JavaScripts through the OleAutoClient class.

Although ActiveX controls are not nearly as platform-independent, secure, or elegant in design as Java, they do have some distinct advantages. Because they are not required to be platform-independent, ActiveX controls can take direct advantage of any Windows components. This allows them to easily work with native controls that might not be available on other platforms. ActiveX controls can be created through many languages including C++, J++, and Visual Basic. J++ is Java with some extensions specifically geared toward ActiveX.

Because you can use C++ to create ActiveX controls, there are no security layers that prevent direct memory allocation or low-level calls. It is very difficult to create a virus with Java, but it is simple with an ActiveX control. An advantage is that a well-written ActiveX control can almost always outperform the Java counterpart.

The ActiveX security scheme is more a matter of trust than a technical solution. When you download a new ActiveX control, Internet Explorer asks you if you trust the person or company from which you are downloading the control. Independent credential verification companies such as VeriSign ensure that a control provider has a valid address and phone number. Figure 18.10 shows the confirmation dialog that appears when downloading the ActiveX popup control from Microsoft.

Figure 18.10.

The ActiveX security scheme in action.

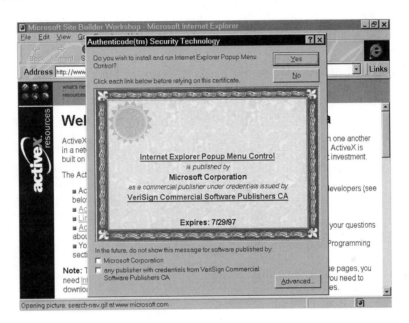

Perhaps the biggest advantage of ActiveX over Java is that Microsoft is committing a tremendous amount of talent and resources to establish ActiveX. Microsoft is by far the most influential software company in the world today, and its push toward ActiveX is almost guaranteed to make it a ubiquitous standard.

To see what ActiveX controls can do, visit the Microsoft ActiveX resource area. This page is the ActiveX equivalent of the JavaSoft site and Gamelan combined into one. Here you will find a wealth of information on ActiveX, some great free downloads, and links for ActiveX developers. The complete URL for the ActiveX resource area is

```
http://www.microsoft.com/activex/
```

TIP   You can use the ActiveX Web site shortcut file that comes with IntraBuilder to quickly locate the ActiveX resource center. The ActiveX URL file is located in the IntraBuilder samples folder. The IntraBuilder Explorer shows URL files in the Custom tab. You can also drag this file to your desktop for more convenience.

The example in the section uses the Popup Menu control. To see how the control works, locate it in the ActiveX gallery. From there you can download the control and run a page that contains the control. Figure 18.11 shows the Microsoft Web site with the ActiveX popup control.

Figure 18.11.

Running the ActiveX popup control from the Microsoft Web site.

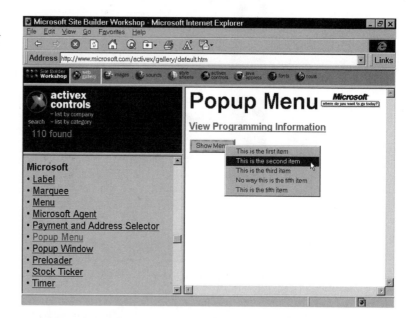

After trying out the popup menu, locate and download the ActiveX Control Pad. This utility shows all the ActiveX controls registered on your system. It also shows the properties associated with each ActiveX control. This utility makes ActiveX controls easier to work with than Java applets. You do not need any extra documentation or source code to determine the valid values for each property.

See what properties are available for the popup menu. Open the ActiveX Control Pad and select Edit|Insert. This displays a list of all the ActiveX controls registered on your machine. Select Microsoft IE30 Popup Menu Control. This opens a Properties window, as shown in Figure 18.12. Each property represents a name-value pair for the params array.

Figure 18.12.

Exploring the properties of an ActiveX control.

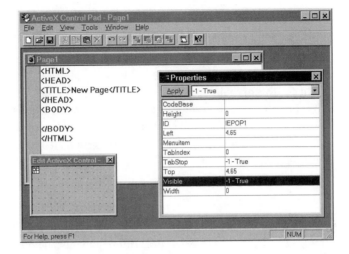

You can also use the ActiveX Control Pad to find the CLSID for a control. The CLSID is a GUID that represents the control in the registry. You need the CLSID when defining the ActiveX control in the IntraBuilder Form Designer. The CLSID for the popup menu is 7823A620-9DD9-11CF-A662-00AA00C066D2.

 A *GUID* is a global unique identifier. All OLE and ActiveX controls have a unique GUID. The GUID is used in place of a control name to prevent problems that might occur when two developers create controls with the same name.

The only name-value pair you will need to use is the Menuitem property. This property represents the text of each menu item. The property takes an array and cannot be set through the Property window of the ActiveX Control Pad.

 TIP

You can quickly add standard ActiveX controls through the ActiveX custom component library. You can add this set of components to your control palette through the Set Up Custom Components dialog. The library is called activex.cc and can be found in the following folder:

C:\Program Files\Borland\IntraBuilder\Custom

Adding a Popup Menu to a JavaScript Form

The Popup form opens from a button, much like the example shown in the ActiveX gallery. The popup presents options for changing the color of the current page to a color of the U.S.

flag. The red, white, and blue options fire server-side events to change the color. The last option, yellow fringe, fires a client-side event to say that the option is not implemented.

This form demonstrates passing values from an ActiveX control to the IntraBuilder Server. It also shows how to incorporate a hidden control and VBScript into a JavaScript form. The form consists of four controls: a pushbutton, an ActiveX popup menu, an HTML control, and a hidden control. The button fires a client-side VBScript command that opens the popup. The HTML control contains the actual VBScript and tags linking it to the button. The ActiveX is the popup with a set of name-value pairs for defining the menu items. The hidden control contains a value corresponding to the menu selection and is accessible from both client and server events.

WARNING

This example requires Internet Explorer. It will not run correctly in Netscape Navigator. Although you can add ActiveX support to Navigator using a plug-in, the plug-in does not add support for the VBScript shown here.

The following steps guide you through the first incarnation of the Popup form. Here, you make sure that you can open the popup from the button. Later, you will add the color changing server-side method.

1. Open the Form Designer to create a new form called popup.

   ```
   _sys.forms.design("popup.jfm") ;
   ```

2. Add a button and set the properties, as shown in Table 18.6. Do not directly link any events to the button.

Table 18.6. Properties for the pushbutton.

Property	Value
name	pushbutton
text	colors
left	0
top	0
width	10

3. Add an HTML control below the pushbutton. You can leave the text property as a default. Fill out the other properties, as listed in Table 18.7.

18

Table 18.7. Properties for the `vbscript` HTML control.

Property	Value
name	vbscript
height	1
left	0
top	3
width	60

4. Add an ActiveX control below the `vbscript` HTML control. Unlike most ActiveX controls, the position of this control doesn't really matter. The client-side script that opens the popup determines where it appears. Name the new control `popColors` and set the `classId` property to the following:

   `CLSID:7823A620-9DD9-11CF-A662-00AA00C066D2`

   You must include the `CLSID` prefix in the `classId` property. Remember that the `CLSID` is obtainable from the ActiveX Script Pad.

5. Open the Params Property Builder and enter the four array elements shown in Table 18.8. Defining name-value pairs for an ActiveX control is identical to defining name-value pairs for a Java applet. Figure 18.13 shows the four menu items in the Params Property Builder.

Table 18.8. Name-value pairs for the popup control.

Name	Value
Menuitem[0]	Red
Menuitem[1]	White
Menuitem[2]	Blue
Menuitem[3]	Yellow Fringe

6. Inspect the HTML control, and create and link a new method for the `onServerLoad` event. Enter the method shown in Listing 18.6. When you're done, save the form and try it out in Internet Explorer.

Figure 18.13.

Entering name-value pairs for the popup control.

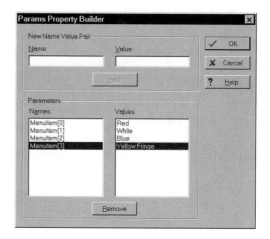

INPUT **Listing 18.6. The `vbscript_onServerLoad()` method.**

```
1: function vbscript_onServerLoad()
2: {
3:     if (((new NetInfo()).userAgent).indexOf("MSIE") > -1) {
4:         this.text =
5:         '<script for="pushbutton" event="onClick" language="VBScript">'+
6:         '    popColors.popup 10,60' +
7:         '</script>' ;
8:     }
9:     else {
10:        this.text = "<H1>This form requires Internet Explorer.</H1>";
11:    }
12: }
```

ANALYSIS This method checks to see whether the current browser is Internet Explorer. Line 3 looks for the string `"MSIE"` in the `userAgent` property of a `NetInfo` object. Notice that the `NetInfo` object is never assigned to a variable. If the current browser is Internet Explorer, lines 4 through 7 define a block of VBScript. Any other browser causes the HTML control to act as a message line.

Line 5 associates the following VBScript commands with the `onClick` event of a control called `pushbutton`. Notice the language parameter that sets the language to VBScript. The default scripting language for Internet Explorer is JavaScript.

The VBScript command appears on line 6. This is a method call with two parameters. In VBScript, parameters are passed to the method without enclosing them in parentheses. The `popup()` method of the ActiveX popup control causes the popup to open. In JavaScript, the statement would be

```
popColors.popup(10,60)
```

If you run the form now, the popup opens correctly but a white box appears where the ActiveX is defined. Figure 18.14 shows the box under the button. If you select any of the menu items, the form is submitted to the server.

Figure 18.14.

Viewing the ActiveX definition area in the Internet Explorer.

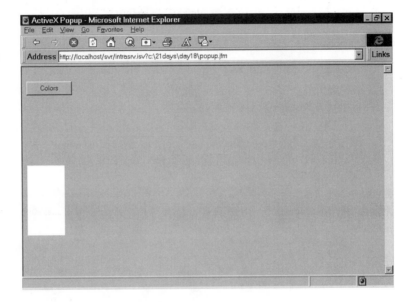

Passing Menu Selections Back to the Server

The last task of the day is to pass the menu selection back to the server so that it can take the appropriate course of action. To do this, you add two methods and a hidden control to the form. The first method is a client-side JavaScript method that is linked by name to the popup `onClick` event. The second method is linked to the `onServerSubmit` event and handles changing the form color. Here are the steps to complete the Popup form:

1. Open the Popup form in the Form Designer.
2. Add a hidden control onto the form. Change the name of the control to `hiddenColor`. It does not matter where you place the hidden control.
3. Change the `form.title` property to `ActiveX Popup`.
4. Create and link a new method to the `form.onServerSubmit` event. Use the following code to complete the method. This method changes the form color based on the menu selection. See the analysis following Listing 18.7 for more information on this method.

```
function Form_onServerSubmit()
{
    if (this.hiddenColor.value == "red") {
```

```
         this.color="red" ;
   }
   else if ( this.hiddenColor.value == "white" ) {
      this.color="white" ;
   }
   else if ( this.hiddenColor.value == "blue" ) {
      this.color="blue" ;
   }
}
```

5. Inspect the ActiveX control and add the following code block to the onServerLoad event. This code block prevents the white box from appearing in the browser.

   ```
   { ; this.width = 0 }
   ```

   At this point, your form should resemble the one shown in Figure 18.15. Keep in mind that the onServerLoad event does not fire when opening the designer. The Form Designer continues to display the ActiveX area for easy selection.

Figure 18.15.

Redesigning the Popup form.

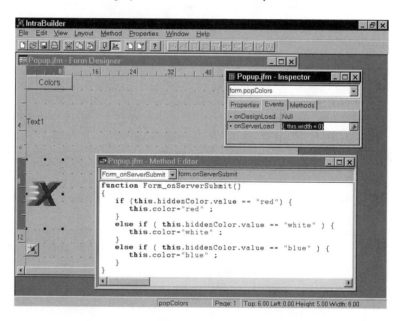

6. From the menu, select Method|New Method to create a method that is not linked to any event. Rename the new method popColors_Click(). Add an nPopItem parameter and complete the method as shown on lines 69 through 87 in Listing 18.7. When you are done, save the form and try running it through Internet Explorer.

18

Listing 18.7. The `popup.jfm` JavaScript form file.

```
1: // {End Header} Do not remove this comment//
2: // Generated on 01/02/97
3: //
4: var f = new popupForm();
5: f.open();
6: class popupForm extends Form {
7:     with (this) {
8:         onServerSubmit = class::Form_onServerSubmit;
9:         title = "ActiveX Popup";
10:     }
11:
12:     with (this.pushbutton = new Button(this)){
13:         width = 10;
14:         text = "Colors";
15:     }
16:
17:     with (this.vbscript = new HTML(this)){
18:         onServerLoad = class::vbscript_onServerLoad;
19:         height = 1;
20:         top = 3;
21:         width = 60;
22:         color = "black";
23:         text = "Text1";
24:     }
25:
26:     with (this.popColors = new ActiveX(this)){
27:         onServerLoad = {; this.width = 0};
28:         height = 5;
29:         top = 6;
30:         width = 8;
31:         classId = "CLSID:7823A620-9DD9-11CF-A662-00AA00C066D2";
32:         params["Menuitem[1]"] = "White";
33:         params["Menuitem[0]"] = "Red";
34:         params["Menuitem[3]"] = "Yellow Fringe";
35:         params["Menuitem[2]"] = "Blue";
36:     }
37:
38:     with (this.hiddenColor = new Hidden(this)){
39:         top = 12;
40:         value = "";
41:     }
42:
43:     function vbscript_onServerLoad()
44:     {
45:         if (((new NetInfo()).userAgent).indexOf("MSIE") > -1) {
46:             this.text =
47:             '<script for="pushbutton" event="onClick" language="VBScript">'+
48:             '    popColors.popup 10,60' +
49:             '</script>' ;
50:         }
```

continues

Listing 18.7. continued

```
51:        else {
52:            this.text = "<H1>This form requires Internet Explorer.</H1>";
53:        }
54:    }
55:
56:    function Form_onServerSubmit()
57:    {
58:        if (this.hiddenColor.value == "red") {
59:            this.color="red" ;
60:        }
61:        else if ( this.hiddenColor.value == "white" ) {
62:            this.color="white" ;
63:        }
64:        else if ( this.hiddenColor.value == "blue" ) {
65:            this.color="blue" ;
66:        }
67:    }
68:
69:    function popColors_Click(nPopItem)
70:    {
71: // {Export} This comment causes this function body to be sent to the client
72:        if ( nPopItem == 1 ) {
73:            document.forms[0].hiddenColor.value = "red" ;
74:            document.forms[0].submit() ;
75:        }
76:        else if ( nPopItem == 2 ) {
77:            document.forms[0].hiddenColor.value = "white" ;
78:            document.forms[0].submit() ;
79:        }
80:        else if ( nPopItem == 3 ) {
81:            document.forms[0].hiddenColor.value = "blue" ;
82:            document.forms[0].submit() ;
83:        }
84:        else if ( nPopItem == 4 ) {
85:            alert("Sorry, the yellow fringe is not implemented.")
86:        }
87:    }
88:
89: }
```

ANALYSIS   The Popup form demonstrates the integration of JavaScript, VBScript, and an ActiveX control. Like all IntraBuilder components, the form is a JavaScript class. One simple VBScript command is defined within an HTML control. The ActiveX control is a popup menu that passes information back to the IntraBuilder Server.

Lines 26 through 36 define the ActiveX control and assign name-value pairs to the control. Notice that the array defined in lines 32 through 35 is out of sequence. The order of the name-value pairs is rearranged when you save the form in the Form Designer. This order does not affect the appearance of the popup when run through Internet Explorer.

18

The hidden control defined on lines 38 through 41 creates a property that you can reference in both client-side and server-side events. The control is not visible to the browser user. This control holds the current color selection.

An `onServerSubmit` event fires when a client-side event calls the `submit()` method. It does not fire when you press a button linked to an `onServerClick` event. Lines 56 through 67 contain the `Form_onServerSubmit()` method. This method checks the contents of the hidden variable to figure out what color to use for the form background. It only responds to settings of red, white, and blue. The color strings are set in the `popColors_Click()` method.

The name given to the method on line 69 creates an implicit link between the `popColor` control's `Click` event and the `popColors_Click()` method. Although this style of linking makes it difficult to reuse the same method for different controls, it does provide for self-documenting code. IntraBuilder does not use this implicit style of linking and requires the comment on line 71 to export the method to the browser. For explicit links, IntraBuilder automatically exports methods linked to client-side events.

The ActiveX control passes the selected item number as a parameter to the `click` event. As a client-side event, the `popColors_Click()` event refers to the current form as `document.forms[0]` rather than `this.form`. If the user selects Yellow Fringe from the popup, the form is not submitted. Instead, line 85 opens an alert to inform the user that the option is not implemented. (See Figure 18.16.)

Figure 18.16.

The Yellow Fringe alert.

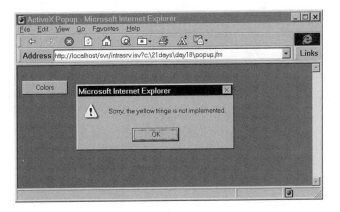

If the user selects Red, White, or Blue, `popColors_Click()` sets the `hiddenColor` value and submits the form. This fires the `Form_onServerSubmit()` method that uses the `hiddenColor` value to change the form color. Figure 18.17 shows the ActiveX popup open on a form that changed from the default silver to white.

Figure 18.17.

Selecting White from the ActiveX popup.

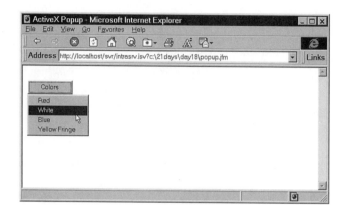

Summary

Today you learned how to integrate Java applets and ActiveX controls into JavaScript forms. Along the way, you learned about the strengths and weakness of Sun and Microsoft strategies. Both control types let you expand the capabilities of your applications far beyond what is possible with pure HTML.

The day began with an exploration of Java on the Web. Your first Java-enhanced form was the Duke form. This enabled you to take the Java mascot, Tumbling Duke, and place him in a JavaScript form. If you were using a Netscape browser, you might have taken advantage of LiveConnect to control the Java applet from client-side JavaScript.

Your second Java-enhanced form was the Grid form. This demonstrated how to integrate IntraBuilder data with a Java applet. The Grid was based on JavaSoft simplified spreadsheet control.

By the end of the day, you moved from Sun's Java to Microsoft's ActiveX. You learned how Microsoft is using ActiveX to leverage OLE technology to create a tight bind between Web applications and the Windows platform. You worked with the ActiveX popup control and client-side VBScript to create a form that could pass popup menu selections back to an IntraBuilder Server.

Q&A

Q What is JBuilder, and how can I use it with IntraBuilder?

A JBuilder is a Java development environment that you can use to create a wide variety of Java applications. It can create complete Java database systems using JDBC, as well as small applets that you can integrate with an IntraBuilder application.

Q I see how to use ActiveX controls and Java applets, but what about Netscape plug-ins? How can I embed a plug-in into a JavaScript form?

A All you need to do to embed a plug-in is create an HTML control with the appropriate <EMBED> tag. The following form works with the popular Shockwave plug-in. It runs the James Borland Shockwave file from the IntraBuilder Web site within a JavaScript form. This form works within both Netscape Navigator and Internet Explorer.

```
var f = new pluginForm();
f.open();
class pluginForm extends Form {
   with (this.plugin = new HTML(this)){
      height = 1.24;
      width = 10;
      text=
   '<EMBED SRC="http://www.borland.com/intrabuilder/jamesb.dcr"'+
   ' width=176 height=252>';
   }
}
```

Workshop

The Workshop section provides questions and exercises to help you get a better feel for the material you learned today. Try to answer the questions and at least think about the exercises before moving on to tomorrow's lesson. You'll find the answers to the questions in Appendix A, "Answers to Quiz Questions."

Quiz

1. Give two reasons why Java has quickly gained widespread industry support.
2. Which browser supports LiveConnect, and what does it do?
3. When working with a Java applet, what is the difference between the `code` and `codeBase` properties?
4. What are the file extensions for Java source and compiled files?
5. What class works with the `params` property?
6. Microsoft refers to its own implementation of JavaScript as what?

Exercises

1. Download the JavaGRID and use it to create a new grid form. Try populating the JavaGRID with the data from the Invoice table. You can download the control from the following URL:

   `http://www.vincent.se/Products/JavaGRID/JavaGRID.html`

2. If you have a Java development environment such as JBuilder or Visual Café, try modifying the JavaSoft spreadsheet class. If you examine the `SpreadSheet.java` file, you see that the `cellWidth` is set to `100` and cannot be overwritten by a parameter. This fixed width is too small to display the Title field from the Titles table. Modify the `init()` method to accept `cellWidth` as a parameter and adjust the Grid form to use your new Java class.

Day 19

External Server Objects and Functions

by Ted Graham

The ActiveX and Java controls described in yesterday's lesson allow you to deliver external objects to the client. In addition, you can utilize external objects on the server. These extend the capabilities of the server while never having to be delivered to a client machine. The server also utilizes external functions to extend the built-in capabilities of the server.

Today you will learn about the following topics:

- [ ] How to access external objects using OLE automation servers.
- [ ] How to use OLEnterprise to access remote server objects.
- [ ] How to access external functions.
- [ ] How to exchange structures with external functions.

OLE Automation Objects

By now, you have created objects using IntraBuilder's many built-in classes. You have also created objects from custom classes defined in JavaScript. Today, you will create objects from classes that are completely foreign to IntraBuilder.

Objects are shared among Windows applications using a technology known as OLE automation.

NEW TERM *OLE automation* is part of the OLE 2.0 standard. This standard defines the sharing of objects between separate applications. In particular, OLE automation allows a client application to execute commands inside a server application. IntraBuilder provides an OleAutoClient class for working with OLE automation servers.

IntraBuilder acts as an OLE automation client (or container). Other applications such as Word, Excel, and OLEnterprise act as OLE automation servers. To establish a link between IntraBuilder and one of these servers, you must know the program identifier (ProgID) of the server.

NEW TERM A *program identifier* is a unique name for an OLE server application. Client applications use the program identifier to search the system registry. The registry contains the information necessary to access the server application.

As an example, Microsoft Excel surfaces several different OLE automation servers. Their program identifiers include Excel.Sheet and Excel.Chart. The identifiers for the OLE automation server should be documented by the server vendor. You can also use a tool such as OLEnterprise to locate servers on your system.

Creating an OLE Automation Client Object

All OLE automation servers are accessed using the OleAutoClient class in IntraBuilder. This is a non-visual class like the built-in Date and Array classes. This means that you instantiate these objects in your script, but you do not work with them using the visual tools in the Form Designer.

The OleAutoClient class takes a single parameter. This parameter is the program identifier of the desired server. To create an IntraBuilder object representing an Excel spreadsheet, use the following command:

```
var excel = new OleAutoClient("Excel.Sheet");
```

This command creates an object named excel. The properties and methods of excel are entirely dependent upon the server application. The dynamic nature of the IntraBuilder object model makes it possible to create objects with properties and methods that IntraBuilder never anticipated. This capability allows almost unlimited extensions to the IntraBuilder product.

After creating the client object in IntraBuilder, you interact with it just like any other IntraBuilder object. For example, you use the Inspector to look at its properties and methods. If you have Excel installed on your system, try running this simple program:

```
excel = new OleAutoClient("Excel.Sheet");
_sys.inspect(excel);
```

This shows the excel object in the Inspector. Feel free to browse the properties and methods to become familiar with the capabilities of the object. For more information about the objects that Excel (or any other OLE automation server) surfaces, including their properties and methods, check the documentation that comes with the server application. For Microsoft Excel 7.0, you look in the online help for a definition of the properties and methods. From the help file's Contents page, select the Microsoft Excel Visual Basic Reference book.

Using Automation Objects

Surely you want to do more than inspect these powerful objects. After creating the object, you manipulate the properties and execute the methods to control the behavior of the server application. The Excel object creates spreadsheets, charts values, and performs calculations. One of Excel's many strong points is the extensive array of financial calculations available. Rather than duplicating these functions in IntraBuilder, you can use OLE automation to have Excel perform the calculations.

Calling an Excel Method

Consider a Web page that calculates the amount of a monthly loan payment, based on the loan amount, period, and interest rate entered on the form. Rather than calculating the monthly payment in IntraBuilder, you could use an OleAutoClient object to access Excel. Excel has a built-in function to calculate the payment. Although this example might be analogous to using a pile driver to push in a thumbtack, it does illustrate the basics of OLE automation.

One of the many methods that the Excel.Sheet server surfaces is called evaluate. This method evaluates any Excel expression and returns the result. The following example calculates the payment for a 36-month loan of $20,000 at 10 percent annual interest:

```
var xl = new OleAutoClient("excel.sheet");
var pmt = xl.evaluate("pmt(10/1200,36,20000)");
```

19

Storing Values in Cells

To make this code a little more dynamic, store the three initial values to cells on the spreadsheet and store the formula to a fourth cell. Then update the cell values to experiment with different payment schedules. The formula cell will always contain the current payment amount. The following example demonstrates the use of cells:

```
var xl=new OleAutoClient("excel.sheet");
xl.range("A1").value = 10/1200;
xl.range("B1").value = 36;
xl.range("C1").value = 20000;
xl.range("D1").value = "=PMT(A1,B1,C1)";
var pmt = xl.range("D1").value;
```

Then to see what the monthly payment would be at 9 percent interest, you simply change the value of A1:

```
xl.range("A1").value = 9/1200;
pmt = xl.range("D1").value;
```

Creating a Loan Calculation Form

This technique is used in the loan calculation form shown in Figure 19.1. The Calculate button's onServerClick() event code contains the call to the OLE automation server to calculate the monthly loan payment.

Figure 19.1.

A loan calculation form in Navigator.

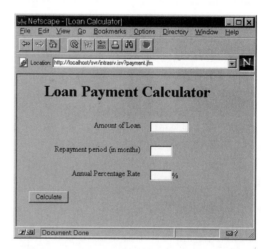

When this form is submitted to the IntraBuilder server, it actually uses Excel to perform the calculation and then report the result back to the browser. The user does not need to have Excel on the client machine; all of the communication between the OLE automation client (IntraBuilder) and server (Excel) takes place on the Web server machine. The source for this form is shown in Listing 19.1.

19

Listing 19.1. `Payment.jfm` **using OLE automation with Excel.**

```
1: // {End Header} Do not remove this comment//
2: // Generated on 02/14/97
3: //
4: var f = new paymentForm();
5: f.open();
6: class paymentForm extends Form {
7:     with (this) {
8:         onServerLoad = class::form_onServerLoad;
9:         height = 14;
10:        left = 5;
11:        top = 0;
12:        width = 63;
13:        title = "Loan Calculator";
14:    }
15:    with (this.html1 = new HTML(this)){
16:        height = 2;
17:        left = 2;
18:        width = 52;
19:        alignHorizontal = 1;
20:        text = "<h1>Loan Payment Calculator</h1>";
21:        pageno = 0;
22:    }
23:    with (this.html2 = new HTML(this)){
24:        height = 1;
25:        left = 2;
26:        top = 3;
27:        width = 30;
28:        alignHorizontal = 2;
29:        text = "Amount of Loan ";
30:        pageno = 0;
31:    }
32:    with (this.amount = new Text(this)){
33:        left = 34;
34:        top = 3;
35:        width = 10;
36:        value = "";
37:        pageno = 0;
38:    }
39:    with (this.html3 = new HTML(this)){
40:        height = 1;
41:        left = 2;
42:        top = 5;
43:        width = 30;
44:        alignHorizontal = 2;
45:        text = "Repayment period (in months) ";
46:        pageno = 0;
47:    }
48:    with (this.period = new Text(this)){
49:        left = 34;
50:        top = 5;
51:        width = 5.5;
52:        value = "";
53:        pageno = 0;
54:    }
```

continues

Listing 19.1. continued

```
 55:    with (this.html5 = new HTML(this)){
 56:        height = 1;
 57:        left = 2;
 58:        top = 7;
 59:        width = 30;
 60:        alignHorizontal = 2;
 61:        text = "Annual Percentage Rate ";
 62:        pageno = 0;
 63:    }
 64:    with (this.rate = new Text(this)){
 65:        left = 34;
 66:        top = 7;
 67:        width = 5.5;
 68:        value = "";
 69:        pageno = 0;
 70:    }
 71:    with (this.html6 = new HTML(this)){
 72:        height = 1.2;
 73:        left = 40;
 74:        top = 7;
 75:        width = 4;
 76:        alignVertical = 1;
 77:        text = "%";
 78:        pageno = 0;
 79:    }
 80:    with (this.calcButton = new Button(this)){
 81:        onServerClick = class::calcButton_onServerClick;
 82:        left = 2;
 83:        top = 9;
 84:        width = 12;
 85:        text = "Calculate";
 86:    }
 87:    with (this.backButton = new Button(this)){
 88:        onServerClick = {;form.pageno = 1};
 89:        left = 2;
 90:        top = 11;
 91:        width = 14;
 92:        text = "Back";
 93:        pageno = 2;
 94:    }
 95:    with (this.html7 = new HTML(this)){
 96:        height = 1;
 97:        left = 2;
 98:        top = 9;
 99:        width = 30;
100:        alignHorizontal = 2;
101:        text = "Monthly Payment ";
102:        pageno = 2;
103:    }
104:    with (this.paymentHTML = new HTML(this)){
105:        height = 1;
106:        left = 34;
107:        top = 9;
```

19

```
108:        width = 12;
109:        pageno = 2;
110:    }
111:    function form_onServerLoad()
112:    {
113:        this.xl = new OleAutoClient("excel.sheet");
114:        this.xl.range("A1").value = 0;
115:        this.xl.range("B1").value = 0;
116:        this.xl.range("C1").value = 0;
117:        this.xl.range("D1").value = "=PMT(A1,B1,C1)";
118:    }
119:    function calcButton_onServerClick()
120:    {
121:        var f = this.form, xl = f.xl;
122:        xl.range("A1").value = parseInt(f.rate.value)/1200;
123:        xl.range("B1").value = parseInt(f.period.value);
124:        xl.range("C1").value = parseInt(f.amount.value);
125:        f.paymentHTML.text = "" + (-xl.range("D1").value);
126:        f.pageno = 2;
127:    }
128: }
```

ANALYSIS Lines 1 through 110 define the controls on the payment form. The form_onServerLoad() method beginning on line 111 creates the OLE automation object xl as a property of the form. It then initializes the spreadsheet cell values.

The calcButton_onServerClick() method, beginning on line 119, passes the values from the form to the spreadsheet (lines 122 to 124). Line 125 takes the calculated value from spreadsheet cell D1 and displays it on the form. Finally, line 126 changes the form to page 2, displaying the payment controls and the Back button.

The backButton control defined on lines 87 to 94 simply changes the page number back to 1 (line 88).

Remote OLE Automation Server Objects

The OLE 2.0 specification allows client applications to access server applications on the same machine. But what if you want to access an OLE automation server on a different machine? For example, you might have several different machines that act as Web servers, each running IntraBuilder. Or you might have several different machines hosting IntraBuilder agents that all service a single Web server. (Remote IntraBuilder agents are possible with the client/server version of the product.) You might want to set up a single application server running your OLE automation server that would service all of the IntraBuilder server machines.

Although this type of distributed OLE is not currently possible with Windows and IntraBuilder itself, there is a product that bridges the gap and makes it possible. OLEnterprise

19

from Open Environment Corporation (a subsidiary of Borland) gives IntraBuilder access to OLE automation servers on remote machines.

Remote Procedure Call (RPC) Servers

Not only does OLEnterprise give you access to remote OLE automation servers, but it also gives you access to any remote server application that conforms to the DCE RPC specification. This gives IntraBuilder access to application servers and database servers on UNIX or even mainframe systems.

OLEnterprise registers the RPC server and then acts as a middleman between the RPC server and IntraBuilder. OLEnterprise presents the RPC server to IntraBuilder as if it were an OLE automation server.

NOTE

To find out more about OLEnterprise, check out the Open Environment home page at www.oec.com.

External Functions

You can extend the capability of the IntraBuilder server not only through the use of external objects, but also through the use of external functions. There are many things that IntraBuilder is simply not designed to do, but other vendors do these things very well. These vendors often make libraries of functions available in the form of an add-on DLL. These DLLs are used by any development tool, such as C++, Delphi, or Visual Basic. Function libraries are available for a wide variety of purposes, including data collection, communications, fax and e-mail, and credit card validation.

IntraBuilder allows you to prototype external functions and then call them just like you call internal functions such as alert() or parseInt(). The prototyping tells IntraBuilder the name and location of the function, as well as the data type of the return value and any parameters. This is necessary so that IntraBuilder can call the external function and exchange data in a compatible format.

The extern Command

You use the extern command to prototype the function in IntraBuilder. The extern command uses several data type keywords to indicate the type of the return value and the

19

parameters. These type keywords are the generally recognized base types in C++ and most other programming languages, such as int for 32-bit integer values and short for 16-bit integer values. The types are modified by the keyword unsigned if the integer value is used for positive values only. The keywords are also modified with an asterisk if the return value or parameter is a pointer to the specified type.

As an example, consider the MessageBeep() function. This function is contained in the USER32.DLL file that ships with Windows. The functions in the Windows DLLs are collectively referred to as the Windows API. According to the Windows API documentation, MessageBeep() plays a sound. The function takes one parameter of type unsigned int and returns a boolean type value indicating whether the function is successful.

Using this information, you prototype the function using this extern command:

```
extern boolean MessageBeep(unsigned int) "user32.dll";
```

After prototyping the function, call it just like a built-in function:

```
var result = MessageBeep(64);
```

NOTE
There is one difference between calling an IntraBuilder function and calling an external function. IntraBuilder functions such as parseInt() can take optional parameters. External functions, however, require an exact number of parameters. Because MessageBeep() is prototyped with one parameter, you must pass one and only one parameter each time you call the function.

19

Calling Conventions

The extern command shown earlier is pretty basic. For instance, it does not specify the calling convention. The calling convention is a predefined standard by which programs exchange information. There are three calling conventions supported by the extern command: cdecl, pascal, and stdcall. Before prototyping any function, you need to know the calling convention that it uses. Most 32-bit programs use the stdcall convention, which is the IntraBuilder default.

The following extern for MessageBeep() shows the inclusion of the calling convention:

```
extern stdcall boolean MessageBeep(unsigned int) "user32.dll";
```

Keep in mind that stdcall is the default calling convention, so you don't actually need to specify it in this case. Almost every one of the functions in the Windows API uses the stdcall convention. But you might run into other libraries that use a different convention.

Renaming External Functions

You also use the extern command to assign a different name to the external function. You use this capability to access two different functions that happen to have the same name, or to simplify the name in IntraBuilder.

You might also want to rename functions when the documented name does not match the actual name of the function. For example, the Windows API documents a function named MessageBox(), but the actual function name is MessageBoxA(). You use the extern command to rename the function in IntraBuilder to match the documented name:

```
extern int MessageBox(void*,          // owner window
                      char*,           // message text
                      char*,           // title text
                      unsigned int     // style
                      ) "user32.dll"
                      from "MessageBoxA";
```

This assigns the documented name MessageBox() to the function in IntraBuilder. When you call the MessageBox() function, IntraBuilder actually calls the MessageBoxA() function in USER32.DLL.

> **TIP**
>
> Many of the Windows API functions are documented under aliases. Trying to prototype the documented name produces an error. This is normally the case if the function takes any strings or structures as parameters. If you do encounter an error prototyping the documented name, try adding a capital letter "A" to the end of the function name.

After you have prototyped the function, you call it with the new name:

```
var result = MessageBox(0, "Save File?", "Extern Sample", 35);
```

This function call opens a dialog box, as shown in Figure 19.2. You see the title and text that were passed as parameters. The style parameter, 35, tells the function to add the question mark and buttons for Yes, No, and Cancel.

Figure 19.2.
The dialog box generated by MessageBox().

Data Type Keywords

The previous examples showed the use of several data type keywords, such as int, char*, boolean, and unsigned int. The complete list of data type keywords is shown in Table 19.1.

Table 19.1. Data type keywords for the extern command.

Keyword	IntraBuilder Data Type	External Data Type
char	Numeric	8-bit character
unsigned char		
short	Numeric	16-bit integer
unsigned short		
int	Numeric	32-bit integer
unsigned int		
long		
unsigned long		
float	Numeric	32-bit floating-point number
double	Numeric	64-bit floating-point number
long double	Numeric	80-bit floating-point number
boolean	Boolean	8-bit Boolean value
void	None	N/A
char*	String	Null-terminated string
void*	String	Structure of unknown type and length
...	N/A	Variable number of parameters

19

In addition to the types shown in Table 19.1, there are pointers to each of these types.

 A *pointer* is a data type in languages such as C, C++, and Pascal. Rather than containing an actual value, a pointer contains the memory address of a value. All pointers are 32 bits in size because that is the size of a memory address.

Prototyping a Pointer

To indicate that a return type or parameter is a pointer to a particular data type, put the asterisk after the data type. Table 19.1 shows two pointer types: char* and void*. In addition to these, there are pointers to all the other types as well.

As an example, if an external function returns a pointer to a 16-bit integer, prototype it as short*. Likewise, if a parameter is a pointer to an unsigned long value, prototype it as unsigned long*.

Parameter-Only Keywords

The last two items shown in Table 19.1, void* and . . ., are used for parameter types but not for return types. While void indicates that there is no return type or parameter, void* is used to indicate a pointer to an unknown data type. The typical use of void* is to indicate that a parameter is a structure. Structures are explained later in this chapter.

These IntraBuilder data type keywords correspond to the base data types in the C programming language. If you are familiar with C or C++, you will be able to prototype functions in IntraBuilder by simply determining the base type for any parameters and the return value. If this is the case, you might want to skim over the next few sections.

Creating a Function Prototype

The last few sections showed you how to use the syntax of the extern command and the data type keywords used by the command. But when prototyping external functions, this is only part of the battle. Before you prototype a function, you must check the documentation from the function's vendor. In some place, the vendor will show the function prototype. However, this documentation is usually written for C programmers and might appear a little cryptic to the rest of us.

The next few sections give you some tips on turning this type of function documentation into an IntraBuilder prototype.

Using the Documentation

Most function libraries come with some sort of documentation. If you are using the Windows API itself, you'll need to get documentation. The official source of information is the Windows SDK, available from Microsoft. The Microsoft Developer Network CD also contains a wealth of information. Development products such as Borland C++ also contain documentation on the Windows API. And numerous books are available on this subject.

Figure 19.3 shows a typical function definition that comes from the Borland C++ help file.

Figure 19.3.

Borland documentation for the MessageBox() *function.*

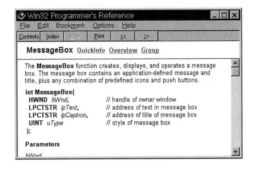

The documentation gives you the function name and identifies the return type as int. The QuickInfo link shown in Figure 19.3 indicates that the function is contained in the USER32.DLL file. So the documentation provides the function name, the number of parameters, and possibly the base type of the return value and parameters.

This documentation indicates that the base type of the return value is int. However, the parameter types are shown as HWND, LPCTSTR, and UINT, which do not match any of the IntraBuilder data type keywords. These custom data types are simply different names for one of the base data types. You have to turn to other sources to determine the base data types.

Using Header Files

When you get an external function library, it usually contains a header file along with the DLL. Among other things, the header file contains the function prototype (so, if it's not in the documentation, it will be here) and definitions of the custom data types.

The header file is intended to be used by C programmers. The programmers simply include the header in their program, and then they have access to the functions and the custom data types.

19

Custom Data Types and `typedef`

As an IntraBuilder programmer, you also use the header file to determine the base data types of the custom types. Open the header file in an editor that allows you to do text searches (such as Window's Notepad), and search for the data type. For instance, the Windows API header file WINDEF.H defines the MessageBox() UINT data type:

```
typedef unsigned int        UINT;
```

In C, `typedef` defines a new data type. This simply indicates that the type (or types) on the right are synonymous with the type on the left. So UINT is just another name for unsigned int.

Multiple Layers of `typedef`

Sometimes you have to look through several `typedef` commands to find the base data type. For example, the Windows API header file WINNT.H defines the LPCTSTR data type:

```
typedef LPCSTR LPCTSTR;
```

This indicates that LPCTSTR is another name for the LPCSTR type. Elsewhere in the file, LPCSTR is defined:

```
typedef CONST CHAR *LPCSTR, *PCSTR;
```

This defines both *LPCSTR and *PCSTR as CONST CHAR types. The CONST is a C keyword indicating that a parameter cannot be modified by the function. Ignore this keyword when trying to determine the base data type. The asterisk before each of the type names indicates that it is a pointer type. Therefore, LPCSTR is a pointer to a CHAR. The CHAR type is also defined in this header file:

```
typedef char CHAR;
```

The `typedef` defines CHAR to be another name for char, which is one of the IntraBuilder data types. From these three lines you can determine that the LPCTSTR data type is just a fancy name for a pointer to a char. You can express a pointer to char as char* in the extern command.

Other Type Definition Techniques

Other data type definition techniques are used in the header files. For example, the HWND is defined by this line in WINDEF.H:

```
DECLARE_HANDLE        (HWND);
```

To see what the DECLARE_HANDLE macro does, you have to look in WINNT.H:

```
typedef void *PVOID;
typedef PVOID HANDLE;
#define DECLARE_HANDLE(name) typedef HANDLE name
```

The type definition of HWND relies on the preprocessor macro DECLARE_HANDLE as well as the typedef commands. The macro evaluates to a typedef for a HANDLE type. HWND is a HANDLE, which is itself a PVOID type. Because PVOID is a pointer to a void type, HWND is a pointer to a void. This is prototyped as void* in the extern.

This type of detective work in the header file reveals the base data type for any of the custom data types in function definitions. Of course, in the worst case, you can contact the function library's vendor to request information about the base data types in question.

Structures and Enumerated Constants

Two custom data types that you might encounter are not based on one of the IntraBuilder base data types. These data types are structures and enumerated constants.

Later in this chapter, you will see the GetDateFormat() function. One of the parameters to this function is of type SYSTEMTIME. The definition of this custom type is located in the WINBASE.H header file:

```
typedef struct _SYSTEMTIME {
    WORD wYear;
    WORD wMonth;
    WORD wDayOfWeek;
    WORD wDay;
    WORD wHour;
    WORD wMinute;
    WORD wSecond;
    WORD wMilliseconds;
} SYSTEMTIME, *PSYSTEMTIME, *LPSYSTEMTIME;
```

The heading typedef struct indicates that this is a structure type.

 A *structure* is a custom data type that combines multiple data types. The individual members of the structure are just like the individual properties of an IntraBuilder object.

Structures are covered in depth near the end of this chapter.

 TIP

All structure parameters are prototyped as void* in the extern command.

The other custom data type that you might encounter is enum. For example, the WINNT.H file defines a custom data type named TOKEN_TYPE:

```
typedef enum _TOKEN_TYPE {
    TokenPrimary = 1,
    TokenImpersonation
    } TOKEN_TYPE;
typedef TOKEN_TYPE *PTOKEN_TYPE;
```

19

The heading `typedef enum` indicates that this is an enumerated constant type.

 An *enumerated constant* is a custom data type that can take any of a set of predefined values. The values are identified with a constant name.

The enumerated constants have integer equivalents. By default, the first constant has the value of `0`, and each subsequent constant has a value one larger than the previous. In the `TOKEN_TYPE` enumerated constant, the first value is explicitly defined to have a value of `1` instead. The subsequent constant is one greater than this, so it has a value of `2`.

You have two options when handling these enumerated constants. The first is to pass the equivalent integer value. For instance, you would use a value of `1` in any place that the documentation for `TOKEN_TYPE` indicates you should use the value `TokenPrimary`. The other option is to use the preprocessor to define constants for these values:

```
#define TokenPrimary        1
#define TokenImpersonation  2
```

Then you use the constant names just as the documentation would indicate.

 TIP

All enumerated constant parameters are prototyped as `unsigned int` in the `extern` command.

Using `WINDEF.H` for Windows Base Types

The preceding examples apply to determining the base type for any custom data type. Because the most common source of external functions is the Windows API, IntraBuilder includes a JavaScript header file that defines the most common data types for you. This file, `WINDEF.H`, is located in the `IntraBuilder\Include` folder.

To use this header file, simply `#include` it in your script before prototyping a Windows API function. Here is the `MessageBox()` prototype using this header file:

```
#include "windef.h"
extern int MessageBox(
    HWND,      // handle of owner window
    LPCTSTR,   // address of text in message box
    LPCTSTR,   // address of title of message box
    UINT       // style of message box
) "user32.dll"
  from "MessageBoxA";
```

This header does not include all of the Windows data types—just the most common types. If you encounter a Windows type that is not defined in the header file, use the techniques shown earlier to determine the base data type.

Parameter Values

The function definition in the documentation also tells you what values are acceptable for each of the parameters. Some parameters, such as the text and title in the MessageBox(), are left up to your choosing (as long as the value is the correct type). Others require specific values. Figure 19.4 shows more of the MessageBox() documentation. This section defines each of the parameters.

Figure 19.4.

Parameter definitions for MessageBox().

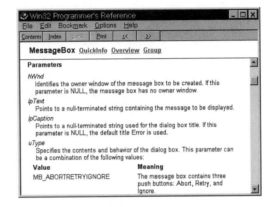

null **Values as Parameters**

One type of value that you might encounter is a NULL value. For example, Figure 19.4 shows that hWnd can have a value of NULL.

Although IntraBuilder supports a null value of its own, you should never pass an IntraBuilder null to an external function. Instead, you pass a zero to an external function that is expecting a C type NULL value. Each of the MessageBox() examples has used this technique to pass a NULL value for the hWnd parameter.

Symbolic Constant Values

The function documentation might also indicate that certain parameters take symbolic constant values. For example, the documentation in Figure 19.4 began to list the possible symbolic constants for the uType parameter. Figure 19.5 shows more constants that can be used for the uType parameter.

The examples so far have used the literal value 35, rather than one of the symbolic constants, for the uType parameter. This was only a temporary trick until the constants were introduced. The value 35 is a combination of two constants, MB_ICONQUESTION (seen in Figure 19.5) and MB_YESNOCANCEL.

Figure 19.5.

Parameter constants for the uType *parameter.*

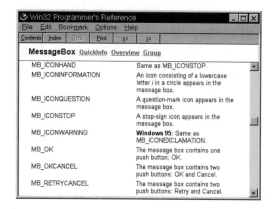

Determining the Value of Symbolic Constants

The symbolic constants are defined in the same header files that contain the data type definitions. When you encounter a symbolic constant in the documentation, search the header file to find the value.

After you find the value for the constant, you have two choices. First, you could simply use the value in place of the constant, as you did with the 35 earlier. Or you could cut and paste the constant declarations from the C header file to your JavaScript program. Then you use the constants as indicated by the documentation.

Here are the two lines from WINUSER.H that define the MessageBox() styles that the examples have been using:

```
#define MB_YESNOCANCEL              0x00000003L
#define MB_ICONQUESTION             0x00000020L
```

This syntax is almost exactly like the JavaScript syntax for defining preprocessor constants. The L at the end of the hexadecimal values indicates that the numeric constant should be stored as a long type. This is not used by JavaScript, so remove the L if you copy this type of line to your own script.

Using Correct Parameter Values in MESSAGE.JS

Listing 19.2 combines what you have learned in the last few sections. It contains the constant definitions that are copied from the C header file. It uses WINDEF.H to simplify the prototyping of the MessageBox() function. It calls the MessageBox() function and evaluates the result.

19

INPUT **Listing 19.2. Using** `MessageBox()` **in** `MESSAGE.JS`.

```
 1: #include "windef.h"
 2: /*
 3:  * MessageBox() Flags
 4:  */
 5: #define MB_OK                    0x00000000
 6: #define MB_OKCANCEL              0x00000001
 7: #define MB_ABORTRETRYIGNORE      0x00000002
 8: #define MB_YESNOCANCEL           0x00000003
 9: #define MB_YESNO                 0x00000004
10: #define MB_RETRYCANCEL           0x00000005
11: #define MB_ICONHAND              0x00000010
12: #define MB_ICONQUESTION          0x00000020
13: #define MB_ICONEXCLAMATION       0x00000030
14: #define MB_ICONASTERISK          0x00000040
15: #define MB_ICONWARNING           MB_ICONEXCLAMATION
16: #define MB_ICONERROR             MB_ICONHAND
17: #define MB_ICONINFORMATION       MB_ICONASTERISK
18: #define MB_ICONSTOP              MB_ICONHAND
19: /*
20:  * Dialog Box Command IDs
21:  */
22: #define IDOK        1
23: #define IDCANCEL    2
24: #define IDABORT     3
25: #define IDRETRY     4
26: #define IDIGNORE    5
27: #define IDYES       6
28: #define IDNO        7
29: #define IDCLOSE     8
30: #define IDHELP      9
31: extern int MessageBox(
32:     HWND,       // handle of owner window
33:     LPCTSTR,    // address of text in message box
34:     LPCTSTR,    // address of title of message box
35:     UINT        // style of message box
36:     ) "user32.dll"
37:     from "MessageBoxA";
38: var result = MessageBox(0, "Save File?", "Extern Sample",
39:             MB_ICONQUESTION | MB_YESNOCANCEL);
40: switch (result) {
41: case IDYES:
42:     alert("File Saved");
43:     break;
44: case IDNO:
45:     alert("File Not Saved");
46:     break;
47: case IDCANCEL:
48:     alert("Exit aborted");
49:     break;
50: }
```

19

Line 1 includes the JavaScript header file, WINDEF.H. This contains the data type definitions for the extern command beginning on line 31.

Lines 2 to 18 contain constant definitions that are copied from the C header file WINUSER.H. When you copy these sections of constants to the JavaScript file, it is easier to change the look of the MessageBox() at a later time. Lines 19 to 30 are also copied from WINUSER.H. These define the constants that are returned from the MessageBox() function. These constants are used in the switch block beginning on line 40.

Lines 31 to 37 prototype the external function that is used on lines 38 and 39. Notice the use of the style constants in the function call. The pipe symbol is used to combine multiple constants. Lines 40 to 50 display a different alert for each of the three possible values returned by the MessageBox() function.

Structures

One of the C data types that you will encounter deserves some extra attention. Structures are custom data types that combine multiple base data types. There is no equivalent data type in IntraBuilder, which makes working with structures challenging.

Structures can be thought of as primitive objects. A structure is a single entity that includes multiple members, just like an object includes multiple properties. Each member of an object contains a distinct piece of data.

One of the many structures used by the Windows API is called SYSTEMTIME. The definition of this structure is shown in Figure 19.6.

Figure 19.6.

The definition of the SYSTEMTIME *structure.*

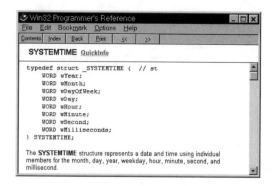

The SYSTEMTIME structure contains eight members. Each member is of type WORD, which is a custom data type equivalent to an unsigned short. Table 19.1 indicates that an unsigned short is a 16-bit (2-byte) integer value. The entire size of the structure is the sum of the member sizes. Therefore, this structure is a total of 16 bytes in size.

Passing Structures in IntraBuilder

Two Windows API functions that use the SYSTEMTIME structure are GetSystemTime() and GetDateFormat(). GetSystemTime() takes a single parameter, which is a pointer to a SYSTEMTIME structure. It stores the current date and time to the various members of the structure. The GetDateFormat() function takes a SYSTEMTIME structure as one of its parameters. It creates a string representation of the SYSTEMTIME value based on the other parameters.

You prototype these two functions just like other functions. To indicate that a parameter is a structure, use the void* data type keyword in the extern command.

Before calling the external function, you must initialize an IntraBuilder string to hold the structure value. This string must be at least as large as the structure itself.

Listing 19.3 shows a script file that prototypes the two functions just mentioned and passes the structure created by one to the other.

INPUT   **Listing 19.3. Using the SYSTEMTIME structure in DATE.JS.**

```
 1: #include "windef.h"
 2: // C prototype:
 3: // VOID GetSystemTime(
 4: //   LPSYSTEMTIME   lpSystemTime // address of system time structure
 5: // );
 6: extern VOID GetSystemTime(
 7:   LPSTRUCTURE      // address of system time structure
 8: ) "kernel32.dll";
 9: // C prototype:
10: // int GetDateFormat(
11: //   LCID  Locale,        // locale for which date is to be formatted
12: //   DWORD  dwFlags,      // flags specifying function options
13: //   CONST SYSTEMTIME * lpDate,  // date to be formatted
14: //   LPCTSTR  lpFormat,   // date format string
15: //   LPTSTR  lpDateStr,   // buffer for storing formatted string
16: //   int  cchDate         // size of buffer
17: // );
18: extern int GetDateFormat(
19:   LCID,        // locale for which date is to be formatted
20:   DWORD,       // flags specifying function options
21:   STRUCTURE,   // date to be formatted
22:   LPCTSTR,     // date format string
23:   LPTSTR,      // buffer for storing formatted string
24:   int          // size of buffer
25: ) "kernel32.dll"
26: from "GetDateFormatA";
27: var Locale    = 0;  // null pointer
28: var dwFlags   = 2;  // long date format
29: var lpDate    = new StringEx().replicate(" ", 16);
30: var lpFormat  = 0;  // null pointer
31: var lpDateStr = new StringEx().replicate(" ", 80);
32: var cchDate   = lpDateStr.length;
```

continues

Listing 19.3. continued

```
33: // get current date
34: GetSystemTime( lpDate );
35: // pass lpDate structure to GetDateFormat
36: var len = GetDateFormat( Locale, dwFlags, lpDate,
37:          lpFormat, lpDateStr, cchDate );
38: // display the formatted date
39: alert(lpDateStr.substring(0,len-1));
```

 ANALYSIS This script file, DATE.JS, has three basic sections. Lines 1 to 26 prototype the external functions. Lines 27 to 32 initialize the variables. And lines 33 to 39 perform the action of the script.

Line 1 includes the WINDEF.H header file. This file contains the type definitions for the Windows data types used in the extern commands.

WARNING

The WINDEF.H that ships with IntraBuilder 1.0 and 1.01 contains incorrect type definitions for several pointer types, including pointers to structures. The CD that comes with this book contains an updated copy of the header file that corrects this problem. Be sure to use the updated copy when running the scripts in this chapter.

Lines 2 to 5 show the documented prototype for the GetSystemTime() function. Lines 6 to 8 contain the IntraBuilder prototype for this function. Notice that the LPSYSTEMTIME parameter on line 4 is prototyped as LPSTRUCTURE on line 7. The LPSTRUCTURE type is defined in WINDEF.H as a void*.

Lines 9 to 17 show the documented prototype for the GetDateFormat() function. Lines 18 to 26 contain the IntraBuilder prototype for this function. Notice that the CONST SYSTEMTIME * on line 13 is prototyped as STRUCTURE on line 21. WINDEF.H defines the types STRUCTURE, PSTRUCTURE, and LPSTRUCTURE, which are all interchangeable.

Lines 27 to 32 initialize variables for each of the parameters of the GetDateFormat() function. The variable names are taken from the suggested names in the C prototype on lines 11 to 16. This makes it easier to coordinate the script with the actual documentation.

Pay particular attention to line 29. This line initializes the lpDate variable. It is initialized as a string containing 16 spaces. This length matches the length of the SYSTEMTIME structure itself. This string is then passed to the GetSystemTime() function on line 34. After line 34 executes, lpDate contains the data associated with a SYSTEMTIME structure.

19

WARNING

It is vital that you initialize variables that will hold structures. They must be initialized to a size at least as large as the structure itself. If you have trouble determining the size of the structure, initialize the variable to a large size. If you do not properly initialize the variable, an external function could write to an inappropriate place in memory. This could cause IntraBuilder or the external function to crash.

The `lpDate` structure is then passed to the `GetDateFormat()` function on lines 36 and 37. Notice that you never need to know the contents of the structure in this script. One function fills it, and you simply pass that structure to another function. This will be the case in many circumstances.

The `GetDateFormat()` function stores a string version of the date to the `lpDateStr` variable. This variable is then displayed by the alert on line 39. The return value from `GetDateFormat()` is the number of bytes written to `lpDateStr`. This return value is used on line 39 to trim `lpDateStr` to the correct length. The length is actually trimmed to one less than the return value, because the C function would have written and counted a terminating `null` character.

The final result of the function is an Alert dialog showing the current date in a text format. The result will look similar to that shown in Figure 19.7.

Figure 19.7.
An Alert dialog showing the result of `GetDateFormat()`.

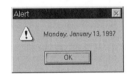

Interpreting Structures

The script in Listing 19.3 did not need to know the contents of the SYSTEMTIME structure. There are times, however, when you do need to determine the individual member values in the structure. Simple integer values like those in SYSTEMTIME can be determined using IntraBuilder methods, but more complex data such as floating-point numbers or pointers require the use of the structure parsing functions described in the next section.

The structure contains the internal representation of each member value. For example, the `unsigned short`, or `WORD`, type is represented by two bytes. Each byte contains a value from `0` to `255`. The first byte represents multiples of 1, and the second byte represents multiples of 256. So the number `5` is represented by the bytes `5` and `0`, in that order. The number `260` is represented by the bytes `4` and `1`, because it contains one multiple of 256 with four multiples of 1 left over.

Knowing this, you convert an unsigned short value stored in a structure to the actual number that it represents. You use the asc() method of the StringEx object to determine the value stored in a particular byte.

The reverse is also possible. You use the str() method of the StringEx object to create a character string value representing a byte value.

Listing 19.4 contains a function that uses this technique to increment the year member of a SYSTEMTIME structure.

Listing 19.4. Manipulating a SYSTEMTIME member in

INPUT ADDYEAR.JS.

```
 1: function addYear (stStruc)
 2: {
 3:     // Create var to simplify calling the asc()
 4:     // and str() methods of StringEx()
 5:     var str = new StringEx();
 6:     // Year is first WORD value in structure
 7:     var year = (str.asc(stStruc.substring(0,1)) +
 8:                 str.asc(stStruc.substring(1,2)) * 256 );
 9:     // Increment the year
10:     year++;
11:     // Create new structure containing the new year
12:     // and the rest of the stStruc structure
13:     stStruc = str.chr(year % 256) +
14:               str.chr(parseInt(year/256) % 256) +
15:               stStruc.substring(2,16);
16:     return (true);
17: }
```

ANALYSIS The addYear() function takes a SYSTEMTIME structure as the parameters (in line 1). This function uses the methods of StringEx to manipulate the structure string stStruc. Line 5 creates a StringEx object for this purpose.

Lines 7 and 8 use the first two bytes of the string to determine the year value. The first byte is taken at face value, and the second byte is multiplied by 256. The sum of these two bytes represents the year member.

This year value is incremented in line 10. Lines 13 to 15 create a new SYSTEMTIME structure using the incremented year and the balance of stStruc.

The technique shown in Listing 19.4 is useful for unsigned integer values of all sizes. An unsigned long value is stored using four bytes. The first byte contains multiples of 1 (256 to the power of 0), the second contains multiples of 256 (256 to the power of 1), the third contains multiples of 65,536 (256 to the power of 2), and the fourth contains multiples of 16,777,216 (256 to the power of 3).

The IntraBuilder Structure Parsing Library

For most of the non-integer data types, you cannot easily parse the structure string to determine the value. To parse these types of structure members, you can use the structure parsing library that ships with IntraBuilder. This collection of functions is contained in a file named STRUCMEM.DLL in the IntraBuilder\Samples folder.

The prototypes for these functions are contained in a script named STRUCMEM.JS, which is also in the IntraBuilder\Samples folder. To use these functions, you need to include the STRUCMEM.H header file. It defines the constant values that are used for various parameters. This file is located in the default IntraBuilder\Include folder.

The structure parsing library contains functions to retrieve values from the structure as well as store values in a structure string. The functions prototyped in STRUCMEM.JS are described next.

GetStructNumber(<structure>, <offset>, <type>)

This function returns the value of type <type> located at position <offset> in the structure string <structure>. The <offset> is zero-based, so the first member is at offset 0. The offset of each member is determined by the size of the members before it. The <type> can be one of the type constants defined in STRUCMEM.H:

- [ ] TYPE_CHAR
- [ ] TYPE_UCHAR
- [ ] TYPE_SHORT
- [ ] TYPE_USHORT
- [ ] TYPE_INT
- [ ] TYPE_UINT
- [ ] TYPE_LONG
- [ ] TYPE_ULONG
- [ ] TYPE_FLOAT
- [ ] TYPE_DOUBLE
- [ ] TYPE_LDOUBLE
- [ ] TYPE_BYTE
- [ ] TYPE_WORD
- [ ] TYPE_DWORD
- [ ] TYPE_BOOL

19

The types UCHAR, USHORT, UINT, and ULONG indicate unsigned values of the indicated type. The last four items in the list are Windows data types, which can be used in place of their actual base type for convenience.

In addition to these constants, there are also size constants. They match these names, except that TYPE is replaced by SIZEOF, as in SIZEOF_INT and SIZEOF_ULONG. These size constants are useful when calculating the <offset>:

SetStructNumber(<structure>, <offset>, <type>, <slen>, <value>)

This function writes the value <value> of type <type> at position <offset> in the structure string <structure>. The <slen> parameter indicates the length of <structure>. This is necessary to make sure that SetStructNumber() does not write past the memory allocated for this string. The types are the same as those used by the GetStructNumber() function. The function returns the number of bytes written to <structure>.

GetStructString(<structure>, <offset>, <length>, <target>, <tlen>)

This function copies the string at offset <offset> of length <length> in the structure string <structure> to <target>. The <tlen> parameter indicates the length of <target>. Structures rarely contain strings; they usually contain pointers to strings, which are handled by another function. However, this function is useful for retrieving structures that are members of other structures. The return value is the number of bytes written to <target>.

SetStructString(<structure>, <offset>, <slen>, <value>, <vlen>)

This function copies <vlen> bytes from the string <value> to the offset <offset> of string <structure>. The <slen> parameter indicates the size of <structure>. The return value indicates the number of bytes written to <structure>.

GetStructCharPointer(<structure>, <offset>, <length>, <target>, <tlen>)

This function writes <length> bytes to <target> from the string pointed to by the pointer at offset <offset> in the structure string <structure>. The <tlen> parameter indicates the size of <target>. Structures usually contain pointers to strings rather than strings themselves. This function retrieves the string pointed to by such a pointer. If the pointer points to a null-terminated string, you set <length> to 0. The return value indicates the number of bytes written to <target>.

SetStructCharPointer(<structure>, <offset>, <slen>, <value>)

This function writes a pointer to the structure string <structure> at offset <offset>. The pointer points to the variable that is passed as the <value> parameter. The <slen> parameter indicates the size of <structure>. You must pass a variable to the <value> parameter. You cannot pass a constant because the purpose of this function is to store the pointer to the variable in the structure. The variable <value> must remain in scope throughout the life of this structure. The return value indicates the number of bytes written to <structure>.

A few other functions are prototyped in STRUCMEM.JS. They are primarily intended to work with the Unicode version of IntraBuilder released in the Asian markets. Check out the STRUCMEM.JS file itself for information on these functions.

Using the Structure Parsing Library

The addYear() function shown in Listing 19.4 can be modified to use the structure parsing library instead of dissecting the structure itself. The updated version of addYear() is shown in Listing 19.5.

INPUT **Listing 19.5. The structure parser at work in addYear().**

```
 1: #include "strucmem.h"
 2: function addYear (stStruc)
 3: {
 4:    // prototype the structure parsing functions
 5:    _sys.scripts.run(_sys.env.home() + "samples\\strucmem.js");
 6:    // Year is first WORD value in structure
 7:    var year = GetStructNumber(stStruc,0,TYPE_WORD);
 8:    // Update the structure string with the incremented year
 9:    SetStructNumber(stStruc, 0, TYPE_WORD, stStruc.length, ++year);
10:    return (true);
11: }
```

ANALYSIS Line 1 includes the STRUCMEM.H header file. This header defines the type constants used in lines 7 and 9.

Line 5 runs the script that prototypes the parsing functions. This version runs the script in its default location. You can duplicate this in your own script, or you can copy the STRUCMEM.JS and STRUCMEM.DLL files to your application folder. Then you don't need to include a path in line 5.

Line 7 uses the GetStructNumber() function to determine the value stored in the year member. Because year is the first member in the structure, its offset is 0. If you wanted to get the month member, the offset would be SIZEOF_WORD. To get the third member, the offset would be SIZEOF_WORD*2.

Line 9 uses the SetStructNumber() function to store the incremented year value back to stStruc. Again, the offset is 0 and the type is TYPE_WORD.

19

Summary

Today you learned about extending the functionality of the IntraBuilder server through the use of external objects and functions. External objects are accessed through OLE automation. IntraBuilder acts as an OLE automation client, and other applications such as Word, Excel, and OLEnterprise act as OLE automation servers. After an OLE automation object has been created, you use it just like any internal non-visual IntraBuilder object.

External functions are created using another programming tool such as Borland C++ or Delphi. These functions are prototyped in IntraBuilder using the extern command. After the function has been prototyped, you use it just like an IntraBuilder function such as parseInt() or encode(). IntraBuilder supports the basic C data types. When prototyping an external function that uses custom data types, you need to determine the base data types. If the custom data type is a structure, you can use the structure parsing library to manipulate the member values.

Q&A

Q How do I determine the program identifier for an OLE automation server?

A The product documentation should provide this information. If it doesn't, you can check with the product vendor. Another option is to use a tool called the Object Explorer, included with OLEnterprise. This tool lists all of the applications that have registered themselves as OLE servers. You can look for the program identifier and even test whether the server responds to OLE automation commands.

Q Why does the OLE automation example work in the IntraBuilder IDE, but not in the IntraBuilder Server?

A If the payment form does not work in the server, you are probably using IntraBuilder version 1.0. You should get the 1.01 update to get problem-free execution of OLE automation in the server.

Q How many functions are in IntraBuilder?

A There are surprisingly few functions in IntraBuilder. alert(), decode(), encode(), eval(), inspect(), parseFloat(), and parseInt() make up a total of seven.

Q Why is there a discrepancy between the documented name and the actual function names in the Windows API?

A The Windows API supports two different character sets: ANSI and Unicode. Functions that take strings or structures as parameters are implemented twice— once for each character set. The MessageBox() function is actually implemented twice—once as MessageBoxA(), and once as MessageBoxW(). The header files used by the C programmers define the documented name to reference the appropriate function depending on the character set used by the application.

Q Are function prototypes case-sensitive?

A Yes. The function name used in the extern command must exactly match the name of the function in the external program. For instance, you receive an error if you try to prototype a function called MESSAGEBOXA() in USER32.DLL because the case of the function name is incorrect.

Workshop

The Workshop section provides questions and exercises to help you get a better feel for the material you learned today. Try to answer the questions and at least think about the exercises before moving on to tomorrow's lesson. You'll find the answers to the questions in Appendix A, "Answers to Quiz Questions."

Quiz

1. Is IntraBuilder an OLE automation client, server, or both?

2. How do you create an OLE automation object named wrd from an application whose product identifier is word.basic?

3. How are external functions different from IntraBuilder functions?

4. What is the function prototype for MadeUp() in MADEUP.DLL? The function takes a string and a pointer to a long and returns an enumerated constant.

5. What is wrong with this prototype?

```
extern void* SomeOtherFunction(void) "MADEUP.DLL";
```

6. How large is the following LOGBRUSH structure?

```
1: typedef unsigned int   UINT;
2: typedef unsigned long DWORD;
3: typedef long          LONG;
4: typedef DWORD         COLORREF;
5: typedef struct tagLOGBRUSH { // lb
6:    UINT     lbStyle;
7:    COLORREF lbColor;
8:    LONG     lbHatch;
9: } LOGBRUSH;
```

19

Exercises

1. Here is some information from the Windows header files about the MessageBeep() function in the USER32.DLL file. There is also information about four of the symbolic constants that are used for the uType parameter. Using this information and the WINDEF.H header file, write a script that duplicates the symbolic constants, prototypes MessageBeep(), and calls it using the symbolic constant MB_ICONEXLAMATION.

```
#define MB_ICONHAND              0x00000010L
#define MB_ICONQUESTION          0x00000020L
#define MB_ICONEXCLAMATION       0x00000030L
#define MB_ICONASTERISK          0x00000040L
BOOL MessageBeep(
    UINT  uType         // sound type
    );
```

2. The following information comes from the IDAPI.H header file that ships with the Borland Database Engine (BDE). Use this information to prototype the IDAPI32.DLL function DbiGetRecord().

```
 1: #define DBIFN    __stdcall
 2: #define UINT16  unsigned short
 3: #define UINT32  unsigned long
 4: typedef unsigned char  BYTE;
 5: typedef unsigned char  BOOL8;
 6: typedef short      BOOL16;
 7: typedef UINT16     DBIResult;    // Function result
 8: typedef UINT32     hDBIObj;      // Generic handle
 9: typedef hDBIObj    hDBICur;      // Cursor handle
10: typedef BYTE       far *pBYTE;
11: typedef enum                     // Lock types
12: {
13:     dbiNOLOCK        = 0,        // No lock (Default)
14:     dbiWRITELOCK     = 1,        // Write lock
15:     dbiREADLOCK      = 2         // Read lock
16: } DBILockType;
17: typedef struct {
18:         UINT32            iSeqNum;
19:         UINT32            iPhyRecNum;
20:         UINT16            bRecChanged;
21:         BOOL16            bSeqNumChanged;
22:         BOOL16            bDeleteFlag;
23: } RECProps;
24: typedef RECProps far *pRECProps;
25: DBIResult DBIFN DbiGetRecord (
26:     hDBICur           hCursor,
27:     DBILockType       eLock,
28:     pBYTE             pRecBuff,
29:     pRECProps         precProps
30: );
```

Exercises 3 through 5 refer to the following script. You should also refer to the script in exercise 2 to complete these questions.

```
 1: #include "strucmem.h"
 2: // prototype the structure parsing functions
 3: _sys.scripts.run(_sys.env.home() + "samples\\strucmem.js");
 4: // prototype the BDE function
 5: extern unsigned short DbiGetRecord(unsigned long,
 6:                     unsigned int, char*, void*) "idapi32";
 7: // initialize the structure
 8: recprop = new StringEx().replicate(" ",  Ex3  );
 9: // create a query object
10: q=new Query("select * from biolife.dbf");
11: // get the record properties for this record
12: DbiGetRecord(q.rowset.handle, 0,  Ex4  , recprop);
13: // get the physical record number from the structure
14: var recno = GetStructNumber(recprop,  Ex5  , TYPE_ULONG);
15: // display the record number
16: alert("Record Number " + parseInt(recno));
```

3. What value would you use in place of Ex3 on line 8 in the preceding code?

4. The pRecBuff parameter to DbiGetRecord() takes a pointer to a buffer that will contain the record data. Because this script does not use the record data, a null pointer should be used. What value do you use in place of Ex4 on line 12 to pass a null pointer?

5. The record number is contained in the iPhyRecNum member of the RECProps structure. What value should you use in place of Ex5 on line 14? Use one or more of the SIZEOF constants from STRUCMEM.H.

19

Day **20**

Mastering Object-Oriented Programming

by A. A. Katz

Today you'll concentrate on gaining an in-depth understanding of object-oriented programming. In previous days you've used these concepts to build forms and applications. However, to take advantage of the remarkable productivity offered by object-oriented programming, you'll need to get truly comfortable with the terminology and concepts that power IntraBuilder's OOP language.

JavaScript, as originally conceived by Netscape, is an object-based (not object-oriented) language. In client-side JavaScript you can use and manipulate existing objects, but you can't create new objects nor derive objects from existing ones. These limitations are imposed by JavaScript's design as a browser-based HTML language. There's just no place to build or store a sophisticated library of custom objects.

Because IntraBuilder runs on the server, it doesn't suffer from the same limitations. Borland has equipped it with a robust, fully object-oriented language whose innate reusability can cut your programming time by half—or more.

Let's start with the three main characteristics that define a truly object-oriented language such as IntraBuilder JavaScript: encapsulation, inheritance, and polymorphism.

Encapsulation

All true objects must be encapsulated. They should be self-sufficient, self-contained, and totally protected from any other object. Encapsulation is a common-sense issue. You can't have a button on one form accidentally show up on three others. You can't have data entered into one input form leak onto another. All the data within a form is encapsulated by the form, and contained and protected from all other objects. Without encapsulation, you can't even have more than one button in an application. Imagine clicking one button on a form and having all buttons fire! Though they share the same form, each button is totally encapsulated from every other button. That doesn't mean that they're not visible or addressable. They are. But changes made to one button do not impact any of the others.

 TIP

> When you design your IntraBuilder programs, give serious thought to encapsulation. The rules have changed. In procedural programming, it was considered a sin to code a function more than once. In object-oriented programming, every stand-alone function creates one more external dependency, one more breach in your wall of encapsulation. At certain times (particularly with large reusable functions), you will want to use callable non-class functions because they're too complex or too reusable to paste into every form that requires them. Just remember that any object that uses external functions is that much less portable than one that doesn't!

Inheritance

Inheritance is the characteristic that provides the most benefit in object-oriented programming. In the past, you reused code as much as possible. Most of us built huge shared function libraries. Although they saved a good deal of typing, they had a major drawback: Their reusability was severely restricted. To adapt a function for a new use, you had to rewrite the function with special tests for the new use or copy the code to create an entirely new function.

Rewriting a long-working function requires a whole new test cycle, and not just for the code that's been changed. You've got to test the rewritten code against legacy applications in which the original function was used in order to be sure you haven't broken anything. Copying code to adapt for a new use loses most of the benefits of a function library. Every time you make a change (or correct an error), you have to find every far-flung copy of the function and make the changes over and over again.

Inheritance, on the other hand, lets you reuse an object without touching the original code. All of the characteristics of any object are brought forward to its child, its grandchildren— to all the generations derived from it. The parent object contributes all its attributes and behavior to each succeeding generation, yet remains an independent entity.

What a huge improvement over the old function library! You can create an entirely new use for an object without risking any legacy uses. You don't copy any code; in fact, you only code the attributes and behaviors that have changed.

As in human inheritance, characteristics are not just inherited from the prime predecessor, but they can also be obtained from any of the generations between. A child can inherit blue eyes from a parent, even though the grandparent's eyes were brown. The same is true for JavaScript objects. Each object you create through inheritance can stand as the parent of your next level of inheritance. Figure 20.1 shows the different levels of inheritance.

Figure 20.1.

Deriving custom button classes.

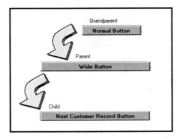

In Figure 20.1, Wide Button inherits all the attributes and behaviors of Normal Button: 3-D, gray background, black HTML, and clicks when pressed. The only attribute that has changed is the width of the button. You now have two objects: Normal Button and Wide Button.

The Next Customer Record Button is derived from Wide Button. It inherits all the characteristics of Wide Button, including its width, as well as all the characteristics of Normal Button not overridden in Wide Button. This new object includes a method to move the rowset forward one row in the Customer table. It has behavior new to its own generation.

Keep in mind that although two of these buttons inherited characteristics from their forebears, they remain totally independent entities. If you were to try to change the width of

20

the Next Customer Record Button, it would be that button's width you're changing, not the width of the Wide Button from which it is derived. You would be accurate if you thought of inherited characteristics as defaults—because they are.

NEW TERM Three terms are used when discussing inheritance. An object created through inheritance from another object is said to be *derived* from its parent object. A derived class is called a *subclass*. The parent class is called a *superclass*. In the following class declaration, MyCustomForm is derived from Form, MyCustomForm is a subclass of Form, and Form is the superclass of MyCustomForm:

```
class MyCustomForm extends Form
```

TIP

> You've already encountered one of the biggest benefits of inheritance when you created your custom form class. Because objects are derived on-the-fly in IntraBuilder, any change made to the parent, grandparent, or any previous generation will be carried through automatically to the current object. Inheritance makes global changes incredibly simple. If, for example, you change your logo or a toolbar menu used on all of your forms, you need to change only the property at the highest level, and that change will trickle down to all objects derived from it and its descendants.

Polymorphism

Polymorphism (which means, literally, *many shapes*) is the ability of objects to alter inherited behavior. Let's take automobiles and helicopters as an example. Assume that you already have defined an automobile object and you want to create a helicopter object. Many attributes and behaviors of an automobile are applicable to a helicopter. Sounds like a good case for inheritance. (You wouldn't have to write much code to describe the differences.) Unfortunately, the differences between helicopters and automobiles are not just attributes, but behaviors as well. Automobiles start, but helicopters take off. Polymorphism lets you take the start behavior of automobile and morph it into the take-off behavior of helicopters without having to create a whole new entity from scratch.

In IntraBuilder, polymorphism is accomplished by giving you the ability to override an inherited behavior. The same start behavior that turns over the engine in an automobile can be overridden in the child helicopter object. Telling the object to start means something entirely different in the child than it did in the parent. Polymorphism gives you increased flexibility to base objects on other objects that might not, at first, appear to be a perfect fit.

What's an Object?

Now that you've learned about the characteristics of objects, you should probably learn their definition. Although objects are more easily described than defined, I don't think it would be too far off to say that an object is a self-contained entity that has built-in attributes and behaviors. An automobile is an object. It has attributes: length, height, width, body style, color, and weight. It has behaviors: start, go forward, go backward, accelerate, decelerate, and stop.

An IntraBuilder form object has attributes and behaviors not all that dissimilar to an automobile object. It has height, width, and color. It opens, closes, and releases.

 Property is the programming term for an attribute of an object. *Method* is the programming term for the behavior of an object.

Properties

The attributes of any object are variables. The `color` property of a control can be selected from any number of predefined colors. Listing 20.1 shows how to set property values using a `with` block.

INPUT

Listing 20.1. Creating an HTML control and setting properties in a `with` block.

```
1: with (this.html1 = new HTML(this)){
2:     height = 1;
3:     left = 17;
4:     top = 2;
5:     width = 10;
6:     color = "black";
7:     text = "<H2>Hello</H2>";
8: }
```

ANALYSIS The `with` block in Listing 20.1 creates an HTML control and sets several properties. Line 2 sets the `height` property to 1. Just like procedural variables, properties can have any value assigned to them within an acceptable range. An error would occur if line 4 tried to set the `top` property to a date value.

NOTE You can find source files for each listing in the Day 20 folder on the CD-ROM. The listings in this chapter are script files. The naming convention for the scripts works as follows: Listing 20.1 is `l20_1.js`, Listing 20.2 is `l20_2.js`, and so on.

20

The difference between properties and variables is that properties are attached to their parent object and are only visible from within the object itself. For all intents and purposes, properties are static variables scoped to an object.

Methods

The behavior of an object is defined the way behavior has always been defined in programming languages—as functions. Just as a variable becomes a property when it's attached to its parent object, functions that define the behavior of the object become methods. Listing 20.2 shows how to create a Form_onServerSubmit() method within a class. Also like properties, methods are both attached to and visible only through their parent objects. Methods are static functions scoped to an object.

INPUT

Listing 20.2. A form class definition containing a single method.

```
1: class TestForm extends Form {
2:    with (this) {
3:       height = 20;
4:       left = 36;
5:       top = 6;
6:       width = 60;
7:       title = "";
8:    }
9:
10:    function Form_onServerSubmit() // a method of TestForm
11:    {
12:     if ( this.hiddenAction.value == "LOOKUP" ) {
13:       _sys.forms.run( "LOOKUP", parseInt( this.hiddenMsg.value ) );
14:     }
15:    }
16: }
17:
18: function Hello()
19: {
20:    alert("Hello World") ;
21: }
```

ANALYSIS   A function becomes a method just by being included within a class block. Lines 10 through 14 define the Form_onServerSubmit() function as a method of the TestForm class. Line 16 ends the class block. Any functions defined after line 16 are not methods. Lines 18 through 21 define a Hello() function that is not a method.

NEW TERM   Methods that are called automatically in response to built-in events are called *event handlers*. Because you neither run nor call these methods, they are said to be *fired* when IntraBuilder automatically runs them. The onServerLoad event-handler is fired when the application is loaded at the server.

Events and Function Pointers

As I'm sure you realize by now, events are triggers that fire under certain predetermined circumstances. But you might not realize that events are also properties. The onServerLoad event is a *property* of all IntraBuilder form controls. It's not a method; it doesn't *run*. It just tells the form where to find the code to fire when onServerLoad is triggered. It points to a method that contains the actual behavior you expect the object to execute.

That wouldn't be possible without function pointers. Like all other pointers (including variables and properties), function pointers contain the address of something else—in this case, code to be executed when a function is *called*. All methods and functions in IntraBuilder automatically generate a function pointer in memory by storing their address to an internal variable with the same name as the function. Just as form.MyFirstName contains the address of John, MyFunction contains the address in memory where the function MyFunction code is located.

```
function MyFunction()    // Generates Function Pointer MyFunction
(
   return ("Hello") ;
}
```

Because a function pointer contains the address of the object and not the executing code itself, it can be stored to another property, passed as a parameter, or overridden by another function pointer with the same name just like variables and properties.

```
form.Function2(form.MyFunction)    \\Send FP as parameter

form.Function2 = form.MyFunction   \\Store FP to another property

function MyFunction()              \\ Override with another method
{
   return 'Good-Bye' ;
}
```

WARNING

You cannot send parameters to a function pointer any more than you can send parameters to a variable or property. Parameters can be sent only at runtime, when a function pointer is executed. Therefore, if you want an event to trigger a method with parameters, assign a code block instead of a function pointer to the event. The following statement does not create a function pointer:

```
onServerLoad = CLASS::MyFunction("Hello")
```

You can use a code block to pass parameters as follows:

```
onServerLoad = { ; form.MyFunction("Hello") }
```

20

To get a function pointer to execute its code, just add parentheses after the function pointer name: `form.MyFunction()`.

Classes

Although by now you're familiar with classes, because they are the cornerstone of IntraBuilder's server-side JavaScript, they probably merit a closer look.

Classes are the blueprint from which objects are created. IntraBuilder has a real-time object model. The actual working objects don't exist at design time. They are created at runtime as required from the plan described in the class.

NEW TERM An *instance* of a class is a single object created from a class blueprint. Using the same class, you can create a virtually unlimited number of *instances* just as you can build any number of houses from the same plans. Each button on a form is another instance of the `Button` class. Object and instance are synonyms. The process of creating an object (or instance) from a class is called *instantiation*.

Borland's implementation of classes is interesting. Although some of the class code that defines an object executes, it doesn't execute when the disk file is run. That's an important distinction. Call a function, and it executes; run a script, and it executes. That is, until it sees the keyword class, at which time it returns without running the class code.

That's because classes have to be instantiated, not called or run. Remember that classes are not executable; they are not functions, nor are they methods. A class is just a blueprint. The class code is executed only when you call the new operator. The following statement uses the new operator to create an instance of the `TestForm` class:

```
var f = new TestForm() ;
```

The class constructor runs only until it encounters the first method (or the end of the class block, whichever comes first) and then stops. This is part of IntraBuilder's dynamic object model. Listing 20.3 shows the class constructor of a simple IntraBuilder `.jfm` file.

INPUT **Listing 20.3. The structure of the `.jfm` file.**

```
1:  // {End Header} Do not remove this comment//
2:  // Generated on 02/21/97
3:  //
4:
5:  var f = new testForm();
6:  f.open();
7:
8:  class testForm extends Form {
9:    with (this) {
10:      height = 20;
```

20

```
11:        left = 32;
12:        top = 0;
13:        width = 60;
14:        title = "";
15:    }
16:
17:    with (this.button1 = new Button(this)){
18:        left = 38;
19:        top = 3.5;
20:        width = 10.5;
21:        text = "OK";
22:        onClick = class::button1_onClick;
23:    }
24:
25:    with (this.checkbox1 = new CheckBox(this)){
26:        height = 1.2
27:        left = 38;
28:        top = 5.5;
29:        width = 15;
30:        text = "Save Data";
31:        checked = false;
32:    }
33:
34:    with (this.hidden1 = new Hidden(this)){
35:        left = 38;
36:        top = 8;
37:        value = "";
38:    }
39:
40:    function button1_onClick()
41:    {
42:      if ( form.checkbox1.checked ) {
43:        form.hidden1.value = 'SAVE';
44:      }
45:    }
46
47:}  // This is the end of the Class block.
```

ANALYSIS In Listing 20.3, five areas of the .jfm are indicated, and each area has its own use, execution rules, and *streaming* rules for the design tools. Lines 1 through 3 signify the end of the header. Any lines you add above line 1 are part of the header. Lines 5 and 6 are the bootstrap section. The constructor spans from lines 8 through 38. The constructor ends with the first method definition on line 40. The methods section is from lines 40 through 46. Any lines you add after line 47 reside in the general area.

NEW TERM *Streaming* refers to the process of code generation by the IntraBuilder design tools. Whenever you save a form in the Form Designer, IntraBuilder *streams* out brand new source code based on the visual components, properties, and methods you designed using the visual tools. Streaming is of particular concern because the new source code generated can overwrite your own code if you're not careful.

20

The following list describes each area of a JavaScript source file. As you read through each item, note how the sections differ by execution requirements. That is, some sections must execute for a form to open, while others are optional.

- **Header area:** If you use _sys.forms.run() to load your forms, this is a convenient place to put any code that you want to execute before the form is instantiated.

  On the other hand, if you don't use _sys.forms.run() to load your forms, this area can be very useful for design-time–only code. You might be setting up your environment, #including other scripts, loading .DLLs, or initializing global variables at the startup of your program. However, when you design and test from within the Form Designer, your startup code might not be available to the form you're working on. The Header area of the .jfm is a handy place to store this code.

  Code that you put in the Header area executes only if you explicitly call the .jfm with _sys.forms.run() (or if you run your form from the IntraBuilder Explorer).

  IntraBuilder does not overwrite code written in the Header area of the .jfm.

- **Bootstrap:** The bootstrap creates an instance of the form class. It executes when you call _sys.forms.run() or launch a form from the IntraBuilder Explorer. This code is streamed every time a form is saved, so you cannot write any of your own code in this section.

- **Constructor:** The constructor defines the form and its components. It executes when you create an instance of the class using the new operator.

  Any executable source code or custom properties that you write in this area will be overwritten when IntraBuilder streams out the code for the form. However, you can write or change any of the built-in properties and their values with impunity. IntraBuilder will not overwrite them.

- **Method area:** Any functions written in this area become methods attached to the form class and are encapsulated within the method area. Methods in this section can be called directly or executed when a linked event fires.

  IntraBuilder will not overwrite any code that you write in this section. However, any changes made in the IntraBuilder Method Editor will be streamed out when the form is saved.

- **General area:** You can use this area for defining functions outside the class. Functions written in this area execute when they are explicitly called. IntraBuilder will not overwrite any code in this section.

NEW TERM IntraBuilder provides two keywords for use with classes to implement polymorphism: class:: and super::. The class:: and super:: operators are called *scope resolution operators*, which is just a fancy way of saying that these powerful keywords specify which class's method you're addressing. The class:: operator means that you should look in this class (the subclass) for the method. The super:: operator tells IntraBuilder to look in the parent (or superclass) for the method. In addition to the built-in keywords, you can also

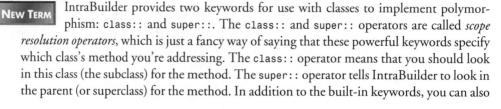

use any object reference variable (see following sections) as a scope resolution operator by adding the scope resolution symbol, the double colon, like this: `form.nextform::open()`. Scope resolution operators work only with methods, not with properties.

You'll remember from the beginning of today's discussion that IntraBuilder implements polymorphism by overriding methods. As a result, you can have an `onServerLoad` method of the subclass that's totally different from the `onServerLoad` method of the superclass. Overriding a method doesn't destroy the original. It leaves it both intact and accessible. There will come a time when you'll want the choice of accessing the superclass `onServerLoad` or the subclass `onServerLoad`. The scope resolution operators help you specify which one you want to execute.

One important use of overridden methods is to replace built-in methods with your own. A good example is `Form::open()`. IntraBuilder has no `PreOpen` or `Init` method, so what do you do if you need to set a property before the form opens? You override the built-in `Form::open()` method with one of your own. Then, when your method has done its work, you use the scope resolution operators to invoke the built-in open method of the `Form` superclass. Listing 20.4 shows an example of overriding the `Form::open()` method in order to set a date in real time.

INPUT   **Listing 20.4. Using `super::` to override a method.**

```
 1: // {End Header} Do not remove this comment//
 2: // Generated on 02/21/97
 3: //
 4: var f = new SuperForm();
 5: f.open();
 6: class SuperForm extends Form {
 7:    with (this) {
 8:        height = 20;
 9:        left = 0;
10:        top = 0;
11:        width = 60;
12:        title = "Super";
13:    }
14:
15:    with (this.html1 = new HTML(this)){
16:       height = 1.2;
17:       left = 16;
18:       top = 5;
19:       width = 10;
20:       color = "black";
21:       text = "Text1";
22:    }
23:    function open()  // overrides form's open() method
24:    {
25:     form.html1.text =  new Date().toLocaleString().substring(0,8);
26:     super::open(); // now invoke the superclass open()
27:    }
28: }
```

20

ANALYSIS   In Listing 20.4, check out function open() on line 23. Declaring this function within
a subclass (in this case, SuperForm) causes IntraBuilder to override the built-in open()
method (from class Form) with yours. However, the superclass open() method still exists and
is still accessible. In line 25 you set the html1.text property to the current date, and in line
26 you call super::open() to activate the form. This code allows you to create your own pre-
open type of event, setting properties before the form is activated.

Classes of Classes

IntraBuilder supports five distinct types of classes, each of which has a distinct source code
file format:

☐ **Standard classes:** Built-in classes, such as Form, Button, and HTML are called standard classes. You use them by creating subclasses. (Class MyCustomform extends
Form.) They can be used in either script files (.jpg) or, in the case of the Form class,
in a .jfm file.

☐ **Base class (custom form classes):** Base classes are the superclass forms you create
to use as templates for your forms. You can select a base class through the File|Set
Custom Form Class menu option in the Form Designer. Each time you create a
new form, it is derived from your base class. Base form classes are stored in a .jfm
file. They do not execute. They are used solely as the template from which to derive
new forms.

☐ **Custom controls:** Custom controls are classes you create from standard classes for
reuse across forms and applications. Examples are custom buttons, HTML classes,
and so on. They are normally stored in a custom control (.cc) format.

☐ **From scratch classes:** You can write your own classes from scratch using the
simple syntax Class Classname. You can define their properties and methods
(although there's no mechanism for creating events that fire automatically). From-
scratch classes are excellent for utilities, processing code, or any non-visual component you create. These are also usually stored in .cc (custom control) files. Listing
20.5 shows an example of a from scratch class with a method that returns the
current time in military format.

INPUT   **Listing 20.5. A from-scratch class.**

```
1: class Time {
2:    function MilTime()  // returns current time as military time
3:    {
4:       this.dDate = new Date();
5:       this.hour = ''+this.dDate.hour;
6:       this.minute = ''+this.dDate.minute;
7:       if (this.minute.length == 1) {
```

```
 8:            this.minute = '0'+this.minute;
 9:       }
10:      if (this.hour.length == 1){
11:          this.hour = '0'+this.hour;
12:       }
13:      return  this.hour+':'+this.minute;
14:    }
15:    function AmPmTime()  // returns current time as Am/Pm format
16:    {
17:      this.cDate = new Date().toLocaleString();
18:      return this.cDate.substring(9,14)+' '+this.cDate.substring(18,20);
19:    }
20: }
```

ANALYSIS Listing 20.5 is an example of a simple from-scratch class. The Time class's MilTime() method (in line 2) converts the current time to military time (23:30). The AmPmTime() method (in line 15) converts the current time to AM/PM format. This kind of utility is a perfect candidate for a from-scratch class. It has no visual elements, but the code is highly reusable.

Although each type of class sports its own file extension, you are not restricted to the specified file type. In fact, all of the source file types are nothing more than scripts. How IntraBuilder treats each type depends on the contents, not on the extension. However, having the various extensions makes organizing your work much easier and allows the IntraBuilder Explorer to find appropriate files for each tab.

WARNING

> You cannot add parameters to standard classes, just like you cannot add parameters to any built-in method. The standard class Form takes only a single parameter: title. Check IntraBuilder's online help for each class for the parameters that the standard class accepts.

Instantiation

20

Instantiation is the process of creating an instance—an actual working object—from the specifications of its class. There's really only one way of launching an object in IntraBuilder, and that's using the new operator.

When you instantiate an object, IntraBuilder returns the address of the object to a variable, property, or array element. (See the "Object References in Variables" section, later in this chapter.) Follow these three basic steps to create and access an object:

1. Load code into memory. The source code for the class must be loaded into memory before you can derive an object from the class. There are three methods

for loading source code from a disk file. You can tell IntraBuilder to load a JavaScript file into memory with the `_sys.scripts.load()` method. You can `#include` a file within another, which loads both when the first one is loaded. When you run a form using `_sys.forms.run()`, IntraBuilder automatically loads the `.jfm` script.

2. Create an instance (instantiate) using the `new` operator, like this:

```
var f = new MyObject() ;
```

3. Activate or access the object. If the object is a form, calling its `open()` method activates the form. Or the object might not have any visual components, in which case you can read and write properties or execute its methods as soon as the object is instantiated.

This multi-step process for creating objects from classes is the core of IntraBuilder's dynamic object model. Older object-oriented environments stored static objects in binary format. The values of properties could be changed after the objects were instantiated, but new properties and methods couldn't be added. In a dynamic object model, you can easily add custom methods or properties as soon as the object has been instantiated—before it has been activated or used.

Although some OOP purists claim that this violates the rules of encapsulation (and it does, to some extent), the benefits of dynamic objects far outweigh any disadvantages. If you want to add a simple property to a single instance of a form, you don't have to create a whole new class; just add the property dynamically. It saves the overhead of loading a new disk file plus the handles associated with an additional class and its components. The same is true for methods. You might want one single instance of a maintenance form to perform one single action for this particular application. No problem. Just add a new method to the form after it has been instantiated, and the method will work exactly as it would if it had been included in the original class. Listing 20.6 shows how to add a property and a method to an existing form instance.

INPUT   ## Listing 20.6. Dynamic properties and methods.

```
1: function CallMyForm()
2: {
3:     _sys.scripts.load('My.Jfm');
4:     form.MyForm = new MyForm();
5:     form.MyForm.User = form.User; //create custom property
6:     form.MyForm.Form_onServerLoad = class::Form_onServerLoad;
7:     form.MyForm.open()
8: }
```

ANALYSIS   Listing 20.6 assumes that you're launching a second form from within one that is already open. Line 3 loads the new form's class script (`.jfm`) into memory. Line 4 instantiates, storing the form's address in a custom property of the first form, `form.MyForm`.

Then, before opening the second form, line 5 adds a custom property to the second form. Line 6 adds a new method to the second form that wasn't in its original class definition— the same method you are using on the original form.

TIP

> It takes some experience to determine what works well as a class or dynamically. If there is any possibility of reuse, create a new subclass. If you need only a single instance of the object to be changed for a single application, the dynamic model of creating properties and assigning methods can be very useful. Another major use is tools. One example is an application manager class—a class that automates instantiation and controls your application. This manager class might need to add a new identification property to each form it opens. Without the dynamic object model, you would have to add this property to every form in your library.

Managing the Object Reference

You can't master object-oriented programming without mastering the object reference. This *handle*—a variable, property, or array element that contains the address of an object—is absolutely key to managing your objects.

As you become more experienced writing IntraBuilder applications, you'll find that you need to access objects from within other objects. This talk between objects is called *interprocess communication*. Interprocess communication can be as simple as instantiating a simple business class and setting properties, or as complex as stringing forms together to build your application. In any case, the object reference is the handle you use to identify each object.

Therefore, where you store your object references can be critical. Variables, properties, and arrays all have scope. Depending on where and when they are declared, and whether they're attached to objects, they might be visible at some times and invisible at others. In the case of variables, they can disappear entirely.

Let's look at the instantiation code that the IntraBuilder Form Designer streams out for each form:

```
var f = new MyCustomForm()
```

IntraBuilder declares a variable, f, in which it stores the address of this instance of MyCustomForm(). If you plan to ever address this form from anywhere except within the form itself, this code won't work. The variable f only exists for the few milliseconds in which instantiation takes place and then goes out of scope. The minute the object has been fully created in memory, f no longer exists, leaving no way to identify this form from anywhere else in your application!

WARNING

> Because variable f has no scope outside of the instantiation process itself, it is highly recommended that you don't launch your forms using _sys.forms.run(), which executes the Form Designer's bootstrap code. This built-in instantiation (and, for that matter, the ability to run a .jfm) was designed strictly for development and testing purposes—for launching forms from the IntraBuilder Explorer or the Script Pad. It was never intended that you should run a .jfm from within a program—unless your program is so simple that no form or object needs to talk to any other form or object.
>
> Instead of _sys.forms.run(), use the multi-step process of loading the .jfm into memory (_sys.scripts.load()), and then instantiate the object yourself using the new operator. This approach gives you more control over your objects and lets you determine what will be in memory at any given point, rather than relying on IntraBuilder.

So where should you store object references? There are several solutions, depending on circumstances.

Object References in Variables

Variables should be used only for quick-and-dirty instantiation. In object-oriented languages, the scope of variables is so limited (within a method or function) that they're difficult to manage and useless for interprocess communication.

Object References in Properties

A property can be an excellent place to store your object reference. However, once again, you have to be careful about scope. Don't store an object reference in another object that's about to be released. Properties are an excellent way to chain your forms together in an application, as shown in Listing 20.7.

INPUT   **Listing 20.7. Instantiating into a form property.**

```
1: function LookupButton_onClick()
2: {
3:    _sys.scripts.load("Lookup.Jfm");
```

20

```
4:    form.Lookup = new LookupForm();
5:    form.Lookup.HTML1.text = form.UserName;
6:    form.Lookup.open();
7: }
```

ANALYSIS Line 4 instantiates class `LookupForm` into a custom property of the current form, `form.Lookup`. Using that object reference, you set the value of a property in `LookupForm` based on the value of the `UserName` property in the current form. By using this method for tying your forms together, you can easily pass data along from form to form as they are launched.

Object References in System Properties

In the previous example, you stored the object reference in a property of a form. The limitation to that style of instantiation is the scope of the property: It cannot be seen from any other form or procedure outside of the form, except using the form's own object reference. So, where can you store an object reference that is visible to every object and function in your IntraBuilder application? You store it in a custom property of the global `_sys` object. Listing 20.8 shows how to add a property to the `_sys` object.

INPUT **Listing 20.8. Instantiating into a `Custom` `_sys` property.**

```
1: function LookupButton_onClick()
2: {
3:    _sys.scripts.load("Lookup.Jfm");
4:    _sys.Lookup = new LookupForm();
5:    _sys.Lookup.HTML1.text = form.UserName;
6:    _sys.Lookup.open();
7: }
```

ANALYSIS Listing 20.8 is almost identical to Listing 20.7, except that the object reference for this instance of `LookupForm` is stored in a custom property (which is created in line 4 during instantiation) attached to the built-in global `_sys` object. What is the advantage? Every object and function can see and address this property. The disadvantage is that the form can only be opened once into this property; a new form will overwrite an existing one.

20

Object References in Arrays

Array objects give you the most flexibility for managing object references. Because you can add new elements as needed or reuse empty ones, arrays don't suffer from some of the scoping and overriding issues of variables and properties. Furthermore, as classes, you can imbed management code to instantiate, open, and close forms right in the array class itself. Listing 20.9 shows how to create a global array.

INPUT **Listing 20.9. Instantiating into a global array object.**

```
 1: function LookupButton_onClick()
 2: {
 3:     _sys.scripts.load("Lookup.Jfm");
 4:     _sys.scripts.load("Form2.Jfm");
 5:     _sys.aManager = new Array(1);
 6:     n1 = _sys.aManager.length-1;
 7:     _sys.aManager[n1] = new LookupForm();
 8:     _sys.aManager.add(1);
 9:     n2 = _sys.aManager.add(1)-1;
10:     _sys.aManager[n1].open();
11: }
```

ANALYSIS   Listing 20.9 pre-instantiated two different form classes (LookupForm and Form2Form), stored their references in two different elements of a global array (_sys.aManager), and opened only one of the forms. Note that you used add()-1 as the array subscript to identify your forms. The call to aManager.add() on line 5 returns the total number of elements in this one-dimensional array. But array subscripts start at 0, not at 1. Hence, if add() returns 1 (one element), the subscript for that element is 0 (the first element in an array object). Therefore, you use add()-1 to identify each form.

> **TIP**
>
> Pre-instantiation (or creating instances before you need them) brings possible performance advantages. The process of dynamically building a form from its class involves significant overhead. Depending on how many forms you have and how complex they are, it's sometimes advisable to instantiate your forms all at once at the beginning of your IntraBuilder program. Your initial program will load a bit slower (because there's more for the Agent to do), and it uses more memory, but subsequent form openings should be considerably faster.

Using array assignments for object references, you can build an automatic form manager that cuts out a lot of the coding required to instantiate and open forms. Listing 20.10 shows an example of a form manager. It is included on this book's CD as Manager.cc in the Day 20 folder.

INPUT   **Listing 20.10. Manager.cc: A rudimentary form manager.**

```
1: class Manager extends Array() {
2:     function Instance(cFileName)
3:     {
4:         cClassName = cFileName.substring(0,cFileName.indexOf('.'))+'Form';
5:         n = this.add(1)-1;
6:         _sys.scripts.load(cFileName);
```

```
7:          eval("this[n] = new "+cClassName+"()");
8:          return n;
9:       }
10:      function Open(cFileName)
11:      {
12:         n = this.Instance(cFileName);
13:         this[n].open();
14:         return n;
15:      }
16: }
```

ANALYSIS   Listing 20.10 defines a simple, two-method form management class. The `Instance()` method loads the form's source file into memory (in line 6), adds a new element to this global array object (in line 5), and instantiates your form, storing its object reference in the new array element (in line 7). Note that you used the `eval()` function to execute an expression with the new operator. The `eval()` function evaluates an expression much like the macro-interpreters of some other languages. Because you cannot hard-wire a classname as in `f = New MyCustomForm()`, you need to use `eval()` to expand the `Classname` variable. When the expression on line 7 (the instantiation) is evaluated, it is also executed.

The `Open()` method both instantiates and opens the form. If you call `_sys.Manager.Open()`, you don't have to call `Instance()`.

`MANAGER.CC` should be instantiated at the beginning of your program, either in a startup script or in the header of your first form. It only takes two lines of code:

```
_sys.scripts.load('Manager.Cc');
_sys.Manager = New Manager();
```

Then, instead of using the built-in object management keywords, you use the methods of this custom array class to instantiate forms. The simplest way is to call its `Open()` method:

```
n = sys.Manager.Open('test.jfm');
_sys.Manager[n].release();
```

A call to the `Open()` method is all that's needed to open a form using `MANAGER.CC`. The call to `release()` demonstrates that you can reference a form opened in `MANAGER.CC` using the subscript n.

This simple version of the Form Manager assumes that you're not changing the class names generated automatically by the Form Designer. `MANAGER.CC` obtains the form's class name from the source filename (the name you saved it as) plus the word `form`. So, `Test.Jfm` usually has a class name of `testForm`. Because JavaScript is case-sensitive, be sure to use lowercase only when sending the filename to methods. Or, you can update `MANAGER.CC` to force the parameter `cFileName` to lowercase.

```
n = _sys.Manager.Instance("test.jfm");
_sys.Manager[n].UserName = form.UserName;
_sys.Manager[n].open();
```

This code uses the form manager to open the test form. Before the form opens, a custom property is added. The first line calls the form manager, the second line creates a custom form property, and the last line opens the form.

WARNING

> The _sys object is global only to a single IntraBuilder Agent. When you are running applications with more than one IntraBuilder Agent, you cannot share information through the _sys object.

Getting Rid of an Object

Getting rid of an object might not be as simple as you think. A number of the IntraBuilder standard classes include a `release()` method to inactivate the object and remove it from memory. However, some objects don't have explicit `release()` methods, and your custom from-scratch classes won't have release methods. However, you can ensure that objects don't linger past their time by controlling their object references.

IntraBuilder does reference-counting. Each time you open a form, a counter is incremented for that particular instance. Each time you store the object reference to another variable, the counter is also incremented.

```
var f = new testForm();   //counter = 1
var n = f;                //counter = 2
form.oForm = f;           //counter = 3
form.oForm.release();     //counter = 2
```

You'll note that the counter never gets down to 0, which means that your form remains in memory, even though it was explicitly released. This can cause havoc in your applications. The solution is to be sure to eliminate each and every reference. This can be done in a variety of ways:

- **Calling `Form::release()`.** Calling `oForm.release()` removes a single reference.
- **Reassigning the reference to a `null` value.** This stubs out the reference by changing its type, and looks like this:

  ```
  oForm = null
  ```

- **Losing scope.** References stored in variables can be removed by letting them go out of scope. When the method in which it was declared completes execution, the method's variables no longer exist. When the variable goes out of scope, the reference counter is automatically decremented.

  ```
  _sys.scripts.load("Lookup.Jfm");
  f = new LookupForm();  // counter increments by 1
  f.open(); // f goes out of scope, counter decrements by 1
  ```

20

Internal Object References

In addition to the external object reference that results from calling the new operator, IntraBuilder sports two internal object references that are generated and managed automatically.

Each form has its own internal object reference stored in an internally generated variable called form. There are two reasons for having a generic reference variable. First, it makes sure you don't orphan a form when you stub out external references without releasing the form; and second, it provides a wonderful generic variable that can be passed and referenced by any object or method on the form. Here are some examples:

```
form.height = 20;    // reference a property

form.close();        // call a method

f = new MyForm()
f.oParent = form     // sent to another form as a property
f.update(form)       // sent to a method as a parameter
```

The form reference is identical to the external reference and can be used in the same way any external object reference is used, with one exception. It can only be used from within the form.

The other object reference generated automatically is this. The this reference points to the current object. In other words, whereas form always refers to a single object (the form itself), this is a moving target. During instantiation, this refers to the class itself, as shown in the following constructor code:

```
class TestForm extends Form {
    with (this) {
    height = 20;
    left = 32;
    top = 3;
}
```

In this code, the this reference refers to the form. In the following code, this is sent as a parameter to a constructor of the Text class:

```
with (this.text1 = new Text(this)){
    left = 8;
    top = 5;
    onChange = class::text1_onChange;
}
```

Within an event-handler method (such as text1_OnChange), this refers to the object that called this method. In the following method, this refers to the object that called text1_onChange—in this case, form.text1:

```
function text1_onChange()
{
    this.value = this.value.toUpperCase()
}
```

20

It's important to note, however that `text1_OnChange()` could have been called by any object. Its function pointer could have been assigned to any event. The object that `this` references will be entirely different depending on which one called this procedure when its event fired.

The `form` and `this` references are important as generic variables for building black-box classes. If you want to create a thoroughly reusable class that can respond to any object, you can use `this` in place of the actual reference (such as `form.Text1`) in your methods. Then you can use the same method regardless of the object that calls it, which is more elegant OOP design.

Containership

IntraBuilder supports several containers, including the `Form` class, `Query` class, and `Report` class. Containers are objects that can contain other objects. A form contains `HTML` objects, `Button` objects, and `Java` objects, among others. The form is said to be the parent of those contained objects. Each object has a read-only parent property that points to the next container up in the hierarchy.

When you need to generically reference the container of a reusable class, use the built-in parent variable, like this:

```
this.text1.value = this.parent.text1.value
```

Don't let all these hierarchies confuse you. I talk an awful lot about parent/child in object-oriented programming, but I'm not necessarily talking about the same things all the time. It makes sense because inheritance is such a key feature of OOP. Sometimes superclasses are referred to as parents, or a form that calls another form is called a parent. However, containership is not inheritance, although it relies on a similar metaphor. The only true parent property in JavaScript is the one that identifies the container of a given object.

Building an Object Library

The fundamental goals of object-oriented programming are to build powerful applications in which you hand-code only unique business rules; to deploy robust, full-featured, bug-free programs in weeks instead of months; and lastly to make software development easier, faster, and cleaner with the more applications you ship.

In fact, that's the power that IntraBuilder brings to Internet/intranet development. Its elegant object model and easy-to-use Rapid Application Development tools are designed to revolutionize the way you create software. But they're only as valuable as your knowledge of them and your willingness to use them. To turn this fantasy into a competitive advantage, you have to stop thinking of functions and `.jfms` as the basis of your application design, and start thinking about objects as the building blocks of a new and better *component architecture*.

Generation by generation, programming languages have become less and less granular. From assembler (with its voluminous low-level instructions) to today's sophisticated object-oriented development platforms (such as IntraBuilder), the clear trend is toward building more powerful applications from fewer components. Productivity is about *leverage*, deriving greater output from less effort. Instead of writing each application with line after line of code, your goal should be to build a robust, high-level object library—to drag and drop your future applications, not write, run, and debug them.

Objects or Functions?

When should you write functions? Probably never. There is nothing you can write as a function that you can't write as a method of a class. Starting right now, at Day 20, everything you write should be a class. You can't inherit a function. You can't easily adapt a function—and if you do, you might find that you've broken a slew of legacy code. Inheritance poses no such risk.

Instead of thinking of your applications as flowcharts, think of your applications as having sockets. Analyze your project before you build it. Take apart each functionality you plan to implement and designate it as a *socket*, a place where you can plug in a reusable class. Then, see how many of the sockets you can fill by existing classes. When that is done, see how many of the sockets you can fill by inheriting from classes that are close to the functionality required. Only when that is done should you consider writing new classes from scratch. After a few outings with IntraBuilder, you'll find fewer and fewer sockets that require new classes. Eventually, you'll build most of your applications without writing any source code except for business classes and queries unique to the project.

Organizing Your Object Library

The following are the general categories of classes that you'll want to include in your object library:

☐ **System classes:** These are important classes because they apply to almost every application you'll develop in IntraBuilder. These are the management tools you'll use over and over again to make the development process easier. Examples are a forms-manager class or a good error-handler class.

☐ **User-interface classes:** Most of us, as a matter of course, reuse certain design elements in most of our projects. When you design a Web page, you probably use certain conventions—combinations of HTML tags to create title text, body text, lists, and so on. This is a commonly overlooked area of leverage. Imagine never having to set HTML tags again; you can just drag and drop custom HTML components from the IntraBuilder Component Palette. Another good example is a

20

custom image class consisting of the logos of credit card companies whose cards you accept. Yet another example is navigation images.

☐ **Custom query classes:** If you think about it, you'll probably find that you use the same basic queries over and over again in your applications. Customer queries, invoice detail queries, and employee queries are good examples. You'll save a huge amount of time over the years by keeping the same table and field names consistent from application to application. You can reuse queries again and again with only minor modifications.

☐ **Report classes:** There is huge leverage in building a library of generic report classes, considering the amount of detail required to put together any good report. Try to create a *person* report class that you can inherit into customer, vendor, or employee classes just by modifying a handful of properties. This is another good reason to keep field names consistent across databases.

☐ **Custom form classes:** Custom form classes have already been discussed extensively, but you might want to think of them in a larger context—not just creating custom form classes for a particular application, but perhaps creating custom form classes with your logo and generic navigation toolbar for use across most or all of your applications. You'll not only save a huge amount of development time, but you'll also give your users a consistent user interface.

☐ **Business classes:** These are the gems that will pay for the learning curve of object-oriented JavaScript. You can pack the power of processing, updating, posting, and closing into stand-alone from-scratch classes that will serve you well for years. You can inherit and override to make those little adjustments you'll need to suit the particular application, but you might never again have to write A/R aging, fixed assets depreciation, or loan amortization. Write a General Ledger class with methods to handle all aspects of creating, posting, and closing accounts. Write edit classes that remove a line item from an invoice, sales order, or purchase order, and update the client, vendor, inventory, and G/L automatically. You're limited only by your imagination.

☐ **Third-party classes:** This is probably the ultimate leverage—writing no code at all. IntraBuilder supports ActiveX and Java objects. Why reinvent the wheel, when you can integrate components already written and tested by experts in the field? The same is true for OLEAutomation. You might want to write a class using an out-of-process OLE server to process credit card payments in real time. Or fax confirmations automatically from the server to the customer or vendor. There is huge power here for the asking.

Summary

Using IntraBuilder's tools combined with its server-side JavaScript object-oriented language, you can achieve a productivity you probably never before imagined. The better your object library is, the more advantage you'll take and the more benefits you'll reap from this true RAD (Rapid Application Development) environment for dynamic Web sites.

Q&A

Q Why not just run the `.jfm` file to launch a form?

A You can do that if you want. But the instantiation code streamed by the Form Designer puts the form's object reference into a variable (`f`) that disappears instantly. Because there is no external reference remaining for the form, you can never address its properties or methods from any other place in your application.

Q Should everything I write be written as classes instead of functions? Doesn't that make a lot more work?

A Initially, it sure does. You don't have to define and set properties in functions, and they're a bit more forgiving than classes. You don't have to instantiate functions. As a whole, they involve less code than classes.

But that advantage exists only for a one-time use. The greatest benefit of object-oriented programming is reusability. The next time you need the same, or even similar, functionality in another form or another application, you really start to see the benefits. Because you never know what you'll need in an application years down the road, it makes sense to create classes for anything that has even a remote possibility of reuse.

Q Why can't I send parameters to a form?

A Because `form` is a built-in standard class in IntraBuilder. It has a single designated parameter (`Title`). You can't add parameters to `aArray.Add()` or `dDate.toString` or any other built-in method. Instead of using parameters, instantiate your forms and declare custom properties before opening.

Q Why can't I send parameters to a function pointer?

A Because a function pointer is a pointer; it's a variable or property containing an address, and it's not a function call. You can't send a parameter to a variable.

20

Workshop

The Workshop section provides questions and exercises to help you get a better feel for the material you learned today. Try to answer the questions and at least think about the exercises before moving on to tomorrow's lesson. You'll find the answers to the questions in Appendix A, "Answers to Quiz Questions."

Quiz

1. How do properties and methods differ from variables and functions?
2. What is an object reference?
3. What is an object reference variable?
4. What is interprocess communication?
5. What are the internal references in a form?
6. What are the generic scope-resolution operators?
7. What is the difference between a class and an object?
8. What is the difference between an instance and an object?

Exercises

1. Expand on the form manager to force the first half of `cClassName` to lowercase. Add a `Release()` method that scans the array elements to find the current instance and release it. Add a `CloseAll()` method that loops through all the array elements, finds active references, and closes and releases their forms.
2. Create a custom business class from scratch. Port some existing business code (if you have some) for a posting routine or an update customer routine. Define properties and methods.
3. Create a small library of derived HTML custom components. Set color, attribute, and size tags to make a useful set of HTML controls that matches your normal style in page design.

20

Day 21

Building Client/Server Applications

by Paul Mahar

The Professional and Client/Server editions of IntraBuilder include native links to high-performance data servers. In this chapter, you learn how easy it is to create applications that bring server data to the Web. If you are using the standard edition of IntraBuilder, you can take the day off or read through the chapter to get an overview of the other editions. The Standard edition restricts data connections to dBASE, Paradox, and ODBC data sources. Here is the final topic list for the week:

☐ **Setting up the Local InterBase Server:** The Local InterBase Server provides big server features within a small memory footprint. You can run the Local InterBase Server along with your browser, Web server, and IntraBuilder to create a complete SQL development environment on a single PC.

The first task of the day is to set up the server with a database that you can use with IntraBuilder. The Local InterBase Server comes with the Client/Server editions of IntraBuilder, Delphi, and C++ Builder.

☐ **Migrating the shopping cart application:** The shopping cart application created during Week 2 relies exclusively on dBASE tables. Today you will take the application as it was on Day 14 and move the tables to a database server. As you modify the application, you will learn some of the differences between local and server data.

NOTE

> Although the examples used throughout this chapter use InterBase as the database server, the same techniques also apply to any servers connected through a native BDE SQL-Link. The Client/Server edition comes with SQL-Link drivers for Oracle, Informix, InterBase, DB2, Sybase, and Microsoft SQL Server.

☐ **Partitioning application logic with stored procedures:** High-performance database servers let developers create procedures and triggers that execute on the server. Routines that execute on the server can take advantage of internal server features and optimizations. The last task of the day, week, and book will be to move some of the data processing logic out of one of the shopping cart's JavaScript forms and into an InterBase database.

The term client/server was coined for database applications that split data processing between a server, where data resides, and the client, or user, machine. Today, the term also applies to Web applications where the client is the browser and the server is a Web server that serves up HTML pages. To add to the confusion, applications such as IntraBuilder are both clients and servers. IntraBuilder is a server in the Web sense and a client in the database model. The Client/Server in IntraBuilder Client/Server refers to the database model. All editions of IntraBuilder support the browser clients and Web servers.

Although the promises of the client/server architecture were starting to be trumpeted to the PC world in the late 1980s, it took years for client/server applications to become mainstream. One of the difficulties that client/server developers have continually encountered has been the complications and expense of configuring database drivers on client workstations.

Both the expense and configuration management of client workstations are nonexistent in an IntraBuilder application. The requirements for the client are nothing more than a Web browser. Database drivers need only reside on machines running the IntraBuilder Server. By the end of the day you will be ready to leverage the Web as the most affordable platform for client/server applications.

21

The Local InterBase Server

Before you can create a client/server application, you should be familiar with a database server and some front-end development tools. For the past 20 days, you have been familiarizing yourself with the front-end development tools of IntraBuilder. If you already have a database server installed and are comfortable with its administration, you can skip to the next section. In this section, you will learn how to set up and administer the Local InterBase Server.

Installing the Local InterBase Server

You can find the setup program for the Local InterBase Server on the IntraBuilder Client/Server or the IntraBuilder Professional CD. The Local InterBase Server is not included with trial or standard versions of IntraBuilder. To work with IntraBuilder, you need only the Program Files and InterBase Windows Tools. I recommend that you also select the InterBase Help, InterBase SQL Tutorial, and the example files when installing. If you want to save disk space, do not install the ODBC driver, the command-line tools, or SDK support. You can select what components to install from the setup dialog, shown in Figure 21.1.

Figure 21.1.

Installing the Local InterBase Server from the IntraBuilder Client/Server CD.

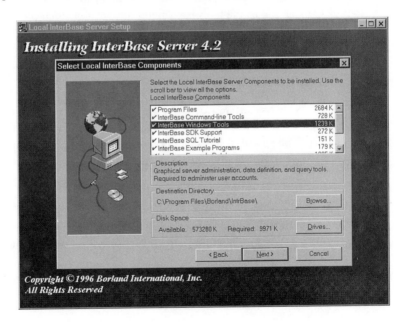

As with other database servers, IntraBuilder can use either ODBC or a SQL-Link to connect to InterBase. The SQL-Link provides superior performance and requires less overhead than the ODBC driver.

When you first install InterBase, the default configuration is to have InterBase start up when you start Windows. Loading InterBase at startup is appropriate when using InterBase Server for NT in a production environment, but consider switching to manual startup for the Local InterBase Server.

WARNING

> The Local InterBase Server comes with a single user license. It will not allow more than three simultaneous connections and is not appropriate for a production environment.

Exploring the InterBase Tool Set

The InterBase tool set consists of the server and four utility applications. The utilities are the Communication Diagnostic Tool, the Configuration dialog, the Server Manager, and Interactive SQL, which are described in the following sections. You can start each tool from an icon in the InterBase program folder. Most of the tools require a running server to be fully functional. Several of the tools have menu options to launch other tools.

InterBase Communication Diagnostic Tool

Use this tool to check that you can make a valid connection to a database. The InterBase Server must be running to complete the DB connection test. To validate a new install, start the InterBase Server and test a connection to the `employee.gdb` example database, as shown in Figure 21.2. The default User Name for `employee.gdb` is `SYSDBA`, and the password is `masterkey`. The password is case sensitive and must be entered in lowercase.

The DB connection test is the first test to try when you have trouble accessing an InterBase database. The test uses direct calls to the server. If the DB connection test fails, the problem resides with the InterBase Server, the GDB file, the user, or the password.

If the DB connection passes and you are unable to connect using IntraBuilder, check the BDE configuration. IntraBuilder requires a BDE InterBase driver and alias to connect to an InterBase database.

Figure 21.2.

*Testing a DB
connection to the
Employee example
database.*

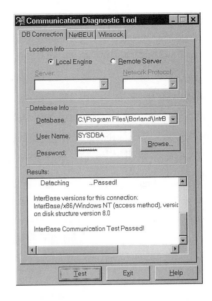

InterBase Configuration

You can open the InterBase Configuration dialog from a program icon or by selecting Startup Configuration from the server shortcut menu. The options presented depend on the current operating system. Figure 21.3 shows the dialog as it appears in Windows 95.

Figure 21.3.

*Configuring the server
for manual startup.*

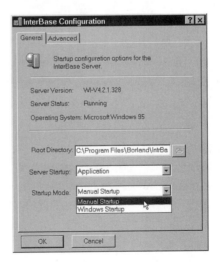

21

If you are running Windows NT, you can set up the server as an NT service and set a priority. The optimum configuration for the InterBase Server for NT is to be a service. If you are using the Local InterBase Server, run the server as an application with a manual startup.

InterBase Server

You can start up the server by selecting InterBase Server in the InterBase group. When the server is running, an icon appears in the status area of the task bar. You can open the server property sheet by right-clicking the icon. The property sheet displays the user license count and connection information. Figure 21.4 shows the server property sheet. If you are having trouble making a connection with the Local InterBase Server, check this sheet to see whether the connections have reached the maximum of three.

Figure 21.4.

Checking the number of server connections.

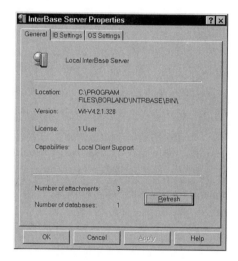

InterBase Server Manager

You can use this utility to perform routine maintenance and administration tasks. Use this utility to manage users, generate statistics, and optimize your databases. Before you can do anything with the Server Manager, start up the server and log in as the system administrator. The system administrator account has the user name SYSDBA, and the password defaults to masterkey. After you log in to the server, you can open multiple databases without reentering a user name or password.

InterBase requires a user name and password whenever you open a database through IntraBuilder. You can force a user name and password using the loginString property of a Database object. If you do not set the loginString property, IntraBuilder uses the pass_sql JavaScript form to get the information from the user.

You can create user accounts by selecting Tasks|User Security from the Server Manager. After creating accounts, you can use the owner account of each database to grant access rights. Any user can open a database, but only those with granted rights can read data from tables within the database.

If you are having trouble with a single database, you can verify the integrity of the file from the Server Manager. Figure 21.5 shows the validation dialog while selecting the knowledge base solution GDB file that comes with IntraBuilder Client/Server and IntraBuilder Professional.

Figure 21.5.

Validating the structure of a GDB file.

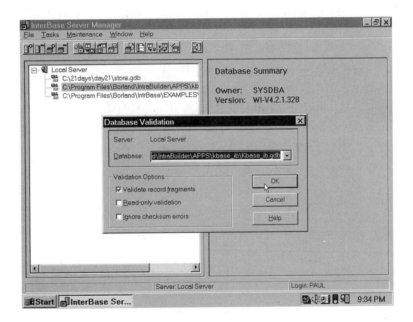

The Database Sweep optimizes database files in much the same way that the Database::pack() method can optimize Paradox and dBASE tables. When you sweep a database, the server recovers space occupied by changes that were rolled back. You do not need to take a database offline to perform a sweep.

The backup and restore options can help you move a database between operating systems. The InterBase backup format is transportable and takes up less space than the standard GDB format.

21

TIP

> You can also make routine backups using any standard backup utility
> such as Cheyenne Backup. All the objects of any one database are
> contained in a single GDB file. The same GDB file will work with the
> single-user Local InterBase Server and the multi-user InterBase Server
> for NT.

You can open the Interactive SQL utility from the Server Manager. If you select a database
in the Server Manager before opening the Interactive SQL utility, it opens with a new
connection to the selected database.

InterBase Interactive SQL

The last utility works like a Script Pad for InterBase. You can enter SQL commands in a text
area control, and view results appear in another. The Interactive SQL utility also lets you view
metadata. You can use Interactive SQL to test SQL statements before embedding them in
an IntraBuilder `Database::executeSQL()` method. Figure 21.6 shows the results of running
a simple `SELECT` command.

Figure 21.6.

*Using Interactive
SQL to try a* SELECT
command.

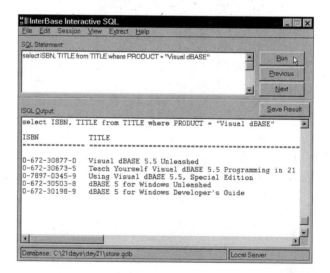

NEW TERM   *Metadata* refers to information that InterBase keeps in system tables. This includes
index definitions, stored procedures, triggers, and generators. Data that you enter
into standard tables is not metadata.

The metadata options provide the complete structure of a database. You can create a quick reference by saving the metadata for a database to a text file. This can come in handy when you need the name of an index or stored procedure for a JavaScript method.

The View option works better for getting metadata from complex database structures. The View option helps you pinpoint specific objects. Extract options are more effective for simple structures such as the knowledge base GDB.

WARNING

> The InterBase utilities do not share connections. If you open two databases with the Server Manager and load the Interactive SQL, you will create three active connections. When using the Local InterBase Server with more than one database or utility, you can quickly run out of connections.

Migrating the Shopping Cart Application

In this section, you will learn how to replace the shopping cart application's dBASE tables with an InterBase database. The shopping cart is a Web bookstore that allows shoppers to search for and purchase books through a browser. The application consists of eight JavaScript forms—one custom form class, one report, and six tables. Although the modifications are simple, you will need to make changes to the custom form class, the report, and all but one of the JavaScript forms.

Before you modify any of the JavaScript files, you need to get all the data into an InterBase database. InterBase, BDE, and IntraBuilder provide all the tools you need to replicate the data on the server.

Setting Up the Store Database

The goal is to have an InterBase database that contains the same six tables that are currently in dBASE format. Let's call the new database STORE and name the InterBase file store.gdb. There is a three-step process for migrating the tables. First, you must create the store.gdb file using the InterBase Interactive SQL utility. After creating the database file, you can define a BDE alias for the gdb. The last step is to pump the data from the dBASE tables to the InterBase database.

NOTE

> If you have C++ Builder or Visual dBASE Client/Server, you can also use the Data Pump Expert to copy dBASE tables into an existing InterBase database. The Data Pump Expert is not provided with IntraBuilder because this functionality is built directly into the `UpdateSet` class.

Creating the Store Database File

You can use the InterBase Interactive SQL utility to create the `store.gdb` file. When you create a new database, InterBase creates a 200KB file containing system tables for storing metadata. IntraBuilder applications do not require direct references to the physical location of a GDB file. In this exercise, you place the file in the store folder along with the other JavaScript forms. Here are the steps for creating the store database:

1. Start the InterBase Server.

2. Open the Interactive SQL utility by selecting the InterBase Windows ISQL item from the InterBase program folder.

3. Select File|Create Database.

4. Select the Local Engine radio button. If the option is not enabled, restart the InterBase Server.

5. Enter the following options, as shown in Figure 21.7, and click OK.

   ☐ Database: `C:\Program Files\Borland\IntraBuilder\Store\STORE.GDB`

   ☐ User Name: `SYSDBA`

   ☐ Password: `masterkey`

Figure 21.7.

Creating the Store database.

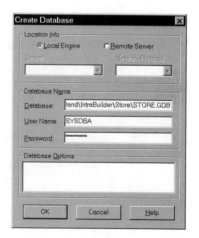

6. Close the Interactive SQL utility.

WARNING

> It is a little too easy to permanently erase a database by selecting File|Drop Database from the InterBase Interactive SQL menu.

Defining the Database to BDE

Without a BDE alias, the database is invisible to IntraBuilder. To create an alias for an InterBase database, you must have the InterBase SQL-Link installed. If INTRBASE does not appear as a BDE driver, you can install the SQL-Link from either the IntraBuilder Professional or the IntraBuilder Client/Server setup program. The setup program's Custom selection allows you to install a single SQL-Link without reinstalling any other components. The BDE InterBase driver is not an option of the Local InterBase Server setup program.

If you have the InterBase SQL-Link installed, the following steps can be used to create an alias for the Store database. The Local InterBase Server does not need to be running to complete this process.

1. Open the BDE Configuration Utility. This utility can take up to a minute to load, depending on the complexity of your configuration.

2. Confirm that INTRBASE is listed on the drivers page.

3. Select Pages|Alias.

4. Click on New Alias.

5. Enter STORE as the alias name. Select INTRBASE, as shown in Figure 21.8, and click OK.

Figure 21.8.

Creating the STORE *alias.*

6. Change the following two parameters, as shown in Figure 21.9.
   - ☐ SERVER NAME: C:\Program
     Files\Borland\IntraBuilder\Store\STORE.GDB
   - ☐ USER NAME: SYSDBA

Figure 21.9.

Setting BDE parameters for the STORE *alias.*

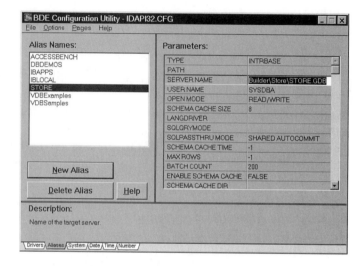

7. Select File|Save and exit the BDE Configuration Utility.

TIP

If you are using any 16-bit BDE applications, you can optimize BDE by not checking the Configure Win3.1 menu option. When this option is checked, the BDE utility saves driver information to the CFG file instead of the Windows Registry. Alias definitions are always saved to a CFG file.

Pumping the Data from a dBASE Table to InterBase

IntraBuilder contains an UpdateSet class for moving data between different table types. After establishing a link to the Store database, you copy the dBASE tables to InterBase through the UpdateSet::copy() method. Although this method will copy table structures and data, it will not re-create index definitions on the server.

dBASE tables follow an index scheme that is incompatible with most servers. When working with dBASE tables, the index is tied to the table and not to a database. dBASE index names need to be unique only to the table. The most common index name for a dBASE index is the name of the field. For instance, the index for the ISBN field in the Cart table is named ISBN. The same index name is also found on the Title table.

InterBase requires every index to have a name that is unique to the database. To create unique index names for InterBase, you can include the table name as part of the index name. Using this convention, CARTISBN is the name of the Cart table's ISBN index, and TITLEISBN is the Title table's ISBN index.

You can use the TableDef class and the Database::createIndex() method to gather index definitions from the dBASE tables and create a new index for the InterBase database. To automate the process, you can create a script that does the job for you.

Before committing any thoughts to JavaScript, make sure you can get a connection from IntraBuilder to the Store database. Here are the steps:

1. Start the InterBase Server.
2. Start IntraBuilder.
3. View the IntraBuilder Explorer and select the Tables tab.
4. Select STORE from the Look In drop-down list, as shown in Figure 21.10.

Figure 21.10.

Connecting to the Store database.

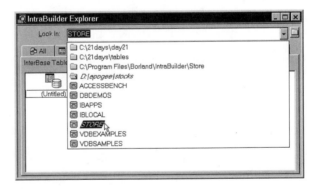

5. Enter SYSDBA as the User Name and masterkey as the Password.

After making a connection, you see either a single (Untitled) icon or many tables that begin with RDB$. InterBase uses the RDB$ prefix for system tables. Avoid making changes directly to any system table from the IntraBuilder Explorer. You can control the display of system tables from the application property sheet of the Desktop Properties dialog.

Create a new script, as shown in Listing 21.1. Save the script as pumpup.js. Run the script to upload the six dBASE tables into the Store database. You might need to modify the #DEFINE statement to refer to the location of the dBASE tables on your system.

21

INPUT   **Listing 21.1. The Pumpup script.**

```
 1: #DEFINE TABLEFOLDER " C:\\PROGRAM FILES\\BORLAND\\INTRABUILDER\\STORE\\"
 2:
 3: var db           = new Database() ;
 4: db.databaseName  = "STORE" ;
 5: db.loginString   = "sysdba/masterkey" ;
 6: db.active        = true ;
 7:
 8: CopyUp(db, "CART") ;
 9: CopyUp(db, "CUSTOMER") ;
10: CopyUp(db, "INVOICE") ;
11: CopyUp(db, "LINEITEM") ;
12: CopyUp(db, "TITLE") ;
13: CopyUp(db, "PRODUCT") ;
14: return ;
15:
16: function CopyUp( db, cTable )
17: {
18:    var up = new UpdateSet() ;
19:    up.source = TABLEFOLDER + cTable + ".DBF" ;
20:    up.destination = ":STORE:" + cTable ;
21:    up.copy() ;
22
23:    var tSource = new TableDef() ;
24:    tSource.database = _sys.databases[0] ;
25:    tSource.tableName = up.source ;
26:    for (var i = 0 ; i < tSource.indexes.length ; i++ )
27:    {
28:       var idx = new Index() ;
29:       idx.fields = tSource.indexes[i].indexName ;
30:       idx.indexName = cTable + idx.fields ;
31:       db.createIndex( cTable, idx ) ;
32:    }
33: }
```

ANALYSIS   The Pumpup script starts on lines 3 through 7 by establishing a connection to the Store database. The db variable contains a reference to the Store database. The reference is passed to the CopyUp() function along with the name of the table to copy. The parameters for CopyUp() are as follows:

```
CopyUp( <object reference>: database to copy to>, <expC: table to copy> )
```

NOTE   You might need to modify the first line of the Pumpup script before running it on your system. Verify that the TABLEFOLDER string points to the location of the dBASE tables for the shopping cart application.

21

Lines 8 through 13 call CopyUp() for the shopping cart application's six dBASE tables. The script ends with the return statement on line 14 after all the tables have been copied to the Store database. The return statement is optional. Without a return, the script ends after executing the last statement outside a function or class block. In this case, the return is the last statement outside a block.

The CopyUp() function has two sections. Lines 18 through 21 copy the table to the server. Lines 23 through 31 comprise the second section. The purpose of the second section is to create index definitions on the server based on existing dBASE index tags.

Unlike other database classes, UpdateSet is not tied to any single database reference. The source and destination properties can point to different databases. UpdateSet selects the appropriate database by examining the string assigned to the source and destination properties. If a string does not begin with an alias name delimited by colons, the table is assumed to be a native BDE dBASE or Paradox table. Line 19 specifies a local dBASE table without supplying an alias.

The ":STORE:" prefix on line 20 requires that a connection be available to the Store database. When the destination property is set, the UpdateSet object establishes a link to the database object created on lines 3 through 6 without making an explicit reference property. An error would occur if the database was not already active.

Lines 23 through 25 create a TableDef object that contains table structure and index definitions for the dBASE table. Line 24 sets the database property to the default system database. This prevents errors that could occur when the current database does not support native dBASE and Paradox tables. Setting the tableName property activates the object and causes the rest of the structure to fill in with values related to the current table.

The for loop, on lines 26 through 32, executes once for each index tag defined on the dBASE table. The idx object defines an equivalent SQL index. Line 30 concatenates the table name to the dBASE index name to ensure an index name that is unique to the Store database.

After running the Pumpup script, open the Title table from the IntraBuilder Explorer to view the InterBase version. Figure 21.11 shows one of the rows for the Title table. The character, memo, and image fields display just as they did in the dBASE tables. The date and numeric fields appear to have different values than the dBASE counterparts. The Pubdate field includes time information. Although no information was lost, you will need to explicitly suppress the time portion of the value when using it in a form or report.

The changes to the Price field look more disturbing. The Price field shows values rounded to the nearest whole number. Whereas the price was 29.95 in the dBASE table, it displays as 30 in the InterBase table. Although it looks bad in the Table run window, the true value is still in the table.

21

Figure 21.11.

Running the InterBase version of the Title table.

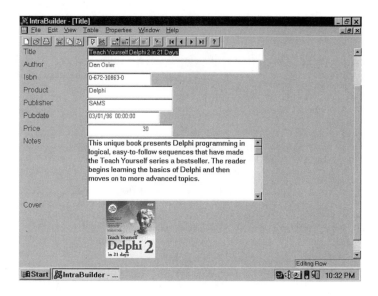

Tip

To edit decimal values in an InterBase table, use the Form Expert to quickly generate a form and set the `template` property for Text controls linked to numeric values. Changing the `template` property for the Price field to `999.99` lets you see and edit the values as they are stored in the table.

Updating the JavaScript Source Files

With the database in place, you're ready to begin the task of updating the custom form class, the JavaScript forms, and the report that comprise the source code of the shopping cart application. To get the application up and running with the Store database, you need to modify only properties of the database objects. The underlying logic for each form remains the same as it was for dBASE tables.

Before you make any changes to the application, you need a working copy of the source files as they were at Day 14. Copy the following files into your working folder. The exercises assume that your working folder is `C:\Program Files\Borland\IntraBuilder\Store`. Table 21.1 lists the files you will need to complete the InterBase version of the shopping cart application.

21

Table 21.1. The InterBase shopping cart file list.

File	Name	Purpose
cart.jfm	Cart Form	Shows contents of the shopping cart
checkout.fjm	Checkout Form	Data entry form for customer
detail.jfm	Detail Form	Shows information from Title table
help.jfm	Help Form	Describes toolbar buttons
index.htm	Store Index	Home page for the bookstore
keyword.jfm	Keyword Form	Provides complex search of Title table
logo.gif	Store Logo	Image map for Store Index
message.jfm	Message Form	Streams an HTML alert
quick.jfm	Quick Form	Provides simple search of Title table
receipt.jrp	Receipt Report	Displays when an order is committed
results.jfm	Results Form	Lists titles resulting from a search
store.gdb	Store Database	InterBase database containing Cart, Customer, Invoice, Lineitem, Product, and Title tables
store.h	Store Header	Precompiler file for including forms
toolbar.jcf	Toolbar	Custom form class used by all forms
vcr.gif	VCR Buttons	Image map for the Detail form

Remove all dBASE tables from your working folder. This causes all the forms but the Message form to generate runtime errors as the forms try to open tables that do not exist. The Message form does not use any tables. When you complete the modifications, the runtime errors will disappear. If you leave the dBASE tables in the same folder, it becomes more difficult to determine what forms have been converted to work with InterBase.

Adding the Database to the Toolbar Custom Form Class

Seven of the forms need a Database object to work with the Store database. You could add the Database object directly to each of the forms, but there is an easier way. All of the forms in the shopping cart application derive from the Toolbar custom form class. If you add the Database object to the Toolbar custom form class, all the other forms automatically inherit the new object.

You can quickly add a Database object through the Custom Form Class Designer. The other modifications you will make to the application will be through source code. Here are the steps for adding a Database object to the Toolbar custom form class:

21

1. Check the task bar to confirm that the InterBase Server is running.

2. Double-click on `toolbar.jcf` in the IntraBuilder Explorer to open it in the Custom Form Class Designer.

3. Open the Component Palette and locate the database object. If the Palette is showing tabs, the database object will be on the Data Access tab.

4. Drop a database object in one of the upper corners of the form.

5. Inspect the new database object and use the drop-down list to select STORE as the `databaseName`.

6. Set the `loginString` property to SYSDBA/masterkey.

7. Double-click on the `active` property to toggle it to `true`. This sets the `driverName` and `handle` properties as shown in Figure 21.12. The `driverName` is the BDE driver name for which the alias is defined. The value of the `handle` is generated as a unique number that identifies the current BDE connection. You can use the `handle` to make BDE API calls use the IntraBuilder extern system.

Figure 21.12.

Adding the Store database to the Toolbar custom form class.

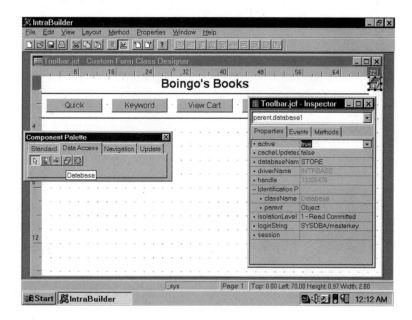

8. Close the Custom Form Class Designer and save your changes.

When you add Data Access objects from the Component Palette, IntraBuilder assigns generic names like `query1`, `query2`, and `database1`. You can provide more intuitive names by replacing the references in the script file. If you right-click on a custom form class and select Edit as Script, you can use the Script Editor to locate and replace references. Open `toolbar.jcf` in the Script Editor and locate the following code:

21

```
with (this.database1 = new Database()){
   left = 70;
   top = 0;
   databaseName = "STORE";
   loginString = "SYSDBA/masterkey";
   active = true;
}
```

Replace the `database1` reference with `dbstore`, like this:

```
with (this.dbstore = new Database()){
   left = 70;
   top = 0;
   databaseName = "STORE";
   loginString = "SYSDBA/masterkey";
   active = true;
}
```

Those are all the modifications that are required to give all the forms access to the Store database. The next task will be to modify the query definitions in each form.

Updating the Help Form

You can use IntraBuilder's debugging tools to locate, fix, and optimize queries. To locate queries that need fixing, simply run the shopping cart application and watch for runtime errors. When a table cannot be found, IntraBuilder displays an alert, as shown in Figure 21.13. You can select Fix to open the form in the Script Editor near the line where the trouble is.

Figure 21.13.

Using runtime errors to locate queries that need to be modified.

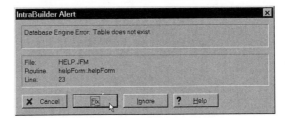

To run the shopping cart application, you must first start with the Help form. Run the Help form and locate the first problem query. If you click on Fix, the Script Editor opens near the following code:

```
with (this.cart1 = new Query()){
   left = 72;
   top = 0;
   sql = 'SELECT * FROM "cart.DBF"';
   active = true;
}

with (this.cart1.rowset) {
   indexName = "CARTUSER";
}
```

The following problems exist with this and all the queries in the shopping cart application:

☐ The table name is enclosed in quotes and has a DBF extension. Fix this by removing the period, extension, and quotes around the table name. Leave the single quotes that enclose the SELECT statement.

☐ The database property is not set. The dBASE tables use the default database and do not require that the property be set. To work with the Store database, set the database property to the parent.dbstore reference created in the Toolbar custom form class.

☐ The name of the index does not match unique names created by the Pumpup script. You can fix this by prefixing the table name to the existing dBASE index name.

The following shows the fixed sql, database, and indexName properties. These changes allow the form to work, but not as well as it could work.

```
with (this.cart1 = new Query()){
   left = 72;
   top = 0;
   sql = 'SELECT * FROM CART';
   database = parent.dbstore;
   active = true;
}

with (this.cart1.rowset) {
   indexName = "CARTCARTUSER";
}
```

Whenever you issue a SELECT against a server, the SQL-Link driver uses an ORDER BY clause to control the row sequence. IntraBuilder executes the SELECT as soon as the active property of the query is set to true. If you do not specify an ORDER BY, the SQL-Link driver adds one. Setting the indexName property forces IntraBuilder to reissue the SELECT command if the indexName calls for different order. You can avoid the overhead of multiple SELECT commands by substituting an ORDER BY clause and removing any explicit settings of the indexName property.

Setting the requestLive property to false can also help optimize queries that use SQL-Link drivers. If a rowset is live, you can update values in the rowset. By default, IntraBuilder tries to make every query result in a live rowset. When requestLive is set to false, IntraBuilder creates a read-only rowset. Queries that perform joins and aggregate operators can result in a read-only rowset, regardless of the requestLive property.

The Help form does not require a live rowset. To fully optimize the cart1 query for the Help form, modify the properties for the cart1 query and rowset as shown here:

```
with (this.cart1 = new Query()){
    left = 72;
    top = 0;
    sql = 'SELECT * FROM CART ORDER BY CARTUSER';
    database = parent.dbstore;
    requestLive = false;
    active = true;
}

with (this.cart1.rowset) {
}
```

The IntraBuilder Desktop Properties dialog contains two options that you can use to gather detailed information on what the SQL-Link driver is doing. The SQL Trace option causes all SQL-Link operations to echo to the results pane of the Script Pad. This lets you see the differences between the SELECT commands in your scripts and the SELECT commands that run on the server. The output of SQL Trace is often too voluminous to work with in the Script Pad. The Output Log option captures all output to the Script Pad in a text file. By combining the SQL Trace and Output Log options, you can create a text file that gives detailed information on how your application is working with the server.

The script shown in Listing 21.2 demonstrates the optimization that happens when you specify an ORDER BY clause rather than an indexName. Before running the script, select Properties|Desktop Properties to set the SQL Trace and Output Log options. The SQL Trace option is on the Application page. Figure 21.14 shows the Output Log set to sqltrace.txt.

Figure 21.14.

Enabling an Output Log.

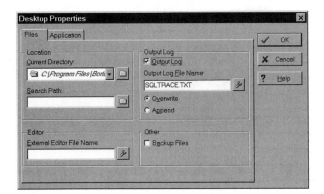

WARNING

The SQL Trace and Output Log options degrade system performance. Disable both options in a production environment.

21

INPUT **Listing 21.2. The SQLTrace script.**

```
1: //
2: // To track and compare SQL operations,
3: // check SQL Trace and set an Output log
4: // file in the Desktop Properties dialog.
5: //
6:
7: clear ;
8: var db = new Database()
9: db.databaseName = "STORE" ;
10: db.loginString = "SYSDBA/masterkey" ;
11: db.active = true ;
12:
13: // Prep database
14: var q = new Query() ;
15: q.database = db ;
16: q.sql = "SELECT * FROM CART" ;
17: q.active = true ;
18:
19: TraceSelect(db, "SELECT * FROM CART") ;
20: TraceIndex( db, "SELECT * FROM CART") ;
21: TraceSelect(db, "SELECT * FROM CART ORDER BY ISBN") ;
22:
23: function TraceSelect(db, cSelect)
24: {
25:     ShowStart(cSelect) ;
26:     var q = new Query() ;
27:     q.database = db ;
28:     q.sql = cSelect ;
29:     q.active = true ;
30:     ShowEnd(cSelect) ;
31: }
32:
33: function TraceIndex(db, cSelect)
34: {
35:     ShowStart(cSelect + " (with indexName setting)") ;
36:     var q = new Query() ;
37:     q.database = db ;
38:     q.sql = cSelect ;
39:     q.active = true ;
40:     q.rowset.indexName = "CARTISBN" ;
41:     ShowEnd(cSelect) ;
42: }
43:
44: function ShowStart(cSelect)
45: {
46:     _sys.scriptOut.writeln() ;
47:     _sys.scriptOut.writeln("// Start Trace of " + cSelect);
48:     _sys.scriptOut.writeln() ;
49: }
50:
51: function ShowEnd(cSelect)
52: {
53:     _sys.scriptOut.writeln() ;
54:     _sys.scriptOut.writeln("// End Trace of " + cSelect);
55:     _sys.scriptOut.writeln() ;
56: }
```

ANALYSIS   The SQLTrace script works with the SQL Trace and Output Log options to create a text file that shows the differences between three similar query operations. Two sections of code prepare IntraBuilder for the comparison. Lines 8 through 11 define a database object that is used throughout the script. Lines 14 through 17 activate a query without adding any extra logging information.

The first query that activates for a database triggers dozens of extra lines of SQL Trace output. For this reason, the first active query is not comparable to subsequent query operations. Lines 19 through 21 call functions to create the queries that perform the following operations:

☐ The first query is a simple SELECT without an ORDER BY clause or an indexName setting. This represents the query that the Form Designer creates when you drop a table from the IntraBuilder Explorer onto a form.

☐ The second query uses a SELECT without an ORDER BY clause and sets the indexName property. Such an operation occurs when approaching SQL queries in a manner more suited to dBASE or Paradox tables.

☐ The last query is optimized for SQL by using an ORDER BY clause and not setting the indexName property. Use this technique to set the row sequence without executing any extra SELECT commands.

Lines 23 through 31 define the TraceSelect() function for tracing queries that do not set the indexName. The db and cSelect parameters refer to the active database and SELECT command used to create the query.

The TraceIndex() function is almost identical to the TraceSelect() function. The only differences occur on lines 35 and 40. An extra string indicating that an indexName is being used is added to the ShowStart() call. The ShowStart() function inserts custom output into the output log.

After running the SQLTrace script, you will not be able to view the log file until you disable the Output Log option from the Desktop Properties dialog. If you open the sqltrace.txt file in a text editor, you can see the differences between the three queries. The first portion of the file contains all the SQL operations that occur when the initial query becomes active:

OUTPUT
```
SQL Prepare: INTRBASE - select RDB$OWNER_NAME, RDB$RELATION_NAME,...
SQL Vendor: INTRBASE - isc_dsql_allocate_statement
SQL Vendor: INTRBASE - isc_start_transaction
SQL Vendor: INTRBASE - isc_dsql_prepare
SQL Execute: INTRBASE - select RDB$OWNER_NAME, RDB$RELATION_NAME,...
SQL Vendor: INTRBASE - isc_dsql_execute
SQL Stmt: INTRBASE - Fetch
SQL Vendor: INTRBASE - isc_dsql_fetch
SQL Stmt: INTRBASE - Fetch
SQL Vendor: INTRBASE - isc_dsql_fetch
SQL Stmt: INTRBASE - EOF
SQL Transact: INTRBASE - XACT Commit
SQL Vendor: INTRBASE - isc_commit_transaction
SQL Stmt: INTRBASE - Close
SQL Vendor: INTRBASE - isc_dsql_free_statement
```

21

```
SQL Prepare: INTRBASE - select R.RDB$FIELD_NAME, F.RDB$FIELD_TYPE,...
SQL Vendor: INTRBASE - isc_dsql_allocate_statement
SQL Vendor: INTRBASE - isc_start_transaction
SQL Vendor: INTRBASE - isc_dsql_prepare
SQL Execute: INTRBASE - select R.RDB$FIELD_NAME, F.RDB$FIELD_TYPE,...
SQL Vendor: INTRBASE - isc_dsql_execute
SQL Stmt: INTRBASE - Fetch
SQL Vendor: INTRBASE - isc_dsql_fetch
SQL Stmt: INTRBASE - Fetch
SQL Vendor: INTRBASE - isc_dsql_fetch
SQL Stmt: INTRBASE - Fetch
SQL Vendor: INTRBASE - isc_dsql_fetch
SQL Stmt: INTRBASE - Fetch
SQL Vendor: INTRBASE - isc_dsql_fetch
SQL Stmt: INTRBASE - Fetch
SQL Vendor: INTRBASE - isc_dsql_fetch
SQL Stmt: INTRBASE - EOF
SQL Transact: INTRBASE - XACT Commit
SQL Vendor: INTRBASE - isc_commit_transaction
SQL Stmt: INTRBASE - Close
SQL Vendor: INTRBASE - isc_dsql_free_statement
SQL Prepare: INTRBASE - select I.RDB$INDEX_NAME, I.RDB$UNIQUE_FLAG,...
SQL Vendor: INTRBASE - isc_dsql_allocate_statement
SQL Vendor: INTRBASE - isc_start_transaction
SQL Vendor: INTRBASE - isc_dsql_prepare
SQL Execute: INTRBASE - select I.RDB$INDEX_NAME, I.RDB$UNIQUE_FLAG,...
SQL Vendor: INTRBASE - isc_dsql_execute
SQL Stmt: INTRBASE - Fetch
SQL Vendor: INTRBASE - isc_dsql_fetch
SQL Stmt: INTRBASE - Fetch
SQL Vendor: INTRBASE - isc_dsql_fetch
SQL Stmt: INTRBASE - Fetch
SQL Vendor: INTRBASE - isc_dsql_fetch
SQL Stmt: INTRBASE - Fetch
SQL Vendor: INTRBASE - isc_dsql_fetch
SQL Stmt: INTRBASE - EOF
SQL Transact: INTRBASE - XACT Commit
SQL Vendor: INTRBASE - isc_commit_transaction
SQL Stmt: INTRBASE - Close
SQL Vendor: INTRBASE - isc_dsql_free_statement
SQL Prepare: INTRBASE - select R.RDB$FIELD_NAME, F.RDB$VALIDATION_BLR,...
SQL Vendor: INTRBASE - isc_dsql_allocate_statement
SQL Vendor: INTRBASE - isc_start_transaction
SQL Vendor: INTRBASE - isc_dsql_prepare
SQL Execute: INTRBASE - select R.RDB$FIELD_NAME, F.RDB$VALIDATION_BLR,...
SQL Vendor: INTRBASE - isc_dsql_execute
SQL Stmt: INTRBASE - Fetch
SQL Vendor: INTRBASE - isc_dsql_fetch
SQL Stmt: INTRBASE - Fetch
SQL Vendor: INTRBASE - isc_dsql_fetch
SQL Stmt: INTRBASE - Fetch
SQL Vendor: INTRBASE - isc_dsql_fetch
SQL Stmt: INTRBASE - Fetch
SQL Vendor: INTRBASE - isc_dsql_fetch
SQL Stmt: INTRBASE - Fetch
SQL Vendor: INTRBASE - isc_dsql_fetch
```

```
SQL Stmt: INTRBASE - EOF
SQL Transact: INTRBASE - XACT Commit
SQL Vendor: INTRBASE - isc_commit_transaction
SQL Stmt: INTRBASE - Close
SQL Vendor: INTRBASE - isc_dsql_free_statement
SQL Prepare: INTRBASE - SELECT CARTUSER ,CARTDATE ,ISBN ,QTY  FROM CART
                 ORDER BY  CARTUSER ASC
SQL Vendor: INTRBASE - isc_dsql_allocate_statement
SQL Vendor: INTRBASE - isc_start_transaction
SQL Vendor: INTRBASE - isc_dsql_prepare
SQL Execute: INTRBASE - SELECT CARTUSER ,CARTDATE ,ISBN ,QTY  FROM CART
                 ORDER BY  CARTUSER ASC
SQL Vendor: INTRBASE - isc_dsql_execute
SQL Stmt: INTRBASE - Fetch
SQL Vendor: INTRBASE - isc_dsql_fetch
SQL Stmt: INTRBASE - EOF
SQL Transact: INTRBASE - XACT Commit
SQL Vendor: INTRBASE - isc_commit_transaction
SQL Stmt: INTRBASE - Close
SQL Vendor: INTRBASE - isc_dsql_free_statement
```

The first query of the comparison appears after the first Start Trace comment line. Notice that the asterisk of the original SELECT has been replaced by an explicit field list. The resulting SELECT also has an ORDER BY CARTUSER clause that was not present on the original query. The simple SELECT query results in 13 SQL operations:

OUTPUT

```
// Start Trace of SELECT * FROM CART

SQL Prepare: INTRBASE - SELECT CARTUSER ,CARTDATE ,ISBN ,QTY  FROM CART
                 ORDER BY  CARTUSER ASC
SQL Vendor: INTRBASE - isc_dsql_allocate_statement
SQL Vendor: INTRBASE - isc_start_transaction
SQL Vendor: INTRBASE - isc_dsql_prepare
SQL Execute: INTRBASE - SELECT CARTUSER ,CARTDATE ,ISBN ,QTY  FROM CART
                 ORDER BY  CARTUSER ASC
SQL Vendor: INTRBASE - isc_dsql_execute
SQL Stmt: INTRBASE - Fetch
SQL Vendor: INTRBASE - isc_dsql_fetch
SQL Stmt: INTRBASE - EOF
SQL Transact: INTRBASE - XACT Commit
SQL Vendor: INTRBASE - isc_commit_transaction
SQL Stmt: INTRBASE - Close
SQL Vendor: INTRBASE - isc_dsql_free_statement

// End Trace of SELECT * FROM CART
```

The next query results in a much more extensive set of SQL operations. It begins by creating a query that is identical to the one of the simple SELECT. A new SELECT is later executed with order set to match the index. By specifying the order with indexName, what were 13 SQL operations become 26 SQL operations. The first SELECT is discarded when the indexName is set:

21

OUTPUT

```
// Start Trace of SELECT * FROM CART (with indexName setting)

SQL Prepare: INTRBASE - SELECT CARTUSER ,CARTDATE ,ISBN ,QTY  FROM CART
              ORDER BY  CARTUSER ASC
SQL Vendor: INTRBASE - isc_dsql_allocate_statement
SQL Vendor: INTRBASE - isc_start_transaction
SQL Vendor: INTRBASE - isc_dsql_prepare
SQL Execute: INTRBASE - SELECT CARTUSER ,CARTDATE ,ISBN ,QTY  FROM CART
              ORDER BY  CARTUSER ASC
SQL Vendor: INTRBASE - isc_dsql_execute
SQL Stmt: INTRBASE - Fetch
SQL Vendor: INTRBASE - isc_dsql_fetch
SQL Stmt: INTRBASE - EOF
SQL Transact: INTRBASE - XACT Commit
SQL Vendor: INTRBASE - isc_commit_transaction
SQL Stmt: INTRBASE - Close
SQL Vendor: INTRBASE - isc_dsql_free_statement
SQL Prepare: INTRBASE - SELECT CARTUSER ,CARTDATE ,ISBN ,QTY  FROM CART
              ORDER BY  ISBN ASC
SQL Vendor: INTRBASE - isc_dsql_allocate_statement
SQL Vendor: INTRBASE - isc_start_transaction
SQL Vendor: INTRBASE - isc_dsql_prepare
SQL Execute: INTRBASE - SELECT CARTUSER ,CARTDATE ,ISBN ,QTY  FROM CART
              ORDER BY  ISBN ASC
SQL Vendor: INTRBASE - isc_dsql_execute
SQL Stmt: INTRBASE - Fetch
SQL Vendor: INTRBASE - isc_dsql_fetch
SQL Stmt: INTRBASE - EOF
SQL Transact: INTRBASE - XACT Commit
SQL Vendor: INTRBASE - isc_commit_transaction
SQL Stmt: INTRBASE - Close
SQL Vendor: INTRBASE - isc_dsql_free_statement

// End Trace of SELECT * FROM CART
```

The last query operation shows an exact match between the original SELECT command and the one that executes on the server. In this case, the ORDER BY and asterisk field specification do not change. The result is 19 lines with a single execution of SELECT:

OUTPUT

```
// Start Trace of SELECT * FROM CART ORDER BY ISBN

SQL Prepare: INTRBASE - SELECT * FROM CART ORDER BY ISBN
SQL Vendor: INTRBASE - isc_dsql_allocate_statement
SQL Vendor: INTRBASE - isc_start_transaction
SQL Vendor: INTRBASE - isc_dsql_prepare
SQL Vendor: INTRBASE - isc_dsql_sql_info
SQL Vendor: INTRBASE - isc_vax_integer
SQL Transact: INTRBASE - XACT (UNKNOWN)
SQL Vendor: INTRBASE - isc_commit_retaining
SQL Execute: INTRBASE - SELECT * FROM CART ORDER BY ISBN
SQL Vendor: INTRBASE - isc_dsql_execute
SQL Stmt: INTRBASE - Fetch
SQL Vendor: INTRBASE - isc_dsql_fetch
SQL Stmt: INTRBASE - EOF
SQL Stmt: INTRBASE - Reset
SQL Vendor: INTRBASE - isc_dsql_free_statement
```

21

```
SQL Transact: INTRBASE - XACT Commit
SQL Vendor: INTRBASE - isc_commit_transaction
SQL Stmt: INTRBASE - Close
SQL Vendor: INTRBASE - isc_dsql_free_statement

// End Trace of SELECT * FROM CART ORDER BY ISBN

SQL Connect: INTRBASE - Disconnect GENERAL
SQL Vendor: INTRBASE - isc_detach_database
```

SQL Trace statements vary by SQL-Link driver. Whenever you change database servers, use SQL Trace to check for differences in performance-critical operations.

Updating More Queries

When you have made the Help form operational, you can update the query definitions for the following JavaScript forms: Cart, Checkout, Detail, Keyword, Quick, and Results, which are covered in the following sections. Use the Script Editor to edit each JavaScript form as a Script. Change each form as shown.

Cart Form

The Cart form requires more than just a change to the table name and the database property. The Cart form relates the Cart and Title tables on the ISBN field. For dBASE tables, the relation is set through the indexName, masterRowset, and masterFields properties. To optimize the query for SQL, all three properties must be unspecified. Each line in bold needs to be revised or removed.

Here are the original Cart form queries for dBASE tables:

```
with (this.cart1 = new Query()){
   left = 70;
   top = 1;
   sql = 'SELECT * FROM "cart.DBF"';
   active = true;
}

with (this.cart1.rowset) {
}

with (this.title1 = new Query()){
   left = 70;
   top = 2;
   sql = 'SELECT * FROM "title.DBF"';
   active = true;
}

with (this.title1.rowset) {
   indexName = "ISBN";
   masterRowset = parent.parent.cart1.rowset;
   masterFields = "ISBN";
}
```

21

The key to creating efficient SQL relations is the masterSource property. You can use the masterSource property to create an SQL parameter that relates one query to another. The WHERE clause of the SELECT command works with parameters to ensure that the rows of one query relate to rows in another. In the case of the Cart form, the WHERE clause of the Title query needs to restrict the rowset to rows where the ISBN matches the current ISBN in the Cart query.

The Cart form allows updates to the Cart and requires a live rowset for the cart1 query. The Title table is never directly modified by the shopping cart application. You can always optimize Title queries by setting requestLive to false.

Here are the revised Cart form queries for SQL tables:

```
with (this.cart1 = new Query()){
   left = 70;
   top = 1;
   database = parent.dbstore;
   sql = 'SELECT * FROM CART';
   active = true;
}

with (this.cart1.rowset) {
}

with (this.title1 = new Query()){
   left = 70;
   top = 2;
   requestLive = false;
   database = parent.dbstore;
   masterSource = parent.cart1.rowset;
   sql = 'SELECT * FROM TITLE WHERE ISBN = :ISBN ORDER BY ISBN';
   active = true;
}

with (this.title1.rowset) {
}
```

Checkout Form

The Checkout form has more queries than the other forms you modified already, but there are no new changes. The Customer, Invoice, and Lineitem queries only need to have the database property and revised table names added. There are no index or relation issues with the first three queries.

Here are the original Checkout form queries for dBASE tables:

```
with (this.customer1 = new Query()){
   left = 70;
   top = 1;
   sql = 'SELECT * FROM "customer.DBF"';
   active = true;
}
```

```
with (this.customer1.rowset) {
}

with (this.invoice1 = new Query()){
   left = 70;
   top = 2;
   sql = 'SELECT * FROM "invoice.DBF"';
   active = true;
}

with (this.invoice1.rowset) {
}

with (this.lineitem1 = new Query()){
   left = 70;
   top = 3;
   sql = 'SELECT * FROM "lineitem.DBF"';
   active = true;
}

with (this.lineitem1.rowset) {
}

with (this.cart1 = new Query()){
   left = 70;
   top = 4;
   sql = 'SELECT * FROM "cart.DBF"';
   active = true;
}

with (this.cart1.rowset) {
}

with (this.title1 = new Query()){
   left = 70;
   top = 5;
   sql = 'SELECT * FROM "title.DBF"';
   active = true;
}

with (this.title1.rowset) {
    indexName = "ISBN";
   masterRowset = parent.parent.cart1.rowset;
   masterFields = "ISBN";
}
```

The relation between the cart1 query and the title1 query is identical to the one in the Cart form. You can copy and paste the same modifications into the Checkout form. As with the Cart form, the Checkout form updates all tables except the Title table.

Here are the revised Checkout form queries for SQL tables:

```
with (this.customer1 = new Query()){
   left = 70;
   top = 1;
   database = parent.dbstore;
   sql = 'SELECT * FROM CUSTOMER';
   active = true;
}
```

21

```
with (this.customer1.rowset) {
}

with (this.invoice1 = new Query()){
   left = 70;
   top = 2;
   database = parent.dbstore;
   sql = 'SELECT * FROM INVOICE';
   active = true;
}

with (this.invoice1.rowset) {
}

with (this.lineitem1 = new Query()){
   left = 70;
   top = 3;
   database = parent.dbstore;
   sql = 'SELECT * FROM LINEITEM';
   active = true;
}

with (this.lineitem1.rowset) {
}

with (this.cart1 = new Query()){
   left = 70;
   top = 4;
   database = parent.dbstore;
   sql = 'SELECT * FROM CART';
   active = true;
}

with (this.cart1.rowset) {
}

with (this.title1 = new Query()){
   left = 70;
   top = 5;
   requestLive = false;
   database = parent.dbstore;
   masterSource = parent.cart1.rowset;
   sql = 'SELECT * FROM TITLE WHERE ISBN = :ISBN ORDER BY ISBN';
   active = true;
}

with (this.title1.rowset) {
}
```

Detail Form

In the Detail form, the Cart query is not related to the Title query. The Cart query is used only when a shopper adds the current title to the shopping cart. A live rowset must be available for the Cart query.

Here are the original Detail Form queries for dBASE tables:

```
with (this.cart1 = new Query()){
   left = 70;
   top = 1;
   sql = 'SELECT * FROM "cart.DBF"';
   active = true;
}

with (this.cart1.rowset) {
}

with (this.title1 = new Query()){
   left = 70;
   top = 2;
   sql = 'SELECT * FROM "title.dbf"';
   active = true;
}

with (this.title1.rowset) {
   autoEdit = false;
}
```

You can remove the autoEdit property from the title1.rowset block. The property has no effect on the Detail form in either the dBASE or SQL version. The autoEdit property comes into play only when the form contains a control with a direct datalink to a field. No such controls exist on the completed version of the Detail form.

Here are the revised Detail form queries for SQL tables:

```
with (this.cart1 = new Query()){
   left = 70;
   top = 1;
   database = parent.dbstore;
   sql = 'SELECT * FROM CART';
   active = true;
}

with (this.cart1.rowset) {
}

with (this.title1 = new Query()){
   left = 70;
   top = 2;
   requestLive = false;
   database = parent.dbstore;
   sql = 'SELECT * FROM TITLE';
   active = true;
}

with (this.title1.rowset) {
}
```

21

Keyword Form

The changes to the Keyword form are the simplest yet. The form contains only one query. There are no indexes or relations to worry about.

Here is the original Keyword form query for dBASE tables:

```
with (this.title1 = new Query()){
   left = 70;
   top = 1;
   sql = 'SELECT * FROM "title.DBF"';
   active = true;
}

with (this.title1.rowset) {
}
```

Like all other instances of a Title query, you can set requestLive to false. You could also delete the with block for the rowset. If you remove the empty with block, the form runs the same. However, if you open and resave the file through the Form Designer, IntraBuilder reinserts the empty with block.

Here is the revised Keyword form query for SQL tables:

```
with (this.title1 = new Query()){
   left = 70;
   top = 1;
   requestLive = false;
   database = parent.dbstore;
   sql = 'SELECT * FROM TITLE';
   active = true;
}
```

Quick Form

The only required changes for the Quick form are adding the database assignment and revising the table name. Because the form does not update any tables, you can also set requestLive to false for the form's two queries.

Here are the original Quick Form queries for dBASE tables:

```
with (this.product1 = new Query()){
   left = 70;
   top = 4;
   sql = 'SELECT * FROM "product.dbf"';
   active = true;
}

with (this.product1.rowset) {
}

with (this.title1 = new Query()){
   left = 70;
   top = 5;
```

```
      sql = 'SELECT * FROM "title.dbf"';
      active = true;
}

with (this.title1.rowset) {
}
```

Here are the revised Quick Form queries for SQL tables:

```
with (this.product1 = new Query()){
      left = 70;
      top = 4;
      requestLive = false;
      database = parent.dbstore;
      sql = 'SELECT * FROM PRODUCT';
      active = true;
}

with (this.product1.rowset) {
}

with (this.title1 = new Query()){
      left = 70;
      top = 5;
      requestLive = false;
      database = parent.dbstore;
      sql = 'SELECT * FROM TITLE';
      active = true;
}

with (this.title1.rowset) {
}
```

Results Form

The last standard query block to change is a simple Title query for the Results form. This query is identical to the Title query of the Keyword form.

Here is the original Results Form query for dBASE tables:

```
with (this.title1 = new Query()){
      left = 70;
      top = 1;
      sql = 'SELECT * FROM "title.dbf"';
       active = true;
}

with (this.title1.rowset) {
}
```

Here is the revised Results Form query for SQL tables:

```
with (this.title1 = new Query()){
      left = 70;
      top = 1;
      requestLive = false;
```

```
    database = parent.dbstore;
    sql = 'SELECT * FROM TITLE';
    active = true;
}

with (this.title1.rowset) {
}
```

After changing the query definitions in each of the five forms, you can run the shopping cart application with the InterBase database. There are still three problems that will keep the application from running as it did with dBASE tables. See whether you can locate the forms that do not respond correctly. One form has a cosmetic problem and a logic error. Another form has a button that can lead to a runtime error. The next two sections will show you how to correct these problems.

Fine-Tuning the Detail Form

If a shopper searches the Titles and opens the Detail form, excess time information displays along with the publication date. If a shopper clicks on the Add to Cart button, the book goes into the cart with a null quantity. To better equip the Detail form for working with SQL tables, the date display and the add operations need modification. Figure 21.15 shows the Detail form before removing the time from the publication date display.

Figure 21.15.

The Detail form with extra time information.

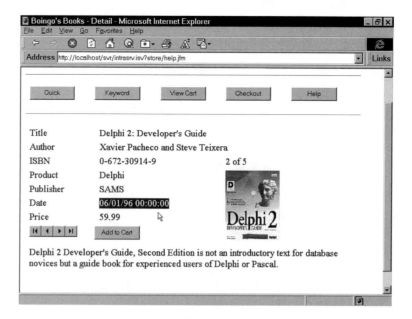

To fix the Detail form, edit the `detail.jfm` file as a script and adjust the `UpdateValues()` and `buttonAdd_onServerClick()` methods as shown in Listings 21.3 and 21.4. The lines that require modification are shown in bold.

INPUT   **Listing 21.3. The revised `UpdateValues()` method.**

```
 1: function UpdateValues(thisForm)
 2: {
 3:     var fTitle = thisForm.title1.rowset.fields ;
 4:     thisForm.valueTitle.text     = fTitle["TITLE"].value ;
 5:     thisForm.valueAuthor.text    = fTitle["AUTHOR"].value ;
 6:     thisForm.valueISBN.text      = fTitle["ISBN"].value ;
 7:     thisForm.valueProduct.text   = fTitle["PRODUCT"].value ;
 8:     thisForm.valuePublisher.text = fTitle["PUBLISHER"].value ;
 9:     thisForm.valuePubdate.text   = fTitle["PUBDATE"].value.getMonth() +
10:                            "/" + fTitle["PUBDATE"].value.getYear() ;
11:     thisForm.valuePrice.text     = fTitle["PRICE"].value ;
12:     thisForm.valueNotes.text     = fTitle["NOTES"].value ;
13:     thisForm.htmlPosition.text =
14:         thisForm.currentRow  + " of " + thisForm.titleCount ;
15:     thisForm.imageCover.visible = (! (fTitle["COVER"].value == "")) ;
16: }
```

ANALYSIS   The `UpdateValues()` method fires when the Detail form loads and whenever the row navigation occurs. The method synchronizes what the user sees with the values from the current row. Lines 9 and 10 replace the following statement:

```
thisForm.valuePubdate.text = fTitle["PUBDATE"].value
```

The original version uses whatever value is in the field as the display value. For the dBASE table, the field value contained only a date. InterBase can store date and time information in a single field. The time is not relevant to a publication date. The only essential information for publication date is the month and year. Because the `value` property of a date field is a date object, you can use methods from the `Date` class to extract the month and year. Line 9 extracts the month, and line 10 appends the year in the format *MM/YY*.

The second problem with the Detail form does not manifest itself until the Cart form opens. When a shopper adds a book to his shopping cart, the Cart form shows the `Qty` set to zero. The actual `Qty` in the table is a null. A `Qty` of one should appear in the table and in the browser. Figure 21.16 shows how the total and grand total are blank when the `Qty` is null. You can add one line to the `buttonAdd_onServerClick()` method to fix the problem. Listing 21.4 shows the new line in bold.

21

Figure 21.16.

The Cart form with a null value in the Qty *field.*

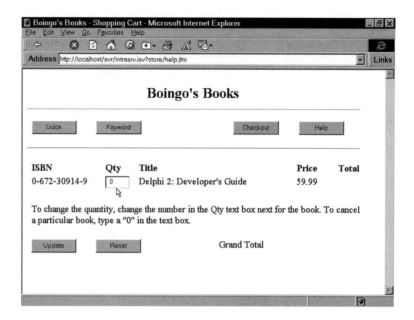

Listing 21.4. The revised `buttonAdd_onServerClick()` **method.**

```
1: function buttonAdd_onServerClick()
2: {
3:    var rCart  = this.form.cart1.rowset,
4:        rTitle = this.form.title1.rowset ;
5:    rCart.applyLocate(
6:      "ISBN = " + "'" + rTitle.fields["ISBN"].value + "'"
7:      + "AND CARTUSER = " + "'" + this.form.user + "'" ) ;
8:    if ( rCart.endOfSet )
9:    {
10:      rCart.beginAppend() ;
11:      rCart.fields["ISBN"].value = rTitle.fields["ISBN"].value ;
12:      rCart.fields["CARTUSER"].value = this.form.user ;
13:      rCart.fields["CARTDATE"].value = new Date() ;
14:      rCart.fields["QTY"].value = 0 ;
15:    }
16:    rCart.fields["QTY"].value++ ;
17:    rCart.save() ;
18:    rCart.active = false ;
19:    nextForm = new cartForm() ;
20:    nextForm.user = this.form.user ;
21:    nextForm.open() ;
22:    this.form.release() ;
23: }
```

ANALYSIS When you append a row to a dBASE table, all numeric fields default to zero. The same operation on most other table types results in null values in the numeric fields.

Any computation involving a null value results in a null value such that 1 + null = null. Line 16 has no effect if the value is a null. To allow the initial value to increment, the Qty field must be set to a non-null value. Line 14 replaces the null with a zero, making the function work the same for both InterBase and dBASE tables.

Updating the Checkout Form

The Checkout form contains two queries that are defined within methods rather than in the constructor. Both queries become active when a shopper clicks on the Buy button and the data has been validated. The queries duplicate existing queries for the Custom and Invoice tables. The secondary queries help calculate the next available primary key value.

Determining the next available key value is a native feature of many table types, including Paradox and InterBase. The dBASE table format does not have any such functionality and requires the calculation to happen at the application script level. Paradox and Access tables have auto-increment fields that have self-generating unique key values. InterBase provides stored procedures, triggers, and generators that allow developers to define server-side functions that track key field values.

To get the shopping cart application up and running with InterBase as quickly as possible, you can keep the dBASE logic intact. The last topic of the day explains how to replace some of the existing logic with database server routines. To make the dBASE logic work for InterBase, edit the Checkout form as a script and update the SaveCustomer() and SaveInvoice() methods as shown in Listings 21.5 and 21.6.

INPUT   **Listing 21.5. The revised SaveCustomer() method.**

```
 1: function SaveCustomer( thisForm )
 2: {
 3:     var customer2   = new Query() ;
 4:     customer2.requestLive = false ;
 5:     customer2.database    = thisForm.dbstore ;
 6:     customer2.sql         = "SELECT * FROM CUSTOMER ORDER BY CUSTOMER" ;
 7:     customer2.active      = true ;
 8:
 9:     var customer1Row = thisForm.customer1.rowset,
10:         customer2Row = customer2.rowset ;
11:     if ( thisForm.radioVisa.value )
12:     {
13:       customer1Row.fields["CARD"].value = "VISA" ;
14:     }
15:     else if( thisForm.radioMC.value )
16:     {
17:       customer1Row.fields["CARD"].value = "MC" ;
18:     }
19:     else
20:     {
```

21

continues

Listing 21.5. continued

```
21:         customer1Row.fields["CARD"].value = "AMEX" ;
22:    }
23: //   customer2Row.indexName = "CUSTOMER" ;
24:      customer2Row.last() ;
25:      customer1Row.fields["CUSTOMER"].value = customer2Row.endOfSet ?
26:          1 : customer2Row.fields["CUSTOMER"].value + 1 ;
27:      customer1Row.save() ;
28:      customer2.active = false ;
29: }
```

ANALYSIS   The SaveCustomer() method saves a new row in the Customer Table. When the
Checkout form loads, the Rowset::beginAppend() method creates a row buffer that
is discarded unless the shopper clicks on the Buy button and all the entries are validated. All
but two of the fields in the customer table have direct datalinks to controls on the Checkout
form. The two that do not are the Card field and the Customer field. Lines 11 through 22
determine the value for the Card field. The rest of the logic calculates the appropriate
Customer value. Lines 3 through 7 replace the following statement:

```
var customer2 = new Query("select * from customer") ;
```

The shortcut approach that was used with the original form does not work when using a table
that is not contained in the default database. Another change from the original code appears
on line 23. This line is commented out in the InterBase version.

INPUT   ## Listing 21.6. The revised SaveInvoice() method.

```
1: function SaveInvoice( thisForm )
2: {
3:     var invoice2     = new Query() ;
4:     invoice2.requestLive = true ;
5:     invoice2.database    = thisForm.dbstore ;
6:     invoice2.sql         = "SELECT * FROM INVOICE ORDER BY INVOICE" ;
7:     invoice2.active      = true ;
8:
9:     var customerRow = thisForm.customer1.rowset
10:         invoice1Row = thisForm.invoice1.rowset,
11:         invoice2Row = invoice2.rowset ;
12:     invoice1Row.beginAppend() ;
13:     invoice1Row.fields["CUSTOMER"].value =
14:        customerRow.fields["CUSTOMER"].value ;
15:     invoice1Row.fields["ORDERDATE"].value = (new Date()) ;
16: //   invoice2Row.indexName = "INVOICE" ;
17:     invoice2Row.last() ;
18:     invoice1Row.fields["INVOICE"].value = invoice2Row.endOfSet ?
19:         1 : invoice2Row.fields["INVOICE"].value + 1 ;
20:     invoice1Row.save() ;
21:     invoice2.active = false ;
22: }
```

21

ANALYSIS   The SaveInvoice() method contains much of the same logic contained in SaveCustomer(). The primary differences in this method are that the fields do not have datalinks and the rowset was not already in append mode. Line 12 places the invoice1 query into append mode, whereas the customer1 query was already in append mode in the previous method. The changes for InterBase are essentially the same as the change made to SaveCustomer().

NOTE   The files for Day 21 contain two versions of the Checkout form. The check1.jfm file contains the methods shown in Listings 21.5 and 21.6. You copy the check1.jfm file over checkout.jfm to run the application without any stored procedures. The checkout.jfm file, contained in the Day 21 file set, relies on the stored procedures presented in the section "Application Partitioning with Stored Procedures."

Updating the Receipt Report

The Receipt report needs many of the same modifications that you have already made to the forms. To make the report run with InterBase, each query needs the database setting and revised table names. Unlike the JavaScript forms, the Receipt Report does not inherit a dbstore database from the Toolbar custom form class. You need to add a definition for the dbstore database before the first query definition. Edit the receipt.jrp file as script and modify the query definitions to match Listing 21.7. All modifications are in bold.

INPUT   **Listing 21.7. The revised queries for the Receipt report.**

```
 1: with (this.dbstore = new Database()){
 2:    left = 0;
 3:    top = 0;
 4:    databaseName = "STORE";
 5:    loginString = "SYSDBA/masterkey";
 6:    active = true;
 7: }
 8:
 9: with (this.invoice1 = new Query()){
10:    left = 1000;
11:    top = 0;
12:    requestLive = false;
13:    database = parent.dbstore;
14:    sql = 'SELECT * FROM INVOICE';
15:    active = true;
16: }
17:
18: with (this.invoice1.rowset) {
```

continues

21

Listing 21.7. continued

```
19: }
20:
21: with (this.lineitem1 = new Query()){
22:    left = 2000;
23:    top = 0;
24:    requestLive = false;
25:    database = parent.dbstore;
26:    masterSource = parent.invoice1.rowset;
27:    sql = 'SELECT * FROM LINEITEM WHERE INVOICE = :INVOICE ' +
28:            ' ORDER BY INVOICE';
29:    active = true;
30: }
31:
32: with (this.lineitem1.rowset) {
33: }
34:
35: with (this.customer1 = new Query()){
36:    left = 3000;
37:    top = 0;
38:    requestLive = false;
39:    database = parent.dbstore;
40:    masterSource = parent.invoice1.rowset;
41:    sql = 'SELECT * FROM CUSTOMER WHERE CUSTOMER = :CUSTOMER ' +
42:            ' ORDER BY CUSTOMER';
43:    active = true;
44: }
45:
46: with (this.customer1.rowset) {
47: }
48:
49: with (this.title1 = new Query()){
50:    left = 4000;
51:    top = 0;
52:    requestLive = false;
53:    database = parent.dbstore;
54:    masterSource = parent.lineitem1.rowset ;
55:    sql = 'SELECT * FROM TITLE WHERE ISBN = :ISBN ORDER BY ISBN';
56:    active = true;
57: }
58:
59: with (this.title1.rowset) {
60: }
```

ANALYSIS   The Receipt report contains four related queries for the Invoice, Lineitem, Customer, and Title tables. The Lineitem table controls the detail band. The page header displays fields from the Invoice and Customer tables. Only fields from the Lineitem and Title tables appear in the detail band.

The query code in Listing 21.7 is part of the constructor code for the report. In the receipt.jrp file, the database and query definitions come before any report object definitions. Lines 1 through 7 show the database definition that is entirely new to the InterBase version of the report. All the query and rowset objects also exist in the dBASE version.

The Invoice query contains three modifications on lines 12 through 14. Because reports are almost always read-only operations, you can set requestLive to false for all the queries in the report. You can see the setting repeated for the other queries on lines 24, 38, and 52.

The indexName, masterRowset, and masterFields properties were removed from the Lineitem, Customer, and Title rowset definitions. The masterSource properties set on lines 26, 40, and 54 act as SQL equivalents to the dBASE masterRowset property settings. The ORDER BY clauses found on lines 28, 42, and 55 work in place of the indexName values. The masterFields property settings are replaced in lines 27, 41, and 55 by WHERE clauses.

After incorporating all the changes in Listing 21.7, you run the Receipt report with the Store database. When you do, one more problem appears that is reminiscent of something you recently dealt with on the Detail form. The order date displays with a time value, as shown in Figure 21.17.

Figure 21.17.

The Receipt report with time display.

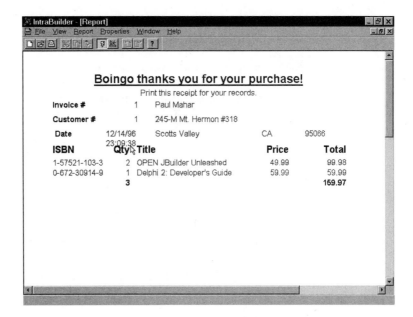

The time value wraps in the Report Designer and can lead to other problems when run through a browser. You can remove the time portion of the order date with the following steps:

1. Open the Receipt report in the Designer.

2. Create a new method and open the Method Editor by selecting Method|New Method.

3. Remove the {Export} comment and rename the method OrderMYD().

21

4. Enter the JavaScript statements, like this:

```
function OrderMDY()
{
  var vDate = this.form.invoice1.rowset.fields["ORDERDATE"].value ;
  return (vDate.getMonth() + 1 + "/" +
          vDate.getDate() + "/" +
          vDate.getYear() ) ;
}
```

5. Press F2 and then Shift+F2 to verify the report and load the new method into the Designer.

WARNING

If you do not reload the report in the Designer, IntraBuilder might encounter an error when you reference the new method in a self-evaluating code block.

6. Select the date field and press F11 to inspect `form.pageTemplate1.orderdate`.

7. Change the text property to `{||this.form.OrderMDY()}`, as shown in Figure 21.18.

Figure 21.18.

Updating a code block with a method call.

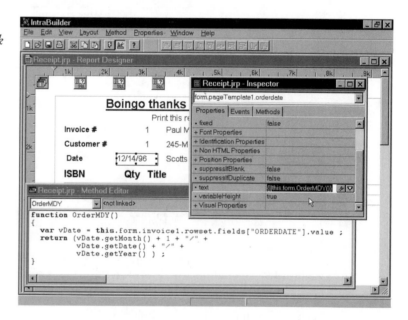

That is the last modification for the Receipt report. You can run the report to view the receipt without time information. The shopping cart application now functions just as it did with dBASE tables. You can stop here or continue to learn how to further optimize the application using stored procedures.

Application Partitioning with Stored Procedures

You can use stored procedures to harness the native processing power of a database server. IntraBuilder supports stored procedures with Oracle, Sybase, Informix, DB2, InterBase, and Microsoft SQL Server. Each server has proprietary syntax for developing stored procedures, but the JavaScript calling system is consistent across vendor platforms.

NEW TERM *Application partitioning* occurs when processing is spread across several systems. By nature, every IntraBuilder application does some partitioning between the IntraBuilder Server and client browsers. Adding client-side JavaScript increases the level of partitioning by offloading some of the processes to client browsers. Another way to partition an application is to move logic from IntraBuilder to a database server. The goal of partitioning is to move processes to the systems most adept at the task. For example, database servers are often better equipped at generating unique key values than IntraBuilder or a browser.

In this section, you will learn how to create stored procedures in the Store database from an IntraBuilder script. After testing the stored procedures, you can simplify and optimize the Checkout form by adding calls to the stored procedures.

Adding Stored Procedures to the Database

To see where stored procedures can be beneficial, let's review the key values of each table in the Store database. Table 21.2 lists the keys that uniquely identify each row for the six tables in the database. An examination of the key values reveals that two tables contain self-referencing keys. The Customer and Invoice tables contain unique key values that have no meaning outside the table. Other tables use values from existing entities such as a session ID, product name, or ISBN.

Table 21.2. Key values.

Table	Key	Origin of Value
Cart	CARTUSER	Netinfo.sessionID
Customer	CUSTOMER	One greater than last Customer value
Invoice	INVOICE	One greater than last Invoice value
Lineitem	INVOICE + ISBN	Invoice from Invoice table and ISBN from Title table
Product	PRODUCT	Unique product names
Title	ISBN	Provided by publisher

21

The Customer and Invoice keys are well suited to the InterBase generator feature. An InterBase generator is a value maintained by the server that you can increment and access through stored procedures. Generators are a remarkably efficient way to track and create key values. Listing 21.8 contains a Generate class to help create, use, and remove InterBase generators.

INPUT   **Listing 21.8. The genclass.js auxiliary class file.**

```
 1: //
 2: // class Generator
 3: //
 4: // Provides methods for working with InterBase generators.
 5: //
 6: // Syntax:
 7: // <oRef> = new Generator(<oRef: database>,<expC, generator name>)
 8: //
 9: // Methods:
10: // make(<expN> start value>)
11: //
12: //      Creates a generator and a stored procedure in <oRef: database>.
13: //      The generator is named <expC: name>. The stored procedure is
14: //      named NEXT<expC: name>. The stored procedure increments the
15: //      generator and sets GNEXT to the new value.
16: //
17: // call()
18: //
19: //      Calls a generator named NEXT+<expC: name> and returns the value
20: //      form GNEXT.
21: //
22: // drop()
23: //
24: //      Removes a generator named <expC: name> and a stored procedure
25: //      named NEXT<expC: name>.
26: //
27: class Generator(db,cName)
28: {
29:     this.db   = db ;
30:     this.name = cName.toUpperCase() ;
31:
32:     function make(nInit)
33:     {
34:         var CRLF = (new StringEx().chr(13))+ (new StringEx().chr(10)),
35:             q    = new Query() ;
36:         q.database = this.db ;
37:         q.sql = "SELECT * FROM RDB$GENERATORS "
38:             + "WHERE RDB$GENERATOR_NAME = '" + this.name + "'" ;
39:         q.active = true ;
40:         if ( q.rowset.count() == 0 )
41:         {
42:             this.db.executeSQL("CREATE GENERATOR " + this.name) ;
43:             this.db.executeSQL("SET GENERATOR " + this.name + " TO " +
44:                     Math.int(nInit) );
```

21

```
45:                 this.db.executeSQL("CREATE PROCEDURE NEXT" + this.name + CRLF+
46:                     "RETURNS (GNEXT INTEGER)"              + CRLF +
47:                     "AS"                                  + CRLF +
48:                     "BEGIN"                               + CRLF +
49:                     "  GNEXT = GEN_ID(" + this.name + ",1);" + CRLF +
50:                     "END" ) ;
51:         }
52:     }
53:
54:     function call()
55:     {
56:         var s = new StoredProc() ;
57:         s.database      = this.db ;
58:         s.procedureName = "NEXT" + this.name ;
59:         s.active        = true ;
60:         return ( s.params["GNEXT"].value )  ;
61:     }
62:
63:     function drop()
64:     {
65:         this.db.executeSQL("DROP PROCEDURE NEXT" + this.name) ;
66:         this.db.executeSQL("DELETE FROM RDB$GENERATORS "
67:                 + "WHERE RDB$GENERATOR_NAME = '" + this.name + "'") ;
68:     }
69: }
```

ANALYSIS   The Generate class makes it easy to work with InterBase generators. This class consists of two properties and three methods. The properties are values that you must pass to the constructor. The db property is an object reference to an InterBase database. The name property is the name of the generator. Line 30 converts the name to uppercase, making the name case-insensitive.

The Generate::make() method is the most complex of the three. This method takes one parameter for the initial generator value. Lines 35 through 40 check to see whether the generator already exists. InterBase stores generators in the RDB$GENERATORS system table. This table contains the names and values of all generators in the database. If the generator already exists, the method ends without making any modifications.

If the query has a count of zero, the generator is undefined and the method executes three SQL commands. The following JavaScript statements use the Generate class to create a generator called MYGEN with an initial value of 5:

```
_sys.scripts.load("genclass.js") ;
var db = new Database() ;
db.databaseName = "STORE" ;
db.loginString  = "SYSDBA/masterkey" ;
db.active       = true ;
var gen = new Generator(db,"MYGEN");
gen.make(5);
```

21

When the Generator.make() method is called in the MYGEN example, the following SQL statements are passed to the InterBase server. The CREATE GENERATOR command adds a row to the RDB$GENERATORS table and sets the value to zero, and the SET command changes the value to 5. The CREATE PROCEDURE command defines a new stored procedure on the server:

```
CREATE GENERATOR MYGEN

SET GENERATOR MYGEN TO 5

CREATE PROCEDURE NEXTMYGEN
RETURNS (GNEXT INTEGER)
AS
BEGIN
  GNEXT = GEN_ID(MYGEN,1);
END
```

TIP
InterBase lets you define much more complex stored procedures than are shown in this chapter. See the InterBase Help file for a complete list of statements and functions that you can use in a stored procedure.

The Generate::call() method is one you can call anytime you need to increment and retrieve a value from a generator. This method calls the stored procedure defined in the Generate::make() method. Line 56 creates an instance of the StoredProc class. The stored procedure executes when the active property is set to true on line 59.

The StoredProc object makes it easy to pass and receive parameters from a stored procedure. For the generator, there is only one parameter, and it is passed back to IntraBuilder on line 60. IntraBuilder retrieves values from a stored procedure as associate arrays. The GNEXT parameter contains the current generator value. The following statements increment the MYGEN generator and return the new value. This calls a stored procedure with the name NEXTMYGEN:

```
_sys.scripts.load("genclass.js") ;
var db = new Database() ;
db.databaseName = "STORE" ;
db.loginString  = "SYSDBA/masterkey" ;
db.active       = true ;
var gen = new Generator(db,"MYGEN");
_sys.scriptOut.writeln(gen.call());
```

The last method removes a generator and associated stored procedure from the database. InterBase does not support a DROP GENERATOR command. To remove a Generator, lines 66 and 67 delete the row defining the generator from the RDB$GENERATORS system table. The following lines remove the MYGEN generator and NEXTMYGEN stored procedure from the Store database:

21

```
_sys.scripts.load("genclass.js") ;
var db = new Database() ;
db.databaseName = "STORE" ;
db.loginString  = "SYSDBA/masterkey" ;
db.active       = true ;
var gen = new Generator(db,"MYGEN");
gen.delete();
```

The following SQL commands execute when calling `Generate::delete()` for the `MYGEN` generator:

```
DROP PROCEDURE NEXTMYGEN
```

```
DELETE FROM RDB$GENERATORS WHERE RDB$GENERATOR_NAME = 'MYGEN'
```

Using the `Generate` class, you can create stored procedures and generators for the Customer and Invoice tables. The `addproc.js` script in Listing 21.9 uses `Generate::make()` to set up the generators with initial values that correspond to the highest key value in each table.

INPUT **Listing 21.9. The `addproc.js` script.**

```
 1: _sys.scripts.load("genclass.js") ;
 2: var db = new Database() ;
 3: db.databaseName = "STORE" ;
 4: db.loginString  = "SYSDBA/masterkey" ;
 5: db.active       = true ;
 6:
 7: KeyIt(db, "CUSTOMER") ;
 8: KeyIt(db, "INVOICE") ;
 9:
10: function KeyIt(db, cKey)
11: {
12:     var q = new Query() ;
13:     q.database = db ;
14:     q.sql = "SELECT * FROM " + cKey + " ORDER BY " + cKey ;
15:     q.active = true ;
16:     q.rowset.last() ;
17:     var gen = new Generator(db, cKey) ;
18:     gen.make(q.rowset.fields[0].value) ;
19: }
```

ANALYSIS Run the `addproc` script to create the generators and stored procedures for the Customer and Invoice tables. When you run the script, the first line opens the `genclass.js` file to get access to the `Generate` class. Lines 2 through 5 establish a connection to the Store database. The function calls on lines 7 and 8 pass a reference to the Store database and a key field name to the `KeyIt()` function.

21

Although the KeyIt() function appears somewhat generic, it makes some broad assumptions about the table and key fields. Line 14 executes correctly only if the table contains a field with the same name as the table. Line 18 also relies on the same key field as being the first field in the table structure. Fortunately, the assumptions are correct for the Customer and Invoice tables.

After running the addproc script, you can use the InterBase Interactive SQL tool to verify that the generators and methods were created correctly. Here are the steps for checking metadata with the Interactive SQL tool:

1. Start the InterBase Interactive SQL tool and verify that the InterBase Server is running.

2. Open the Store database by selecting File|Connect to Database and entering the following options:

   □ Database: C:\Program Files\Borland\IntraBuilder\Store\STORE.GDB

   □ User Name: SYSDBA

   □ Password: masterkey

3. To see the Procedures, select View|Metadata Information, and select Procedure from the list, as shown in Figure 21.19.

Figure 21.19.

Getting a list of procedures.

You can also use the View|Metadata Information option to get a list of generators and the definition of a single stored procedure. If you select Procedures and enter NEXTINVOICE, the ISQL Output area displays the commands and parameters that make up the procedure. Figure 21.20 shows the ISQL Output area.

Figure 21.20.

Viewing the definition of the NEXTINVOICE *stored procedure.*

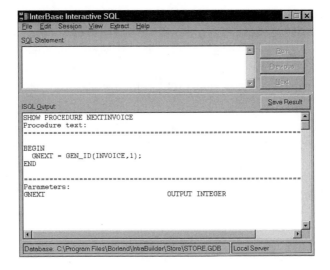

Partitioning the Checkout Form

It is now time to update the Checkout form to take advantage of the stored procedures. Only the SaveCustomer() and SaveInvoice() methods need modification. Edit the Checkout form as a script file and make the changes shown in Listings 21.10 and 21.11. These changes eliminate the redundant queries and ensure valid keys across any number of IntraBuilder Agents.

INPUT

Listing 21.10. The SaveCustomer() **method with a stored procedure call.**

```
 1: function SaveCustomer( thisForm )
 2: {
 3:    _sys.scripts.load("genclass.js") ;
 4:    var gen        = new Generator(thisForm.dbstore, "CUSTOMER"),
 5:       customer1Row = thisForm.customer1.rowset ;
 6:    if ( thisForm.radioVisa.value )
 7:    {
 8:       customer1Row.fields["CARD"].value = "VISA" ;
 9:    }
10:    else if( thisForm.radioMC.value )
11:    {
12:       customer1Row.fields["CARD"].value = "MC" ;
13:    }
14:    else
15:    {
16:       customer1Row.fields["CARD"].value = "AMEX" ;
17:    }
18:    customer1Row.fields["CUSTOMER"].value = gen.call() ;
19:    customer1Row.save() ;
20: }
```

21

ANALYSIS The new version of the SaveCustomer() method is about one third shorter than the one that relied on the dBASE key generation technique. See Listing 21.5 for a comparison. All references to customer2Row are gone. Only lines 3 and 4 are new. Line 3 loads the script containing the Generate class. IntraBuilder ignores the statement if the script is already in memory. Line 4 creates an instance of the Generator class using the Store database and the Customer table.

The real action happens on line 18. The gen.call() expression executes the NEXTCUSTOMER stored procedure on the InterBase Server. The return value is a valid unique key.

INPUT **Listing 21.11. The SaveInvoice() method with a stored procedure call.**

```
 1: function SaveInvoice( thisForm )
 2: {
 3:    _sys.scripts.load("genclass.js") ;
 4:    var gen        = new Generator(thisForm.dbstore, "INVOICE"),
 5:        customerRow = thisForm.customer1.rowset,
 6:        invoice1Row = thisForm.invoice1.rowset ;
 7:    invoice1Row.beginAppend() ;
 8:    invoice1Row.fields["CUSTOMER"].value =
 9:        customerRow.fields["CUSTOMER"].value ;
10:    invoice1Row.fields["ORDERDATE"].value = (new Date()) ;
11:    invoice1Row.fields["INVOICE"].value = gen.call() ;
12:    invoice1Row.save() ;
13: }
```

ANALYSIS The new SaveInvoice() method is about half the size of the one in Listing 21.6. All references to invoice2Row are gone. The new lines are 3 and 4. As the form is currently written, line 3 will always be ignored because SaveCustomer() always executes before SaveInvoice() and SaveCustomer() also loads the genclass script. Line 11 contains the stored procedure call.

Moving the key generation process to the database server can improve the performance and reliability of the Checkout form. The difference becomes more noticeable as the table grows larger and more users access the system simultaneously. The improvement might not be detectable with only one client or when working with small tables such as those provided with the book.

Summary

Today you learned how to leverage IntraBuilder applications by adding connections to database servers such as Oracle, Informix, InterBase, DB2, Sybase, and Microsoft SQL Server. The exercises shown throughout the chapter used InterBase to demonstrate effective access methods that apply equally well to any database server that you connect to through a SQL-Link driver.

The day began with a quick overview of the Local InterBase Server. This small footprint server is ideal for single-station development, and it comes with the Client/Server version of IntraBuilder, Delphi, and C++ Builder. You can use the Local InterBase Server to prototype a database for later deployment with Oracle, Sybase, Microsoft SQL Server, or InterBase Server for NT.

Today's main task was updating the custom form class, a report, and JavaScript forms to replace the dBASE table connections with SQL database connections. The changes for each form included adding a database object and updating the query object. To optimize the queries for SQL, you removed `indexName`, `masterRowset`, and `masterField` settings from the rowset definitions. In their place, you added `ORDER BY` and `WHERE` clauses to the SQL commands and `masterSource` properties to related queries.

By the end of today's lesson, you were partitioning the shopping cart application by moving process out of a JavaScript form and onto the database server. To create unique key values on the server, you defined generators and stored procedures that you could call from IntraBuilder.

Q&A

Q The final version of the Checkout form calls a stored procedure to generate a unique key value when appending rows. Wouldn't it be easier to create a trigger on the server that automatically fired when a row was added?

A Client applications are not notified of changes made by a trigger. If an IntraBuilder method appends a row to a table, values altered by any related triggers are not posted back to the IntraBuilder application. This can result in a mismatch between the IntraBuilder row buffer and the current database image. So, although it is possible to generate unique keys through a trigger, it is not recommended.

Q I need to create an audit trail of all transactions. What is the best approach when using a database server?

A Triggers offer the most efficient way to track changes to a table. When creating an audit trail, the audit table modified by the trigger is distinct from the table causing the trigger. Row buffers are not in danger of becoming corrupt when a trigger does not modify the table causing the trigger.

Q I have IntraBuilder Professional and Delphi Client/Server. Is it okay to use the InterBase version bundled with Delphi as a server for IntraBuilder?

A Yes. The InterBase Servers are not tied to any specific client product. The version bundled with Delphi also allows more connections than the one that comes with IntraBuilder.

21

Q **I have completed the dBASE and InterBase versions of the shopping cart application, and I'm having problems running both at the same time. It seems like IntraBuilder keeps running the wrong version. What can I do to run both applications on the same agent?**

A IntraBuilder agents cache class definitions and script files. If you try to load more than one class or script that has the same name, the agent recognizes only the first version. If you want to run the dBASE version and the InterBase versions of the shopping cart applications, you need to make the form and class names unique across both versions. If you prefix the names in the InterBase version with the letter I, the applications will run simultaneously.

Workshop

The Workshop section provides questions and exercises to help you get a better feel for the material you learned today. Try to answer the questions and at least think about the exercises before moving on to the answers. You'll find the answers to the questions in Appendix A, "Answers to Quiz Questions."

Quiz

1. What is metadata, and where is it stored?
2. How can you improve the performance of a SQL query that contains an `indexName` setting?
3. When is it better to use `masterRowset` to relate queries?
4. What command can you use to remove a generator from an InterBase database?
5. How do you reference a database when working with the `UpdateSet` class?
6. What tools are available for debugging problems with SQL connections?

Exercises

1. If you have another database server such as Oracle or Microsoft SQL Server, create a new version of the shopping cart application for the other server. The modifications will be very minor if you delete the InterBase `STORE` alias in BDE and create a new `STORE` alias that uses your server's driver.
2. Compare the performance of native BDE tables to your database server. Modify the bench scripts from Day 10 to work with a SQL database, and chart the results.

21

WEEK
3

15

16

17

18

19

20

21

In Review

Week 3 covered several advanced topics, with an emphasis on reusable components. Day 15 started things off with an in-depth look at customizing the IntraBuilder Designer. Debugging and exception handling took center stage on Day 16. The next four days focused on reusable components. Day 17 described the reusable components that come with the business solution applications. On Day 18, you learned how to integrate Java applets and ActiveX controls into your JavaScript forms. Day 19 took reusability to the operating system level with examples of OLE automation, remote procedure calls, and using the Windows API. Object orientation is the key behind reusability in IntraBuilder applications. Day 20 provided a tour through the dynamic object model. The week ended with a day devoted to the SQL connectivity features found in the IntraBuilder Professional and IntraBuilder Client/Server.

APPENDIX

A

Answers to Quiz Questions

Day 1

1. You can create and modify JavaScript forms through the Form Designer.
2. The IntraBuilder Explorer lets you view, run, and design the files that comprise a JavaScript application.
3. IntraBuilder Professional supports Microsoft SQL Server and InterBase.
4. IntraBuilder Client/Server supports Oracle, Sybase, Microsoft SQL Server, InterBase, Informix, and DB2. The retail version contains SQL-Link drivers for all supported servers. The trial version supports but does not contain SQL-Link drivers. You can use the trial version with 32-bit SQL-Link drivers from C++ Builder or Delphi.
5. IntraBuilder can connect to Microsoft Access tables through ODBC.

Day 2

1. Shift+F2 opens the currently selected file in design mode. F2 runs the file.
2. All versions of IntraBuilder come with the Knowledge Base, Security Administration, Contact Manager, Phone List, and Guest Book applications. IntraBuilder Professional and IntraBuilder Client/Server also include Web utilities and an InterBase version of the Knowledge Base.
3. The default location of the Solution Application home page is

   ```
   C:\Program Files\Borland\IntraBuilder\Apps\Index.Htm
   ```

4. The Knowledge Base Search is not case sensitive.
5. The default Web server port is 80.
6. A document alias lets a Web server work with files outside the root document folder.
7. The Sample forms each demonstrate a single JavaScript concept, while the Solution Applications provide turn key systems that combine many JavaScript techniques.

Day 3

1. The options property determines what values appear in a select list.

2. The form background property lets you set a background image for a form.

3. When you move past the last row in a table, the cursor is at end of set.

4. The Database component lets you work with tables through SQL-Link drivers.

5. The dataLink property links a Text control to a field.

Day 4

1. Custom components can contain property values, linked events, and custom methods.

2. You can create a custom form class in any of the following ways: selecting File|Save as Custom when designing a standard form, programming the custom form class with JavaScript, or using the Custom Form Class Designer.

3. You can select multiple controls by dragging a rectangle around them in the Designer. You can also select one control, hold down the Shift key, and click on additional controls.

4. Before saving a multiple page form, set the current form page to page one.

5. Page zero is the "global page." It shows all controls on all pages. Also, anything you place on it shows up on all other pages.

6. Anything that you can add or set on a standard form can be inherited from a custom form class.

7. The easiest way to add a custom component to the Component Palette is through the Set Up Custom Components dialog.

8. Controls on page zero are visible on all form pages of the form.

9. You can set the current form page through the form's pageno property.

10. Custom form classes provide an easy way to establish a common look and feel to your application.

11. All components are visible when viewing page zero.

Day 5

1. The Report Expert creates detail and summary reports.

2. You can choose between tabular or columnar layouts.

3. Place page heading controls within the page template but outside of the stream frame.

4. Moving a field value within a detail band may not move the field heading if the field was not added through the Field Palette.

Day 6

1. Server-side JavaScript executes entirely on your Web server. Applications that are completely server-based require only that users have browsers supporting HTML 2.0.

   Client-side JavaScript requires Web browsers that support JavaScript.

   For maximum accessibility, your applications should be primarily server-based.

   You should supplement server-side JavaScript with client-side JavaScript as necessary.

   The trade-off is this: Even though exclusively using server-side JavaScript makes your applications more accessible, they will be less functional than apps that include client-side code. The answer is to not pick one approach over the other. Rather, you should build as much of your app as possible in server-side JavaScript, and then supplement it as necessary with client-side code.

2. The _sys object contains methods that execute when you work with the IntraBuilder Explorer.

3. The Script Pad lets you quickly try out JavaScript statements and expressions.

4. The Script Editor lets you edit the JavaScript that defines a form or report. You can also use any other text editor for the same purpose.

5. You can use the Method Editor to create and modify methods from within a designer.

Day 7

1. dBASE table security enables the creation of user- and group-level encryption.
2. The `Query` object provides access to tables, while the `Database` object provides access to SQL connections.
3. When you run a table, IntraBuilder displays a data entry form with Text controls for each field.
4. You can assign a password to a Paradox table through the Database Administration dialog.
5. You can load an existing SQL script or build the SQL statement visually using the Query Builder.

Day 8

1. On secure pages, the address starts with `https` instead of `http`.
2. The *m* and *p* in *mcp* stand for Macmillan and Publishing.
3. Indexes greatly enhance the speed of quick searches when you are looking for complete values rather than substring matches.
4. The HTML editor is available only with the Gold version.
5. Navigator Gold supports GIF and JPEG images.
6. Enter `JAVASCRIPT:` as a location to open Netscape Navigator's Script Pad.

Day 9

1. The start tag for a list item is `<LI>`. The end tag is `</LI>`.

2. By opening the Form in the script editor and using search and replace to replace all references to the `Query` object. There is no way to modify a query reference name through the Form Designer.

3. After dropping a table onto the Form Designer, remove the full path from the new `Query` object's `sql` property.

4. The `filter` property is part of the `Rowset` class.

5. An object is an instance of a class. The class is only a definition of something.

6. The scope resolution operator is `::`, as in `class::Form_onServerLoad`.

Day 10

1. The most user-friendly `filterOptions` setting is `3 - Match partial length and ignore case`.

2. The most performance-unfriendly `filterOptions` setting is `3 - Match partial length and ignore case`.

3. `Database::executeSQL()` is the only method that can create a primary key on a Paradox table. You can define a primary key by passing a `CREATE TABLE` command that includes the `PRIMARY KEY` option to the `Database::executeSQL()` method.

4. Query by form calls the `Rowset::applyLocate()` method that searches for a value without restricting the current rowset. Filter by form adds a filter to the rowset and allows navigation to only those rows that match the filter expression.

5. An IntraBuilder application can include JavaScript expressions, SQL expressions, and dBASE expressions. SQL expressions are allowed in `Database::executeSQL()`, `Rowset::applyLocate()`, and the `filter` property of the `Rowset` class. dBASE expressions are allowed in the `expression` property of the `DbfIndex` class.

6. From fastest to slowest: dBASE, Paradox, Access. Faster speeds are achievable through data sources such as Oracle and Microsoft SQL Server when using SQL-Links with IntraBuilder Client/Server. Refer to Day 21 for more information on creating fast applications for SQL databases.

Day 11

1. Prefix any single quote that occurs within a lookup value with a triple backslash when using the `Rowset::applyLocate()` method or the `filter` property.

2. The `onImageServerClick` receives the top and left position of a mouse click on the image. You can use these parameters to determine what region of the image was clicked.

3. If the `dataSource` of an image is empty, the IntraBuilder Server substitutes a black-and-white image that says "IntraBuilder."

4. A binary field is empty if its value is equal to an empty string.

5. JavaScript: `this.form.title1.rowset.next(-1)`

   English: Move the row pointer to the previous row for the `Title1` query that belongs in the current form.

6. The `autoEdit` property lets you toggle a form between read-only and read-write with a single method call.

Day 12

1. The Form Designer always streams out the `height`, `width`, `color`, and `text` properties for an HTML control. If the color is set to `"black"`, you can remove the `color` property without altering the appearance of the control because the default color is `"black"`.

2. Arrays are zero-based. Length returns a value that is one higher than the highest valid index to the array.

3. Functions defined within a class are methods. Functions defined after the closing class bracket that appears at the end of a JavaScript form file are standard functions, not methods.

4. If the Text control's `value` property is outside of the range of the template, it evaluates to zero.

Day 13

1. Use `this.parent.parent` to refer to a form from a rowset event. The parent of the rowset is a query, and the parent of a query is a form.

2. `<BR>` is the HTML tag for line break.

3. The `groupName` property determines how to group radio buttons. If you create six radio buttons, you can break them into two groups of three by assigning one `groupName` to three of the controls and another `groupName` to the remainder.

4. Little `d` and big `BASE`.

5. Trick question. There are actually two classes with `toUpperCase()`: `String` and `StringEx`.

6. In Navigator 3.0, you can select Options|General Preferences and check the Always Use My Colors option to force Web pages to use a custom browser defined color scheme. The same option is available in Netscape Communicator by selecting Edit|Preferences|General Preferences.

Day 14

1. Controls on page zero appear on all other pages. If you want toolbar buttons to appear on every page of a form, placing the controls on page zero eliminates the need to move them when you change pages.

2. To create a bulleted list in HTML, you need to use the `<LI>` and `<UL>` tags. The `<LI>` tag delimits items in the list. The `<UL>` tag goes around the entire list of items.

3. The Paradox `AutoIncrement` field type creates unique numeric key values when you append new rows to a table.

4. If you pass the SQL command to the constructor of a new `Query` object, IntraBuilder sets the `sql` property to the SQL command and activates the query.

5. You can use a report's `preRender` event in much the same way that you use a form's `onServerLoad` event.

6. The `Group::agSum()` method can sum field values in a self-evaluating code block.

Day 15

1. `IREG0009.DBF` is the custom component registry table. You can use this table to specify toolbar images and tabs for custom components. The table resides in the designer\forms folder. Note that the last four digits of the table name correspond to the country code and will vary in international releases of IntraBuilder.

2. The Desktop Properties dialog lets you specify an alternate script editor.

3. The Toolbars and Palettes dialog lets you configure the look and position of the toolbars.

4. The Application tab of the Desktop Properties dialog contains an option for suppressing the Expert prompt. You can also avoid the prompt by opening the designers from the Script Pad.

5. You can check the multi-user lock option in the Desktop Properties dialog to prevent other users from modifying tables that you are currently using.

6. The View menu has an option for controlling the status bar.

Day 16

1. During Script development you can use the Script Pad for many purposes, including the following:

   ☐ Testing statements and expressions.

   ☐ Listing debug information to the results pane by embedding `_sys.scriptOut.writeln()` statements in your script.

   ☐ Opening, running, and compiling scripts with `_sys.scripts.design()`, `_sys.scripts.run()`, and `_sys.scripts.compile()`.

2. In the Custom folder.

3. The output is 4.

   On line 5, the preprocessor substitutes the value 4 for `OUTPUT_HTML`, which is defined in `Intra.h`. Because `DEBUG` is never defined, line 5 is the only line that is sent to the compiler.

4. It allows you to display dates and times using string names for months, days, and so on. The Windows Control Panel settings determine the display of date and time strings.

5. You can manage the security options for users, groups, resources, and policies.

Day 17

1. From the Form Designer, you can select File|Set Up Custom Components to add `.cc` files onto the Component Palette.

2. The `ActiveX.cc` file is located in the Custom folder. The default location for the Custom folder is

   ```
   c:\Program Files\Borland\IntraBuilder\Custom
   ```

3. The following script causes a runtime error when `alert(OUTPUT_HTML)` executes. `OUTPUT_HTML` is defined as a numeric `5` in the `intra.h` file, and `DEBUG` is not defined. The `alert()` function requires a character string parameter.

   ```
   #include "intra.h"
   #ifdef DEBUG
   alert("Debugging");
   #else
   alert(OUTPUT_HTML);
   #endif
   ```

4. The `DateEx` class contains several methods that make it easier to get formatted date strings. These include `DateEx::getSDate()`, `DateEx::getSDay()`, `DateEx::getSMonth()`, `DateEx::getSTime`, and `DateEx::getSTimezone()`.

5. The application security components allow you to manage users, groups, resources, and policies.

Day 18

1. Three reasons for Java's fast and widespread acceptance are as follows: Java is cross-platform. Java has simple object orientation. Java is secure.

2. LiveConnect is a feature of Netscape Navigator. It allows interaction between JavaScript and Java applets.

3. The `code` property names the Java class, and the `codeBase` property identifies where the class can be found.

4. Java source files have a `class` extension. The source files end in a `java` extension.

5. The `params` property is an associative array.

6. Microsoft refers to the Internet Explorer version of JavaScript as JScript.

Day 19

1. IntraBuilder is an OLE automation client only.

2. `wrd = new OleAutoClient("word.basic");`

3. You must pass the exact number of parameters that are contained in the function prototype. This does not apply to functions whose parameters are defined with the ... data type keyword.

4. `extern unsigned int MadeUp( char*, long* ) "madeup.dll";`

5. The type `void*` cannot be used for the return value. Because a pointer is a 32-bit memory address, use the `long` type instead.

6. The structure contains 12 bytes. The `UINT` data type is the same as an `unsigned int` (line 1), which is four bytes. The `COLORREF` is a `DWORD` (line 4), which is an `unsigned long` (line 2), which is four bytes. The `LONG` is a `long` (line 3), which is also four bytes. Refer to Table 19.1 for the size of each base type.

Day 20

1. Properties and variables are attached to objects. Variables are scoped to methods, and methods can be called from anywhere as long as they're in memory. Properties and methods are encapsulated within objects.

2. An object reference is the address of an object.

3. An object reference variable is the variable, property, or array element in which the address of the object is stored.

4. Interprocess communication is the sharing or transfer of data between objects. An example of interprocess communication is setting a property in a second form to match a value in a property on the first form.

5. The `form` reference is the automatically generated internal reference; it contains the address of the form. The `this` reference is an internal reference to the current object.

6. The generic scope resolution operators are `class::` and `super::`.

7. The class is the blueprint; the object is the actual functioning entity.

8. There is no difference between an instance and an object.

Day 21

1. Metadata is the data that defines the table structures, indexes, procedures, and other items that make up a database. You can re-create an empty database using the metadata from another database. Metadata is stored in system tables.

2. SQL queries perform better when the sequence is defined through an ORDER BY clause rather than an indexName property.

3. Use masterRowset to relate the native dBASE and Paradox table types. Otherwise, use masterSource.

4. You can use a SQL DELETE FROM command to delete the appropriate row from the RDB$GENERATORS system table. InterBase 4.2 does not support a DROP GENERATOR command.

5. The source and destination properties of UpdateSet work with colon-delimited string values to differentiate between database connections.

6. IntraBuilder contains SQL Trace and Output Log options that record all interactions between the SQL-Link driver and the database server. The InterBase Communication Diagnostic tool and InterBase Server Manager can detect connection problems and database corruption.

APPENDIX

B

The Undocumented
IntraBuilder

In this appendix, you will discover some of the undocumented features found in IntraBuilder 1.01, including classes, properties, and configuration settings. You are sure to find some of the undocumented features useful for managing indexes and debugging JavaScript applications.

Disclaimer

The features described in this appendix are undocumented yet functional in IntraBuilder 1.01. As with most new Internet tools, IntraBuilder is going through a period of frequent revisions. As of this writing, there have been two updates since the initial 1.0 release. Version 1.01 added significant client/server features such as the ability to call stored procedures. Version 1.01a provided compatibility with the OEM release of Windows 95b. Be sure to check the IntraBuilder Web site periodically to get the latest release news.

WARNING

> Use of some undocumented features might lead to resource loss and cause IntraBuilder to become unstable.

With each revision, undocumented features may change, become documented, or cease to exist. Do not rely on any undocumented feature in a mission-critical application. Technical support is also unlikely to be available for any of these features.

Class DbfIndex

A class object used to display a current index definition or serve as a parameter to the Database::createIndex() method. This class works with dBASE tables. The DbfIndex class has no methods or events.

Syntax:

```
[<oRef> =] new DbfIndex([<parent>])
```

Table B.1. Properties of DbfIndex.

Property	Default	Description
className	Index	Read-only value that identifies the object as an instance of the Index class.
descending	false	Determines sort direction. If false, the direction is ascending (A, B, C, and so on).

Property	Default	Description
expression	Empty string	dBASE expression supported by BDE. This is the sort key. It can contain dBASE functions such as UPPER() and DTOS().
forExpression	Empty string	Logical dBASE expression used to create high-performance filter sets.
indexName	Empty string	The name of the index.
parent	null	Object passed to constructor.
unique	false	If true, duplicate values are not shown in the table.

Listing B.1. An example of class DbfIndex: DBFINDEX.JS.

```
 1: var idx = new DbfIndex() ;
 2: idx.indexName     = 'VDB' ;
 3: idx.expression    = 'UPPER(title)' ;
 4: idx.forExpression = 'PRODUCT="Visual dBASE"' ;
 5: _sys.databases.current.createIndex("title.dbf",idx) ;
 6:
 7: var q = new Query("select * from 'title.dbf'");
 8: q.rowset.indexName = "VDB" ;
 9: _sys.scriptOut.clear() ;
10: while (! q.rowset.endOfSet )
11: {
12:    _sys.scriptOut.writeln(q.rowset.fields["TITLE"].value) ;
13:    q.rowset.next() ;
14: }
15: q.active = false ;
```

ANALYSIS This script creates a new index on the Title table. Line 3 makes the index case insensitive through the dBASE UPPER() function. The forExpression limits the index to displaying only rows where the expression is true. Lines 7 through 15 display the dBASE titles in the Script Pad's results pane. Using an existing index with a forExpression is the fastest way to filter rows in a dBASE table. Note that the forExpression only hides rows. It does not enforce any integrity or delete rows from a table.

Class Index

A class object used to display a current index definition or serve as a parameter to the Database::createIndex() method. This class works with Paradox and SQL tables. The Index class has no methods or events.

Syntax:

```
[<oRef> =] new Index([<parent>])
```

Table B.2. Properties of `Index`.

Property	Default	Description
caseSensitive	true	Determines whether sort order is case sensitive.
className	Index	Read-only value that identifies the object as an instance of the Index class.
descending	false	Determines sort direction. If false, the direction is ascending (A, B, C, and so on).
fields	Empty string	One or more comma-delimited fields that make up the index.
indexName	Empty string	The name of the index.
parent	null	Object passed to constructor.
unique	false	If true, duplicate values are not allowed in the table.

Listing B.2. An example of class `Index`: `INDEX.JS`.

```
1: var idx = new Index() ;
2: idx.indexName = "Location" ;
3: idx.fields    = "Location" ;
4: _sys.databases.current.createIndex("employee.db",idx) ;
```

ANALYSIS The preceding script adds a new index to the Employee table that comes with IntraBuilder. You can find the Employee table in the apps\data folder within the main IntraBuilder folder. The index is ascending, not case sensitive, and it allows duplicate values.

Class `TableDef`

A class object that represents the structure of a table. You can use the `TableDef` class to examine the indexes and fields of a table. The field information is the same as you get through a rowset. The index and table type information is unavailable through any other class. To date, the `TableDef` class has no methods or events.

Syntax:

```
[<oRef> =] new TableDef([<parent>])
```

Table B.3. Properties of `TableDef`.

Property	Default	Description
className	TableDef	Read-only value that identifies the object as an instance of the `TableDef` class.
database	sys.databases.current	Database to which `TableDef` is assigned.
fields	null	Array of field objects in row. Same as found in class rowset.
indexes	null	Array of index objects.
ldName	Empty string	BDE language driver.
parent	null	Object passed to constructor.
primaryKey	Empty string	Paradox or SQL primary key. Blank for level 5 dBASE tables.
recordCount	0	Number of physical rows in a table.
tableName	Empty string	The table to extract structure information from. This is the only property you should write to.
tableType	Empty string	DBASE, PARADOX, or SQL.

Listing B.3. An example of class `TableDef`: **TABLEDEF.JS.**

```
1: var tDef = new TableDef() ;
2: tDef.tableName = "TITLE.DBF" ;
3: _sys.scriptOut.clear() ;
4: for ( var i = 0 ; i < tDef.indexes.length ; i++ )
5: {
6:     _sys.scriptOut.writeln(tDef.indexes[i].indexName) ;
7: }
```

ANALYSIS The preceding script lists all the indexes of the Title table to the results pane of the Script Pad. Open the Script Pad before running the script to see what happens. You could use a similar technique to populate the options of a select control with index names.

The Credits

On Easter morning, bright-eyed children look high and low for hidden treats. The children learn that treasures await those who have the patience and persistence to be steadfast in their exploration.

Today, computer-hacking kids of all ages stay up all night seeking hidden treasures in computer software. Many CD-ROM games are full of hidden screens and messages. Commercial software also contains hidden dialog boxes with information such as the programmer's name.

IntraBuilder contains hidden credits. As with most Windows software, the IntraBuilder Easter egg is in the About box. To see a list of the many people who brought you IntraBuilder, follow these steps:

1. From the menu, select Help|About.
2. Press Alt+I. When you hold down the Alt key and press the letter I, the dialog starts scrolling the long list of credits, as shown in Figure B.1.

Figure B.1.

The credits.

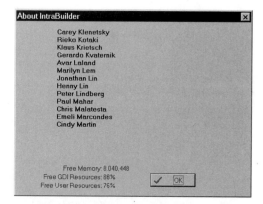

3. You can click the OK button during or after the scroll of the credits. Clicking OK closes the dialog box.

SET PREKEEP=ON

IntraBuilder recognizes one DOS environment variable, PREKEEP. If PREKEEP is equal to ON, IntraBuilder does not delete any temporary files created during compilation.

When IntraBuilder compiles a script, it first processes any compiler directives and creates an intermediate source file. IntraBuilder compiles the temporary source file into an object file.

Normally, IntraBuilder deletes the temporary file as the last step of the compilation process. You can use PREKEEP to prevent IntraBuilder from erasing the intermediate source file. This file is extremely useful for debugging preprocessor directives.

1. Close all programs and erase all files from the Windows temporary file folder. The default location is C:\Windows\Temp. You can override the default by setting the TEMP environment variable.

2. Open a DOS window in Windows 95. You can open a DOS window by choosing Run from the Start menu and entering COMMAND.

3. Use the DOS SET command to create the PREKEEP variable. You also use SET to view all current DOS variables. In the DOS window, enter the following:

```
SET PREKEEP=ON
```

4. To make IntraBuilder recognize this variable under Windows 95, you must open IntraBuilder from the DOS window. You must be in the BIN folder before loading IntraBuilder. Enter the following in the Script Pad (as shown in Figure B.2):

```
CD "\Program Files\Borland\IntraBuilder\Bin"
INTRA.EXE
```

Figure B.2.

Opening IntraBuilder from a DOS window.

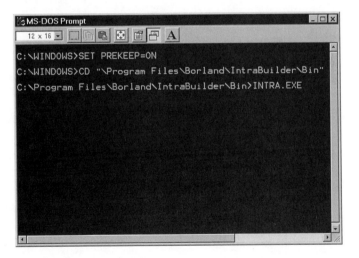

5. When you are in the IntraBuilder Designer, you can verify the existence of PREKEEP with the _sys.env.getEnv() method. Open the IntraBuilder Script Pad and enter the following:

```
? _sys.env.getEnv("PREKEEP") ;
```

If you see ON in the results pane, you are ready to compile something. If there is no output, IntraBuilder does not recognize the DOS variable.

6. Compile a script that contains preprocessor directives. You can use the `prekeep.js` file as follows:

```
_sys.script.compile("prekeep.js") ;
```

7. Use the `_sys.os.dir()` method to locate temporary files that start with INT. IntraBuilder creates the intermediate source files in the temporary folder and begins the filename with the letters INT. In the Script Pad, enter the following:

```
_sys.os.dir("C:\\Windows\\Temp\\INT*.*") ;
```

8. When you have the filename, you can open it with the Script Editor. Before you can read the file in the Script Editor, you have to open the Script Editor properties dialog and select Interpret Text as DOS Text. Until you do this, the characters appear as vertical bars. Figure B.3 shows the file open in the Script Editor after loading in from the Script Pad.

Figure B.3.

Checking for an intermediary compiled file.

The first two characters remain unreadable after setting the DOS Text option. Do not try to modify or run this file. Use it only to help you work with the pre-processor.

WARNING

Any program you compile in the current session of IntraBuilder will create another INT*.* file. You should close IntraBuilder and restart Windows to avoid creating unwanted temporary files. Likewise, do not place SET PREKEEP=ON in your AUTOEXEC file. Doing so prevents IntraBuilder from properly disposing of temporary files.

B

serverEcho

The serverEcho property and registry setting are debugging tools. You can use them to force an IntraBuilder Agent to draw windows as a designer session. The following steps show how you can use serverEcho to cause an IntraBuilder agent to echo form display within a designer as it also streams HTML to a browser:

1. Open the Windows Registry Editor.

2. Locate the following key:

   HKEY_LOCAL_MACHINE\SOFTWARE\Borland\IntraBuilder

3. Add a new string value by selecting Edit|New|String Value. Name the new key serverEcho, as shown in Figure B.4. Close the Registry Editor when done.

Figure B.4.

Adding the serverEcho key to the registry.

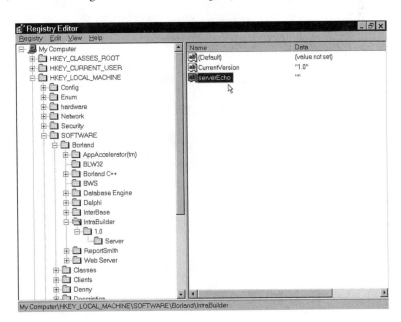

The second part of serverEcho is the property. This is a hidden form property that defaults to false. If you set it to true before a form opens, the echo happens. The property does nothing when set after the open. To set the serverEcho property, add initialization code into the header as shown in Listing B.4.

Listing B.4. Using the serverEcho property.

```
 1: var f = new echoForm();
 2: f.serverEcho = true;
 3: f.open();
 4: return null;
 5:
 6: // {End Header} Do not remove this comment//
 7: // Generated on 02/14/97
 8: //
 9: var f = new echoForm();
10: f.open();
```

ANALYSIS   The Form Designer generated lines 9 and 10. Both lines are duplicated in the header as lines 1 and 3. The serverEcho property assignment occurs on line 2, after creating an instance of the form but before opening it. Line 4 contains a return to prevent the form from opening twice.

If you have both the serverEcho registry setting and the serverEcho property set, you can see forms open in the agent and the browser. Figure B.5 shows the form in Netscape Navigator and the echo image in an IntraBuilder agent.

Figure B.5.

Viewing an echoed form.

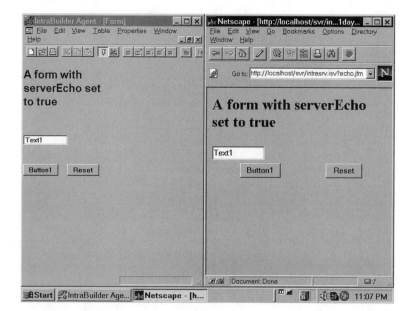

WARNING

Never use `serverEcho` in a production environment. This feature consumes Windows resources that are unnecessary when JavaScript forms are running through a browser.

Also never try to work with design tools through an agent. Doing so could lead to undesirable results.

allowDupSessions

The IntraBuilder Server optimizes communications by reusing existing form definitions if a form is repeatedly requested from the same IP address. This is done by using the IP address to take precedence over the session ID. Although this is beneficial in most situations, it might cause undesirable results if you want to run an application through multiple browsers that share a single IP address.

If you are developing a new application, you might want to fire up a few browsers on a single workstation to try out some row locking code. This does not truly emulate multiple workstations using the default IntraBuilder Server settings. You can use the `allowDupSessions` registry key to force the IntraBuilder Server to treat each session on a single machine as an independent connection. Like the `serverEcho` key, the `allowDupSessions` registry key needs to exist only as a string value key. The actual string can be left blank. The IntraBuilder Server looks for this key in the following location:

```
HKEY_LOCAL_MACHINE\SOFTWARE\Borland\IntraBuilder\1.0\Server
```

DBSYSTEM INI Setting

If you are working with encrypted dBASE tables, the password and encryption keys are stored in a file called DBSYSTEM.DB. Despite the extension, this is not a Paradox table. By default, this file resides in the IntraBuilder BIN folder.

```
C:\Program Files\Borland\IntraBuilder\Bin
```

You can change where IntraBuilder looks for the DBSYSTEM.DB file with the INI setting shown in Listing B.5. Add the setting to INTRA.INI for the IntraBuilder Designer and INTRASRV.INI for IntraBuilder agents.

Listing B.5. The DBSYSTEM setting for INTRA.INI and INTRASRV.INI.

```
1: [CommandSettings]
2: DBSYSTEM=M:\TSHARE
```

clear

The clear command clears output from the results pane. This is synonymous with the _sys.scriptOut.clear() method. This is one of two Xbase commands that make it easier to work with the Script Pad's results pane. The other command is the question mark, which is documented. You can use the Xbase output commands as shortcut versions of _sys.scriptOut methods. Figure B.6 shows how you can use the commands to quickly evaluate simple expressions.

Figure B.6.

Using Xbase stream-ing output commands.

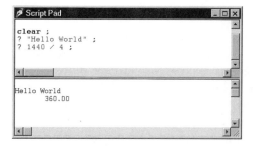

Syntax:

clear

The Xbase CHARACTER option is not supported.

INDEX

Teach Yourself Borland C++ Builder in 21 Days

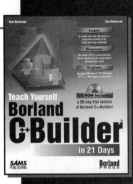

—Kent Reisdorph & Ken Henderson

Following the format of the best-selling *Teach Yourself* series, this step-by-step guide makes learning Borland C++ Builder programming a breeze. It's the perfect learning tool for beginning programmers who want to develop their own programming capabilities, and for developers who want to get up to speed with C++ Builder quickly and easily. Workshops, Q&A sections, and Do and Don't sections reinforce the information found in each chapter. The book also provides coverage of C++ Builder development tools, the C++ Builder IDE, debugging, structured programming, program flow control, DLLs, branching, data manipulation, and pointers.

$39.99 USA/$56.95 CDN   *User Level: New–Casual*
ISBN: 0-672-31020-1   *800 pages*

Delphi 2 Developer's Guide, Second Edition

—Steve Teixeira & Xavier Pacheco

This book empowers the reader with the ability to capitalize on the growing movement toward applications based on GUIs (Graphical User Interfaces). The reader will become adept at exploiting Delphi 32's tools and commands and will learn how to create object-oriented programs. The book's CD-ROM contains product demos and all of the source code from the book. This book also demonstrates practical applications through the use of step-by-step written procedures. It details Delphi 2's tools for efficient OOP.

$59.99 USA/$81.95 CDN   *User Level: Casual–Accomplished–Expert*
ISBN: 0-672-30914-9   *1,368 pages*

Tom Swan's Mastering Borland C++ 5, Premier Edition

—Tom Swan

The new release of Borland C++ 5 includes valuable tools that developers are craving—tools such as new object-oriented scripting, a new C++ language environment that lets you control the IDE completely, and debugger control. With all those and many other new features, developers will turn to *Mastering Borland C++ 5, Premier Edition* to receive the latest and most accurate information on how to exploit these new features in their programs. The book's CD-ROM includes source code from the book and powerful utilities. This book provides a complete introduction and thorough coverage of intermediate and advanced topics, and it includes hundreds of working examples.

$59.99 USA/$81.95 CDN   *User Level: Casual–Accomplished–Expert*
ISBN: 0-672-30802-9   *1,088 pages*

Database Developer's Guide with Borland C++ 5

—Mike Cohn, Jay Rutten, Kristen Hill, Mark Gee, & James Moran

Database Developer's Guide with Borland C++ 5 helps all programmers get the most from Borland's latest version of C++. Readers quickly learn, through the use of real-world applications and examples, the tricks and techniques necessary to efficiently enhance their programs. Exhaustive detail is given to every subject—from Windows extensions such as MAPI, TAPI, OLE2, and NetDDE, to cross-platform programming. This is the most detailed book on developing programs with Borland C++. The book's step-by-step instructions cover every detail. This book also provides coverage of advanced C++ extensions such as MAPI, TAPI, OLE2, and NetDDE. The included CD-ROM contains source code from the book and sample applications.

$59.99 USA/$81.99 CDN   *User Level: Accomplished–Expert*
ISBN: 0-672-30800-2   *736 pages*

Delphi 2 Unleashed, Second Edition

—Charlie Calvert

This book helps every programmer get the most from the latest version of Delphi. And it reveals all the latest information, including how to develop client/server applications, multimedia programs, and advanced Windows programming, in an easy-to-understand style. The included CD-ROM contains source code from the book and sample applications. It also teaches the components of object-oriented programming and covers Windows 95 and multimedia programming.

$59.99 USA/$81.95 CDN　　　　*User Level: Accomplished–Expert*
ISBN: 0-672-30858-4　　　　　　*1,440 pages*

Teach Yourself Delphi 2 in 21 Days

—Dan Osier, Steve Grobman & Steve Batson

This unique book presents Delphi programming in the logical, easy-to-follow sequences that have made the *Teach Yourself* series a best-seller. The reader begins learning the basics of Delphi and then moves on to more advanced topics. *Teach Yourself Delphi 2 in 21 Days* guides the reader through a system for learning a programming language in a set period of time. The book's question and answer sections answer the most commonly asked questions. This book also includes a detailed study of looping, records, arrays, branching, data manipulation, and more.

$35.00 USA/$47.95 CDN　　　　*User Level: New–Casual*
ISBN: 0-672-30863-0　　　　　　*800 pages*

Database Developer's Guide with Delphi 2

—Ken Henderson

This is the only book to focus on advanced database development, and in it readers learn the intricacies involved in developing robust database applications with Delphi 2. Comprehensive coverage of how to create distributable database applications is included. This book explains all of Delphi's database development tools, and the CD-ROM includes all of the source code from the book, sample applications, and demo software.

$55.00 USA/$74.95 CDN　　　　*User Level: Accomplished–Expert*
ISBN: 0-672-30862-2　　　　　　*912 pages*

Teach Yourself Borland C++ 5 in 21 Days, Third Edition

—Craig Arnush

This updated and revised book shows readers how to use the language and how to write beginning-level programs. The author is a member of Team Borland and has access to the most frequently asked questions from the Borland help line. The book uses the successful *Teach Yourself* elements, including Workshop and Q&A sections, quizzes, and shaded syntax boxes.

$39.99 USA/$53.99 CDN　　　　*User Level: New–Casual*
ISBN: 0-672-30756-1　　　　　　*864 pages*

Add to Your Sams.net Library Today
with the Best Books for Internet Technologies

ISBN	Quantity	Description of Item	Unit Cost	Total Cost
0-672-31020-1		Teach Yourself Borland C++Builder in 21 Days (Book/CD-ROM)	$39.99	
0-672-30914-9		Delphi 2 Developer's Guide, Second Edition (Book/CD-ROM)	$59.99	
0-672-30802-9		Tom Swan's Mastering Borland C++ 5, Premier Edition (Book/CD-ROM)	$59.99	
0-672-30800-2		Database Developer's Guide with Borland C++ 5 (Book/CD-ROM)	$59.99	
0-672-30858-4		Delphi 2 Unleashed, Second Edition (Book/CD-ROM)	$59.99	
0-672-30863-0		Teach Yourself Delphi 2 in 21 Days	$35.00	
0-672-30862-2		Database Developer's Guide with Delphi 2 (Book/CD-ROM)	$55.00	
0-672-30756-1		Teach Yourself Borland C++ 5 in 21 Days, Third Edition	$39.99	
		Shipping and Handling: See information below.		
		TOTAL		

Shipping and Handling: $4.00 for the first book, and $1.75 for each additional book. If you need to have it NOW, we can ship product to you in 24 hours for an additional charge of approximately $18.00, and you will receive your item overnight or in two days. Overseas shipping and handling adds $2.00. Prices subject to change. Call between 9:00 a.m. and 5:00 p.m. EST for availability and pricing information on latest editions.

201 W. 103rd Street, Indianapolis, Indiana 46290

1-800-428-5331 — Orders   1-800-835-3202 — Fax   1-800-858-7674 — Customer Service

Book ISBN 1-57521-224-2

MACMILLAN COMPUTER PUBLISHING USA
A VIACOM COMPANY

Technical ---- Support:

If you need assistance with the information in this book or with a CD/Disk accompanying the book, please access the Knowledge Base on our Web site at **http://www.superlibrary.com/general/support**. Our most Frequently Asked Questions are answered there. If you do not find the answer to your questions on our Web site, you may contact Macmillan Technical Support **(317) 581-3833** or e-mail us at **support@mcp.com**.

Installing the CD-ROM

The companion CD-ROM contains all the source code and project files developed by the authors, plus an assortment of evaluation versions of third-party products. To install, please follow these steps:

Windows 95/Windows NT 4 Installation Instructions

1. Insert the CD-ROM into your CD-ROM drive.
2. From the Windows 95 or NT 4 desktop, double-click on the My Computer icon.
3. Double-click on the icon representing your CD-ROM drive.
4. Double-click on the icon titled `setup.exe` to run the CD-ROM installation program.

This program creates a program group with the icons to run the programs on the CD. No files will be copied to your hard drive during this installation.

NOTE If you have Windows 95 and the Autoplay feature is enabled, the `setup.exe` program is executed automatically when the CD-ROM is inserted into the drive.

Windows NT 3.51 Installation Instructions

1. Insert the CD-ROM into your CD-ROM drive.
2. From the File Manager or Program Manager, choose Run from the File menu.
3. Type `<drive>\setup.exe`, where `<drive>` corresponds to the drive letter of your CD-ROM drive, and press Enter. For example, if your CD-ROM drive is D:, type `d:\setup.exe` and press Enter.
4. Installation creates a program group named `TY IntraBuilder`. This group will contain icons to browse the CD-ROM.